Greece under Socialism

A NATO ALLY ADRIFT

Greece under Socialism

A NATO ALLY ADRIFT

Edited by
Nikolaos A. Stavrou

Introduction by
Matthew Nimetz

Published by
Aristide D. Caratzas
ORPHEUS PUBLISHING INC.
New Rochelle, New York

Aristide D. Caratzas, Publisher
ORPHEUS PUBLISHING INC.
30 Church Street
P.O. Box 210
New Rochelle, New York 10802
U.S.A.
Telephone: (914)632-8487

Greece under socialism
Includes index.
1. Greece--Politics and government--1974
2. Panellenio Sosialistiko Kinema (Greece)
I. Stavrou, Nikolaos A. 1935–
DF854.G7 1988 949.5'076 88-28985
ISBN 0-89241-460-X

Printed in the United States of America

Contents

Preface

When the publisher of this compendium, Aristide D. Caratzas, asked the question, "has sufficient time passed since PASOK's assumption of power for an in-depth analysis of its domestic and foreign policies," I told him that it was possible but I had no inkling of the complexities involved in editing such a volume. It was and remains my considered judgement that the advent of socialism in a society noted for its individualism and entrepreneurial spirit was a legitimate subject of scholarly research and analysis. A casual review of publications in western languages on Greek socialism revealed an obvious lack of studies about Greek politics since 1981 and no interdisciplinary study of the origins, evolution, rise, and current status of the Panhellenic Socialist Movement (PASOK). Several doctoral dissertations have been written on aspects of the Panhellenic Socialist party, and several more are in the works, but as dissertations go, most are written from a narrow, often selective perspective. Aimed at satisfying a committee of diverse scholars rather than at enlightening the public at large, they are subject to methodological constraints.

While there is a lack of any interdisciplinary evaluation of PASOK's rise to power in English, there is an inordinate amount of material published in the Greek language about the party. The Ministry of Press and Information is the major producer of "raw data" on the subject . Its goal is usually to improve the image of the party and to make its leader "charismatic" and capable of winning elections.

Government-produced publications no doubt are useful to historians and other researchers. They provide "packaged date" on ideology, personalities, trends, and problems, but they can hardly be characterized as neutral.

PASOK has been in power for approximately seven years, freely elected twice by substantial majorities of the electorate. Before its victory, it was an opposition party for seven years, and a "liberation movement" for slightly more than six years.

20 years may or may not be sufficient time for social scientists to offer a macro-analysis of a political movement. Our experience with this project has shown that it is neither unusual nor without reward to attempt certain generalizations about a political phenomenon on the basis of its record and the empirical evidence that has accumulated in a relatively short span of time. I am, of course, aware of the perennial socialist argument, "don't judge us yet, we are in transition to a higher stage." Still I believe that PASOK is ripe for a thorough review of its policies and a preliminary attempt to determine whether *promises* match *performance.*

Neither I nor the publisher have any pretences that this volume is comprehensive, or that it exhausts all the issues that could have been researched and included. But I do hope we have succeeded in raising new questions about socialism in Greece and, in some small way, contributed to the debate about the course of Greek politics under socialism. We hope that other scholars will add to the literature on post-1974 Greek politics and correct the errors that are bound to occur when something as volatile as contemporary Greek politics is being analyzed. As the future unfolds and PASOK's record receives greater scrutiny, some of our conclusions will naturally be modified.

We knew from the outset that any evaluation of contemporary Greek affairs could not avoid displeasing some individuals or some groups. During the past two decades in which I have studied and published work on contemporary politics, I have come to realize that all scholarly work about contemporary Greece is subjected to an ideological acid test no matter how innocent or objective the work might be. The post-1974 Greek society, unfortunately, has been split into warring ideological camps, locked in endless monologues with no chance for calm voices to reach wide audiences and bridge the political rifts. That much is obvious in the daily headlines of the Greek newspapers, which in some instances cover half of the front page. Political discourse in the land of Socratic dialectics has been replaced by the cacophony of street agitators who sound like Christmas tree vendors eager to sell their product before 10 P.M. on Christmas eve. Some of them are in control of the electronic media and thus possess the means to make arguments in a louder pitch. They give their opponents reason to adopt the same methods. In the interest of military bases, the polemics are seldom countered in the West, and the officially sanctioned ideological warfare remains widespread. I have thus made a conscious effort to develop methods that would make our undertaking more objective. I have tried to give our work the best chance of *appearing* as well as *being* as objective as humanly possible.

Toward this end, I made the following decisions at the conceptual stage of this volume: 1) that there should be a mix of Greek and foreign contributors to the compendium; 2) that no active or retired politicians would be invited to contribute, even though some first-rate minds and scholars are involved in Greek public life; 3) that all authors should be given wide latitude to develop their arguments, with the sole condition that they emphasize the post-1981 period; 4) that all contributors *let the evidence* make their case, not the other way around; 5) that as a matter of principle and responsibility I would retain the right to include or exclude an essay. In other words, *no* contributor could in any way dictate who was to be included. Invitation to write an essay for this volume did not ensure final inclusion; basic standards of quality and scholarship had to be met. At the minimum such standards include adequate support of assertions and arguments, dispassionate analysis of issues and, above all, no attempts at "political hatchet jobs."

The issues studied and included in this volume were identified and agreed upon by editor and publisher. Decisions to include or exclude were made solely by the editor, and I make no apologies for the selections. Yet choices are not always easy, particularly when friends and associates are involved. When most of the pieces were in place, I decided to exclude two chapters, which, even though well documented, could have seemed politically motivated. One was called "The Politics of Corruption under Socialism," the other "The Para-State of a Ruling Party." I hasten to add that an inordinately large number of articles, studies and parliamentary debates have already been devoted to these two issues. But, I rejected both chapters primarily to avoid possible false perceptions, which could have been derived from their lack of a comparative basis.

A chapter on Greek-Turkish relations, promised by a prominent scholar, was not produced for "personal reasons." As matters turned out, it was just as good in light of the 180-degree reversal of Andreas Papandreou on fundamental causes of the Greek-Turkish disputes.

Some authors (Robert Pranger, Charles McCaskill, and Bill

Shepard) augmented their analyses with an American perspective of some of the issues that have distorted U.S.-Greek-Third World relations.

A chapter of the legal aspects of the Aegean dispute was rejected for poor quality, shallow documentation (or no documentation at all), and overall poor scholarship.

Thus, the reader will find a compendium that covers what the editor thought to be the critical issues influencing Greek political trends during PASOK's tenure in opposition and in power. It is written by a diverse group of scholars and experts of high integrity and impeccable credentials. Although I made an editorial decision to exclude politicians from this volume, an exception was made in favor of the Socialist government. I invited the alternate minister of foreign affairs, the Honorable Yannis Kapsis (a former Editor-in-Chief for the daily *Ta Nea,* a newspaper for which I wrote dozens of articles, mostly at his invitation) to contribute a key chapter on the "Philosophy and Goals of PASOK's Foreign Policy." The rationale for the exception is simple: first, Mr. Kapsis is a non-elected member of the cabinet, in other words not a professional politician; second, it was only fair that if scholars engage in evaluating a government's foreign policies they should at least provide that government with an opportunity to offer an authoritative overview of what these policies are.

I have decided to retain the Kapsis piece despite its methodological weaknesses, which simply could not be corrected since it constitutes an official document, formally submitted through appropriate diplomatic channels. It is hereby published in its entirety and unedited.

In preparing this volume I have become indebted to many friends and associates. Dr. Ngozi C. Kamalu read several of the manuscripts and made useful suggestions for their improvement. He was particularly helpful in reviewing the piece on the Aegean dispute, which was ultimately rejected. Ambassador Richard W. Boehm, Diplomat in Residence at Howard University and former Ambassador to Cyprus, read several essays and made useful suggestions for their improvement. Young Christopher Pranger pursued with enthusiasm and scholarly persistence sources and documents of U.S.-Greek relations, which were useful to several contributors.

The Department of Political Science was generous in providing a grant for manuscript preparation and technical support. Mrs. Mildred Mason labored hard and long in typing many of the edited and re-edited essays. Here I express my profound appreciation for her invaluable support in difficult moments. Three associates and friends who love their country, Greece, and who have dept the faith with the original ideals of the Panhellenic Socialist Movement, the ideals of genuine democratic *allage* (change) read with critical eyes my own manuscript on the ideological foundation of the party and made useful suggestions for its improvement. I cannot thank them by name to avoid "inevitable political reprisals," as I was told, but they know who they are and have my deep gratitude for their unwavering support of truth and fairness.

This volume would have not been possible without the steady cooperation and assistance of Aris Caratzas and the meticulous editorial work of John Emerich and his associates. They had the painful tasks of making sure that the final product is of the highest technical and stylistic quality. Finally, a collective thanks to all of the contributors to this volume for venturing into an area of Greek life that is bound to cause at least a heated debate, and perhaps even denunciations of our attempt to evaluate a new phenomenon of Greek politics, "the third road to socialism."

Nikolaos A. Stavrou
Howard University
February, 1988

Publisher's Note on Transliteration

The transliteration of Modern Greek into Latin characters is a problematic and confusing matter. A number of systems compete in the newspapers, periodic literature and books of the English-speaking world. In Greece itself, disorder appears to be the dominant rule, as any traveler to that country will attest: the road, street and store signs, so imaginatively transliterated, provide a constant source of both amusement and bewilderment.

Given the absence of a generally accepted transliteration system, writers and editors must maneuver between the Scylla of phonetic reproduction and the Charybdis of traditional orthography. The editors of this house have decided to adopt the following approach in dealing with this task.

1. The basic guide is the Library of Congress system (cf. Georg F. von Ostermann, *Manual of Foreign Languages*, 4th edition, New York: Central Book Company, 1952, reprinted 1970, p. 109 ff; also, *A Manual of Style*, 12th edition, Chicago: The University Press, p. 231 ff). It is based on the practices of transliterating the classical language. Its main merits include practicality and integrity. It is practical because it is based on the concept of direct equivalence between Greek and Latin characters; thus, alpha is *a*, gamma *g*, delta *d*, etc. It is faithful, furthermore, to the orthography of the ancient language, which in large part is preserved in the modern. Certain of the conventions derive from longstanding transliteration practice from Greek to Latin, i.e., phi is *ph*; the diphthongs alpha/epsilon/omicron-upsilon are *au*, *eu* and *ou* respectively; the initial rho is *rh* (unless the recently-adopted modern monotonic/no-breathing system prevails in the Greek original); the rough breathing is retained as an *h*, again unless the Greek original uses the monotonic system. Finally, chi is *ch*, as in the German *ich*.

2. Some modifications to the Library of Congress system have been made to conform with phonetic changes from classical to modern Greek. Thus the beta is transliterated as a *v*; the modern mu-pi combination as a *b* or *mb*; nu-tau as a *d*, etc.

3. Names represent a major challenge to the editors and they are treated as follows:

a. Well-known figures in the political and cultural life of modern Greece whose names have gained wide currency in the English-speaking world: the most common form of accepted transliteration used in some of the more authoritative newspapers (i.e., *The Times* of London, *The New York Times*) and in the scholarly literature is adopted; hence, Karamanlis, Rallis, Theodorakis etc. (not the more consistent Karamanles, Rhalles, Theodorakes).

b. The first names of well-known figures usually use established Latin/English equivalents unless a specific version of the Greek original is commonly used. Hence, Constantine Karamanlis, George Rallis, etc. However, Giannes (not John) Aleuras. As with last names, if the first name of a particular individual has gained wide currency in the English-speaking world in a nonstandard form, then this form is retained. Thus, Yannis Kapsis (not John or the more correct transliteration, Giannes).

c. The names of authors and scholars frequently published in the English-speaking world: the version of the name most commonly appearing in the literature. Thus, Couloumbis not Kouloumbes

d. Greeks living abroad whose names have been legally transliterated in characters that are not consistent with the above. Example, Caratzas not the more correct Karatzas, etc.

e. An effort has been made to cross-index orthographic variants for ready reference, or to include them in parentheses within an entry of the index.

4. Some sources of potential confusion: certain Latin letters have been used to transliterate more than one Greek letter. The *e* has been used to transliterate both the eta and the iota, while the *o* is used for both the omicron and the omega. The exigencies of typography have not permitted the use of the long mark (-) above the letter to distinguish the eta and omega from iota and omicron. The *u* is been used instead of the *y* in transliterating the upsilon in diphthongs, in keeping with traditional usage in Latin and English.

Introduction

Matthew Nimetz

In October 1981, in free and democratic elections, the Greek people chose the Panhellenic Socialist Movement (PASOK) to govern their country, ending over three decades of conservative rule that commenced with the defeat of communist insurrection. The assumption of power by a socialist party in a NATO country was not unique: socialists in Italy, France and West Germany had successfully governed their respective countries and played a constructive role in the Western alliance.

The Greek "Socialist" party was different and raised concerns among those who believe that Greece is an important member of the Western community. PASOK's leader, Andreas G. Papandreou, an American-educated economist, fought the election on a political platform that promised the removal of U.S. bases from Greek soil, withdrawal from NATO, a referendum to decide whether Greece should remain a member of the European Community, and a vague promise of a "third road to socialism." From an American perspective, there was introduced a new uncertainty about the future of U.S.-Greek relations and apprehension about the promised internal transformation of Greek society. Most of these concerns were derived from the self-definition of PASOK and the theoretical premises upon which the 1981 electoral contest was fought.

The Panhellenic Socialist Movement is not a social democratic party shaped in the Western European mold. It was in 1981 and to a large extent remains today a *personalist* entity which incorporates a number of centralist features that are more characteristic of monolithic third world models than its Western counterparts. This characterization pervades the founding charter of the party and the pronouncements of its founder: Prime Minister Andreas Papandreou has gone to some lengths to differentiate his party from the social democratic traditions of Western Europe.[1]

Drawing from Marxist and socialist thought since the Paris revolt of 1848, Papandreou sees capitalism as being both the major cause of all human problems and in a state of permanent crisis. The "crisis of capitalism" theme pervades his theoretical arguments and often his political statements. Thus, in a recent article he renews this theme and in the process attempts to "correct" Marx as well. "I would have to give a newer interpretation to capitalism's problems than Marx did," he said. "Capitalism is in deep crisis not because it is blocked from development but because of the self-destruction caused by its dynamism. On a global scale, capitalism has to be held responsible for the more nefarious ills of mankind," he concluded.[2]

In his efforts to carve a distinct personality and to underscore the fact that PASOK was not part and parcel of Eurosocialism, Papandreou put distance between his party and West European social democrats whom he has dismissed as "dupes of capitalism" and who by their conciliatory philosophies have protracted the life of the bourgeois system, rather than "radically change it."[3] His lack of commitment to traditional social democracy (and by extension to the Center Union, the political party that his father led to two electoral victories in the sixties) stemmed from his belief that social democrats were "piecemeal socialists," who fostered "reforms whose goal was to cover up the weaknesses and contradictions of the system."[4] In his view these were not steps toward socialism but a measure of staving it off. In contrast, PASOK was in favor of "radically changing the socio-economic relations of Greek society."

Naturally, this type of rhetoric raised concerns among Western policy-makers, who for forty years considered Greece an important member of the Western Community. Papandreou's political rhetoric, which seven years ago justifiably raised concerns in the United States and Western Europe,was heightened by the contrast between the new Greek leader and the recently elected President of the United States, a conservative Republican with a history of hostility to leftist philosophies and causes.

The central question of the 1980s for the two countries was whether two allied national leaders, democratically elected but ideologically at opposite ends of the political spectrum, could find a way to cooperate in the interest of their two nations and the Western alliance. The experience of the past seven years has given a more positive answer to that question than many had expected. As some of us anticipated, the relations between the two countries, shaped by multiple ties, common ideals and shared interests, had acquired an enduring quality, which was not easily disrupted by the power of personalities no matter how charismatic they might be. Yet, despite the dynamics of continuity in U.S.-Greek relations, political trends set in motion by the advent of socialism, and sustained by complex foreign policy issues and carefully managed "ambiguity" on the part of PASOK, underscore the need for dispassionate scholarly investigation of the entire spectrum of post-1981 Greek policies. The present volume that I have been asked to introduce to the American reader was conceived and undertaken with the purpose of rendering an evaluation of PASOK's performance during the past seven years in areas that constitute the core of its public policy.

Greece under Socialism: A NATO Ally Adrift is the collective product of 13 prominent academics, journalists and practitioners of Greek politics from both sides of the Atlantic, edited by Dr. Nikolaos A. Stavrou. The contributors to this volume represent diverse disciplines and viewpoints, and offer a broad analysis of domestic, economic, military, foreign policy and social issues. Each was asked to research, analyze and evaluate the impact of PASOK's policies in their respective areas of expertise and respond to the question "what has changed," if anything, in Greece since the advent of PASOK to power.

This volume is not about U.S.-Greek relations; yet by its very nature and depth, the question of the U.S.-Greek relationship pervades most of the essays. Although the book's contributors do not dwell on why a socialist party was elected to power in a country known for its entrepreneurial spirit and individualism, it is quite obvious that foreign policy issues played a critical role in the elections of 1981 and 1985. Effective exploitation of national issues, appeals to popular misconceptions about the role of the Western alliance in the Cyprus debacle, obviously orchestrated anti-Americanism and vague promises of a "third way to socialism"--all carefully packaged under the slogan "allage" (change) contributed heavily to the margin of victory for Andreas Papandreou.

It would be fair to say that PASOK's electoral victory in 1981 did not prove to be the cataclysmic event that many analysts had predicted. Despite the rhetoric, which resembled that of more flamboyant and radical third world leaders, a modus operandi was achieved with the United States and NATO. An agreement on the status of bases was successfully concluded in 1983 and the two sides are in the process of renegotiating that arrangement. Greece has remained a member of the Western alliance and an active participant in the European Economic Community.

Although U.S.-Greek relations improved steadily since the 1985 Greek elections, it would be an error to take this positive trend for granted. Indeed, several contributors to this volume seem to have reached independently a consensus on a fundamental point, namely, that the foundations of U.S.-Greek relations have been steadily narrowed to the point that they appear dependent on the status of military facilities. In my view the emphasis on military facilities undermines and distorts other areas of common interest. (This was true to some extent in the pre-PASOK period as well, when Karamanlis and Rallis were unable to successfully renegotiate the U.S. base agreement.) The emphasis on military bases tends to lessen interest in other areas of relations, such as political cooperation, economic ties and cultural and scientific projects, which in the long term are far better assurances of future stability. Unfortunately, the excessive preoccupation of the Reagan administration with military relationships was a perfect foil to Papandreou's excessive preoccupation with the same subject.

Contrary to perceptions that "little has changed in Greece, despite the rhetoric," most contributors argue persuasively that indeed deep changes have taken place in Greek society and that these changes will eventually be reflected in domestic and foreign policies. Several scholars argue convincingly that PASOK's tenure in power has dramatically altered the perceptions of the Greek people about threats from the North and has brought about a profound alteration of traditional values and institutions. In a more concrete instance of change, PASOK legitimized the antidemocratic forces of the forties that sought to impose a totalitarian system upon the Greek people and redefined the concept of political participation in a manner that may ultimately limit the basis of contractualism in the relationship between citizen and state.

Thus, while on the surface U.S.-Greek relations have somewhat improved in a step-by-step fashion during the past three years, their narrow focus does not guarantee their stability or future growth. No doubt there are legitimate issues affecting ties between the two countries. At least three deep-seated issues influence the foreign and domestic politics of Greece and contribute to the acceptance of the slogan "change." These were themes in Greek politics during the pre-PASOK period as well, but have achieved a higher level of legitimacy under Papandreou's skillful exploitation. These issues are, first, the perception that the U.S. promoted, or facilitated, the Greek military coup of 1967; second, that the integration of Turkish forces into, and subsequent division of, Cyprus in 1974 was engineered by Washington; and third, that Greek-Turkish tensions over Cyprus and the Aegean are also managed surreptitiously by an American hand, with an American and NATO tilt toward Turkey.

While there is agreement among the contributors about the centrality of these issues, the majority of them reject the "devil theory," and see the Papandreou government as accentuating the differences between his country and the Western alliance, rather than encouraging areas of agreement and friendship. An atmosphere of negativism has pervaded Greek society for the past seven years, and it is the opinion of several of the scholars who have analyzed Greek public life that this atmosphere is fostered by the ruling party and reflects ongoing attempts to alter Greece's relations with her traditional allies under the guise of the appealing slogans: "national independence; popular sovereignty; social liberation; and democratic progress..."

Let me add a few words on the three "issues" that have played a role in the qualitative change in U.S.-Greek relations. It has been a recurring article of faith among Greek elites that the 1969-74 Greek dictatorship was, if not established, at least tolerated by the United States. This claim has been incorporated into PASOK's overall theoretical premises and has been effectively exploited to portray Greece as a nation under limited sovereignty. (I was told several times by "conservative" Greek leaders that Greece had been dominated first by the Ottoman Turks, then by the British, then by the Americans.) A few brief remarks are worth making about this claim.

It is the conclusion of the majority of the contributors to this volume that the United States neither encouraged, supported, nor unduly tolerated the Greek dictatorship. Several of the contributors were among those who as American citizens and academics opposed the Greek dictatorship and were instrumental in influencing American policy vis-à-vis the Papadopoulos junta. It is also worth noting that only the United States suspended military assistance promptly after the coup occurred and withdrew its Ambassador from Athens for more than two years. Furthermore, the United States Congress and many of its distinguished members were in the forefront of those supporting the full restoration of democracy in the land of its birth. No other country, East or West, did as much in support of democracy in Greece. Although perceptions of support for the Greek junta were often unavoidable, since Greece and the U.S. were members of the same alliance, our overall record was unsurpassed. Yet the issue of "the U.S. role during the dictatorship" seems to be embedded in the political agenda of the ruling party and in the minds of left-wing intellectual elites and this has, rather than diminishing over time, remained a cancerous tumor in the bosom of U.S.-Greek relations.

The Cyprus problem, with all of its complexity, has also played a central role in domestic Greek politics since the mid-fifties and has been a major distorting factor in U.S.-Greek relations. In the final analysis, the Cyprus problem is one for the two communities to work out, with the constructive support of the two metropoles—Greece and Turkey. Yet by its sheer presence in the area and the history of relations with Greece and Turkey, the U.S. is expected to play a catalytic role in its solution. And here lies a paradox: on the one hand, Washington is viewed by the ruling socialist party as a "dominant force" that should be precluded from influencing Greek affairs (to maximize "national sovereignty"), but on the other, we are expected to interfere and resolve issues that to a great extent are of local creation and require a local solution. As one who has played a small role in seeking—unsuccessfully—to assist in resolving the Cyprus problem, I know too well that there are no heroes in the Cyprus problem. A workable solution is difficult enough to find, even if all the actors are working wholeheartedly for a fair resolution; how frustrating, then, the manipulation of those who for ideology, power politics, personal advancement or other goals, prevent serious negotiation.

Aegean problems and other disputes with Turkey have also become a persistent irritant in U.S.-Greek relations. This issue is not American made or American encouraged. The United States does not take any pleasure in seeing valued allies at the brink of hostilities. The territorial integrity of Greece has never been and should never be questioned. But to be straightforward about it, the solution of the Aegean problem lies in a direct dialogue between the two neighbors and in fair application of principles of international law. Unfortunately, both Greece and Turkey see our influence as omnipotent—if applied on the other side. Yet the truth is that allies do not go about bullying their friends into submission. It would therefore be an error of immense proportions for either party in the Aegean dispute to try to coax the United States to take sides, or, failing that, to deduce that we have abandoned our strong support for the territorial integrity and security of existing borders.

In the past two decades Greek-Turkish relations have been burdened with issues whose roots go deep in the history of the two nations. Nevertheless, there is an apparent realization by the leaders of both countries that bilateral issues have a better chance of being resolved via a direct dialogue and without the involvement of powers external to the region. The January 1988 meeting at Davos, Switzerland, between Prime Minister Andreas Papandreou and his Turkish counterpart, Turgut Ozal, underscores the value of direct contacts as a means of resolving problems. Prime Minister Papandreou showed exceptional courage, statesmanship and political maturity in commencing such a dialogue.

It would not be unfair to conclude that the history of the past twenty years in U.S.-Greek relations needs calm evaluation and perhaps revision. Too much has been said by Greek commentators about U.S. "involvement" in domestic affairs even though the evidence does not support such a blanket conclusion. Certainly the evidence accumulated in this volume points in the opposite direction. The need for serious analysis of domestic and foreign policies is partially filled by this volume, which I hope will precipitate a new look into Greek political trends and U.S.-Greek relations, based on intellectually responsible research.

In the chapters that follow, scholars and specialists from different political perspectives have groped with the question: How has PASOK behaved while in power? What factors have shaped or modified its behavior and what are the prospects for pluralism in Greece? The central question—what has changed" in Greece during the past seven years—guided the contributors in their research and conclusions. I shall not attempt a critique of the various contributions—but a few generalizations are warranted.

First, it is obvious that U.S.-Greek relations have largely endured the tests and strains that were caused by PASOK's pre-electoral slogans. The endurance of the bilateral relationship is a testimony to the depth of these ties (cemented by a vibrant Greek-American community), and the fact that the people of both countries have an affinity for each other, which serves as a safety valve in times when their governments attempt abrupt changes of direction. Not many issues found solutions during the seven years of PASOK's being in power; in fact, many divisive issues were created or accentuated. In the area of U.S.-Greek relations, there are two points of agreement: first, that the bilateral relationship is not on a firm basis when it is narrow in scope and has as its core element the issue of military facilities; second, although the two countries have managed to reintroduce a degree of calm ("warm waters," or "step-by-step diplomacy"), in their dealings, the deep changes in values and social attitudes in Greek society, intensified by deliberate PASOK policies, will have a long-term effect on the course of U.S.-Greek relations. Regrettably, disinformation, deception and heavy-handed leftist propaganda have undermined traditional Western values and attitudes that link Greece with other Western democracies.

There is a third area on which the contributors seem to have reached a consensus: namely, that despite external perceptions that PASOK's "rhetoric has not matched reality" there have occurred real changes in the perceptions of the average Greek citizen about the role of government. Changing values, "historical revisionism" (particularly as it relates to the forties), desensitization of the Greek people to any fear from the Soviet-dominated North and a heavy and continuous dosage of anti-Western rhetoric fomented by the government-controlled mass media, will inevitably alter public policy. Changes in defense doctrine (here examined effectively by Gen. George Tsoumis), introduction of the concept of "total peoples defense" (borrowed from the Yugoslav model), revival of a policy of Balkan "integration" despite the deep systemic differences among Greece's neighbors, infatuation with Qaddafi and Arafat, and the assault on such important institutions as the Church and the Presidency of the Republic, are viewed here as dramatic changes with unpredictable consequences, undertaken by the ruling party to achieve what its leader calls "socialist transformation."

Finally, and more positively, there is consensus among the contributors about the importance of the EEC-Greek connection. This historic link, achieved by Constantine Karamanlis, is viewed as a safety valve in the Greek political system. In a more practical way, the EEC has been the saving grace in PASOK's economic policies (which have been detrimental to overall growth and development), and its subsidies to Greek agriculture have been presented as evidence of the party's interest in the well-being of the Greek peasants. Also, by providing the Greek people with an institutional link with the European democracies, the European community serves as a sort of antidote to the provincialism and isolationism that has always been an important factor in Greek politics and has now been intensified by PASOK.

This volume, *Greece under Socialism: A NATO Ally Adrift*, raises provocative questions about the future of Greek politics through its examination of critical areas of Greek public policy. I hope that this compendium will precipitate a serious discussion on the nature of Greek socialism and U.S.-Greek relations and that it will encourage further research in this important field.

NOTES

1. Andreas G. Papandreou, *Metabase sto Sosialismo: Problemata kai Strategike gia to Elleniko Kinema.* (Transition to Socialism: Problems and Strategy for the Greek Movement) (Athens: Aichme, 1984, 5th edition): 9.

2. Andreas G. Papandreou, "If capitalism can't, can socialism?" *New Perspective Quarterly* , vol. 4, no. 3 (fall 1987): 52.

3. A. Kokkos and A. Mourike-Kostopoulou (Editors), *Metabase sto Sosialismo* (Athens: Aletri Publishers, 1981): 12-13.

4. Andreas G. Papandreou, "He Diaphores mas me te Sosialdemokratia." (Our Differences With Social Democracy) in *Gia mia Sosialistike Koinonia* (For a Socialist Society) (Athens: Aichme, 1984): 12-13. [This volume re-issues and apparently reaffirms earlier statements made by Andreas Papandreou.]

Ideological Foundations of the Panhellenic Socialist Movement

Nikolaos A. Stavrou

The Panhellenic Socialist Movement (PASOK) has been in power in Greece since the landmark elections of 18 October 1981. Although its pre-electoral rhetoric promised radical changes in all facets of Greek society, thus far PASOK has not done away with political pluralism, if by pluralism we mean the perpetuation of a multiparty system. Six years after the accession to power of a socialist movement that by its own definition does not belong to the Western European category, the Greek party system has remained quite stable. Coalition of political forces into fewer and fewer parties has been in progress since the middle sixties. Currently, three major parties represent in excess of ninety-five percent of the electorate in Parliament. The remaining five percent is claimed by several splinter groups formally chartered as parties, but in reality they are merely pressure groups.

The existence of pluralism, however, does not imply social stability or general acceptance of the basic rules of pluralistic democracy. Indeed, some political movements and parties reject routine participation in the political game and do not accept the existing social system. They have as the centerpiece of their ideology the goal of fundamentally transforming society. The Greek Communist party (KKE), for example, espouses radical change of the socio-economic system to be achieved through class struggle.[1] Nor does the Panhellenic Socialist Movement fit the mold of traditional pluralistic parties. Its founder did not intend it to be a usual party conforming to Greek reality, and it has not functioned as one either in opposition or in power. It is a new phenomenon in Greek society, with a monolithic ideology, a centralized organizational structure and mass membership. Neither its charter, behavior nor program justifies its classification as a centrist party or as the heir to the Greek liberal tradition.[2] Its ideology especially precludes that possibility.

In this essay, we will attempt to offer the reader the rudiments of PASOK's ideology, broadly analyzing its philosophical underpinnings. We hope that our essay will orient the reader as he considers the essays of the other contributors to this volume. Our work is based by and large on the writings of PASOK's founder and on secondary sources relating to them, most of which appeared in the Greek language. Although on numerous occasions we have expressed specific views about the Panhellenic Socialist Movement and its impact on Greek pluralism, it is not our intention here to choose one side or the other in the debate concerning the political preferences of the Greek people.[3]

Conceptually, we shall pursue our objectives by:

1) examining the theoretical content of the "third road" to socialism, the keynote of Papandreou's pronouncements;

2) attempting to link, if linkable, the overall theory of Greek socialism to the Greek experience;

3) comparing (and delineating) differences or similarities between PASOK and other socialist parties that function in pluralistic societies.

The areas of our interest cannot be fully analyzed without considering PASOK's organizational characteristics and its perception of the role of the state and the masses in the political process. At the outset, we should stress that any examination of PASOK's ideology is essentially an examination of Papandreou's own philosophy of government. In fact, since its formation on 3 September 1974, the party has been managed from above with an iron hand. An American-educated professor metes out ruthless discipline and treats his underlings as an ivy-league snob would treat bothersome intellectual mediocrities.

Papandreou's ideology and idiosyncracies are central components of the party's existence. Although a separate chapter examines the personality of the leader, we must note here briefly that the founder of PASOK is a complex individual. He is the product of two cultures, but does not feel comfortable in either of them. He is still in search of acceptance in the West, or at least notice, anywhere.

Papandreou's formative intellectual years were spent in such American universities as Harvard, Northwestern, Minnesota and Berkeley. His political odyssey, however, commenced while still a law student at the University of Athens. While there, he joined an active Trotskyite group.[4] In 1939, he was arrested by the Chief of Metaxas Secret Police,

Constantine Maniadakes, imprisoned and tortured. Through the intervention of his father, who was already an important figure in the Greek political establishment, Andreas Papandreou was released, and his family sent him to the United States to pursue his educational goals. He returned to Greece permanently in 1960 at the invitation of Constantine Karamanlis, again through the intervention of his father. It is risky for us to suggest that Papandreou's personal experiences in the hands of the Metaxas secret police brought about his eventual drift in the direction of a Marxist interpretation of society. At the same time, we cannot ignore the fact that on numerous instances in history, personal events have shaped a leader's character. Lenin became an avowed atheist, for example, when his father, whom he had idealized, died prematurely. In his young mind, God was unfair to deprive a young boy of his idol. Later he resolved to become a professional revolutionary after his brother Alexander was hanged for his participation in the assassination attempt against Tsar Alexander III.[5]

So for Andreas Papandreou it is likely that his experience as a Trotskyite during the heady days of the Third and Fourth (Trotsky's outfit) Internationals and his involvement in revolutionary work left an imprint. Members of his inner circle, who later defected, intimate that Papandreou often referred to his early experiences at the University of Athens as significant for his later identity.[6] This may be, but the central position taken in this essay is that the core of Papandreou's philosophical content was derived from his experience in American academia, of which he was an important member. More specifically, his and his party's ideology reflects the economic analysis of a small group who for lack of a better term will be called neo-Marxist, or theorists of the *dependencia* (dependence) school of thought.

PASOK's social analysis is in many respects a reworking of the positions of several social thinkers, among whom are André Gunde Frank, Hans J. Axt, Samir Amin, Bartel Olman and the neo-Marxist economists Paul Sweezy and Paul Barran. The common thread that links the thinkers of the dependence school of thought, which Papandreou has taken up, is the division of the world into an "exploitative center" (or "metropolis") and an "exploited periphery," a division that introduces a new wrinkle in orthodox Marxist class analysis.

Central in the "metropolis versus periphery" theories is the existence of "capitalist crisis," which can only be alleviated by imperialist expansionism and control of resources. In other words, in the dependence theories the world is seen as divided between rich countries, which control the means of production, and the poor countries of the periphery, which *possess* but do *not* control the raw materials needed by the industrial centers.[7] In such a situation it is the "metropolis" that determines the value of labor and of raw materials, and in our era it does so on a global scale. In this new situation, vaguely predicted by Marx, class divisions and, by extension, class struggles must be understood in the context of new economic realities brought about by technological advances and shrinking markets and not within the context of nation-state. The theorists of dependence argue that not only development, but also independence must be redefined. In their scheme of things, achieving political independence or sovereign status does not mean "liberation," since self-determination without the means for self-sufficiency falls short of true liberation.

The theoretical formulations of the center-periphery (or metropolis-periphery) are central in PASOK's ideology. Even after PASOK in 1985, prodded by the International Monetary Fund, announced what amounts to its own version of a "new economic policy," the party did not reject its earlier positions, which claimed that unequal development stemmed from capitalist accumulation. The dependence theory remains a critical component in PASOK's analysis of current international developments, "correlation of forces" and Greece's foreign policy. In Papandreou's view, determining *where* a country belongs in the new international division of classes is the critical basis of an effective strategy for modernization and national liberation. This position has not been modified since its formulation in the early 1970s.

In his book *Paternalistic Capitalism* Papandreou adopted the central theses of the metropolis versus periphery theory, but he also attempted some additional innovations in his analysis of the new form of class struggle that pits the rich North against the poor South.

In what Papandreou considers a new situation caused by unequal development, the old Marxist interpretation of class alienation and therefore of class struggle loses its meaning. In Papandreou's view, which is shared by other neo-Marxists, the working class in developed countries does not feel allegiance with its counterparts in the developing nations; neither can working class attitudes in Third World countries be modified by the social welfarism that has become the trademark of Western European socialist parties. For economic reasons the politics of social welfare is not possible in non-industrial societies. In other words, neither Eastern socialism, nor its Western variant are relevant in explaining the new division of labor in the North versus South configuration. A *third way* must be pursued. What explains this discrepancy in the Marxist "scientism"?

In Papandreou's view, which has been imposed on or accepted by the core members of PASOK, improvement of conditions of the working class in the capitalist metropolis is possible, while the same improvement in Third World countries is neither possible nor permissible, because such improvement would reduce profit margins. In a true Leninist inversion (though he rejects Leninism as dogmatic Marxism), Papandreou attributes the higher standard of living in the advanced countries to the accumulation of surplus value (i.e., profit) made possible by the exploitation of cheap labor in the Third World. In spite of their wealth he does not see the capitalists making any significant concessions, even in the advanced countries. Thus he believes the way is open to future development of an international class consciousness. In his view:

> Improvement in the working conditions of the working class in the capitalist society is possible with some *encroachment* on the surplus value, but a more proper Marxist answer would have to be that the increase in the standard of living reflects an increase in the *social cost* of performing the duties of a wage earner in an increasingly complex society.[8]

Espousing a Leninist interpretation of why the working class in the industrial society is non-revolutionary, Papandreou sees manipulation of class relations through an old trick of the capitalists: the monopolies use part of the surplus value (created by exploitation of third world countries) to bribe the working class in advanced societies, achieving two goals simultaneously: first, they render it non-revolutionary; second, they separate it from its counterpart in developing societies. That being the case, different analyses must be utilized to explain many obvious Marxist fallacies, and different strategies must be devised to achieve socialist transformation. Whatever the nature of the differences in analysis and application, the core of Papandreou's explanation of current conditions remains Marxist, in its terminology if not in reality.

The periphery, in which Papandreou has placed Greece, is

forced by externally imposed conditions to pursue two goals simultaneously: first, to terminate its dependence on advanced countries (i.e., achieve national liberation) and, second, to acquire the economic means needed to raise the standard of living of its working class to the level of capitalist societies. Once the second goal is achieved, international class allegiance is possible and Marxist dialectics reacquire their applicability.

Papandreou is not optimistic of achieving these two interrelated goals easily, since part of his strategy is dependent on what every neo-Marxist or old Marxist calls the "impending crisis" of the capitalist society.[9] According to every self-respecting Marxist, capitalism has been in "crisis" since 1848, but it is still thriving and predictions about its impending demise are grossly exaggerated.

Papandreou sees the United States at the center of the metropolis-periphery analysis: "Following the setbacks of the seventies, marked as they were by the Vietnam debacle, international isolation and a regrouping of the countries in the periphery," the United States has become more aggressive in determining world economic trends.[10] Only because of "internal contradictions," Papandreou argues, has the United States been forced to recast "the relationship between capital and labor, so that the stagnant global product [can] be addressed."[11] But the whole effort is a sham, he believes, since its real goal is "the institutionalization of *epikyriarchia* (domination) of the United States over the global economy, and by extension the securing of its role as manager of development." Although the capitalist mode of production affects both center and periphery, the capitalists never permit it to become dominant in the periphery. This region of the world is condemned to the "pre-capitalist mode of production," characterized by cottage industries, handicrafts and a vicious cycle of product recycling in a supposedly free market. In other words, the "periphery is never allowed to develop into a self-sufficient economic or political system."[12] For this reason, development and liberation are inseparable. It is in this formulation that we trace Papandreou's heavy emphasis on national liberation for Greece.

The founding charter of PASOK, speeches before the Central Committee, "programmatic statements" before the Parliament, and effusive praise of East European and Third World Marxist states all indicate a consistent admiration of Marxist theoretical formulations. Having copied a page from neo-Marxist theorists, Papandreou has internalized a belief that the capitalists are hell-bent on maintaining a state of underdevelopment in order to maximize their profits or surplus value, which is needed to keep their own working class pacified. Underdevelopment and cheap labor are perpetuated by a deliberate maldistribution of income within Third World countries, accomplished by means of bilateral entanglements of small countries in regional or global alliances and by "corrosive" practices. Corrosion (co-opting or winning over) of local elites, is preferred to the metropolis in the opinion of PASOK ideologues. It is carried out by identifying and co-opting local individuals willing to play the role of overseers for capitalist enterprises. Greece fits the model of a Third World country, according to PASOK's ideology, even though orthodox Marxists would have difficulty with that classification. In their view the country has been subjected to systematic corrosion and alliance entanglements, except for a "brief period when E.A.M. [National Liberation Front, the Communist-dominated organization] [was dominant] during the resistance of the forties."[13]

The above excursion into the basics of Papandreou's world view should provide a framework for the interpretations of his party's foreign policy platform, which despite occasional dilutions (and American illusions) has not changed in any substantive way since PASOK came to power; it only changes in tactics.

Greece, being a developing Southern European country and desirable for its strategic location, bears all the consequences of corrosion and military entanglements, according to socialist and KKE interpretation of modern Greek history. An elite, dependent on foreign support and traditionally "toeing the line" of the protector power, began governing in 1832. NATO and the United States, the latest actors in the Greek political drama, entered the scene at the invitation of this elite, which "did not hesitate to plunge the country into a civil war." Not surprisingly, a central position of PASOK while in opposition was its opposition to NATO and the American bases. Papandreou wanted Greece out of NATO and the European Economic Community (EEC) and the bases out of Greece. That was one of the planks of his platform in the 1981 elections and (with less emphasis) in the 1985 elections:

> Greece must withdraw not only from its military alliance with NATO, but its political alliance. And all bi-lateral agreements which have allowed the Pentagon to turn Greece into an outpost of its expansionist policies must be nullified.[14]

However, he sees problems with "corrosion," which must be addressed first:

> Behind NATO, behind the American bases are the multinational monopolies and their domestic agents. This is why social liberation and socialist transformation constitute the cornerstone of our movement.[15]

Obviously, PASOK's foreign policy has been shaped by the ideological formulations of its leader, which show a remarkable degree of consistency since he entered Greek politics in the early sixties. The essential core of this position is that in order for Greece to achieve national liberation, it must deal with the problem of elite co-option and terminate the linkages that perpetuate such a state of affairs. Thus, Papandreou argued, "military bases, be it in the form of joint military groups, NATO membership, or bi-lateral ties must be abrogated,"[16] an aim at the heart of the founding document of his party, the Declaration of 3 September 1974, which he considers "non-alterable" and something that "can only be overthrown by revolution."[17]

Papandreou began with a Third World perspective when he constructed his foreign policy agenda, linking in deliberately vague manner four principles. These principles at face value seem inoffensive, but are quite revealing if placed in the historical context of their implementation. They are:

1) *National independence*, which we discussed to some extent above and will return to later;

2) *Popular sovereignty*, which is pregnant with meaning, but as practiced seems to suggest coercion of masses into a role that de facto converts them into an extension of the party;

3) *Social liberation*, which has hardly been defined by party ideologues, except to say that it is achievable through class conflict;

4) *Democratic processes*, which in application, overlap with so-called "social liberation" and certainly with sovereignty.

As stated earlier, PASOK does not accept the acquisition of de jure sovereignty of a nation as evidence of its independence; neither does it view decisions by national elites as legitimate, if such decisions necessitated linkages with major powers. Thus, the freely exercised option of the post-war Greek governments to seek (often with stern opposition from American officials, such as George Marshall) assistance from the United States in resisting internal armed aggression fomented by Yugoslavia, Albania, Bulgaria and the Soviet Union is not perceived as a decision dictated by the conditions of the times, but as a means to bring into the Greek scene "American imperialism."[18] It is worth noting in this context that textual analysis of PASOK's ideological output does not reveal similar concern about "foreign interventions" in Greek affairs, if the source of such intervention is a non-capitalist state. Thus, in his keynote address to the first and only congress of his party, Papandreou went to extreme lengths to define the meaning of intervention and threats to national independence by clearly distinguishing between "monopoly capitalism," which threatens Greek sovereignty, and Soviet state capitalism, which he absolved as non-expansionist and therefore non-threatening. Thus he states:

> A condition for the survival of capital is the incessant pursuit of the greatest profit, the subjugation of every other goal on the altar of investment, unbridled expansionism. This key characteristic does not correspond to the Soviet reality. For exactly this reason, *it is not possible for one to term the Soviet Union an imperialist power.* [19] (Emphasis supplied)

As with national sovereignty, the principle of "national liberation" is viewed by the founder of PASOK as achievable only if and when the masses become part of the governing process. When that occurs, then and only then can one talk about the existence of democratic process. However, if PASOK considers mass participation and democratic processes the cornerstone of pluralistic democracy, then the *contractual origin of the state* must be rejected outright and the totality of the body politic must be brought into the governing process (By whom? The ruling party). This perception of popular sovereignty and democratic processes, more common in Eastern European models, inflicts two serious blows to the notion of pluralistic democracy as we know it: it merges a party (or, better, superimposes it) with the social life of the country, and it frees the government from accountability/responsibility for its actions since the government can always defend itself by arguing the all-too-familiar position—the people govern, therefore, don't blame us.

The notion of social liberation is also imbued with Marxism. According to PASOK interpretation, alienation is a prerequisite to social liberation, and social liberation is achieved only through class struggle. In fact, the whole notion of social liberation in PASOK ideology is cast in terms of "working class domination," a concept which, if carried to its logical end, would mean the imposition of the dictatorship of one class over another.

Even theoretically the principle of social liberation is more difficult to justify in Greece than in Third World societies. The latter have suffered through periods as colonies, while Greece, an independent state since 1832, has in general fared no better or worse than many European states. The country did not go through the deep traumas of the industrial revolution or the classic form of class conflict that Marx envisioned, based on his experience in England. It would be ludicrous for PASOK or even the KKE (which is even more inventive in redefining Marxism) to suggest that Greek society, noted for its individualist character and entrepreneurial spirit, could be neatly divided into oppressed and oppressors, and is therefore in need of "social liberation." Yet the inability of scholars or politicians to build a theory on empirical evidence does not always prevent them from adopting the Hegelian aphorism "to hell with the facts, my theory still stands."

After taking power in 1981, the ruling Socialist party realized that there was a glaring inconsistency between theoretical principles and Greek reality. It had to "discover" a "new class" that would bridge the gap between the "oppressors" (the wealthy bourgeoisie), and the "oppressed" (the poor). The new class that has since become a fixture in the "culturistic" Greek political terminology (and is the source of endless situation comedies) is the "micro-middle class" (*mikromeseoi*) . It is defined as non-oppressive and therefore an ally of the proletariat. Yet even this interjection of another economic class (economic level is the only objective means of defining classes) makes little sense in the Greek context. In terms of real income, the *mikromeseoi* of Konitsa stand far below the street cleaners of Athens, but quite high in the social political ladder; and the wealthy of Metsovo are hardly exploitative, since their wealth is usually measured by the number of sheep they maintain, not in the number of workers they employ. Usually they employ none.

Yet PASOK defined itself as the party of the working class even though that class has been for 100 years the ward of communist parties. Defining itself on this basis, PASOK cuts itself off from Greek socio-economic reality, which cannot be explained by socialist formulations, old or new. Close socialist advisors to Papandreou and his party have serious difficulties with contemporary attempts to explain dialectically the state of socio-economic development in Greece. Such an explanation is made even more difficult by the center-periphery addition to a Marxist doctrine that has already suffered innumerable mutations.

Some scholars, among them James Petras, have noted Papandreou's propensity to define development (and liberation) in classical Marxist terms, and are sceptical about the classification of Greece in the periphery of capitalism. Such a classification, in Petras's view, is valid only if one accepts industrialization as the sole means to measure capitalist accumulation and is prepared to discard other segments of the economy, such as shipping and the tourist industry, as irrelevant. If shipping is taken into account in any measurement of development, then Greece is hardly your typical Third World or "peripheral" country.

But PASOK gains in two ways by relegating Greece to the periphery: first, the center-periphery analogy is useful to the party as an explanation of its deviation from traditional Western European socialist practices; second, it can rationalize its postponement of the socialization of wealth promised in the party's charter. It can be argued that PASOK's political platform while in power bears little resemblance to its ideological promises while in opposition. In any case, what was said, done or promised had one practical consequence: it chilled the economic environment in Greece and caused foreign investors to avoid placing their money in a country where the ruling party could not decide what its priorities were. Should it seek foreign capital in order to expedite development and ensure "national liberation," or should it keep "monopoly capitalists" out, because their involvement entails dependence. The upshot has been that PASOK's two primary goals "national liberation" and "development," which leads to it, have neatly cancelled each other out.

The behavior displayed by the Socialist party while in power shows inconsistency only in applying its pre-electoral positions to both domestic and foreign policy issues. It has adhered to its philosophy. No comprehensive efforts were undertaken by the PASOK leadership to match post-electoral performance with pre-electoral promises, but the articulated goals have yet to be revised. Depending on one's perspective, the failure of PASOK to "deliver" can be reassuring or dismaying. It is reassuring to those who always thought that Papandreou never meant all those bad things he was saying on the road to power (the look-at-what-he-is-doing-not-what-he-said, thesis); it is dismaying to the Left wing of his party who realize that their suspicions that Papandreou was a pseudo-Marxist, with intellectual roots in the America academia of the sixties were well-grounded. In their view the PASOK leadership has displayed gross unreliability and a willingness to be co-opted by the political establishment.

Predictably, the Left-wing followers of PASOK accused Papandreou of right-wing deviation.[20] Stathis Panagoulis, an early believer in Papandreou's charisma but not necessarily in his message, mocks the prime minister's superficiality in redefining class relations in Greek society and his generous attempt to absolve the Greek industrialists from any exploitative sins, classifying them as middlemen in a complex economy.[21] Others felt betrayed by the leader's abandonment of positions, which critically weakens the entire theoretical formula on which the dependence theory and the concept of "liberation" and "sovereignty" were based. In fact, the critics go as far as arguing that Papandreou has caused as much dependence (both economic and military) on the powers that in the 1970s he decried as detrimental to Greece. Thus Petras laments:

> After five years of Papandreou government Greece still exports apples and imports apple juice from West Germany; it imports feta cheese from Denmark, lamb from New Zealand and calamari from the Peoples Republic of China.[22]

No doubt many of the contradictions between pre-electoral promises and post-electoral practice were forced upon PASOK by factors beyond its control such as economic exigencies originating beyond Greek borders. But there are compromises that have all the characteristics of political opportunism, which at least in the short run seem to cancel all pretenses to a "proud Greek foreign policy," one conceived by Greeks and not by external powers. Petras, perhaps the most articulate critic of post-1981 policies, sees "an historic compromise" between Papandreou and Washington at the expense of both national liberation and sovereignty. "In exchange for office," he argues, "[Papandreou] sacrificed the program of his party... the U.S. got status quo; the people got balcony rhetoric."[23] Few people, liberal or conservative, however, believe that the "compromise," if in fact true, is irreversible. Given Papandreou's track record, it can legitimately be said that the only thing predictable about him is his unpredictability.

Before we leave national liberation, independence and

sovereignty, an attempt must be made to place these concepts in the context of Greek reality and East-West competition for dominance. After all, Greece has been a prime example of the intense efforts made by the Soviet Union to expand its control over the area and has served as the critical test in the implementation of the Truman Doctrine.

As stated, Papandreou and the followers of the dependence school regard susceptibility to penetration and corruption of elites as the central problem of countries in the periphery. PASOK has not offered concrete solutions to these "evils." In fact, Papandreou has appointed more American-educated people to government positions than any other post-war government, but still has opted to put ideological *distance* between Greece and the capitalist metropolis as the best substitute for policy. In practice, distance means preventing the Greek economy from becoming structurally integrated with advanced capitalist enterprises, which quite often tend to promote the political interests of their own governments. Furthermore, integration of unevenly developed states invariably means dependence of the weaker on the stronger and perpetuation of underdevelopment.

However, this aversion to economic integration with capitalist economies (more explicitly manifested in PASOK's pre-1981 anti-EEC posture) is not reflected in the party's attitudes towards integrating Greece's economy with Eastern European and Soviet enterprises. Dealing with the capitalist West, PASOK ideologues argue, is a far more serious matter because the pursuit of profits becomes a cause of domination and because the state becomes "a cog in the process of private planning by the corporate establishment."[24] In their view, profit leads to expansion. The capital-state relationship is viewed as the motor "behind expansionism and national subjugation," and economic dependence of any duration must be avoided. "For free-market capitalism," Papandreou argued, "the state's role was limited to providing the legal framework for its operation, as well as, of course, to assisting its expansion beyond the nation's shores in imperialist adventures."[25] He does not see a similar risk of dependence in dealings with socialist states. In fact, attempts by the Soviet Union at dominance are viewed as qualitatively different; they are never seen as a threat. A brief comparison of positions on this matter is in order.

In his address to the 1984 party congress, Papandreou

offered the following assessment of U.S. and Soviet roles in contemporary affairs:

> The U.S. is attempting to establish and consolidate a new international division of labour, by pursuing and applying new methods and options. Using its rich and long-term experience, it is reshaping the world correlation of power, while adapting to specific local conditions. *With all the means at its disposal, its strategy is aimed as it has always been, at expansion and domination. The continual propagation of the Imperium* .[26] (Emphasis supplied)

The condemnation of the United States contrasts sharply with the favorable assessment of the Soviet Union's role in world affairs. Besides absolving Moscow of any exploitative characteristics, Papandreou has also re-defined "dominance," as applied to the Soviet Union, so that it is no longer pejorative:

> The USSR dominance does not spring from economic necessity, from the operational framework of its socio-economic system, as is the case of the U.S., *but from its strategic needs, and therefore from its strategic aspirations* .[27] (Emphasis supplied)

Making a clear distinction between the United States' motives for expansion and the Soviet Union's, Papandreou proceeds to rationalize Soviet incursions in the periphery as reactions to imperialist moves. In his view, such incursions "could be interpreted as a result of its [the Soviet Union's] efforts to guard itself against U.S. expansionism."[28]

There is no doubt that the core of PASOK's ideology is derived from the untested and, one could say, failed theories of the dependence school of neo-Marxist thought. This ideological ball of wax provides the movement with a theoretical ambiguity that permits it to adopt a Marxist analysis without using the analysis as a guide for action. PASOK avoided adopting the Leninist revisions of Marxism, which were conveniently dismissed by Papandreou as "dogmatism." Adoption of the Leninist variant of Marxism would have alienated the military and other institutional groups from PASOK. These groups have fought for generations with the overwhelming support of the Greek people to ally their country with the advanced Western democracies and against the bloc that takes inspiration from Lenin. Although this thesis needs further testing, the writer believes that the "rejection" of Leninist dogmatism by PASOK, in light of its overall view of the Soviet Union, can be interpreted as a tactical maneuver.

To compensate for the tactical rejection of Leninist praxis and to entice the generation of the forties into his political camp, Papandreou has unashamedly laid claim to the ideological heritage of the [Greek] National Liberation Front (E.A.M.)--the umbrella resistance organization created in 1942 with instructions from Comintern and the help of Marshall Tito of Yugoslavia.

Papandreou not only considers the resistance put up by E.A.M. and the communists in the forties heroic but also as the "sole instance" in modern Greek history that national sovereignty was achieved in its true form. The PASOK leader who missed both the war and the resistance (and from the safe haven of America romanticized it) fashions himself the successor of E.A.M. In an article on the subject, published in *Exormese* (PASOK's theoretical organ), the continuity between E.A.M. and PASOK is stressed.[29] He repeated the same theme in his programmatic statement before the Greek Parliament on 21 November 1981. The continuity theme goes further than simple ideological sympathy. Papandreou appointed 17 people from E.A.M. to ministerial or sub-ministerial posts in his first cabinet and almost all remain in important posts in today's party apparatus. Among them are Paraskeuas Augerinos (former minister of welfare), Giannes Skoularikes (former minister of public order, who as a youth was active in E.P.O.N., E.A.M.'s branch for the young), Eustathios Alexandres (former minister of justice), Apostolos Lazares (minister to the prime minister) and Euangelos Couloumbis (minister of environment). The latter two were members of E.P.O.N.[30]

PASOK expressed an affinity for the ideological heritage of E.A.M.--an organization controlled from the outset by the Greek Communist party—is a deliberate attempt to separate itself from the liberal center. The center was too constraining for Andreas in the sixties, since it had in its ranks established political personalities of impeccable democratic credentials, who were unwilling to accept Papandreou's centralistic and authoritarian style of leadership. Many of them felt offended to have someone who had been absent from the critical struggles of the nation impose a new form of paternalism.

In Papandreou's designs, the only value the liberal center had was to serve as a source of moderate party members, whom he could use as evidence of his party's broad appeal and who would assure his wavering voters that PASOK was a legitimate choice. Under no circumstance would he lead a party of the center, which was philosophically the equivalent of Western European social democracy. Thus, in 1974, when Giannes

Aleuras (later president of the Parliament) presented Papandreou with a letter signed by 124 former deputies of the Center Union party asking him to assume its leadership for a second time in six years, he turned down the offer.[31] In 1968 his father had asked him to represent his party abroad. He rejected the idea because he viewed the Greek problem as solvable through a national liberation struggle, similar in character to that of E.A.M., not through the political process of free elections.[32] In 1974, the reasoning was similar: Papandreou would not assume the leadership of a bourgeois party which had too many members considered unreliable and which would therefore not advance the cause of national independence. He would rather create a new party structured in accordance with principles of democratic centralism and based on the ideology of the only movement in modern Greek history that he viewed as "having a Greek perspective," namely, E.A.M. It is not a coincidence that among the "operational sources" close to the leader's desk are the following two books: *What is E.A.M. and What Does It Want?* (Ti Einai kai ti Thelei to E.A.M.) and Mao Zedong's: *On Democratic Centralism.*[33] Papandreou went so far as to legalize communist participation in Greek politics, formally rehabilitating E.A.M. in 1982. When he legitimized the Left en masse, the entire opposition walked out of Parliament.[34] No distinction was made between E.A.M. supporters and K.K.E. members, who had been responsible for a bloody civil war that almost turned Greece into a Soviet satellite. In 1985, the commander of ELAS (the Communist Liberation Army), General Markos Vafiades, returned the favor to Papandreou: he organized approximately 300 *kapetanioi* (chieftains) of the Greek Communist resistance to campaign for PASOK.[35]

One can argue that Papandreou's affinity for E.A.M. ideology is connected to his overall theory of economic determinism, mostly borrowed from contemporary neo-Marxists. The Balkan experience of Communist-dominated resistance to the Nazis and Fascists could not be fully explained in usual Marxist terms, unless nationalism and national liberation could be somehow fused into the Marxist core. The turn of events in the forties, the premature attempt by the Greek Communists to seize power in December 1944 in a coup d'état, and the advent of the cold war did not leave much room for theoretical innovations in the East or West. The whole idea of Third World was rejected in 1948 by the Zhdanov Doctrine.

Stalin's heir apparent neatly divided the world into two camps. The Stalinist fallacies and their Western counter-fallacies were "corrected" by Nikita Khrushchev, who took another look into the "periphery countries" and introduced a few innovations of his own concerning the process of transition to socialism. Among Khrushchev's innovations was the acceptance of national democracy as another form of socialist state wedged between the capitalist system and the system of the countries known as people's democracies. Following the revisions of Khrushchev, a number of Western theoretical experimentations were undertaken, including the so-called center-periphery analogy. These innovations, merging class struggle and nationalism, were given an additional push forward with Lin Biao's and Mao Zedong's revolutionary theory, which comes even closer to the dependence viewpoint.[36] It is worth noting that the analysis based on the center-periphery theory was carried out even as the non-aligned movement was emerging and competition between the Soviet Union and China was growing, with each seeking to influence the course of events in the southern hemisphere.

Linking E.A.M. ideology to the post-1960 ideology of liberation leaves little room for PASOK to behave as a traditional Western European socialist movement. On the contrary, Papandreou sees social democracy as regressive and detrimental to the causes of national liberation and popular sovereignty and persists in maintaining the theoretical and practical distinctiveness of his party as compared to its Western European socialist counterparts. Such a distinctiveness is essential for a successful implementation of his program of change, which in his view must encompass, among other things: a change in the value system; re-distribution of wealth; removal of American and Western influences; creation of a neutral Balkan zone free of nuclear weapons and military bases; and a re-definition of the relationship between party and state.

These fundamental changes, contrary to assertions of "bourgeoisification" of PASOK, have been pursued consistently but with tactical finesse during the past six years. Such policy goals could not have been possible if social democracy had been accepted as an alternative.

Papandreou has criticized the weaknesses he sees in social democracy and the members of the Second International (the organization that Karl Marx helped establish in 1864 and the only one he formally belonged to). In particular, he does not accept, as the social democrats do, peaceful transition to socialism, reallocation of wealth via progressive taxation, rather than outright seizure, and assumption of power by the working class. These issues had separated Lenin from Bernstein and Kautsky. The latter two believed (and proved to be correct) that the working class does not have to go through the traumas of another Paris Commune to achieve equality or assume political power. The examples of French socialists, West German social democrats and British labourites confirm the correctness of Bernstein and Kautsky, and stand in sharp contradiction to the Leninist theory that revolution is the only road to socialism.

Papandreou's objection to social democracy depends on a Leninist interpretation of Marxism, but he accepts only half of such an interpretation: the dialectical analysis without the dogmatic praxis. Thus it is ironic that, disposing of Lenin's dogmatic praxis himself, Papandreou should claim to reject social democracy as his model because Western European social democrats have forsworn Leninist dogmatic praxis. He dismisses social democracy as the caretaker of capital. He has come closer to adopting Eurocommunism because it at least maintains that class struggle as one of the methods to socialist transformation is not inevitable. As Santiago Carrillo explained and Papandreou agrees, "Eurocommunism proposes to transform capitalist society, not to administer it; to work out a socialist alternative to the system of state monopoly capitalism, not to integrate in it and become one of its governmental variables."[37] Papandreou started from exactly the same position in his search for power and has not deviated from it. This Eurocommunist thesis is the essence of *allage* (change) and it is on this crucial point that Papandreou and social democrats have parted company. To the extent that cooperation now takes place, it is not ideological but pragmatic. The crucial differences between PASOK's ideology and social democracy have been summarized by Papandreou as follows:

> Social Democracy does not aim at the abolition of exploitation of man by man but at the amelioration of class differences with a view to maintaining the system, to consolidate and maintain the monopoly and imperialist capitalism. For this reason the marginal reforms social democracy advances, reforms whose goal is to cover up the contradictions and weaknesses of the system, *are not steps towards socialism but measures of staving it off.*.[38] (Emphasis supplied)

However, his party is different:

> In contradiction, our socialist movement is based on the principle that *we must pass beyond capitalism to a socialist transformation. Which means that the social relations of production must change fundamentally* .[39] (Emphasis supplied)

In order to avoid any doubts about what distinguishes PASOK's ideology from social democracy, Papandreou has dealt with the subject on numerous occasions and in various publications (both before and after his assumption of power). He has set a course for his party that is distinct from that of European social democratic parties. We may summarize the core of his differences as follows: first, social democratic parties advocate *reform* (which Papandreou perceives as support of capitalist accumulation of wealth), whereas PASOK seeks transformation; second, social democrats do not reallocate wealth in their own countries, even though they have had ample opportunity in government, but PASOK does; third, social democrats accept the notion that the state is a *neutral actor* in the governing process and serves as arbitrator of social contradictions, but PASOK sees the state as an *instrument* in the hands of the working class or the party that represents it, to be used in "socialist construction." The state, in PASOK's analysis, is the critical agent that can be used either by reactionaries to postpone socialist transformation or by a workers party to attain socialism.

In his pre-1981 elaboration of the process of transition to socialism, Papandreou castigated Western European social democracy for its deceitful tactics and for its postponement of the socialist agenda. "Social democracy must not be judged by its declarations, but by its actions," he argued. "What is its praxis? It supported monopoly capital, monopoly capitalism in Western Europe; and it is substantially reformist, renewed capitalism with a better face."[40] Social contradictions, PASOK believes, cannot be overcome with the acceptance of social democracy's faulty logic. "Within the social democratic logic the marginal reforms taking effect in countries governed by labor and social democratic parties simply change and modernize the form of capitalism; they do not, however, change its fundamental structure."[41] PASOK's policy is aimed at changing capitalism fundamentally. And here we note a serious contradiction in the party's ideology.

The main problem that Papandreou has with the Mitterrands or the Willy Brandts is similar to the problem that Lenin had with Kautsky and Bernstein, namely, reformism versus radicalism. If PASOK's radicalism, as opposed to the social democrats' reformism, is the central element of disagreement, then PASOK is actually propounding something like Leninism. Its rejection of Leninism is thus meaningless and must be viewed either as a rhetorical scheme intended to pacify those in Greek society who find Leninism repugnant, or it may simply be an exercise in hair-splitting. No matter what the intent, the question remains in the minds of supporters and opponents alike: Is PASOK a Marxist party or at least a Marxist variant? Instead of extrapolating a response from the totality of the party's ideological output, we will refer the reader to Papandreou's pre-1981 positions, which thus far have neither been rejected nor amended. We must note, however, that a favorite indoor game of intellectuals is under way in Greece. With the help of American sympathizers (including some members of the U.S. Congress), they amuse themselves by playing down the strident ideology of the pre-1981 period, dismissing it as electoral exaggerations. They redefine Papandreou as a politician in the mold of the post-Vietnam American generation. The "give-him-the-benefit-of-the-doubt" school of thought advises that we evaluate earlier positions in the context of policy output. That advice, besides being overly charitable, ignores the fact that PASOK as a party has never abandoned earlier ideological positions. On the contrary, its leader keeps reminding his followers that only tactics change, that goals never do, and that the "Declaration of 3 September 1974 can only be overthrown by revolution." Answering directly the question about PASOK's being a Marxist party, Papandreou said:

> The next question is: Are we Marxists, yes or no? There is no reason to leave these questions dangling... If with the term *Marxist* we mean the method of historical analysis that we have inherited from Marx, who talks about the struggles of classes, about the structure of the state, about dialectical determinism, if that is what we mean, we are obliged as a socialist party to say yes. And for that reason our opposition to liberal thought is absolute, such as for example that the state is a neutral entity .[42]

Following the 1985 elections the Panhellenic Socialist Movement has modified its earlier views about its class character and its ideological relationship to Marxism. These changes, according to some, were dictated by economic difficulties coupled with an intense effort to correct image problems that have kept investors away from the Greek market, causing high unemployment and double-digit inflation.[43] However, even with these modifications, there is a consistent pattern between early and current PASOK ideology. Any careful evaluation of theory and practice would reveal that the Socialist party has not deviated in any meaningful way from its core tenets. Though Greek pluralism has remained more or less the same during the past six years, anti-pluralistic tendencies of the ruling party have become widespread (some have even become institutionalized), which raises fears of future political irregularities.[44] Fears of non-democratic practices (i.e., violation of laws, arbitrary invasion of privacy, telephone tapping, de facto expropriation of private property, interference in church affairs, and so on) as a rule are traceable to PASOK's theory on the role of state.

As indicated earlier in this essay, one of the fundamental differences between PASOK's ideology and social democracy concerns the role of the state. Social Democracy, as well as other pluralistic parties, view the state as a neutral entity that arbitrates conflicts and resolves disputes among competing interests. All social democratic parties have accepted the contractual origin of the state and the basic principles under which contractualism operates. Central among these principles is the idea that governments ought to be constrained by explicit rules (i.e., constitutions) in their exercise of power.[45] Papandreou and his party reject the concept of a neutral state. With the exception of dialectical analysis, Leninism has been repudiated as dogmatic Marxism, yet Papandreou has embraced the Leninist view of the state as an instrument in the hands of a ruling class (or party) to be used to neutralize its opposition and impose its rule on society.[46] Concerned that his cadres would be disappointed if he abandoned this central thesis after he assumed power, Papandreou assured them that PASOK would not fall into the trap of social-democratic praxis; it would not be reduced to the level of manager of class interests, instead it would be an instrument of socialist transformation:

> I wish to give my personal assurances to the cadres and the members of the movement that we have no desire for PASOK to be a simple expressor, or another manager of the interests of the establishment. *I do not forget for a moment—neither do my associates—that we are a socialist movement and our goal is the socialist transformation of society*.[47] (Emphasis supplied)

In pursuit of social transformation Papandreou has imposed the party's will on the state and the government in ways that would be viewed as totalitarian in pluralistic societies. In the first meeting with PASOK cadres after the 1981 election, he all but formally announced the principle that his party is "the leading force" of both the state and society. To preserve that role he warned his followers to beware of three risks that could undermine its status as leading force: first, "at all costs the absorption of the PASOK organization by the state authority" must be avoided because "something like that would have led quickly to its wilting and to its transformation into either an electoral mechanism or to a structure that simply prepares some technocrats to participate in power."[48] Simply put, the party should be the force that uses the state to obtain the socialist transformation; it should not *supplant* the state. Second, while the party must remain above the state (and use it), its cadres should not to be too shy about being involved in directing the state. The party should not "free itself from the governmental policy [and see it] as if it were the governmental policy of another movement, or another party."[49] Third, he advised the cadres not to be too zealous by making the "movement the policeman of the government in the sense that it will replace the governmental functions in the daily clashes and developments."[50]

The third admonition is strikingly similar to Soviet views on the role of the party. Article 60 of the Rules of the Communist Party of the Soviet Union states: "Party organizations operate within the framework of the USSR Constitution; they do not *supplant* Soviet, trade union, cooperatives and other public organizations."[51] But, as in the Soviet Union, in no instance is PASOK to abandon its "tasks" of spearheading the transition to socialism. Emphasizing the significance of PASOK in governing the country and underscoring its hierarchical structure, Papandreou reminded his cadres who is the boss: "the general framework of PASOK's activities is formulated through the organs of the Central Committee, the Politburo and its chairman."[52] Following through on his view of the role of the state, Papandreou has all but obliterated the function of the Greek Parliament. Almost a year elapsed after he assumed power before he met with his parliamentary group.[53]

Papandreou's view of the state is evident in several other areas: in the functions of the Parliament and the constitution; in the relationship of the state he inherited to "parastate" that he espouses as essential; and in the role of the state in mobilizing the masses to pursue the ultimate goal of socialism.

In an important 1979 interview, Papandreou insisted that even the constitution of a country must reflect class relations and under no circumstances must be viewed as beyond the reach of the Socialist party. After all, he argued, constitutions, too, reflect economic interests; attempts to change them are therefore legitimate:

> In our country today there is a Constitution which defines the institutions with capitalist social structures in mind. It is however, natural, that when PASOK comes to power to push for a revision of constitutional provisions, so as to secure new foundations, which will facilitate the socialist transformation of society.[54]

Six years after he spoke these words, Papandreou changed the Greek constitution, reducing the powers of the presidency (thus eliminating a safety valve in the system), and changed the electoral law to make it legal for the leader of the party and the Politburo to select all candidates for elections to Parliament. Thus he superimposed the party on the Parliament and the state, as Lenin did in November 1917.

Consistent with Papandreou's perception of the state is his view that the party needs special mechanisms to protect itself from class enemies, even when it is in power. In an interview given in 1974, only three months before the downfall of the junta, he advocated unequivocally creation of extra-legal mechanisms for the control of power, which would be needed during the inevitable clash with the forces of conservation. In preparation for such a clash, he advised:

> The electoral victory of the Left does not mean assumption of power. You will find us in Ministries, and what would you do afterwards? The government must be conquered by people who defend themselves and possess the means of coercion.... We must know it, that the clash will be unavoidable and we must start preparing for that now. We must immediately create striking teams, able to resist to the violence of the bourgeois state and to impose the legitimate power of authority. We must create independent means of communications, administration at several levels, men determined and trained. [55]

This principle, calling for the creation of independent means of defense *after* assumption of power, has been partially carried out during the past six years. In excess of 3,000 mass PASOK organizations function in all structures of society, often supervising state organs. Wiretapping of telephones has been widespread during the past six years according to Constantine Mitsotakis, leader of New Democracy, and Leonidas Kyrkos, leader of the United Left party. Moreover, traditional means of communications between party and state have been superseded. An informal inner party, above Parliament and cabinet determines and executes policy. Party organizations have been established even within the armed forces (see the chapter on Defense Policies).

The role of the party and its determination to treat the state as its tool is acutely visible in PASOK's policies concerning the socialization of wealth through the introduction of the idea of "self-management." Self-management, a concept borrowed from Yugoslavia, serves the purpose of collectivization and socialization, without raising undue fears among the *mikromeseoi*, the bourgeois class that is included in his dialectical analysis of socialist transformation. However, Papandreou has tried to improve on the Yugoslav model by including the state in the management of the enterprise, be it an agricultural cooperative or a factory. In introductory remarks to his book *Transition to Socialism* (Metavase Sto Socialismo), Papandreou "modifies" the Yugoslav model as follows:

> We [in PASOK] add that not only is it necessary for the workers to participate in management; they must also take part in local government. The local government or the municipality has responsibility for any productive activity [business or factory] depending on the relative size of the enterprise, taking place in a specific area.[56]

The Yugoslav model leaves the government out of the process of managing an enterprise. PASOK, on the other hand, wants to institutionalize the management of productive forces, which, in Papandreou's view of economics as the foundation of a future without monopoly capitalism, are too important to be left outside of party control. Towards this end two troublesome legislative decrees were adopted: the first constrains labor union activities (Legislative Decree 1264/1987) and the second establishes "social controls" to oversee the operation of enterprises (Decree 1385/1983). Thanks to direct involvement of the party, Papandreou envisions "the replacement of the capitalist mode of production" by a socialist one. This process will free the working class from conditions of dependency and exploitation and will lead to national liberation. Thus, his ideological edifice culminates in the socialization of production, control of the state by the party, and creation of special security organs that guard against an inevitable conservative reaction. The state at the same time is used to create the "socialist man."

All these add up to what even politicians who are not conservatives (for example, George I. Rallis) see as abuse of the state mechanism for ideological ends:

> The PASOK government, in an anxious effort to uproot the liberal consciousness as soon as possible, conducts a systematic Marxist propaganda in schools and universities with the help of "drafted teachers" and "revised" textbooks. It introduces Marxist dialectics, distorts history and persists in separating the youth from our national and Christian heritage, trying to create the "model" of socialist man.[57]

Any careful examination of PASOK's ideology, even in brief, as is the case here, shows that it is at variance with pluralism and is akin to orthodox Marxism. It is true that the party has been pragmatic, carefully avoiding any actions that would provoke Western powers. Nevertheless, a consistent and rational process towards single-party domination has been launched, which may gain sufficient momentum to continue after Papandreou's career is over. The empirical evidence accumulated thus far suggests the institutionalization of deep changes that will affect government policy for years to come.

Certain effects of PASOK's ideology should be noted. First, PASOK's undermining of the legislative branch is regressive in a country that has had some form of parliament for 125 years. Most reputable centrist figures have been passed over as candidates for office because they are labelled "unreliable" or "capable of creating alternative centers of power."

Second, consistent with his views on the role of the state, PASOK has reduced the cabinet to rubber-stamp status. Only those who have both party and state positions influence policy.[58] Eight cabinet changes have been made in less than seven years—107 officials have been shuffled. Government instability and management by an upper echelon of party members (a changeable group epitomizing the politics of musical chairs) tends to spread responsibility for failures. It also emphasizes the pre-eminence of the party over Parliament and the executive. Cabinet members, the logic goes, tend to acquire prominence if they stay too long in their posts, and prominence undermines centralism.

Third, the emphasis on classical Marxist class struggle in a society known for its individualistic tendencies has encouraged social antagonisms that hamper the management of a modern economy. Furthermore, emphasis on cooperative and collective principles, overt and covert relations with Eastern European states (which seem to be closer with the two most regressive regimes, Romania and Bulgaria), and expansion of party-to-party relations between PASOK and the Communist Party of the Soviet Union have made the Greek public oblivious to any threat from the north. If trends continue, the rationale for Greece's alliance with NATO and the United States becomes dubious.

Fourth, PASOK has, in the name of "total" democracy, adopted the concept of mass participation in politics, which in its application tends to negate the philosophical foundations of pluralism and institutionalize the superimposition of the party on the state, the Parliament, the cabinet and the masses. By its adoption of mass participation PASOK, in the manner of East European parties, has affirmed the idea that it possesses a "natural" right to be the leading force in society. The bent of PASOK's ideology was revealed in a poll of PASOK Central Committee members. Of 25 respondents only three saw French socialism as a worthy model, 11 chose the Yugoslav League of Communists as their model, while the rest were split between Iraq's Baath Party, and similar third world structures.[59]

In sum, cumulative evidence supports the argument that PASOK's ideology shows consistency, whereas its praxis is characterized by pragmatism and careful balancing of pertinent variables. Changes have indeed been brought about in Greek society at all levels, but they are more pronounced in the fundamental relationship between the state and the individual. The government has expanded its role under PASOK. The individual Greek citizen is compelled by policies, ideology and economic needs to accommodate himself to a new system that has renounced the neutrality of the state and reduced the rulemaking bodies to party instruments.

Since the 1985 elections, PASOK has entered a phase of deradicalization, ideological disorientation and decline. Deradicalization of socialist and Marxist movements is a predictable phenomenon and is explainable by several factors such as: success of party or movement in stabilizing its power and neutralizing challenges to it; co-option of elites and longevity in power. In PASOK's case moderation can also be seen in its increasing tendency to reject its former slogans. It has been prompted by severe economic problems. The party is now searching for appealing, less threatening policies to broaden its base and entice foreign investments. The party's decline is reflected in ideological disarray and a rather curious attempt to define itself as the Greek Left par excellence.[60] But, while the party manifests all the characteristics of a movement in decline, its leader remains pivotal in the Greek political scene and an effective tactician in explaining away the massive contradictions that have beset his version of socialism.

NOTES

1. "Theseis tes Kentrikes Epitropes to KKE gia to Dodekato Synedrio" (Theses of the Central Committee of KKE for the 12th Congress), *Rizospastes* , 8 February 1987.

2. Andreas G. Papandreou, "Ti Einai to PASOK?" (What Is PASOK?) in his *Gia mia Sosialistike Koinonia* (For a Socialist Society), (Athens: Aichme, 1984) 21-28. For an effective comparative analysis of PASOK's ideology and politics see Spyros C. Phillippas, "The Panhellenic Socialist Movement: Ideology and Politics" (Ph.D. Dissertation, George Washington University, 1986).

3. Nikolaos A. Stavrou, "PASOK and Greek-American Relations," *Greek Accent* , Vol. 6, No. 4, February 1986.

4. Demos M. Botsaris, *Apokalypto tous Koryphaious tou PASOK* (I Expose PASOK's Top Leaders), (Athens: Isokrates Publishers, 1983) 47. See also Nicholas Gage, "The Paradoxical Papandreou," *New York Times Magazine* , 21 March 1982.

5. Louis Fischer, *The Life of Lenin* (New York: Harper and Row Publishers, 1964): 17.

6. Gage, "The Paradoxical Papandreou," 74.

7. Samir Amin, *Accumulation on a World Scale: A Critique of the Theory of Underdevelopment* (New York: Monthly Review of Books, 1974) and Herb Addo (editor), *Transforming the World Economy: Nine Critical Essays on the New International Economic Order* (London: Hodder and Stoughton, 1984).

8. Andreas G. Papandreou, *Paternalistic Capitalism* (Minneapolis: The University of Minnesota Press, 1972): 59.

9. Andreas G. Papandreou, "Speech to the 19th Plenum of the [PASOK] Central Committee," *ANA Daily Bulletin* , 1 September 1986, 1.

10. Panhellenic Socialist Movement, *Hoi Theseis tes Kentrikes Epitropes tou PASOK gia to Synedrio* (Theses of the Central Committee of PASOK for the Congress) (Athens: Aichme, 1984) 7. This document was widely circulated for public debate, prior to the first and only PASOK Congress of 10-12 May 1984).

11. Stelios Kouloglou, *Sta Ichne tou Tritou Dromou* (On the Tracks of the Third World) (Athens: Odysseas, 1987): 42.

12. Andreas G. Papandreou, "Metropolis, Periphery, Independent Development and Social Change" in *He Metavase sto Sosialismo: Problemata kai Strategike gia to Helleniko Kinema* (Transition to Socialism: Problems and Strategy for the Greek Movement) (Athens:

Aichme, 1984) 50-62. Thereafter referred to as *Transition to Socialism: Problems and Strategy*.

13. Andreas G. Papandreou, *Democracy at Gunpoint: The Greek Front* (New York: Doubleday and Company, 1970) 62-79. See also *Exormese* (official organ of PASOK Central Committee), 9 September 1977.

14. *PASOK: The Organizations* (Athens: International Relations Committee Series A. Publication) No. 1, (September 1975): 5.

15. *Ibid.*, 5.

16. *Hoi Theseis tes Kentrikes Epitropes tou PASOK gia to Synedrio*, 28.

17. *Ibid.*, 7. See also Kouloglou, *Sta Ichne tou Tritou Dromou.* and "Speech of Andreas Papandreou, President of PASOK, at the Meeting of the Provisional Central Committee" (9 January 1975) in *PASOK, The Organization*, 5 ff. In that speech Papandreou made the following statement, which he has not revised: "There is no legitimate process within the Movement which would permit the overthrow of a single one of the principles which were formulated [in the Declaration of] 3 September."

18. Papandreou, *Democracy at Gunpoint*, 67-68.

19. Papandreou, *Full Text of Speech By Prime Minister and PASOK President Andreas Papandreou at the PASOK Congress* (Athens: *ANA* Feature Stories, No. 158): 11. See also *New York Times* and *Washington Post*, 11 May 1984.

The U.S. Department of State formally protested this assertion by Prime Minister Papandreou, who in turn rejected the protest since he was speaking as party leader, not as prime minister.

20. Stathis Panagoulis letter to Prime Minister and President of PASOK Comrade Andreas G. Papandreou, 24 August 1982. In a thirteen-page letter (a copy of the original is in the possession of the author), Mr. Panagoulis castigates the "bourgeoisification" of PASOK and Papandreou's rejection of the principle "government with the people, not on their behalf."

21. *Ibid.*

22. James Petras, "The Crisis of a Crumbling Populism," *Against the Current* Nos. 4 & 5 (1987): 17.

23. *Ibid.*, 17.

24. Papandreou, *Paternalistic Capitalism*, 91.

25. *Ibid.*, 90.

26. Papandreou, "Speech to the [PASOK] Congress," 10-12 May 1984, 2.

27. *Ibid.*, 12.

28. *Ibid.*

29. *Exormese*, 9 September 1977.

30. For biographical statements about PASOK top leaders see

Mesembrine , 16 October 1981; *Rizospastes*, 29 August 1982; and *To Vema* , 29 August 1982 and 1 January 1980, which list all members of the Politburo of PASOK.

31. Kouloglou, *Sta Ichne tou Tritou Dromou*, 34.

32. Andreas G. Papandreou refused to participate in the second congress of EDIN (The Center Union Youth) held in Vienna in 1971. He sent a representative to make his position clear, i.e., that the "Greek problem" could only be solved by a national liberation struggle, not by politics as usual. In 1967, he turned down his father's offer to assume the Center Union's leadership, but still claimed to represent it abroad in order to prevent George Mylonas from assuming the leadership. See Kouloglou, *Sta Ichne tou Tritou Dromou* , 10.

33. Kouloglou, 45.

34. *Praktika Boules* (Parliamentary Minutes). Third Period Session A. 19 August 1982, 703-722.

35. "Who Doesn't Remember Markos' Support for Papandreou?," *National Herald*, 18 September 1987.

36. Lin Biao, "Long Live the People's War," *Peking Review* , September, 1964. See also Herbert J. Ellison (editor), *The Sino-Soviet Conflict: A Global Perspective* (Seattle: Washington University Press, 1982): 16-22.

37. Santiago Carrillo, *Eurocommunism and the State* (Westport, Conn.: Lawrence & Hill Co., 1978): 103-104.

38. Andreas G. Papandreou, "Hoi Diaphores mas me te Sosial Demokratia" (Our Differences With Social Democracy) in A. Kokkos and A. Mourike-Kostopoulou (editors) *He Metavase sto Sosialismo* (Transition to Socialism) (Athens: Ekdoseis Aletri, 1981): 45-46.

39. *Ibid.*, 45.

40. *Ibid.*

41. *Ibid.*, 12.

42. Andreas G. Papandreou, *Gia mia Sosialistike Koinonia, Koinonekopoiese, Autodiacheirise, Apokentrose, Topike Autodioikise, Syndikalismos* (Athens: 1977). (For a Socialist Society: Socialization, Self-Management, Decentralization, Local Self Government, Syndicalism), 37. See also George Katephores, "Greece: The Empiricist Socialism of PASOK," *Socialist Economic Review* (London: The Medin Press, 1983) 53.

43. Andreas Andrianopoulos, "Politike Physiognomia tou PASOK" (Political Profile of PASOK) *Epikentra* , July-August, 1978, 25-30. See also Euangelos Averoff-Tossizza, *Allage: Nai, PASOK: Ochi* (Change: Yes, PASOK: No) (Athens, 1981): 14.

44. "Mitsotakis Fears PASOK Will Cause Constitutional Problems," *National Herald* 4 October 1987, 1. Constantine Mitsotakis is the leader of the opposition party New Democracy.

45. Brian R. Nelson, *Western Political Thought: From Socrates to the Age of Ideology* (Englewood Cliffs, N.J.: Prentice-Hall, 1982): 159-190.

46. V. I. Lenin, "State and Revolution" in *Selected Works, Vol. 2* (Moscow: Progress Publishers, 1970): 289-292.

47. Andreas G. Papandreou, *Speeches of Prime Minister Andreas G. Papandreou, 1981-1982* (Athens: General Secretariat of Press and Information, 1982): 94.

48. *Ibid.*

49. *Ibid.*

50. *Ibid.*

51. Donald D. Barry and Carol B. Barry, *Contemporary Soviet Politics: An Introduction* (Englewood Cliffs, N.J.: Prentice-Hall, 1987): 370.

52. Papandreou, *Speeches,1981-82* , 92.

53. Stathis Panagoulis, "Letter to the Prime Minister and President of PASOK Comrade Andreas G. Papandreou," 24 August 1982, 3.

54. *Auge*, (Organ of the Communist Party of the Interior), 4 November 1979, 1.

55. Gus Sitbon, "Interview with Andreas Papandreou," *Nouvel Observateur,* 1 April 1974.

The prime minister was challenged in Parliament by the leader of the opposition to state whether he had rejected these earlier views. He declined to do so.

See also *Praktika tes Boules, Synedriasis PMD* (Athens, 30 May 1987): 7267.

56. "Eisagogikes Paratereseis tou Proedrou Tou PASOK Andreas G. Papandreou" in Kokkos and Mourike-Kostopoulou, *He Metavase sto Sosialismo* , 15.

57. *Kathemerine* , 27 November 1984, 1.

58. The first PASOK delegation to Moscow was led by Karolos Papoulias (then member of the Politburo for International Affairs) currently foreign minister. He is also the architect of all pro-Third World initiatives. Following the first visit to Moscow, several exchanges took place on a *party-to-party* level between PASOK and the Communist Party of the Soviet Union. For a text of the first communiqué on PASOK-CPSU cooperation, see *Eleutheros Kosmos* , 8 May 1981, 1 and 3.

59. Kouloglou: *Sta Ichne tou Tritou Dromou* , 42-43.

60. See speech of Andreas Papandreou at the 24th Plenum of the [PASOK] Central Committee, *Eleutherotypia* , 8 November 1987.

The Philosophy and Goals of PASOK's Foreign Policy

Yannis Kapsis

Editor's Note: Because this essay represents a Greek governmental elaboration on the philosophy and goals of PASOK's foreign policy (as requested in the letter of invitation of 24 March 1987; see appendix), no editorial or substantive changes have been made other than to correct obvious misprints and to standardize names to conform with the remainder of this work. The entire text is published as originally submitted on 19 October 1987. The editor apologizes for any stylistic errors that might be present. It must also be noted that the essay was written and submitted prior to Papandreou's abrupt reversal in his policy vis-à-vis Turkey, underscored by several meetings between the prime ministers of the two countries. Proofs of the text were submitted for final review through the Greek embassy, but they were returned unopened and without any changes whatsoever.

The strictly methodological analysis of the PASOK Government's foreign policy stumbles on three specific and "sui generis" difficulties that are not met in the development of the foreign policy of any other government or state. First of all, it should be emphasized that the term "foreign policy of the PASOK Government" is not the right one, or certainly not the best. In general, a country's foreign policy is determined by the political and ideological principles of the government which shapes it. But, in the case of Greece, the foreign policy which the PASOK Government implements mainly reflects the political maturity and social integration achieved by the Greek people. The PASOK Government endeavors to shape and express this reality according to the needs and possibilities of the present time. In other words, the Government of PASOK does not follow a policy which it has itself chosen, but a policy imposed on the country's political life by the Greek people themselves.

So, when Andreas Papandreou asserts that our foreign policy is a "Greek foreign policy," he is not engaging in political propaganda: he is making a statement of objective fact. Nor is it accidental that this policy, at least in its basic elements, has the support even of the Opposition. Obviously, such a policy, which is determined more by the people than by the government, cannot be very flexible.

Greece enjoys a unique, if unfortunate, distinction among the rest of the countries of Europe: she began life as a modern free State—after shaking off the Ottoman yoke—with three political parties: the English Party, the French Party and the Russian Party. The very names of these parties demonstrate the degree of Greece's dependency on the Great Powers of the time.

This status of dependency on the dominant powers in the Mediterranean survived until after the second World War: it was so "recognized" by the dictator Metaxas, a declared admirer of the Kaiser's Germany, on whose side he wished Greece to enter the first World War. It was Metaxas who in 1936 established a fascist regime with ideological affinities to Mussolini's movement. However, he did not dare overlook the geopolitical realities of the region (the guarantor of the interests of the superpowers of that time was the then Royal House of Greece) or the wishes of the Greek people, who, above and beyond its anti-fascist sentiments, had accepted Greece's dependency on Great Britain as a political 'modus operandi.'

The replacement in 1947 of Britain by the United States as the influential power in the region was an important development affecting Greece and Turkey and the control at the Mediterranean. However, from 1947 onwards, the dependency took on a different and stronger character politically, or otherwise. American influence left its imprint even on aspects of everyday life. With this background in mind, the current Ambassador in Athens, Mr. Robert Keeley, in his confirmation hearings testified before the Foreign Relations Committee of the Senate, on July 25, 1985: "We did a great deal for Greece and came to their rescue after World War II and did a great deal to help that country get back on its feet. But inevitably that creates somewhat of a client relationship, a dependency relationship and they want to get away from that. And they quite rightly should because it is a country that is much stronger economically and militarily in every way and can take better care of its own security."

On a smaller scale, a similar phenomenon was observed in the other countries of continental Europe. Ruined and lacking political, economic and social organisation, these countries accepted, along with massive American economic aid, the

American socio-economic model. However, as these countries matured socially, there was a return—not without friction, sometimes of a serious nature—to their national ways of life. Thus, we had in France the "De Gaulle phenomenon" and the "Brandt phenomenon" in Germany, which, more or less rocked the boat of the "allies." In Greece, we have the "Papandreou phenomenon."

This social maturity came late to Greek society and coincided with the achievement of political maturity. Since the catalyst in these developments was the invasion of Cyprus—a direct consequence of Greece's dependency on foreign centers of decision-making—it is surprising that the friction has not been more serious.

This preliminary introduction serves to demonstrate the first difficulty in the methodological approach to an understanding of Greek foreign policy: the complexity of the historical background and its constituent elements.

It is well known that the colonels' regime was imposed by foreign decision-making centers. This fact is disputed even by Americans with the best of intentions towards Greece. But their denials fly in the face not only of Greek documentary evidence but also of the official Congressional Record of the United States.

I had recent experience of this mistaken approach. An eminent American of Greek descent handed me a book about the CIA's activities which he said he had read with great interest. The book, he said, disproved allegations of CIA involvement in the colonels' coup. And yet, that same book quotes the testimony of William Colby to the House Foreign Affairs Committee, according to which the leader of the junta, George Papadopoulos, had been receiving funds from the CIA since 1952.

This typical example points to the second difficulty in the development of Greek foreign policy: the fact that people abroad are ill-informed, not only about the underlying causes and historical background of this policy, but even about contemporary and often obvious facts.

This lack of information is closely linked to the third difficulty in the understanding of Greek foreign policy, namely an extensive and well-orchestrated disinformation campaign which has repeatedly caused difficulties not only to the Greek Government but even to the State Department itself.

This campaign consists of a variety of false allegations ensuing reactions which vary from anger (as in the case of the Greek-Bulgarian communiqué, which was described as "a secret political agreement") to amusement, as in the case of the claim that the Papandreou Government does not permit the military personnel of the American bases in Greece to repair their bathroom fittings, (note: the permission of the Greek Government is required, by virtue of the 1983 DECA, *only* for those works which increase the operational capacity of the bases). To the extent that such allegations slander Greece alone, they are of concern to Greece. But when they mislead the Congress itself, the problem becomes an internal political problem for the USA.

JULY 20, 1974 - THE CATALYST

The date July 20, 1974 was a catalyst, at least in the shaping of Greek foreign policy. The broader consequences for the balance of power in the Eastern Mediterranean are still to be seen. The Turkish invasion of Cyprus was a painful awakening for the Greek people, who in the space of a few days were forced to re-assess the convictions and orientations of centuries.

The Cyprus issue, it is true to say, began to play this catalytic role in the political life of Greece back in 1948, when the people of Cyprus, under the leadership of Archbishop Makarios, almost unanimously manifested their will for self-determination.

The devious incitement of the Turkish minority by the British colonial power, at a much later date, served to shrink the demand for self-determination to one for the creation of an independent State of Cyprus, with full guarantees for the Turkish Cypriot minority. But in July 1974, even this status of the Republic of Cyprus was destroyed.

Here we should point out a dramatic coincidence: the right to self-determination as a principle of international law was formulated and elevated to the status of international practice by Eleutherios Venizelos, the innovator of modern Greek State, at the Paris Conference of 1919 and was eagerly adopted by President Wilson in the context of the establishment of the first independent Armenian state, which was to serve as the first bridgehead of American influence in the Middle East. The price which the Armenian people paid for that *temporary* American support is common knowledge: 1,500,000 Armenians were mercilessly slaughtered. The painful question for the average Greek with knowledge of history and a good memory was this: would the Greeks of Cyprus (whose claim since 1960 has been not self-determination but simply the independence of their state) share the fate of the Armenians?

Apart from the emotional reactions, a rational view to the invasion led to certain incontrovertible conclusions: First, the U.S., by refusing to intervene and prevent the invasion of Cyprus, had abruptly and on their own initiative severed the bond of dependency and protection which until then existed in Greek-American relations. The Johnson (and later the Kissinger) "letters" ceased to be in effect—a fact confirmed by the American negotiator on the issue on the American bases in Greece, Reginald Bartholomew, who said that these letters "are shelved in the their archives." Indeed it was immediately obvious (and subsequently confirmed by the official investigation) that the puppet regime of the junta had tolerated the July 1974 invasion after receiving the promise that it would lead to the implementation of a variation of the notorious Acheson plan which would lead to the "cantonisation" of Cyprus. Consequently, it is obvious that relations with the U.S. were entering a new phase which is still today in the process of evolution.

The second disturbing experience was that of NATO. The Turkish invasion of Cyprus was carried out by an army that belongs to NATO, with NATO weapons and by officers and men trained by the Alliance. And yet the Alliance displayed not the slightest reaction. It was obvious that the famous NATO "umbrella" did not protect Greece from attacks coming from outside the Warsaw Pact countries. This conclusion became official in December 1981 at the NATO Defense Ministers Council. At that meeting Greek Prime Minister Andreas Papandreou made a brave attempt to bridge the gap by proposing that Article 5 of the Atlantic Charter should be interpreted with the clarification that the Alliance would hasten to protect its members "against any attack of whatever origin."

Turkey vetoed this proposal, thus admitting by inference that she might possibly attack Greece. Moreover, Turkey was indirectly supported in this reaction by the U.S. Defense Secretary, who in so doing made clear the priorities of American foreign policy in Eastern Mediterranean. The period between 1974, the year of the Turkish invasion of Cyprus, and 1981, the year when PASOK came to power, had permitted a full evaluation of the real meaning of that invasion: it was the starting-point for a dynamic expansion westwards—an attempt to resurrect the Ottoman Empire—and the invasion was the first rehearsal for a policy of 'faits accomplis' in order to test the reactions of the international community. Additional evidence which supports (and goes a long way towards proving) this interpretation was provided by a whole series of claims against Greece raised by Ankara at this time. In particular Lemnos: Ankara suddenly voiced objections to the inclusion in NATO exercises of the island of Lemnos, which is of vital importance for the defence of the Aegean, on the grounds that by virtue of the Montreux Convention the island should be demilitarised. If Greece has accepted this argument by joining in NATO exercises which excluded Lemnos, she would have been accepting 'de facto' the unfounded Turkish claims. The Turkish arguments are indeed outrageous, since, apart from the text of the Montreux Convention—which does not leave the slightest doubt that the demilitarised status of Lemnos was ended at the same time as that of the Straits—we also have the statement of the then Turkish Foreign Minister Rusdi Aras before the Turkish National Assembly, who said: "The provisions concerning the islands of Lemnos and Samothrace, which were demilitarised in application of the Treaty of Lausanne of 1923, are also abolished by the Convention of Montreux and we are very glad of that. I avail myself of this opportunity to stress once more that one of the features of the policy of the new Turkey is to wish for her friends what she wishes for herself and not to wish for her friends what we would regard as an injustice for ourselves...." There is also an official letter of the Turkish Ambassador in Athens to the Greek Prime Minister of the time to the effect that "...Turkey would look favourably upon every measure that the Greek Government might consider it necessary to take to ensure the security of the islands that are under the sovereignty of Greece... The militarisation of the islands to take place is that of the islands of Samothrace and Lemnos. We absolutely agree to the militarisation of the two islands and at the same time to that of the Straits." These documents fully confirm the Greek position.

Last but not least, not only has the legal department of NATO vindicated Greece but the Supreme Allied Commander Europe (SACEUR) reacted strongly against the Turkish claim, though without any success.

Thus, Greece had no choice but to decline to take part in NATO exercises as long as Lemnos is not included in them, in order to prevent the amendment by custom or acquiescence of the Montreux Convention.

Airspace: The Greek Government extended its airspace to ten miles as early as 1931. In doing so it was exercising the right given by the Chicago Convention; Article 1: "The contracting States recognize that every State has complete and exclusive sovereignty over the airspace above its territory." Article 2: "For the purpose of this Convention the territory of a State shall be deemed to be the land areas and territorial waters adjacent thereto under the sovereignty, suzerainty, protection or mandate of such State." This "Status Quo" was accepted by Turkey, which respected Greek sovereignty over the ten-mile airspace for half a century. This is proved by a large number of Turkish NOTAMS regarding Turkish air force exercises in the air, which state: "No (Turkish) aircraft is to approach Hellenic territory closer than ten (10) nautical miles." These NOTAMS exist in the files of the Greek Ministry of Foreign Affairs.

And yet, without warning, the Turks in 1974 unilaterally announced that they did not recognize Greek airspace beyond six miles and began systematically violating Greek sovereignty.

Continental shelf of the Aegean: On 28 March 1987, the two countries came to the brink of war because of the attempt by Turkey to conduct drilling operations on the Greek continental shelf. The dispute over the continental shelf issue began in 1973. In that year the Ankara government issued permits for oil prospecting on the Greek continental shelf. The Turkish claim is based upon Ankara's refusal to accept that islands have their own continental shelf, in spite of the fact that the 1958 Geneva Convention states explicitly that: "The term 'continental shelf' is used as referring to the seabed and subsoil of similar submarine areas adjacent to the coasts of islands." Furthermore, the UN Convention of 1982 on the Law of the Sea provides that: "... The continental shelf of an island is determined in accordance with the provisions of this Convention applicable to other land territory."

By her arbitrary interpretation of international law, Turkey claims half of the continental shelf of the Aegean. Lying above this are scores of Greek islands in the Aegean archipelago. An attempt on the part of the Karamanlis Government to have the dispute referred to the International Court at the Hague (1976) foundered when, at the last moment, Turkey backed out by declining to sign the compromissum, or joint document of recourse.

If, for the sake of argument, we were to suppose—though such a thought is not entertained in Greece even as a hypothesis—that a Greek Government accepted the Turkish claims "in toto," we should be faced more or less with the following situation: the Greek islands would be sitting on the Turkish continental shelf; their airspace would belong to the area of responsibility of the Turkish Air Force; and civil aircraft, which carry out scores of flights each day to the islands, would have to seek clearance from the Istanbul air traffic control, because Ankara is even seeking a change in the boundaries of the Flight Information Region.

It is obvious to any bona fide observer that under such circumstances the Greek islands of the Aegean, which are the home of one-fifth of the country's population, would not remain Greek for very long. Moreover, as if to remove any doubts as to her intentions, Ankara has assembled a powerful armed force—known as the Fourth Army of the Aegean—which consists of her most efficient units of parachutists, commandos, helicopters and tanks. It is deployed along the Turkish coastline opposite the Greek islands. In addition, she has assembled a fleet of 130 landing craft, ready at a moment's notice to carry this army to the Greek islands on the pattern of the invasion of Cyprus.

To support this direct and actual Turkish threat to Greek sovereignty, the government in Ankara has devised a geopolitical foundation. As early as 1975, well before the Greek Government formulated its own defense doctrine, the War History Department of the Turkish General Staff published a booklet entitled "Turkish-Greek Relations and the Great Idea," which forms part of regular instruction courses in the Turkish Army. It is simply the Turkish military doctrine. Its most recent edition, revised by General Hamnei Erturk and Staff Colonel Okse, and edited by Colonel Yuzel Aktar, was published in 1985.

Outlining Turkish aims in the Aegean, the booklet propounds the "logic" that Greece is not in a position to defend her islands against the aggression of a "third party"—obviously the Soviet Union and its allies—and, therefore, that Turkey should undertake that task. It is ironical that, at the same time, Turkey, by virtue of the Lausanne Treaty, denies Greece the right to fortify the islands in order to protect them against foreign aggression.

From this brief summary of the historical, social and defense factors which at a given moment (the day of the invasion of Cyprus) served as the catalyst of events, it will readily be seen that Greek foreign policy, in the form it has taken today, is not purely and simply a choice of the PASOK Government, but a mandate from the Greek people. It is not an ideological and political option, but a necessity for national survival. Thus, the first priority of Greek foreign policy is to safeguard our national interests and our national sovereignty; that is to say, to secure the territorial integrity of our country. This priority is absolute and takes precedence over any other considerations.

Furthermore, the direct and serious threat from Turkey, together with the unwillingness of Greece's traditional allies to use their influence to discourage these designs upon our country, calls for the creation of a new political and defence balance. In particular, the preservation of the balance of power in the Aegean is the cornerstone of Greece's national policy. In these circumstances, policies in each particular area of interest have evolved along more or less predetermined lines.

GREEK-U.S. RELATIONS

The problem in Greek-U.S. relations, as Prime Minister Andreas Papandreou has repeatedly explained to American officials, can be divided into two main categories: a) strictly bilateral problems, and b) issues which are rooted in the triangular relationship between Athens, Washington and Ankara.

As far as the bilateral level is concerned, people often fail to realize that the present Government has achieved more than any of its predecessors towards a solution of these long-standing problems.

However, the most important contribution of the PASOK Government's policy in this area has been the endeavor—which has had considerable success in spite of certain difficulties—to redefine the relations between the two countries on the basis of equality and mutual cooperation, as is the case with the relations of the United States with other countries in the West, and to put an end to what the U.S. Ambassador in Athens, Mr. Keeley, has described as a client relationship.

Relations with Greece and the U.S.A. have very deep roots. Particular events in history and individual personalities have created the framework of historical and emotional bonds between the two nations: the common experience of the struggle for independence; the great wave of American philhellenism during Greece's War of Independence in the 19th century; the vast flow of Greek immigrants to the United States; political figures of the stature of President Wilson and the Greek Prime Minister Eleutherios Venizelos, who co-operated to implement the famous 14 points of that great American idealist and to establish the post-war League of Nations; the affection shown towards Greece by President Roosevelt, who never ceased to express his admiration for the sacrifices and efforts of Greece during the Second World War. All this has contributed to what might be called "a special relationship" between the Greek and the American people.

It was, however, after World War II that, under special psychological circumstances and, indeed in the context of the real fears produced by the spectre of the Cold War, that the criteria of U.S. foreign policy became purely strategic and geopolitical. All those who have studied American policy during this period are agreed on this analysis. Ideological considerations and the memories of the struggles for freedom shared by the two nations gave place to an exclusively and, alas, uncritically, strategic assessment of the relative value of the potential of Greece and Turkey for the effective containment of the Soviet Union.

It was obvious that the scales weighed in favour of Turkey in U.S. post-war assessments. For this reason, the Greeks saw to their disappointment that on the outbreak of the anticolonial struggle in Cyprus (1955) American policy inclined initially in favour of Great Britain and subsequently of Turkey.

America ignored Greek national susceptibilities, sacrificing them on the altar of East-West confrontation. Even when, in 1964, President Johnson addressed his famous letter to Turkish Prime Minister Inonu, seeking to avert a Turkish attack upon Cyprus, his message was worded according to the same reasoning: as Lyndon Johnson wrote: "The NATO Allies might well reconsider whether they have an obligation to protect Turkey from the Soviet Union if Turkey takes a step which results in Soviet intervention, without the full consent and understanding of its NATO Allies."

In the light of such a view on the part of the U.S., it was

inevitable that certain positions of the new Greek Government of 1981 would not find favor in Washington.

The multidimensional foreign policy of the new government in Athens was bound to be seen as heretical, given that for the first time Greek positions were emancipated from outdated cold war attitudes which would have been more appropriate to the immediate post-war years.

In spite of this, in the six years of PASOK government there has been considerable progress towards the resolution of bilateral problems. The turning point was the agreement of 1983 on the military bases, which was concluded after negotiations of only nine months, while previous negotiations which lasted for nine years had failed to reach an agreement. This agreement, which is still in force today, replaced an outdated and complex plethora of legal and military agreements, going back to 1947, and contractually reaffirms the 7:10 ratio in American aid to Greece and Turkey respectively, thus reflecting Greece's strong concern for the preservation of balance of forces in the region.

The same period has seen other positive steps, including:

*The conclusion of a Defense Industrial Cooperation Agreement (DICA).

*The signing of a civil aviation agreement.

*Purchase of the F-16 aircraft.

*Drawing up a technical text for the renewal of the agreement on the Voice of America facilities.

*Promotion of commercial exchanges and American investments in Greece.

*Effective co-operation between the appropriate authorities of the two countries on combating terrorism.

Of course, there have also been serious retrograde events, such as the travel advisory of President Reagan in June 1985 and other unfortunate statements by U.S. officials.

Nevertheless, the visit of the U.S. Secretary of State, Mr. George Shultz, to Athens in May 1986 was of decisive importance. It was followed by a visit (July 1987) of the Undersecretary of State for Political Affairs, Mr. Michael Armacost, which set the stage for the beginning of new negotiations on the future of the U.S. facilities in Greece after 1988, when the current 5-year agreement expires.

In a recent interview, the Greek Premier reiterated that the top priority of Greek foreign policy is the security of the country. He stressed that the content of the new agreement on the bases will be linked with the crucial issues of national importance which face Greece. Speaking in Parliment last May, he also said that if the talks lead to an agreement, this will be put before the Greek people for approval, to be expressed through a referendum—a position which the U.S. Assistant Secretary of State for European Affairs, Mrs. Rozanne Ridgway, testifying before Congress, described as understandable.

In a region beset by so many contradictions, with problems deeply rooted in the historical evolution of Eastern Mediterranean, it would be surprising if, in the area of Greece's foreign relations, there were not at least some apparent contradictions. The step-by-step improvement in Greek-American relations has been universally welcomed by the Greek people, who also receive hundreds of thousands of American tourists each year with warmth and sincere cordiality.

This could hardly be otherwise, given that the ten million Greeks, who regard the family as the primary social bond, have more than three million relatives in America. And yet, for example, the visit of an American aircraft carrier to a Greek port is capable of producing a hostile reaction on the part of a section of the population.

It is such reactions which are given undue prominence by the U.S. media. It indicates a failure to understand that the friendly welcome given to American visitors reflects the relationship between the two peoples, while the reaction to the visit of an aircraft carrier is the response to some unfortunate pronouncements on the part of the U.S. Administration—for instance, U.S. Defence Secretary Weinberger's statement that the Turkish occupation troops in Cyprus are there for defensive purposes. This, however, is a distinction which is perfectly clear to the average Greek, who has a high degree of political awareness and maturity, is extremely well-informed and actively participates in public affairs as urged by Pericles 2,000 years ago. On the other hand, traumatic experiences of contemporary history have made him highly sensitive to national issues. Understanding on both sides of the way the other reacts is one of the most essential prerequisites for the establishment of close relations.

THE TURKISH FACTOR

Greek policy towards Turkey is expressed very simply in the words of Prime Minister Andreas Papandreou: "Greece makes not the slightest claim on Turkey, but is not prepared to yield an inch of her own land, air or sea territory." Behind this brief sentence is a whole philosophy—that of legitimacy in international affairs. Greece's only objective is the maintenance of the "status quo" which was established by the Treaty of Lausanne of 1923, which ended the war between the two countries and determined relations between them—relations which were perfectly normal for some 60 years. This policy was conveyed officially to Turkey in November 1985 by a memorandum, which did not, however, receive any substantive reply.

In spite of the fact that Greece, while not making any demands herself, has to face a series of expansionist claims on the part of Turkey, the Greek Government agreed initially with Ankara on a moratorium which would permit a dialogue on uncontentious issues (tourism, trade, etc.), thus working towards discussion of the more thorny problems of the Aegean. This effort, however, was stillborn. The repeated provocative violations of Greek airspace and the unilateral and unlawful proclamation of "Independence" of the pseudo-state of Denktash in occupied Cyprus (November 1983) damaged the moratorium and ruled out any possibility of a dialogue. However, the Greek side kept calm and continued to base its attitudes towards Ankara on the principles of good neighbourliness and of international law and on the rights which derive from the legal "status quo" as established by international conventions.

In conformity with the legal *status quo* in the Aegean, Greece maintains that there is only one problem of a legal nature between herself and Turkey: the delimitation of the continental shelf. Following the international outcry over the latest (March 1987) provocative act of Turkey, in announcing that the oceanographic vessel "Piri Reis" could sail into the Aegean, thus provoking a strong reaction on the part of Greece which placed her armed forces on the alert, Ankara seemed not to rule out the referral of the dispute to the International Court at the Hague. This would be an acceptance of the previous proposal of the Greek side, recently renewed by the Greek Premier in a message to the Prime Minister of Turkey. The exchange of messages between the two Prime Ministers is still continuing, and it is to be hoped that we are now seeing a new and realistic approach on the part of Ankara—one that is not another tactical manoeuvre designed to allay international concerns over Turkey's provocative policies in the Aegean.

CYPRUS, THE CATALYST

Many references have already been made to the Cyprus issue as the catalyst in post-1974 developments. This is a problem of unusual complexity dominated by the continuing occupation of almost 40 percent of the Republic of Cyprus by Turkish troops. This protracted occupation alone, with its disregard for the repeated resolutions of the Security Council and General Assembly of the United Nations as well as other international bodies, is a challenge to the international rule of law. It is disturbingly reminiscent of the provocative rejection of the decisions of the League of Nations on Ethiopia by Benito Mussolini—the exploit which undermined the first attempt to establish an amphictyony of the peoples of the world.

In an attempt to cut through this Gordian knot, Prime Minister Andreas Papandreou has proposed the replacement of the Turkish armed forces in Cyprus by a strong international force which could even be constituted by troops from Muslim countries; Greece, by no means a wealthy country, would be prepared to bear the cost. This proposal was rejected by Turkey, which thus no longer has any justification for claiming that her troops are there to protect the Turkish community. This explains the strong reaction of the Greeks—Government and people alike—to the statements of U.S. Defense Secretary Weinberger and Assistant Secretary Perle, who told Congress in March 1987 that the purpose of the presence of the Turkish troops in Cyprus was defensive. The Greek side is also opposed to the modernization of the Turkish M 48 tanks in Cyprus with new up-to-date American equipment.

This is also the reason why Greece applauded the subsequent decision of Congress, which confirming existing American legislation, again included an amendment in the foreign aid legislation for FY 1988 forbidding the transfer of U.S. military equipment for the use of the Turkish army of occupation in Cyprus.

The importance which Greece attaches to this matter was emphasized by the Prime Minister in a speech before the Greek Parliament on December 6, 1985. Mr. Papandreou stated categorically that the continuing presence of Turkish troops in

Cyprus is damaging to the immediate national interests of Greece herself, since "from the moment that the Turkish occupation of Cyprus is legitimized the threat in the Aegean becomes more immediate and more pressing." The Premier also stated expressly, during a debate on a vote of confidence on May 22, 1987, that any move made by the Turkish forces towards the unoccupied part of the island would be deemed a "casus belli" and would provoke a military response from Greece. This position is justified not only by reason of Greece's moral support for the Cypriot nation with which Greece has links of brotherhood, and by Greece's legal rights as a guarantor power of the Republic of Cyprus, but also by considerations affecting the security and defense of Greece itself.

Greece has always upheld the indivisibility, integrity and sovereignty of the Republic of Cyprus, in accord with the United Nations Charter and international conventions. It also supports any solution which would safeguard the so-called "three freedoms" of settlement, movement and property ownership and ensure the withdrawal of the Turkish army of occupation.

Unfortunately, the Turkish side has cynically stated that, under any solution, a part of the Turkish army will remain in Cyprus and that Ankara will insist on a system of guarantees which will give her a right to unilateral military intervention. For these reasons Greece supports the proposals submitted by President Kyprianou on June 10, 1986.

It should be noted, that in Resolution 3212 (XXIX) of the General Assembly of the United Nations, Resolution 365 (1974) of the Security Council and paragraph 7 of Resolution 37/253 of the General Assembly it is expressly stated that: "The General Assembly regards the withdrawal of all the occupation forces from the Republic of Cyprus as a substantive basis for a speedy and mutually acceptable solution to the Cyprus problem."

Apart from insisting on the withdrawal of the Turkish troops, Greece also denounces the attempt to alter the demographic composition of the population of Cyprus by the transfer and establishment of more than 60,000 settlers from Turkey on the island.

NATO

When Greece joined NATO in 1952, this was welcomed by the other member countries as a development of great importance for the completion of allied defense. And for 30 years Greece was regarded as an exemplary, loyal and obedient partner in the Atlantic Alliance. The part she played in the Alliance was a matter of pride for the pre-1967 conservative governments. A fact, however, which has not been given its due weight is that it was the Karamanlis conservative Government which in 1974, taking the measure of popular reaction and expressing the disapprobation of the whole country, decided to withdraw from the military wing of NATO in protest against the invasion of Cyprus.

Responsibility for the mistaken interpretation of this step on the part of Greece does not rest solely with her Atlantic partners: she herself must shoulder a considerable share of the blame. Her extreme and unquestioning devotion to the Atlantic Alliance, and somewhat romantic readiness to come to the aid of her allies, had given rise to the belief that "the Greeks never protest, never disagree," to quote the words of a former member of the U.S. Administration to this writer.

Greece's position and policy in NATO may be summarized as follows:

*NATO statistics show Greece as holding first place in the Alliance in defense expenditure (7.1% of Gross National Product) and in the contribution of military and civilian personnel.

*NATO installations in Greece, e.g., the firing range in Crete, the Souda base, etc., are of an importance which can hardly be exaggerated.

*Greece's territory, and particularly the Aegean, is, according to NATO studies, of primary importance. Without it Turkey could not properly function and play her role in the Eastern wing and the existing balance in the Balkans could not be maintained. To the question: What problems Greece has with NATO, it would be possible honestly to answer "none." And yet: Greece does not take part in NATO exercises in the Aegean: This is because Turkey, by exercising her veto, will not accept the inclusion of the island of Lemnos in these exercises.

*The 7th ATAF, that is the Larissa Headquarters, has not yet been set up: this, too, is the result of Turkey's refusal to accept the implementation of the Agreement on Greece's re-entry into the military structure of NATO in 1980, which clearly provides that: "The mission of the Greek Armed Forces is to defend jointly with Allied Forces and on the basis of agreed operational plans, the land, sea and airspace for the defense of which they were responsible before August 1974."

Both the Rogers Agreement and the Greek replies to the Open-Ended Group clearly provide that all the arrangements in force prior to 1974 will continue to apply.

GREECE AND THE MIDDLE EAST

Foreign policy, has its own dynamic, which is determined, more or less equally, by those who plan it and by the degree to which it is understood often in the face of deliberate misrepresentation—as well as the extent to which it is successful. The relations of Athens with the countries of the Middle East provide a typical example: they have been misunderstood perhaps more than any other area of Greece's foreign relations and the degree of understanding has been profoundly affected by a series of mistakes on the part of most of the countries which aspire to play some role in the region.

The bonds between the Greek people and the peoples of the Middle East were not forged only yesterday: They go back to antiquity. Geographical proximity has inevitably led to interaction, both in times of peace and in periods of general tension in the area. Trading relations, the existence of flourishing Greek communities in these countries, and the presence there of the Greek Orthodox Patriarchates, have always been factors in promoting friendship and close cooperation.

Indeed, in recent years, the support which Greece has regularly received from the Arab countries on the Cyprus issue has been an additional and important reason for closer ties and increased mutual support. The result has been that Greece has played a part in the area of Middle East inversely proportionate to its size—geographical or economic—and this is recognized today.

The positions adopted by Greece have, in the recent past, occasioned surprise, though they have always been vindicated by events. Thus, for example, in 1982 Greece maintained, within the framework of EEC Political Cooperation, that Yasser Arafat should be regarded as the sole representative of the PLO and that any weakening of his position, would enable more extreme groups to gain the upper hand leading to an upsurge of terrorism. Not only was Greece not listened to: she was sharply criticized by circles. But today, of course, the policy of

Greece has proved to be justified: the West accepts Arafat and is trying to reestablish a dialogue with him.

Greece also argued that Syria should not be cold-shouldered as an interlocutor and as the sole remaining channel for treating the burning issues of Lebanon and the Western hostages. This view was regarded as ill-advised. But today, the countries of the West, without exception, are "building bridges" and seeking to re-establish communications with Syria.

The key to the Middle East is the Palestinian issue. Greek policy clearly favors the recognition of the lawful rights of the Palestinian people—whose legitimate representative is the PLO—including the right to self-determination and the establishment of an independent Palestinian state.

GREECE AND ISRAEL

What has been said about the links between Greece and the peoples of the Middle East also, of course, applies to Israel. The shared experiences of two ancient neighbouring peoples and similar painful memories from the period of Nazi occupation form a bond here. Although the whole people of Greece suffered under the occupation of the Axis powers, it did not fail to do its duty in rendering every assistance to the most heavily persecuted Jewish community of Greece.

Although, up to the present, Greece has not recognized "de jure" the State of Israel, it has nevertheless accorded it "de facto" recognition since its foundation in 1948. Both countries maintain diplomatic representation with each other, headed by a diplomat of ambassadorial rank. Greece's recognition of the rights of Israel is much more than theoretical: when the expulsion of Israel has been proposed in various international organizations, Greece has voted against. Since 1983 there has been a constant acceleration in the improvement and expansion of Greek-Israeli relations.

Of particular importance was the visit to Athens of the General Secretary of the Israeli Ministry of Foreign Affairs (January 1986). During the subsequent visit (May 1986) of Israel's Minister of Tourism further cooperation on tourism and joint tourist programs for third countries were decided upon. This visit was returned by the Deputy Minister of National Economy responsible for matters of tourism, Mr. Roumeliotes, and by the Chairman of the National Tourism Organization of

Greece, Mr. Kyriazes, who visited Tel-Aviv during 1986.

Visits have also been paid to Athens and Tel-Aviv respectively by the General Secretaries of the Agriculture Ministries of the two countries (1986). Two members of the Israeli Parliament have visited Athens as guests of the Greek Minister of Foreign Affairs, Mr. Karolos Papoulias, while the Speaker of the Greek Parliament, Mr. Aleuras, is expected to visit Israel in the near future.

Cultural exchanges are also on the increase, with the renewal of an educational protocol, the appearance for the first time of Israeli dance companies at the 1987 Athens Festival and a visit by the President of the Athens Academy to Israel.

The success of the recent meeting of the European Jewish Congress in Athens has been one more tangible expression of the trust which the international Jewish community places in Greece.

All these contacts have now prepared the ground for a visit, already announced, by the Greek Foreign Minister, Mr. Papoulias, to Israel. This will undoubtedly be a major step in the process of constant improvement in Greek-Israeli bilateral relations.

RELATIONS OF GREECE WITH THE USSR, EASTERN COUNTRIES AND THE BALKANS

Greece's relations with the USSR, the Eastern countries and the Balkans lagged behind considerably in the cold war atmosphere of the attitudes prevailing after World War II.

A scheduled official visit to Russia by the then Prime Minister of Greece, Mr. George Papandreou, in 1964 was opposed by the Allies and never took place, in spite of the fact that all the countries of the West had by then initiated normal political and economic relations with the Soviet Union and the countries of the Eastern bloc.

Greece's first high-level contact was the visit of the then Premier, Mr. Karamanlis, to Moscow as late as 1979. After the restoration of legitimate government in Greece in 1974, a policy of technical and economic cooperation with the Balkan countries was put into effect continuing a cautious opening made by the "Centre Union" Government in 1964.

Within the framework of its multidimensional foreign policy, the Andreas Papandreou Government attempted, from 1981 onwards, to put Greece's relations with the Eastern European countries on the level of those which other Western countries maintained with them.

This is because—and this should be emphasized—even today Greece's bilateral relations with these countries have not advanced as far as those of other Western states. This can be clearly seen from the table of bilateral economic relations.

Furthermore, commercial exchanges between Greece and the Soviet Union remain at a very low level.

Particularly in the political field, the relations of Greece with the Soviet superpower have always been dictated by a recognition of the historic role long played by the Russian, and then the Soviet, State in developments in the Balkans.

The present intensity of activity of the Soviet Union throughout the neighbouring region makes it necessary for Greece to monitor carefully any Soviet contacts which might have repercussions on her vital national interests. The constant development, for example, of privileged relations with neighbouring Turkey is something to which Athens cannot remain indifferent.

PEACE AND NUCLEAR DISARMAMENT

The basic guidelines of Greek foreign policy which have been set out above could well serve to interpret, but also to vindicate, the positions adopted by the Government of Andreas Papandreou on the whole range of international problems and regions of the world. What we see is simply the realisation of the multidimensional foreign policy of PASOK, which, in the given circumstances, over and above any ideological option, means a policy of survival for Greece.

There is, however, one area of world politics where Greece and her Prime Minister personally, have risen above petty interests and calculations and have taken up the cause of mankind and of world peace: this is the struggle for nuclear disarmament.

Greece, faithful to the principles enshrined in the U.N. Charter, spares no effort to encourage all endeavours tending to the safeguarding of international peace and security. In particular, shortly after PASOK assumed power in 1981, the Greek Government actively promoted the idea of establishing a zone free from nuclear and chemical weapons in the Balkans. The establishment of such a zone in the Balkans and possibly of others in the Nordic area and Central Europe is considered to be a most appropriate confidence-building measure within the framework of the East-West dialogue, a measure that diminishes the risk of military confrontation between the NATO and the Warsaw Pact countries and constitutes an important step towards the elimination of nuclear weapons in Europe.

Furthermore, Greece follows the negotiations for banning chemical weapons and hopes that the U.N. Disarmament Conference will agree on a treaty to that effect within 1987. In that spirit, Greece was a co-sponsor of the U.S. draft resolution adopted with a large majority at the 41st session of the General Assembly of the United Nations. Pending the conclusion of such an agreement. Greece firmly believes that the proposal recently made by the President Zhivkov of Bulgaria and the President Ceaucescu of Romania for the establishment of a chemical weapons free zone in the Balkans is an important step in the right direction.

The positive outcome of the Stockholm Conference on disarmament in Europe has bolstered the hope that the Vienna review meeting of the Conference on Security and Cooperation in Europe (CSCE), with its broader mandate, will lead to further tangible results.

As the destructive capability of conventional weapons has reached terrifying proportions, Greece supports efforts for the reduction of such weapons to the lowest possible level, taking into account the security interests of states. A reduction of conventional weapons would also reduce the risk of nuclear confrontation, while liberating funds which could be devoted to the economic and social progress of all peoples and especially the less-developed nations.

As a firm opponent of the proliferation of nuclear weapons, whether horizontal or vertical, Greece is firmly committed to the treaty of non-proliferation of nuclear weapons and shares the view that the International Atomic Energy Agency actively contributes to the limitation of armaments and to disarmament, namely through its efforts to improve the system of safeguards, which would facilitate the verification of non-proliferation commitments of various countries.

Greece subscribes to all initiatives aiming at the gradual and mutual reduction of nuclear weapons of both East and West to the lowest possible level, with a view to their total elimination, and supports all efforts to seek effective mechanisms of verification.

Particularly concerned by the threat posed by the ever-accelerating nuclear arms race, the continuation of nuclear testing and the possible militarization of outer space, Greece actively participates in the initiative of the Six Leaders for Peace and Disarmament, an Initiative launched on May 22, 1984 by the President of Argentina, Mr. Raul Alfonsin, the late Prime Minister of India, Indira Gandhi, the President of Mexico, Mr. Miguel de la Madrid, the First President of Tanzania, Mr. Julius Nyerere, the late Prime Minister of Sweden, Olof Palme and the Prime Minister of Greece, Mr. Andreas G. Papandreou. The place of the late Indira Gandhi and Olof Palme in the Initiative has been taken by their successors, Mr. Rajiv Gandhi and Mr. Ingvar Carlsson respectively.

The initiative of the Six has repeatedly urged the two Superpowers, first in 1984, to resume negotiations on the nuclear arms reduction with a view to ultimately achieving nuclear disarmament. Moreover the Leaders of the Initiative have repeatedly stressed, as explicitly stated in their first Joint Declaration, the Delhi Declaration, the necessity of taking two steps of high priority: The immediate halting of all nuclear tests and the prevention of an arms race in outer space.

It is to be noticed that during their 1986 Summit meeting in Mexico and with a view to facilitating the conclusion of a Comprehensive Test Ban Treaty, the Six Leaders made a concrete offer to assist verification of a bilateral moratorium on the halting of nuclear tests by placing the seismological networks of their countries at the disposition of the two superpowers. This offer, as affirmed in the most recent statement of the Six, issued on May 22, 1987, is still valid.

The Six through their messages have constantly called the Leaders of the two superpowers to live up to their obligations towards humanity and put an end to the mindless outpouring of world resources spent today for ameliorating and stock-piling nuclear weapons and other means of destruction when famine, illiteracy and disease are the everyday experience of hundreds of millions of people.

The recent agreement in principle between the U.S. and the Soviet Union to eliminate medium and shorter-range nuclear weapons in Europe—giving rise to hopes of still further reductions of nuclear arms in future—was warmly welcomed by Prime Minister Papandreou on behalf of the Greek people, in a statement congratulating President Reagan and Secretary-General Gorbachev.

Andreas Papandreou: [Political] Portrait of a Modern Socialist

Jeffrey Schaffer

Probably no Western political leader in modern times has been more of an enigma to the outside world than the present prime minister of Greece, Andreas Papandreou. The Greek-born Papandreou received much of his higher education in the United States, and acquired both U.S. citizenship—which he held for more than 20 years—and an American wife. Yet during his six years of leadership, the traditional pro-Western, pro-American orientation of Greece has been seriously undermined, as Papandreou has embarked on a campaign seemingly aimed at discrediting the American image with the Greek public. In carrying out this campaign, he has indulged in a strident, anti-American rhetoric more typical of an Ayatollah Khomeini or a Colonel Qaddafi than the leader of a long-time U.S. ally.

How to explain this seeming contradiction? Many critics see Andreas Papandreou as an unprincipled opportunist, who has simply ridden the waves of a resurgent anti-Americanism among the Greek electorate. Still others, noting that he is a self-proclaimed Marxist, charge that he is determined to eventually lead Greece out of the Western camp in order to align Greece with the Third World, "neutralist" bloc of nations.

On the other hand, supporters insist that Papandreou is a true Greek patriot, who sincerely believes that the long-time Greek "subservience" to the United States and NATO is inimical to fundamental Greek interests. He is, they maintain, determined to do what is best for Greece, regardless of how much his actions may offend the United States and other Western countries. Finally, some observers note that despite the harshness of his criticism of the United States and his fulsome praise of the Soviet Union, there has been no fundamental change in Greece's foreign policy alignment, with membership in NATO and the European Community (EC) continuing, and the U.S. military bases agreement still in force (albeit under renegotiation as of this writing).

However, as an American journalist noted recently, even if Andreas Papandreou's continual criticism of the U.S. is not followed by commensurate actions, it is, nevertheless, "not only subverting Greek minds, particularly those growing up under his government, but also creating a mood towards Greece that is of itself a new political reality."[1]

To the American observer, familiar with the long-standing, friendly relationship between the United States and Greece, it is indeed unsettling to listen to Andreas Papandreou's harsh denunciations of the United States for its alleged sins, both past and present. His attitude towards the Truman Doctrine, (the American program of economic and military assistance to Greece during the 1947-49 effort of the Soviet-backed Greek Communists to seize power), was set forth a couple of years ago in an interview with the CBS program "60 minutes." In that interview, Papandreou said that he felt no gratitude for American aid to Greece after World War II, nor would he answer the question of whether Greece would have fallen into the Soviet camp if the United States had not come to Greece's aid.

Papandreou's oft-quoted statements at PASOK's party conference in 1984 are enough to shake the confidence of any Western government relying on Greece to be a loyal member of the NATO alliance. At that conference, the Greek leader referred to the United States as the "metropolis of imperialism," (a term Papandreou has often used to refer to the United States) and asserted that "the Soviet Union cannot be called an imperialist power like the United States.... It is a force against imperialism and capitalism."[2] Papandreou has repeatedly differed with his counterparts in the EC on issues involving East-West relations. For example, he refused to go along with an EC resolution condemning the Polish government's suppression of Solidarity, and he declined to join in the Community's condemnation of the Soviet Union for downing a Korean passenger plane in 1983 with the loss of over 300 lives. As Andreas told the "60 Minutes" reporter, the Greek Air Force would have shot the airliner down had it intruded into Greek air space!

To try to understand the paradoxes of Papandreou's behavior, it is necessary to look in some detail at his background to determine the major influences on his character and personality. One key to explaining his actions as prime minister during the 1980s and his ambivalence towards the United

States can be found in his years of residence in the United States.

Another important—if not the most important—factor in the development of Andreas Papandreou's character was his relationship to his father, George. The relationship was nearly shattered after Andreas's first entrance into Greek politics in the 1960s. This was the only period of their lives that Andreas and his father had much contact with each other. I have thus focused my study on the events of that period and the experiences Andreas Papandreou underwent during what turned out to be an unsuccessful entry into Greek politics, ending with the overthrow of Greek democracy and the imprisonment of Andreas and his father.

To gather the necessary information for such an examination, I have read most of the significant literature on Andreas Papandreou's past. In addition, I have drawn extensively on Andreas's own version of the Greek turmoil of the 1960s, as set forth in his book *Democracy at Gunpoint* , and, to a considerably lesser extent, on the book on the same subject written by his wife, Margaret, entitled *Nightmare in Athens* .

As could be expected, the views of both authors reflect a strong bias in support of their own roles in the events under discussion. Nevertheless, the books are valuable both for what they say and what they do not say. As Erik Erikson has pointed out, if one knows at what age and under what circumstances a public figure has written his memoirs, then one can judge "the less conscious motivations, which may have led the autobiographer to emphasize selectively some experiences and omit other equally decisive ones; to profess and reveal flamboyantly some deed or misdeed and to disguise or deny equally obvious commitments; to argue and to try to prove what seems to purify or confirm his historical role and to correct what might spoil the kind of immortality he has chosen for himself."[3]

Fortunately, the conditions under which Andreas Papandreou has written his first memoirs are known, and thus the views he expresses—or does not express—can be examined in that context. Since he was writing in 1970, only three years after the military coup d'état that overthrew Greek democracy, his memory of the experiences leading up to the coup could be expected to be fresh in his mind. Even more significantly, in 1970, when he wrote his book, Andreas Papandreou had no certainty that he would ever be able to return to Greek political life—or, for that matter, even to Greece; this would depend on the longevity of the Greek colonels' rule. Therefore he was undoubtedly more open than would be the case were he expecting to soon resume his political life. Not knowing what the future might bring, he probably wanted to set the historical record "straight," at least as seen from his perspective. As will be seen, his description of the break with his father, and the reasons for it, are strikingly frank.

Let us take a brief look at the basic facts of Andreas Papandreou's early life. He was born in Greece in 1919, the son of Greek politician George Papandreou and his first wife, whose family name was Mineiko, of Polish-Greek origin. While growing up, Andreas hardly knew his father, since his parents were separated and he lived with his mother. If we are to accept Andreas's account of his formative years, as told to the American writer Nicholas Gage, he was deeply affected by the condescending attitude towards Greeks displayed by the British, American and other foreign families residing in the fashionable Athenian suburb of Palaio Psychiko, where Andreas grew up. According to Andreas, this foreign attitude "aroused great hostility in me," and out of this experience, he asserts, emerged his slogan "Greece for the Greek."[4]

Andreas became active in politics at an early age, joining a Trotskyite organization then popular among some students at Athens University, where Andreas was studying law. In 1939, when he was only 20 years old, he was arrested by the Greek security police and reportedly revealed to the police the names of some of his fellow student Trotskyites. In his book, Papandreou insists that he gave to the police only information they already possessed, and asserts that even this was given only after he was tortured and his jaw broken.[5] In any event, his arrest and alleged torture by agents of the Metaxas regime had an important impact on Andreas's subsequent attitudes towards the Greek establishment.

With war on the horizon, in May of 1940 the Papandreou family send Andreas abroad, to the United States. (A number of other young Greeks left during that period to study in the United States and several were to return again in the early 1960s to join Papandreou's economic research council.) Having completed his law studies at Athens University, he entered Harvard's graduate school, and in 1943 obtained a PhD in economics. He joined the U.S. Navy that same year, serving as medical corpsman until his discharge in 1946. While in the navy, he became an American citizen.

Following his discharge from the navy, Andreas returned to Harvard as an instructor in economics, and subsequently moved to the University of Minnesota. In Minnesota he met his wife-to-be, the American Margaret Chant. Andreas was then married to a Greek-American, Christina Rassias, and Margaret at the time was involved with another man, whom she later married. Margaret later got a divorce (after six months of marriage) as did Papandreou, and they were married in Nevada in August 1951. Shortly thereafter, Andreas returned to Greece on a visit for the first time since his departure in 1940.

While at Minnesota Andreas took his first plunge into American politics, supporting the 1948 presidential candidacy of Henry Wallace, leader of the leftist Progressive party, and then, in 1952, the Democratic party presidential candidate, Adlai Stevenson. The Papandreous moved to the University of California at Berkeley in 1954, where for a time Andreas was chairman of the economics department.

Meanwhile, Andreas's father, George Papandreou, had been having an active and largely successful political career in Greece. By the end of World War II, George Papandreou had become head of the Greek government in exile in Cairo; in the fall of 1944 he returned to Greece as prime minister. With British backing, he fought off the initial Communist takeover attempt in December 1944. Throughout the forties and into the early fifties, he was a member of various governments, serving in several ministerial capacities.

In 1959 Andreas decided to take temporary leave of absence from the University of California to return to Greece on a Guggenheim and Fulbright fellowship to undertake a study of the Greek economy. An underlying purpose was to see his father, whom he had seen only once in the previous 20 years. In his book, Andreas describes the purpose of his visit as follows:

> My principal reason for returning, however, was a purely personal one. I wanted to get to know my father again, this time in a mature way. I had always had a deep respect for George Papandreou, of course, as well as an abiding filial love. But I had never gotten to know him really well. My memories of him were those of an adolescent, and my thoughts of him were circumscribed by the limitations that that context imposed.[6]

Andreas's study of the Greek economy made a favorable impression on the then prime minister, Constantine Karamanlis, leader of the conservative National Radical Union Party (ERE), who asked the young Papandreou to set up an economic research center in Athens that would assist in the modernization of the Greek economy. Andreas agreed, and he returned again to Greece in 1961.

By this time, George Papandreou had become the leader of Greece's largest opposition party, the Center Union (EK), and in the November 1963 parliamentary elections, his party won a plurality at the polls and George Papandreou was named prime minister. The elder Papandreou had tried, following his son's initial return to Greece, to persuade Andreas to enter Greek politics, but his efforts met with no success, since Andreas was well aware of the vagaries of Greek political life, and had little desire to abandon his secure academic position at Berkeley for an uncertain political future—particularly since he had never even run for a major political office.

However, his father's electoral victory in 1963 changed the picture considerably; George Papandreou was now prime minister, and since he was unable to obtain a lasting majority in Parliament, new elections were scheduled for early 1964. Given the "bandwagon" psychology that his upset victory in November 1963 was expected to engender in the forthcoming elections, it was considered a near certainty that Papandreou's Center Union party would be returned to office with an even larger margin of victory.

It was at this stage, when he was 44 years of age, that Andreas Papandreou made the crucial decision to enter Greek politics, which necessitated resigning his tenured post at Berkeley as well as (ultimately) relinquishing the American citizenship that he had held for more than 20 years. Entering Greek politics might appear to have been a difficult and risky undertaking since Andreas Papandreou was relatively unknown in Greece at the time, but a major build-up was undertaken to create a positive image for him. It was decided that he would stand for Parliament in his father's home constituency of Patras (Achaia), while George Papandreou, who was sure of reelection wherever he ran, would campaign out of Athens. The result was never in doubt; the party achieved a majority nation-wide and Andreas led the party's ticket in Patras. The younger Papandreou was then appointed minister to the prime minister in his father's cabinet in March 1964.

In naming his son to the cabinet, George Papandreou had promoted Andreas over the heads of many in the party who had been his supporters over the years, and who had far more political experience than Andreas who, in fact, had none. Yet there was initially relatively little opposition within the party to the appointment, which seemed quite natural to most Greeks. It was frequently noted by Papandreou supporters that only a couple of years earlier, U.S. president John F. Kennedy had named his brother to a post in his cabinet; moreover, nepotism had traditionally been more or less accepted in Greek political life as a natural spoil of victory.

Moreover, Andreas Papandreou's cabinet appointment was welcomed by many Greek and foreign observers as a positive development, suggesting as it did a break with "politics as usual." Given his training in economics, Andreas seemed well qualified to assist Greece's economic and social development. It was anticipated that he would attract around him a number of young, bright, Western-trained economists who could assist him in coping with the problems that had hindered Greece from emerging fully from the status of a developing nation. Expectations were high, and some even suggested that with Andreas and his coterie, Greece would have its own version of "Camelot."

TROUBLE BEGINS

However, it was not long before problems began to arise which were to dissipate the initial enthusiasm greeting Andreas's entry into Greek politics. As might have been anticipated, one of the problems centered on Andreas's lack of political experience. In his book he describes his first few days as a minister, when he was confronted by hordes of constituents seeking jobs, work permits, and other such favors which, because of the traditional ineptness of the government bureaucracy, frequently required the intercession of a member of Parliament or at least the use of his name. As Andreas describes in his book his reactions to these importunities:

> I was not quite ready for this torrent of personal requests. I agreed to do what I could, always subject to the proviso that the request was legitimate, but deep down I had a sinking feeling. Was this what politics was about? And were I to fritter away my time in this fashion would I be able to contribute anything to the vision of a new Greece that had led me into politics? I slept little....[7]

A hallmark of Andreas Papandreou's style from the outset of his entry into politics was a tendency towards confrontation rather than accommodation or compromise when meeting opposition. This tendency not only placed him in continuing controversy with his opponents outside the party, but also made him a disruptive force within the party.

Thus, Andreas began feuding with various Center Union figures, including some close to his father. It was also at this point that Andreas's proclivity to view political dynamics in a conspiratorial framework began to manifest itself. Those who made their living peddling rumors around the Athenian political world soon learned that Andreas was an avid consumer of such reports, particularly when they concerned him, as they often did. This tendency towards a "conspiracy" theory of politics is rather puzzling, since it seems completely at variance with the rigorous, scientific approach expected of a prominent economist. In any event, Andreas's behaviour gradually began to strain his relations with some of the Greek-American social scientists who had followed him to Greece.

It was also at this time that Andreas Papandreou became embroiled in a dispute with the American government over U.S. broadcasting rights in Greece, rights that had been obtained by agreement with a previous government, and in exchange for which the United States had supplied Greece with a major share of its transmitting equipment. The details of the controversy are too complicated to be discussed in detail, but the affair was a clear indication that with Andreas Papandreou playing a major role in the new Greek government, the traditionally close U.S.-Greek relations would be strained.

Because of the broadcasting dispute, the director of the United States Information Service (who was on home leave) was discouraged from returning to his post; as Margaret Papandreou described it in her book, (with more than a small trace of pride), "it was the first time since World War II that an American official had become persona non grata in a Western European country."[8] However, some observers suggested that because of his 20-odd years of American residence (and his U.S. citizenship), Andreas needed to demonstrate that his allegiance was to Greece and not to the United States, and the dispute over broadcasting rights provided the opportunity.

THE CYPRUS ISSUE

American relations with Andreas Papandreou were further strained by the long-simmering Cyprus problem, which had flared up again in December of 1963, and which was to plague the government of George Papandreou throughout its term in office. In his book, Andreas suggests that it was in large part due to the Cyprus problem that the Papandreou government was forced to leave power a little more than a year after coming into office. As Andreas described it:

> The threat of war over Cyprus was to absorb much of the attention and effort of George Papandreou. Furthermore, it was destined to bring the Center Union government into sharp conflict with Washington and thus pave the way for its eventual overthrow by the king.[9]

The disagreement with the United States over Cyprus during the mid-sixties can be briefly summarized as follows: Greek-Turkish tensions over Cyprus were intensifying; the United States, anxious to avoid a war between two NATO allies (which would be fought with equipment supplied by the United States to deter a Warsaw Pact attack), developed the "Acheson Plan," which provided for union (*enosis*) of Cyprus with Greece in exchange for a leased Turkish military base on the island.

Negotiations in Geneva on the Acheson Plan took place under the shadow of Turkish preparations to invade the island. (Indeed, the Turkish Air Force carried out bombing raids on the island in early 1964.) For a time it seemed that agreement was near on the plan, but at the last minute Prime Minister George Papandreou rejected the plan and the Geneva negotiations were broken off.

Of principal interest in this history is Andreas's role in persuading his father to reject the Acheson Plan, which in retrospect appears to be far more favorable to Greek and Greek/Cypriot interests than any settlement Greece could hope to achieve today. In an interview in October 1964 with a journalist from the French journal *Le Monde*, Andreas revealed that he had been instrumental in securing the rejection of the Acheson Plan. This admission attracted considerable attention in Greek political circles, since it seemed to confirm the suspicion that Andreas was more than just one of his father's advisors—he was *the* advisor, even on matters of foreign policy. Andreas himself has written that, as a result of the furor over his role in the Cyprus question, "there was no doubt that I had put the prime minister in a difficult position just as there was no doubt that I was becoming a source of serious friction between the government and the Americans in Greece."[10]

While Andreas Papandreou undoubtedly scored points with sectors of the Greek electorate by "standing tall" on Cyprus and rejecting any compromise with Turkey over the island, the reality was that only the United States could deter the larger and more powerful Turkey from invading Cyprus. To do this, the United States exerted considerable pressure on Ankara not to move militarily, and this pressure was exerted at considerable cost to the United States' reputation in Turkey.

ANDREAS PAPANDREOU RESIGNS

In October of 1964, Andreas Papandreou surprised the Greek political world by announcing that he was resigning from his father's cabinet, and would henceforth be only a member of Parliament. There was considerable speculation in political circles as to the reason for the abrupt resignation; as Margaret Papandreou wrote in her book, "It was one of the few times in modern Greek history that a minister resigned voluntarily."[11] However, the resignation occurred following allegations in an anti-government journal that Andreas had given a government contract to a close friend and former business associate without competitive bidding. The same paper also published innuendoes about Andreas's relationship with the wife of the same man. (Rumors of womanizing have followed Andreas Papandreou throughout much of his career.)

In explaining his abrupt resignation, Andreas Papandreou does not allude to the awarding of the contract nor the sexual innuendoes. Instead, he cites American pressure! As he relates in *Democracy at Gunpoint*:

> While it was not true that the Americans had asked for my resignation, it was true that my clashes with them had created an atmosphere between them and our government that, given the prevailing power relations, were working to the disadvantage of our government.[12]

Whatever the true reason, the fact was that after only eight months in office, the neophyte politician had quit a cabinet headed by his own father under bizarre circumstances. This recourse to unexpected, dramatic moves was to become the hallmark of Andreas Papandreou's political style over the years; when faced with a crisis, Andreas would do the unexpected, surprising friend and foe alike. Former Greek president Constantine Karamanlis was to learn this to his regret some 20 years later, when Papandreou, contrary to his assurances, suddenly and dramatically removed his support for Karamanlis's continuation in office as president.

THE PROBLEM OF SUCCESSION

From the outset of its victory at the polls in early 1964, a key issue affecting the future of the Center Union government of George Papandreou was the question of who would succeed the prime minister when he stepped down from office. By the mid-1960s, George Papandreou's health was failing. There were politicians around the elder Papandreou who had supported him loyally during his years in opposition and in his own struggle for leadership of the center forces against his long-time rival Sophocles Venizelos, who had died in early 1964. The most prominent contender for succession was Constantine Mitsotakis, who as minister of finance in the Papandreou cabinet had already clashed with Andreas Papandreou over the government's economic policies. As suspicion deepened among Mitsotakis and his supporters (who included the publisher of the pro-government daily *Eleutheria*) that George Papandreou was grooming Andreas as his eventual successor, the struggle for succession became more intense.

In early 1965, this issue entered the public arena when *Eleutheria* charged in a front-page story that Andreas had helped Cypriot president Archbishop Makarios wreck the Acheson Plan and thus prevent *enosis* with Greece. With the publication of this story, relations between Andreas Papandreou and Constantine Mitsotakis deteriorated rapidly, to the point that they were no longer on speaking terms.

ANDREAS RETURNS TO GOVERNMENT

In April of 1964, George Papandreou reappointed his son to the cabinet as alternate minister of coordination, the same position he had abruptly left only a few months earlier. Surprisingly, Andreas in his book attributes his reappointment to his father's concern that Andreas was becoming too popular outside of the government! As Andreas writes, George Papandreou was concerned that "being outside the cabinet, I would have the freedom and license to tour the country, magnify my political following, and create concern among the other party leaders that they might be overshadowed by me."[13]

Ironically, Andreas was subsequently to view his return to his father's cabinet as a "strategic mistake," since he had now become the specific target of the opposition's general attack on the government. According to Andreas, ERE had become "openly venomous" toward him. As he explains it, "I had taken strong, hard stands against them. Furthermore, they knew that I meant what I said when I committed myself publicly to dismantling the structure of special privilege which impeded the economic, social and political development of the country."[14]

THE OUSTER OF THE PAPANDREOU GOVERNMENT

In May of 1965, General George Grivas, commander of Greek forces in Cyprus and leader of the earlier Cypriot resistance to the British, reported to Petros Garouphalias, the Greek defense minister, that he had uncovered the existence of a secret organization of officers among the Greek forces on Cyprus, with the code name "Aspida." According to Grivas, the organization was linked to Andreas Papandreou, who had visited the island the previous fall, following his resignation from the government. Although the organization was reputed to hold somewhat vague neutralist tendencies, its exact purpose, other than loyalty to Andreas Papandreou, was unclear.

Any charge of a conspiracy in the Greek military—whether well-founded or not—was bound to have serious repercussions in Greece. Since traditionally the Greek royal family had identified with the armed forces, the alleged existence of an illegal secret organization within the military would be seen by young King Constantine as a direct challenge to the crown's preeminent position with the armed forces.

Recognizing the sensitivity of the issue, Prime Minister George Papandreou ordered an immediate investigation, headed by a senior officer in the military judicial branch. After a brief inquiry, the investigators concluded that only a handful of junior officers were involved. However, King Constantine apparently considered the investigation a whitewash, and ordered a full-scale inquiry. Relations between the prime minister and the king rapidly deteriorated, as the king seemed convinced that Aspida was a serious conspiracy, whose ultimate goal was the overthrow of the constitutional government and the imposition of a Nasser-type dictatorship, whereas George Papandreou was ready to dismiss Aspida as an insignificant pocket of discontent.

A deadlock ensued between the king and the prime minister, which ended with resignation of the Papandreou government in mid-July, 1965. For the next two months, Greece was without a parliamentary-supported government, as the king's first two choices to form a new government failed to secure a majority in Parliament due to the opposition of the Papandreou-led Center Union. Finally, on September 15, while demonstrators outside the Parliament shouted their support for George Papandreou, Stephanos Stephanopoulos, who had been deputy prime minister in Papandreou's government, succeeded in forming a narrow majority in the 300-member Parliament.

To form the Stephanopoulos government, some 30-odd deputies had bolted the Papandreou ranks to form the new government, which had to depend for support in Parliament on the opposition ERE party and a handful of deputies from the tiny Progressive party. What motivated the "apostates" (as they were henceforth to be called) is difficult to say. The stated concern of many of them was that Andreas Papandreou was pushing the country to a confrontation between the king and the government that could result in the destruction of Greek democracy. It is indeed plausible that this was the true motivation of a number of those who deserted the Papandreou ranks.

The true story of Aspida may never be known. Although Andreas was formally indicted during the dictatorship of George Papadopoulos, he was never brought to trial. In his book, Andreas is somewhat ambiguous about the existence of Aspida; although he acknowledges the charge regarding the organization "had a grain of truth in it," he denies strongly that he personally was in any way involved.[15] However, the end result was that because of real or fabricated activities of Andreas Papandreou, the elected government of George Papandreou was forced out of office and Greece entered a period of political instability, which terminated with the April 1967 coup d'état.

THE CONFLICT BETWEEN FATHER AND SON

Following the ouster of the Center Union government, Andreas Papandreou was to emerge more and more as the leader of the party's leftist wing, which numbered perhaps 40 out of the approximately 120 deputies remaining in the Center Union party. He also formed a youth organization, the Democratic League, which was personally loyal to him rather than to the party as a whole.

As described by Andreas in his book, the Democratic League was an "extra party, militant, democratic organization which in the case of elections was to support the progressive, anti-establishment candidates of our party in preference to those who, belonging to the center-right (of the Center Union), would be willing to come to terms with the establishment. In the case of a military coup, they were to form the nuclei, neighborhood by neighborhood, of the forces opposing the would-be dictators."[16]

It appears that following the revelations about Aspida and the ouster of his government, George Papandreou began increasingly to have doubts about his son's actions and political judgement. The elder Papandreou had become prime minister in 1963 after struggling for almost a generation to unite the center forces and challenge the right wing parties which had ruled Greece for a large part of the period following World War II. Now Andreas, at his father's urging, had entered Greek politics, but instead of slowly developing as George Papandreou's eventual heir, he had jeopardized not only his own future but that of his father by his confrontational tactics and intemperate rhetoric .

Moreover, despite being ousted through his disagreement with the king, George Papandreou hoped to once more become prime minister. By the end of 1966, however, it must have become increasingly clear to him that his son posed a potential threat to his achieving that goal.

Both Andreas and his wife have written at some length about the emerging conflict between father and son. Noting that his father resisted his efforts to provoke a confrontation with the power structure in Greece, Andreas asserts that George Papandreou:

> ... did not wish to preside over the dissolution of his party.... he was willing, while I was not, to make accommodations that would postpone such a confrontation (between the left and right wings of the party).... He did not believe that we could defeat the establishment in a frontal confrontation, and he retained the hope that the establishment would get around to recognizing that, after all, we were not as great a danger as they had seemed to think we were.[17]

C. L. Sulzberger reports a conversation that he had with Andreas Papandreou shortly after his father's ouster from office. According to Sulzberger, Andreas told him:

> My father loves me as a son, but my unbending tendencies have caused him trouble. I am a tough nut. He felt I was going overboard. He has not supported me politically as his successor. In fact, he has gone the other way. After George Papandreou, I have the widest popular base in Greece. I do not need George Papandreou![18]

A strong argument can be made that the growing rift

between the two men stemmed from the father's rejection of his son's confrontational politics, which could threaten the party's chances of returning to power. Yet both Andreas and his wife suggest another reason for the rift: George Papandreou, seeing his own strength slipping away, was jealous of the growing power of his son. As Margaret Papandreou writes in her book:

> It was at this stage that a conflict between father and son began to smoulder. It was a conflict in its classic form. A father jealous of his son's ability to gain power, his youth, his virility, his productive energy. Side-by-side existed also a pride in what his son was achieving. But the old man had all his life been stage center; he was unable to play a supporting role.... Under these circumstances, it was natural that Andreas assumed a leadership role, often making decisions without consulting his father. Andreas's father considered him ungrateful, impulsive, and disrespectful."[19]

Margaret Papandreou became the focal point of the two men's rivalry; both tried to convince her of the rightness of their positions. Inevitably, Margaret was to side with her husband and against her father-in-law. Nevertheless, George Papandreou would frequently seek her out to voice his complaints about Andreas, hoping that she would agree to persuade Andreas to change his views. Margaret Papandreou describes how on one occasion George Papandreou angrily accused Andreas of being "secretive and impulsive." He added, "These are Mineiko traits."[20] (Mineiko was the family name of Andreas's mother, George's first wife.) Margaret adds that with the passing of time, her father-in-law "began complaining not only to me but to close friends, and it was soon understood that a conflict existed between father and son."[21]

THE OPEN BREAK

However, the conflict between father and son did not burst into the open until December 1966, when, without informing his son, George Papandreou reached a three-way agreement with the king and the leader of the conservative party, Kanellopoulos, to give his support to an interim, non-political government that would remain in power for six months. The purpose of this temporary government—to be headed by the deputy governor of the Bank of Greece (Paraskeuopoulos)--would be to reduce the tension of Greek political life, in effect to let the country "cool down." In return for George Papandreou's support, the king promised that the country would go to elections by the end of May 1967.

According to their accounts, Andreas and Margaret Papandreou were thunderstruck when they learned for the first time of the agreement through the radio. Referring to her father-in-law as the "enemy within," Margaret Papandreou comments in her book, "By now my anger had turned into hurt and pain. The conflict between father and son, with all its psychological, emotional, and political components, had burst into the open."[22]

After his initial shock, Andreas Papandreou acted swiftly, issuing a public statement denouncing the agreement and insisting that he and his followers would vote against the Paraskeuopoulos government and, hence, against his father. In addition, he wrote his father a letter (they were no longer on speaking terms) asserting, "I could not follow him in what I considered a radical departure from principle, from the substance of our struggle for a new Greece."[23] George Papandreou's response was brief and to the point: Any deputy in the party who did not vote in favor of the Paraskeuopoulos government would automatically be expelled from the party. He further insisted that all attacks upon King Constantine must cease immediately.

Meanwhile, the parliamentary members of the party were busily occupied choosing sides for what promised to be a final showdown between father and son, with roughly two thirds of the deputies lining up behind party leader George Papandreou and the remaining one-third supporting Andreas.

In *Democracy at Gunpoint* , Andreas describes how he was in a terrible dilemma at this point; should he stand up for principle and thus involve himself in a fight to the finish against his father, or should he accept the authority of his father (and party leader) and thereby—in his view—compromise his principles? After considerable hesitation, Andreas decided to withdraw his opposition to the agreement; however, as he notes in his book, the effect of the dispute on relations between father and son "was to last a long time."[24] To be sure, Andreas's reluctance to break irrevocably with his father is understandable. As Margaret Papandreou points out, "in a culture like Greece, a schism between father and son was repugnant and incomprehensible."[25]

Though a final break between George and Andreas Papandreou had been averted at the eleventh hour, the public conflict had placed a tremendous strain on party unity as well. Andreas Papandreou continued his "crusade to the people," which featured sharp criticism of the king, the Greek establishment and the United States. For its part, the conservative ERE party and the "apostates" from the Center Union intensified their personal attacks on Andreas. In short, despite the agreement to support the Paraskeuopoulos government, the Greek political situation did not become calmer.

With elections tentatively scheduled for late May 1967, the conservative forces became increasingly concerned that the Center Union would repeat its 1964 electoral triumph. And a victory for the Center Union meant, in their eyes, that Andreas Papandreou would eventually come to power—it was widely believed that the ailing senior Papandreou could not long maintain the party leadership, and would bequeath power to his son. Since there were no longer any real competitors for succession within the party, this was a logical conclusion.

In her book, Margaret Papandreou has described the atmosphere that prevailed in early spring 1967, as rumors grew of an impending coup. "How does one stop a military coup? The snowball had been pushed and we were rolling down the hill, speeding towards disaster at the bottom. We were shouting, but our words were heard only by us, echoing our desperation."[26]

By this point, events were moving rapidly towards a dénouement. On 10 March 1967 the Aspida court martial, which had been meeting since the previous fall, rendered its verdict: 15 officers were convicted and given prison terms ranging from two to 18 years. To forestall any effort to bring Andreas to trial for his alleged part in the affair, the Center Union introduced an amendment to the electoral law that would extend parliamentary immunity through the electoral period. However, the ERE refused to go along with the amendment, an impasse developed and, when no agreement seemed possible, the Paraskeuopoulos government resigned.

The crisis was now full-blown. The king's attempt to form a government of national unity, which would govern the country until autumn to allow passions to cool, was rejected by George Papandreou, who insisted that the country proceed to elections, as originally agreed. Instead, the king offered the mandate to ERE leader Panagiotes Kanellopoulos, with instructions that if he was not able to obtain majority support in Parliament, he could dissolve that body and hold elections.

George Papandreou immediately denounced the king's action, charging that it was a betrayal of the December agreement to support the Paraskeuopoulos government.

Meanwhile, tensions were rising, and police clashed with Papandreou supporters in the streets of Athens. As expected, Kanellopoulos was unable to obtain a majority in Parliament. The king then made one last effort to form a government of national unity; when this failed because of Center Union opposition, Kanellopoulos dissolved Parliament on 14 April and proclaimed elections for 27 May.

But the elections were never to take place. In the early morning hours of 21 April, a group of Greek colonels seized power and the lights of Greek democracy were extinguished for seven long years.

It can be fairly argued that the overthrow of Greek constitutional government on 21 April 1967 was in no small part caused by Andreas Papandreou. By almost single-handedly polarizing Greek political life, Andreas Papandreou created the psychological atmosphere that emboldened the colonels to make their fateful move to overthrow constitutional authority. His inflammatory rhetoric, his thrust for primacy within his own party, his attacks upon the Greek establishment in general had convinced many people that an electoral victory for the Center Union party, enabling him to play a major role in governing the country, would create an intolerable situation for Greece. Although Andreas spoke repeatedly of his vision of a "new Greece," the many enemies he had made believed an Andreas victory promised only divisiveness, confusion, and the destruction of their values.

Greece, of course, had been a democracy—admittedly, an imperfect one—since the withdrawal of Nazi forces in the closing days of World War II. It had survived a civil war that had threatened to bring it under communist control. Furthermore, it had been robust enough to undergo transfers of power from right to center, including the victory of George Papandreou in 1963, which brought an end to 8 years of conservative rule. But the fabric of Greek democracy was apparently not strong enough to withstand the strains placed upon it by the confrontational politics of Andreas Papandreou. Andreas's style apparently so aroused the fear and hatred of his opponents in the Greek establishment that they were prepared to countenance a dictatorship rather than risk his coming to power. It is significant that there was no spontaneous outpouring of resistance to the colonels from either the Greek elite or the general public on 21 April.

In retrospect, it appears that Andreas Papandreou made little effort to alleviate the concerns of his opponents regarding the consequences of a Center Union return to power. On the contrary, his refusal to brook compromise or to make accommodations, his constant references to conspiracies and intrigue, and his assertion that a victory for his forces would not be simply an electoral triumph but would constitute a radical transformation of the Greek body politic, all contributed to raise Greek political passions, already at a high level. In short, by "going for the jugular," Andreas polarized Greek politics beyond the limits of traditional Greek political rivalry.

Some observers suggested that it was Andreas's political inexperience that was at the root of the problem. As Elizabeth Drew, writing a year after the coup, put it: "Brilliant, arrogant, charming, given to demagogy, and particularly at the beginning, politically inept, Andreas Papandreou fought all his battles at once and thereby managed to antagonize concurrently the palace, the military, the conservative circles and the American establishment (sic) in Greece."[27] A writer sympathetic to Andreas, Harry Psomiades, has written that "political ineptness on the part of the younger Papandreou ultimately arrayed the traditional political establishment (some even say his own father) and the army against him, pushed him towards the left, and thus further polarized Greek politics."[28]

However, inexperience cannot explain why Andreas pushed matters to the point where it was clear even to him and his wife that a coup was likely. The question arises as to whether there was some flaw in his personality, perhaps a "self-destruct" syndrome, that drove him inexorably towards conflict and disaster in 1967.

There is a seeming parallel in the career of the brilliant and controversial U.S. president Woodrow Wilson, whose compulsive behavior in the latter days of his administration destroyed his goal of bringing the United States into the League of Nations. Alexander George, the brilliant biographer, described Wilson's behavior as self-defeating: "[he] stubbornly persisted in his course and helped bring about his own personal defeat and the defeat of worthwhile measures which he was championing."[29]

More recently, the American presidential aspirant Gary Hart, by his flouting of conventional American social behavior (and challenging the American press to "watch" him), in essence destroyed his own political career. It may be that, like Wilson and Hart, Andreas, relentlessly moving into conflict with forces that his reason must have told him he could not defeat (and that his father and others warned would crush him), was acting out an inner compulsion to press forward until checked.

In his work, George describes the psychology of a neurotically compulsive person as follows:

> What is usually called stubbornness in the behavior of adult persons is an attempt to use other persons as instruments in the struggle with the super ego. By provoking people to be unjust, they strive for a feeling of moral superiority which is needed to increase the self-esteem as a counter balance against the pressure of the super ego.... The stubborn behavior is maintained the more obstinately the more an inner feeling exists that it is impossible to prove what needs to be proven, and that one is actually in the wrong.... The feeling that whatever I do is still less wicked than what has been done to me is needed as a weapon against the super ego, and if successful, may bring relief from feelings of guilt.[30]

A paragraph in George's biography of President Wilson describing Wilson under stress could fit perfectly the way Andreas Papandreou dealt with political crisis. George writes:

> In the heat of battle, he would recognize no legitimate, intermediate position, and could tolerate no ambiguity. He tended to lump together all his opponents. In such crises, therefore, his leadership was strongly divisive rather than unifying. He alienated the potential support of moderate elements who strove to sympathize with his general aims....[31]

In Andreas's case, the more his opponents reacted to his rhetoric or actions, the harder Andreas counter-attacked. And as the intensity of his attacks escalated, his opponents hit back in every possible way, which eventually led to the coup d'état.

Andreas was aware of the forces coalescing against him. He and his wife undertook some rather rudimentary security measures. Margaret Papandreou described these measures in her book: "It was during this time that Andreas purchased guns in case of a sudden attack or assassination attempt. It was not unusual for me to be at a social gathering dressed in evening wear, necklace and dangling earrings, carrying a revolver in my beaded purse."[32] Andreas and a group of associates had worked out a complicated set of arrangements to conceal their comings and goings. He described in his book how, by the spring of 1967 he was keeping "several apartments available for concealment in the event of a coup or an assassination attempt. Coups occur only at night and for the last few nights I have not slept at home."[33]

It is interesting to note that Andreas Papandreou believed that his rather amateurish efforts at concealment and the establishment of a rudimentary resistance organization could thwart a determined effort by the armed forces to take action against him; as we know from Andreas's writings, friends in the American embassy, his associates, and even his father had warned him that his actions were polarizing Greek political life and causing his enemies to coalesce against him. Obviously, prudence would have dictated an effort to calm the situation, lest tensions result in a coup effort.

In retrospect, it is clear that Andreas grossly overestimated the strength of his own following and the willingness of his supporters to resist when faced with the overwhelming might of the Greek military. In his book, he reveals his bafflement following his arrest:

> What had gone wrong? Both he (Aleuras, a close friend, detained in the same room) and I had expected a violent confrontation. And we had taken the steps, had laid the foundations for a massive popular reaction. Was it taking place at this moment?... Somewhere we had failed.[34]

Later, in prison, he ruminates: "Time and time again we had asked the citizens to be ready for a military coup. Our solution had been simple and straightforward: A general strike. It was the obvious response." Still later, Andreas wonders: "Above all, what were the people doing? Was there nowhere a clash, nowhere a confrontation?"[35]

Near the close of his book, Andreas takes himself to task for neglecting to set up an effective resistance organization. Significantly, his self-criticism is limited to the lack of proper management of resistance efforts; he does not consider the possibility that some action on his part might have prevented the coup. In his view, he had been remiss only in not devoting more time to clandestine activities. As he put it:

> ... had we given serious attention to the establishment of a clandestine, resistance-oriented organization, had we given clear instructions for action in response to a coup, had we distributed radio transmitters and mimeograph machines, and had we rented apartments under cover to protect the leadership of the organization, then possibly we could have frustrated the coup within the first few hours. And while it was true that I organized the Democratic League and gave them this type of assignment, it must be admitted candidly that neither I nor my immediate circle chose to concentrate our energies in this direction.... All the same, the leadership should have done more than it did. This, too, therefore, is our responsibility.[36]

It is revealing that this is the only point in his entire book that Andreas Papandreou acknowledges his own responsibility for developments surrounding the coup d'état. Missing is any suggestion of political steps that might have been taken to ameliorate the deepening crisis. Nor is there any realization on his part that the paramilitary activities he states he should have undertaken might have been incompatible with his role as a democratic political leader.

THE PROBLEM OF IDENTITY

Any effort to understand Andreas Papandreou's personality must take into consideration his role of living within two cultures, American and Greek, but not being fully assimilated into either, of being what sociologists refer to as a "marginal man." The contradictions inherent in such a role are evident. Thus, although Andreas had been born in Greece and had lived there the first 20 years of his life, his higher education had been largely obtained in the U.S., where he was to live another 20 or so years. His wife was (and is) American, his children were raised as Americans, the language of the home was (usually) English, and his research and writings in economics were in English. On the other hand, by 1959 he was back in Greece, once more using his mother tongue, establishing a close relationship for the first time with his Greek father and, finally, embarking on a new career in which the concepts and language were exclusively Greek.

It would not be surprising, therefore, if the transitions between the two cultures placed a strain on Andreas's sense of self-identity. This point is made several times by his wife; as she notes at one point in her book, "Andreas was leading a schizoid life in many ways. Greek by birth, American by naturalization, he would see events one day through the eyes of a Greek, the next through the eyes of an American."[37] But following the coup, Margaret noted how Andreas reverted to his Greek character. As she commented, "As he was once quite completely American, he became quite completely Greek—even his language and his gestures changed."[38]

This identity struggle may have been the major factor in Andreas Papandreou's eventual rejection of his American background and his subsequent accusations that it was the United States—not the king, the Greek establishment nor even the Greek junta—that was ultimately responsible for the coup of 1967. (This theme, of American responsibility for Greece's ills, first evidenced in his denunciation of the U.S. role in Cyprus in 1964, has recurred throughout Andreas Papandreou's career, including his current charges of American complicity with Turkey in frustrating Greece's legitimate interests in Cyprus and the Aegean.) As Andreas phrased it in his book:

> Thus the Greek military regime has apparently taken over the country in order to deliver it on a platter to the economic and strategic interests of the U.S. industrial military complex, to the private-public bureaucratic establishment of the metropolis. Greece, in this context, as a result of the military take-over, has become an industrial-military satellite of the United States.... Thus it is quite fair to think of the Greek military regime as falling in the category of the Latin American banana republic regimes.[39]

The theme that the Greek colonels acted in behalf of U.S. interests is repeated time and again in *Democracy at Gunpoint* . For example:

> And by now, every Greek, civilian or military, understands the coup and the regime for what they really are: Putsch to subjugate the Greek nation to the interests of Big Brother (the U.S.) For the coup and the regime are as anti-nationalist, as anti-reformist as possible. The colonels' uniforms are Greek, but neither their thoughts nor their actions are Greek....[40]

Andreas Papandreou has repeatedly denounced alleged U.S. interference in Greek affairs throughout his career, both during his years in exile in the late 1960s and early 1970s, and later when he returned to Greek politics, first in opposition and then as leader of the government.

Ironically, in Andreas Papandreou's hour of need it was to the United States that he turned for assistance and protection. Thus, when he was seized and imprisoned by the junta, it was thanks mainly to U.S. efforts, including significant pressure from American academic circles, that Andreas Papandreou was eventually freed to enter into exile.

For a time, Andreas's wife and his supporters in the United States raised the possibility that Andreas Papandreou still retained his American citizenship (since he had never formally renounced it), which could provide a possible means of securing his release. It was indeed an ironic twist of fate that the Greek political leader who had made anti-Americanism the hallmark of his political career and who had most strongly attacked U.S. "interference" in Greek political life, should attempt to invoke U.S. influence in Greece for his own welfare.

In any evaluation of Andreas Papandreou's career and his historical significance, two questions come to mind: First, have Andreas Papandreou's continuing denunciations of the United States during his years in opposition and in power led to a permanent realignment of Greece's fundamental relationship to the United States? Second, have Andreas Papandreou's foreign policies—and particularly his efforts to move Greece away from its traditional, close relationship with Washington—contributed positively to Greece's national interests? In this writer's view, a considered answer to both questions must be no.

In responding to the first question, it must be acknowledged that largely in response to the years of anti-American rhetoric of the prime minister and his supporters in politics, the media and academia, the prevailing sentiment today among a large number—perhaps a majority—of Greeks is highly critical of the United States. Nevertheless, some observers, such as *New York Times* journalist Henry Kamm, have argued that the many ties between Greeks and Americans, of more than a half century's standing, cannot be severed by the policies of one Greek administration, however anti-American it may be.[41]

Certainly, the unfavorable picture of the United States painted in the strident rhetoric of Andreas Papandreou contrasts strikingly with the experience of millions of Greeks who have immigrated to the United States and been successfully absorbed into the American mainstream. Many of them have risen to the highest positions in the business, academic, and political worlds of their adopted country. The continuing interaction between Americans of Greek origin and their relatives and friends in their motherland have created bonds that would seem to be of an enduring nature, not subject to the vagaries of specific administrations, either in Greece or the United States.

To be sure, the "American experience" of Andreas Papandreou differs from that of the average Greek immigrant, who came from a farm or city where he was of very modest means and who left for the United States like other European immigrants in search of opportunity not available in his own country. Papandreou was a member of that small, elite group of educated Greeks who either left Greece (as he did) because of World War II or, in the decades since the war, to obtain additional training in their fields of specialization. The reaction of Andreas Papandreou to his years of U.S. residence may be seen as the exception which proves the rule. For the most part, this cadre of professional Greeks who received post-graduate or other training in the United States represents a significant pro-American element in Greek society.

With regard to the impact of the Papandreou policies on Greek youth, it seems clear that the young people of Greece have been strongly influenced by the anti-U.S. attitudes pervasive in the universities and in much of the mass media. This is particularly true of the students in universities who have been exposed to the "revisionist" teachings of the left regarding U.S.-Greek relations since World War II. According to one observer, professors who do not give a Marxist perspective to their teachings are often intimidated and even blocked by radical students from entering their classrooms.[42]

Having said this, it is necessary to point out that Greek youth, like those of the rest of Western Europe, are equally exposed to the "pull" of popular American culture as represented in cinema, music, dress and life styles. It is certainly possible that, assuming that Greece remains an open, democratic society, the pendulum will eventually swing back towards a more balanced view of the United States, irrespective of the regime in power; after all, Greek young people share youth's universal challenging of whatever theories their elders attempt to foist upon them.

In sum, it is probable that even after years of anti-American rhetoric and propaganda, the legacy of Greek-American common interests, and even friendship, will endure.

Answering the second question, it is questionable whether Andreas Papandreou's foreign policy—and particularly his seeming determination to distance Greece from the United States and NATO—has been beneficial to Greece.

Andreas Papandreou has mobilized public opinion in a way that no Greek leader in recent times has been able to do, with the possible exception of his father. His militant rhetoric against American policies, reminiscent of that used by campus radicals in the United States in the 1960s, has succeeded in eroding the image of the United States and the credibility of American policies among thousands of Greek citizens, even if only temporarily. It is hard to see how this has benefited Greece, other than to make its citizens more cynical about Greece's allies.

For Greece, a nation of less than 10 million people, surrounded on the north and east by potential adversaries, is not in a position to successfully pursue its national aspirations in Cyprus or elsewhere without the support of powerful friends; unlike many of the smaller nations of the Third World, Greece is not a member of a larger ethnic group, such as the Arabs or Slavs, with which it can identify and from which it can seek support. As a Western nation with a long Christian tradition, Greece has far more in common with the democracies of Western Europe and the United States than it does with nations to the east and south.

During his years in office, Andreas Papandreou has played the "Turkish card" successfully, whipping up Greek public opinion against Turkey when it has suited his foreign or, more frequently, his domestic purposes. But by exploiting the ever-present anti-Turkish sentiment of the Greek public and the very legitimate Greek complaints about Turkey's occupation of Cyprus, Andreas has played for high stakes, since a miscalculation could plunge Greece into a war from which no one—not Greece, not Turkey, not the Western alliance—would benefit. In appealing to the nationalist sentiments of the Greek people, Andreas has successfully diverted public attention from some of the failures of his domestic policies. But the dangers of miscalculation are ever present.

As is often pointed out, Greece has traditionally been aligned with the Great Power controlling the Mediterranean; before World War II, that was Great Britain; since the war, the United States. Andreas Papandreou's efforts to look to the Third World nations for support, other than as a voting bloc in the United Nations, seem a poor substitute for the real protection and assistance offered by close ties with the nation to which it is linked by common values and tradition—the United States. To the extent that Andreas Papandreou has isolated Greece from her natural allies, he has performed a disservice to the Greek state and the Greek people.

NOTES

1. Henry Kamm, "Papandreou: The Politics of Anti-Americanism," *New York Times Magazine*, 7 April 1985, 18.

2. Nikolaos A. Stavrou, "Harry Would Have Given Papandreou Hell," *Wall Street Journal*, 27 Sept. 1986.

3. Alexander George, "Some Uses of Dynamic Psychology in Political Biography: Case Materials on Woodrow Wilson," *A Source Book for the Study of Personality and Politics* (Chicago: Markham Publishing Co., 1971).

4. Nicholas Gage, "The Paradoxical Papandreou,"*New York Times Magazine* , 21 March 1982, 45.

5. Andreas Papandreou, *Democracy at Gunpoint: The Greek Front* (New York: Doubleday, 1970): 45. In an interview a few years ago with Nick Gage, Papandreou related how when he returned to Greece for the first time in 1951-52, he received a call at his father's home in Kastri from the security official who had broken his jaw (Maniadakes), and the next day his jaw broke again—at exactly the same place. It was not clear if Andreas meant the story to be apocryphal. See Gage, "The Paradoxical Papandreou," 74.

6. *Ibid.*, 99.

7. *Ibid.*, 120.

8. Margaret Papandreou, *Nightmare in Athens* (Englewood Cliffs, N.J.: Prentice-Hall, 1970): 71.

9. A. Papandreou, *Democracy*, 129.

10. *Ibid.*, 38.

11. M. Papandreou, *Nightmare*, 78.

12. A. Papandreou, *Democracy*, 138.

13. *Ibid.*, 146.

14. *Ibid.*, 146.

15. *Ibid.*, 152.

16. *Ibid.*, 185.

17. *Ibid.*, 186.

18. C. L. Sulzberger, "Greece Under the Colonel," *Foreign Affairs* (January, 1970): 301.

19. M. Papandreou, *Nightmare*, 102-3.

20. *Ibid.*, 193.

21. *Ibid.*, 109.

22. *Ibid.*, 122-3.

23. A. Papandreou, *Democracy*, 199.

24. *Ibid.*, 204.

25. M. Papandreou, *Nightmare*, 123.

26. *Ibid.*, 132.

27. Elizabeth Drew, "Democracy on Ice," *Atlantic Monthly*, July, 1968, 57.

28. Harry Psomiades, *Journal of International Affairs* 24, no. 1 (1970).

29. George, "Some Uses of Dynamic Psychology," 91.

30. *Ibid.*, 91.

31. *Ibid.*, 94.

32. M. Papandreou, *Nightmare*, 125.

33. A. Papandreou, *Democracy*, 16.

34. *Ibid.*, 19.

35. *Ibid.*, 26.
36. *Ibid.*, 347.
37. M. Papandreou, *Nightmare*, 61.
38. *Ibid.*, 229.
39. A. Papandreou, *Democracy*, 330-331.
40. *Ibid.*, 334.
41. Kamm, "Papandreou," 46.
42. Stavrou, "Harry Would Have Given Papandreou Hell."

The Defense Policies of PASOK

George J. Tsoumis

From 1980 on, Greece has undergone a gradual but perceptible change (*allage*) in the social, economic, productive, and even spiritual aspects of life. Inevitably these changes have influenced the domestic, foreign, and defense policies of the country. At this stage we are not sure whether *allage* was successful or not. The reply to this question will be given by the Greeks in the next general elections, but in some areas the results of *allage* are obvious.

The size of the gross national product and the per capita income has dropped, international relations and national prestige have also deteriorated, and, in the view of this writer, the effectiveness of the Hellenic armed forces has been negatively affected.

Whether *allage* has failed or succeeded will be better examined by other specialists in this volume. In this chapter the impact of PASOK's policies on national defense will be analyzed in the context of the overall policies of the Socialist government and compared with the post-1974 defense doctrine of New Democracy.

THE DEFENSE POLICIES OF NEW DEMOCRACY

With the fall of the Greek junta in 1974, the National Unity government of Karamanlis and the subsequent government of the New Democracy party found the Hellenic armed forces with low morale and inadequately prepared in most material areas. The obsolete equipment and structure of the armed forces were the result of a long embargo by the United States against the military junta, which was endorsed by most Greek politicians as a means towards bringing an end to the dictatorship. Only Evangelos Averoff opposed the embargo in several communications to congressional committees, strictly for national security reasons and not in support of the junta.

The low morale of the armed forces was the result of their being blamed for the defeat in Cyprus, even though they had not been engaged in combat against the Turks. Although the military was criticized for inadequate mobilization, it is well known that this state of affairs was the result of hasty decisions made by the junta in the absence of professional soldiers. The armed forces were further demoralized by the strategic blunder of the exit of Greece from the military wing of NATO in 1974. Karamanlis withdrew from the alliance because of "the pressure of public opinion," and without proper consultation of any national military leadership, which at that time did not exist. By withdrawing all its armed forces from the NATO Joint Command, Greece lost the operational control of the Aegean Sea, which was gladly assumed by the Turks.

The first defense decision of the Karamanlis government, after concerted diplomatic actions aimed at isolating the Turkish government internationally and portraying it as the aggressor, was to demobilize the Hellenic armed forces, and to disengage them from the political affairs in which they had been active during the seven years of military rule. The second decision was to acquire the military equipment urgently needed to overcome the Turkish superiority in matériel.

After the personal appeal made by Karamanlis to President Giscard d'Estaing of France, Greece purchased thirty-three Mirage F-1 fighters and thus achieved a limited air superiority in the Aegean Sea. At the same time the air force acquired from the U.S. Navy fifty A-7 bombers, twelve C-130 Hercules cargo planes (a considerable number), and from Olympic Airlines six Japanese YS-11-200 transport aircraft. In addition a number of helicopters of different types and capabilities were also purchased. The navy, too, was reinforced. Two Kontanael frigates and fourteen Combattand missile boats with Exocet and Penguin missiles were acquired on an urgent basis. To counter the mass of Turkish tanks in Thrace, the army was provided with 250 AMX French tanks, 240 AMX armored personnel carriers (APC), a number of antitank MILAN and TOW missiles and other accessories, and more than ninety helicopters. With immediate material needs taken care of, the attention of the political leadership turned to the psychological factor.

Defense Minister Averoff succeeded in raising the morale of the armed forces by involving the senior officers and the cadres of the army in central decisions and by exploiting the spirit of revenge against the Turks. This approach proved to be effective, although PASOK, as the opposition party, was quite critical of the armed forces and especially of the officers corps, which in its view eroded the discipline of the army and indirectly caused the Cyprus debacle.

Averoff's position, reflected in the political directives of the government to the military and in the slogan "Not one foot of national territory is negotiable" improved both discipline and morale. The armed forces then adopted the doctrine of the "forward strategy with flexible response against any possible invasion." This became the defense doctrine of New Democracy. It met the needs of the situation and made best use of the nation's capabilities.

The specific measures taken to implement that doctrine were the following.

1. The bulk of the armed forces were posted in the Aegean Islands and Thrace. A considerable number of reserves were kept back, ready to be introduced at any threatened point of the extended border line, by airlift, by sea ferries, or through improved routes and railways.

2. The national guard battalions were reorganized to defend critical points, and the manual Political Planning of Urgent Situations was revised and upgraded under laws No. 17/1974 and 1977 (despite PASOK's opposition).

3. The air force was reinforced to provide necessary air cover, to wage interdiction operations and close air support, and to strike targets of military and economic importance deep in Turkey.

The navy was to be the dominant power in the Aegean Sea and remain a constant threat to Turkish shores and ports. In addition to developing its readiness against the Turks, with its reserve forces Greece was able to fulfill its obligations to NATO (even though it was not technically under NATO unified command) and to counter any threat from the north.

From a significantly strengthened position, the Karamanlis government began negotiations for the reintegration of the military into NATO. The result was the Rogers Plan, which was characterized as a "monument of obscurity," but was a sensible formula for the country's reentry into NATO and a step in the direction of regaining operational control over the Aegean Sea. When Karamanlis moved from the position of prime minister to that of president in 1980, the weak Rallis government, under pressure from the political opposition, slowed down modernization and relaxed discipline. For instance, after a five-day workweek with continuous eight-hour days had been introduced in the civil service and the armed forces, both were then targeted by PASOK agitators and left-wing ideologues who clamored for their "democratization." From that point on, profound changes occurred in the armed forces, with great side effects in training, discipline, well-being, and morale. Disparities in training and readiness became endemic.

Units that, in accordance with their mission, were to be on constant alert and in hard training, had to train more hours without rest, while units and headquarters in the interior behaved as ordinary civil servants, often insisting on a nine-to-five schedule. Because of political interference, the frontline units began to lose status, while the interior units augmented theirs. As a result new morale and discipline problems emerged. Those were the first results of PASOK's defense policies, offered against a weak Rallis cabinet that tried to please all, but in the end satisfied no one.

SOURCES OF INFLUENCE ON PASOK'S DEFENSE POLICIES

The dramatic changes in the defense posture of the country under PASOK reflect the contradictory history of the party's origin and sources of influence. Many of its key cadres were participants in the politics of marginal movements in the West, while others admired the totalitarian ideology of the East. Thus upon its assumption of power in 1981, PASOK put in doubt the age-old belief—reinforced by Karamanlis's policy since 1974—that Greece belonged to the West.

PASOK's cadres brought to Greece the "anti-imperialist" mentality that was spawned by the anti-Vietnam war movement and expressed in theories ranging from pacifist to outright anarchist. European and American academic cadres were dominated by socialist agitators and the Third World, nonaligned movement was perceived as an alternative to bloc the political alliance. More specifically, the NATO alliance was the target of left-wing agitation. The anti-establishment or "flower" culture that had been rampant in Europe and the United States in the 1960s and early 1970s was transplanted belatedly to Greece by PASOK in 1974.

PASOK's cadres brought that thinking to Greece. Members of the Socialist cabinet had even adopted counterculture attire; some returned to Greece wearing robes of the flower children, and others hippie haircuts. The leader of the party, reflecting his rejection of convention, would enter Parliament without a necktie, wearing a turtleneck collar and long sideburns, flouting decorum.

With the legalization of the Greek Communist party, a considerable number of the civil war rebels who were refugees in communist countries also returned to Greece. They were divided into different warring factions, such as Orthodox Communists, Eurocommunists, Heretics, Maoists, and Reformists. Some of them, including the commander-in-chief of the Communist rebel forces, Markos Vafiades, a brigade commander with the nom de guerre Ypsilantes, and others, supported the PASOK movement. They were trained in Boulkes, Yugoslavia, from 1945 to 1946 for the purpose of seizing power by force, and their combat experience was in guerrilla warfare. Although they did not occupy governmental posts, they became advisors to the ministries, including the Ministry of Defense.[1]

Another faction of PASOK's cadres who influenced the defense policies were ex-military officers, such as the vice-president of the government, the minister of foreign affairs, Giannes Charalambopoulos (now defense minister), who had retired from the army as lieutenant colonel of the Engineering Corps in the early sixties. Similarly, the deputy minister of defense and now minister of public order, Antones Drosogiannis, was an ex-lieutenant colonel of the infantry. The vice-director of the Central Intelligence Agency (KYP) and the present director of the Military Office of the Presidency were lieutenant colonels of the artillery. More important, the director of the Hellenic Telecommunications Organization, responsible, as the rumors say, for communications tapping, was an ex-captain of the Signal Corps.[2] All of the above were promoted to the rank of general retroactively without the essential military training, education, and spirit, but with a strong background in covert actions and political manipulations.

The last faction of PASOK's cadres involved in the formulation of defense policies comes from the military branch of PAK, the predecessor of the PASOK movement, whose members trained in Libyan and Palestinian camps. They include the general-secretary of the Ministry of Interior (currently the director of the National Intelligence Agency, or EYP, formerly KYP), PASOK's ambassador to Libya, and many other lesser personalities.[3]

It goes without saying that all of the above factions, often espousing contradictory goals, influence Papandreou's defense doctrine, which neither is "doctrine" nor defends anything. In fact, these factions convinced the prime minister that Greece faces no threat from the north.

THE THREAT FROM THE NORTH AND THE EAST

With the ascent of PASOK to power, after the elections of October 1981, Andreas Papandreou concluded that the threat from the east (Turkey) was not necessarily a security problem but a political one, which in turn could be used for domestic political objectives. Contrary to the assertions of some, the professionals in the military were not consulted. Instead PASOK concluded that Turkey would attack Greece only if the Americans wanted the Turks to overthrow PASOK's government, or if the Greek military wanted to create a crisis in order to seize political power again. Oddly enough, PASOK turned for information on the Turkish threat to Palestinians, Libyans, and Cypriots, who continuously exaggerated Turkish intentions but said very little about the Turkish military build-up. They always wanted to appear as though they were offering their good services to PASOK, but in reality they were bringing Greece and Turkey closer to a collision for reasons of their own.

On the other hand, the threat from the north, Papandreou believed, was an exaggerated assessment by the military and NATO. The solution merely required withdrawal from NATO and relaxation of tensions with Bulgaria. New Democracy's opening to the Balkans was not enough in PASOK's view. They firmly believed that if they adopted a nonaligned posture, Greece would not have to counter any threat from the north. Willingly or not, Papandreou placed Greece squarely within the perimeter of the Andropov "buffer zone" (see map in the appendix at the back of this volume).

According to Soviet doctrine, the security of the USSR was more feasible with the creation of a "buffer zone" between the Western and Eastern blocs, consisting of nonaligned countries rather than satellite states, which often created problems for the USSR. For the creation of such a zone, only two countries were useful: West Germany and Greece.

Greek military specialists, including the writer,[4] are convinced that the assignment of Andropov's son (an expert on Finnish affairs) as ambassador to Greece was intended to promote the nonaligned policy that had been adopted by PASOK as early as 1974. PASOK declared that no threat from the north existed and was universally applauded by Greek leftists. This "discovery" provided the party with the opportunity to move "dangerous" or unreliable forces from the mainland to the islands and Thrace, thus allaying its own fears of a military intervention.

Despite these political manipulations and force redeployments, PASOK remained distrustful of the officers corps. Retirements for political reasons increased. After cumulative purges of approximately 1,100 senior officers through 1984, the National Intelligence Agency (NIA or EYP in Greek) and the Military High Command finally gained the trust of PASOK, and the government attempted to address real defense problems.

PASOK at last realized the threat from the east was not simply a case of political posturing by Turkey, but a serious problem for Greek national security. Similarly, the threat from the north, dismissed until 1984, suddenly reappeared when the Yugoslavs revived the "Macedonian problem," the Rumanians had difficulties accepting the propositions for a nuclear-free zone in the Balkans, and the Bulgarians pressed to open routes to the Kavala and Alexandroupolis ports and turned a deaf ear to suggestions for the distribution of the waters of the Nestos River.[5] Meanwhile, no reduction of the Warsaw Pact forces was observed, and no change in their offensive disposition occurred. Yet PASOK's policy became that of an ostrich: the threat from the north existed, but would not be declared; the threat from the east was "imminent," but NATO, the European Community, and the American bases in Greece would de facto protect the national interests of the country, while Greece would not even acknowledge their role. Instead, Papandreou would pursue the Third World connection.

THE BALANCE OF POWER: BEFORE AND AFTER PASOK

When PASOK assumed power, the Hellenic armed forces had a slight superiority over the Turkish military in the air force and navy, and with their support the land forces could have successfully waged a defensive war. Defense Minister Evangelos Averoff (of New Democracy) had done a remarkable job in building the capabilities and morale of the armed forces following the Cyprus debacle.

The PASOK government, after the basic transition briefings, was so impressed with the status of the armed forces, that Papandreou, as prime minister and minister of defense, expressed his unreserved satisfaction with the excellent job done by the New Democracy government and properly congratulated the military leadership for its professionalism. But the military was not critical in his schemes, and he turned his attention to political issues.

On the other side of the Aegean, Turkey continued to improve its military power by exploiting the new tensions in the region (i.e., the Gulf War) to its advantage. The result was a decline in the relative power of Greece compared with that of Turkey.

The International Institute of Strategic Studies in Great Britain (IISS) has tabulated data on the balance of power in 1986 between the two countries (see table in the appendix at the back of this volume).

The balance of power until 1984 was significantly in favor of Greece in all branches of the armed forces, making it possible for the country to wage successfully a defensive war applying the doctrine of forward strategy and flexible response. In 1985 the balance of power began to shift, as Turkey made operational the 180 F-104 Starfighters that were transferred from the air forces of West Germany and other NATO countries, thus increasing Ankara's air capabilities. The acquisition of the F-104s enabled Turkey to reevaluate her tactical doctrine and to adopt NATO's Air-Land Battle tactics successfully. The new Turkish defense posture will be fully operational when Turkey receives the first 160 F-16s in conjunction with the modification of the rest of its M 48 tanks to M 48A5 and some other improvements in its infantry, artillery, and antiaircraft defense. Great progress was also noted in the naval forces, especially in their amphibious capabilities, while Greece was vainly searching for a defense doctrine to complement a political ideology that was in many instances antithetical to NATO's raison d'être.

PASOK AND THE GREEK MILITARY

As indicated in other chapters of this volume, PASOK's policies vis-à-vis the military were influenced by its stance towards the NATO alliance. As an opposition party PASOK denounced some aspects of the alliances and treaties of previous governments, such as the agreements for the American bases and the country's entry into the Common Market. The pre-1981 slogans included "Out the American bases of death," and "NATO and EEC the same syndicate." This posture ran against the common sense of the armed forces, which did not believe that the slogans merely represented preelection promises. As the date of the 1981 elections approached, PASOK was preoccupied with the fear that even if it won the contest, some "dark power" would prevent it from assuming office. The belief among the party's left wing was that if it insisted on enforcing its policies, it would be overthrown by a combination of military and allied opposition.

Mitigating such fears was Papandreou's belief that President Karamanlis's sense of democratic fair play would ensure the support of the High Command of the armed forces. Yet questions remained in his mind about the attitudes of the lower echelons, especially at the rank of colonel and below. The rank of colonel had acquired a bad reputation in the years of the junta, but it also has a special meaning in the Greek armed forces because it is the critical rank for shaping the higher echelons. Only one-third of all colonels are promoted; the others end their career at that rank.

Although no officers of any rank or command had any intentions of disrupting the democratic process, due to their experience during the military regime, or being unfaithful to their duties, some PASOK advisers who pretended to be experts on military matters cultivated the idea that a large number of officers would actively oppose the Socialist government in order to prevent it from applying its "socialist transformation" program. The self-proclaimed advisers (mainly ex-officers seeking to gain power in the inner circles of PASOK) approached the armed forces as they approach labor unions. In the first instance, they created within the officers corps a PASOK branch (*kladike*), intended to be the party's eyes and ears in the military. A number of dissatisfied officers, whose careers had slowed down because of professional deficiencies, or who had personal or political connections with PASOK's cadres, and opportunists of every situation, were recruited into this political commissariat. Into this branch organization were inducted officers from the deputy chief of the Armed Forces General Staff down to the colonels of the District of Athens Command (to which belong the various training centers and military schools) along with officers of the air force and naval bases, as well as officers of the headquarters of Larissa and Thessalonike. Lastly, at least one colonel from every major garrison was involved.

As these officers had anticipated, in later years they were

promoted and assumed high positions in the armed forces (including political positions), irrespective of their professional or educational capabilities, becoming part of the PASOK nomenclature. In this manner the party secured itself politically and militarily and proceeded now towards complete consolidation of power. Although the army had been politically neutral since 1974, the Socialist government created a special situation in the armed forces, where the officers were politically and morally divided into professionals and party commissars. The political leadership would now take the advice of their men in the armed forces when critical issues of defense arose. And that advice was not always the best.

The second psychological complex of PASOK was that the "dark forces," like the CIA, would create a crisis in the Aegean, exploiting the Turkish desires to remove PASOK from power. To prevent such an occurrence, the government devised extra-military safety valves, always depending on dubious advice from its chosen core of officers.

When Papandreou assumed power, he was briefed and rebriefed by the General Staff and was "satisfied" that the army had the capabilities to wage a successful defensive war and that the navy and air force, with a slight superiority over Turkey, were a strong deterrent against such a war. On that premise, the PASOK government felt secure in moving to the eastern borders both combat units and the most professional officers, who, of course, were not politically involved in party organizations, while PASOK branch officers remained in the interior to safeguard the government. Parallel to redeployment of troops for political reasons, Papandreou gave some privileges to the officers and soldiers in the form of rent subsidies, better food, and occasional "moral rewards."

The last danger that the Socialist government had to counter was the possibility of a surprise attack from the east. The suspicion of "dark forces" at work never left Papandreou's calculations. Turkey, the CIA, "domestic reactionaries"--all figured in his evaluation as enemies ready to bring him down. To counter this "threat," PASOK improved its intelligence capabilities by exploiting its connections with Third World countries (especially Arab socialist states like Syria, Iraq, and Libya) and with the PLO.

The Arabs, of course, did not have extensive intelligence capabilities in Turkey, but they pretended they did and were often believed. As matters turned out, they provided false information that prompted many alerts and even partial mobilizations. Moreover, the cooperation with the socialist Arabs created some side effects in other areas. Greece's relations with conservative Arabs deteriorated, and the Greek government was accused of tolerating terrorist actions by underground Arab organizations.

Having succeeded in co-opting the leadership of the Greek armed forces and thus safeguarding its flanks, the PASOK government adopted a hard line in the diplomatic field. At first it shelved both the implementation of the Rogers Plan and the dialogue with Turkey, which was held at a low diplomatic level. As could have been expected, the Turks began their own countermeasures, with constant violations of Greek airspace and territorial waters. The Hellenic Air Force and Navy intercept every Turkish attempt, thanks to Greece's air superiority. Tension characterizes the relations between the two countries.

Step by step, the Turkish leadership built up the combat readiness of its armed forces, improved its international position, and adopted a more provocative stand vis-à-vis Greece. Turkish violations of Greek territory were more frequent under PASOK, and in 1983 the Turks raised the matter of the demilitarization of the Greek islands, especially Lemnos. In this situation PASOK softened its position towards NATO, and correctly sought to use the alliance to ensure the protection of the country's sovereignty and secure the flow of assistance. There was an about-face towards Washington as well.

In November 1983, the government signed a new treaty ensuring the continuing presence of U.S. bases in Greece, while attempting to hide behind the ambiguity of the term "terminable," which was interpreted as "terminated" in the Greek text. With this basic agreement in place, Papandreou proceeded with his "diplomatic program" in other directions: he expanded "contacts" with the countries of "actual socialism," meaning Eastern Europe, in pursuit of the status of an international pacifist leader capable of bridging the East-West gap. In pursuit of this dream, the party cadres decided to purge "non-Socialist officers" from key positions in all branches of the armed forces.

In the spring of 1984 this purge of "professionals" was implemented. Within one year the government changed two chiefs of the army's General Staff, as well as senior officers from the rank of colonel and above. The objective was twofold: not only to find faithful PASOK officers, but also to find officers willing to propagandize the party's policies openly, irrespective of their professional capabilities.

Meanwhile, Turkey continued to improve its defense capabilities, its economic situation, and its international prestige and position, especially its relations with the moderate Arab states.[6] Moreover, its standing in its alliances grew immensely, and its geostrategic significance was enlarged by the rise of Muslim fundamentalism and the deterioration of the Iranian situation. While Turkey cashed in on its opportunities, PASOK persisted in its socialist dogmatism. With theatrics aimed at concealing the country's economic decline, PASOK proceeded to elections in the summer of 1985, which it won with the help of the Greek Communist party. But the economic problems that had accumulated prior to the elections and had intensified afterwards forced the suspension of critical military modernization programs.

GOVERNMENTAL DIRECTIVES ON DEFENSE

In a series of meetings held during the winter of 1985-86 under the auspices of the Governmental Council on Defense and Foreign Policy (with the input of party apparatchiks), the Socialist government produced a series of directives on defense matters, which, in modified form, were later presented to the Parliament.[7] These directives, which one can say represent the "governmental philosophy" on matters of national security, are interesting for two reasons: first, they are comprehensive in nature and carefully linked to the ruling party's ideological predisposition and, second, their content is an obvious departure from traditional Western defense doctrines. Furthermore, the directives begin with several basic assumptions that, in retrospect, seem erroneous.

First, the government states without qualification that "an augmented international tension and détente is on the retreat"; and second, it maintains that Greece's defense posture is subject to influences related to the problems in the Middle East, which include the "lack of respect for Palestinians' rights," the situation in Lebanon, the Iran-Iraq war, and the Cyprus problem.

Within this context, the government declared its own strategy to be based on the slogan "We do not claim anything, we do not concede anything." But this was hardly a strategy.

In pursuit of this so-called strategy, the government listed a number of key requirements, which at best are impractical and at worst are empty reflections of party ideology. The "means" for a national strategy based on the slogan "We do not claim anything, we do not concede anything" centered on a need for national preparedness and development of defense capabilities, coupled with "unanimity, unity, nationalistic and patriotic conscience." In a redundant manner, the government also proposed to "mobilize the Greeks in diaspora" in pursuit of its national strategy—an idea that could have immense consequences for the welfare of this group. Finally, PASOK proposes "full fortification of democracy and freedom" as a prerequisite for an effective national defense strategy.

Certain "external influences" affecting the implementation of the PASOK defense policy were identified as needing to be "neutralized." Central among them are heavy investment by the United States in Turkey, which in turn "stirs up Turkish chauvinism," the "negative role of NATO due to its attitude during the dictatorship," and the Cyprus problem and NATO's inclination to lean towards the Turkish side on Aegean issues. Although NATO is viewed as a "negative external influence" on defense matters, the directives also state, "Our remaining in the political wing of NATO will have as target improving the chances for the cessation of cold war, which undermines détente." As stated elsewhere in this volume, the ultimate objective of PASOK's policy is complete independence from "imperialist circles." In this respect, the "final separation and recovery of our independence from the United States" is seen as an important goal, directly related to "securing territorial integrity," according to the currently operative defense directives. Readjustment of relations with the West and particularly with the United States is imperative, from the point of view of PASOK defense planning. This can be expedited with the creation of "a Balkan peace zone." Appropriate utilization of resources, careful implementation of the proposed strategy, and understanding of the external influences will, in the opinion of the governing elite, "ensure the independence of the country from military blocs which contribute to the polarization of the world and serve foreign military interests."

The specific guidelines issued in pursuit of the national defense and foreign policy objectives represent a political potpourri, heavily ideological in nature but short on specifics. They are the following.

1. Independence and a multifaceted foreign policy must be preserved through the development of friendly relations on a worldwide scale, especially with the people of the Balkans, the Mediterranean, West and East European countries, and the Arab nations.

2. The external policy of Greece is to be peaceful and realistic and promote solidarity.

3. The defense policy aims at securing territorial integrity with the maintenance of a high level of readiness and defensive capabilities.

4. Success of these targets will be achieved step-by-step.

5. The primary target is the continuous modernization of the armed forces with parallel development of Hellenic Military industries and the diversification of arms procurement to avoid partial dependence.

6. The further aim of the policies in the European area is that Europe should not be one-directional (neither Eastern nor Western), the Balkans are to be a non-nuclear zone, and the Aegean and Cyprus are to be areas where Greece's sovereignty and rights are secure.

7. In a case of collision with Turkey, it is expected that the United States and NATO will intervene politically to deter or immediately terminate the conflict. Therefore the hostilities will be on a small scale and the time available to supply the armed forces will be limited. Therefore the existence of large stocks of equipment is absolutely essential.

8. The training and the organization of the armed forces should be adapted to conform to these circumstances.

9. In the expression of defense policies the *human factor* should be carefully manipulated to develop coherence and morale.

From this socialistic terminology we conclude that the further objectives of the armed forces, as PASOK sees them, are to protect Greek "freedom" and promote a nonaligned policy that could convert Greece into a buffer zone between East and West, and simultaneously to secure the country from any threat without relying on friends and allies and with limited national resources.

The military made some efforts to operationalize and to apply the set of directives issued by the Parliament, but time was lost because of economic deterioration and because PASOK cadres and commissars interpreted the directives differently from the way the military hierarchy did.

For example, in the beginning of 1986, an active general suggested a more careful handling of the problems Greece had with the alliance, and the inclusion of the Greek Orthodox Church in the military strategy and in the fulfillment of the preconditions of the declared national strategy (unity, unanimity, patriotic conscience). He was characterized as a "conservative" and was retired during the annual spring promotions and retirement session of the defense council.

PASOK's plan for a "Hellenic defense" ran into another dilemma: how to apply the guidelines of the party in light of the American proposal to the NATO countries for the production and disposition of advanced chemical weapons in Europe, due to the threat of the Warsaw Pact's tremendous capabilities in Chemical Biological Radiological (CBR) warfare. On 18 May 1986 the alliance accepted the American proposals, and the Greek government, although it could have blocked this decision together with Holland, Norway, and Denmark, made only a perfunctory announcement referring to the Geneva protocols of 1948 and 1974, which restrict the use of chemical weapons.

The NATO decision legitimized Turkish efforts to enter the club of nations with CBR capabilities. Turkey and Pakistan had long ago entered into a technological agreement involving research in chemical weapons, and had succeeded in isolating the yellow fever virus and proceeded to the production of Yellow Rain. Currently Turkey has equipped its armed forces with gas masks and organized CBR disinfectant/decontamination units. The Greek armed forces lacked any capability not only to wage CBR warfare but also to provide absolutely necessary anti-CBR equipment and training. Paradoxically, the establishment of the CBR warfare school was assigned to the Ministry of Justice and only recently found a roof of its own.

To counter the great capability for CBR warfare possessed by the Warsaw Pact countries and Turkey, the Socialist government tried to address the problem in the context of its policy for a "non-nuclear Balkans zone," but reference to chemical warfare in political documents is scarce. The government still believes that it has eliminated the CBR threat from the north and east, although the whole armed forces and the population of Greece remain unprotected.

In pursuit of military modernization, the government finally decided in 1987 to equip the air force with modern aircraft to counterbalance the Turkish acquisition of 160 F-16 fighters. After long deliberations, and supposedly after implementing the directive for "diversification of sources of weapons," the government decided to undertake what it called the "purchase of the century." The military leadership suggested that the deal involve only the purchase of one type of advanced fighter aircraft with the best possible options. It was obvious then, as it is now, that any type other than the F-16 (such as the Tornado, the Mirage, or the Swedish SAAB) would be unaffordable. Furthermore, the government had kept intact the FMS (Foreign Military Sales) credits, which by 1988 would amount to about $2 billion, but could only be used to buy U.S. equipment.

Indeed, it would have been a good deal, if the Socialist government had opted to procure one type of aircraft. For example, at the beginning it could have considered the relatively inexpensive F-20, chosen by Taiwan and Korea, which could have been manned promptly by the already available trained personnel who operate the similar F-5 aircraft of the Hellenic Air Force. At a later stage, Greece could have acquired the F-18, which is superior to the F-16, and in the process could have obtained offsets for the construction of an air industry for maintenance and parts production of the Northrop plane. This solution had the "political" disadvantage, however, of perpetuating dependence on the United States.

With "diversification of sources" in mind the PASOK government decided to buy with FMS credits only 40 F-16s, of exactly the same type as those purchased by Turkey and with the same offsets. This action antagonized Ankara because Greece could now compete with Turkey in offering aircraft maintenance services to Middle Eastern countries. But in order to vary its arsenal resources, the government also decided to buy another 40 F-2000 Mirages from France, using scarce funds from the national defense budget and saddling itself with the burden of two maintenance systems.[8]

This exercise in socialistic dogmatism will cost Greece more than $600 million at the beginning and more than $1 billion in the long run because of the operational use of two different types of planes. Furthermore, the 40 F16s, since they were purchased on a commercial basis, will cost $150 million over what they would have cost had they been purchased on a government-to-government basis. The offset provisions of the contract include coproduction by Hellenic Aerospace Industry of fuselage sections ($60 million), engine components ($40 million), radar and electronic components ($10 million), and provision of upfront capital of $50 million to establish a "development" company in Greece. The sum total of these offsets exceeds the amount that could have been saved by a direct government-to-government purchase. True to its credo, the government bluntly stated that the purchase was "based on political decisions" for which it assumed full responsibility. But the 40 F-16s and 40 Mirages could hardly counterbalance Turkey's 160 F-16 fighters.

Another area that PASOK's defense policies neglected was manpower. According to the magazine *Europaish Werhkonde*, the strength of the frontline infantry units is 50 percent of the level of authorized personnel, that of the mechanized and armored units is 53 percent, and that of the other active units is 10 to 35 percent, which means the army must depend on efficient and expeditious mobilization in time of crisis.[9] Similar problems exist in the air force and navy. The air force has only 90 percent of its authorized personnel, and the navy, with a manpower of 13,500, just 50 percent. In comparison, the Turkish armed forces have 90 percent manning in the second line units and 110 percent in the frontline units.

This serious problem was not ignored by the government, but it grew worse due to the policy that allows every student to postpone his conscription until his thirties, thus causing bottlenecks in training and inconsistency in the supply of manpower. The result was not only the low level of the authorized strength of the units but the absence of the most vigorous youth from those units. To solve the problem, PASOK reacted "politically." After it lost the majority in the elections of the student organizations in 1986, it forwarded a draft law (in August 1987) revising conscription, including exemptions and postponements, and in the process alienated more students. Those policies that derived from the governmental defense directives confused the mission of the armed forces and inevitably politicized the officers corps.

But there were other problems as well, related to the modernization programs. The FMSFUS credits not utilized for the "purchase of the century" (the purchase of 40 F-16s and 40 F-2000 Mirages) were all allocated to the air force. The other two branches received no FMSFUS credits, causing difficulties in their modernization. Naturally this contributed to disputes among the chiefs of the Defense General Staff (consisting of an air force general and the chiefs of the Army and Navy Staffs), but the air force's viewpoint prevailed.

The chiefs of the Army General Staff since January 1985 have been weak personalities, with the result that this service, in addition to suffering from the low level of the authorized strength of its units, was equipped with obsolete armor and artillery and a primitive communications and command system. The chief of the Navy General Staff fought more stubbornly for the neglected navy, but he was purged.

Although the PASOK government and especially the Defense Ministry was briefed about the extent of the modernization of the Turkish armed forces since 1983, and especially concerning the air force and navy, and the army's amphibious capabilities, it still hesitated to act. With the deterioration of the Greek economy and a "socialistic" view on defense policy, the tested doctrine of flexible response can no longer be applied against Turkey. Under the circumstances, the government sought other solutions, which have an East European sound to them.

THE DOCTRINE OF TOTAL POPULAR DEFENSE: A NEW CONCEPT FOR GREEK DEFENSE

According to Army Regulations 320-5, doctrine is defined as a combination of the principles, policies, techniques or procedures by which the armed forces or elements thereof, guide their actions. It is derived from approved developmental concepts, from experience or from theory and represents the best available thought that can be defended by reason. It is taught authoritatively as guidance but requires judgement in application.

We offer this definition because the word *doctrine* is translated in Greek as "dogma" and means something other than religious or political beliefs, but we doubt whether the PASOK cadres make the proper distinctions.

The acceptance of doctrine depends on the following considerations: the organization, strength, equipment, and training of the armed forces; the possible theater of operations and the social and economic status of the population; the morale, esprit de corps, will to fight, and the leadership of the armed forces, of the civil administration, and of the whole nation; and the doctrine of the possible opponent, as well as the capabilities and intentions of that opponent.

As we have stated earlier, the Hellenic armed forces lack the means to implement the doctrine of the forward strategy and flexible response, due to the Turkish buildup, and due to the inability of the military to counter multiple threats. Under the circumstances, an old idea surfaced from deliberations of the PASOK Central Committee and the Executive Office—the doctrine of "Total Popular Defense."

Total Popular Defense was derived from the experience of the patriotic guerrilla warfare of Tito's forces in Yugoslavia during World War II. It was developed by authors like Army General Nicolai Ljubicic, former federal secretary for national defense of Yugoslavia, and Admiral Branco Mamula, chief of the Yugoslavian General Defense Staff and current defense minister.[10] But more important, the concept was introduced to PASOK cadres who were trained in Camp Boulkes by General Markos and Brigadier Ypsilantes of the Communist rebel forces of the Greek Civil War, both of whom are unofficial advisers to PASOK political bodies.

The doctrine of Total Popular Defense was announced by the Governmental Council of Defense and External Policy in January 1985, with great fanfare, and introduced to the legislature in the summer of 1987. It provides for the creation of popular units of two kinds: the Local Units of Popular Defense and the Reserve Units of Popular Defense.

The Local Units are under the control of local authorities of every village or small town, which in the majority are currently controlled by the ruling party.

They consist of men sixteen to eighteen and fifty-one to sixty-five years old, and those eighteen to sixty years old who have not been drafted into the regular army or the national guard; of women eighteen to fifty years old; and of volunteers, visitors, or capable men over sixty-five years old. These units—theoretically under the command of mayors or the village chiefs—will defend their towns or villages against any invasion. The Reserve Units of Popular Defense are organized on the level of county or region and cannot act outside the region, the limits of which are defined by the Defense and Public Order ministries.

This doctrine—even if it does not have political effects such as the creation of an Orwellian state, as many politicians and intellectuals believe it does—does not meet the needs of effective defense that we have outlined at the beginning of this paper, for the following reasons.

1. In the Aegean islands and the border villages, there are not enough people, men or women, to form such units. On the contrary, the rural population is declining and is quite mobile nowadays. It has been confirmed by various crises in the

Aegean, and especially in the last crisis of March 1987, that the rural families move—by any means, such as tractor trailers and small boats—from the potential war zone to the interior. The structure of Greek society is quite different from that of Yugoslavia and of pre-Civil War Greece. Furthermore, the potential enemy is very different from Hitler's Wehrmacht (if the model defense is supposed to be the Yugoslavian resistance or the battle of Crete during World War II), and its intention is also different. Turkey, for example, not only wants to occupy Greek islands or regions, but eventually to colonize them with a Turkish population, as it did in Cyprus, and to annex the occupied territory, as it did with Alexandretta.

2. If an enemy conquers an area defended by its own population, it would theoretically be able to justify taking the entire population as "prisoners of war," according to international law, to expatriate them, and, after that, to resettle the territory with new settlers. Obviously, in case of invasion, the invading forces are usually select units. They are by definition more formidable and powerful enemies than any World War II army. The destructive capabilities of modern air forces are much greater, leaving the weak, untrained Popular Defense units of young and old people to the mercy of a superior, modern enemy.

After the announcement of the doctrine of Total Popular Defense, the Turkish government, in a special meeting on the night of 26 to 27 January 1985, responded by adopting the NATO doctrine of the Air-Land Battle. A few words on the Air-Land Battle plan are in order to demonstrate the futility of the PASOK doctrine of popular defense.

As it is stated in the U.S. Army Field Manual 100-5, the Air-Land Battle doctrine takes a nonlinear view of the battle. It enlarges the battlefield area, stressing unified air and ground or sea operations throughout the theater. Secondly, it distinguishes the operational level. It recognizes the nonquantifiable element of combat power, especially the maneuver, which is as important as the firepower. It acknowledges the importance of chemical weapons and of electronic warfare, and their effects on operations. Most importantly, it emphasizes the human element—courageous, well-trained soldiers and skillful, effective leaders. To ensure success, the Air-Land Battle doctrine concentrates on (1) indirect approaches, (2) speed and violence, (3) flexibility and reliance on the initiative of junior leaders, (4) rapid decision making, (5) clearly designated main effort, and (6) deep attacks.

Air-Land Battle offensives are rapid, violent operations that seek the enemy's soft spots, remain flexible in shifting the main effort, and exploit successes promptly. The attacker creates a fluid situation, maintains the initiative, and destroys the coherence of the enemy defense. Using support and reserve units flexibly, the attack must continue for as long as it takes to ensure victory, which hinges on fully synchronized combat forces. The air force is an equal partner in the Air-Land Battle. The doctrine specifies support for the battle with counter-air and air interdiction operations.

Counter-air operations achieve necessary air superiority and ensure that enemy air forces cannot interfere with the operations of air or ground forces. The counter-air tasks belong to F-16s in Greece's case; the ratio of which is two to one in Turkey's favor.Air interdiction operations destroy, isolate, neutralize, or delay the enemy's military potential before it can influence friendly operations, which is obviously the task of the 220 F-104 Strikers. Offensive air support is that portion of offensive air power in direct support of ground operations, and consists of tactical air reconnaissance (the task of the more than thirty plus F-4Es). Close air support is the task of forty F-100s together with 60 F-5s, as well as different combinations of other types of aircraft.

Comparing the two doctrines, particularly the defensive nature of the Total Popular Defense and the offensive nature of the Air-Land Battle, it is obvious that the initiative of the operations belongs to the Turkish side. It is easy, therefore, to understand the basis of a depressing conclusion: the effectiveness of Greek defense has been undermined by party sloganeering and catchy clichés.

IMPLICATIONS

According to the PASOK directives on national defense policy, "in a case of collision with Turkey it is estimated that the USA and NATO will politically intervene for the deterrence or the immediate termination of the hostilities, which will be of a small scale." This assessment is correct. But it assumes that the Turkish leadership and the Turkish General Staff could have a "free hand for few days" to crush the Hellenic armed forces. Since 1974, Turkish defense planners have relied on a conflict of two weeks or of fifteen days. In the first week they have even included a local and artificial "failure" of their offensive so that the Hellenic armed forces, and especially the air force, would expend its energy. After this, the plan envisions the exploitation of the weaknesses of the Greek force, by using massive power and fresh troops. However, the Turks now believe that fifteen days is optimistic and that international intervention might stop the hostilities earlier, leaving the possibility open that Turkey will suffer the cost of the war.

Since 1983 the time frame of fifteen days has been continuously reduced by Turkey's buildup and PASOK's neglect of defense modernization, causing a change in the balance of power between the two countries. The question is, how quickly would the Turks be able to achieve their objectives now, or how much time does NATO need to intervene? More important, how can Greece rely on NATO intervention when the country does not belong to NATO's military wing, but remains in the political wing solely for the purpose of putting an end to the cold war—that is, in order to "expedite the process for the elimination of military blocs."

The PASOK strategy entails even more dubious assumptions about the role of the United States in case of a Greek-Turkish conflict. The first error, of course, is that PASOK expects Washington to intervene at all. The second error is the belief that the United States will intervene in time to contain the conflict and save the Greece from grievous losses. Here, we must note an antinomy in the PASOK thinking: on the one hand, the government prides itself on its ability to fend off "foreign interventions," but on the other, counts on the "foreign factor" to intervene in critical times. Sober minds ought to assess the current attitudes in Washington toward a government that has, for almost five years, made it a practice of "bashing" the "world imperialists," before it is assumed that the same "imperialists" can be viewed as a critical element of a national defense policy. It is obvious that the links between Greece, NATO, and the United States are loosening as the country drifts towards becoming a buffer zone between East and West. In other words, preparing the country for a "short" war and counting on timely intervention of foreign powers does not constitute a serious strategy. Yet, that is exactly what has emerged under PASOK, coupled with the romantic notion that a 1940-type guerrilla war is still possible in a country that has been thoroughly urbanized, and in which the backbone of guerrilla war—the peasant—is fast disappearing.

It is obvious that in any Greek-Turkish conflict—the only conflict that is perceived as likely by the majority of the Greek people—the only credible deterrent remains the ability for direct, quick action to repel any invasion at its early stages and to retaliate effectively so as to shift the burden of the conflict onto the other side. Such a strategy could only be operationalized with flexible, efficient, powerful, and well-trained units with high morale and an air force and navy capable of not only intercepting the enemy but also of retaliating. Units with less than 50 percent of their authorized strength are neither powerful nor flexible. Complicating matters further, mobilization is not always high enough to respond to all potential threats simultaneously. The Popular Defense units may have a democratic name, but they are not substitutes for a professional soldiery.

Any thorough and professional evaluation of the situation would reveal the obvious: there is a need to redefine Greek defense priorities, to reorganize the armed forces, to depoliticize their ranks, and to modernize them. The Greek borders, unique as they are, given the combination of continental and island territory, can only be defended by a forward-looking strategy, not with political exorcisms or reversion to Tito-style partisan warfare.

The Turkish army in Thrace and Cyprus has been in a state of high readiness, and the warning time is limited in both situations. Frequent alerts are not the solution to a defense gap, because, as soldiers know, both the population and the enemy get used to them, too. In concrete areas, the defense preparedness has declined during the past six years. Greece's airlift and sealift capabilities are dangerously limited. The available equipment, purchased during New Democracy's rule (1974-81) is fast becoming obsolete. CBR warfare protection is nonexistent, and no one has even considered what would happen if the opponent simply faked the use of chemical warfare by wearing masks to fool the Greek forces. Although improvement in these areas is essential—they have been neglected long enough—the Greek defense policy needs a deeper revision: it must revert to the basic principles of flexible response. It cannot count for help on an alliance in which it is not a full participant, nor can it be constructed upon the sandy foundations of pro-Arabism and tacit understandings with Bulgaria. Greece must, at least, learn from its history: it defeated the Ottoman Empire in the Balkan wars by allying with other Balkan states, but soon thereafter it had to fight another war to sort out remaining differences.

A small country, like Greece "without brotherhood," as the Greek president characterized it, must take defensive measures against all potential enemies and inevitably must depend on trusted allies to defend her sovereignty. Since 1981 the threat from the north and the threat from the east have not received equal attention. A political ideology coupled with political action have combined to desensitize the Greek nation to any threat from the north. And we know, from history once again, that attitudes are as difficult to change as are self-propelled policies.

NOTES

1. In the June 1985 elections approximately 300 guerrilla leaders, including the Communist Army leader Markos Vafiades, campaigned actively on behalf of PASOK.

2. The issue of wiretapping of private telephones by the state-owned telecommunications agency emerged on several occasions during the past six years. The latest incident was reported in October 1987. See *Anti*, 23 October 1987, and *Auge*, 7 October 1987.

3. Several high-ranking members of the PASOK government admitted their presence and training in Palestinian or Syrian camps, but argued they were there in order to oppose the junta more effectively.

4. The author served as military attaché to Ankara from 1981-83 and was also accredited to Iran.

5. During the March 1987 "crisis" in the Aegean, Foreign Minister Karolos Papoulias made a hurried trip to Sofia, Bulgaria, to consult with the Bulgarian leader, Todor Zhivkov. See Associated Press for 26 March 1987. See also "To the Brink in Athens," *New York Times*, 30 March 1987.

6. For an excellent study on the "third option" to socialism, see Stelios Kouloglou, *In Search of the Third Road: PASOK, 1974-86* (in Greek) (Athens: Odysseas Publishers, 1986).

7. *Parliamentary Minutes*, Meeting NH, 23 January 1987; 23 October 1983, 2 November 1983 and 3 November 1983. [Editor's Note: Proceedings of the meeting of the Council of Defense and Foreign Policy were routinely published in selected pro-government newspapers as they occurred.]

8. *House Committee on Foreign Affairs, Hearings on Greece, Spain and the Southern NATO Strategy*, 100th Cong., 1st sess.

9. *Europaish Werhkonde*, No. 3/85.

10. For a comprehensive study of the Yugoslav model of Total Popular Defense see General Nicolai Ljubicic, *Total National Defense* (Belgrade: Book Series of Socialist Thought and Practice, 1987).3

Soviet Manipulation of the Press and Political Opinion in Greece 1974-88

Paul Anastasi

"To speak the truth is a petty bourgeois prejudice. To lie, on the other hand, is often justified by its ends."

Lenin[1]

"Disinformation is not just lying: it is expected to serve as a subtle means of inducing another government to do what the Kremlin wants it to do or to frighten or bluff a foreign government into inaction or into making a concession to the USSR."

Statement by a former KGB officer[2]

"We have to influence non-communists if we want to make them communists or if we want to fool them. So we have to try to infiltrate in the big press, to influence millions of people."

Igor Bogolepov, a Soviet foreign ministry defector[3]

"We do not publish all news items, and when news comes in we take a decision as to whether we will publish it or not publish it. We always decided that. With what criteria do we decide? According to whether it promotes or not the aims of the Movement. If they pose an obstacle, we put them aside. It's clear-cut."

Charilaos Florakis, secretary-general of the Greek Communist Party, explaining the party's use of the news and the press[4]

The above quotes are intended not only to illustrate the historical continuity of the Soviets' interpretation of journalism as an instrument to promote their ends but also to show that the practical application of this notion is also espoused by Greece's Communist party.

The object of this chapter, however, is not limited to an examination of the obvious use that Communist parties make of journalism as an instrument of policy. The chapter also examines the growing evidence that in Greece the same methodology has gone far beyond the communist press, into the non-communist, center-leftist, neutral, and even right-wing media. It analyzes how, through the manipulation of the mainstream media, public opinion and government actions in Greece have been considerably influenced—indeed, influenced to such an extent that a Soviet campaign in the Greek media, though not of course the *only* factor, is responsible to a considerable degree for turning Greece into the most anti-Western country in Europe since the end of the Second World War.

There is now substantial documentary evidence, as well as first-hand accounts from KGB defectors and former official Russian propagandists, pointing to the conclusion that the Greek Communist party and the Soviet Union undertook a joint, concerted effort from 1949 onwards to achieve in Greece, through covert political warfare, what they had failed to achieve by force during the 1946-49 civil war. There is also documented evidence that these operations have been financed by the Soviet Union. Statements by Russian leaders themselves (such as Brezhnev and Gorbachev) reveal that Moscow's strategy is to use economic, cultural and political means to bring about a communist regime in Greece. They have even boasted of their success. We will examine the evidence in this essay.

In more general terms, and well beyond the Greek experience, there is also specific testimony and evidence that the Soviet Union, at the highest level, decided in the early 1960s to infiltrate and to manipulate the non-communist press of Western Europe and the developing world through a process known as Active Measures and Disinformation. This process is a more developed form of what has traditionally been referred to as political or psychological warfare, and it is designed to alter the correlation of social and political forces in other countries to Moscow's advantage. It is designed to influence the political process in a way that is beneficial to Soviet foreign policy goals, without allowing Soviet involvement to be easily identified or traced.

KGB defectors and Western foreign policy experts now recognize that Greece has been one of the weakest links in the Western alliance and is a primary target of the Soviet effort. In brief, they say the goal of the Soviets is to generate anti-Western sentiments on such a scale as to bring about the loosening of Greece's ties with the West and ultimately its Finlandization.

The aim of this chapter is not to examine the overall Soviet subversion effort in Greece. It is to examine how and to what extent the country's ideological Finlandization has been achieved through media manipulation and what repercussions this may be having on public opinion and on the country's foreign policy orientations.

FIRSTHAND TESTIMONY

Ilya Dzhirkvelov, an Active Measures specialist and KGB defector who fled to the West in 1980, recently told a London court that in 1960 the Central Committee of the Communist Party of the Soviet Union (CPSU) decided to increase its propaganda and disinformation campaigns in the West and the Third World, and that Greece was a primary target. He said that he personally participated in such operations, the main goal of which was to manipulate non-communist, neutral and even right-wing newspapers so as to generate anti-Western and pro-Soviet sympathies. He explained that the reason for this was that the Soviet hierarchy realized that the influence of the Communist press alone was minimal among the broader public. Dzhirkvelov also revealed that he participated in the setting up and financing of the pro-Soviet daily *Patriot* in India as a platform for Soviet disinformation and anti-American propaganda and that there was a plan to set up a similar newspaper in Greece.

More specifically, Dzhirkvelov said:

> I try to very briefly explain what happened at the end of 1950's-1959-1960, I don't remember very correctly. It was decision of the Central Committee of the Communist Party of the Soviet Union to increase our ideological influence in the West especially and in developing countries. We started to use new term like "Active Measures,".... the most important was to plant this disinformation in foreign newspapers, usually neutral or right wing newspapers because we believe that it is very difficult to believe that we can create public opinion using the communist newspapers. It is covert active measures....there was a Central Committee decision, as I have already mentioned, about intensifying our ideological activities against the West and a decision about making more use of organs of the western press.[5]

Dzhirkvelov said that Greece was one of those countries targeted by the Central Committee. He knew personally of the decision to set up a newspaper in Greece, which had been made by his colleague and superior, Colonel Vasili Sitnikov, whom he identified as the deputy director of the KGB Disinformation Department—as he had been identified by several other defectors and specialists. Dzhirkvelov said the plan was the same as that applied in India, where in 1962 he and Sitnikov participated in the setting up and financing of the pro-Soviet daily *Patriot*. The aim in both Greece and India was the same, he said, namely, "so that we should have a publication which could publish our ideas and fulfill our purpose in trying to compromise American policy, and in order to publish disinformation."[6]

There is ample documentation, including photographs, showing that Colonel Sitnikov was the Soviet official who travelled to Greece on a number of occasions in the 1970s and early 1980s and met and negotiated with several Greek newspaper executives and interested book publishers.[7] Ultimately, he negotiated and signed interconnected commercial and publishing agreements with George Bobolas—the publisher of the *Great Soviet Encyclopedia*, several propagandistic Russian books, and later the daily newspaper *Ethnos*. Mr. Bobolas denies that *Ethnos* is related to these agreements and says that its contents, if pro-Soviet, are the result of free editorial choice.

Though Dzhirkvelov himself fled to the West one year before the launching of *Ethnos*, he said that his study of all of that paper's foreign commentaries (published in the seven-month period from September 1981 to April 1982, the main period under consideration at the London trial) led him to the firm conclusion that *Ethnos* faithfully applied Soviet disinformation techniques. He said its contents were unequivocally pro-Soviet, to a degree unparalleled in any other Western newspaper.

Explaining the broader political goals of the USSR in Greece, Dzhirkvelov also said:

> The Central Committee was, apart from Austria, which was neutral and apart from Finland, up in the north of Europe, we needed to have a non-Socialist country which would be a very close ally of ours in our attempts to break up the North Atlantic Alliance and get rid of American bases and at the same time drive a wedge between relations in the Western European countries and the United States of America.[8]

A similar observation has been made by Stanislav Levchenko, a KGB defector who fled to the West in 1979 and who also specialized in Active Measures and Disinformation. He said:

> Disinformation in Greece is very important for the Soviets because they have realized that Greece is one of the weakest links in the NATO alliance. They are therefore trying with every means to use your country against the interests of the USA by aggravating the anti-Americanism which exists amongst a section of the population. Apart

from that, they are trying to cultivate anti-NATO sentiments as much as possible among the public.[9]

And Lord Chalfont, former British Labour minister of foreign affairs, made the point at the London hearing that it was the rise to power of PASOK in 1981 that provided Moscow with a particularly good opportunity to increase its influence in Greece. The overall result, he said, is that the Greek public has been conditioned into thinking that the West is to blame for the country's domestic and foreign problems.[10]

THE TESTIMONY OF FORMER PROFESSIONAL PROPAGANDISTS FROM GREECE

Equally enlightening are the personal experiences of former propagandists and activists from Greece who worked for the Soviets. Kostas Mavropoulos, a former broadcaster with the Greek section of Radio Moscow, revealed at the same trial in London that he participated in propaganda planning sessions in Moscow in which instructions were given on how to increase pro-Soviet and anti-Western propaganda themes in Greece. The effort was to begin in the early 1970s.[11] Moscow's heightened interest in influencing Greek political affairs at that time, and particularly as the rightist dictatorship began to lose its grip, became obvious to Mavropoulos when Radio Moscow increased its daily broadcasting hours to Greece to levels comparable to those for such key countries as West Germany.

In a written statement about these planning sessions, in which he participated with positively identified Soviet disinformation and propaganda experts, Mavropoulos said:

> Throughout these meetings, great emphasis was placed by Pankin, Sitnikov and Semenikhin on making greater use of the Greek press to propagate Soviet propaganda. The thrust of the proposals was to adopt methods beyond the usual propaganda practices or channels. The usual channels were, of course, Radio Moscow, the Greek-Soviet Friendship Association, the left-wing Greek press, and the Soviet embassy. The publication of the *Great Soviet Encyclopedia* was considered to be a step in the creation of a new platform for the dissemination of propaganda in Greece. I understood this to mean that new conduits of Soviet propaganda had to be created which would not be overtly tied to communist interests.
>
> Messrs. Pankin and Sitnikov were the two principal characters who came to these meetings in order to impart information to us and in order to inform us of the new direction to be taken in relation to Greece and the matters which were to be stressed.
>
> It was the one central theme of all of these meetings that the

USSR should seek to exploit as fully as possible the existing conflicts and problems in Greece. The themes most constantly played upon in relation to Greece and which were relayed to me personally at these meetings were as follows:

1. That NATO is an aggressive organization;

2. That the Warsaw Pact is a defensive alliance established in response to the threat posed by NATO;

3. That the United States is an aggressive, imperialistic force primarily responsible for many Greek problems;

4. That the U.S. was to blame for the seven-year (1967-74) rightist dictatorship in Greece;

5. That the U.S. was directly responsible for the 'Cyprus tragedy', i.e. the Turkish invasion of Cyprus in 1974;

6. To pursue Greece's withdrawal from NATO;

7. To secure the removal of the U.S. bases from Greek territory;

8. To improve the image of the USSR in Greece and to increase the influence of the USSR in Greece.[12]

In addition to such testimony, information from former Greek Communists with expert knowledge on Greek affairs is also valuable. One such analyst is Ilios Yannakakis, a former Communist party veteran who sought refuge in Czechoslovakia at the end of the Greek civil war in 1949, but who subsequently became a Dubcjek supporter and sought asylum in France following the Soviet invasion of Prague in 1968. In Yannakakis's view, the Soviet propaganda and disinformation offensive in Greece was facilitated by the unique political conditions that prevailed in the country in the mid-1970s, conditions that provided a fertile environment unmatched in any other Western country.[13]

Yannakakis points out that a unique opportunity was presented to the Soviets and their allies with the collapse of the rightist dictatorship in Greece in 1974 and the Turkish invasion and occupation of northern Cyprus, as well as by the continuing tension between the two neighboring NATO members. He says that on the one hand the Left was able to come out of the ghetto the Right had imposed after the Communists' defeat in the 1944-49 civil war, and on the other Greece's experience under the dictatorship and the military humiliation over Cyprus provided an excellent opportunity to point an accusing finger at the United States as the guilty party. It became convenient for the Greeks to put all the blame on a foreign scapegoat, and the Soviets actively and very easily fuelled this notion. It was not long before anti-Americanism assumed enormous and sometimes violent dimensions. This gradually developed into pro-Sovietism, or at the very least into a greater toleration of or receptiveness to Soviet positions.

Yannakakis wrote that after the pro-Moscow Greek Communist party was legalized in 1974, it received massive economic assistance from the USSR and other Eastern bloc countries. He said it then put into action many new and skilled professional militants, set up a vast organizational network, and developed the country's most modern publishing facilities. "Gradually," he wrote, "it introduced its members into the non-Communist press, took control of mass organizations, exercised a considerable influence on intellectuals and, through them, on the broader public."[14]

Another key development, Yannakakis pointed out, was the informal alliance that developed between the Communist party and the Socialist party of Andreas Papandreou, especially after the latter's election victory in 1981. This, he says, extended the former's influence well beyond its electoral strength, which has always been limited to between 10 and 14 percent of the electorate.

Most noteworthy is the fact that the Communist party and PASOK shared similar views in the field of foreign policy, at least where their anti-Nato platforms were concerned. In power, PASOK on several occasions carried pro-neutralist or pro-Soviet arguments into NATO and EEC forums, in a way that neither the KKE nor the Soviet Union could ever have hoped to accomplish on its own. Not surprisingly, therefore, the Soviet Union was more interested in seeing PASOK in power—a PASOK that shared certain principles and policies with the KKE—than in actually backing solely the interests of the Communist party.

This becomes very clear in the address by Boris Ponomarev, the former head of the International Department of the CPSU's Central Committee, to the Eleventh Congress of the KKE in Athens in December 1982, in which he openly called for cooperation between the KKE and PASOK. This, of course, is also part of Moscow's now evident policy worldwide of trying to promote its interests through social-democratic parties, after it had realized that such front tactics are more realistic and effective than relying on the very remote possibility of a Communist party coming to power in a Western country.

The value of all this testimony is that we now have

firsthand reports from people who actively participated in the Soviet propaganda and disinformation effort targeted on Greece. Four basic conclusions can be drawn from their evidence:

1. That the USSR made a specific decision and carried out a disinformation and propaganda blitz in Greece, which was intensified in the early 1970s, when the end of the rightist military junta was in sight;

2. That it was decided that the best means of achieving this was through the non-communist Greek media;

3. That the radical, anti-Western platforms of PASOK created the preconditions for its cooperation with the pro-Moscow Communist party, an alliance that was actively encouraged by the Soviet Union because it made it possible to influence the Greek political process well beyond the capabilities of the KKE and the USSR alone;

4. That Greece's particular political experiences, especially the rightist dictatorship and the Cyprus debacle, and weak social and economic conditions in Greece created a unique opportunity and fertile territory to exploit the Greek public's frustrations and to direct them against the West;

THE GREEK PRESS TODAY AND THE MAIN DISINFORMATION THEMES

In view of the above, it is not surprising that most of the Greek press today, not only Communist party organs but also the center-leftist press, accuse the United States of dominating and manipulating the Greek political scene since the end of the Second World War in such a way as to hinder the evolution of a healthy democracy. The result has been a "witch-hunt" by the press against the West. The McCarthyism of the Right, which existed in the late 1950s and 1960s, has now been supplanted by the McCarthyism of the Left.

As Chares Bousboureles, editor of the centrist newspaper *To Vema* said: "There is a 'demon' conspiracy complex in the Greek press....Whatever happened then in the post-civil war period of the 50s and 60s was attributed to a supposed Communist conspiracy. Today, whatever happens is the work of the CIA."[15]

These trends have intensified since the collapse of the rightist dictatorship and restoration of democracy in 1974, which was brought on by the Turkish invasion of Cyprus following the junta's coup against the Nicosia government of

Archbishop Makarios. The center-leftist Greek press and politicians (foremost among the latter, the current prime minister, Andreas Papandreou) have encouraged each other in the argument that the United States is responsible for a number of "crimes" against Greece. These allegations can be grouped into five main themes, which are worth noting because Soviet disinformation efforts can be traced to these same five ideas:

1. The West in general and the United States in particular are responsible for hindering Greece's democratic evolution through military and economic intervention against the Communists in the civil war and through later interference in the Greek political process.
2. The United States masterminded the 1967 coup and the seven-year dictatorship.
3. The United States masterminded the Greek junta's July 1974 coup against Makarios.
4. The United States assisted Turkey a few days later in its invasion of Cyprus and subsequent occupation of the northern 40 percent of the country.
5. The United States is orchestrating the continuing tension between its NATO allies Greece and Turkey, pushing them towards armed confrontation so as to enrich itself with the sale of more military hardware, and has actively assisted Turkey to defeat Greece in the event of war.

The U.S. government categorically denies these accusations, saying that they are the result of a Soviet-backed disinformation blitz designed to weaken Greece's ties with the West.

The official argument of the United States in particular, and of the West in general, is that Western military and economic assistance for the defeat of the Communist armies in the civil war was the determining factor in keeping Greece a parliamentary democracy and in preventing its absorption into the Soviet bloc. Similarly, it is maintained that Western aid was vital to Greece's evolution from a poor and backward country to an advanced democracy. Furthermore, American officials have stated that the United States was not involved in the colonels' coup in 1967 or in the 1974 coup in Cyprus, nor did it orchestrate or support the Turkish invasion of Cyprus. Western officials say that the last thing they would want in Greece is a fragile democracy, as this would facilitate the activity of the extreme Left and its Soviet bloc patrons. Nor would they want a war between two of their NATO allies that would disrupt the alliance's southeastern flank.[16]

They say that it is the *Soviet bloc* that has no interest in supporting Greece's evolution as a healthy democracy, that it is the only side benefiting from the promotion of such anti-Western disinformation themes in Greece, and in particular that it alone benefits from military tensions within NATO that stem from the Greek-Turkish conflict.

Indeed, the United States finds itself caught in the middle of a dispute between the two allies, a dispute involving not only argument but the threat of war. The historic resentment between Greece and Turkey creates a situation in which it is easy to fan existing tensions and to invent a foreign scapegoat. It is a situation that the Soviets—not surprisingly—have hastened to exploit. The fact is that those who condemn the United States for its alleged involvement in the 1967 coup have failed so far to present hard evidence supporting their claims. The same is true for the Cyprus coup and for the argument that the United States is assisting Turkey against Greece. Yet the center-leftist politicians and press have repeatedly and vehemently made this claim, apparently basing their statements on prejudice and propaganda rather than on any real evidence.

The United States *did*, in fact, actively intervene in 1964 and 1967 and prevented a Turkish invasion of Cyprus during similar periods of tension. In sharp diplomatic moves, President Johnson warned the Turks against invading the island. In 1974, however, it did not. This is hardly surprising, considering that the Greeks' coup in Cyprus was viewed not only by the Turks but also internationally as a move designed to impose a local dictatorship and to unite the island forcibly with Greece. This provided an unprecedented opportunity and "legitimacy" for the Turkish invasion and occupation of 40 percent of the island republic. Ankara quickly exploited the situation to make what it hopes will be permanent territorial gains.

Perhaps the most realistic approach for Greece in its effort to reverse the situation in Cyprus is to seek support in the West for its position. In the meantime, however, Greek resentment over the United States' inability to resolve the dispute was easily exploited and developed into the argument that the

United States was responsible for the whole crisis in the first place.

Similarly, it has become just as easy to exploit the fact that the West, though exercising considerable pressure on the 1967-74 dictatorship to restore democracy, did not work actively enough against the junta, nor did it move to oust the junta by force. It therefore appeared to be tolerating the dictatorship. It took only one more step for skilled propagandists to argue that the West *actively supported* the dictatorship, and one step further to claim that it *established* the dictatorship in the first place.

Western arguments get far less airing in Greece today than those of the other side, with inevitable repercussions on Greek public opinion. Not surprisingly, recent opinion polls show that the majority of the Greek public still appears convinced that the West in general, and the United States in particular, are to blame for Greece's domestic and foreign policy problems.[17]

Lord Chalfont said at the London trial cited above that throughout his long career in politics and foreign affairs he never came across any evidence of U.S. involvement in the 1967 coup or the Turkish invasion of Cyprus. As already noted, he said that the Greek public has simply been "conditioned" to think that way, and that the advent of PASOK, both as an opposition party and as the party in power, rendered Greece particularly fertile ground for Soviet destabilization efforts.[18]

U.S. UNDERSECRETARY DERWINSKY ON THE GREEK PRESS

Disinformation in the Greek press and the damage it has caused to U.S.-Greek relations were deplored in an even more outspoken manner by U.S. Undersecretary of State Edward Derwinsky. Speaking to Greek daily *Kathemerine* early in November 1987, he said: "The U.S.A.'s relations with Greece have suffered very serious blows, more so than with any other country. And this because of the coverage of the Greek press, which has been full of fantasies. It would be good if the tone of these reports, as well as the level of fantasies, was somewhat reduced."

According to *Kathemerine,* the U.S. government is concerned over the role of the Greek press because it believes that "its exaggerated and often inaccurate involvement with Greek-American relations renders their improvement difficult."

This statement, inevitably, came under vicious attack by the Communist press (*Rizospastes, Auge,* and *Prote*), and by pro-Soviet daily *Ethnos*, as unacceptable American pressure on the Greek "democratic process," designed to intimidate and silence it so that the Greek government will submit to American demands on the military bases.[19] These same newspapers tried to exert pressure on deputy government spokesman Soteres Kostopoulos to condemn Derwinsky's statement. While they did not succeed with him, they were successful with official government spokesman Giannes Roubatis. He criticized the remark as unfounded, characterized it as unwarranted interference in the Greek press, and implied that it was the United States that was the source of disinformation: "The American undersecretary should look elsewhere—and certainly not in the Greek press—for the causes of the problems created in relations between the two countries over the last years," Roubatis said, adding: "Maybe Mr. Derwinsky should address himself elsewhere to discover the country where imaginary scenarios are fabricated, leaked and made public."[20]

It is hardly surprising that Roubatis defended the Greek press from accusations of fomenting anti-Americanism. For as a long-time foreign correspondent for the Lambrakes press group in Washington, he had contributed through his dispatches to the "American-conspiracies-against-Greece" syndrome. His willingness to fan such notions became evident at the end of 1987, when he published a book in Greek on U.S.-Greek relations, based on his thesis at Johns Hopkins University. The English version was titled, simply, *Tangled Webs, The U.S. in Greece 1947-1967*. To the Greek version, however, he gave the sinister title of *Trojan Horse, American Infiltration of Greece 1947-1967* , which was given considerable attention in the center-leftist press. Therefore, the official spokesman of a Western government proved that in Greece anti-Americanism can be officially aggravated and then marketed. Between the anti-Western rhetoric of Andreas Papandreou, and an official spokesman like Roubatis, Greece's "official voice" can hardly be anything but anti-Western.

THE KEY SOVIET PROPAGANDA THEMES AND THEIR ECHO IN THE GREEK PRESS

It has been conclusively proved that the Soviet bloc has set up a vast apparatus to conduct propaganda in the West and the Third World. Its main instruments are the International

Department; the International Information Department, which has been absorbed by other organs; and Service A (which stands for Active Measures) of the KGB's First Chief Directorate, i.e., the foreign intelligence branch.[21]

The main objectives of Soviet propaganda and disinformation activities have been identified by defectors and western experts as follows:

1. To influence American, European and world opinion to believe that American military and political policies are the major cause of international conflict and crisis;
2. To demonstrate that the United States is an aggressive, militaristic, and imperialistic power;
3. To isolate the United States from its friends and allies (especially those in NATO) and to discredit those countries that cooperate with the United States;
4. To discredit the American and NATO military/intelligence establishments;
5. To demonstrate that U.S. policies and objectives are incompatible with the interests of Third World countries;
6. To confuse and mislead world opinion about the objectives of Soviet foreign policy and to create a favorable environment in the West for the projection of Soviet interests.[22]

THE GREEK PRESS

An analysis of the Greek press that I have conducted over the past five years has led me to the firm conclusion that all of the themes listed above are very prominent in most of the Greek media. In addition to these general propaganda themes, specific accusations against the American role in Greece, as explained above, are also very prominent. Indeed, the general themes and specific accusations are interconnected. Allegations against U.S. activity in the world in general are often easily manipulated by the media to draw parallels with the United States' alleged activity in Greece in particular (e.g., reports about the CIA's destabilization activities in South America are often presented as "proof" that the United States did the same against hostile governments or politicians in Greece).

My conclusions are based on a very detailed analysis of *Ethnos*, Greece's largest circulation daily, from its launching in September 1981 to the present; an analysis of the influential investigative weekly *Pontiki* over the past two years; spot analyses of several other center-leftist newspapers and magazines; and a detailed analysis of the daily *Ta Nea*, the largest circulation newspaper during the critical period 1974-76, when anti-Western sentiments were at their height.

PRO-SOVIETISM BECOMES A NORMAL PHENOMENON IN THE GREEK PRESS

The conclusions I have reached as a result of my analysis of the Greek press are similar to those arrived at earlier by John Demetriades in his book *The Soviet Infiltration of Greece*. He argues that by going beyond the traditional communist outlets and by manipulating the non-communist press, the Soviets have achieved a qualitative increase in their propaganda effort in Greece. As a result, he concludes, an estimated 65 percent of those who read newspapers in Greece read publications that, to varying degrees, "convey Soviet propaganda on an almost daily basis." He says that to this should be added state radio and television, which have also become a major conduit for such propaganda and disinformation since PASOK came to power in 1981.

Three years before KGB defectors went on record and revealed the Soviet propaganda offensive in the non-communist Greek press, Demetriades had already written the following:

> For the past decades propaganda has constituted one of the most important weapons of Soviet foreign policy. The Soviets quickly realized that the existence of a well-orchestrated propaganda machine within the countries of their ideological and social opponents, in combination with the pressures which the USSR could exercise, produces remarkable results.
>
> Soviet propaganda in Greece, until recently, was expressed through channels controlled exclusively by the Communists. That is, the legal or at one time illegal communist press, and the Greek-language radio programs broadcasted by the 'socialist' countries. In recent years, however, and I am compelled to stress that I refer to the period after the 1981 elections (i.e. when Pasok came to power), one noted a serious qualitative change in the Soviet propaganda directed to Greece. This is due mainly to the fact that it has now been given the opportunity to express itself through media which are under the control of the state or of private individuals, and the main characteristic of which is that they are not communist.
>
> Through this qualitative leap the USSR achieves a broader dissemination of its views. Even more significant is the fact that it succeeds in having its views heard by a non-communist audience.[23]

Besides *Rizospastes* and *Auge,* the official organs of the two Communist parties in Greece and therefore traditional outlets for Soviet viewpoints (both with limited impact), Demetriades identified mass-circulation *Ethnos* as the most thoroughbred Soviet propaganda instrument in Greece. He also noted that the phenomenon, though not as intense and systematic as in *Ethnos,* can be seen to a serious extent in such major publications as *Ta Nea*, which currently is the second largest circulation daily in Greece and the largest circulation publication of the Lambrakes group publications. (Chrestos Lambrakes originally had the rights to publish the *Great Soviet Encyclopedia,* granted jointly to him and Communist party member Giannes Yannikos by Sitnikov. But the rights fell through due to disagreement over the indirect financing mechanism pursued by Sitnikov, who, apparently unknown to Lambrakes, was the deputy director of the KGB Disinformation Department. Lambrakes had insisted on a direct, interest-free loan of about $5 million for the advertising and publishing costs of the *Great Soviet Encyclopedia* . But Sitnikov had pursued the establishment of companies for trading purposes and the granting by Moscow of advantageous commercial deals, the profits from which would be used to finance the Greek publishing operation. When the negotiations with Lambrakes collapsed, this formula eventually was accepted and implemented by George Bobolas.)

Other publications listed by Demetriades as carrying pro-Soviet propaganda and disinformation include the daily *Eleutherotypia*, the weekly *Pontiki* (a publication that recently became the focus of a number of trials concerning its alleged Soviet, Cuban, and Nicaraguan connections), *Eleuthere Gnome* and *Romiosyne* (two newspapers that have since shut down), *Exormese* (the official organ of the ruling Socialist party), and a number of other, lesser publications.[24] One could now also add *Auriane* and *Demokratikos Logos*, newspapers owned by publisher George Koures, which have fabricated some of the most outlandish anti-Western stories circulated in Greece in recent years. Finally, there is the daily *Prote*, which was launched in April 1986 and which has repeatedly been described as—and does not deny being—the afternoon press organ of the Communist party.

It is worth noting that following the launching of *Prote*, there was a drop in the circulation of Greece's two most pro-Soviet afternoon dailies, *Ethnos* and *Ta Nea*. On the other hand, *Eleutherotypia*, a paper occasionally carrying pro-Soviet disinformation but generally striking a more balanced and respectable tone, rose in circulation over the same period.

Indeed, *Ethnos*'s publisher, George Bobolas claimed at the London trial between the newspaper and the *Economist* magazine that at the end of 1985 the Communist party issued a specific order to its members not to buy his paper. This, he said, led to a 10-percent drop in circulation.

Auriane, in a front-page editorial on 5 May 1986, said the rift at the time between *Ethnos* and the Communist party was due to the fact that *Ethnos* would not always blindly toe the Moscow line. This, the editorial argued, angered the Communist party, which subsequently decided to publish *Prote* . *Auriane* said the KKE had made an identical move in 1981, when it instructed its followers to abandon *Ta Nea* and to buy the newly launched *Ethnos*, which "sold leftism in bagfuls."

This editorial, coming from a center-leftist populist paper, gives credence to the argument that the circulation and therefore financial well-being of such mass-circulation papers as *Ethnos* and *Ta Nea* rely in part on the patronage of the pro-Moscow Communist party. This was indirectly confirmed by the publisher of *Ethnos* himself, in court.

Whatever the behind-the-scenes financing or the circulation battles among Greece's center-leftist dailies, the fact remains that *all* these newspapers—*Prote*, *Ethnos*, *Ta Nea*, *Auriane* , and *Eleutherotypia*—continue to carry Soviet disinformation and propaganda in varying degrees. The multiplicity of outlets for Soviet propaganda gives credibility to the argument—used at the London trial (which was historic because it publicized Soviet disinformation techniques) that pro-Sovietism is a *natural* phenomenon in the Greek media and reflects Greece's particular political climate. After conditioning Greek public opinion through Soviet disinformation techniques, the propagandists turn the argument around to claim that pro-Sovietism in the Greek press is simply a reflection of Greek public opinion!

The extensive use of Soviet material in the Greek press, some of which is openly identified as such but most not, has led to the view that it is quite a normal and acceptable phenomenon. It has been given a "scientific" explanation and an aura of legitimacy, or a "rational, economic" justification, since it secures a Communist readership and therefore a higher circulation.

The same argument was used, with unexpected results, at the London trial between *Ethnos* and the *Economist* . *Ethnos* 's publisher and editor, George Bobolas, seeking to defend the paper against allegations of being a paid Soviet mouthpiece, and arguing that there was nothing unusual in the paper's pro-Soviet contents, hastened to present a large amount of even more pro-Soviet material published by *Ethnos* 's two arch rivals, *Ta Nea* and *Eleutherotypia*. In trying to defend the paper against the charge that it was unique in its "slavishly pro-Soviet" articles, Bobolas exposed the two papers' own pro-Soviet propaganda and disinformation.

Bobolas inadvertently admitted that Soviet influence in the center-leftist (non-communist) press was so extensive that it had permeated the entire political climate, making anti-Western and pro-Soviet sentiments the norm. More specifically, Bobolas said:

> Both papers [*Ta Nea* and *Eleutherotypia*] do contain anti-United States articles and propaganda from the center-left. I have never heard it said that either of these two newspapers are slavishly pro-Soviet....these articles [i.e., scores produced from *Ta Nea* and *Eleutherotypia*] express the same sort of views as articles from *Ethnos and often one would find similar articles in right-wing newspapers* [my emphasis].... It is quite usual to see these types of articles in the Greek press. Indeed, some of those in *Eleutherotypia* and *Ta Nea* are rather harder-hitting than *Ethnos*.[25]

Early in 1982, the Soviets themselves were beginning to express publicly their satisfaction with the greater use of Soviet-origin material by the Greek press. According to the 29 April 1982 issue of *Foreign Report*, the *Economist* magazine's subscription-only newsletter:

> Russia's satisfaction with Greece has been voiced by several commentators. The Athens correspondent of the Soviet foreign affairs weekly *New Times*, Nikolai Miroshnik, reported that, though foreign news was still drawn largely from western agencies and "avowedly anti-Soviet publications," the Soviet news agency Tass and the newspaper *Pravda* were now quoted in Greek news reports: "The important thing is that the Iron Curtain in the sphere of information, with which the Greek mass media have fenced themselves off from the Socialist world for years, is being lifted."[26]

Demetriades explains that the Soviet propaganda offensive is also successfully conducted through a number of other channels, such as cultural and tourist exchanges, front organizations, and book publishing. While there is little room to examine this phenomenon fully in the present context, it is worth noting Demetriades' comments on book publishing and on radio and television, for these media also play a significant role in shaping public opinion. On the subject of pro-Soviet book publishing, he writes:

> The "Golden Age" began after the collapse of the dictatorship and restoration of democracy. It is estimated that almost 30 percent of the books published over the past ten years serve the political, social and economic reality expressed by the Soviet Union and its allies. Indeed, it should be noted that this is about twice as high as that prevailing in Italy and France, two other Mediterranean member states of the European Economic Community.[27]

Of the state-controlled radio and television networks, he notes:

> While in the press one now sees the results of years of efforts, in radio and television matters developed over a very short period. In this case Soviet propaganda relied both on specific individuals, as well as on the attempt of the government not to rely on the traditional western news agencies. As a result, as of mid-1982 viewers and listeners literally started being bombarded with a range of news of particular interest to the Soviets.[28]

As the author remarks, the sudden increase in pro-Soviet propaganda over the state-controlled radio and television networks provoked a considerable reaction, which the government could not ignore. This is not the case with newspapers, which are privately owned and therefore remain the best medium for manipulation. Demetriades writes:

> The press constitutes the most fertile terrain for Soviet propaganda, as a means of conveying a number of themes of interest to the USSR. The main ones are the condemnation of NATO, the weakening of the country's traditional ties with the West and the creation of a pro-Soviet climate. This latter issue is particularly significant. Many Greek analysts often mention that the USSR's objective is the Sovietization of the country. Perhaps so in the long term. In the short and medium term, however, the aim is not the creation of communists but of citizens with pro-Soviet inclinations.

Finally, Demetriades points out that Soviet infiltration of the Greek press has been achieved through various means:

> It begins with the open offer of money and reaches up to the supply of a whole series of facilities. For example, papers which cannot meet the high costs of maintaining a permanent correspondent in Moscow are offered exclusive reports from Tass correspondents or, more usually, from Novosti, as well as their link-up to these news agencies at a very low cost for coverage of international and Soviet affairs. One such example is the daily *Ta Nea*, whose correspondent in Moscow is a Novosti editor. The services of the same agency are occasionally also used by other Greek publications.[29]

The paradox of the overwhelming success registered by the extreme Left and pro-Soviet elements in manipulating newspapers owned by wealthy Greek capitalists, and through them manipulating public opinion and the government, has been well presented in an analysis by the moderate conservative weekly *Antilogos* . In an article titled "Why Greek Newspapers Are Leftist-oriented," it said:

> One of the major questions hanging over our political life today is how extreme Left political formations, while not attracting more than 15 percent of the electorate, have succeeded in luring the overwhelming majority of mass circulation daily newspapers.
>
> Therefore, according to undeniable circulation figures, about 60% of the total circulation of newspapers in terms of news and slogans cover the most extremist left-wing and pro-Soviet positions.
>
> ... This situation takes on both tragic and comical dimensions when one considers that such idolatrous, leftist texts are published in Greek newspapers which belong to prominent businessmen who are soaked in riches afforded to them by the western lifestyle... a provocative lifestyle of flashy villas, expensive cruises, casinos, limousines, etc.... They [the publishers] secure all these luxuries by selling through their pages the deceptive drugs provided by leftist rhetoric.
>
> In that way they confirm Lenin's highly applicable observation that the capitalists will provide the rope with which to hang themselves.
>
> The Greek Communist Party has taken good advantage of this situation, and in various ways supports the bourgeois newspapers which, in this way, accept to play the role of the rope for their own neck.... By securing the economic survival of all [the pro-leftist bourgeois newspapers] it succeeds in giving the impression that the Greek press is in the hands of the Left and that Greek society, therefore, is also moving to the Left.[30]

THE EVIDENCE REGARDING SOVIET-BACKED DISINFORMATION IN THE GREEK PRESS

There is considerable evidence to support the firsthand testimony of experts in the field as to the Soviet and Communist party influence-mechanisms in the Greek press. There are also several factors besides Greece's recent domestic and foreign political experiences that make this particular NATO-member country far more prone to Soviet penetration than any other Western country. Here we simply outline the main reasons for Greece's vulnerability:

—Greece's modern history, with forty-five years of right-wing rule (including a seven-year dictatorship and often some questionable democratic practices) facilitated an understandable backlash from the Left that the Soviets could easily exploit.

—A right-wing guilt complex followed, driving the conservatives often to adopt left-wing policies so as to appear more progressive than their past record showed them to be; this also meant avoiding anti-Soviet positions and sometimes going so far as to appear pro-Soviet.

—A policy of extreme caution and a low profile was maintained by the United States and NATO so as not to give rise to further criticism of the West's alleged wrongdoings. This in turn facilitated the upgrading of the Soviet image in Greece, to the point where Moscow's friendship could be presented as a better alternative for Greece.

—A financially-strong Communist party (it has been conclusively proved that its publishing operation was financed by East Germany), capable of using its resources to develop an extensive newspaper, magazine and book publishing network, and able to lure non-communist journalists with financial incentives.

—A history of Communist party journalists working for the non-Communist Greek press, who had found their way into newspapers when excluded from the state controlled mass media, or media-related jobs, and who could be activated for party and Soviet interests when necessary.

—The growth of PASOK and its advent to power, with its anti-Western platforms often overlapping those of the Communist party, resulting in an extremely fertile climate for Soviet Active Measures. Indeed, anti-Americanism and pro-Soviet sympathies became common under PASOK and almost became part of state ideology.

—The low standards of education in general and of journalism in particular; journalists are less scrupulous in Greece than in other western countries.

—Greece's proximity to the Eastern bloc countries and the post-civil war situation. After the civil war, 100,000 Greek communists fled to the East bloc and settled as political refugees; the majority have now returned home, thereby creating a significant flow of friends and relatives across the borders. Also, proximity and the low cost of living there make it much cheaper for Greeks to go to the Eastern bloc for holidays, health treatment and education, which, in turn, facilitates what are known as "influence operations" on the visiting Greeks.

—Unlike the U.S. and West German governments, which on a regular basis expose Soviet-bloc Active Measures and Disinformation campaigns, no Greek government, including those of the conservatives when they were in power, has appeared willing to take any action, because of the present ideological climate in favor of the Left.

—Finally, the Soviet-bloc countries and their local operatives are relatively free to exploit the open societies of the West—not only through the press, but also through the legal system (for example, there are no laws in the West against disinformation) and the open channels of communication in general. On the other hand, Western countries hardly have any access to the closed societies of the Eastern bloc for a free competition in ideas. (An excellent account of this enormous imbalance between East and West is provided by Jean-François Revel in his book *How Democracies Perish*.)

Similarly, in this context we can only briefly examine the growing amount of evidence regarding Soviet and Communist party involvement in the mainstream Greek media. Such evidence includes:

—the financing through East Germany of Typoekdotike, the Greek Communist party's publishing plant, and its various offshoots in Greece, which include newspapers, magazines, books, bookshops, a video-club, posters, pamphlets, and liaison agreements with non-Communist publications;

—the activities of the Greek branch of the International Organization of Journalism (IOJ), a major Soviet-front organization based in Czechoslovakia;

—the large number of Communist party journalists now working in the non-communist press;

—the employment of Soviet journalists as correspondents for Greek newspapers, and the extensive use of Soviet press agency material in the Greek media, to a degree unparalleled in any other Western country;

—*Ethnos*, Greece's largest circulation newspaper, which has developed into the best-documented example in the West of a newspaper that consistently uses Soviet propaganda and disinformation, of a paper staffed by commentators almost all of whom are members of Greek and foreign communist parties or of Soviet front organizations, and whose publisher first entered the publishing business through interconnected commercial and publishing agreements with officials of the KGB Disinformation Department; and

—the very large amount of Soviet propaganda and disinformation that has been uncovered in other mainstream publications, mainly in the center-leftist (non-Communist) political spectrum.

Upon examination, one cannot help but conclude that the contents of a majority of Greek newspapers and magazines, and radio and television news reflects those same Soviet aims identified by defectors and other specialists who had firsthand involvement in the plan—namely, to carry out a far-reaching disinformation operation in Greece so as to alter the political climate radically, and to do this by influencing the non-communist media.

THE SOVIETS' FORGERY AND FABRICATION OFFENSIVE IN THE GREEK PRESS

Now let us examine some of the hard evidence available on Soviet tampering. Namely, the use of forged documents planted in the Greek media, and cases where Soviet officials or agents have actually been discovered interfering with the Greek press.

Disinformation is sometimes difficult to trace because it is either false information disguised as truth or half-truths weaved into an actual event. Whatever the case, it delivers a deceptive message, the exact origins of which are difficult to pinpoint. Forgeries, on the other hand, are specific documents that disinformation experts actually sit down to fabricate with the purpose of creating a specific impression. Text, letterheads, and signatures can all be fabricated. Such documents have, quite aptly, been described as the most extreme manifestation of disinformation, and the most tangible, so it is important and valuable to expose forgeries when they are discovered.[31]

It is also important to track down forgeries because of their potentially damaging impact. Documents are always convincing both to the unsuspecting journalist and to the reading public, since they are presented as tangible proof of a story's validity. According to Kathleen C. Bailey, a U.S. deputy assistant secretary of state, responsible for coordinating efforts to expose Soviet forgeries and other Active Measures, forged U.S. government documents are being spotted "increasingly and in higher quality in various parts of the world, with adverse effects on U.S. foreign policy."[32]

Strictly speaking, forgeries could be traced to their origin if authorities or newspapers insisted on knowing journalists' sources. In this way, the network that provided forged documents could be exposed. In practice this seldom happens because of the privilege the press enjoys in protecting its sources.

The author's research has shown that more forgeries of documents have appeared in the Greek press than in that of any other Western country.[33] Since these forgeries constitute some of the strongest proof of Soviet disinformation efforts in Greece, it is worth listing them in detail. I must point out that those cited below come from only a spot analysis covering the thirteen-year period 1974-1987, and from occasional disclosures made by Western governments. Therefore, they can by no means be considered a complete listing of the undoubtedly large number of Soviet-origin forgeries, or fabricated reports, planted in the Greek media. Briefly, they are the following:

1. 1974—Reports that U.S. jet fighters intercepted Greek Phantom jets to prevent them from assisting Cyprus during the Turkish invasion, and numerous reports since then that the whole Cyprus debacle was an American operation intended to establish military bases there.[34]

2. 1978—A forgery in the authoritative centrist daily *To Vema*, citing Defense Intelligence Agency (DIA) instructions to monitor the activities of certain Greek political organizations.[35]

3. 17 March 1978—Socialist party leader (and current prime minister) Andreas Papandreou brought a document to Parliament that purported to be a 1976 State Department telegram by U.S. Secretary of State Henry Kissinger. Entitled "Greek-Turkish Differences in the Aegean," it was designed to show that the U.S. favored Turkey in its disputes with Greece. Papandreou, in the middle of a stormy foreign policy debate, presented it as a "bombshell" designed to prove his constant argument that the United States and NATO were conspiring against Greece and that therefore Greece should leave the alliance.

Constantine Karamanlis, who was then premier, declared in Parliament that his government "knows nothing of the existence of this document." Papandreou responded that "it came into my hands by chance." (Reference: official records of Parliament, 17 March 1978; also reprinted in weekly *Pontiki* , 15 April 1988) The U.S. government immediately and repeatedly denied the contents of the telegram and stated that it was a forgery. To this date Papandreou (like all the Greek publications that have used forgeries) has not revealed where he got it. (Reference: see "Soviet Covert Action, the Forgery Offensive," Hearings before the Subcommittee on Oversight of the Permanent Select Committee on Intelligence, House of Representatives, 96th Congress, 2nd Session, 6 and 19 February 1980; "Soviet Active Measures: The Propaganda War," by David Rees, The Institute for the Study of Conflict, London, 1984; and State Department Report to Congress on Active Measures, 6 April 1988).

4. 1979—Another forged document passed to *To Vema*, which was rejected after being identified as such by the U.S. embassy; soon after, however it surfaced in *Eleutherotypia*. [36]

5. 1982—A forgery sent to Greek provincial newspapers, purporting to be a State Department plan for a coup in Greece in order to safeguard the U.S. bases.[37]

6. One of the best-known forgeries internationally, published by *Anti* magazine—namely, an alleged U.S. Army field manual--(FM 30-31B), giving guidance to army intelligence as to how to suborn officials in countries where it appeared that Communists were about to gain government posts.[38]

7. 1983—A report, published in *Ethnos* and based on three forgeries, that inferred that Glafkos Clerides, the conservative candidate in the Cyprus presidential elections, had been groomed as an agent by the Nazis; the forgeries were republished by the Cypriot daily *Eleutherotypia* the next day; after a three-year legal battle, the Cypriot paper retracted, apologized and admitted that it had unwittingly fallen victim to forgeries. Former Cyprus government officials later admitted that these forgeries had been planted on none less than Cypriot President Kyprianou.[39]

8. 1985—A report, published in *Pontiki* and based on a forged letter from the Department of the Air Force to U.S. Secretary of Defense Caspar Weinberger, "revealing" that Cyprus would be used as a refuge for American personnel in the case of a limited nuclear war in Europe and that better use should be made of Turkish-occupied Cyprus for that purpose; the report was published even though the forgery had been exposed as such a month earlier in the Cyprus press; the forgery was first published in the Cypriot conservative daily *Semerine* , and was responded to within a day by U.S. authorities.

THE UNITED STATES MAKES A MAJOR POLICY DECISION TO EXPOSE DISINFORMATION IN GREECE

Early in 1987 the U.S. government decided to include Greece in a policy (which apparently dates from 1981, the year of the formation of the Interagency Committee on Soviet Active Measures) of publicly exposing Soviet forgeries or "blatantly false and potentially damaging" press reports. Prior to that, a cautious policy of virtual silence had been applied, in the belief that public reaction from the U.S. embassy would be criticized in the Greek press as further proof of American interference in Greece's domestic affairs and as a threat to "the freedom of the Greek democratic press."

This long overdue policy change resulted in new exposures. During the 100-day period from 10 April to 27 July 1987, the U.S. embassy issued announcements and provided on-the-record information that exposed eight forgeries or fabricated stories. They were the following:

1. On 29 November 1986, pro-Socialist government daily *Demokratikos Logos* published a "world exclusive" on the Irangate affair, based on alleged taped conversations between Iranian officials and U.S. National Security Advisor Robert McFarlane. It claimed to show that promised U.S. military aid to Iran amounted to $5 billion and that $2 million was paid to a terrorist group as ransom for the release of American hostages. Investigations showed that the paper, in fact, had no tapes or transcripts and that the dialogue was fictitious.[40]

2. On 6 April 1987, the pro-Communist daily *Prote* published a forged U.S. State Department telegram purporting to show that the United States was considering using Turkish-occupied Cyprus as an alternative to Greece for the establishment of its bases should Greece leave NATO and close down the U.S. bases.[41]

3. On 10 April 1987, *Demokratikos Logos* stated in a banner-headline that the U.S. base at Nea Makri jammed Greek naval telecommunications during the Greek-Turkish crisis in March 1987, a confrontation that almost led to war in the Aegean between the two NATO members. (Such allegations—of the U.S. *actually assisting* Turkey against Greece in a conflict situation—always succeed in stirring up anti-American sentiment among the Greeks and, not surprisingly, constitute a very common theme employed in the Greek press from 1974 to the present.)

A U.S. embassy announcement, dated 10 April dismissed the report as a "total fabrication," and it was also denied by the Greek government. Despite this, the allegations continued to surface in *Auriane* , *Ta Nea*, and *Ethnos* .[42]

4. On 18 April 1987, *Auriane* claimed that the recent dispute between Greece and Turkey over oil exploration rights in the Aegean was part of a U.S. plan to pressure Greece and to make it compromise. The U.S. Embassy yet again dismissed the claim as a "total fabrication."

5. On 7 May 1987, *Ta Nea* provided more "details" of U.S. interception of Greek military communications to assist Turkey during the Aegean crisis, a report that drew yet another categorical denial from the U.S. embassy.[43]

6. From October 1986 to the present, a large number of Greek publications, but primarily *Ethnos*, made use of the Soviet-fabricated allegation that the AIDS virus was invented by the Pentagon as part of its preparations for biological warfare. The reports picked up such momentum that a group of Greek left-wing "peace activists" went so far as to initiate legal action against the U.S. government before an international court. The development was strongly criticized in a U.S. embassy announcement dated 22 May 1987.

7. On 28 May 1987, the center-leftist weekly *Kalami* published a forgery purporting to show that NATO had planned a coup to prevent Papandreou from coming to power in 1981, and that it had an alternative government ready. The communication was allegedly sent to Greek conservative politician Stephanos Stephanopoulos, the supposed leader of the would-be junta, by Dr. S.I.P. van Campen, the chef de cabinet for Joseph Luns, NATO's secretary-general in 1981.

The U.S. embassy did not issue a formal announcement on this because, as an embassy spokesman explained, this particular forgery was so clumsy in its formulation that it was not necessarily of Soviet bloc origin. Neither did the Greek Socialist government give the report any credibility. However, *Counterpoint*, a monthly bulletin produced by two KGB defectors and one that specializes in exposing Soviet Active Measures, concluded in a recent article that it was indeed a Soviet-bloc forgery, however clumsy in its formulation.[44]

8. In what appears to be one of the most extreme examples of combined fabrications and forgeries, between June and July 1987, *Demokratikos Logos* and *Auriane* produced a series of reports alleging that the United States was orchestrating acts of

terrorism in Greece and was attempting to murder Papandreou and to overthrow the government. The accusations were focused on Michael Ledeen, a U.S. government adviser in security affairs, whom the papers specifically identified as the alleged leader of the conspiracy. The allegations were also published in *Pontiki*, *Ta Nea*, and *Ethnos* and ultimately gave rise to two U.S. embassy announcements describing them as "vicious falsehoods" designed to harm U.S.-Greek relations. The Greek government also stated that it had no such information, while Ledeen himself in an interview provided his own answers as to what appeared to be a well-orchestrated disinformation campaign (see *Acropolis*, 13 September 1987).

On this occasion the U.S. embassy response was particularly strong, in that it directly accused the Greek press of fabricating reports designed to spread the notion that the U.S. government was involved in hostile acts against Greece and the Greek government. Similarly, in its very first announcement on a forgery under its new policy of exposure (10 April 1987), the U.S. embassy had stated the following:

> We note that the U.S. has been the target of numerous efforts in recent years aimed at driving a wedge between us and our NATO allies and friends. While we do not know who is behind the forgery in question, it is evident whose interests are served by this kind of fraudulent enterprise, as an inordinate number of these stories appear in communist newspapers and those which support Soviet policies.

HOW FORGERIES PROVE THE BROADER SOVIET DISINFORMATION OFFENSIVE

These forgeries, or blatant fabrications, uncovered over the relatively short period examined, lead us to the following conclusions:

1. That the five main themes of anti-Western propaganda and disinformation have appeared in the Greek press with a persistent regularity from 1974 to the present

2. That a far greater number of forgeries and fabricated stories have been exposed since the U.S. government reversed its earlier policy of silence

3. That the forgeries provide some of the strongest evidence of Soviet involvement in cultivating these key disinformation themes

4. That the publications that have been used in this way (*Ethnos, Ta Nea, Pontiki, Auriane, Anti, Kalami, Prote, Auge, Demokratikos Logos, Rizospastes,* and *Eleutherotypia*) *cover the*

entire spectrum of center-leftist newspapers and mainstream publications , and are the same ones that often carry pro-Soviet propaganda and disinformation.

Considering that the total circulation of national daily newspapers in Greece is about 950,000, one cannot but agree with the estimates cited earlier that about 65 percent of the total circulation is represented by publications which, to varying degrees, regularly carry pro-Soviet propaganda and disinformation.

5. Finally, that the Soviets have not even hesitated to exploit Greek political leaders in their forgery offensive, demonstrating their contempt for Greece's political maturity and the extent to which they are prepared to go to cultivate the desired political climate. Their success is palpable: Greece and Cyprus are the only known examples in the West of political leaders actually falling victim to Soviet forgeries. In Greece, as we have seen, Papandreou was unwittingly manipulated with the "State Department document" he brought to Parliament. In Cyprus, forgeries published in 1983 in *Ethnos* and *Eleutherotypia* were in fact first planted on President Spyros Kyprianou. The president then leaked them to the press, as admitted publicly by Nikos Rolandis, Kyprianou's foreign minister at the time, and by Stauros Ambizas, his former parliamentary spokesman. (Reference: See "Kyprianou involved in the Fraud concerning the Forged Documents," *Aletheia* 5 February 1988.) Rolandis said he had advised the president against making use of the "documents."

When the April 1988 congressional report again included the incident of the forgery involving Papandreou, a section of the pro-government press this time reacted strongly. So did government spokesman Giannes Roubatis, who together with the newspapers implied that it was yet another American conspiracy designed to pressure the government over the negotiations on the U.S. military bases. However, he did not attempt to deny that Papandreou had fallen victim to a forgery. Some newspapers noted this, but others persisted in their conspiracy theory (for example, see "Another Provocation" in *24 Hours*, 16 April 1988.)

The state of mind or "thought conditioning" of the average Greek newspaper was typified by a question asked by a reporter of the centrist daily *24 Hours,* who participated in a live press conference broadcast on 15 April by the Worldnet satellite television service of the United States Information Agency

(USIA) in which reporters posed questions to a panel of experts on Soviet Active Measures and Disinformation.

The Greek reporter asked: "As you know, Greece and the U.S. are having talks on a new agreement for the American bases in Greece. A few days ago, a ten-year-old report of the USIA was used in the State Department report to Congress to accuse the Greek prime minister of being a victim of Soviet disinformation.

"Given the fact that the talks on the bases are very delicate and there are great tensions between the two parties, do you think that this foregrounding of a very old report was anything but a way of the Americans to pressure the Greeks?"

Herbert Romerstein, the specialist responding on behalf of the USIA, denied any U.S. pressure on Greece concerning the military bases and explained that "we were both the victims of this Soviet forgery, and that is the point. We should not allow Soviet forgeries to divide us, even ten-year-old Soviet forgeries, let alone current ones. We should make sure that such things unite us so that we join together in exposing the forgeries."

The Greek journalist pressed on: "Your agency has accused Greece, and especially its very outspoken press, of being vulnerable to Soviet disinformation. Do you think this is true? If yes, could you give us some examples?"

Romerstein replied: "First of all, our agency has not accused Greece of anything. A private scholar [Ed. note: he was referring to Steven Schwartz, the scholar who researched the cases of forgeries floated by the Soviet bloc, and whose findings were listed in the State Department's report to Congress of 6 April 1988], in analyzing a series of forgeries of the past, indicated that Greece and a number of other countries were targets of Soviet disinformation and forgeries. That does not make Greece a criminal. It makes Greece a victim.

"... I make the offer to you, sir, if you have a document that is supposedly an American document and it is embarrassing to the United States, contact us. If it really is an authentic document and it is embarrassing, we will tell you that it is authentic. If it is a forgery, we will give you the evidence that it is a forgery." (Reference: official transcript, USIA, Worldnet broadcast on disinformation, 15 April 1988)[45]

* * * *

The U.S. change in policy was long overdue; the previous policy of extreme caution had verged on timidity, had given rise to interpretations of "a guilty silence" on the part of the United

States, and only had the snowball effect of encouraging increasing disinformation and fabricated reports that in volume were already unparalleled in any other Western country. The falsehoods went mostly unanswered for thirteen years (1974-1987), resulting in a considerable buildup of unjustified anti-Western resentment that will take considerable time to dispel.

A good analysis, and perhaps the only currently available comment on U.S. policy in Greece on the subject, was made by George Savidis, a researcher at Boston University's Center for the Study of Disinformation. In notes for his master's thesis, he wrote:

Although the U.S. initiated a policy of studying and in some cases exposing disinformation in the early 1980s, the policy is still handicapped by several factors. Firstly, many reports are issued with seminal facts deleted or blacked out, which is a common practice employed to protect "sources and methods." As a result, the reports and related press releases lack objective evidence, and subsequently can appear to be merely political pronouncements.

Moreover, in countries such as Greece, the U.S. is ironically the victim of its previous refusal to recognize the effectiveness of Soviet propaganda and disinformation. With the success of disinformation, and the general public convinced that Greece's post-war political hardships are the result of U.S. conspiracies, input from the U.S. authorities concerning disinformation is the object of suspicion by a good deal of the Greek public. The vicious circle of decreasing U.S. credibility has created a situation in which more and more vitriolic anti-American stories can be planted. The United States Information Agency (USIA), which is responsible for issuing responses to disinformation in the Greek press, is now responding to the most extreme cases of forgeries or blatantly fabricated reports. But it is not countering the majority of (false) stories, for fear that efforts to set the record straight all the time might be characterized as interference in the free press or democratic process within Greece.

Unfortunately, what is really needed is a clear refutation each time an example of disinformation surfaces. Included in any press announcements should be an indication of the possible sources of the story, and a reference to those who might be benefiting from it (usually the same party). Although the U.S. has recently had some bad experiences sharing intelligence information with the government of Greece, as exemplified by Greece's failure to act in a meaningful manner on information supplied by KGB defector Sergei Bokhane (he defected from his Athens post to the U.S. in May 1985), long-term aggressive efforts at exposing Soviet activities within Greece should be continued. Additionally, information concerning clear-cut disinformation examples, such as forgeries, should be shared with journalists.[46]

While the change in America's policy on how to deal with the disinformation problem in Greece was late in coming, it has still proved effective. Not surprisingly, it drew some sharp epithets from publications and journalists publicly identified as responsible for such activity.[47] But it also encouraged those journalists and researchers who are concerned about the effects of the problem to become more active in combatting it.

Indeed, continuing investigation and exposure based on careful research remain the most effective means of combatting disinformation. As Lawrence Eagleburger wrote in 1983: "Soviet Active Measures need to be countered by public exposure. They are infections that thrive only in darkness, and sunlight is the best antiseptic."[48]

SOVIET ATTITUDES TOWARDS GREECE AND THE GREEK PRESS

It is not surprising that the success achieved by the Soviets has made them feel more confident and has encouraged a brazen approach towards Greek affairs in general and the Greek press in particular. For example, several journalists have spoken to me of the aggressive approach used by former Soviet press attaché Eugeny Chistiakov in attempting to befriend Greek writers so as to promote pro-Soviet material. Chistiakov was the main Soviet official in Athens who synchronized the publishing and commercial agreements between Moscow and George Bobolas and Alexander Filippopoulos—the publisher and editor respectively of *Ethnos* and the *Great Soviet Encyclopedia*. Chistiakov was found to be an intelligence agent and was expelled from Greece in July 1980 when caught *in flagrante delicto* in an espionage operation against the NATO department of Greek Naval Headquarters.

Perhaps even more illustrative of Soviet arrogance in attempting to manipulate the Greek press was the unusual confrontation between the Soviet embassy's press attaché, Vladimir Prygin and *Nea Poreia*, the official press organ of the conservative (New Democracy) government.

According to a letter sent to the New Democracy party's leadership by the paper's editor, Titos Athanasiades, Prygin paid him a courtesy call during which the Soviet official attempted to pressure him to stop publishing articles critical of the Soviet bloc:

Specifically, Mr. V. Prygin strongly protested over the contents of the articles of *Nea Poreia* on issues dealing with the domestic and foreign policies of the USSR, "It is not possible," he said, characteristically, "for *Nea Poreia* to be an organ of the governing party and to exercise such intense criticism of the USSR, the government of which has good relations with the Greek government."

"The articles of *Nea Poreia*," he continued, "undermine the good spirit prevailing between the two countries. The polemics conducted by *Nea Poreia*," he added, "are directed against the USSR, its relations with its sister socialist countries, the third world, and the Arab states." Mr. V. Prygin also referred to the Polish issue, going as far back as the 1939 period, to Afghanistan, etc. and stressed: "If you want to criticize, you can do so on the theory of Marxism and Socialism, but not on the practice."[49]

The Greek government at the time considered lodging a protest with the Soviets over this incident, but ultimately refrained from doing so.

If a Soviet official felt so self-assured as to attempt to censor the official press organ of the ruling conservative government, then it is not difficult to imagine how comfortable Moscow feels in its contacts with the center-leftist Greek press.

Indeed, Soviet confidence concerning its gains in Greece was perhaps most clearly illustrated recently, not only where the press is concerned, but at the very highest government level—that of close contacts between the two countries' leaders. On 3 July 1987, *Pontiki* carried an exclusive report revealing the contents of an exchange of letters between Soviet leader Mikhail Gorbachev and Prime Minister Andreas Papandreou. In his letter, which provoked considerable reaction from the conservative opposition in Greece, Gorbachev went so far as to advise Papandreou on how to handle the closing of the U.S. bases, pending termination of the present agreement. He claimed that this was the "unanimous demand of the Greek people." The Soviet leader also felt confident enough to refer to Papandreou as a "fellow ideologue." Again, if the Soviets felt that they had achieved such close relations with Greece's leadership that they could advise the Greek government on how it should conduct itself on a key issue of foreign and defense policy, then how easy they must have found it to manipulate the Greek press.

THE ULTIMATE PRODUCT OF DISINFORMATION: TERRORISM

Disinformation is not just an academic exercise in which Soviet intelligence officers try to dupe the Western press into publishing pro-Soviet propaganda. Above all, it is designed to bring political results favorable to the Soviet Union. In this regard, it seeks to cause friction, misunderstandings, and tension; to upset relations between the Western allies; and even to fuel riots. The violent anti-American demonstrations that have been a common feature of Greek life have undoubtedly also been encouraged by media disinformation. Similarly, disinformation has also encouraged terrorism.

A prominent example of how the Greek press has been manipulated, with very serious repercussions, was a story that appeared in the English-language daily *Athens News* .

In late November 1975, the newspaper published a list of CIA agents, sent to it by the so-called, and previously unheard of, Committee of Greeks and Greek-Americans to Prevent Their Country and Fatherland from Being Subverted to the Uses of the CIA. It included the phone numbers and home addresses of the alleged agents. The story denounced the CIA for destroying democratic freedoms and pledged to expose its "evil work" in Greece through subsequent reports.[50] The list and story had obviously come from Eastern bloc intelligence operatives, or persons manipulated by them.

A week later, the *Athens News* was sent a similar report exposing ten alleged KGB agents; it was signed by the "Committee to Keep Greece Greek." The action was apparently intended to counter what was seen as a move by the KGB to cause harm to its intelligence adversaries, and no doubt came from American intelligence sources.[51]

Indicative of the attitudes of the time, however, the *Athens News* did not publish the list of KGB agents. Three weeks later, CIA station chief Richard Welch was assassinated outside his home by the November 17th terrorist group. After all, his identity and address had been published in the *Athens News* .

A similar incident, linking disinformation with terrorism, occurred more recently. On 24 April 1987 the same terrorist organization staged a bomb attack against a Greek air force bus carrying U.S. military personnel home from work. Seventeen servicemen were injured. The ensuing proclamation from November 17th explained that this action was aimed against American imperialism in Greece. Moreover, the reasons it gave included all the disinformation themes prominent in the Greek media in the past 13 years; namely, that U.S. bases constituted an "occupation force" in Greece, that the United States was responsible for the Cyprus tragedy, that the U.S. bases in

Greece were intended for Turkish interests in the case of a military confrontation between Turkey and Greece in the Aegean Sea, and that America was encouraging Turkish territorial ambitions against Greece. It also blamed the Communist party for failing to stage a mass uprising against the Americans during the recent Greek-Turkish confrontation in the Aegean.[52]

There was, however, something unusual in the group's proclamation. It said that the text had been finalized when *Demokratikos Logos* carried a banner-headline story on 10 April that the U.S. telecommunications base at Nea Makri had jammed and thereby blacked out Greek naval communications during the recent confrontation with Turkey in the Aegean Sea. This, the terrorist organization said in a postscript to its proclamation, "fully confirms" its own information that the U.S. bases in Greece serve as support for Turkey. As discussed above, the report in *Demokratikos Logos* was totally fabricated, and was exposed as such by the American embassy. But Soviet disinformation has been so successful in encouraging anti-American sentiments that even public exposure of an obvious fabrication cannot halt the most extreme result of disinformation—terrorism.

THE REPERCUSSIONS OF DISINFORMATION ON THE GREEK POLITICAL PROCESS

It was October 1949. The Greek Communist guerrilla forces had just been defeated and driven back behind the Iron Curtain after a four-year civil war. But in the small town of Bourelli, in neighboring Albania, a plenary meeting of the Greek Communist party (KKE) was convening to decide on the course of action henceforth. Here it was decided that the best means of regaining ground lost as a result of the civil war was to wage political and psychological warfare. The effects of this decision, as well as of others which followed soon after, can be traced to the ideological climate prevailing today in Greece.

The plenum rejected the proposal of Mitsos Partsalides to continue the armed struggle, and instead adopted that of Nikos Zachariades, who was then party secretary-general. In brief, he argued that the Communists would now have to continue their struggle through political, economic, social, trade-unionist and ideological means.[53]

This decision was pursued further in subsequent meetings of the party. Vasiles Barzotas, at the second plenum of the

Central Committee of the KKE in October 1951, suggested the following:

> We need to form a strong ideological front. To organize the dissemination and study of Soviet literature, of Soviet films and music. Our cultural work must be organized and based upon a specific plan.[54]

Leonidas Stringos, at the fourth plenum of the KKE's Central Committee in December 1953, took the plan for ideological warfare several steps further. He proposed:

> A greater development of the mechanism, the means and the methods of communist propaganda. To fight and to destroy anti-communism. To counter the theories of European and Greco-Christian civilization. The systematic publication of the archives of the KKE and the writing of a history for it. Popularizing the National Resistance. Combating reformism. Exploitation of Neo-Hellenic history based on Marxist interpretations. The development of left-wing literature, the arts, of popular music and the works of progressive artists. The strengthening of the work of writers and of intellectuals and scientists in general, for all these play a significant role in the shaping of public opinion. Combating reactionary theorists. A general attack on the ideological and propagandist front.[55]

The defeated and demoralized Greek Communist forces, however, could hardly have hoped to achieve even a fraction of these goals without foreign support. This was particularly so given that the party remained outlawed in Greece until 1974 and that its excesses in the Civil War had led to the development of formidable popular opposition to left-wing propaganda and ideology.

THE SOVIETS' POSITION ON RECORD

Covert political activity and financing through front organizations was the answer. There is now clear evidence, from the time of defeat in the Civil War to the present, showing that the Communist party and the Soviet Union pursued a long-term plan of political, economic and cultural infiltration in Greece as a means of turning the correlation of forces in their favor. This is in line with Soviet activity worldwide. However, in Greece the Soviets' infiltration has had more success than in any other Western country.

Former Soviet leader Leonid Brezhnev illustrated the Soviet approach to Greece in a work that was translated and published in Greek: "Our friendly ties and relations of good neighborliness will prove to the advantage of peace in Europe and the whole world," he wrote. "One of the links in the chain which leads to this goal, and which we should seize hold of, are the cultural exchanges between Greece and the Soviet Union.... Of course, cultural ties alone will not bring Spring. But when these are transformed into a systematic pattern, when ties are developed in the fields of politics and the economy, then we can say that a new climate is being created."[56] Close cultural ties with Greece were only a prelude to close economic and political ties.

Soviet persistence in pursuing cultural and economic inroads in Greece as a means of developing political and intelligence-gathering opportunities was made evident yet again by the terms Moscow tried to impose on Greece as a condition for diplomatic support in the United Nations over the Cyprus issue.

According to recently available British Foreign Office records disclosed at the end of England's 30-year secrecy rule, the Greek conservative government at the time rejected the three Soviet conditions, which were:

1. Re-establishment of diplomatic relations between Greece and Albania;

2. Abstention by Greece from voting against Soviet bloc interests at the U.N. at the time, especially during debates over the Eisenhower doctrine;

3. Development of relations between Greece and the Soviet Union and its allies in the cultural and economic sphere.[57]

Paradoxically, the Soviet bloc managed to lay the firm foundations for all these demands during the rightist military dictatorship, which ruled Greece between 1967-74. It did so by taking advantage of the diplomatic isolation the Greek regime found itself in when under pressure from the West to restore political liberties. At various times between 1967 and 1974 Greece re-established diplomatic relations with Albania, East Germany established a commercial mission in Greece, economic and cultural agreements were made with Rumania and Bulgaria, and ministers visited Greece from both Rumania and Bulgaria.[58] After the junta collapsed in 1974, left-wing sentiment rose, and the seeds planted by the Soviets and East Europeans during the dictatorship took root in fertile soil and grew in the years that followed.

With the advent of the Socialist government of Andreas Papandreou in 1981, the Soviet bloc enjoyed relations with a Western government which not only drew closer to it than any other European country, but which went so far as to support some of Moscow's key foreign policy interests within Western platforms such as NATO and the EEC (e.g., over the Polish issue, the downing of the South Korean passenger jet by the Soviets, and East-West disarmament issues).

GORBACHEV'S LETTER TO PAPANDREOU

Indeed, over the next few years, the Soviet Union had every reason to be pleased with the fruits of its efforts. This became evident, in a most embarrassing way for both the Soviets and the Greek government, when the contents of a letter to Papandreou from Gorbachev, delivered to him on 14 May 1987 were disclosed. Gorbachev, among other things, said: "I cannot but express my satisfaction with the steadily rising course of Soviet-Greek cooperation in many fields, especially the better mutual understanding in the political field. The deep confidence established between our countries, the closeness or identity of our positions concerning the most significant issues of our time, the frequent contacts and rich dialogue—all these constitute undeniable proof of the steadiness and liveliness of the traditional friendship existing between our peoples for the past many centuries."

Gorbachev expressed his concern that commercial and economic relations were not developed enough between the two countries and called for even more cooperation in joint enterprises and scientific and technological cooperation. (Not surprising in view of the growing evidence that Greece and Cyprus were developing into major platforms for the theft of Western military-oriented technology by the Bulgarians, acting on behalf of the Soviet bloc.)[59] The Soviet leader also said there was greater scope for "the development of cultural and scientific cooperation."

Turning to the political outlook and actions of the Papandreou government, especially on disarmament issues, Gorbachev specifically praised the difference between Greece and its Western allies. "It is noteworthy that both Greece and you personally, Mr. Papandreou... demonstrate a broadness of vision and a desire for cooperation, independent of the political and ideological positions of your partners in the talks."

It was at this point that Gorbachev revealed that he felt confident enough to attempt to instruct Papandreou to expel the U.S. bases from Greece, claiming that this was the "unanimous" wish of the Greek people, and to praise him as a "fellow-ideologue." He wrote in his letter: "Your desire to pursue the removal from Greek territory of the military bases existing there, after the termination of the relative agreement, is known to us. We share your view that these bases, in accordance with the unanimous demand of the Greek people, must be removed from the country.... Mr. Papandreou, we see in you and your government our fellow-ideologue concerning the problem of turning the Mediterranean into a zone of peace, security and cooperation, free from nuclear weapons and the presence of foreign armed forces."[60]

As regards the Greek Communist party, its dogmatically pro-Soviet stance and the scarcity of its means of raising money make it obvious that it must rely on economic support through the covert mechanisms of the Soviet Union. The financing of the party's vast publishing and propaganda apparatus through a front company set up in Luxembourg by East German intelligence has already been proved and documented. But as previously stated, defecting KGB officials and former Russian propagandists who were directly involved in the Soviet efforts have now provided even more impressive evidence on such covert operations in Greece.[61] One such example is that given by Ilya Dzhirkvelov, a former KGB colonel, who, as mentioned earlier, defected in 1980. He recently provided a startling insight into the covert financing mechanisms used by the Soviets in Greece. In a statement made to *The Economist* before its trial with *Ethnos*, he spoke of his personal involvement in sending 50,000 dollars to Greece in 1960, which was to be used, among other things, to finance the defense of 42 leftists who were being tried on charges of subversive activity.

Dzhirkvelov elaborated on this incident in an interview with Greek journalists in Paris in October 1987, explaining how advertisements were placed in two French newspapers, calling for support of the Greek leftist Manoles Glezos, one of the 42 on trial. He said a bank account in Paris was established for donations and that it was also used by him to bring in 50,000 dollars from Moscow, which was funnelled to Greece. Dzhirkvelov, acting on the orders of his immediate superior, KGB Colonel Pavel Gevorkian, personally sent the money through Moscow's State Bank (GOSBANK). Both Dzhirkvelov and Gevorkian operated under the cover of being senior officials of the International Department of the Soviet Union of Journalists. They specialized in active measures and disinformation.[62]

We thus see that evidence is mounting about large-scale Soviet involvement in Greece. The evidence ranges from the Communist party's resolutions at the end of the Civil War and the formation of front organizations in Greece under the PASOK government to the recent Gorbachev diplomatic offensive.[63] It is the central contention of this essay that manipulating public opinion and short-circuiting government actions through influence over large sections of the media has been key to Soviet success.

The continuing worldwide Soviet propaganda effort, which entails considerable costs at a time of growing difficulties for the Soviet economy, proves that Moscow attaches a great deal of importance to its worldwide disinformation and propaganda campaigns. They are not simply an exercise in narcissism but a form of political or psychological warfare that is designed, above all, to have political effect.[64]

While locating and exposing disinformation activities may be relatively easy, measuring their effect on public opinion and government actions is far more difficult. Still, there is little doubt that the cumulative impact of disinformation, especially through the process of repetition, does have an effect on the political climate of a country and its pro-Western, neutralist, or pro-Soviet orientations. This has been observed in the case of India, for example.[65]

Similar results can be detected in Greece. Thirteen years after the initial outpouring of anti-Western sentiments, no factual evidence pointing to Western responsibility for the country's woes has surfaced. On the contrary, there is growing evidence that the anti-Western sentiments among the Greek public are more the result of a well-orchestrated campaign conducted by the Soviet Active Measures apparatus and its local operatives.

Unfortunately, one is compelled to admit that the Soviets' efforts have succeeded to a considerable extent. Active Measures and disinformation have worked in Greece, and their results have been startling. Although Greece has legitimate foreign policy grievances against Turkey for its occupation of northern Cyprus and its claims in the Aegean, the Soviets have actually managed in Greece to invert reality, to confuse and disorient public opinion, and to direct public grievances against the West. *They have succeeded in making the Greek public and many politicians think what they want them to think.* As already pointed out, it would be difficult to find any other Western country, in the entire post-World War II period, that has developed such anti-Western positions in the press, in public opinion, and in government.

The use of opinion polls to measure the impact of specific or cumulative Soviet disinformation efforts is relatively new. The results of comparative international polling, measuring the effect of disinformation on public opinion, are difficult to come by, as are estimates of the proportion of the public that actually believes a particular floated falsehood.[66]

Polls taken in Greece, however, have repeatedly confirmed an anti-Western trend. With regard to specific incidents, we can look at the surprising results of a poll dealing with such themes as terrorism and American and Soviet policy toward Greece. An opinion poll conducted by ICAP-Gallup on behalf of the independent magazine Epikaira showed that a large section of the Greek public at that time believed that the United States was involved in, or was to blame for, some of the most extraordinary developments in the country. Nineteen percent believed that the assassination attempt on labor leader George Rautopoulos (30 June 1987) was CIA-engineered to destabilize Greece, as compared to only 6 percent who thought that perhaps the Eastern-bloc intelligence services were responsible. Twenty-nine percent said it represented a reaction to the government's economic austerity measures, while 37 percent did not know or would not reply. Responsibility for the assassination attempt in fact was claimed by an ultra-leftist terrorist group, and there is little reason to attribute it to anyone else. But this most plausible explanation was believed by only 29 percent of the persons polled.

As to the U.S. allegations and evidence that Greek government officials had contacts with Arab terrorists and that the latter had based some of their activities in Greece, only 7 percent replied that the Americans were probably right. Nearly half (47 percent) replied that it was an American ploy to exercise pressure on Greece for a favorable outcome in the base negotiations. (How such a connection can be made is difficult to understand.)

Finally, as to the notorious Gorbachev letter to Papandreou, in which the Soviet leader gave advice on how the Greek prime minister might get rid of the U.S. bases, and stated that this was the "unanimous demand of the Greek people," only 31 percent considered the letter an interference in Greek domestic affairs, while 46 percent did not. Indeed, 45 percent agreed with Gorbachev's opinion that the Greek public wanted the bases to go, while 34 percent disagreed with the Soviet leader's assessment.[67]

In more general terms, the Greek Opinion polls, regularly published by Panayote Dimitras, also confirm that a majority of the Greek public suspects and disapproves of what it believes to be the West's intentions toward Greece, and has become more sympathetic toward Soviet-bloc positions.

This trend was also confirmed by a comparative inter European poll dealing with public attitudes toward the United States and the USSR. It was conducted simultaneously by nine institutions in nine European countries. The results, published in the Italian magazine *Espresso*, showed that Gorbachev's public relations campaign has born fruit in Europe, and especially in Greece.[68]

According to the poll, 32 percent of Europeans believe that the USSR is working more for peace than the United States is, while only 11 percent believe the United States is working more for peace than the USSR. 44 percent believe that the superpowers are making equal efforts. Greece, with 54 percent, headed the list of those believing more in the USSR, far ahead of the European average of 32 percent.

51 percent of Greeks polled believed that human rights are respected in the Soviet Union. The Italians followed, but at a considerable distance—37 percent believed that human rights are respected in the Soviet Union. In the other European countries polled, only 13 to 14 percent responded positively, a clear condemnation of the Soviet record on human rights.

Finally, Greeks, like most Europeans, expressed confidence in Gorbachev's declared intentions to carry out reforms in the Soviet Union. The Italians, with 87 percent, expressed the greatest confidence in Gorbachev, followed by the British with 83 percent, West Germans with 77 percent, the Dutch with 72 percent, and Greeks with 69 percent. The French, with 34 percent, clearly were the most skeptical among Europeans as to Gorbachev's declared intentions.

Yet another inter-European opinion poll, published in the weekly newsletter *Gramma*, showed that there was greater anti-American sentiment in Greece than in any other European country. Forty percent of Greeks questioned expressed the conviction that the USSR defends human rights better than the United States. The same number, 40 percent, considered the Soviet Union a democratic country, compared to an average of only 12 percent subscribing to that view in the rest of Western Europe. Only 22 percent of Greeks polled said the United States defends human rights more effectively than the USSR, compared to 67 percent in France and Germany and 76 percent in Britain. Similarly, 56 percent of Greeks polled said their country, though a member of NATO, was threatened more by the United States than by the USSR, compared to only 29 percent who saw the USSR as the greater danger.[69]

Gramma concluded:

> The above results, especially where Greece is concerned, are particularly significant. For they demonstrate that Soviet propaganda and disinformation have registered a high degree of success in our country, which ideologically has already become the Finland of the Balkans.[70]

The very latest opinion polls confirm all the general trends described above; they also show that Greek public opinion may be becoming less susceptible to Soviet manipulation.

A poll conducted by Eurodim for *Chronos* magazine (published in issue of 4 April 1988) showed that as many as 19 percent of the Greek electorate, or one in five Greeks, still consider the United States the main threat to Greece; only one percent sees the Soviet Union as the main threat. 68 percent see Turkey as the main threat. However, the number of those seeing the United States as the main threat has dropped markedly from the 28 percent recorded in 1984. Furthermore, the number of Greeks in favor of the maintenance of the U.S. bases has risen to 54 percent compared to 48 percent only five months earlier, and the number of Greeks wanting total severance of ties with the U.S. dropped sharply from 29 percent recorded in 1981 to only 11 percent.

Some might argue that this means that though the Soviet Union is registering continuing success in embellishing its image in Greece—as indeed throughout the world—its anti-American disinformation in Greece might be faltering. Others might conclude that the Greeks, while maintaining the prejudices implanted upon them, are more pragmatic when it comes to the final choice.

THE FIRST CASE OF SUBVERSION OF A WESTERN COUNTRY THROUGH DISINFORMATION?

A number of writers, both Greek and foreign, have reached the conclusion that what we are witnessing in Greece today is the country's "ideological Finlandization." Two who hold this opinion are Ilios Yannakakis and Fergus Bordewich.

Yannakakis who was, as mentioned earlier, a former Communist party activist, points out that an "ideological reign of terror" currently prevails against conservatives in Greece. "For example," he writes, "criticism of the Eastern Bloc on human rights issues is regarded as a 'rightist conspiracy'... there is a climate of intellectual terrorism...it is no exaggeration to speak of an ideological Finlandization of the country."[71]

Fergus Bordewich also detected this "ideological Finlandization" in his analysis of Greece.[72] He does not believe that Greece will go so far as to drift into the Soviet camp, or that it will sever its military, political, and economic ties with the West, for he believes that Soviet interests are "perhaps better served by a troublesome and unreliable ally in the NATO camp than by a breakaway state that might encourage similar thoughts of independence by nations of the Warsaw Pact." What did impress Bordewich about Greece, however, was the ideological domination by the Left and by pro-Soviet elements. Focusing on the Ethnos case, he wrote:

> As the case has unfolded, over the intervening three years, it has also revealed the degree to which leftist dogma has come to influence the political life of Greece, the ease with which the crudest Soviet propaganda may be purveyed here....[73]

In conclusion, it is perhaps appropriate to note the views of Michael Ledeen, a man who has studied the phenomenon of disinformation in Greece and who also has become a victim of it. Ledeen, who over the years has advised various U.S. administrations on the issues of terrorism and disinformation, was recently accused by the Greek press of conspiratorial activities against Greece. Among other things, he is said to have secretly based himself in Greece in 1987, reorganized the U.S. intelligence agencies to make them more capable of overthrowing the government, organized a disinformation and terrorism network in Greece, and actually participated in plans to murder Prime Minister Andreas Papandreou.

The fact that Ledeen was singled out by the Greek press for this extraordinary disinformation campaign may not come as a surprise—at least not to those who already knew why he may have been unpopular among the disinformation specialists on the other side. For two years earlier, perhaps prophetically, he had written the following:

> The Greek operation of the USSR Committee on State Security (KGB) from the mid-1970s to the present may eventually be recognized as the most ambitious example of political subversion of a West European country. The Greek case exposes the KGB at its most

arrogant and aggressive, generally not even bothering to carefully hide its own direct involvement in the internal affairs of Greece. Even today, without the usual lag in our understanding of such matters, we can see the broad outlines of the design and many of the details of the operational plan: first, restructuring the national political debate in such a way that all discussion occurs within the comfortable context of Moscow's worldview; to achieve this, establishing maximum possible control over the mass media; and, once this has been accomplished, ruthlessly attacking those who dare to challenge this cultural hegemony....Consequently, the country that gave democracy to the world may now have given us another innovation: the first case of the political subversion of a Western country through disinformation. If this outcome is to be averted, it will require all the courage and imagination of the West; commodities that have not been in abundant supply in the past decade.[74]

NOTES

1. Vladimir Volkoff, *La Désinformation Arme de Guerre* (Paris: Juillard, 1986); from a memorandum addressed to Tchitcherine, Lenin's foreign affairs commissar, as quoted by Y. Annenkov in 1921.

2. Chapman Pincher, *The Secret Offensive* (London: Sidgwick and Jackson, 1985), 172; cited in the *U.S. Military Review* .

3. Igor Bogolepov, testimony to the U.S. Senate Internal Security Subcommittee.

4. Charilaos Florakis, speech to the Athens Union of Journalists, 31 March 1977.

5. Ilya Gregorovitch Dzhirkvelov, testimony in *Ethnos* v. *Economist*, London, 24 March 1987.

6. *Ibid.*

7. Photographs, correspondence and copies of court records in the possession of the author.

8. Dzhirkvelov, testimony.

9. Stanislav Levchenko, interviewed in *Kyriakatike Apogeumatine*, 31 May 1987.

10. Lord Chalfont, testimony in *Ethnos* v. *Economist* , London, February-April 1987; see also his *Specialist's Report*, submitted at the trial.

11. Kostas Mavropoulos served with the Greek Section of Radio Moscow from 1961 until his return to Greece in 1976.

12. Kostas Mavropoulos, in a written statement for the *Economist*

attorneys and in testimony in *Ethnos* v. *Economist*, London, February-April 1987; Mavropoulos said that those participating in the propaganda planning sessions on Greece included Vasili Sitnikov, the deputy director of the KGB Disinformation Department, and Sergei Bokhane, another intelligence agent, who defected from Athens to the U.S. in May 1985 after serving in Greece for a total of eight years.

13. Ilios Yannakakis, "La Grèce de Papandreou," *L'Express*, 13 April 1984 .

14. *Ibid.*

15. "Press and Mass Media," *Anti*, 27 June 1986; from Bousboureles's remarks at a two-day conference on the Greek press, organized by *Anti*, in December 1985.

16. Among the main sources cited by U.S. authorities, which explain the U.S. position and make clear that there was no involvement or intention to harm Greek foreign or domestic interests, are the following U.S. government publications:

— Senate Committee on Foreign Affairs, *Situation in Cyprus: Report to Accompany S. Res. 381*, 15 August 1974, Publication 08385 1092.

— Subcommittee to Investigate Problems Connected with Refugees and Escapees, *Crisis on Cyprus, 1974: Study Mission Report*, 93rd Cong., 2d sess., 14 October, Publication 05519.

— Subcommittee to Investigate Problems Connected with Refugee and Escapees, *Crisis on Cyprus, 1975: One Year After Invasion*, 94th Cong., 1st sess., 20 July 1985, Publication 17331.

— Committee on Foreign Affairs and Subcommittee on Europe, *Cyprus, 1974* , 93rd Cong., 2d sess., 19 August and 20 August 1975, Publication 11098.

Also cited were the hearings before the House Subcommittee on Europe and the Middle East, Committee on Foreign Affairs, 98th Cong., early November 1983.

17. For example, see the Eurodim ("Greek Opinion") reports, which specialize in opinion polls and are published by Panayote Dimitras. The latest such report, confirming the persisting—though somewhat reduced—anti-Western trends, was published in the Greek press early in 1988.

18. Lord Chalfont, testimony.

19. For example, see daily *Prote*, 10 November 1987, article titled "Sharp Reaction Against Derwinsky," by Communist party cadre and editor George Delastik.

20. *Ibid.*

21. David Rees, "Soviet Active Measures: The Propaganda War," *Conflict Studies*, 169 (London: The Institute for the Study of Conflict, 1984); summarized from Richard H. Shultz and Roy Godson, *Dezinformatsia: Active Measures in Soviet Strategy* (London: Pergamon-Brassey).

22. *Ibid.*

23. John Demetriades, *The Soviet Infiltration of Greece* (Athens: ROES Publications, 1984).

24. *Ibid.*

25. George Bobolas, testimony in *Ethnos* v. *Economist*, London, March 1987.

26. *Foreign Report*, 26 April 1982.

27. Demetriades, *Soviet Infiltration.*

28. *Ibid.*

29. Demetriades; the *Novosti* editor who was a correspondent for *Ta Nea* was Boris Korolev. Paradoxically, one year after the publication of this book, Korolev's cooperation with the paper was abruptly terminated when the Athens Union of Journalists strongly protested an insulting article he had written. Specifically, he had accused Greek conservative newspapers of "serving their bosses" by casting doubts on the economic value of Greece's exchanges with the USSR and on the agreements that Prime Minister Papandreou had made following an official visit to Moscow. The dangers inherent for the Greek press in associating with Russian "writers" subsequently became more evident when it was discovered that Korolev was a KGB agent who a few years before had been expelled from a Western country.

30. "Why Greek Newspapers Are Leftist-oriented," *Antilogos*, 6 September 1986.

31. "Forged U.S. Documents are Said to Complicate Nation's Foreign Policy," *New York Times*, 4 June 1987, *Herald Tribune*, 4 June 1987; also see House Subcommittee on Oversight of the Permanent Select Committee on Intelligence, *Soviet Covert Action, the Forgery Offensive: Hearings*, 96th Cong., 6 February and 19 February 1980; House Permanent Select Committee on Intelligence, *Soviet Active Measures* , 13 July and 14 July 1982; and *U.S. Policy Towards East Europe, West Europe and the Soviet Union: Hearings before the Subcommittee on European Affairs and Political Refugees.*

32. "Forged U.S. Documents Are Said to Complicate Nation's Foreign Policy," *New York Times*, 4 June 1987, and *International Herald Tribune*, 4 June 1987.

33. The author has established an office focusing on this subject, the Greek Center for the Study of Disinformation, through which research is conducted on Soviet Active Measures and disinformation in Greece.

34. *Ta Nea*, 24 August 1974.

35. Rees, " Soviet Active Measures."

36. Demetriades, *Soviet Infiltraion,* 196.

37. This particular forgery has been given exposure in many official and unofficial publications. For the most complete details about it, see the *Specialist Report* by Lord Chalfont. (See note 10 above.) This report even explains in detail the linguistic mistakes committed by the Russians in preparing the English text of the forgery.

38. Rees, "Soviet Active Measures"; Demetriades, *Soviet Infiltration*

39. See *Ethnos* and *Eleutherotypia* (Athens) and *Aletheia* (Nicosia) 11 February and 12 February 1983, as well as *Aletheia* on the following days. The apology and retraction by *Eleutherotypia* in Cyprus was published three and a half years later, on 9 August 1986, in a front-page boxed announcement. The whole affair has also been described in National Strategy Information Center, *Disinformation, Soviet Active Measures and Disinformation Forecast* Summer 1987, No. 6 and in *Swiss Press Review and News Report*, 9 March 1987.

40. *Demokratikos Logos*, 29 November 1986; see also reports from Athens by the Associated Press on the same day, quoting the Greek daily, and a news item in the *New York Times* the following day. The whole disinformation operation was exposed soon after in an article by Andrew Borowic of the *Washington Times.*

41. *Prote*, 6 April 1987; see also the U.S. embassy announcement, Athens, 10 April 1987 and the subsequent reaction by *Prote* over the next four days.

42. See these three dailies, May-August 1987.

43. U.S. embassy announcement, Athens, 7 May 1987.

44. *Counterpoint*, September 1987.

45. Official transcript, USIA, Worldnet broadcast on disinformation, 15 April 1988.

46. George Savidis, Master's thesis, Boston University, Center for the Study of Disinformation.

47. See, for example, *Prote*, 14 April 1986, and the editorial by Kyriakos Diakogiannes, "An Announcement from Apes for Chimpanzees," *Auriane* , 29 July 1987.

48. Senate Committee on Foreign Relations, *U.S. Policy Towards East Europe, West Europe, and the Soviet Union: Hearings before the Subcommittee on European Affairs*, 99th Cong., 1st sess., 12 September and 13 September 1985, 202-206; originally published as "Unacceptable Intervention," *NATO Review*, vol. 31, 1983.

49. Titos Athanasiades, letter of 26 March 1981, published in Paul Anastassiades, *Take the Nation in Your Hands* (in Greek) (Athens 1983): 238.

50. *London Times*, 4 December 1975; *Financial Times*, 4 December 1975.

51. *Ibid.*

52. *Eleutherotypia*, headline story, "17th November: We Strike Against the U.S.," 25 April 1987.

53. See decision of the 6th plenum of the Central Committee of the KKE, "The New Situation and Our Duties," a KKE publication, 1950, page 5, as cited in article by Ath. Georgiades titled "Facing the Ideological Terror of the Left," *Prote Gramme* magazine, Athens, October 1987, 18.

54. Ath. Georgiades, "How the Ideological Takeover of Greece was

Organized," *Prote Gramme* , Athens, November 1987.

55. *Ibid.*, Georgiades quotes a study by Leonidas Stringos, published in *Neos Kosmos*, July 1963 issue, the ideological publication of the KKE.

56. Introduction by Brezhnev to the Greek version of his book titled *Peace Is the Priceless Right of the People*, Moscow, 18 July 1978, and published in Athens by Akademos. This publishing house is owned by George Bobolas, publisher of the *Great Soviet Encyclopedia* and of *Ethnos*, Greece's pro-Soviet mass circulation daily.

57. British Foreign Office document Number RGC 10338/2, letter from British ambassador in Athens Sir Roger Allen to the Foreign Office. A brief item on this, without comment, also appeared in daily *Ethnos*, 7 January 1988, 19.

58. *Ibid.;* Demetriades, *Soviet Infiltration.*

59. See the author's articles in the *New York Times*, October 28 and 29, 1987, *International Herald Tribune*, 29 October 1987, and *New York Times*, 30 November 1987.

60. Gorbachev's letter was revealed exclusively in weekly *Pontiki,* 3 July 1987, and inevitably was branded by the conservative opposition and press as unprecedented Soviet interference in Greek domestic affairs.

61. One such major source is Sergei Bokhane, the deputy director of the Soviet Military Intelligence (GRU) branch in Greece, who defected from Athens to the U.S. in May 1985. Some of this evidence was given to Greek authorities and led to limited administrative and legal action against the alleged Greek agents. But most of Bokhane's information, which is apparently invaluable considering his position and his eight years of service in Greece, is still classified. Furthermore, it primarily involves military espionage rather than the areas of Active Measures, political warfare and the press.

62. See *Sunday Acropolis*, November 1987, *Prote Gramme* monthly magazine, December 1987 and January 1988 issues, and T.V. Press video news service, 15-30 January 1988. Glezos never attempted to deny the reports.

63. Front organizations are active today in the peace and trade union movements, the women's and youth movements, as well as among doctors, lawyers and scientists. More recently, Greek branches of Soviet international front organizations have become active even in the church and the military. At the time of writing this essay, their key objective has been to put pressure on the government to expel the U.S. bases in Greece. This, after all, has also been the expressed wish of Soviet leader Mikhail Gorbachev.

64. For a discussion among U.S. experts on the political effect of Active Measures, see Senate Committee, *Soviet Active Measures: Hearings*, 99th Cong., 1985 and Senate Committee, *U.S. Policy*

Towards East Europe, West Europe and the Soviet Union: Hearings, September 1985.

65. See Jiri Hochman, "Politics of Calumny: Soviet Disinformation Campaign in India, 1985," Ohio University, School of Journalism, Center for Slavic and East European Studies.

66. The National Strategy Information Center in Washington, D.C., conducted such polls within the United States, and was pleasantly surprised by the limited effect it had on Americans. On the other hand, similar polls conducted in Greece confirmed the effect the media is having in developing anti-Western and pro-Soviet sentiments.

67. For a brief presentation of the results of the Gallup poll by ICAP, which were published in *Epikaira*, see *Gramma*, 22 July 1987.

68. *Espresso* , 13 July 1987; see also dispatches of the Athens News Agency for 14 July 1987. The news agency's dispatches were published in the Greek press.

69. *Gramma*, 26 November 1986.

70. *Ibid.*

71. Yannakakis, "La Grèce de Papandreou."

72. Fergus Bordewich, "Democracy Adrift," *Atlantic Monthly*, December 1985

73. *Ibid.*

74. Michael Ledeen, "The Political Subversion of Western Europe," *Public Diplomacy: U.S. vs. USSR* (Hoover Institute on War, Revolution and Peace) .

Pressure Groups under Pressure: Socialist Policies towards the Church and Labor

Spelios Speliotopoulos

The purpose of this essay is to provide an evaluation of the Socialist policies towards two important interest, or pressure, groups in Greek society, the church and labor. It is not our intention to engage in a broad historical review of church-state or state-labor relations in modern Greece, but to offer a case study of the most critical developments in these relations since the assumption of power by the Panhellenic Socialist Movement.

CHURCH-STATE RELATIONS UNDER PASOK

Relations between the state and the Orthodox Church of Greece have reached their lowest point since the reign of King Otto. Now as then, the central issue dividing the two institutions is the property that the church has accumulated through the bequeathals of its faithful over centuries. This property now includes a high percentage of the arable land in Greece. In 1852 the Bavarian king proceeded to confiscate nine-tenths of the land owned by the church. A few years later, owing to massive popular opposition, he was dethroned.[1] In 1985, the Greek Socialist government, for different ideological reasons, initiated a process aimed at divesting the church of its property, even though the latter had, over the years, engaged in outright redistribution of land to landless peasants.

Our essay will commence with a consideration of the current condition of church-state relations, created by attempts by the Socialist government to seize church property without compensation and without the involvement of the ecclesiastical authorities in the distribution of the "reformed lands."

On 14 October 1985, Minister of Education and Religious Affairs Antones Tritses introduced a bill called Regulation of Matters Concerning Monastery Property in Parliament. According to the proposed bill, if there are no "recognized" titles of property, the property is to be taken over by the state and distributed to agricultural cooperatives. The operative, but problematic term is "recognized." The hierarchy of the Greek Orthodox Church was ignored when this bill was drafted, but sent a memorandum to the prime minister in which it expressed "its astonishment" and concern because this "unilaterally taken step" created the possibility of conflict between church and state.[2] Moreover, offering good-faith criticism of the proposed bill and wishing to contribute to the materialization of the government's social and agricultural policies, the hierarchy of the church suggested three alternatives for divesting monastic properties and turning them over to the state in return for certain state concessions that would enable the church "to carry out an independent and respectable living." After the minister's counterproposals, the church submitted its "final" offer to the government, which entailed among other things health and pension benefits for the lower clergy. But in a meeting of representatives of the church and the government to discuss the church proposals, the minister informed the church hierarchy of the government's decision to carry out its original plan without taking the church's opinion into consideration. This decision, the minister said, was in conformity with his government's overall socialist program. But for the church it meant the confiscation of its property.

As expected, the conflict intensified. In a meeting between the archbishop of Athens and the prime minister, which was called to "soothe the tension," it was agreed that the text of the bill, after "necessary adjustments," should be given to the hierarchy for its consideration. The hierarchy was also to make recommendations for the bill's improvement. However, despite the premier's promise, the minister of education and religious affairs stopped the negotiations with the church, changed the agenda of the proposed talks, and expanded the scope of negotiations to include not only the monastery property but the whole property of the church. Despite the repeated but futile attempts of the hierarchy to reach a compromise, on 12 March 1987, the government suddenly introduced a new bill, the contents of which it had kept a secret during the talks with church representatives. The second bill, entitled Regulation of Matters Concerning Church Property, was similar to the first bill in title only. Its aim now was, apart from an immediate takeover of monastery property and its transfer to agricultural cooperatives (euphemistically termed "utilization of property"), the takeover of urban real estate belonging to the church or church entities as well as the takeover of church assets with "touristic value." All these objectives were obvious violations of the country's constitution, canons, and church tradition.

An avalanche of complaints and many mass meetings against the government's massive assault on the church were followed by a heated parliamentary debate. The Nea Demokratia party attacked the bill, stating that it was "predatory, dishonest, anti-constitutional and demagogic" and aimed at the subjugation of the church by the state.[3] Furthermore, the opposition demanded to know the motivation for the attempt to confiscate not only monastery property but also other church possessions such as legitimate enterprises owned and managed by the church. The New Democracy party correctly saw ideological and political motives in both instances. Let it be noted at this point that both the church itself and the New Democracy party supported the distribution of monastery property to indigent peasants; moreover, they did not have any objection to bringing into use church property, but wished it to be done through a "consensus procedure" and always according to the law.[4] In fact, their main accusation against the government was that it set up the church as a convenient scapegoat to renew the initial revolutionary image of PASOK and to quickly achieve some kind of property regulation, but without the consent of the church, in order to "advertise" its own "reformist" initiatives and contrast them to the "reactionary" attitude of the church. Thus it would be able to present "something important" in the Kileler celebration.[5] Furthermore, the government wanted a quick fix to influence the elections that were going to take place in the agricultural cooperatives.[6]

Nevertheless, despite the strong reaction of a majority of the Greek public, despite a statement by the ecumenical patriarchate in the form of a synodic resolution, despite the steps taken by the World Church Organization and numerous independent bodies in many countries, and despite the mass mobilization of the clergy and laity in Greece, the bill was finally approved by the governing majority in the Parliament and became a law.

This situation, legal from now on, forced the Church of Greece to seek protection from the ecumenical patriarchate and to consider at the same time the possibility of ending its 137-year old autocephalous existence by recognizing the patriarch as its supreme head once again. The church made two appeals to the High Administrative Court,[7] questioning the constitutionality of Law No. 1700/1987 and of the first order issued by the minister of education and religious affairs on the basis of that law. By this order a new central council of the Church Property Management Organization (ODEP) was formed, without the participation of the archbishop of Athens, who was its head until then. As far as the formation of this new council was concerned, even Law No. 1700/1987 was violated by the ministerial order because neither a cabinet meeting had taken place on the matter nor had the church been consulted.[8] The law required both.

The Holy Synod of the Church of Greece, in a last-ditch effort "for justice, legality and for the restoration of the moral order," proceeded to take several steps. The last of these was a letter appeal by the archbishop of Athens, addressed to the country's political leadership, as well as to high judicial and university authorities. In it, Primate (Archbishop) of Athens and All Greece Seraphim said:

...The Church is saddened because, even if it wished to, it could not enforce, under any circumstances, Law No. 1700/87 . And by the Church we hereby mean both the clergy and the laity. Nor does the Church accept to resort to the lay courts in order to claim its rights, like a poor beggar; these remain unadulterated for centuries because they are an integral part of its sacred substance and the component elements of its mission. On this matter the Church of Greece is not in violation of the State's law. The Church of Greece is attempting to go beyond the law only in the philosophical sense of the term. In other words, it determines in advance the terms under which in fact, it will continue to exert its authority. The Church of Greece spurns slavish submission. It proclaims its immovable faith in its God-given liberty and it declares that it will fight for it.

The Hierarchy of the Church of Greece, based on the above, is possessed by the sincere desire that a way be found so that the continuation of the conflict between it and the State would end. The Church however surmises that, if the conflict continues, the consequences for the unity and for the spiritual and the national life of the Greek people will be disastrous. In the name of the pious people faithful to the Church and in conformity with its Founder's, Jesus Christ's, instruction to preserve peace, seeks a peaceful way to resolve the deadlock. For this reason it addresses itself to you, the responsible, competent and public persons of our country. We propose to you and we invite you to contribute directly and positively in the search for a solution of the most acute ecclesiastic problem. When good intentions prevail in the conscience of men, especially those who are charged with being the responsible functionaries of a democratic regime and who are the decision makers in the more general political life of our country, then there exist no insoluble problems. Help us to bring peace, so that the Church and people of God shall be pacified. The chasm opened by the upheaval must be closed with the breath of evangelical peace. This is the best way in which we will be guided as a Church and as a Nation "from the bondage of corruption to the freedom of the glory of the children of God"(Romans, 8:21)[9]

AN ATTEMPT AT POLITICAL CONTROL OF THE CHURCH: LAW NO. 1700/1987

Law No. 1700/1987, governing church property and, in effect, church-state relations, which was passed by the Greek Parliament on the initiative of the minister of education and religious affairs, is perceived by the faithful as a major assault on the institution of the church. What is more important, it is also of questionable constitutionality. In preparing this law, the government ignored important sources and legal precedent. Critical church documents, even legal opinions, were not considered in the preparatory stage of the law, raising questions about its intent, character and constitutionality.

A committee of four canonic scholars, or theologians, at the University of Athens, had reservations about the constitutionality and legitimacy of the law, which was entitled Regulation of Matters Concerning Church Property.[10] In the committee's opinion, the following pertinent documents were ignored in the law's preparation and adoption by the Greek Parliament:

1. At least eight constitutional articles, including Articles 72, 87, and 109, which define church-state relations and the autonomy of the former
2. Important clauses of the 1850 *Synodic Tome* (which has the validity of applicable law) on the autocephalous status of the Church of Greece and the 1928 patriarchal and synodic acts concerning the church's self-governance
3. Articles 1 and 2 of the charter of the Church of Greece (as defined by Law 590, enacted in 1977) and the Holy Rules (deriving from the apostolic and ecumenical synods), which the Church of Greece feels bound to observe

The committee's opinion is that the failure of government officials and of the parliamentary committee that drafted Law No. 1700/1987 to consider the sources mentioned above is unreasonable, since this law concerns the basis of relations between church and state. In the opinion of the academic experts, the law is unconstitutional in all its aspects, and misleading, since, apart from matters of property, it also regulates other independent functions of the church, such as the management of temples, religious schools, and welfare foundations. In other words, the law sanctions the interference of state authorities in the affairs of the church. The hierarchy's refusal to accept the law, the committee concluded is legally and morally valid and well-founded.

The Holy Rules, which are incorporated in the Holy Tradition and the 1850 *Synodic Tome*, are explicit on church-state relations. They envision an administration of the church "according to the Holy and Sacred Rules, independent of any secular intervention." This independence is thrice reaffirmed by the Constitution of the Hellenic Republic: (1) separately and verbatim in Article 3; (2) in the Holy Tradition, which is reaffirmed by Article 1; and (3) by the long-standing practice of the independence of the church, which relies on texts that safeguard human rights and specifically freedom of religion (Article 13).[11]

Thus the academic committee concluded that any secular intervention in the administration of the church is clearly unconstitutional. Church authorities feel that they are not obliged to accept this kind of interference since theoretically they must "obey God rather than men." More explicitly, judicial authorities are not obliged by Article 87 of the constitution to adopt laws violating fundamental aspects of church autonomy.

The arbitrary confiscation of church property, accumulated through the centuries thanks to donations made by monks or by members of the laity, does serious violence to Articles 3, 4, 5, 12, 17, and 18 of the constitution, which guarantee the protection of private property, and to Article 109, which assures the right of donors to dispose of their possessions to the church and not to the state. This law effectively expropriates property already owned by the church and also affects future donations, because people will know henceforth that the state will not respect their wishes and will eventually take away what they leave to their parishes.

The academic committee advanced numerous other arguments regarding Law No. 1700/1987 that reinforced the reaction of the church. The committee's conclusion is forceful.

This law already voted is, for the reasons stated above, in many aspects unconstitutional, since it violates fundamental articles of the constitution of the Republic, as well as fundamental Holy Rules, according to which the basis of the administration of the Church are the decisions of the Holy Synods and of the Bishops.... The election or appointment of Church authorities without the consent of a bishop or of the bishops, is quite inadmissible.[12]

As a result of intense criticism and in light of its obvious lack of constitutional basis, the law was suspended through a technicality: the presidential decree that would have led to the establishment of a government-controlled body to manage church property, ODEP, was withheld. This "reversal" was initially perceived by the public as a retreat by the government. Upon closer examination, however, when the rapporteur of the Council of State recommended that the judicial body consider the constitutionality of the entire law, it became clear that the decree had been suspended only temporarily. The rapporteur's own opinion was that the law was indeed unconstitutional. But it appears that the government had its plans in place: a new presidential decree was issued, with only slight modifications, as soon as the composition of the Council of State was changed, with new members favorable to the ruling party. In addition, a new rapporteur was appointed by the minister of justice. Not surprisingly, he offered a different opinion of the law than his predecessor.

The hierarchy of the church returned to its unrelenting struggle, accusing the government of political and ideological harassment. Furthermore, Primate of Athens and All Greece Seraphim, head of the Committee on the Northern Epirus Struggle, (established to defend the human rights of the Greek minority in Albania), denounced the government for trying to get even with the church by abandoning Greek Christians to the mercy of the Albanian Communist regime when Papandreou unilaterally terminated the state of war with Albania on 28 August 1987.

The battle has been joined, and the tensions continue. But a retrospective examination of PASOK ideology indicates that the government's moves should not have surprised anyone. The Declaration of the Third of September (the founding charter of PASOK) states clearly the party's intention to "collectivize" estates and church property.[13]

Understandably, it is difficult to gauge the political implications of the church-state split that has been masterminded by the ruling Socialist party. It would be safe to say, however, that the church's role as a unifying force in the Greek nation has been seriously undermined. As far as the conservative and moderate forces of Greece are concerned, the method used by the ruling party to expropriate church property and the disposition of the expropriated lands, which have been given only to self-managed cooperatives, usually controlled by PASOK followers, reflect a deep ideological cleavage in Greek society. This interpretation acquires validity if one considers the fact that historically the church has been conscious of its role and obligations to the poor and on several occasions, without government interference, has ceded lands and other assets to fulfill its mission. It has also used its resources to fund hundreds of educational and social institutions.

If church-state relations have deteriorated during the past six years, the situation is even worse in the labor movement. As we shall see in the following pages, the Socialist government has engaged in relentless efforts to convert the labor organizations into political fronts and their members into followers. Legislative decrees and ordinary ministerial orders have combined to undermine the independence of trade unionism and its organizational self-sufficiency.

PASOK AND LABOR: A SHAKY RELATIONSHIP

Since immediately after the 1981 elections, the PASOK government has been systematically attempting to subvert the socio-economic structures of Greece, using "democratization" as its pretext. Its real aim, however, is to impose upon practically every aspect of life its vision of the future, through an already omnipotent state and a pervasive party mechanism. The economy was, of course, the first "victim" of PASOK's socialization efforts, since it was chosen as the primary vehicle for achievement of short-term political goals. The impact of PASOK's economic policy has been painfully felt by the Greek people in ways described in the chapter on PASOK's economic policies. The government's acrobatics in economic matters, that is, its alternation between orthodox Marxism and Third World socialism, have had the greatest impact on working men and women, the very people that the party has paternalistically claimed as its wards. Inconsistent policies, enactment of restrictive laws, and high unemployment caused serious friction between PASOK and labor. Since the party could not satisfy the basic demands of the workers, it opted to colonize the labor unions in an intense competition with the Communist party.

The workers have borne the cost of government experimentation with the economy. In 1982, in an attempt to "spark up" the frustrated market, the government introduced a wage policy that included an automatic cost of living readjustment, thus presenting itself as concerned about the prosperity of the working class. However, this measure was immediately followed by a severe market decline and business immobility. Consumers used their increased buying power to obtain imported durable goods, causing balance of payments problems and underlining a lack of faith in the future of the economy under socialism. The result of PASOK's "social policy," aimed at helping working men and women, and initially welcomed by the working class, was massive trade imbalances and an equally massive decline in investment prospects. Greek and foreign businessmen were discouraged by the rise in labor costs. However, the automatic cost of living increase adopted in 1982 was the first PASOK measure to gain approval among members of the working class. With it, PASOK displaced the Greek Communist party, with whom it had been in intense competition for labor support. This policy, in conjunction with laws affecting private enterprises, served the purpose of the Socialist party in seeking to alter market relations in Greece and to shift the economy in the direction of state ownership. As a first step, the government sought to bring into management functions the workers in all public enterprises and in enterprises classified as "of common benefit."

Co-opting of the working class into false managerial roles meant among other things that the workers could not strike, since, after all, they now had no one to strike against. They "owned the corporations" and they managed them. In reality, the corporations are managed by carefully selected party hacks, the majority of whom have neither the experience nor the ability to handle a modern economy.

We shall not attempt to make any direct correlation between the decline in the standard of living and the state of labor unions under socialism. But in general terms, one can argue that scarcity of goods, lack of employment opportunities, and a general decline in the standard of living affects the behavior of employees towards employers and usually converts the state into some kind of arbitrator. In the case of Greece, the state is also the largest employer by far and therefore maintains a vested interest in controlling the activities and demands of the working class. For the first time since the end of the Second World War, according to the *Wall Street Journal* , the standard of living in Greece has declined precipitously, making labor unrest and government manipulation of labor activities daily occurrences.[14]

To deal with the inevitable labor problems, the Socialist government introduced a controversial bill on labor relations and utilized its parliamentary majority to restructure labor unions. Its goal seems to have been to secure labor peace. In the following pages, we shall attempt to delineate the governmental policy towards labor by reviewing the most important so-called frame-laws, introduced and enacted for the purpose of controlling union activities.

Not accidentally, the main thrust of the government, to regulate labor activities, was made simultaneously with its efforts to socialize private corporations, as it had originally promised in the declaration of the party's founding. Law No. 1365/1983, on The Socialization of Companies Characterized as Public or of Public Benefit, was introduced and enacted by the ruling Socialist party. This law de facto meant that more workers would come under the auspices of the government as more companies were "shielded" from strike activities by the government's invocation of its "public interest" clauses.

Legislative Decree 1365 provided for the creation of workers councils, which would ensure "participation" in the management of corporations, and therefore workers welfare. However, as indicated earlier, "participation" degenerated into a prohibition of the right to strike, which is the ultimate weapon used by workers to secure their economic interests. The law on corporations must be examined in two other contexts: first, in the context of a 1982 governmental act (Law No. 1264/1982), which was aimed at "democratizing labor unions," and second, in the context of the government's failure to put the idea of workers councils into operation, even after it enacted legislation dealing with "public corporations." Furthermore, we must note that the PASOK government never ratified International Labor Convention No. 135, which assures labor freedom from governmental interference. In addition, without solving the critical problems of unemployment and inflation, PASOK imposed upon the workers a ceiling of 4.4 percent in any salary increases.[15] The inflation rate hovered in the vicinity of 20 percent during the first five years of PASOK's rule. As matters stand now, the notion of free bargaining between employers and employees has been rendered meaningless, since the employee worker is now viewed as part of the management and de facto part of the state, which he/she supposedly controls under a socialist system.

The law, The Socialization of Companies Characterized as Public or of Public Benefit, was perceived at the time of its enactment (perhaps correctly so) as a deliberate move on the part of the government to rescue its image among the left-wing members of its party. Regardless of the government's motives, the law was and remains a controversial act for a number of reasons besides the fact that it deprives the working people of their most effective weapon, the right to withhold their labor when deemed necessary to earn a better living.

First, it was heralded during the parliamentary debate as evidence of "socialist transformation" and the fulfillment of PASOK's promise. Socialist transformation, the government argued, was achieved through the workers' participation in the "self-management" of public entities, which were state-owned to begin with. In other words, the Socialist government decided to socialize corporations it already owned, but whose workers, under previous laws, had the right to strike in defense of their economic interests. The logic of the governmental action is still unclear. One cannot understand the reasons for socialization of already nationalized corporations, unless one is prepared to accept the idea that PASOK has commenced the "withering away" of the state.

The second observation about the controversial law concerning public corporations is that it increased dramatically the number and categories of workers who *could not strike*. Article 4 of the law is quite explicit in its restrictions of workers rights and of bargaining processes.

The enactment of this law, indicated quite clearly that the motive of the government was not socialization (unless it did not trust itself to run these public, already nationalized corporations), but the limitation of workers rights and the restriction of the independent labor movement. The urgency to deal with the problem of strikes was underlined by the government's selective approach to the implementation of this sweeping law. The appropriate presidential decrees, implementing the first three articles (dealing with the process of socialization), were postponed for over eight months, but Article 4, which regulates strikes in public corporations, was put into effect immediately, in order to forestall an avalanche of shutdowns planned for the fall of 1983.

As expected, the law was rejected by the public and by the rank and file of the labor unions for two major reasons: (1) the government, as in the case of the church, had no meaningful dialogue with the labor unions prior to the law's formulation and enactment and (2) the prohibition of strikes, as defined in Article 4, effectively abolished a cherished right of workers everywhere, i.e., the right to withhold their labor.[16] Furthermore, labor unions, particularly those controlled by the Left, and nonunionized workers in general opposed the law, because the government had misrepresented its goals. As labor saw matters, the government's principal objective was to increase the productivity of public enterprises, not the participation of workers in the planning and management of public corporations.[17] In other words, the law was a clear contradiction of the party's promise to bring about "self-management" of public enterprises. The law, which is characteristic of PASOK attitudes towards public affairs, in a sense defines what is an acceptable relationship between employer and employee and ignores fundamental principles of free bargaining. The state sets limits on bargaining processes, while pretending that the whole exercise is aimed at the socialization of wealth. As it has worked out thus far, the law has proved to be contrary to the welfare of the workers, as it seriously erodes their purchasing power (wages are controlled, while strikes are curtailed). It exposes once again the true meaning of the Socialists' interest in the working class.[18] Finally, as enacted, the law also proved to be a last, but lost chance for the democratization of labor unions. It did not free labor unions from partisan politics or from governmental control (which in the past was more effectively carried out through governmental handouts), but expanded the government's control to any company that is arbitrarily defined as being in the "public interest"[19]; or to put it differently, it dramatically increased the number of workers whose right to strike was curtailed.[20]

Article 4 of Law No. 1365/1983 caused the most intense parliamentary and public debate. The opposition leader called it "dictatorial" in character and employee organizations protested its undemocratic features. A few additional comments on this article are warranted.

Besides weakening trade unions in the public sector, Article

4 also violates the secrecy of the ballots of union members. Arbitrarily the government commands how a vote on a strike by members of a union should be counted. First, it is no longer the general assembly of a union that decides on job action, but the executive council of the secondary organizations, which is usually handpicked by the ruling or some other party. Secondly, the law mandates that all absentees from a vote on the question of a strike or other job action must be counted as voting against such action, rather than as absent. However, the most serious criticism derives from the fact that Article 4 of Law No. 1365/1983 is in clear violation of the Constitution of the Republic.

The Athens Bar Association, after a long discussion in a meeting on 26 May 1983, expressed the following opinion on the constitutionality of the law:

> For the above stated reasons, the board of the Athens Bar Association, although in favor of socialization, asked that Law No. 1365/1983 be withdrawn and that the elaboration of a new law in cooperation with the workers and all other people concerned be undertaken. Moreover, the bar is asking that Article 4 be withdrawn in its entirety.[21]

Objections to the law came from international bodies as well. A special committee of the International Labor Office (ILO) on trade unions rights, at the invitation of banking industry unions, which brought a charge against the Greek government for adopting Article 4, recommended that the government reconsider its decision, since it was contrary to the principle of free activity of unions and to International Labor conventions nos. 87 and 98, which Greece had ratified.

Nearly four years after the adoption of this unusual labor law, the government interferes in labor matters directly and in disregard of the constitution and of advice from the ILO. It still refuses to comply with the parts of the constitution and legal code pertaining to labor.[22]

THE WORKERS' "PARTICIPATION" IN MANAGEMENT

Law No. 1365/1983 on Socialization, which is PASOK's landmark legislation in labor relations, makes provision for representation of the trade unions on the executive boards of the enterprises and in two recently created councils of planning and control, and for their participation in the formation of the strategies of the socialized companies. At the same time, it makes provision for the participation of four other entities: the state representatives, the municipal authorities, the organizations directly influenced by the activity of the given company, and shareholders. Thus only one-third of the votes is controlled by the trade unions. This composition of the governing councils effectively cancels out the workers' power, simultaneously with the cancellation of their right to strike. In other words, socialization does not serve the workers, but other social classes or even the geographical areas in which the company is established.

Moreover, a key characteristic of Law No. 1365/1983 is its ambiguity as to who represents what in the councils in charge of public enterprises. The three "participants"—state, employer, worker—are not clearly defined. In some cases, workers are identified as "managers"; in other cases, they represent the governmental component; while in other instances, employers are defined as "social organizations" and their interests are viewed as identical to the interests of the workers. Who belongs to what is determined by praxis or by political criteria.

The working people's duty now is not the defense of their interests but the "increase of productivity and of production, the improvement of services offered by the company to the society, the normal and beneficial function of the enterprise and the progressive elimination of their deficits."[23] As the policy is put into practice, "participation" in management has only an economic objective, which ultimately benefits the employer. And, as expected, the principle of coadministration of the companies and of equal participation of the workers in the organs of socialization has not been observed.

The PASOK labor legislation, in a sense, reverses progress that had been made in labor-employer relations since 1944, even as it provides for a workers role in the administration of banks, railways, the Piraeus Port Authority, and other business entities.[24] Previous legislation provided for employees' advice not only on matters of their competence but also on questions of general interest. In some cases, e.g., Trolley-Bus Organization (ILPAP), workers coadministered their company. In short, previous gains were cancelled by the peculiar notion of "self-management," which, according to PASOK, was based on the Yugoslav model, but with "improvements" to provide for a role for the state, the local government, the management, and the worker.[25] Since the first three entities are either the state or state-appointed officials, the worker's role is diluted under the pretext of "participation."

Following the 1985 elections, which PASOK won with a reduced majority, and due to international pressures to restructure loans and reform the economy, the ruling party initiated a debate on whether it should abandon the whole idea of the socialization of private properties or public corporations and by extension release large numbers of workers from the constraints of Law No. 1365/1983. The debate has not gone very far because far too many interests are at stake for a reversal of a policy that was heralded as "evidence of transition to socialism." As a consequence, the labor unions are not expected to regain any semblance of independence any time soon. As we shall see below, the problems created by massive governmental interference in labor affairs are far too many to be corrected in the foreseeable future.

THE STATE AND LABOR UNIONS: A LEGACY OF SOCIALIST CONTROLS

Contrary to the Declaration of the Third of September, which states that "trade unionism is free of dependence on the economic oligarchy and the guardianship of the state" and that the party intends to "establish a free and independent movement and serve the interests of the working people," the policies and praxis of the Panhellenic Socialist Movement point in the opposite direction—they represent a consistent, unrelenting effort to control unions by handpicked leadership and divisive practices.[26]

In cooperation with labor leaders controlled by the two Communist parties (pro-Moscow and Eurocommunist), the PASOK government cancelled the election of the General Confederation of Greek Labor Leadership (GSEE), which was freely elected in 1981, and appointed a new one upon assumption of power. The appointed president of GSEE (a Communist) and the secretary-general (a PASOK member) assumed the responsibility for "democratizing free trade unions" in accordance with governmental policies. A series of laws, related and unrelated to workers welfare, were enacted that were collectively called "measures to cleanse trade unionism." After their enactment, those who spoke of workers rights outside the framework of the "reformed" GSEE were branded "enemies of the people."

A first step towards formal control of labor unions was the enactment of Law No. 1264/1982, titled The Democratization of Trade Unionism and Protection of Trade Union Freedoms of the Workers. However, this law, as applied, did not free the workers from "dependence on the economic oligarchy," or from the "guardianship of the state," but firmly established the latter as the arbiter in natural employer-employee disputes. The law made it next to impossible for employers to adjust their work force in accordance with sound management practices, causing serious harm to the workers' well-being in ways elaborated earlier. When private enterprises were unable to reorganize on the basis of market conditions, more and more of them were declared "problematic," bringing them directly under government control and their workers under the constraints of Law No. 1365, which makes strikes impossible.

With economic conditions deteriorating as foreign firms declined to even consider investing in Greece (since they are deprived of the right to hire and fire personnel), unemployment and scarcity of opportunities dispelled any inclination on the part of workers to demand better conditions and compensation commensurate with their needs and the rise in the cost of living. In times of scarcity, internal labor strife takes over. It would be fair to state that class struggle in Greece under socialism commenced within the labor class, which is now divided between the "healthy" (followers of the party policies) and the "bourgeois-minded," who persist in defending workers rights by traditional western practices, such as strikes, work slowdowns, agitation and marches.

Bitterness prevails in the workplace. Such an atmosphere has contributed inevitably to the emergence of well-organized minority groups that espouse Marxist, class-struggle ideologies. In sum, the PASOK labor legislation accomplished several objectives that, in retrospect, are consistent with the party's goal of "socialist transformation." PASOK supposedly assured workers in private enterprises the right to strike, even for political reasons (such as defense of the Nicaragua regime), but denied to employers the right to regulate their labor force, even if it means closing the enterprise altogether. This, of course, assures the failure of private business, which, in turn, justifies governmental takeover "in order to protect the livelihood of workers."[27] It is indeed, an ingenious method of socialization without compensation.

CONCLUDING REMARKS

This essay is by no means an exhaustive analysis of the impact of PASOK policies on two critical interest groups in Greek society, church and labor. Nevertheless, our research points to certain trends that are apparent in Greece under socialism, which, in conjunction with policies in other areas, are bound to have great impact on the character of the political system.

The Socialist government, as is obvious in Article 8 of its founding charter, considers the church a serious impediment to its goal of "socialist transformation." Throughout its existence the church has played a pivotal role in the survival of the nation and is still perceived by the majority of the people as the essential component that defines Greekness. The legislative assault on the church, couched in appealing terms of "interest" in the Greek peasant, belies the true governmental objective, namely, the increased collectivization of lands and the nationalization of church real estate. Indicative of the government's goal is the fact that the church lands to be confiscated are not granted outright to the poor peasants but to cooperatives. If individual peasants accept such lands, they are automatically made members of the collective.

The next step in attempts by the state to control or neutralize the church seems to be a persistent effort by PASOK ideologues to exclude it from any role in defining school curriculum and from any involvement in the determination of the pedagogical content of higher education. Such a church role has been established for a long time, and its uniqueness is reflected in the fact that Greece is the sole European state with a Ministry of Education and Religious Affairs.

Governmental policies towards labor unions are similar in scope and objective to those towards the church. They aim at controlling the labor organizations even through clearly questionable legislation and intimidation. Thus all legislative acts (particularly Laws No. 1365/1983 and No. 1264/1982), that have been criticized by international organizations and legal scholars as unconstitutional, confirm an authoritarian governmental attitude toward unions. As a footnote to history, it must be noted that the first time the General Confederation of Greek Labor (GSEE) appealed to the International Labor Office was in 1964 (under the government of George

Papandreou, in which Andreas Papandreou was minister to the prime minister). Then as now, the issues were governmental interference in labor affairs, attempts to curtail the right to strike, and selective bribery of labor leaders.[28] The ILO sided with the GSEE then and severely criticized the George Papandreou cabinet.

Although the government has put in place the legal mechanism for the control of labor organizations, the rank and file continues to defy all rules. Strikes occur with higher frequency, thanks to the deteriorating economic situation. Making matters worse, immediately after the June 1985 elections (and after repeated promises of prosperity), the government imposed wage controls and authority measures that further aggravated the economic status of workers. Pitting "friends" against "enemies," the government persists in dividing and controlling unions. These actions prompted the leader of the opposition party to state in Parliament, "We have as Prime Minister an unreliable person and a liar and you cannot be proud of him."[29] Obviously, the battle for control of labor, the neutralization of the church, and the politicization of the armed forces and security is not over yet. But church and labor, two pivotal groups in Greek society, are indeed under political pressure originating in the ideological circles of the ruling party.

NOTES

1. Dimitrije Djordjevic and Stephen Fischer-Galati, *The Balkan Revolutionary Tradition* (New York: Columbia University Press, 1981): 141-142.

2. See the correspondence between the church hierarchy and the government, which makes clear the negative attitude of the PASOK government towards the church as well as the continuous goodwill of the church, *The Holy Synod of the Hierarchy of the Church of Greece, An Attempt to Capture the Church: The Truth on the Church Issue* (in Greek) (Athens 1987).

3. *Parliamentary Minutes*, 30 March 1987, 4866 ff.

4. *Ibid.*

5. *Ibid.*, 2 April 1987, 5059 ff; Kileler is a village in Thessaly, where the poor peasants' uprising against landowners started in 1910. Every year, on its anniversary, the largest mass meeting of peasants in Greece takes place, and political leaders announce agricultural measures in order to attract votes.

6. *Parliamentary Minutes*, 2 April 1987, 5059 ff.

7. The Council of State (official name of the court).

8. According to Article 1 of Law No. 1700/87, the exclusive administration of all the monastery property is turned over to ODEP. ODEP (which henceforth will be a state-run organization, since the majority of its members will be appointed by the government in accordance with Article 8 of the law) is able, according to Article 2 of the law, to transfer to the Greek state, within a period of six months, the ownership of all the land property of the monasteries.

9. The archbishop's letter was circulated in churches throughout the country after it was ignored by the government.

10. Article 2 of the law Regulation of Matters Concerning Church Property states that the use of church property is to be left to cooperatives or to peasants who might not be members of the cooperatives but who on the receipt of property automatically become members. As written, the law is intended to foster the collectivization of agriculture. See also "Aletheia" (in Greek) July 1987.

11. See the text of the academic committee's report in The Holy Synod of the Church of Greece, *An Attempt to Capture the Church: The Truth on the Church Issue* (in Greek). See also "Aletheia" (in Greek) July 1987. It must be pointed out that articles 3 and 13 of the constitution are so important that they cannot be suspended even in "time of siege"; their suspension in peace time is contrary not only to the *ratio legis* but to the letter of the constitution as well.

12. See note 10 above.

13. PASOK, *The Declaration of the Third of September*

14. *Wall Street Journal*, 17 September 1986.

15. Theodoros Theodorou, "Socialization and Regulation of the Strike" (in Greek), *Review of Labor Law* 43 (1983): 571.

16. Compare Law No. 1264/1982, which despite its weak points and exaggerations and the constitutional issue it raised, was finally accepted, since it appeared prima facie to secure the democratization and independence of the trade unions and because the consequences of its application were not yet evident. Nevertheless, later it became obvious that the law had weak points that resulted in the trapping of the labor movement in the labyrinth of the "socialist transformation."

See Giota Kravaritou-Manitake, "Law No. 1365/1983 on The Socialization of Enterprises Considered as Being of Public Character and Labor Relations" (in Greek), *Review of Labor Law*, 42 (1983): 671.

17. Kravaritou-Manitake, 674; see also the introductory note that accompanied law 1365/1983, 434.

18. Kravaritou-Manitake, 678, note 27; there it is revealed that during talks between the minister of national economy and representatives of the trade unions, one of the latter said: "Today hundreds of thousands of workers are on strike as a sign of protest against not only the article 4, but against the whole attitude of the government, which is treating the working people in a most dictatorial

way. We were hoping that there could be at least a discussion on the matters concerning the workers...."

19. Kravaritou-Manitake, 667.

20. In the private sector too, many enterprises were characterized as "problematic" and were put under the control of the Organization for the Economic Recovering of Enterprises (Law No. 1386/1983). Among the "problematic" enterprises were several very prosperous companies. Two examples are A. Pyrkal, S.A., and the Skalistiris, S.A., group of companies. A description of how Pyrkal, S.A., was made "problematic" is indicative of the government's policies: See Giannes Lampsas, *Nomenklatura: Hoi Pronomiouchoi tes Exousias* (in Greek) (The Greek Nomenclature: The Privileged in Power) (Athens: Roes Publishers, 1985): 342. Pyrkal, S.A., the Greek powder and cartridge cases industry, a company of 100 years of successful life in the field of military hardware, had in 1983 8.5 billion Dr of working capital (of which 4.5 billion Dr were from exports) and 4 billion Dr in orders from the Greek army. In order, however, for Pyrkal to be placed under PASOK's control, it had first to be declared "problematic." The government took two actions: first, it delayed for months paying off its debts to the company; second, it cancelled orders coming from abroad (amounting to millions of dollars) on the pretext of "foreign policy" considerations that prohibited the sale of ammunition to certain countries (Syria, for example). Thus the company, with over 5,000 workers, went bankrupt within a year. It was then "socialized." A member of PASOK's Politbureau was appointed as director, and an advance of 1 billion Dr was immediately made for a contract with the Greek army to be signed in the future! The "foreign policy" pretext was abandoned, and an ammunitions contract worth $300,000 was signed with Philippine President Marcos. Moreover, the objection to exports to Syria was soon thereafter forgotten. PASOK started supplying that country with light tanks produced by another company. Nevertheless, despite government protection and financing, the results of socialization during the first six months of 1984 were a management deficit of 574 million Dr, a cash deficit of 3.5 billion Dr, and only 1 billion Dr worth of orders made by the army (instead of the 4 billion Dr orders in the previous year). Complicating matters was factional strife within PASOK for control of major enterprises, which led to colossal losses and the frequent replacement of executives with relatives or friends of the high-ranking party officials. On the Skalistiris case, see *Parliamentary Minutes* , 6 February 1986, 3136.

21. *Review of Labor Law* 47 (1983): 620 ff.

22. See Theodoros Theodorou, "Socialization and Regulation of the Strike" in *Review of Labor Law* 42 (1983) 571 ff.; Alexandros Karakatsanes, "Questions Concerning Article 4"; *ibid.* 580 ff.; Giannes Leixouriotes, Dionyses Spanos, Giorgos Tsatires, "Law and Socialization"; *ibid.,* 584 ff.; Antonios Floros, "The Right to Strike"; *ibid.,* 618 ff.; Leonidas Dassios, "Strike in Enterprises in the Way of

Socialization After the Law No. 1365/1983"; *ibid.* 660 ff.; Giota Kravaritou-Manitake, "Law No. 1365/1983 on Labor Relations and The Socialization of Enterprises Considered as Being of Public Character and on Labor Relations"; *ibid.,* 664 ff. (all in Greek).

Also see the daily papers and periodicals of the period, as well as A. Metropoulos, *The Labor Institutions in Greece* (in Greek) (Athens-Komotine: Editions Sakkoulas, 1985) and Lampsas, 308.

23. See the introductory note that accompanied Law No. 1365/1983 p. 432.

24. G. Leixouriotes, D. Spanos, G. Tsatires, 600.

25. Papandreou modified the Yugoslav model as follows: "We [in PASOK] add that not only is it necessary for the workers to participate in management, but also for the local government," thus bringing the government into the affairs of enterprises twice. (A. Kokkos, A. Mourike-Kostopoulou, *Transition to Socialism* [in Greek] [Athens: Odysseas, 1986] 15.)

26. PASOK: International Relations Committee, *The Organization,* ser. A, 1 (no date): 9.

27. Georgios Vlachos, "Law 1264/1982 on Trade Unionism" (in Greek) (typescript).

28. Nikolaos A. Stavrou, "Pressure Groups in the Greek Political Setting," (Ph.D. diss. George Washington University, 1970): 115-140.

29. *Parliamentary Minutes* , 6 February 1986, 3929.

Socialist Policies and the Free Market: An Evaluation of PASOK's Economic Performance

Judith Kleinman

OVERVIEW

Although now a member of the European Community, Greece remains in many respects a developing country. Structural rigidities pervade her economy, while persistent imbalances in international transactions and stagnating private investment severely hamper its ability to grow. Some developing economies, notably the industrialized countries (NICs) of Southeast Asia, have successfully overcome these problems by encouraging direct foreign investment.

In the 1960s and early 1970s, Greece could rely upon foreign investment to help cope with her chronic trade deficits. But by the mid-1970s, the country became increasingly less attractive to investors from overseas. Structural weaknesses in the composition of her current account began to emerge, namely, the reliance upon shipping and other service industries. This contributed to a deterioration in Greece's external balances despite an increased demand for Greek exports generated by the prosperity of her Arab trading partners. This imbalance in Greece's transactions with the rest of the world persisted throughout the 1980s and, as a consequence, her present economic situation has become a cause for growing concern. In essence, Greece has been buying more goods and services abroad than she has been able to sell to other countries and by margins in excess of the transfers that she receives form her richer partners in the European Community. Such an external imbalance can be directly attributed to Greece's excessively loose fiscal, monetary, and wage policies, policies that raised her rate of inflation, made Greek goods and services less competitive, and swelled a demand for imports far in excess of her ability to pay.

By 1985, it was clear that corrective action—postponed for five years due to political considerations—had to be taken quickly in order to prevent a ruinous loss of Greece's foreign exchange reserves. It was also recognized that some demonstration of economic readjustment would be necessary to restore the confidence of foreign lenders so that Greece could continue to borrow abroad to ease the pressures on her external account. Indeed, a number of forceful measures were taken in 1985 and 1986, under a comprehensive stabilization program, to curb excessive spending at home and abroad, and to improve the country's economic competitiveness. However, as of this writing, not enough has been accomplished. The expansion of key variables such as government expenditure, bank credit, and consumer spending has slowed by less than called for in the stabilization program. Partly because introduction of stabilization had been postponed, the return to equilibrium in international transactions will take longer than initially anticipated.

In the longer run the need to revive private investment spending (i.e., outlays by industry on new plants and equipment) is of crucial importance. Only through substantial new capital investment can the productivity of labor increase sufficiently to sustain rising real incomes for all sectors of the population. To increase private investment, business needs to have both more incentive to invest and more wherewithal with which to do it.

Yet a revival of private investment requires a shift in governmental attitude. Greek governments have historically chosen an interventionist approach to economic development rather than relying on market forces. Among the recent governments, both the centrist, populist Karamanlis administration (1974-1981) and the Socialist administration of Andreas Papandreou (since 1981) have implemented highly interventionist policies. For example, in an attempt to shift income from entrepreneurs toward wage earners, both governments have maintained comprehensive price controls not accompanied by significant wage controls, large increases in the minimum wage (and hence in most wage rates), and the overmanning of industry and commerce through legal restrictions on dismissals of workers or cuts in working hours.

These policies have significantly harmed the profitability of industry, which is a major source of the funds required to carry out investments. The other main source of investment finance is borrowing from domestic banks or in domestic financial markets. Such borrowing has been made more difficult because an increased share of the funds available from these sources has been diverted to the public sector to finance rising deficits of the government and of public enterprises. The interventionist approach to economic development not only has created obstacles for the entrepreneur, but also has limited the flexibility of the economy to adjust.

It remains to be seen if the Greek authorities are disposed to alter their views enough to allow a revival of private investment on a continuing basis. It is mildly encouraging that in 1986, the first full year of the stabilization program, private investment appears to have increased. Yet while some of this increase reflects the improved profitability of industry, much of the investment was in housing and reflects the relaxation of rent controls that led to a "mini-boom" in residential investment.

NATURE OF THE PROBLEM

The problems facing the Greek economy stem partly from deeply rooted structural deficiencies and partly from continuing reliance on loose or expansionary economic policies. A long tradition of subsidization and protectionism and the steady decline in business profits during the 1970s stifled the manufacturing sector and impeded adjustment to external shocks, particularly the oil price rise of 1979. Years of protectionism insulated Greek industry, making the Greek economy vulnerable to the increased competition associated with entry into the European Community in 1981. The formation of capital needed for sustained economic growth was discouraged by extensive regulation of goods and factor markets, aimed at controlling unemployment and inflation.

By increasing direct government intervention in the economy, the Socialist government of Andreas Papandreou precipitated a further deterioration in the business climate. Promises of investment incentives and a five-year development strategy have given way to nationalizations and increasing government involvement in private sector business decisions, including the establishment of workers councils to sit on the boards of firms. Conflicting signals and inconsistent policies deterred domestic entrepreneurs from expanding capacity and foreign investors from seeking investment opportunities in Greece. The deterioration in the business climate is reflected in the acceleration of the flight of capital and the sharp drop in autonomous capital inflows since 1981.[1] Further evidence is seen in the behavior of net private investment, which, having declined since the oil shock in 1973, turned negative in 1984.

PASOK, the Panhellenic Socialist Party, has pursued two dichotomous economic policies since it came to office in October

1981. The first term of the Papandreou administration was characterized by a continuation of the expansionary fiscal and monetary policies of New Democracy. Throughout the first term, the government favored a gradualist medium-term approach to economic development. The alternative, a more forward-looking "adjustment" strategy, would have entailed short-run costs in terms of job loss and a decline in living standards, considered by the newly elected government to be unacceptable and unnecessary. The government acknowledged the problem of widening public sector and current account deficits and attempted to respond with a policy aiming to control central government expenditure on goods and services. However, the administration permitted increases in expenditures on wages, salaries, and pensions. These increases caused such sharp deterioration in the finances of public corporations and public entities (primarily social insurance funds) that the consolidated government deficit (i.e., that of the entire public sector) continued to climb. Private investment declined further, stifled by a monetary policy whose principal function was to accommodate the financing needs of the public sector. Development of the financial sector was stunted by a complex system of primary and secondary reserve requirements applied to commercial banks, and pervasive government intervention in the allocation of credit and the determination of interest rates.

Without sufficient new investment, Greek industry was unable to increase output to satisfy higher domestic demand being generated by rising incomes and stimulative government policy. Import penetration rose accordingly, becoming especially worrisome with accession to the EC. The current account deficit, which had averaged less than 6 percent of the GDP between 1979 and 1984, rose to 10 percent of the GDP in 1985. When neither domestic sources of finance nor autonomous private capital inflows could finance the rising current account and public sector deficits, the Bank of Greece began to borrow heavily on foreign capital markets.

Only when the deterioration in domestic economic conditions threatened Greek access to foreign sources of financing did the government introduce adjustment measures. The program was designed to reestablish enough of a balance in the Greek external accounts, primarily through a reduction of imports, to restore Greek creditworthiness. Additionally, the program was designed to enable Greek authorities to request balance-of-payments assistance from the EC.

In the first year of the program much of the progress achieved in meeting established macroeconomic targets was attributable to external factors, such as the oil price decline, the reduction in global interest rates, and increased grants ("transfers") from the European Community's budget. On the other hand, important signs of adjustment are emerging in the form of factors reducing domestic demand and consumption. Yet sustained adjustment will require greater commitment to private capital formation and a lessening of government intervention.

HISTORICAL PERSPECTIVE

The rigidities that underlie the macroeconomic imbalances in the Greek economy can be traced to a tradition of pervasive government intervention in all facets of economic activity. In the goods market, widespread price controls have all but nullified the traditional relationship between supply and demand, where prices signal consumer preferences and resource scarcity, and this has limited the ability of Greek industry to generate profits for reinvestment. In the financial markets, strict control over the allocation of funds by monetary authorities has impeded private sector access to financial resources as well as the development of viable alternative capital markets. In the labor market, legal restrictions on the release of unnecessary workers, regulations preventing unilateral reductions in working hours by company management, and high severance pay requirements have tended to discourage employers from investing in a job-creating expansion of productive capacity.[2] Sectoral policies of protection and subsidization, which facilitated very strong economic growth in Greece during the 1950s and 1960s, masked the deteriorating international competitiveness of Greek industry. Moreover, subsidization of ailing industries served to perpetuate inefficient and heavily indebted firms.

The strong investment that fostered growth in the 1950s and 1960s also obscured some of the rigidities in the economy. Such rigidities, however, limited the responsiveness of the economy to unanticipated economic developments. When the stability that characterized the global economy in the 1950s and 1960s crumbled under the OPEC oil price shocks of 1973 and 1979, the Greek economy did not have the flexibility to adjust to higher fuel prices and slower global economic activity. Price controls prevented producers, including public sector corporations, from passing on to consumers the increased cost of energy. The squeeze on profits, combined with limitations on private sector access to domestic financial resources, led to an abandonment of investment plans. In 1974, the trend of increasing real fixed investment reversed. From increases averaging 10 percent between 1963 and 1973, real fixed investment fell over 25 percent in the one year following the first oil shock. The decline in investment pulled real growth of the economy as a whole down to 0.2 percent in 1974, following an average rate of increase of 7 percent per year over the previous ten years. Industrial productivity fell even more sharply since employers could not reduce the size of their work force in the face of stagnant output.

The Greek recession was somewhat different from concurrent recessions in other industrialized countries. Greece's export industries were initially sheltered from much of the decline in foreign demand since a large proportion of Greek exports went to Arab markets. As the oil exporters began to use their wealth for infrastructural development, the countries increased their demand for Greek products, such as cement, and for the services of Greek construction and engineering firms. According to the International Monetary Fund's *Direction of Trade Statistics* , between 1974 and 1981 Greek exports to Arab countries increased from approximately 8 percent of total exports to almost 19 percent.

Thus, despite the sharp increase in the value of oil imports, the government had little need to implement external adjustment policies. Instead, the New Democracy government chose to pursue policies that aimed to support the high consumption and employment rates attained in the 1960s and early 1970s. In response to the sharp decline in private investment, which had generated so much of the growth of the earlier period, the government applied stimulative fiscal policies. Surpluses in the accounts of public corporations and social insurance funds initially covered much of the increase in government spending, but rising public sector spending soon began to overwhelm the positive returns on investment generated by the Public Sector Corporations (PCEs). Monetary policy was used to accommodate excess borrowing requirements of the public sector. In an attempt to avoid the potentially inflationary effects of direct credit expansion by the Bank of Greece, the objectives of monetary policy were carried out primarily through the banking sector, which absorbed an increasing share of domestic savings. After inflation accelerated to a 27-percent rate immediately following the 1973 oil price shock, it fell back to an average of 12 to 13 percent between 1976 and 1979.

The second oil shock reverberated more sharply through the Greek economy than that of 1973 due to structural and cyclical factors. Traditional growth industries, most important of which is, perhaps, shipping, were weakened by the global recession. Greek industry began to face increasing competition from other EC countries as Prime Minister Karamanlis sought to accelerate Greece's accession to the EC. Consumption-oriented government policies did not sustain growth as expected, because without new investment, industry lacked the capacity to respond to increasing demand.

These expansionary policies also caused new structural problems, notably the emergence of sustained public sector deficits. Increases in government spending ran countercyclical to the slowdown of output in the Greek economy, but so long as PCEs and public enterprises remained in surplus the deficit on the central government account could be covered. Through 1979, the general government accounts (i.e., central government plus PCEs and public entities) recorded net savings. In 1980 the trend reversed. In 1981 the general government deficit skyrocketed to over 8 percent of the GDP, of which interest payments on the public debt were about 50 percent.

Excess demand, combined with escalating unit labor costs and lagged effects of the oil price rise made inflation increase faster. In 1980 inflation rose to an annual rate of about 25 percent, substantially higher than that of Greece's principal trading partners. The sharp increase in the inflation differential between Greece and its trading partners damaged the competitiveness of Greek exports in foreign markets and made foreign goods seem relatively cheap in Greece.

Lack of a market-determined exchange rate prevented the depreciation of the drachma that would otherwise have resulted from the higher inflation in Greece so as to restore competitiveness. Since the mid-1970s the monetary authorities had pursued an interventionist exchange rate policy (a so-called managed float) more often serving domestic macroeconomic policy objectives than taking the external sector into consideration. In the mid-1970s, following the oil price shock, the objective was to control price increases. Had the exchange rate of the drachma been market-determined, the increase in the inflation differential would have put pressure on the drachma to depreciate in such a way as to bring the prices of imported goods in line with the price increases being experienced by domestic goods, and to prevent domestic inflation from increasing the foreign price of export goods. Instead the drachma became overvalued, exacerbating the reduction in the competitiveness of Greek exports.

The effect on the economy of declining real net exports and declining real investment became so acute that in 1981 real economic growth turned negative. Even unemployment, which had been held to low levels throughout the 1970s, began to rise. By 1981 the rate of unemployment had risen to 4 percent, more than double the rate in 1978.

PASOK ADMINISTRATION: 1981-1985

Rather than address and correct the structural problems that generated the unemployment, economic policy under the Papandreou administration tended to aggravate the decline in productivity. Medium-term plans of the government's gradualist development program were often subordinated to short-term ends depending on the pull of interest groups and political considerations. Highly stimulative fiscal policies aimed at promoting growth compounded problems of the public debt, inflation, and the widening trade and current account imbalances. Reinforcement of price controls and restrictive labor legislation, combined with heightened antibusiness rhetoric, deterred the new investment essential to the generating of economic growth.

POLICY OBJECTIVES

Redistributive or reallocative objectives often underlie the design of economic policies: redistribution of resources to achieve greater equity, or reallocation of resources to promote greater efficiency in production. Alternatively, the need to address persistent economic imbalances may make stabilization of the economy the chief objective of economic policy.

The Socialist government's initial approach appears to have been to combine redistributive and reallocative objectives in an effort to promote rapid real growth and high employment. An early policy of sharp wage increases was to provide the stimulus for higher national output.[3] An implicit assumption was that higher wages would bring forth a larger supply of labor which would produce a substantial increase in output. Under this strong growth assumption, the increase in nominal wages promoted by the government would not necessarily cause prices to rise. Sale of the expanded output would provide industry with extra revenue to pay higher wages. Furthermore, the growth in aggregate supply would obviate the need to reduce aggregate demand through austerity measures—the consequences of which, in terms of higher unemployment and lower living standards, were fundamentally incompatible with government objectives.

In November 1981, within a month of assuming power, PASOK raised minimum wages and salaries by near 50 percent over the level of the previous November.[4] In January 1982, the government increased wages to employees who had not benefited from the boost in minimum wages in November. Incorporating redistributional objectives, these increases were graduated according to the level of earnings. Employees with total pay up to Dr 20,000 per month were awarded an increase of 25 percent. Higher income brackets received smaller absolute increases, and those earning more than Dr 52,000 received no increase.

With a 25 percent rate of inflation inherited from the New Democracy government, it could be seen that any efforts to increase real income among lower income groups would quickly be reduced in terms of the purchasing power of workers. Thus, to preserve the real wage gains, Papandreou implemented an automatic wage indexation mechanism known as ATA. ATA formed the core of the incomes policy introduced into legislation by the Socialist government. Every four months, wages would be increased to compensate workers for increases in consumer prices. The degree of compensation varied according to the level of earnings: the wages of low income groups were fully indexed to the rise in consumer prices, while higher earnings were only partially indexed.[5]

The government periodically modified the scope and timing of the indexation mechanism in an effort to allay its inflationary effects. Initially, the legislation was binding only upon the public sector. In 1983, indexation was made compulsory for the private sector and penalties were instituted for firms granting wage increases in excess of the legal limits for the compensation of inflation. Legislative changes in the following year again exempted the private sector from mandatory compliance. The four-month interval between increases was altered in 1983 to reduce the impact of the most inflationary first months of the year.

Also under the broad rubric of redistributive policy, the new government very quickly raised minimum payments to pensioners, and (of more significant long-term consequence) implemented a policy granting minimum pensions on a universal basis. Pension coverage was extended to farmers, returning emigrants, and others who had never contributed to any social insurance fund during their working life. As the ratio of contributors to pensioners fell, the system was transformed from a social insurance system dependent on contributions into a social welfare system in which benefits granted to a large proportion of the population were increasingly disassociated from contributions. As a result of higher payments and broader coverage, pension expenditures from the social insurance funds rose from about 7 percent of the Gross National Product (GNP) in 1979 to over 11 percent of the GNP in 1982.

The combination of the higher government wage bill and pension payments plus increased budgetary transfers for social services frustrated Papandreou's announced intention to shift the emphasis of government spending from consumption to investment. In 1982 central government current expenditures increased by 27 percent, although this was a significant reduction from the election-year rate of 51 percent in 1981. Payments for wages, salaries, and pensions rose 33 percent—considerably more than in recent years—and were among the major factors behind the overall increase in government expenditure. Public sector investment, meanwhile, increased only 21 percent, implying no change in real terms and representing a marked decline from the 51 percent rate of increase recorded in 1981. Little of the public investment budget was devoted to job-creating in the productive capacity of the economy. Rather, a chief aim of public investment was to improve the "social infrastructure" of the economy. Funds were directed toward improvement of health and education facilities as well as promotion of special projects such as the "kapi" program to develop a network of vacation facilities for pensioners. A large proportion of the investment budget was also devoted to land reclamation.

BOOSTING EMPLOYMENT

Underlying much of Greek economic policy has been a tradition of maintaining low rates of unemployment. The Socialist government assumed office in the midst of a rising trend of unemployment, which originated in the slowdown of economic activity in the late 1970s. Yet despite government efforts to bolster employment through high growth policies and legislation strengthening job protection regulations, the rate of unemployment in Greece has risen every year since 1981. By

1985, the rate of unemployment reached 8.3 percent, more than double the 1981 rate of 4 percent.[6] The increase in unemployment has resulted from continued increases in the labor force and slack private sector demand for labor.[7]

Contrary to the full employment intent of the various policies, their combined effect may have been to stifle private job creation. Higher minimum wages have tended to dampen business demand for labor since the expense of hiring an additional worker is greater than the revenue of the output the worker produces. Increased borrowing needs of the government have crowded private investors out of the shallow capital market, while price controls and tax policies have restricted the accumulation of profit for reinvestment and further limited the ability of private industry to contribute to job creation.

The responsibility for maintaining high employment thus devolved upon the public sector and industrial policy. The Greek government often has been the employer of last resort, but Greece's public sector employment, particularly in PCEs and banking, accelerated considerably during the first years of the PASOK administration. Between 1981 and 1985, central government employment increased an average of 3 percent per year; employment at PCEs increased an average of 3 percent per year, despite severe cash-flow problems; and employment in the banking sector increased an average of 5 percent per year. A short-term public-works program, introduced in 1983, employed some 15,000 workers in projects such as road repair, the building of playgrounds, and the enhancement of public gardens. A youth employment program, partly supported by EC funds, provided subsidies to industry to encourage the hiring of workers under the age of twenty-five.

Industrial policy was largely effected through a policy of subsidization of loans to selected "social preferred" industries. The policy could be implemented on two fronts because monetary authorities exercised direct control over interest rates and the allocation of credit. About 30 percent of bank deposits were earmarked to sectors such as agriculture, construction, mining, textiles, or handicraft industries. Interest rates on the loans, determined by the monetary authorities, varied according to the sector and were often set below the banks' costs on deposits. Under the Investment Incentive Law enacted in 1982, small and medium-sized businesses were added to the list, and in 1983 banks became obligated to earmark 1 percent of new deposits to finance heavily indebted "problematic" firms.

Aid to these problematic firms was institutionalized in 1983 through the enactment of the Ailing Enterprise Law. This law attempted to shift management of problematic enterprises from purely private control to a mixture of public and private control. Direct government intervention was justified by PASOK on grounds of "social responsibility." It was alleged that much of the deterioration in the financial position of these companies was caused by the diversion of profits by owners for personal use. By assuming managerial control, the authorities could prevent such mismanagement of funds.

The rescue program initially involved a state takeover of ailing companies and a freezing of their debts.[8] The troubled companies were grouped under a specially established government authority, the Secretariat of Business Reconstruction Organization (OAE), created to assess their economic viability. If a firm was found viable, a new directing board appointed by OAE took charge of the company's management. The new management group was to design a detailed "rehabilitation" program and to determine how to restructure corporate finances. Arrangements were then made for settlement of the firm's debt. Procedures included compulsory capital increases and negotiation of debt-to-equity swaps. Any remaining debt was rescheduled.

DOMESTIC CONSEQUENCES

Government policies to stimulate economic growth and prevent increases in unemployment created further distortions in financial, labor, and goods markets and compounded existing public sector and external deficits. The increase in consumer demand that resulted from greater consumer income led to a substantial increase in imports, since Greek industry lacked the capacity and flexibility to respond to the demand shock. Where the supply of imports still failed to satisfy Greek consumers, the excess demand created pressure on the goods market for prices to rise.

Added to this "demand pull" on prices was a "cost push" effect created by the higher wages. Without new investment in Greek industry, even if people were willing to work harder, Greek industry would not have the capacity to increase output sufficiently to offset the increase in labor costs. According to an important economic principle known as the "law of diminishing marginal returns," given a fixed capital stock, gains made in output when labor inputs are increased will become smaller and smaller and eventually will become negative (i.e., total output could decline). While people working extra hours or new workers will initially help to increase output, without new machines and equipment at their disposal, these workers will soon encounter, if not cause, bottlenecks in the production process. In the case of Greece, investment had actually been declining since the mid-1970s, so that the Greek economy could not physically increase output fast enough to accommodate the additional cost of higher wages and a larger labor supply.

Another line of economic theory questions whether, in fact, higher wages would induce a greater work effort. It is suggested that the substitution of work for leisure generated by a wage increase, may be offset by an "income effect" whereby with higher wages workers choose to spend more time on leisure activities (that is, work less). A strong "income effect" will thus have "perverse" consequences on the labor market, in that higher wages will reduce the total amount of labor supplied.[9]

A further distortion in the labor market was created by the sharp narrowing of wage differentials among income groups by the graduated nature of the wages policy. By the end of 1985 the average wage was only 1.9 times higher than the minimum wage, whereas in December of 1981 the average wage had been 2.4 times greater than the minimum. The compression of wages was even more pronounced on an after-tax basis. The compression of wage differentials can lead to a decline in the productivity of the economy by discouraging those with higher education or advanced training who see those with substantially less training earning roughly similar salaries. More than just reducing their incentive to work, the compression in wage differentials may influence the more highly educated to emigrate to a country where their training will be more richly rewarded. The resultant "brain drain" has the long-term effect of removing valuable human capital necessary, especially, for the development of more technologically advanced industries. Of equally serious long-term consequence is the effect of the compression of wage differentials on occupational and educational choice. The compression of wage differentials between jobs of diverse levels of education and skill tends to discourage advanced training considering both the direct costs of education and, perhaps more significant, the income foregone during the period of schooling.

FISCAL OUTCOME

Despite increases in government revenue—the key to PASOK's deficit reduction plan—the public sector deficit remained near 10 percent of the GDP. While defense expenditures and items in the investment part of the current budget were trimmed, increases in structural elements such as public sector salaries and pensions (i.e., those that cannot be easily reduced) signaled the emergence of a worrisome trend. Both PCEs and social insurance funds, which had traditionally recorded surpluses sufficient to help finance the central government deficit, began to record deficits. PCEs, which in the early 1970s were able to internally finance investment through surpluses in current accounts, were running deficits on the order of 3 percent of the GDP by the mid-1980s. The PCEs fell into deficit largely because higher fuel costs and sharply increased wage bills had not been compensated for by increases in rates charged for public services.[10] The social insurance funds, which had continued to register surpluses through 1981, fell into deficit in 1982 as a result of substantial increases in pension payments. Thus, despite the cutbacks in current expenditures, the increased deficit of PCEs and the disappearance of the surplus generated by public entities contributed to the maintenance of a high public sector borrowing requirement (PSBR).

MONETARY POLICY

Financing the increasing PSBR at lowest cost has been the foremost function of monetary policy in Greece. To avoid the inflationary impact of monetary expansion, the authorities tended to rely more on obligatory holdings of treasury bills by commercial banks and other financial intermediaries than on money creation by the central bank. With rapidly growing public sector borrowing needs, pursuit of this type of monetary policy siphoned off increasing amounts of domestic savings that otherwise could have been used for productive investment. By the end of 1981, banks were required to devote about 40 percent of new deposits to investment in government paper.

The rapid depletion of domestic savings prompted a shift toward more substantial central bank financing. The share of financing by the Bank of Greece jumped from one-quarter of total public sector financing in 1980 to over one-half of substantially greater public sector financing needs in 1981. Concurrently, financing through the bank's compulsory investment in treasury bills dropped from over 30 percent in 1980 to less than 15 percent in 1981. Concerned that accelerated growth of the money supply was contributing to the maintenance of high rates of inflation, PASOK enacted legislation in 1983 to place a legal limit on Bank of Greece financing. Initial compliance with the law yielded a reduction in central bank financing of the PSBR to only 7 percent in 1983. However, in 1984 central bank contributions again jumped to almost 15 percent.

Public-sector demand for funds soon outpaced the supply of funds provided by depositors and autonomous capital inflows from abroad, and severe distortions were created in the financial markets as a result of this type of monetary policy. In order to reduce the cost of government borrowing, monetary authorities tended to keep nominal interest rates at or below the rate of inflation. Real interest rates (nominal interest rates adjusted for inflation) were maintained at very low levels or even at negative levels (i.e., nominal rates were held below the rate of inflation) so that, in effect, depositors were subsidizing the cost of government borrowing.

Negative real interest rates contributed to a substantial decline in the pool of national savings available for the financial requirements of the government and the investment needs of industry. Gross national savings fell from about 21 percent in 1980 to 18 percent in 1983, although it has risen again since 1984. Capital flight from Greece increased as corporations and individual depositors with substantial assets sent funds abroad, despite capital controls, in search of higher rates of return. The redistributive policies of the government may have compounded the fall in savings, since lower-income groups, to whom wealth was shifted, tend to consume more and save less than higher-income groups.

Another important change occurring in the composition of public sector financing was increased recourse to foreign borrowing. Foreign borrowing had been averted throughout most of the 1970s to avoid higher interest rates on international capital markets, over which Greek monetary authorities had no control. In 1980 the share of foreign borrowing in the financing of the PSBR nearly quintupled from 5 percent to over 24 percent on a cash basis. The proportion fell back to about 14 percent in 1981, but when borrowing from the Bank of Greece was legally curtailed in 1983, the share of foreign borrowing again rose sharply to almost 35 percent of total financing.

EFFECTS ON EXTERNAL ACCOUNTS

Substantial increases in the current account deficit also led to an increase in foreign borrowing under the initial phase of PASOK policy. On the one hand, structural problems and stimulative government policies contributed to the increased trade deficit, both through continued strong demand for imports and continued decline in export competitiveness. On the other hand, largely cyclical factors associated with the global recession caused a deterioration in the nontrade elements of the external accounts that had traditionally financed the trade deficit, namely, shipping, tourism, and remittances of Greek workers living abroad.

Greek export competitiveness was dealt a severe blow by Papandreou's effort to sharply increase minimum wages and salaries. Greek labor costs rose much more rapidly in 1981 than labor costs in competitor countries. Relative unit labor costs rose 10 percent in 1981. The automatic indexation of wages to prices reinforced the feedback effects of wage increases into inflation, so that in 1982 relative unit labor costs rose 20 percent. This institutionalization of a wage-price spiral sustained a more rapid rate of increase in labor costs in Greece than in countries where productivity considerations were incorporated in the wage determination process. The widening of cost differentials caused a real appreciation of the drachma.[11] Between the fourth quarter of 1979 and the fourth quarter of 1982, the drachma (measured by consumer price inflation) appreciated about 14 percent in real, effective terms because the depreciation of the nominal exchange rate did not keep pace with the inflation differential.[12] The appreciation made the drachma-value of imports cheaper, resulting in higher import penetration.

Vacillations in exchange rate policy intensified the deterioration of the trade balance. Exchange rate policy swung back and forth between the objectives of reducing inflation and improving competitiveness. In January 1983, the drachma was devalued 15.5 percent against the U.S. dollar in an attempt to recoup the loss of export competitiveness. The drachma was then pegged to the dollar in an attempt to forestall rapid appreciation. However, the gains in competitiveness against other trading partners were offset not only by continued high rates of inflation, but also by an unanticipated strengthening of the dollar in early 1983. In the seven months after that devaluation, the drachma appreciated 12 percent in real, effective terms against the weighted average of its trading partners. In August 1983 the government announced that the drachma would no longer be pegged to the dollar, but would be more actively managed by monetary authorities in order to hold steady the effective weighted average value of the exchange rate.

Adding to the deterioration in external competitiveness,

earnings on the invisibles account (services and unilateral transfers) declined, and autonomous capital inflows slowed. Invisible earnings (net of interest payments) had historically financed a large part of Greece's trade deficit. However, between 1981 and 1984, invisibles receipts fell 40 percent. The major factor behind the decline in invisibles was the recession in the Greek shipping industry in the early 1980s.[13] Shipping receipts fell some 40 percent between 1981 and 1984, to about $1.1 billion. Another factor contributing to the decline in the invisibles surplus was the fall in worker remittances from abroad as the global recession led to a return home of Greek emigrants employed in other European countries. The worldwide recession in 1981-82 also led to a slowdown in tourist receipts.

In the early 1980s, the net inflow of private capital dropped precipitously. In 1981, net private capital flows financed one-half of the current account deficit. In 1982, only one-third of a somewhat smaller current deficit was financed by private inflows. By 1985, the amount had dropped to about one quarter of the total deficit. The decline in direct foreign investment and the acceleration of capital flight reflected uncertainty and unease regarding the direction of economic policies following the election of PASOK. PASOK appeared to advocate the adoption of investment incentives and the promotion of private investment in its five-year development strategy. Uncertainty was fostered by controversial government moves such as the nationalization of the Heracles Cement Company in 1983.[14] The decline in net private capital inflows also reflected the existence of more profitable real and financial investments abroad as the differential in real interest rates widened in favor of investments in other European countries and in the United States. Between 1980 and 1985, while monetary authorities maintained negative real interest rates for deposits in Greece, real interest rates on U.S. and German capital markets, for example, were not only positive but rising.

From 1981 to 1985, direct foreign investment in Greece fell some 30 percent. During the same period Greek investment in the United States alone rose more than 400 percent to over $20 billion. According to the U.S. Department of Commerce, investments by Greeks in the United States more than doubled between 1981 and 1984 from $44 million to $90 million and doubled again in 1985.

The decline in "non-debt" private inflows precipitated a substantial increase in official foreign borrowing.[15] Official foreign borrowing jumped 60 percent in 1982 to over $1.1 billion. By the end of 1985, official capital inflows had risen to $2.3 billion. The Bank of Greece had generally been responsible for more than half of the borrowing, with public enterprises borrowing the remainder.

The combination of the decline in nondebt capital inflows and the increase in government borrowing requirements and in the associated current account deficit led to a large accumulation of external debt in the early 1980's. Between 1980 and 1985, total external debt rose from about $7 billion (equivalent to 18 percent of the GDP) to almost $16 billion (48 percent of the GDP). Growth of the external debt has been accompanied by rising servicing charges: interest payments have more than doubled since 1980 to over $1.2 billion in 1985 and total debt servicing (i.e., interest and amortization of principal) have risen from $1.5 billion in 1983 to an estimated $2.1 billion in 1985. And, as mentioned above, Greece's ability to service its debt through export earnings fell dramatically between 1980 and 1985. In 1985 almost 30 percent of current earnings on exports of goods and services were used to cover interest and amortization payments on the external debt, compared with the use of only 11 percent of net current receipts to accomplish this in 1980. Interest payments alone were absorbing an increasing portion of total current receipts, making the policy of borrowing abroad less and less sustainable. Despite its increasing inability to meet debt service obligations through export receipts, Greece has managed to remain current in its interest and amortization payments through continued access to international credit markets.

Since first seeking substantial official funds in the early 1980s, the Greek government had been able to obtain needed loans on generally favorable conditions. The late entry of Greece on international capital markets meant that Greece's stock of external debt outstanding (only $5.5 billion in 1979) appeared low compared with other debtor countries. Greece was thus considered an attractive sovereign borrower, and commercial banks were willing to lend at low spreads. U.S. bank exposure to Greece increased from $2.4 billion in 1979 to $3 billion in 1983. However, in 1984 and 1985, total U.S. bank exposure did not change; U.S. banks apparently had concluded that the existing spreads did not justify the risk of lending. In contrast, lending by non-U.S. commercial banks increased 13.2 percent during 1984 and continued to rise rapidly during early 1985 without a tightening of terms. Japanese banks were the most active group in the Greek syndications; Greece provided a welcome opportunity to increase their foreign lending in the European market and was considered by Japanese banks to be a better risk than many other middle-income sovereign borrowers, such as the Latin American countries.

Beginning in mid-1985, however, Greek authorities encountered increasing difficulty in borrowing at reasonable rates on international capital markets. The urgency of the situation became apparent in August 1985, when in coordination with the Bank of Greece the national telecommunications company, OTE, was unable to raise a planned medium-term loan. Finding themselves unable to solicit large syndicated loans, the Greek monetary authorities began to borrow heavily on the market for short-term funds at substantially higher interest rates.

STABILIZATION PROGRAM

The financing needs of the enlarged current account deficit, as well as the continuing declines in invisible earnings and autonomous capital inflows, made continued access to international capital markets essential; however, this required that foreign lenders retain confidence in Greece's ability to pay. By 1985, total external debt had risen to about 50 percent of national income. Interest payments alone on debt were absorbing about 17 percent of export earnings. Maintenance of creditworthiness on world capital markets would have required a substantial and sustained improvement in the current account deficit through higher export earnings and/or lower import payments. Concern over the possible loss of creditworthiness ultimately precipitated the change in Greek government policy in mid-1985.

Furthermore, amortization payments were scheduled to jump sharply starting in 1988, when grace periods on earlier loans would begin to expire. Without a program for refinancing the upcoming maturities, the government would face heavy debt payments starting in 1988 (the year of the next general election) and depletion of foreign exchange holdings. Repayments were scheduled to double from $1 billion in 1986 to about $2 billion in each year from 1988 to 1990. With such large actual and prospective current financing needs, the authorities might have approached the IMF for assistance in the form of a "standby arrangement." Papandreou, however, had rejected recourse to IMF assistance during his electoral campaign because the IMF attaches certain macroeconomic conditions to its loans, which

Papandreou considered a threat to sovereign decision making.

Instead, the authorities used the EC loan mechanism, which was more acceptable politically. A commitment to a macroeconomic adjustment was required for access to the EC loan mechanism, but design of the stabilization program allowed more consultation between domestic policymakers and the lending institution. By taking an EC loan, Greece would not be bowing to a "hegemonic" foreign organization, but rather availing itself of a benefit of EC membership, as had France and Italy in past years.[16]

The EC balance-of-payments support facility was designed to provide loans to member nations struggling with the financing of external imbalances.[17] When a member state has problems independently raising capital on international markets, the EC can initiate fund raising operations on behalf of that member. Money borrowed by the EC, either directly from third countries and their financial institutions or on international capital markets, is then reloaned to the member state. Access to the loan mechanism, however, requires that the borrowing country present the EC Council of Ministers with an economic program that demonstrates a willingness to implement external adjustment measures.

Papandreou took advantage of his success in the June 1985 election to shift the focus of policies toward stabilization of external imbalances. Yet, while the emphasis of policy appeared to shift, the "gradualist" orientation of policymakers toward adjustment seemed to linger. Initial implementation consisted of raising certain administered prices, primarily for imports and services of PCEs, and allowing the drachma to depreciate.[18]

It was not until October that Papandreou announced his intention to take more decisive action. On 11 October 1985, in the prime minister's annual economic policy speech, Papandreou introduced a two-year stabilization program designed to reduce the public sector deficit, control inflation, and narrow the current account deficit. One month later, Papandreou asked the EC to assist the Greek stabilization effort by approving a large balance-of-payments support loan.

A set of ambitious "economic policy targets" was built into the program, which met with the approval of the EC finance ministers. The targets were by and large similar to the conditions attached to IMF programs, but the Greek plan lacked the structural adjustment measures that have become an integral part of most IMF-supported programs. The most immediate objective of the program was to improve the country's competitiveness and to stabilize the external debt. The medium-term goal was to reduce the current account deficit in 1988 to a level that could be financed by the autonomous capital inflows from Greeks living abroad, thereby stabilizing the external debt. The core of the program was a 15-percent devaluation of the drachma intended to encourage manufacturing exports. To discourage imports further, an advance deposit scheme was introduced on "nonessential" imports. Importers were required to deposit 40 to 80 percent of the value of certain imports interest-free with the Bank of Greece for six months as a condition of customs clearance.

The devaluation and the import deposit scheme were intended to increase the price of imports to Greek consumers and thus reduce demand for imported goods. Since under the ATA indexation mechanism import price increases would feed into wage increases and refuel the wage-price spiral, the stabilization program modified the ATA to lessen the pass-through of the devaluation to prices as well as to break inflationary expectations. Under the modified system, wage increases were to be awarded on the basis of the official inflation target, adjusted to exclude the impact of imported inflation (the prices of imported goods were removed from the consumer price index), rather than on the basis of past rates of inflation. In addition to moderating wage increases, inflation was to be checked through a reduction of domestic demand through fiscal and monetary tightening. By December 1986, the consumer price index was to be, at most, 16 percent higher than the level in December 1985—nearly ten percentage points below the level recorded in December 1985. By December 1987, year-over-year inflation was to be reduced to 10 percent.

The program also targeted a reduction of the PSBR by four percentage points per annum for 1986 and 1987. Contraction of the public sector deficit was to be achieved through revenue enhancement with some reduction in government expenditures. The government planned to increase taxes on business profits and crack down more strongly on tax evasion. To allay the cash-flow problems of PCEs, the government increased administered prices on certain public services. Other deficit reduction measures included cuts in selected budgetary appropriations, primarily defense and infrastructural investment, and a reduction in agricultural subsidies.[19] In addition, credit tightening by the Bank of Greece was intended to impose further discipline on deficit spending as well as to reduce overall domestic demand. Bank liquidity was to be reduced by Dr 35 billion ($250 million), equivalent to about 10 percent of the scheduled allocation of credit to the private sector for 1985.

ROLE OF THE EC

Since Greece's accession to the EC in 1981, transfer payments from the EC to Greece have played a significant role in both the external and the public sector accounts of the country. Increases in subsidies from the EC upon accession in 1981 have largely offset the decline in invisibles receipts from more traditional categories, such as shipping and emigrants' remittances. Subsidies from the European Agricultural Guidance and Guarantee Fund (EAGGF) of the EC Common Agricultural Policy (CAP) have helped relieve a major element of pressure on the Greek budget. Subsidies for Greek farmers from the EAGGF increased by Dr 74 billion between 1981 and 1984, corresponding to a Dr 30 billion reduction in expenditures from the central Greek budget on agricultural subsidies.

EC financing also has played an important role in support of the austerity program. A large part of the improvement in the current account resulted from increased transfers from the EC's developmental funds. Concurrently, the balance-of-payments support loan enabled Greece not only to meet current financing needs and to restore access to international capital markets, but also to refinance part of its outstanding debt. On 18 November 1985 the EC finance ministers approved a six-year loan of 1.75 billion Eurocurrency units (ECU), or about $1.5 billion. The loan was to be allocated in two equal installments, with allocation of the second half of the loan contingent upon a review of economic performance under the stabilization program.

The first half of the loan was disbursed in January 1986. The second half of the loan was disbursed a year later, after EC finance ministers and the EC Monetary Committee had found substantial "progress" toward reaching the macroeconomic targets set by the Greek government for inflation, the public sector and current account deficits, and domestic credit growth.

ECONOMIC PERFORMANCE UNDER THE STABILIZATION PROGRAM

Despite some heated opposition by labor unions, the government has so far broadly adhered to its stabilization program. The government's commitment to the demand management objectives has begun to yield some signs of adjustment, although much of the success in meeting the targets measured by the EC was largely facilitated by external factors.

The most concrete signs of adjustment have been the narrowing of the current account and public sector deficits, the deceleration of inflation and monetary growth, the moderation of wage increases and unit labor costs, and some recovery in profits. By making the increase in wages a function of *projected* rates of inflation, rather than past rates, the government helped to break inflationary expectations. Real wages declined 8 percent in 1986 and were expected to decline at least another 3 percent in 1987. The drop in real wages was substantial enough that despite continued stagnation in productivity growth, unit labor costs decelerated to 13 percent in 1986, the lowest rate of increase since 1973. Additionally, agricultural incomes were constrained through policies limiting agricultural price increases.

The reduction in real wages helped to relieve cost pressures, thus facilitating a reduction in inflation to near its 16-percent target. Consumer prices in December 1986 were only 16.9 percent above the level in December 1985. Yet it should be noted that imposition of a price freeze in November 1986 contributed significantly to the apparent success in reaching the inflation target.[20]

While the apparent adjustment of real wages and inflation was largely in response to better government policy, success in reducing the PSBR by the targeted 4 percent of the GDP, and in reducing the current account deficit by 50 percent to within $100 million of its target, was greatly helped by unanticipated international economic developments. The decline in the net oil import bill and higher net transfers from the EC explain a large part of the sharp drop in the current account deficit from $3.3 billion in 1985 (about 10 percent of the GDP) to $1.7 billion (about 4 percent of the GDP) in 1986. The fall in oil prices produced a net savings in the trade deficit of about $900 million, while EC transfers contributed $1.3 billion to the invisibles account.[21] Without these helpful external factors, continued declines in export competitiveness and the strength of domestic demand in the first half of the year would have produced a serious deterioration in the external accounts.

Declines in relative unit labor costs should help to improve the competitiveness of Greek producers against the producers in Greece's major trading partners. The exchange rate policy aims to maintain the improved competitiveness through exchange rate management based on a measure of relative unit labor costs. The authorities chose to follow this policy as a means of disciplining domestic producers to limit price rises and increase efficiency. Exporters, on the other hand, favor a formula that would capture the non-wage-related cost differentials as well and allow for a more rapid depreciation of the drachma. Their argument is based on the fear that the tight wages policy will narrow the differential in the rate of labor cost increases between Greece and its trading partners to less than the differential in the rate of increase of other factor costs. By focusing strictly on labor cost differentials, the exchange rate policy could thus lead to a deterioration in overall competitiveness for Greek exports.

The oil price decline was also responsible for roughly half of the reduction in the public sector deficit. The government oil monopoly appropriated windfall profits on the order of 2 percent of the GDP by not passing on to consumers much of the huge savings realized in oil import costs (i.e., in effect, raising the consumption tax on petroleum products). Without the extra boost to government revenue provided by the extra fuel consumption tax, the reduction in the general government deficit was fairly small. The reduction in the PSBR from 18 percent of the GDP to 14 percent did not result from significantly lower government consumption—the actual reduction, in drachma terms, was not as large as planned in the budget. Policy relied heavily upon increases in revenue through higher taxes and the elimination of tax evasion. Contrary to the tighter fiscal policy stance of the stabilization program, government expenditures on pensions, the wage bill, subsidies, and transfers all increased.

Despite the unanticipated profits of the oil monopoly and the revenue accrued through the effect of fiscal drag, the rise in revenue was below expectations.[22] One reason was that higher rates of taxes encouraged greater tax evasion. In addition, deficits on social welfare funds rose sharply, and the deficit of the PCEs fell less than expected, reflecting the central role of social policy in economic decisions. Further easing of pension eligibility has contributed to a trend of increasing pension payments and a further deterioration in the finances of major social welfare funds.[23] The deficit of the PCEs declined as a result of increases in fees charged for services, cutbacks in real fixed investment, and a reduction in the wage and salary bill in real terms. The reduction in the borrowing requirement of PCEs was substantially smaller than projected as a result of further rises in public sector employment that largely offset the effect of the tight wage norms.[24]

The additional liquidity created by the financing of the PSBR, combined with the rapid growth of private sector demand for credit in the initial months following the devaluation, contributed to an acceleration of the monetary aggregates in the first months of 1986. The disappointing response to the introduction of treasury bills to the nonbank public further frustrated the plans of the monetary authorities. Substantial corrective action was required in order to reduce monetary growth; this was effected primarily through a tightening of credit to the private sector. By the end of 1984, the rate of growth of M3, the broad money supply, was slightly below the target in the monetary program. However, a not insignificant factor in achieving the 1986 target was the draining of liquidity by the import deposit scheme introduced as part of the stabilization program, which siphoned off liquidity into noninterest bearing accounts in the Bank of Greece.

Private consumption, like public consumption, grew more strongly in 1986 than the planners of the demand management program had anticipated. Despite the decline in real income, private consumption grew by 1 percent. The factors behind the strength in private consumption were partly transitory and partly structural. Many consumers initially assumed the austerity measures to be temporary. Thus, to avoid reducing the level of consumption to which they had become accustomed, consumers reduced savings and/or supplemented their income with second jobs.[25] Expectations of further devaluations shortly after implementation of the austerity program contributed to an increase in the purchase of imported goods early in the year, despite the extra costs imposed by the import deposit requirement and the lagged effect of the October devaluation. Later in the year, retail sales surged in anticipation of sharp price rises associated with the introduction of the value-added tax (VAT) in January 1987.[26]

Despite signs of adjustment, realization of the full effect of the demand management will be proscribed by structural obstacles. The demand management program relies almost exclusively on the moderation of wages through the modified indexation mechanism; however, wages constitute less than 50 percent of household income. According to estimates by the independent Institute of Economic and Industrial Research, about one-quarter to one-third of the national income in Greece is derived from the black market. By definition, the authorities can neither regulate nor tax the wages of those employed in the black market. Furthermore, wages in the agricultural sector, which employs about 30 percent of the labor force, have been exempted from the incomes policy.

Even if consumption could be reduced so as to increase the availability of domestic financial resources for investment purposes, direct foreign investment would still be essential as a supplemental source of financial resources and as a primary source of new technology. However, as mentioned above, since 1981 direct foreign investment in Greece has declined about 30 percent. In contrast, during the same time period, direct foreign investment in the Spanish economy, an economy with structural characteristics similar to those of Greece, jumped an estimated 70 percent. The rise in foreign investment, strongly encouraged by the Spanish government, has contributed significantly to Spain's recent economic boom. Anticipating their 1986 entry into the EC and the need to improve the competitiveness of Spanish industry, the Socialist government of Felipe Gonzales took strong disinflationary measures that enhanced the credibility of government policy and fostered the greater profitability of real and financial investments.

Movement toward positive real interest rates in Greece became particularly urgent with the upsurge of capital flight in 1985, whereas the need for long-term reform has been made necessary by the EC program for full integration of European capital markets. If capital flows between European countries are completely liberalized by 1992, as scheduled, Greek financial resources will become even more vulnerable to outflows in search of higher rates of return. In 1986 Greek monetary authorities appeared to have acquiesced to positive real interest rates, contrary to the traditional practice of aiming to reduce interest costs on the government debt. Nominal interest rates on deposits were maintained at 15 percent, while during 1986 the rate of inflation slipped below the 15-percent mark. Compared to international standards, this positive real interest rate was still modest and hardly sufficient to generate a revival of foreign investment or to stop the flight of capital. Additional progress toward liberalization of the banking system and the securing of positive real interest rates was marked by a Bank of Greece decision in February 1987, enabling commercial banks to determine their own interest rates on seven-day and three-month time deposits. Additionally, the 20-21.5-percent ceilings on interest rates on selected loans, which currently account for over 50 percent of total bank credit, have been abolished, replaced by a minimum rate of 21 percent. Also the process of gradually unifying the complex interest rate schedule has been resumed with a one percentage point increase in subsidized rates on loans to agriculture and small manufacturing firms. Commercial banks have been authorized to issue certificates of deposit for amounts of over Dr 5 million with freely negotiable interest rates.

Industrial profitability has improved markedly, particularly in the manufacturing sector, since implementation of the stabilization program. The upturn in profitability was brought about by the steep deceleration in wage costs combined with limited liberalization of price controls. The OECD reported that, excluding the "ailing enterprises," business profits increased by about 50 percent in 1986, and that the profit share of national income was expected to rise by about four percentage points to 32 percent in the two years to 1987. But the improvement in profitability has yet to be reflected in private investment as a whole. Investment improved in 1986 only in construction, while sluggish investment in plant and machinery reflected continued uncertainty. The investment climate improved somewhat with the invitation extended by Papandreou to foreign investors at the world economic forum in Davos, Switzerland, and the extension of repatriation rights to non-EC investors.[27] However, two months later investor confidence was dampened when the government introduced legislation, which was later revoked, to acquire a controlling interest in the North Aegean Petroleum Company (NAPC) on security grounds.

CONCLUSION

With the two-year austerity program approaching its scheduled conclusion, the government has said it intends to move from the policy of "stabilization" to one of "development." While inflation and the public sector and external deficits have shown substantial improvement, few would argue the stabilization of macroeconomic imbalances is a *fait accompli* . Economic adjustment is a long-term process, especially when the rigidities that generated the imbalances are so deeply entrenched in the structure of an economy. Enlargement of the EC to include two keen Southern European competitors makes the adjustment process even more difficult for Greece.

The stabilization program has been criticized for its strict reliance on demand management policies that unduly restrained growth. Political considerations, and the fact that the government was the captive of its own rhetoric, seemed to have prevented introduction of supply-side measures necessary for sustained economic growth, and obviated the reforms in fiscal accounts that will be necessary to ensure a lasting reduction in public sector deficits in order to make room for private sector activity.

While new plans for development should center around investment incentives and removal of the supply-side impediments to growth, pursuit of development objectives cannot ignore the continuing structural problems underlying the public sector and external deficits. If the structural deficits of the public pension funds (IKA and NAT) cannot be contained in the medium-term, any investment plans contained in the development strategy may be frustrated by further financial "crowding out." And, if the inflation differential between Greece and the EC is not reduced, long-term problems can be anticipated by the export sector on which development relies in a small open economy such as that of Greece.[28]

A limited degree of government intervention can be a positive contribution to the development process if it is forward-looking, rather than protective. Policy should be geared toward promoting a shift in resources from consumption to the traded goods sector and to dynamic developing markets, rather than focusing on the propping-up of declining industries. To cite the example of Spain again, rather than bailing out declining industries with new loans, the Spanish government has implemented a policy of *saneamiento* (restoration to health), by which the industry is rationalized and made more efficient through investment in new plants and equipment and reduction of overmanning. Moves by Greek authorities to liquidate a number of heavily indebted industries show some realization of the futility of encouraging the operation of inefficient enterprises.

While it did not achieve all the planned objectives, the stabilization program did lay the groundwork for growth, most significantly through the deceleration of unit labor costs and the improvement in corporate profitability. Returning to the government's initial objective to improve productivity, the opportunity now exists to try a more rational economic approach through the revival of private investment spending. As stated in the introductory premises, only through substantial new capital investment can the productivity of labor increase sufficiently to support higher wages and create new employment opportunities. Promotion of such investment will depend critically upon the ability of interest rates to reflect real rates of return on competing investment opportunities, thereby enabling capital to seek the more productive ventures.

Development of an active capital market in Greece must thus be an integral part of the new development strategy, in terms of both private sector investment and more efficient public sector borrowing. It is important that early moves are made to nurture genuine capital markets (as a substitute for commercial bank intermediation) and to reduce the control on the expansion of bank credit. The gradual liberalization of interest rates and the creation of alternative forms of investment have been important first steps, as has the abolition of the requirement of banks to earmark 15 percent of deposits for special investment purposes. Recommendations made by a special committee established to study financial sector reform focused on allowing market conditions to dictate bank lending rates, dismantling the existing complex system of secondary reserve requirements and regulated interest rates, and limiting central bank policy tools to primary reserve requirements and the rediscount rate.

Liberalization of labor markets in terms of wage determination and hiring and firing practices should also figure prominently in the development strategy. Just as is true in the case of other costs, wages play an important role in the allocation of a scarce resource (here, labor) to more productive industries. Wage indexation, while perhaps an effective temporary tool to reduce inflationary expectations, can in the longer term act as an impediment to the functioning of wages as a determinant of labor demand, since employers in rapidly growing industries cannot raise wages to reflect their increasing needs for labor. This is not to advocate the complete and immediate abolition of the tight wages policy that fostered the reduction in unit labor costs. The *modified* indexation mechanism still has a role to play in continuing to moderate price expectations, at least until inflation reaches the EC average. Yet indexation is an interventionist mechanism, and in a more liberalized economic environment can be gradually phased out to allow wages to promote more productive use of the Greek labor force.

Foreign investment will still be a central element of any development strategy. The stabilization program made possible an improvement of creditworthiness for the Greek government. With the restoration of access to international credit markets in 1987 monetary authorities were able to prepay or refinance several bilateral loans with foreign commercial banks (equivalent to about $700 million). The rescheduling was planned to help smooth out the hump in debt service payments in 1988-89. Yet in the absence of a lasting turnaround in the external account, this rescheduling merely postpones future reckoning with international lenders. Successful and sustained external adjustment will require stabilizing the current account deficit at a level that can be covered through nondebt capital inflows.

The years 1986 and 1987 represented a move *toward* more rational economic management. Considering the long-term nature of the adjustment process and the sensitivity of the business climate to the direction of policy, such a shift should be nurtured in the medium term, while any signs of adjustment fatigue must be immediately arrested. Yet in slowly revealing plans to follow the completion of the Stabilization Program, the government appears to be again falling back on stimulative, politically expedient objectives. The climate of confidence was dealt a severe blow amid fears of a renewed wage-inflation spiral when in late November 1987 Papandreou retracted plans in which the incomes policy was to remain as the anti-inflationary linchpin of stabilization efforts in 1988. It is up to the Greek policy makers to avoid basing plans for development on such short-term goals, but rather to capitalize on the progress it has achieved *toward* stabilizing the economic imbalances.*

**The views expressed in this essay are those of the author and do not reflect those of the Board of Governors of the Federal Reserve or the London School of Economics. The author acknowledges the valuable comments of Alan Cohen, Rodney Mills, and Joerg Dittmer. Their assistance was instrumental to the completion of my work. Any errors should be attributed to the author.*

NOTES

1. The term *autonomous capital inflows* is used by the Greek authorities and the European Commission to cover inflows from Greeks abroad (including seamen) in the form of real estate investment, equity and working capital investment in Greek enterprises (entrepreneurial capital), and foreign exchange deposits with the banking system.

2. Employers are reluctant to employ additional workers during economic boom periods of strong aggregate demand if they are prevented from readily dismissing excess workers during periods of slack demand.

3. The policy also served to promote immediate short-term political objectives of increasing real wages to low-income groups. Despite New Democracy's *ad hoc* indexation of wages, minimum wage rates and minimum salaries had risen less than the rate of inflation in 1979 and 1980, so that low-income groups had suffered losses in real income.

Increases in *average* earnings, on the other hand, exceeded price increases throughout the entire decade.

4. Actual labor costs to business rose even more than 50 percent because Papandreou legislated a reduction in working hours concurrently with the increase in wages.

5. Workers earning up to Dr 35,000 per month received 100 percent of the percentage rise in the consumer price index (CPI) over the previous four months. For workers earning more than Dr 35,000, the portion of earnings between Dr 35,000 and Dr 55,000 per month was increased 50 percent of the CPI increase; the segment between Dr 55,000 and Dr 80,000 per month received only 25-percent compensation; and for increments greater than Dr 80,000 no indexation was provided.

6. Unemployment statistics for Greece are not considered to be highly accurate due to significant underemployment as well as disguised employment in the large agricultural sector.

7. The enlargement of the labor force reflects both higher participation of women (particularly in urban areas) and net repatriation of Greek workers from other European countries as economic growth slowed abroad. The Greek labor force grew at an annual average rate of 1.2 percent in 1982 and 3.4 percent in 1983. The labor force in urban and semiurban areas grew even more rapidly, at an annual average rate of 4 percent in 1982 and 4.3 percent in 1983. Labor force growth appears to have slowed since 1984.

8. Indebtedness alone was not sufficient to qualify a company as "ailing" or "problematic." In addition, it had to meet one of the criteria of 1) suspending operations for economic reasons, 2) ceasing payments to creditors, 3) declaring bankruptcy or being placed under receivership, 4) accumulating total indebtedness five times greater than capital and reserves and showing an evident inability to service its debts, or 5) being declared important for national defense or for development of national resources and being unable to service its debt.

9. The dominance of the income effect over the substitution effect in the labor market produces the phenomenon known in microeconomics as the "backward-bending" supply curve of labor.

10. The PCEs had been dually affected by both increased minimum wages and by the forced absorption of so much new employment.

11. Relative unit labor costs and relative inflation rates are among the factors affecting the exchange rate of a currency. All other things being the same, the currency of a high-inflation country would depreciate (i.e., fewer units of foreign currency would be required to buy a unit of domestic currency) relative to the currency of a low-inflation country, so that the domestic currency price increase would be offset by the (foreign currency) price decrease of the currency itself. Thus the world price of the export good would remain stable and competitive.

The mechanism through which the higher domestic price would affect the exchange rate is the demand curve: at an initially unchanged exchange rate the foreign currency price of the good would rise, foreign demand for the good would decline, and with it demand for the currency with which to pay for the good. Reduced demand for the currency means its equilibrium price would fall, given a free exchange market.

12. Use of other indexes, such as wholesale prices or manufacturing prices, yields an even greater appreciation in real, effective terms.

13. Development of the shipping industry, particularly in newly industrializing countries such as Korea and Taiwan, led to a substantial expansion of world shipping capacity. At the same time demand for shipping services had fallen, primarily as a result of the deceleration in world trade, associated with the global recession of the early 1980s.

14. The Heracles takeover did not reflect the establishment of an explicit government takeover policy. However, the suddenness of the action concerning one of Greece's largest export industries, on what appeared to be trumped-up legal charges against the management of the company, may have scared off would-be investors.

15. "Non-debt" private inflows include such capital account items as direct foreign investment, other long-term "entrepreneurial" capital, and foreign exchange deposits.

16. France had been granted a similar loan by the EC in 1983, although with a less stringent monitoring clause. Italy had requested assistance in 1976 and 1977. Ireland also had approached the EC for assistance in 1976.

17. The loan mechanism, originally known as the "oil facility," was established in 1975 to provide aid to member states experiencing balance-of-payments difficulties associated with the first oil crisis. The mechanism has been modified on two occasions: in March 1981 and in April 1985. The changes have been geared toward increasing the flexibility of the facility. The link between the balance-of-payments difficulties and petroleum product prices was loosened in 1981 and abolished altogether in 1985. The ceiling for borrowing operations was increased to 8 billion Eurocurrency units (the equivalent of $6 billion at current exchange rates) from its original $3 billion (the limit on the 1975 instrument was specified in dollar terms). The choice of borrowing and lending techniques was made more flexible to take better advantage of prevailing market conditions and to allow loans to be more closely adapted to the needs of borrowing member countries. Provisions were also made for the loan to be drawn down in installments and for the borrowing member to request the inclusion of an early repayment clause. With the accession of Britain (1973) and Greece (1981), the quota schedule was also adjusted. Also, in the original formulation, the EC Council of Ministers would develop and attach to the loan a set of economic policy conditions thought necessary to restore external equilibrium. This responsibility to draw up an adjustment program was shifted to the borrowing nation in a series of

modifications to the mechanism made in 1981. The council retained the ability to outline economic policy conditions to be attached to the loan, as well as the option to negotiate additional quantitative targets.

18. Between July and October the real, effective rate depreciated by about 6 percent.

19. Agricultural subsidies were reduced as a function both of the government's lowering of agricultural prices and of larger transfers from the EC agricultural support fund.

20. The price freeze was imposed for the ostensible purpose of preventing profiteering prior to the imposition of the value-added tax (VAT) on 1 January 1987. However, it should be noted that in the months preceding imposition of the price freeze, the twelve-month rate of inflation was running well above the 16-percent target rate for the end of the year.

21. Transfer payments include subsidies and grants from the EC budget and are different from the $750 million received from the loan. Another external factor contributing to the apparent success in reducing the current account deficit was an $800 million increase in remittances from Greek workers living abroad.

22. Unlike wages, tax brackets were not indexed to inflation. Thus, as incomes rose to keep up with inflation, wage and salary earners were pushed into higher income-tax brackets.

23. The combined operating deficit of the PCEs and social welfare funds amounted to 3 percent of the GDP in 1985 and was largely accounted for by the deficits of the two social insurance funds: the Workers' Social Insurance Organization (IKA) and the Farmers' Social Insurance Organization (OGA). The operating deficit of OGA rose by over 50 percent in the first quarter of 1986.

24. Employment in the PCEs rose by about 2.5 percent in 1986.

25. The savings rate dropped sharply from 22 percent in 1985 to 17.5 percent in 1986.

26. Retail sales increased, especially for automobiles and consumer durables that are considered investment items in Greece.

27. EC and non-EC investors have conditional repatriation rights: by a Bank of Greece decree, effective 25 July 1986, dividends and profits from new investments in productive activities made by U.S. and other non-EC investors can be repatriated, provided the investor has properly registered his project with Greek authorities. These supposedly "unlimited repatriation rights" are subject to the approval of the minister of the economy on a case-by-case basis. Furthermore, an across-the-board hold on repatriation can be implemented whenever it is determined that the Greek economy is experiencing a foreign exchange crisis. The repatriation provisions do not become effective before November 1988.

28. Even at the reduced rate of 13 percent, estimated for 1987, the rate of inflation in Greece would still be four times as high as the EC average.

PASOK and the Greek Americans Origins and Development

James G. Pyrros

Editor's Note: In preparing this volume, the editor and publisher had one objective in their selection of scholars and specialists in Greek affairs: that each should offer the best account in the subject area of his or her individual expertise. Neither style nor political perspective would be allowed to interfere with this goal. Thus the reader no doubt will note a diversity of styles and approaches in the essays. Some are strictly academic, others reflect perspectives acquired while the authors served in official capacities in either the U.S. or Greek government, and several others adopt a narrative style that permits a wealth of anecdotal information to be effectively presented.
James G. Pyrros's piece on the origins of PASOK's relations with the Greek American community is an excellent essay, which contains important information on the development of a relationship between Greece and its diaspora. The style is free-flowing, and the informational content superb. It is hoped that Pyrros's anecdotal essay will encourage further studies on a subject that merits closer scrutiny than it usually gets.

I

The year was 1973. It was a warm summer evening in Washington, D.C. A small group of us—exiled Greeks, Greek Americans, Americans, all anti-junta—were gathered for drinks, conversation, and political gossip at The Piccadilly, an outdoor cafe on Connecticut Avenue.

The eldest among us, a wise, retired old State Department hand, Charilaos "Charley" Lagoudakis, asked the question, "What is the single greatest contribution the Greek immigrants have made to America?"

"Their gift for business enterprise," someone ventured.

"No," he said, "although that *is* a considerable contribution. I believe it is the fact that in the course of a few decades, and in less than two generations, they have managed to establish over 450 churches. There is at least one Greek Orthodox church or chapel in every one of the fifty states. That is a remarkable achievement. It is the Greeks who are responsible for establishing the Greek Orthodox Church in America."

A practical and significant consequence of this is that Greek Americans have achieved a presence in every part of the country. Thus, when the Turkish invasion of Cyprus occurred in July 1974, followed by the second Turkish offensive in August, the Greek American community was suddenly agitated, and every member of Congress seemed to know a Greek American in his or her district. Again and again one heard members of Congress describe Greek Americans as friends who have never before asked for anything. During the ensuing legislative battle over a Turkish arms embargo there was, figuratively speaking, someone firing from behind every bush. This added snap and crackle to the case.

The establishment of Greek churches had begun with the first rush of immigration in 1900-10. By the time the Cyprus crisis erupted in 1974, the Greek experience in America had reached into a third and fourth generation. The flavor of the community is changing rapidly. Counting the original immigrants as the first generation, it is fair to say that in the third and fourth generations, the language has been lost and the intermarriage rate is very high. In many communities, priests say, over 80 percent of marriages being performed are between Greek and non-Greek persons. Thus there is a great difference between a fourth-generation Greek American in Denver, Colorado, and a recent Greek immigrant in the Astoria section of Queens, New York. One's grasp of the language and the internal political situation in Greece may be virtually nil; the other may read and talk Greek politics with a passion. Nevertheless, both feel a tug of the emotions where Greece, that ancient and ancestral land, is concerned.

Lagoudakis, who served in the tiny intelligence and research section of the State Department until the late 1960s, was known to us for another reason. True, he had been educated in Greece and the United States, was fluent in Greek and Turkish, and had served with the OSS in the Middle East during World War II. True, he had an encyclopedic knowledge of Greek politics and political personalities and was a close friend of Patriarch Athenagoras. More intriguing, however, was that when he taught at Athens College in the 1930s, one of his students was a very young Andreas Papandreou, whom he later would describe as "my best student" and "a shy boy, very bright."

In 1939, during the Metaxas dictatorship in Greece, George Papandreou had written to his friend Lagoudakis, then in the United States. His son, Papandreou said, had already been arrested and beaten by the dictatorship's security forces. If he stayed in Greece, he would be true to his beliefs and surely get into more trouble. Could Lagoudakis help in getting Andreas into an American university? He did. Harvard.

Lagoudakis would later recall that he wrote a strong recommendation, describing Andreas in glowing terms. Harvard authorities, as he tells it, did not realize that Athens College was only a two-year school and accepted young Papandreou as a graduate student. Nevertheless, Andreas met the academic challenge and excelled at Harvard, and later at the University of Minnesota and the University of California, Berkeley. He entered fully into American academic life and remained happy in its relative isolation for two decades.

When Andreas entered Greek politics in 1964, Lagoudakis applauded. In the 1965-67 *anomalia* period, when Andreas had fallen into deep disfavor with the American mission in Athens, Lagoudakis, to the dismay of his State Department colleagues, would frequently make the prediction, "Andreas will be prime minister of Greece some day." Lagoudakis, a mild man, was friendly with everyone. Retired, with little to do, he occasionally responded to department requests to escort Greek junta officials around the United States on leader-grant tours.

Mutual bad feelings had developed between the Papandreous—Andreas and his wife Margaret—and the U.S. Embassy in Athens in the 1965-67 period. Only one diplomat, a relatively junior officer named Bob Keeley, was friendly in his reporting. A popular diplomatic couple, Monte and Toni Stearns, who had become close personal friends of the Papandreous' when they first moved to Greece from California in 1961, had moved on to another post. Deputy Chief of Mission Norbert Anschuetz was respected by the Papandreous and was regarded as relatively open-minded. When told at a Washington lunch in early December 1967 (at a moment when Andreas was in prison, the colonels' junta was in power, and the king's countercoup was a few days away) that the Papandreous seemed to have a higher regard for him than anyone else at the U.S. Embassy, Anschuetz smiled wanly. "They thought I was the least worst," he said. Then, choosing his words carefully, he characterized Andreas in generally negative terms as a mistake-prone, crisis-inducing guy who was a disappointment as a minister in 1964 "because he preferred *la dolce vita.*"

Anschuetz soon faded from the political scene, becoming a banker. Stearns and Keeley, however, were to be heard from again. Each served as U.S. ambassador to Greece during Papandreou's time as prime minister in the 1980s. It may have been natural selection, for both were experienced diplomats, well-versed in Greek affairs, and fluent in the language. At the same time, their appointments revealed an audacious pragmatism on the part of the State Department, which recommended them, and the Reagan administration, which approved. Without Stearns and then Keeley in Greece, relations between the PASOK government and the United States might have become much worse.

Lagoudakis's only known, postcoup contact with Andreas Papandreou occurred in February 1968. Papandreou had been released from prison in a Christmas amnesty and had flown to Paris with his family. He came to the United States to address an Americans for Democratic Action dinner in Washington. The invitation was arranged by LuVerne Conway, then legislative aide to Congressman Don Edwards (D-Calif.).

When Andreas spotted Lagoudakis at the reception before the dinner, he embraced him and exclaimed, "My old teacher!" Lagoudakis did not live to see his former student attain Greece's highest office; he passed away in the mid-1970s.

In my view, the Lagoudakis vignettes suggest, first, the Greek American community is greatly dispersed and has many sides; second, many of the same people appear and reappear in the story of U.S.-Greek relations; and, third, Andreas Papandreou has old and sentimental ties with the United States and Americans, but even though he has some defenders, he has received sharp criticism from U.S. officials at home and abroad.

II

When the question is asked, What has been the relationship between PASOK and the Greek American community? the answer must be that Greek Americans generally know little of PASOK, but have definite impressions of Andreas Papandreou and his American wife, Margaret. In this they are not very different from the voters of Greece. PASOK is Papandreou.

When Papandreou goes, PASOK will go. Or fragment. Or become something else.

To a casual observer, Papandreou would seem to have natural advantages in dealing with the United States. He is fluent and at ease in English, he is a modern man who is charming in private meetings, and he and his family spent years on American college campuses. It is obvious, however, that he has squandered much of this seeming advantage, partly by design, partly by yielding to whim and impulse. Papandreou has thus accumulated, in pollster terms, "high negatives" among informed Americans. It is the kind of burden his Greek political rivals, past and present—Karamanlis, Rallis, Mitsotakis—neither created nor carried. The negatives play themselves out in the Greek American community as well.

And yet it was not always so. There was a time, well before the Papandreous adopted their mix of spit-in-your-eye, angry, indifferent, or defiant stances, when they cared very deeply about how they were regarded by Americans. In the two tumultuous years of the so-called *anomalia* (1965-67), when Andreas's father, George, the head of the Center Union party, was maneuvered out of the position of prime minister after he had won a landslide election, Andreas and Margaret appealed repeatedly to U.S. senators and newspaper columnists. They sent "packets," written material and arguments, to liberal senators, including Wayne Morse, J.W. Fulbright, Robert Kennedy, Eugene McCarthy, and Mike Mansfield, and to columnists Marquis Childs and Drew Pearson. The theme was that they had found American values and ideals to be one thing at home and quite another abroad, that they were worthy of American understanding and support, that the U.S. mission in Athens was distorting its reports as well as contributing to an atmosphere that denied the sovereign will of the Greek voters. Except for several columns by Drew Pearson, the response was disappointing. It would be well then, when the litany of Papandreou's anti-American rhetoric is examined, to remember that in 1965-67 he and his wife cared about American opinion and made strong and even humbling efforts to be understood and liked.

III

The persona of Andreas Papandreou has taken a long journey in his nearly seven decades. He went from being a Greek to becoming an American to becoming a Greek again.

To become a Greek again made sense for Papandreou politically as well as emotionally. When he returned to Greece in 1961 with his American wife and four American-born children, he had been away for more than twenty years. As *New York Times* reporter Henry Kamm wrote in a brilliant portrait, Papandreou for several years thereafter was much more at ease in an American academic-diplomatic environment than he was in the hurly-burly of Greek politics.[1] Gradually he changed, becoming in some respects "Greekier than the Greeks." At first, however, a political career seemed remote. His father was in a minority political situation: Constantine Karamanlis was firmly in power. (Ironically, it was Karamanlis who invited Andreas to return to Greece and work in an economics research center). Andreas, in sociological terms, was the classic marginal man: not fully at home as a Greek, not fully at home as an American. His social circle was initially quite American and included many from the U.S. Embassy, notably Monte and Toni Stearns.

Indeed, the Stearnses retain a pocket-sized copy of Theodore White's *The Making of the President: 1960* with an inscription from Andreas and Margaret, reading, "To Monte and Toni, who helped see us through the first year of our 'Greek Experience.'" With those words the Papandreous spoke explicitly of Greece as an "experience," not as a place to stay and launch a political career.

The political landscape changed abruptly when George Papandreou's Center Union scored an unexpected success in the national elections of November 1963. In February 1964, the Center Union won with a record 53 percent of the vote, and Andreas, who had run as a deputy from Patras, was swept into office.

For a time Andreas benefited from talk that he was "a Greek John F. Kennedy." The martyred U.S. president was enormously popular in Greece and many Greek voters yearned for similar young and modern leadership.

Soon, however, as Andreas entered more deeply into the reality of Greek political life, he found himself attacked from both left and right as a "parachutist," a man who had dropped into Greek politics at the top, without paying his dues. His supposed influence with his aging father unsettled political rivals. There were also suggestions that, having come from America, he must be an American "agent."

Partly because he needed to show he was his own man and

partly because he was truly bothered by the extent of American influence, Papandreou began to disengage. Old friends were offended. One might excuse the disengagement as a practical necessity; the cheap shots were quite another thing. By mid-1965, his old friends at the U.S. Embassy had become very bitter towards him, and the feeling was reciprocated. That bitterness has never been extinguished.

American diplomats and journalists in Athens came to regard Andreas and Margaret Papandreou's claim that they "knew America" as a mere conceit. Papandreou's speeches and comments repeatedly rang false to American ears. This remained the case in 1987. After all, the Papandreou exile was spent in Toronto, Canada. Papandreou and his wife left California more than a quarter of a century ago. On the West Coast they had lived a typical academic life, something apart from both the mainstream of American life and the mainstream of the Greek American community. And yet Papandreou cannot completely shake the American label, nor avoid a Greek conspiratorial mentality that speculates that he is somehow "an agent."

When the colorful composer-political activist Mikis Theodorakis visited Washington in late 1973, he was clearly chagrined by the success his erstwhile friend, Papandreou, was having with the Greek Left. After his Kennedy Center concert, Theodorakis met with a small group of us. Our conversation stretched into the early-morning hours. Of Papandreou, Theodorakis said, "He's either stupid or he's an agent. And we know he's not stupid."[2]

Theodorakis also said that night that when he and Andreas had been on friendlier terms (presumably around 1965-66), the latter had suggested that they approach the Soviet ambassador in Athens and ask for funds to establish a new Greek political party. According to Theodorakis, the Soviet ambassador turned them down. No confirmation of this story has ever been found, and it must be counted a fanciful tale.

More likely, and not irrelevant in consideration of Papandreou's bouts of political romanticism, is another Theodorakis anecdote. Papandreou, who had spent the war years and the civil war years abroad, enthused to Theodorakis, who had stayed in Greece, "Mikis, wouldn't it be great to go to the mountains and fight, to live in the open, and be revolutionaries?"

"Are you kidding?" snorted Theodorakis, as he related it.

"Next time, let the Right go to the mountains. We'll stay in the cities."

IV

When the colonels' coup occurred on 21 April 1967, friends of the Papandreous' in the U.S. academic community took the lead in intervening with the Johnson administration to put pressure on the Greek junta not to harm Papandreou. The plight of Andreas and of thousands of other political prisoners, as well as the suppression of fundamental democratic rights, spawned anti-junta sentiment in the American press. The original anti-junta groups were "Andreist" and university-based. After Andreas was released from prison eight months later, however, those groups tended to fade away or to take on a wider, multiparty point of view.

The most effective anti-junta entity in Washington was the U.S. Committee for Democracy in Greece, formed in October 1967. Its leaders included Congressman Don Fraser (D-Minn.); Congressman Don Edwards (D-Calif.); labor leader and friend of the Kennedy brothers, Jack Conway; Victor Reuther of the United Auto Workers; and an old socialist pamphleteer, Maurice Goldbloom. Its board included such sparkling New Deal personalities as Francis Biddle and Benjamin Cohen, as well as a little-known but level-headed young Washington economist named Angelo Clones. Unfortunately, Clones, a close friend of Papandreou's and his primary Washington contact, passed away in 1971.

Early anti-junta efforts in the U.S. Senate were led by Senator Claiborne Pell (D-R.I.) and Senator Vance Hartke (D-Ind.). Over the years, Senators Stephen Young (D-Ohio), J.W. Fulbright (D-Ark.), and Henry Jackson (D-Wash.), among others, made valuable contributions. On the House side, Fraser and Edwards recruited their friend Congressman Benjamin Rosenthal (D-N.Y.). In 1971, Rosenthal became chairman of the European Subcommittee of the House Foreign Affairs Committee and began a series of unprecedented hearings on the situation in Greece. The hearings were politically important at the time and provide a rich body of historical information concerning the junta years. Others who played a part in the House of Representatives included the irascible Congressman Wayne Hays (D-Ohio); Congressman Lucien Nedzi (D-Mich.), an important figure in defense matters; and Congressman Ogden Reid (R-N.Y.). Mention must also be made of Cliff Hackett, a committee staffer for Congressman Rosenthal, and Richard Moose, a staffer for Senator Fulbright.

V

The Papandreous established themselves in Toronto, Canada, where Andreas took an academic position at York University. He returned to Washington in the spring of 1968 for a series of meetings. He met with Deputy Secretary of State Nicholas Katzenbach and took a certain grim satisfaction in the fact that the unsmiling notetaker for the department was Daniel Brewster, son of a missionary to Greece, a classmate of his at Athens College, head of the State Department's Greek Desk, and a longtime foe. Papandreou's most hopeful meeting was with Senator Robert Kennedy. The two met in the hours just prior to Kennedy's announcement of his candidacy for president.

Whether it was the death of Bobby Kennedy that symbolically closed all doors, or the lack of encouragement that Papandreou found among those in the executive branch of the U.S. government, or simply the result of a cool analysis of where the Greek electorate was heading, after that Papandreou turned away from the American scene. He visited Washington only once more, in 1969, when the venerable, bombastic Greek American attorney, George Vournas, hosted a fund-raiser for him at the Vournas farm in suburban Maryland.

Slowly Papandreou began to put together a political network of friends and supporters in Europe and North America, and to redefine himself. Although on 10 March 1968, in an appearance on "Meet the Press," he had said, "Socially and economically I am what you might call a New Dealer," he entered into an ersatz socialism, one that passed through many phases.[3] Spurning the social-democratic parties and personalities of Western Europe, he adopted a posture of "Nenni socialism." When he approached the day of assuming power in 1981, he changed course and urged interviewers to regard him as of the same mold as France's Mitterrand. Once in power, he became something else again.

Margaret Papandreou visited Washington more often than Andreas. In 1971 she was an excellent and spirited witness before the European Subcommittee. At other times she was a rather forlorn figure carrying a PAK sign at anti-Vietnam War rallies on the Mall. When Greece returned to democracy, Margaret continued to display her fondness for protest marches.

Year after year, on 17 November she would be in the leading ranks of demonstrators marching on the U.S. Embassy in Athens to mark the anniversary of the 1973 uprising of the Athens Polytechnic students, which had been put down bloodily by the junta security forces and the army. Her role annoyed a succession of American ambassadors, who regarded the targeting of the U.S. Embassy by the demonstrators as hypocritical and selective. The United States was not responsible for the events at the Polytechnic, surely not directly so; the Greek police and the Greek army were. Better to scapegoat the United States, however, than to march on police and army barracks. On the other hand, Margaret did not indulge her yen for demonstrations when it came to human rights for the Greek Epirotes in Albania. It was easier to demonstrate about the situation in Chile and Nicaragua. In her choice of interests, she was still "acting like an American."

All through the junta years, U.S. policymakers and "old Greek hands" continued to criticize Papandreou. Jack Maury, for example, had been CIA station chief in Athens at the time of the 21 April 1967 coup. Maury, a charming Virginian with an ancestor who was the teacher of Thomas Jefferson, had no love for the colonels but retained a fondness for the monarchy. In the early 1970s he became the CIA's liaison officer with the two intelligence committees in the Congress. As a specialist on the Soviet Union, he had been the agency's case officer from Washington in running Colonel Oleg Penkovsky, generally regarded as one of the most important spies ever recruited by the Americans. (Penkovsky provided military documents that proved invaluable during the 1962 Cuban missile crisis.)

Maury tended to treat Greek matters rather more lightly. "How's your friend, Andy Pappy-n-dreou?" he would ask in his slight drawl. "He's through politically, don't you think? Ol' Andy is addlepated."[4] (*Addlepated* is a rarely used word meaning "a confused, muddled fellow.")

Few dismissed Andreas as easily as did Maury.[5] Greek and American specialists speculated constantly on what Papandreou might do and what Papandreou was thinking. There was also an inordinate interest in his reportedly turbulent personal life. Similar speculation went on on the Greek side in the 1974-81 period, when the Karamanlis and Rallis governments were constantly looking over their shoulders, determining their conduct by what Andreas might do.

After 1968, Papandreou was not involved in the anti-junta

struggle in Washington. Other exiles, notably journalist Elias Demetracopoulos and General Orestes Vidalis, a participant in the failed countercoup of 13 December 1967, played far wider and more important roles. To a lesser degree, former Greek Embassy officials John Nicolopoulos and Telis Sismanides also played important roles. None were under any illusions: if and when democracy returned to Greece, the two dominant political personalities would be Constantine Karamanlis and Andreas Papandreou.

VI

When the history of the American response to the Greek junta is written, it will be recorded that the institutions that behaved most honorably and perceptively were the U.S. Congress, the American press, and the academic world. In the academic sector, certain Greek American professors—especially Theodore Couloumbis of American University and Nikolaos Stavrou of Howard University, both in Washington, D.C.; George Anastaplo of Rosary College, Chicago; and Adamantia Pollis of the New School for Social Research, New York—were very much involved.

The U.S. Committee for Democracy in Greece, led by traditional liberàls, was way ahead of the five-man Greek American congressional delegation. As the committee evaluated them, Congressmen John Brademas (D-Ind.) and Paul Sarbanes (D-Md.) were on the anti-junta side, Congressmen Peter Kyros (D-Maine) and Gus Yatron (D-Pa.) were on the pro-junta side, and Congressman Nick Galifianakis (D-N.C.) was completely indifferent. Brademas waited until 1971 to make his first strong anti-junta statement, at the European Subcommittee hearings. The statement was outstanding, if overdue. Sarbanes, who was first elected to Congress in 1970, quietly supported Brademas, but his position was so muted that it went virtually unnoticed and provided no rallying point. As for Galifianakis—Melina Mercouri, meeting him in the U.S. Capitol restaurant for the first and only time, confronted his indifference. She hotly accused him of embarrassing not only his Greek heritage, but even worse, his Cretan forebears!

Once the Turkish invasion of Cyprus occurred in 1974, Brademas, Rosenthal, and Sarbanes emerged as the undisputed leaders in congressional debates on Cyprus and the Turkish arms embargo.

The U.S. Committee for Democracy in Greece had provided

an invaluable foundation for the anti-junta movement in the House of Representatives. Senators Pell, Jackson, and Fulbright had done the same in the Senate. They had made the anti-junta struggle a liberal issue. When the Turkish arms embargo issue came along, it found a large, ready-made base. In addition, a contingent of about thirty conservative Republicans, unhappy with Kissinger's détente policy towards the Soviet Union and seeking a means to punish him, joined those who opposed the junta. And then there were the scores of House and Senate members who were hearing from old Greek friends who had never before asked for anything. The result was one rebuke after another for President Ford and Secretary Kissinger when they attempted to lift the embargo.

The sheer equity of the case could not be overlooked then, nor can it be now. Few, except the self-styled "ambassador from Ankara," Congressman Stephen Solarz (D-N.Y.), would defend the second Turkish offensive on the island. Without the equities, no amount of activity by the so-called Greek lobby would have any effect.

VII

During the junta years (1967-74), the record of what may be termed the Greek American establishment in America, namely, the Church, AHEPA, and the Greek press, was a sorry one.

In a time of moral and political crisis in Greece, the head of the Greek Orthodox Church in America, Archbishop Iakovos, was silent. He held the Clergy-Laity Conference in the junta's Greece in 1968, and maneuvered for Greek and U.S. government support in a futile quest to succeed Athenagoras as patriarch. After more than six years of inaction, he responded to Cretan American friends and finally chanced a private letter to Secretary of State William Rogers regarding the imprisonment of two Greek political figures, one of whom was Cretan. Part of the letter was leaked by a State Department source and reached a *New York Times* reporter. The reporter confronted Iakovos, who reluctantly conceded the letter's authenticity. The junta ritually protested this "interference" in Greek affairs; Iakovos squirmed and, in this curious way, chalked up his only score on the credit side of the anti-junta ledger.

AHEPA, the largest Greek-American fraternal order, was actively pro-junta, both in messages to the U.S. Congress and in frequent trips by delegations to Athens. In seven years, only one AHEPA president, Dr. Michael Spirtos of Warren, Ohio, diverged from this path.

Of the Greek-language dailies, *Atlantis*, under Vlastos, was rabidly pro-junta until it folded for business reasons after many decades. The *National Herald* , under Markettos and Makrias, also supported the junta, but in a less excited manner. Both relied heavily on Greek government advertising. The Boston-based English language weekly, the *Hellenic Chronicle* , edited by Peter Agris, was consistently pro-junta, even distributing buttons in its support. One of its frequent targets was Andreas Papandreou.

Yet the Greek American community, taken as a whole, was not pro-junta. My personal evaluation at the time was that put to a test, the community would vote pro-democracy; without a dramatic, crystallizing event, the community would remain 5 percent anti-junta, 5 percent pro-junta, and 90 percent indifferent. When it came to testimony on Capitol Hill, however, the quality was all on the side of the anti-junta forces, who invoked American and Greek ideals as well as skillful political arguments. The pro-junta testimony, given primarily by a psychiatrist, N. Destounis, and a professor, D. Koussoulas, reads very poorly indeed sixteen years later.

VIII

The dramatic, crystallizing event occurred in August 1974, with the second Turkish offensive.

The 19 July invasion of Cyprus, following as it did the Greek junta-directed coup, the attempt to murder Makarios, and the installation of the notorious Nikos Sampson, did not arouse the passion that the second Turkish offensive in mid-August did. The junta of Greece and Cyprus had fallen by then; Karamanlis was in power in Athens; a cease-fire had been agreed to; and George Mavros, newly freed from prison, was Greece's foreign minister negotiating in Geneva. The Turkish power move was naked and undisguised.

Greek Americans rose up in anger at the Turks and at Secretary of State Henry Kissinger for his handling of the issue.[6] A deep and terrible ancestral memory was stirred. It seemed that nearly everyone had within his or her psyche a sense of Turkish oppression—of family, of fellow Greeks, or of other peoples. More than four hundred years of occupation of Greek lands and the blood spilled in this century on Crete, in the Balkan wars, and in Asia Minor had left their mark. The murder, pillage, and rape that accompanied the Turkish military thrust against defenseless Cypriot civilians triggered the collective memory and reopened old wounds—thus the outrage, the outpouring of letters and telegrams, and the personal visits to members of Congress.

The Cyprus issue united Greek Americans as it did the people of Greece. To this day, even though passions have inevitably subsided, Turkish aggression on Cyprus and the perceived threat to the Greek islands remain a worry. No one has stroked this theme more vigorously than Papandreou. The effect of what he may say on other matters may vary, but the mention of "the Turkish threat" always assures him a favorable response.

IX

It is one of the ironies of Greek-U.S. relations that the normally skillful Henry Kissinger, much criticized for his blundering and self-congratulating performance during the Cyprus crisis, became the inadvertent father of both the Greek lobby and the 10:7 ratio.

Kissinger's conduct in the aftermath of the 15 July 1974 coup against Makarios was made worse by his angry and stubborn efforts in the prolonged series of battles over the Turkish arms embargo. Several groups sprang up and plunged into an informal concert of action in support of certain congressional initiatives. Anger at Kissinger was intense. Thus a Greek lobby was formed where none had previously existed.

Of course, without congressional leadership the Greek lobby's efforts would have foundered. That leadership was provided by Brademas, Rosenthal, and Sarbanes in the House and by Thomas Eagleton (D-Mo.) in the Senate. The primary link to the Greek American community, though not the only link, was provided by Brademas and Sarbanes. Both Rhodes scholars, they were respected in and out of Congress and by the media. Moreover, they addressed the Cyprus issue in American terms and in the context of U.S. foreign policy. While one small English-language Greek newspaper featured the foolish headline "Greek Power Wins" after a congressional vote, those in the know understood that a position on a foreign-policy vote was jeopardized if it was reduced to strictly an ethnic issue.

Greek Americans kept in mind that Kissinger had once scored a temporary public-relations gain at a time when he faced a recalcitrant Israeli position. He had invited a group of American Orthodox Jews to the White House. When they emerged to be interviewed on television, wearing yarmulkes and speaking with accents, they conveyed foreignness that did not help their position. Thus, when Kissinger invited a Greek American group to the White House, they made sure that those who spoke for them were successful public officials and others who looked and sounded as smooth as the smoothest television anchors.

X

As the long succession of votes on the Turkish arms embargo unfolded, many astute political observers were impressed with how quickly and expertly "the word went out" to Greek Americans across the country. The phenomenon Lagoudakis had alluded to was at work. Greek Americans, gathered around their local churches for religious and secular purposes, formed a coast-to-coast communications network.

Several elements combined to form the support group for this immediate and long-term effort. There was the new United Hellenic American Congress (UHAC), with strong ties to the church, headed by Andrew Athens, a respected Chicago businessman prominent among the Greek Orthodox laity. There was a secular, unattached group, the American Hellenic Institute, organized by Eugene Rossides, a former assistant secretary of the treasury. Quiet during the junta, he had been a very active figure in the 1950s in the movement for Cyprus's independence from British colonial rule. Rossides, a street-smart attorney with the powerhouse law firm of Rogers & Wells, was especially adept at organizing legal research and marshalling arguments for the embargo, as well as at raising funds from his Republican party colleagues. A third, smaller, and later effort was mounted by New York-based Greek shipowner George Livanos, who had prospered under the junta. He formed the American Hellenic Alliance. AHEPA, with its scores of local chapters, became active. The American Greek press—including the *National Herald*, the *Hellenic Chronicle*, and the newly formed *Hellenic Times* of New York and the *Western Hellenic Journal* of San Francisco—gave prominent coverage to the struggle.

The practical consequence of the embargo in the near term was that Greece's armed forces, badly out of shape, were given a healthy boost. This put them in better balance with Turkey. The embargo also established the U.S. Congress, in the Greek perception, as a counterweight to Kissinger on Greek-Turkish issues. The congressional votes were a solace to a Greek population seething over the humiliation of Hellenism and troubled by seven years of inaction and the acceptance of the junta by the American executive branch.

The embargo eventually ran its course, but it remained in place for a time even after a maneuver by Kissinger that led to the 10:7 ratio. In 1975, Kissinger, freewheeling architect of U.S. foreign policy under President Ford, in discussing a new base agreement with the Turkish foreign minister, publicly offered the Turks $1 billion in military aid over four years. There was immediate dissent in Congress, for three reasons: first, the embargo was still in existence; second, Congress traditionally did not approve foreign aid for more than one or two years at a time, because it would lose an element of its control over the appropriation of funds; and, finally, the aid package did not depend on Turkish concessions. Brademas was among those issuing statements in opposition.

Kissinger then publicly offered Greece a similar four-year deal with $700 million in military aid. Prime Minister Karamanlis and Foreign Minister Rallis thereupon made a hardheaded decision. Accurately perceiving that after so many votes the embargo would eventually be overturned and fearing that Greece, which did no lobbying in Washington on the issue, would nevertheless be blamed by Turkey, they found the ratio inherent in the Kissinger offer suddenly attractive. Without consulting or informing the government of Cyprus, Karamanlis grabbed the offer.

Thus was formed the basis of the 10:7 ratio passed by Congress soon thereafter, a ratio which continues to this day. It is a ratio more favorable to Greece than Turkey's population advantage (at the time over 50 million to Greece's 9 million) might suggest. In the following decade, the 10:7 ratio became imbedded in congressional attitudes. Powerful veterans like William Broomfield (R-Mich.) and Dante Fascell (D-Fla.) in the House and Joe Biden (D-Del.) in the Senate joined with the steady Sarbanes to maintain the balance. With each year, Congress developed a vested interest in confirming its earlier judgment. Their victories were abetted by Turkish intransigence regarding a Cyprus settlement.

XI

In my judgment, the changing character of the Greek American community was illustrated by what took place in Washington on Sunday, 18 August 1974, a few days after the quick and devastating second Turkish offensive began.

In an unprecedented display, thousands of Greek Americans demonstrated peacefully in front of the White House—in fact, all the way around the White House . Even the marchers were astonished. Organizers, who had put things together in three or four days, expected 2,000 people. Instead, over 20,000 turned out in what the Washington media called "a vast outpouring. " (President Ford, incidentally, was playing golf and did not witness the demonstration.)

Never before had Greek Americans demonstrated in such numbers. Historically, they had been cautious and hardworking, and had kept a low profile. They placed emphasis on getting along in the new land, seeking economic opportunity, and providing an education for their children. The unwritten rule was "Let's not call attention to ourselves." It was akin to the prayers of Jews in the American South who did not want their small communities to be conspicuous. Essayist Harry Golden characterized this attitude with the line "Please send us a blond rabbi."

Before 1965, the Greek immigration quota was a mere 308 a year, a shamefully low figure set by the Immigration Act of 1924, which discriminated against people from eastern and southeastern Europe. The 1965 Immigration Reform Act, proposed by John F. Kennedy and enacted under Lyndon Johnson, changed all that. An average of 12,000 new Greek immigrants a year began arriving; the ranks of the Hellenic community in America were being replenished at last. The newcomers were often urbanized. The street march was familiar and popular with them.

A clear majority of the demonstrators that Sunday in August 1974 were recent Greek immigrants. Many were New York city taxi drivers, an occupation that would have been rare for earlier immigrants. Hundreds drove their own taxis, jammed with friends and family, down to Washington. Others came by chartered bus and plane from Chicago, Detroit, and even San Francisco. Banners were unfurled, slogans chanted, and a near-festive air created. Over the long haul, however, the leadership and legislative moxie came from the American-born.

XII

And what of the Papandreous? Andreas and Margaret, after 1968, had established themselves in Toronto, provided an American education for their children, and kept in touch with their supporters. Andreas earned a living by teaching, lecturing, and writing.

It could not have been easy; the junta had stayed on for a very long time, and the future was uncertain. Andreas, despite a reputation for impulsiveness, made some calculated moves. Instead of building upon his acknowledged strength in the Center Union, he abandoned it and moved left. While in exile, he eschewed coalitions with other political leaders. He formed a movement called PAK. Upon returning to Greece in 1974, he formed a socialist party and named it PASOK. He also played for the long haul, displaying a patience missing in his precoup behavior.

During the 1974-1981 period, Papandreou took pains to distance himself from the United States, and not only in his anti-NATO, antibases rhetoric. Donning a leather jacket and open shirt, passé American New Left trademarks soon abandoned for more conventional garb, he instructed PASOK cadres to have no contact with the men and women of the American mission in Athens. In 1975 he himself refused to receive visiting Congressmen John Brademas and Paul Sarbanes, who were meeting with the top political leadership in both Greece and Cyprus. Papandreou is also known to have shunned his old friend Monte Stearns, American deputy chief of mission, when they both attended diplomatic receptions at other embassies. It was as if Papandreou were constructing a *cordon sanitaire* around himself and PASOK to prevent the reality or appearance of infection.

While it may fairly be said that Papandreou succeeded in building a party of the non-communist Left—no small achievement—it can also be said that he planted seeds of anti-Americanism that festered among the Greek press and public long after a tactical gain had been achieved.

A longtime Washington observer and friend of Papandreou's declared with exasperation: "They say it is 'tactics.' Listen, when the Germans transported Lenin in a sealed boxcar to the Finland Station, that may have been tactically right. But strategically it turned out to be a disaster. They are playing with fire." He added: "Here Greece has a chance at last to join the First World and Andreas acts like he wants to join the Third World. It's ridiculous! How does all that serve Greece's vital interests?"

In 1980, as his ascension to power neared, Papandreou and his PASOK colleagues gradually began seeing Westerners, including Americans. He dropped hints that under certain conditions, and if given better terms, he would consider renewing the base agreements. Regrettably, the disproportionate emphasis the United States has long given to the military bases in its relations with Greece puts the United States in a position where it can be manipulated both in Greek public opinion and in the negotiations themselves.

When Papandreou was elected prime minister in autumn 1981, the American ambassador he found in office was the newly arrived Monte Stearns. Their relations during the next four years proved to be correct, even amiable. Indeed, Stearns was often viewed back in Washington as too understanding, too willing to give Papandreou the benefit of the doubt.

As prime minister, Papandreou has officially received thousands of political visitors from all over the world. Included among them have been an incredible number of American congressmen, diplomats, and representatives of the military. He has also received scores of AHEPA delegations, Greek Orthodox Church officials from the United States, and other Greek Americans.

One of the most important visits was from Congressman Benjamin Rosenthal (D-N.Y.) in January 1982. It came at a time when Papandreou's embrace of Yasir Arafat, the PLO, and bitterly anti-Israeli Arab elements angered and galvanized American's Jewish community. Washington-based journalist Elias Demetracopoulos, a friend of both Papandreou's and Rosenthal's, arranged the visit. The congressman and the prime minister had a long, productive talk. For a time, Papandreou eased his rhetoric regarding the Middle East. Rosenthal, in turn, gave an analytical, restrained, and sympathetic assessment of Papandreou at the Biannual AHEPA Congressional Dinner in Washington.

For the past six years, Papandreou has regularly sent official delegations to the United States. They are often led by his wife Margaret or by their mild-mannered son, George, a PASOK deputy. One wonders if, to use a carnival term, they are "doing a soft con." Margaret's speeches to Greek groups come across as patronizing pabulum. On the other hand, her speeches to purely American audiences have a dissonant sound. The Greece of the Papandreous has regularly hired New York and Washington public-relations firms to influence American opinion. None—including Edelman and Associates, a firm previously used and discarded by Turkey—have lasted very long. Greece also hired George Lois, the advertising genius and Greek American, who turned in a rare flop with his awkward "I'm Going Home to Greece" tourism ads. A slick-paper, English-language "political analysis," produced in Athens by the Greek government and addressed to a select U.S. audience, was so heavy-handed as to be useless. Little seemed to be working.

XIII

Despite his charm and fluency in English, his American academic background, and his American wife, Andreas Papandreou seems fated to have it recorded that it was on his watch that Americans "fell out of love" with Greece.

Why?

Perhaps it is because of Papandreou and his colleagues' insistence that they "know America."

In 1983 I had occasion to dine with John Zigdes, an old friend from Washington, now head of a badly shrunken Center Union Party. In early 1974 he had testified bluntly before the European Subcommittee and had been barred from returning to Greece by the Ioannides junta. Articulate, short-tempered, and contentious, Zigdes was a talented phrasemaker. We met at a time when he was at loose ends, before he was invited to run under PASOK auspices and was able to regain his parliamentary seat.

"You know what the problem is with Greece?" he asked rhetorically. He switched to Greek, "The problem with Greece is that the American-educated call the shots."[7]

We all laughed. It was a nice line, and did reflect the fact that a considerable number of PASOK ministers had received their degrees abroad. Many, like Papandreou himself, have non-Greek wives. No particular significance should be attached to this. After all, love is love. But some attention should be given to the fact that a Greek studying in the United States will not fully understand America if he does not seek to immerse himself in the totality of American life beyond the campus.

America's love affair with Greece goes back to the 1820s, when excited by the Greek rebellion against Turkey, Dr. Samuel Gridley Howe, Daniel Webster, and James Monroe led a wave of American philhellenism. The resurrection of a people with a heritage so fraught with history and learning, a people so long under foreign domination, thrilled like a trumpet call through the young American nation. Those good feelings continued into the twentieth century and were given fresh impetus in 1940, when Greece provided the desperate Allies with their first victories against the Axis. After World War II, there was the Truman Doctrine and service by a small but effective Greek expeditionary force in Korea. The advent of jet travel in the early 1960s opened Greece up to the average American tourist, who spread the word about the beauty of the land, the vitality of its people, and their ardent desire to make a worthy place for themselves among nations.

Why the deterioration of relations? It must be conceded that some elements in Greece had fallen out of love with America, too. There was already the hard-core Left, endlessly nursing the bitterness of its defeat in the civil war. Then there were the junta years and U.S. tolerance of the dictatorship. Finally, there was the tragedy of Cyprus. And constantly, in the four decades since World War II, there were curiously insular American policymakers who viewed the world strictly through the prism of the U.S.-Soviet struggle and regarded Greece as mere convenient real estate. Nevertheless, even Americans initially sympathetic to the Papandreous believed they went beyond the bounds of fair criticism.

A Greek American visitor told Papandreou in 1980: "You can go on kicking the elephant in the shins, and for a long time nothing will happen. But one of these days the elephant might kick back." In 1985, in the aftermath of the TWA hijacking, when U.S. officials were frustrated and outraged by shabby security at Athens Airport and Greek indifference to FAA requests for improvements, the elephant kicked back. Congressman Dante Fascell (D-Fla.), pro-Greek chairman of the House Foreign Affairs Committee, was disgusted. His colleague Congressman Dan Mica (D-Fla.), chairman of a subcommittee dealing with airport security, made it clear that his group regarded Athens Airport operations as lax and Greek officials as uncooperative. American public opinion, aroused by vivid television coverage of the drawn-out hijacking drama, turned unfriendly. President Reagan, who, after all, had a moral and legal obligation to protect American citizens abroad, issued his advisory on travel to Greece.

Fairly or unfairly, Greece became identified in the American public mind with hijackings and a softness towards terrorists. This, combined with what many perceive as a series of gratuitous insults by the Papandreous, led to a definite drop in the esteem in which Greece had long been held by the average American.

The habit of both Papandreous, moreover, of equating the United States and the Soviet Union and then criticizing only the United States, inevitably took its toll. The old John Mitchell line "Watch what we do, not what we say," could not overcome the perception.

XIV

In our era of rapid communications, words tailored for one audience quickly get around. More than most leaders, Papandreou was victimized by this reality.

American diplomats and political analysts do not operate in a vacuum; they readily learn of statements, interviews, and off-the-cuff gaffes. Neither do Greek Americans. When American public opinion soured on Papandreou and Greece, Greek Americans were affected, too. They wearied of constantly being placed on the defensive in efforts to help Greece.[8]

I will discuss three instances, among several, that helped to diminish Greece's standing in American public opinion: first, Papandreou's trip to Jaruzelski Poland; second, the TWA hijacking; and, third, the Diane Sawyer interview on CBS's "Sixty Minutes." In doing so, I will put aside Papandreou's impulsive and untrue charge in 1983 that Korean Airlines Flight 007, shot down by the Soviets with great loss of life, was an American spy plane. Also put aside is his PASOK party conference speech, more suitable for an Eastern bloc gathering, in which he described the United States as "the metropolis of imperialism."

THE PAPANDREOU VISIT TO POLAND

In October 1984, Prime Minister Papandreou made an official visit to Poland. He was, as the Athens News Agency said at the time, "the first leader of a western country to visit Poland since the imposition of martial law there in 1981."[9]

Responding to Greek journalists who accompanied him on the trip, Papandreou said: "It is also quite clear that the great outcry in the West against the dissolution of Solidarity is not because the capitalist regimes of the West wish to have 'Solidarity' in their countries. Especially a trade union organization which has a regional, geographic base, rather than a particular sector, or trade, and takes on a purely political dimension.

"So," he continues, "the reason for the attacks was not their great sensitivity...but rather it was mainly because, in view of the enormous and explosive internal difficulties experienced in Poland, it was thought to be the most suitable link, the weakest link in the eastern bloc, where a policy of destabilization could be used in general, with all that could imply for peace in Europe."[10]

Note that Papandreou questions the integrity of the critics of Poland's Communist government while assuming the integrity of his own opinions. Note also that he describes the Western countries not as free, democratic governments but as "capitalist regimes."

Papandreou faulted Solidarity for failing to "operate within the framework of historical possibilities." This refers to the always looming prospect of Soviet intervention, which he does not mention specifically. The threat of Soviet intervention is the club always used by those Polish Communist leaders in power to turn back efforts to liberalize and achieve a degree of national independence. Beirut used it; so did Gomulka, Gierek, and now Jaruzelski. In this regard, Papandreou is in bed with the much-criticized "Sonnenfeldt Doctrine," named after Kissinger's NSC aide, Helmut Sonnenfeldt. In 1976, Sonnenfeldt created a tempest by telling a group of U.S. ambassadors that Soviet dominance in Eastern Europe should not be disturbed, that no hope should be given to those who felt themselves oppressed by regimes not freely chosen but imposed by the Eastern bloc. Lest the peace of Europe be disturbed, of course. As if internal pressures did not force change; as if continuing an oppressive status quo did not invite explosions.

Papandreou, on the plane trip back from Warsaw, criticized the economic sanctions imposed by Western nations—bound to be temporary anyway—but not the reasons for the sanctions. He even mentioned Jaruzelski "promise as time goes on to give the greatest possible prestige to the role of Parliament in relation to the other political forces and institutions in the country.[11] So what is the Polish Parliament's prestige in 1987-1988? Some promise. Some prestige. A mockery.

Papandreou's comments represented a certain ethical erosion on his part, as well as a lack of sensitivity to Poland's painful history.

In the 1820s, when the Greek War of Independence broke out, it was the liberals of Western Europe and distant America who cheered that heroic development. European governments and officials of that time, especially Metternich, argued against doing anything that might upset the geopolitical balance. In 1969-76, Metternich's admirer, Henry Kissinger, then secretary of state, argued against pressuring the Greek junta and later the Turks, lest in each case the geopolitical balance be disturbed. Now Andreas Papandreou, himself a victim of the junta, uses the geopolitical argument.

The truth is that the people of today's Poland have a sense of permanent grievance. Against the Soviet Union. Against their own rulers. The collective memory cannot be expunged. Again and again the grievance will be shadowed by silence and despair, then it will erupt in hope, spiritual uplift, and euphoria.

In the nineteenth century, the oppressed Poles repeatedly rebelled against the Russians, the Austrians, the Germans. Each uprising created exiles. Among the exiles was a man named Sigmund Mineiko, a Polish army officer who fought against the Russians, was captured, sent to Siberia, escaped, made his way to Greece, married a Greek girl, and had several children.[12] One of Mineiko's children was Sophia, the first wife of George Papandreou and mother of Andreas. In 1984, Andreas, given an opportunity to support the spirit of Polish independence and to honor his grandfather's memory, instead supported communist officialdom.

Polish writer Kazimierz Brandys tells of an argument often advanced in pre-Solidarity days by persons who had been persecuted during the days of Stalinism: "The present evil is the lesser one and shouldn't be provoked. Things were worse before." Yes, says Brandys, "but, in fact, a lesser evil can reach deeper and embrace more..."[13]

Papandreou provided no solace for a people trapped by their geography. He did not recognize their history, their traditions, their efforts to save themselves from spiritual death. In criticizing those who criticize the government of Poland and its Soviet sponsors, it is not the fact of Soviet perfidy and oppression that seems to cause him dread but the fact of their disclosure.

Andreas was not the standard-bearer who would lead the

Polish people to the realization of their hopes and dreams. He was, at best, a messenger of devalued merit, arguing for the status quo. It is virtually certain, however, that Solidarity and what it stands for will outlast both Jaruzelski and Papandreou.

THE TWA HIJACKING AND ITS AFTERMATH

When TWA Flight 847, bound from Athens to Rome and New York, was hijacked by Shiite Moslem extremists in mid-June 1985, it set in motion a train of events that had severe repercussions on Greece's tourist industry and Greece's image abroad.

Day after day the hijack drama, with crew and passengers held hostage in Beirut, made riveting television-viewing around the world. America was on edge and was very troubled by reports that the International Air Transport Association (IATA), the pilots' group, had complained of habitually poor security at Athens Airport. The FAA representatives gave vent to frustration over what they regarded as a lack of cooperation from Greek airport authorities in previous months. It did not help America's mood when the Greek passengers were released and Greek singer Demi Roussos, a passenger, serenaded the hijackers while a young American sailor lay clubbed to death. President Reagan's advisory reflected America's mood as well as the IATA and FAA reports.

Papandreou remained silent during this period. Some close to him explained that he abstained from comment because he believed his controversial personality might make matters worse. It was left to Nikos Skoulas, secretary-general of the Greek National Tourist Organization, to be Greece's spokesman. Instead of taking the obvious step of announcing that Greece would cooperate with the IATA, which is, after all, not an American organization, he appealed "to all U.S. citizens not to pay attention to President Reagan's recommendations and come to Greece."[14] One can hardly imagine anything more inept. Further, Skoulas termed the official U.S. concern as "a defamatory campaign" and "a provocation." By the time Greece finally conveyed an image of cooperation on safety, crucial time had been irrevocably lost. On the hair-raising day when the TWA plane went from Beirut to Algiers and back again, under control of the hijackers, the Greek ambassador to the United States was away from Washington and, in any event, out of sync with the reaction of the man in the street.

Greece's tourism suffered another jolt when the *Achille*

Lauro cruise ship was hijacked, although it was not a Greek ship and not in Greek waters. And again, when four passengers were blown out of the cabin of a TWA plane about to land in Athens. Both incidents were highly visible in the media and devastating for travel in the Eastern Mediterranean. Years of Papandreou's rhetoric; his association with radical Arab leaders Assad, Qaddafi, and Arafat; and several unsolved political assassinations in Athens all came together reinforcing a perception among Americans that Papandreou's Greece was not friendly. Hundreds of millions of dollars were lost. The loss was partly due to sheer ill fortune, but not completely. Years will be required to repair the damage to Greece's economy.

THE DIANE SAWYER INTERVIEW

The CBS program "Sixty Minutes" has the largest viewing audience of any program on American television. In a segment broadcast on 6 January 1984, the attractive coeditor Diane Sawyer interviewed Prime Minister Papandreou in Athens. The overall impression conveyed was unfortunately negative. Greek Americans received flak about it from their American friends over the following days. A dispassionate reading of the transcript reveals that much of the negative impression flowed from editorial commentary dubbed in by Sawyer, in which Papandreou and Greece were described as unreliable, ungrateful, and reluctant allies.

Nevertheless, a persistent Sawyer wheedled some concessions from Papandreou. Yes, he had enjoyed his American college days and the opportunity given him. And:

Sawyer: Are you grateful that Greece is not part of the Soviet bloc?

Papandreou: I would put it this way to you. Yes, I don't want to be in the Soviet bloc. Very clearly.

Margaret Papandreou, in a brief appearance alone with Sawyer, did not help matters with a weak attempt at humor:

Sawyer: In your wildest imagination, could you ever have envisaged that you would be the wife of the Prime Minister of Greece?

Mrs. Papandreou: Well, I've been asked that question before and I say no, I didn't dream that I would be the wife of the Prime Minister of Greece. I dreamt that I would be the prime minister.

Asked about his condemnation of Solidarity and his praise of General Jaruzelski, Papandreou responded: "What would have happened, let's be honest and direct, if Jaruzelski was not there? The Polish Government would be finished for good, any

Polish government, and the Soviet Union would have come in to directly govern the country. That was the only alternative."

In answer to another question, he admitted he had no proof that Korean Airlines Flight 007 was a spy plane, as he had charged. He made matters worse by adding, "The point is that if such a plane came into Greece, we would have downed it."

Papandreou closed: "I want a Mediterranean without the Soviet fleet, without the American fleet, I don't want American bases. I want to be left alone." The actual broadcast broke off at this point. The transcript reveals that Papandreou continued: "This is my notion of Europe. Unfortunately, it's a vision that is not likely to take form and shape during my lifetime."

Thus Papandreou, a charming man, fell victim to the even more charming, seductive Sawyer, who, moreover, controlled the editing. It was not the first time that "60 Minutes" loaded up a segment with stylized editing and commentary. Invariably, interviewees believe they can handle the situation, only to discover too late that they did not. While Papandreou's remarks should not have been overly damaging in and of themselves, the overall message of the broadcast reflected the attitude of much of the American foreign-policy establishment. It had a damaging impact on the reputations of Papandreou, Greece, and PASOK at a time when more negatives were least needed.

XV

When George Rallis, a decent man not given to excess in word or action, ended his short term as prime minister, having succeeded Karamanlis, he left honest elections and a peaceful transfer of power as his legacy. Perhaps that will also be Andreas Papandreou's primary legacy when his tenure comes to an end.

Papandreou's two terms have been burdened by economic woes—high inflation, rising unemployment, a large trade deficit. Nevertheless, PASOK did enact overdue, modernizing social legislation. It also brought into Greece's political life a new, younger generation of men and women, some of whom have much talent and merit.

In the long term, it may be the *process*, and its reinforcement, that count. This seems to be the position of Senator Paul Sarbanes, a central player in the U.S.-Greek equation. The cautious but tenacious Sarbanes has lines to all key players, guards the 10:7 ratio, and takes the long view. He has refused, correctly in my judgment, to be drawn into internal Greek political fights such as the vote to replace Karamanlis with Sartzetakis and PASOK-New Democracy differences over how to deal with Albania. Important congressmen, taking the long view, justify their fidelity to the 10:7 ratio by saying they are looking "beyond Papandreou."

Meanwhile, the fact remains that the base agreements have been renewed once already under Papandreou, Greece has remained in NATO—if grudgingly—and Greece has abandoned talk of leaving the EEC. All of these developments run counter to major portions of Papandreou's campaign speeches.

Many Greek Americans, viewing this zigzag performance, have concluded that they cannot expect Papandreou to "act like an American," nor PASOK to act like an American political party. For them, a certain unpredictability is more typically Greek. On the other hand, some occasionally overreact. For example, former Senator Paul Tsongas (D-Mass.), returning from a business trip to Greece, was given front-page treatment by the *Hellenic Chronicle*: "Former Senator Paul E. Tsongas warned Prime Minister Papandreou of Greece last week that there is a danger of neutralization of both the Greek-American community and members of Congress because of recent events in Greece."[15] He was referring especially to Papandreou's statements about the Korean Airlines incident: "If that were to happen, and if it comes to the point where Greek-Americans have to choose between loyalty to the United States or loyalty to Greece, obviously they would choose loyalty to the United States."[16]

The reference to the ultimate loyalty of Greek Americans is true. But the relationship between Greece and the United States is not so desperate. Tsongas had unnecessarily leapfrogged all the subtleties and in-betweens and reached a final step that few believe will ever be taken.

Greek Americans love America, wish Greece and the United States to be friends and allies, and are surprised and upset when they seem otherwise. Their good feelings flow to Greece, and only indirectly to its representatives of the moment.

The Greek American community, jolted by the Cyprus crisis, learned sophisticated lobbying techniques and realized the depth of its own resources. It does not jump automatically to support every Greek government position. Of course, there are some who will say, "Don't criticize Greece (under any circumstances)," just as there are American Jews who will say

"Don't criticize Israel (under any circumstances)." The Greek American community has matured politically.

Greek Americans, highly individualistic, confident of their place in this society, unashamed of their affection for Greece and their loyalty and love for America, are well-positioned to hold both nations, and their leaders, to high standards of conduct. As they do so, good things will inevitably happen.

NOTES

1. Henry Kamm, "Papandreou: The Politics of Anti-Americanism," *New York Times Magazine*, 7 April 1985. The correspondent, whose roving assignment allowed him to interview Papandreou over a span of two decades, wrote: "Twenty years ago, when his American-campus past was still the more active part of his complex personality, Andreas Papandreou, then a freshman member of the Greek Parliament, seemed more at ease over a drink with an American reporter than in the somewhat levantine ambiance of Greek political antechambers. He was the only man without the ubiquitous worry beads. Now, the Prime Minister twiddles them as though to the manner born, as he is less on his guard before a political crowd than over a drink with an American reporter." Over the years, Kamm added, Papandreou "has refurbished his Greek self."

2. His comment in Greek: *E elithios einai e praktoras. Kai xeroume den einai praktoras.*

3. "My politics can be described in a very few words," Papandreou also said on that "Meet the Press" program. "Politically, I am a fanatic democrat. I believe in the Bill of Rights, in freedom of speech, of syndicalist and political organizations. I believe in a judicial system that is independent of the executive, that can protect the citizen from police and arbitrary executive intervention." It can be fairly said that Papandreou has remained essentially constant to this part of his then-stated creed, while adorning himself abundantly with all sorts of ideological embellishments.

4. Maury was in retirement from the CIA when Secretary of Defense James Schlesinger asked him to return to government as assistant secretary of defense for congressional relations. In that position, he influenced Schlesinger in the latter's spirited differences with Secretary of State Henry Kissinger over the handling of the Cyprus crisis of 1974. If Maury must be accorded a mixed review, then so too must Congressman Ed Derwinski (R-Ill.), who rallied from a much drearier performance. During the junta years, nobody put more pro-junta material in the *Congressional Record* than Derwinski. Other pro-junta congressmen, such as Roman Pucinski (D-Ill.) and Peter Kyros (D-Maine), fell well short of Derwinski's production. When the Cyprus crisis erupted in 1974, however, Derwinski played an

important leadership role in enacting the Turkish arms embargo. All along, he argued that his actions reflected the views of his Greek constituents in Chicago. After he was defeated in 1982, Derwinski, a savvy operator, became a counselor in the State Department. Clearly, the Cyprus tragedy afforded not only American officials but large numbers of Greek Americans an opportunity for redemption.

5. The misreadings were not limited to Papandreou. In 1967-68, the Greek Desk of the State Department dismissed Karamanlis, then sixty-one and in self-exile in Paris, as "too old and completely deaf."

6. On Thursday night, 15 August 1974, the day after the second Turkish offensive began, I heard a CBS radio broadcast as I was driving home from Capitol Hill. The respected reporter Marvin Kalb commented that "the U.S. is clearly showing no pain" over the Turkish action. (Kalb had authored a flattering biography of Kissinger. I knew Kalb was friendly to Kissinger and had ready access to him. In his book he had written, "Our primary source was Henry Kissinger.") I was unable to obtain a transcript of the radio broadcast, but I obtained a transcript of the CBS evening news television program for that night. Kalb, reporting from the State Department, had said: "The United States accepts the partition of Cyprus—the top third to be controlled by the Turks, the bottom two-thirds by the Greeks. Top officials believe that a Turkish stronghold on Cyprus helps keep this island out of the Soviet orbit and provides a kind of base in the event of another Soviet-American confrontation over the Middle East.... Kissinger is known to believe that in the next 24 to 48 hours Turkey will agree to a ceasefire on Cyprus and negotiations will follow to confirm Turkey's military grip over the northern third of the island."

7. In Greek he said: *To problema me ten Hellada einai, dieuthynoune hoi Amerikanospoudasmenoi.*

8. Andrew Athens, UHAC head, in an interview published in the *Chicago Star*, 20 August 1987, spoke admiringly of his good friend Archbishop Iakovos. Athens credited him with saving the 10:7 ratio by intervening with Senator Charles Percy—a questionable conclusion. As for Papandreou, he said, "The relations between the omongenia and Greece were never worse."

9. Release from the the Office of Press & Information, Embassy of Greece, November 1984.

10. *Ibid.*

11. *Ibid.*

12. See Margaret Papandreou, *Nightmare in Athens* (Englewood Cliffs, N.J.: Prentice-Hall, 1970): 103-104.

13. Kazimierz Brandys, *A Warsaw Diary, 1978-1981* (New York: Vintage Books, 1985): 55.

14. Wire from *Athens News Agency*, 21 June 1985.

15. *Hellenic Chronicle,* 21 March 1985.

16. *Ibid.*, 21 March 1985.

U.S.-Greek Relations Under PASOK

Robert J. Pranger

On 21 October 1981 Andreas Papandreou was sworn in as prime minister of Greece, fulfilling a long-held ambition on his part, just nine months and one day after the first inauguration of Ronald Reagan as fortieth president of the United States. While one can hardly imagine two persons more different in terms of ideological persuasion, Papandreou with his pronounced socialist beliefs and Reagan with his devotion to entrepreneurial capitalism, the two leaders have a basic similarity that has marked their two terms of office: both lead movements that have become governments, in Papandreou's case, PASOK, and in Reagan's what is often called "the Reagan Revolution." Their general domestic and foreign policies reflect tensions between movement and government and, more narrowly, these tensions have produced some dramatic results—at times unexpected—in their relations with each other. No more so is this the case than in the area of U.S.-Greek relations since 1981, especially in critical matters concerning the historic defense alliance between the United States and Greece since the end of World War II.

A dispassionate person interviewing either Papandreou or Reagan before their dramatic 1981 electoral victories (one has to admit that most knowledgeable people are anything but dispassionate or neutral about either), would likely hear a similar prognostication from each about their policies in power: the symbols of an ideological movement are necessary for gathering a public following when one is proposing drastic policy changes and, indeed, such symbols are essential for bringing popular support behind any policy. At the same time, however, both Papandreou and Reagan made plain, in advance of their electoral triumphs, that they knew the difference between governing a country and using symbols to achieve and sustain power; after all, both were men experienced in the arts of government as well as electioneering. In other words, despite the extremist tendencies of the movements they led, Papandreou and Reagan were quite prepared to play "the lion and fox" with both friend and foe in the fullest sense of this Machiavellian view of political rule.

The course of U.S.-Greek relations since the advent of Papandreou and Reagan can best be described as an effort by both to achieve some balance between their needs to lead militant ideological movements that would ordinarily place these relations on a collision course, given the nature of the ideologies now governing foreign policy in the two countries, and the requirements of maintaining stable alliance relationships in the postwar continuum between Athens and Washington. It was, after all, the American argument for continuity that kept the alliance intact during the military dictatorship, and this same imperative would now work, as best it could, with the very movement, PASOK, whose anti-Americanism was rooted in U.S. support for the colonels. As one of the most visible victims of the dictators, Papandreou would now be called on to opt for continuity in U.S.-Greek relations or else make decisions no previous Greek leader had done, by moving either toward the nonaligned or Eastern bloc countries, with inevitable confrontation with Washington. The logic of PASOK and the Reagan Revolution could only lead to impasse, but higher political wisdom is, as always, more pragmatic. The course of U.S.-Greek relations since 1981 has been an intricate political and military *pas de deux* between ideological opposites, Papandreou and Reagan, over the terms of a common defense. The results have remained provisional, but under circumstances of ideological enmity, the provisional is always friend of the good, if not the best. However, such accommodation is essentially improvisation and, therefore, subject to reversal; it is not the stuff of stable alliances.

My review of U.S.-Greek defense relations since 1981 will concentrate on five areas of improvisation between PASOK and the Reagan Revolution, as mediated through the political acumen of Papandreou and Reagan: (1) base negotiations; (2) NATO; (3) Turkey; (4) relations with the Soviet Union and East bloc; and (5) the Middle East. In all areas the same accommodation between ideology and pragmatism may be found, as well as a constant tension between stalemate and the provisional. The rich complexity of Papandreou's relations with the United States requires a book for full treatment. In this essay we can only highlight some salient features for illustrative purposes.

I. NEGOTIATIONS ABOUT MILITARY BASES

Andreas Papandreou has not been the first Greek prime minister, nor will he be the last, to challenge the United States on the status of its bases and rights of military access in Greece. The negotiations that take place every five years for renewal of American use of these facilities and the interactions between governments over their ongoing operation provide the best barometer of the state of U.S.-Greek *bilateral* security relations.

For reasons connected with sensitive public opinion, the New Democracy leadership suspended negotiations with the U.S. during June 1981 in a move no doubt tied to the important parliamentary elections of that year which eventually brought PASOK to power, a move also smacking of blackmail since ostensibly pro-American negotiators hinted that a poor showing for Greece in these negotiations might elevate the apparently anti-American Papandreou to the premiership.[1] It was, of course, New Democracy's own domestic failings, not the base negotiations, that led to its defeat in October.

Nonetheless, the pro-American government of Prime Minister George Rallis could hardly ignore strong Greek sentiments against continued American military presence, or at least as that presence had been tolerated in the past. Resentment, stimulated by a volatile combination of anti-Turk, anti-American and anti-nuclear proclivities, crossed party lines. (The preponderance of Greek opinion has no strongly pro-Soviet feelings, but often makes up for this with emotional negativity.) If on one end of the New Democracy spectrum was Defense Minister Evangelos Averoff, firmly committed to the American presence, on the other was Foreign Minister Constantine Mitsotakis, who was not above playing the threat of Papandreou's victory as a means of extracting more American concessions on the bases.

In a sense, therefore, Papandreou's negotiating strategy with the United States after his October election represented simply an increase in horse-trading tactics already exploited, to some extent, by the Rallis government for its own ends in Greek domestic politics. These objectives were very much conditioned by the omnipresent hand of President Constantine Karamanlis in all important matters connected with the non-socialist sector of Greek political life. Indeed, in the case of the 1981 election it was suggested that Karamanlis was dabbling in PASOK affairs as well. The important difference between Papandreou and Rallis, however, was that the former's constituency was PASOK, a well organized and ideologically united movement, while New Democracy had to contend with a less ideological and more amorphous political clientele. Also within New Democracy was Averoff's strong anti-communist position, around which many rallied, whereas in PASOK there was an equally powerful anti-American tendency. In private as well as in public Averoff and Papandreou have been dedicated political enemies.

In his first major speech to Parliament as prime minister on 22 November 1981, Papandreou announced his plans to achieve withdrawal of U.S. military bases from Greece beginning in early 1982.[2] Until total withdrawal, he said, the bases could remain on three conditions: (1) all activities by the U.S. would be monitored by Greece; (2) there would be an annual review of relative agreements; and (3) there would be immediate suspension of any American activities detrimental to Greece's foreign relations. In the same address, Papandreou called for removal of U.S. nuclear weapons from Greek territory, a theme that would continue in his dealings with Americans and with NATO more generally until shelved by the prime minister in 1985. What this amounted to was a declaration that negotiations between Greece and the United States on the bases would henceforth concentrate on an agreement for withdrawal rather than continuation of basing rights.

As of late 1987, the bases remained in Greece, albeit under a threat of termination in December 1988. American activities seemed no better—or worse—monitored than during New Democracy's term in office, and U.S. nuclear weapons apparently stayed in their discreet emplacements within Greek borders at the ready for certain NATO contingencies. In other words, although the six years after Papandreou's inaugural speech in Parliament had witnessed a *Sturm und Drang* over American bases too complex to fully analyze in a short essay, these facilities still stood where they had been since PASOK took power.

The history of negotiations during this six-year period illustrates the ambivalence between movement and government typical of Papandreou's major policy endeavors in foreign relations: the necessity to maintain the symbolism of radical change essential to PASOK's existence on the one hand, and the equally important pragmatic imperative to continue in some way Greece's close ties with NATO and the United States on the other. The miracle is that the ideologically energetic Reagan administration did not respond more vehemently to this sometimes genuine, sometimes mock anti-Americanism, a tribute to the Atlanticist preferences of Secretaries of State Alexander Haig and George Shultz, and to the appointment, by the Reagan administration, of Papandreou's friend as American ambassador to Athens, Monteagle Stearns. There is also no question that those in Washington troubled by Papandreou, most notably in the Pentagon, found a subliminal outlet for their frustrations in greater emphasis on Turkey, a matter that would cause another burst of ideological anti-American enthusiasm from Papandreou, PASOK and other Greeks outside the socialist family. All these tensions, of course, are hardly prescriptions for a healthy, stable alliance relationship. They have not abated and worse may lie ahead.

Signs of unresolved ambivalence and contradiction were everywhere in the base negotiations after 1981. Emerging from his meetings in Athens in May 1982, Secretary Haig saw progress in "key substantial topics involving U.S.-Greek relations," although Papandreou was said to be only partially satisfied with these talks.[3] Yet six months later the Greek prime minister announced in Rumania that he had started an effort that might lead to the "denuclearization of the Balkans," including Greece, a point he insisted remained "totally independent of the U.S. base negotiations."[4] Given Haig's pronounced allergy to nuclear disarmament in NATO, however, one can only wonder whether Papandreou was simply being illogical or disingenuous.

By January 1983 the American ambassador in Athens was summoned to hear Greece's protest over "unauthorized" use by American aircraft of the Suda Air Base in Crete, with Greek authorities making it clear that new base accords must be reached to eliminate such transgressions.[5] The following month, 1,600 Greek employees on U.S. bases, in what was to become a familiar action, staged a strike to protest increased American aid to Turkey—as will be noted, the bases and Turkey seemed inextricably connected in Papandreou's policy toward the United States—while in March, 80,000 Greek leftists staged a rally, organized by PASOK in cooperation with the Communists, to protest the very fact of U.S. bases in their country. (Papandreou and PASOK have few problems in mustering thousands of persons into the streets of Athens for any *cause célèbre* .) In April a visit to Greece by Assistant Secretary of

State Richard Burt was cancelled when it was learned that Papandreou would not receive him because of his "pro-Turkish statements," a cancellation followed three days later by another rally involving thousands of Greeks to protest the U.S. presence.[6] By the middle of May, a second strike by 1,600 Greek employees was staged demanding a 35-percent pay hike and dismissal of 580 American citizens said to be illegally employed at U.S. bases.

On 15 July 1983, however, the United States and Greece signed an accord allowing the U.S. to retain military bases for five years, with Papandreou arguing that this accord demonstrated that Greece had regained power over its own territory. Indeed, he said, Greece could renounce this accord at any time, if the established 7:10 ratio of military aid (seven parts Greek to ten parts Turk) was upset. The accord was further said to limit American use of the bases to "defensive" purposes and to bar interventions by the United States from these bases against countries deemed friendly to Greece, the latter prohibition mainly directed at the Middle East. Greece rejected the U.S. position at the end of the talks that it could remain at the bases beyond expiration of the agreement on 30 December 1988. For the Greeks, a strong incentive in favor of this agreement was undoubtedly the $500 million in military credits promised by the Reagan administration.[7]

In September 1983 the new base accord, assuring that a balance of military power in the Aegean region between Greece and Turkey would not be altered in the near future, was signed and then made public; two months later the Greek Parliament ratified the pact with an overwhelming show of hands on both sides. It was said that the accord could be terminated by either side at the end of five years, if either submitted a request for termination five months before the pact's scheduled renegotiation. In a word, the first half of 1983 was devoted to strident demands that the Americans leave Greece, and the second half to extending the base agreement for another five years under terms similar to those of the previous accord.

During 1984 Greek officers arrived at the American bases, as part of an oversight arrangement established in the September 1983 agreement, an arrival duly noted for its symbolic importance. U.S.-Greek military talks in the spring, which included U.S. Secretary of Defense Caspar Weinberger, were said not to have covered the "touchy" subject of the base negotiations, suggesting that the agreements ratified the previous fall might be provisional.[8] And in July the 1,600 Greek employees at the American bases were on strike again, thereby apparently placing great strain on already weakened U.S. Greek relations. Such weakening of defense linkages was no doubt something like a person first jumping vigorously on one side of a swinging bridge and then on the other, repeating this many times, with the resultant motion leading to vertigo.

As the U.S.-Greek bases relationship entered the 1985 election year in Greece, reports leaked from Washington that the Reagan administration had developed contingency plans to remove these bases in 1988 if Papandreou were reelected prime minister and then continued to act in ways "frowned upon" by Washington (strengthening ties with the communist Balkan states, agreeing with the U.S.S.R. in episodes like the KAL 007 disaster, and so forth). President Reagan denied these reports.[9]

In the wake of his March election victory, which produced a reduced margin for PASOK in the Parliament, Papandreou seemed to hedge on his persistent threat to close the bases in December 1988. He also shelved his Balkans "nuclear free zone" idea for which, at one point, he had even received Soviet backing.[10] During October, when U.S. Undersecretary of State Michael H. Armacost visited Athens for "intensive talks" about the future of the bases, it was announced that the Greek government stood by its commitment to allow the five-year base agreement to expire in December 1988. The U.S. seemed ready to embark on plans to relocate.[11]

Early in 1987 Papandreou informed his Parliament that he would open talks with the United States about the future of its bases in Greece, indicating that the U.S. would have to approach these talks on a "zero basis," as if the facilities would be legally non-existent in December 1988.[12] During its March crisis with Turkey, however, Greece persisted in confrontation with the U.S. over the relative amounts of American funding for bases in the two countries, and asked Washington to suspend all its operations at Nea Makri in protest over alleged American leanings toward Turkey. But American and NATO pressure on the Turks led to Greece's cancellation of the latter request.[13] Ominously, however, protest over the bases moved from strikes and street demonstrations to violence against Americans, when a far-leftist group calling itself "November 17" bombed a bus carrying American military personnel to the Hellenikon Air Base at Athens Airport, an act the Socialist government condemned as abhorrent.[14] Papandreou seemed ready to quiet unrest in Greek-American relations over the preceding years, but then called in May for a national referendum on the U.S. base agreements scheduled for renegotiation beginning in October.

The base negotiations between the United States and Greece under PASOK dramatically illustrate incipient tensions between movement and government in Papandreou's foreign policy. This ambivalence has led to both friction in the past and uncertainty about the future in 1988, a presidential election year in the United States and the time of expiration for the five-year agreement so laboriously produced in 1983. Adding to this inherent ambiguity has been the domestic political and personal difficulties of the prime minister.[15] According to Papandreou's promise during the flush of his 1985 reelection, the base agreement will be left to expire in December 1988 unless supported by a national referendum, one month after a new American president will be fresh from his own electoral victory. Relations with Greece could well be the first order of foreign policy business for a new American administration in January 1989.

II. NATO

It was clear from the start of PASOK's ascension to power that the same security ambivalence that marked Greece's bilateral relations with the United States would extend to its participation in NATO as well. This was evident both in terms of Papandreou's fixation on the Turkish threat to Greece and in his attitude toward the Soviet Union. While these two areas are covered separately in my analysis, they also play a central role in Greece's stormy involvement in NATO since 1981.

With Papandreou's election to prime minister, PASOK vowed to take Greece out of both the European Economic Community (EEC) and NATO. At the December NATO ministerial meetings, Greece demanded that the alliance, in its official communiqué, insure it against Turkish attack, a demand that disrupted the ordinarily uneventful, semi-annual proceedings as other alliance members objected, at which point Papandreou hedged on Greece's NATO commitments, arguing that the chief threat for Athens came from Turkey not the Soviet Union. All efforts at compromise failed. Papandreou declared Greece's military commitment in the alliance limited to command cooperation and participation in staff groups, adding that Greece would extend its sovereignty over the entire Aegean

Sea. Nonetheless, Greece did support those parts of the final communiqué approving plans for medium-range missiles (INF) negotiations coupled with a threat of deployment if negotiations failed, as well as agreeing to Spain's entry into the alliance. Greek refusal to sign certain parts of the final communiqué was rationalized in Athens as a desire to stay clear of what was judged to be an American campaign to smuggle economic sanctions against Soviet bloc regimes into NATO's defense policy.[16]

As the failure of U.S.-Soviet negotiations on INF became increasingly probable and the likelihood of missile deployment more imminent, Papandreou's government rejected the American deployment plan for Pershing IIs and cruise missiles at the June 1983 NATO ministerial meetings, the only alliance member to do so. In the June 10 communiqué, Greece refused to support NATO's reaffirmation of a plan also backed by Papandreou in 1981.[17] Greece repeated its opposition to INF deployment in 1984. By this time it was clear that taking exception to parts of NATO communiqués was becoming a special feature of Papandreou's alliance policy with the prime minister declaring Greek independence from "continual subservience" to the alliance.[18] In collaboration with some other alliance members, Greece also succeeded in blocking mention of the U.S. "Star Wars" program in the June 1985 NATO communiqué.[19]

Part of Papandreou's suspicion of NATO has no doubt been related to his belief that Turkey has generally been favored at Greece's expense, a matter addressed in another section of this essay, but there is also no question that he has been sensitive to what he perceives to be Washington's unhappiness with him being prime minister in the first place. The latter view has probably been reinforced by the Jeane Kirkpatrick notion of "dictatorships and double standards" influential in certain Reagan circles.[20] As 1985 opened, an election year in Greece, Papandreou protested a hypothetical classroom exercise at the NATO Defense College in Rome depicting an overthrow of the Greek government. Greece then withdrew from participation in the school.[21]

Papandreou no doubt remembers NATO's rather effortless accommodation of the Greek colonels (although there were protests from the alliance's weakest members, the Scandinavian states), and its relative insouciance about the fate of democracy in Greece. And it has become a central tenet of socialist faith that behind NATO's acceptance of the Greek military *fait accompli* lay the powerful influence of American *Realpolitik* despite protests from Congress, a view shared in important nonsocialist circles as well. This policy of the United States during the Johnson and Nixon administrations worked against all democrats in Greece or in exile, socialists and nonsocialists alike, creating sensitivities in Athens about NATO—often expressed as anti-Turkish sentiments—across the political spectrum. In this sense, Karamanlis could be as suspicious of the United States as Papandreou. A recurrent Papandreou nightmare might well be that his main foes are within NATO and not in the Warsaw Pact, and that not all these enemies are Turks.

Papandreou's mixed feelings about NATO may also be related to the relatively poor economic performance of Greece under PASOK. This linkage between economics and national security in NATO is frequently ignored by strategists but not by politicians in the member countries. After a severe recession in the early 1980s, NATO Europe staged something of an economic recovery, led by Canada, Norway and Turkey at annual Gross Domestic Product (GDP) growths of over 4%, followed by Great Britain at approximately 3.5%. Greece did less well, achieving only a 1.5% GDP increase in 1985. At the same time, difficulties with inflation persisted in some NATO countries, led by Turkey in 1985 with an annual 40% increase, with Greece and Portugal at rates approaching 20%.[22] In other words, on the scale of both GDP and inflation growth, Greece's performance was among the poorest in NATO, while the growth of Turkey's economy at least offset some of its high inflation rate. By 1986 few NATO countries, including the United States, were maintaining the 3% real growth in defense outlays pledged in 1979.[23] Membership in the exclusive NATO club may simply become too expensive for some countries.

Greece's relative lack of enthusiasm for NATO was matched by others in the alliance, but Papandreou's active animosity to certain alliance policies was not. Again, his eccentricity may be seen as ambivalence based on tensions between his role as leader of a movement advocating radical domestic and foreign policy change on the one hand, and his role, on the other, as prime minister of a country that, since 1952, had its reservations about one NATO partner, Turkey, but none whatsoever about American leadership of the alliance.

III. TURKEY

Long before the events of March 1987, when Greece and Turkey almost went to war over the issue of sovereignty in the Aegean Sea, relations between the two countries have also troubled relations between Athens and Washington. The central issue of Cyprus has been a long-standing source of friction between Greeks and Turks, inevitably involving the United States: during the 1974 Turkish invasion of Cyprus, after a coup on the island sponsored by the military junta then ruling Greece, the American ambassador to Cyprus, Rodger Davies, was killed by sniper fire in his own embassy. Indeed, around the Cyprus issue and matters of controversy with Turkey in the Aegean, Greeks of all political persuasions seem able to unite. What has constrained Athens and Ankara so far has not been their common relationship with the United States, but their membership in NATO, yet there is little doubt that the alliance itself has been threatened on its southern flank, less by Soviet pressure than by the constant potential for armed conflict between these two alliance partners.

Long ago the Soviet Union learned to leave this conflict to its own dynamics, fishing in troubled waters only when the temptation to do so proved irresistible, with a full understanding that these frictions have a long history that is not likely to be settled soon; there is no need to divide and conquer what is already divided. What has saved NATO so far has been a fierce anti-communism of both Greeks and Turks that keeps would-be conquerors from exploiting their division. As will be noted in the analysis of PASOK's relations with the Soviet Union and East bloc countries, however, there has been a notable shift in official Greek attitudes toward the East-West conflict since 1981, a shift that is likely to be even more noticeable with the maturing of Mikhail Gorbachev.

The origins of the March 1987 brinkmanship between Greece and Turkey in the Aegean also have some relationship to PASOK's rise to power in 1981. Ironically, the party most identified with Greek military power (although *not* with any idea of military rule), New Democracy, would also be the most favorably inclined toward friendship with the United States. This has left PASOK in the enviable domestic position of being both leftist and nationalist, with the latter tendency focused on conflict with Turkey. Before entering office in 1981 it was clear that Papandreou saw Turkey as Greece's foremost security problem, not the Soviet Union and its allies to the north. While NATO was northward oriented, he argued, Greece's principal adversary was its eastern neighbor. With a sizeable force in the Aegean, Turkey posed threats, it was thought, to Greek islands claimed by Ankara without any historic right. Competing Aegean claims also included very practical considerations: mineral rights to oil exploration on the continental shelf beneath all Greek islands and a 12-mile limit for territorial waters off each of these islands (the latter claim could be pressed after the December 1982 United Nations Law of the Sea Convention was finalized).

As noted earlier, a Greek demand at the first NATO ministerial meeting attended by the PASOK leadership in 1981, that the alliance insure Greece from Turkish aggression, led to serious disruption in the framing of a joint communiqué. Papandreou then stated to NATO what he had earlier claimed in Greek domestic politics: the chief threat to Greece comes from Turkey not from the USSR. Some leaders of New Democracy, far to Papandreou's right, were also using the Turkish threat in 1981 for whatever domestic political advantage it might produce.

After 1981 Greece continued to use the NATO framework to underline its enmity for Turkey. Papandreou protested to the United States about NATO exercises, in which Greece refused to take part, involving overflights of Greece by American and Turkish aircraft. In 1984 Greece reaffirmed its refusal to participate in a five-nation NATO exercise in the Aegean Sea scheduled for September.[24] A British ship involved in NATO exercises in 1985 was refused permission by Greece to refuel in its ports as part of what Athens termed its on-going "war" against NATO "favoritism" toward Turkey in the Aegean.[25] A week after this incident NATO defense ministers agreed to provide more aid to upgrade Greek armed forces, but within two weeks Papandreou warned again of favoritism toward Turkey in alliance Aegean policy. On 19 December 1986 the Greek-Turkish rivalry reached an ugly stage in something of a preparatory act for the events of March 1987: three soldiers, one Greek and two Turkish, died after an exchange of fire between border patrols on the Evros River, thereby escalating tensions between these two NATO allies.[26]

That NATO provided a convenient context for continuing the long struggle between Greeks and Turks, while at the same time preventing this conflict from reaching outright war, is best illustrated by the events of March 1987 that brought the two sides to high alert. In his controversial remonstrance at his first NATO ministerial meeting in December 1981, on protecting Greece from Turkey in the final communiqué, Papandreou claimed Greek sovereignty over the Aegean Sea, meaning that an extension to 12 miles of territorial waters off each of its 2,000 islands, an extension envisaged under the pending United Nations Law of the Sea Convention finally signed in December 1982 (but not by Turkey), would bring roughly 72% of the area under Greek control with only about 9% Turkish and the remainder international.[27] As 1987 opened, Greece still claimed only 44% and Turkey 7.5% with the rest international, but when Greece seemed, to the Turks, to be moving toward a 12-mile concept of its territorial waters around the Greek island of Thasos, in search of oil, Ankara prepared its research vessel, Sismik I, for sailing into these disputed waters. Playing his American and NATO cards, Papandreou asked the United States to suspend its operations at the communications base of Nea Makri, implying that the U.S. had not exercised enough diplomatic vigor with the Turks over this crisis. Again, the Greek government charged that NATO was once more displaying favoritism toward Turkey in the Aegean Sea. Under pressure from the United States and NATO, the Turkish prime minister, Turgut Ozal, ordered his seismic research vessel to avoid the disputed waters, while Greece was reported to have given assurances to Ankara that it would cease further expansion of oil exploration around the island of Thasos.[28] This easing of tension was widely regarded as a standoff, but Washington was said to be angered by Papandreou's threats to close all American bases if Greece was forced to move closer to war with Turkey; it was pointed out in various circles that the 1983 bases agreement was due for expiration in late 1988 and Papandreou had given no assurances of renewing it. As of the end of 1987, nine months after this crisis, he still had made no commitment about renewal.

It is clearly the case, therefore, that bilateral relations between Greece and the United States and Greece and Turkey are not only inextricably intertwined with each other, in a kind of *pas de trois*, but are also related to NATO affairs. In the resultant confusion of motives and aims it is often very difficult to locate Papandreou's policy priorities and preferences. One suspects this ambiguity may well be by design in Athens and not chance, but this is hardly a sound basis for steady U.S.-Greek relations. If one were pressed to summarize U.S.-Greek relations under PASOK, on the basis of evidence from base negotiations, NATO relations, and the Greek-Turkish conflict, one might characterize these relations as "a policy of unsteady design." Papandreou's approach to East-West relations has compounded this ambiguity, while his Middle East policy has alienated parts of his powerful American liberal constituency.

IV. SOVIET UNION AND EAST BLOC

Tensions between movement and government in Papandreou's relations with the United States are nowhere more clearly evident than in his policies toward the Soviet Union and East bloc, with an added dimension, the economic, also salient. Perhaps equally important as far as the future of PASOK rule in Greece is concerned, it is on East-West issues that one finds a significant contrast between socialists and non-socialists, an important domestic as well as international question for Greeks given the events of the early postwar period. PASOK tends to be influenced by anti-imperialist, anti-American, pro-Third World trends that became *de rigueur* for the European left during the Vietnam War and have persisted since then, whereas New Democracy, while obviously anti-dictatorship, has been dominated by anti-communist, pro-American thinking. Most Greeks are probably somewhere between the extremes of the two parties, with any anti-Americanism largely focused on U.S. support for the military junta in the 1967-1974 period (which coincided with the height of U.S. involvement in Vietnam) and on alleged American "favoritism" toward Turkey.

Surely a large number of Greeks would have difficulty accepting Papandreou's argument that the chief threat to Greece comes not from the Soviet Union but Turkey, yet it has been on the basis of this perspective that the prime minister has engaged in an interesting and perplexing set of initiatives with the Soviet Union and some of its Warsaw Pact allies. While every NATO leader has invented his or her country's own game of confrontation and cooperation with Soviet leaders since 1981, especially with Gorbachev, only Papandreou, in an ostensible effort to appear independent, has openly espoused views that deviate from positions accepted by most members of the alliance.

In January 1982 the Greek government, only three months

into PASOK rule, announced it would resume servicing of noncombatant commercial and naval supply ships of the Soviet Union for "simple economic reasons." This service was discontinued by the Rallis government in 1981 because of American objections. The Reagan administration, exactly one year from its own ascension to presidential power, voiced disapproval.[29] A collision course with the Reagan Revolution on East-West relations seemed inevitable.

The same month of January witnessed an even more serious clash between the United States and Greece over the question of Poland's martial law government. The Greek government notified NATO that while it condemned military rule in Warsaw, it also objected to accusing the Soviet Union of involvement and to imposing economic sanctions. Although this opposition appeared to some as a way of strengthening Greece's hand vis-a-vis the Turks and base negotiations with the U.S., this Papandreou position, along with his opening of Greek repair facilities to Soviet naval ships, was seen by some in Washington—and indeed by Papandreou himself—as an early effort to declare his independence from the Western alliance thought to be dominated by the U.S.[30] This tension would become more apparent over the next several years.

After a November 1982 three-day visit to Rumania, the prime minister said that the two nations would call for a conference of Balkan leaders to discuss a nuclear-free zone in the region within 18 months. In this same statement, he reiterated his position that he wanted U.S. bases out of Greece—eventually.[31]

The Balkan nuclear-free zone idea received predictable Soviet support during a visit to Greece by Prime Minister Nikolai A. Tikhonov in mid-February of 1983. A joint communiqué between Greece and the Soviet Union agreed that nuclear-free zones were an important part of the disarmament process; the same statement indicated that Papandreou had embarked on a more independent stance regarding NATO positions; such alliance positions surely did not include the Balkan idea, as no Warsaw Pact statement had. In addition to security issues, a 10-year economic pact was signed during Tikhonov's visit, as were agreements covering the transmission of Soviet natural gas and electric power, via Rumania and Bulgaria, to Greece; the latter agreements were actually made by predecessor governments in Athens.[32]

By early 1983, therefore, it was clear that Papandreou's

policies toward East-West relations would be influenced by tensions between movement and government on the one hand, and by economic realities on the other. As noted earlier, by mid-1983 Papandreou was insisting that his advocacy of nuclear-free zone talks in the Balkans and his argument that he could expel U.S. nuclear forces from Greece without negotiations of any kind, were positions quite independent of talks underway on the future status of American bases.[33] To give further indication of its independence from Washington pressures, Greece opposed a NATO agreement on a two-week ban of civilian flights in and out of the U.S.S.R. as retaliation for the KAL 007 disaster.[34] The many cynics in Greek politics might have reasoned that these fundamentally contradictory positions allowed Papandreou to satisfy the passions of the PASOK ultra-left and their Communist party allies, while at the same time keeping his NATO commitments and even increasing American military aid.

Having secured a new five-year extension of U.S. bases in late 1983, together with an impressive $500 million package of military aid, the Papandreou government again embarked on its independent course in East-West relations by rejecting American efforts in COCOM (Coordinating Committee for Export to Communist Areas), in January 1984, to apply export controls to oil pumps.[35] By May the U.S. State Department was calling "outrageous" Papandreou arguments labeling the United States an imperialist power and praising the Soviet Union.[36] Reports were circulating of anti-Western positions taken by Greece inside NATO and the EEC.

The economic side of Papandreou's detente with the East bloc was evident in July 1984 when Greece signed a contract with the Soviet Union to purchase $45 million worth of Soviet engineering equipment to be used by the military service for reconstruction work.[37] In the same month Greece and the Soviet Union signed an accord in Moscow for construction of a $450 million alumina plant in Greece with an annual capacity of 600,000 metric tons, 75% of which would be exported to the Soviet Union and Bulgaria in a ten-year agreement.[38]

Papandreou's independence brought forth more acrimonious responses from Washington in 1984, public frictions rare in NATO relations. In October the prime minister visited Poland and described Wojciech Jaruzelski as a "patriot," criticizing, in the course of this praise, Solidarity as "negative and dangerous." He also disapproved publicly in Warsaw of U.S.

sanctions against Poland. The U.S. State Department responded that Papandreou's statement in Poland on U.S. policy indicated "total misunderstanding" of this policy and of the realities of Poland and Eastern Europe.[39] A month later Papandreou insisted that his government was pursuing moderate but independent policies toward the United States.[40] In December the Greek government rejected an American protest over Greek Communist party allegations that the U.S. had been involved in recent bomb attacks in Athens.

Papandreou's independence from Western alliance policy, although in certain eyes anti-Western and pro-Soviet, was probably motivated to some extent, as noted earlier, by important non-aligned tendencies in PASOK and the European left in general. Surely the prime minister himself expressed such views long before entering office. This was also evident in his decision to join the so-called Group of Six world leaders representing Argentina, Greece, India, Mexico, Sweden and Tanzania. In May 1983 they issued their first appeal to the United States and Soviet Union to halt the nuclear arms race and resume arms control talks acrimoniously suspended by the two superpowers in November 1983. This initiative received the endorsement the following day of Pope John Paul II.[41] The Group of Six made its most visible impression to date in August 1986 when it unveiled its Five Continent Peace Initiative in Ixtapa, Mexico, calling for a halt to all nuclear testing under a special verification plan that the group would administer.[42] This initiative, first revealed to the public in April of the same year, again drew the predictable support of Soviet foreign minister Edward A. Shevardnadze, but received only perfunctory politesse from Washington.[43] In December the six leaders urged the pursuit of talks to prevent the arms race in space, terminate it on earth, and ultimately eliminate nuclear weapons everywhere.[44]

Of interest here is the fact that Papandreou's membership, as head of a NATO government, in a highly visible group of world leaders advocating initiatives in nuclear disarmament at variance with American policy—on nuclear testing or arms in space for instance—is unusual, to say the least. Such "independence" is not lightly regarded in Washington nor in Greek domestic politics. In the fall of 1984, Constantine Mitsotakis, leader of the opposition in Parliament, accused Papandreou of "playing with fire" by making anti-American, anti-Western gestures, an accusation made in the same month that Papandreou issued a bitter personal attack on Mitsotakis.[45] In October 1986 the *New York Times* was reporting that "Greek and diplomatic commentators" noted that Papandreou had been trying to appease the anti-U.S. left in PASOK and pro-Soviet Communists by distancing himself from the United States. His losses in the municipal elections of that same month appeared to have "heightened his government's ambiguity over relations with the U.S."[46]

Tensions between movement and government seem to dominate Papandreou's maneuvering between East and West, but the net beneficiaries in Greek politics appear to be conservatives not socialists, with New Democracy scoring gains in both the 1985 parliamentary elections and the 1986 municipal elections.[47] New Democracy's comeback may well have been the result of the poor economic showing of PASOK's domestic policies, but the prime minister's improvisations in the ouster of President Karamanlis in 1985 (protested by U.S. Secretary of Defense Weinberger)[48] and in his foreign policy may also have caused him problems on *both* the left and the right: by 1986 the Communist party would no longer support him in the municipal election run-offs because of increasing strife between its cohorts and PASOK,[49] and he was now locked in a bitter personal feud with Mitsotakis on the conservative side.

In February 1985 Papandreou made his celebrated trip to Moscow for meetings with the Soviet leadership as a follow-up to Tikhonov's visit to Athens two years earlier. He was greeted warmly by the Soviet premier and Andrei Gromyko, then foreign minister. What made an original four-day visit, to be cut short, so newsworthy was the unavailability of General Secretary Konstantin Chernenko who was then in the final days of his rule. On the second and last day of this Moscow visit, however, Greece signed a contract with the Soviet Union for joint financing of the alumina plant and agreed to a joint study of a $1.5 billion gas pipeline. The Soviet Union also accepted a 70% increase in imports from Greece.[50]

The liaison between Papandreou and Chernenko's forces in 1983-1985 was straight Gromyko: an eager Western alliance member, anxious to exercise some independence from the United States in order to appease domestic constituencies, was ripe for divide-and-conquer strategies. The temptation to fish in these troubled waters was all the more appealing to Gromyko's Moscow (and at this point in the Soviet leadership transition no one doubted that, in foreign policy matters, Gromyko did indeed own Moscow), because Papandreou was more seriously anti-Turk than his predecessors and espoused an economic policy that desperately needed outside assistance (Libya's Qaddafi was to do his share as well; see section V of this essay).

With the ascendancy of Mikhail S. Gorbachev and Gromyko's removal as foreign minister, the Soviet interest in Greece's possible "independence" from the West became much less important than Moscow's interest in Ronald Reagan's ambitious disarmament deals with the Kremlin. Similarly, while approving of the Five Continent Peace initiative of the Six at Ixtapa in 1986 for its ideas on verifying compliance of a comprehensive test-ban treaty, Shevardnadze was looking forward to future Reagan-Gorbachev summits where the really serious matters of East-West relations would be settled. If other alliance members were to be involved with such weighty considerations, they would be the likes of Kohl, Mitterrand and Thatcher on the western side, not Papandreou who seemed to have gone out of his way to play the maverick. In a word, what the Soviets wanted after Gorbachev was *stability* in NATO so the alliance would stay united behind Reagan when arms agreements were ratified (see also section VI).

Ironically, Papandreou seemed to improve his relations with the United States after Gromyko no longer controlled Soviet foreign policy and Papandreou's own reelection in 1985 had produced diminished parliamentary strength for PASOK. Some easing of tensions between Athens and Washington were reportedly responsible for the visit of U.S. Secretary of State George Shultz to Greece in March 1986.[51] Such an event could not take place without some sign of protest, however, this time in the form of a bombing of President Harry S. Truman's statue in Athens. And, as noted earlier, when the October municipal elections went against PASOK, there was some speculation that Papandreou would revert to appeasing the movement at the expense of governing his relations with the U.S. in a steady manner. In fact, just before these elections the prime minister signed a nonaggression pact with Bulgaria, a move that could be interpreted by Greeks as either anti-American or anti-Turk. Yet, by January 1987 the Truman statue had been repaired and Athens was in its usual confusion about the future of U.S. bases after December 1988: Papandreou had contrived a "zero basis" strategy for the negotiations where the Americans should assume that, by the end of 1988, they would no longer have any legal claim to these facilities.[52]

As if to illustrate the fundamental conundrums of U.S.-Greek relations under PASOK in the realm of East-West relations, in late January 1987 about 6,000 Greeks massed in front of the American embassy in Athens demanding an end to nuclear tests, encouraged no doubt by the Group of Six initiatives to which Papandreou enthusiastically subscribed, while in March more than 4,000 supporters of Greece's military dictatorship of 1967-74, whose rise to power in the first instance had been justified on the most extreme anti-communist grounds, marched through Athens demanding immediate release of 17 former officers serving prison terms.[53]

V. THE MIDDLE EAST

As noted in Section IV, PASOK tends to be influenced by anti-imperialist, anti-American, pro-Third World trends important for the European left, no more so than on the Middle East. Unlike the French left, however, Greek socialists seem to have little interest in Israel as a progressive polity symbolic of the defeat of anti-semitism in European civilization. Instead, the leanings of Papandreou and his followers in the Middle East move more in directions prevalent in many Third World nations where Libya, Syria and the PLO find so much favor. These leanings have led Papandreou into something of a trap in American policy, however, not only with the Reagan administration but with forces in U.S. politics generally unsympathetic with the Reaganites on East-West relations. His stands on Palestinian rights, Libya's leadership and Arab support of terrorist organizations, positions basically anti-Israel by definition, have threatened Papandreou with loss of valuable support in liberal as well as conservative circles in the United States. In the postwar period, the Greek Left, and Papandreou in particular, has found strong support in an alliance of pro-Israel and pro-Greek individuals and groups among American liberals. In the Middle East, Papandreou's desire for independence from American policy has meant taking sides against Israel. This independent posture may also be influenced by economic considerations of some importance to Greece.

Some of the more dramatic confrontations since 1981 between the U.S. and Greece over policy in the Middle East have occurred on Libya and the related issue of terrorism. The matters of the Palestine Liberation Organization (PLO), Israel and Syria are obviously connected to other policy shifts of PASOK on the Middle East and have, in certain instances, also brought Greece into conflict with the United States.

Libya

In early 1981, when Greece was still governed by the New Democracy party, a Libyan pilot was granted asylum when he landed on Crete in a Soviet-built MiG-23. In retaliation, Colonel Muammar el-Qaddafi cut off Greece's oil supply, a move by Libya that may also have been partly due to a visit to Israel by the Greek minister of agriculture. Scarcely in any policy area did such a sudden and dramatic shift of policy occur in the transition from New Democracy to PASOK as on the question of Libya.

In early April 1982 the Papandreou government announced that Colonel Qaddafi would visit Greece on April 30, a visit subsequently cancelled due to "unforeseen circumstances." Athens noted that the Qaddafi visit was meant to show Greek "independence" from Western policy.[54] This new found independence did not prevent the Papandreou government, however, from formally protesting Libyan interference in Greek domestic affairs after Libya's diplomats in Athens had criticized the Middle East policies of the opposition conservative party.[55]

By 1984 it was clear that Papandreou's new relationship with Libya had economic as well as political motivations; indeed, the idea of Greece's independence from Western policies on Libya was probably supported by a growing *interdependence* between economically troubled Greece and financially solvent Libya. In September the two countries signed a $1 billion economic cooperation agreement in Tripoli: Greece would sell arms to Libya and repair its commercial vessels as well as buy Libyan oil at "unspecified preferential" terms over three years.[56] Amid reports that Greece was protesting possible Qaddafi activities in Athens against Libyan exiles, France's Francois Mitterrand and Qaddafi were meeting on the island of Crete, with Papandreou as mediator, on the Chad issue.

American and Greek policy collided most dramatically after the April 1986 U.S. raids on Libya. During the build-up to this event earlier in the year, U.S. Deputy Secretary of State John C. Whitehead had provoked a diplomatic contretemps in Athens during January where he claimed that Greece had actually known of Qaddafi's role in terrorist attacks, an allegation denied by Greek foreign minister Karolos Papoulias.[57] In the same month an EEC joint declaration condemning international terrorism, an initiative inspired by the United States, removed all references to Libya at the request of France, Greece, Italy and Spain.[58]

After the American air attacks on Libya in April 1986 the Greek government was quick to condemn the bombing and called for a meeting of EEC's foreign ministers. Having voted to support the EEC on diplomatic and economic restrictions on Libya, Greece then fought specific EEC curbs on Libya and its diplomats; in the course of these discussions Greece obtained a concession that Libya would be able to respond to any proposed EEC restrictions before they took effect. Papandreou pronounced as "absurd" the idea that the United States might enter a state of war against Libya to end terrorism; he insisted there existed no "tangible proof" of Libyan involvement with the Berlin discotheque bombings. Western diplomats were reported to say that the U.S. was disturbed by Greek unwillingness to carry out EEC restrictions against Libya even though it had joined in unanimous support of the original measure.[59] By mid-1986, however, American attention had shifted from Libya's to Syria's role in international terror and Papandreou, true to his vow of independence from U.S. domination, moved to a pro-Syrian position as well as one partisan to Libya.

Syria

The visit of President Hafez al-Assad to Athens in May 1986 gave Papandreou yet another opportunity to express a sense of distance between himself and Washington on matters of international terrorism. In a toast at a state dinner in Assad's honor, the prime minister indirectly criticized the American position on terrorism and also renewed his support for "national liberation struggles" such as those against Israel.[60] Perhaps in response to this gesture of independence the U.S. Department of State labelled recent Papandreou criticisms of American policy on combatting terrorism "baseless and unhelpful."[61] In October and November of the same year Greece declined to go along with sanctions imposed by the EEC on Syria in the wake of the El Al airliner incident, saying that Syria should not be put in the same bracket with Libya when it comes to terrorism. By this time the Greek government was discreetly advising the world that the number of Libyan diplomats in Athens had been significantly reduced. Papandreou's strong backing for Libya probably grew out of economic more than sentimental considerations, whereas the support for Syria must have been more purely ideological. But how then would one explain Papandreou's enthusiasm for Yasir Arafat and the PLO who were considered enemies by Assad? This confusion was endemic to Papandreou's foreign policy, trapped between movement and government, and impacted on his more general views about terrorism and the Arab-Israeli conflict. In turn, his quandaries on terrorists—at once the sons and daughters of "national liberation struggles" and yet criminals in his own country as well as elsewhere—affected his credibility as an alliance leader in the eyes of the United States and perhaps in the minds of his countrymen.

Terrorism

No sooner had the PLO forces, with their leader Arafat, been evacuated by Greek ships from the Lebanese port of Tripoli in late December 1983 than terrorist activity erupted in Western Europe and the Mediterranean. The PLO's near disastrous defeat by Israel in Lebanon had seemingly inspired new waves of terrorism against Western targets, although the timing of this upsurge, which began early in 1984, may have been connected with other events in Lebanon and elsewhere as well. Whatever the reasons, terrorism became a central preoccupation of NATO after 1983 and the Athens airport a major focus of international concern.

During the first half of 1984 terrorist activities by Arab groups in Athens escalated. While the Greek government's response to cases of attacks on Libyan exiles was apparently an expression of "deep concern" to Libya's ambassador,[62] its release of a Jordanian member of the "15th of May" group, arrested after having been discovered by U.S. and British experts with bombs in his possession was strongly protested by the United States.[63] American unhappiness with the latter case reached the point where State and Defense Department officials were said to be nearing a decision by mid-year to delay acquisition by Greece of surplus Norwegian F-5 aircraft.[64] These events were mere harbingers of what was to come.

In June 1985 two Lebanese Shiite Muslim gunmen hijacked a TWA jetliner carrying 153 passengers after it had taken off from the Athens airport.[65] This ultimately led to the intense crisis at the Beirut airport and the death of one American sailor. On President Reagan's orders, the U.S. State Department warned travelers in July of the high risk of terrorism at the Athens airport, a warning greeted by a strong Greek protest.[66] An attack on the Glyphada Hotel near Athens wounded 18 British tourists in September: a phone call warned that unless a Palestinian arrested in Athens with a suitcase filled with arms was released, the Black September group would "fill Athens with bombs."[67] In November an Egyptian airliner en route from Athens to Cairo was also hijacked by Arab gunmen, while in December three Greeks were among those killed in simultaneous Arab terrorist attacks on El Al service counters at the Rome and Vienna airports.[68] Clearly, Papandreou's government, supportive of "national liberation struggles," faced serious problems in both international and domestic credibility as far as management of its security policy was concerned.

As noted earlier, an easing of tensions between the United States and Greece opened the door for a Shultz visit to Athens in March 1986. Once there, however, he used the occasion to urge tougher anti-terrorist measures by Greece as well as support for Washington's actions against Qaddafi.[69] The secretary of state no doubt was mindful that his remarks would reach Greek public opinion much more directly if he made them in person in Greece. While the Libyan raid affair brought a sharp downturn in U.S.-Greek relations, it was relatively short-lived. By the end of May, there were reports that Papandreou had shaken up the leadership of Greece's intelligence and security services.[70] Yet in December the interior ministers of the EEC, except Greece, had agreed on which countries support terrorism, although they did not make the list public for security reasons.[71]

Fundamentally the source of much of the Arab terrorism visited upon Western Europe and the Mediterranean in the 1980s has had some relationship to the unresolved Arab-Israeli conflict. Papandreou's strong beliefs in the justice of Palestinian claims in this struggle, as yet unsatisfied, probably explains the ambivalence he and his party feel not only toward control of international terrorism but also toward Israel itself. And on this topic, as no other, Papandreou and the Greek Left risk alienation of powerful liberal support in the United States.

Arab-Israeli Conflict

As if to underline the importance of Palestinian rights for PASOK, within two days of Papandreou's swearing in as prime minister, Greece announced that it would upgrade the status of PLO offices in Athens. At the same time the new prime minister invited Yasir Arafat to Athens. Israel immediately called on Greece to withhold this upgrading and to withdraw its invitation to Arafat. Two months later Greece announced, at the end of a successful visit by Arafat to Athens, that the PLO would be given full diplomatic status.[72]

The following year the PLO was to become a central preoccupation of the new Papandreou government. In June 1982 Greece criticized Israel's invasion of Lebanon in the strongest terms and likened this action against the Palestinians in Lebanon to Nazi crimes against the Jews, a view Israel protested in equally strong terms.[73] During EEC talks on the withdrawal of foreign forces from Lebanon, Greece stressed the importance of the PLO as a "key element" in any future negotiations.[74] Israeli concerns in Greece were sacrificed to protest events in Lebanon. In early September Arafat arrived in Athens for a visit to express his "gratitude" for Greek support.[75] By the end of the year Greek ships had evacuated Arafat and the remaining remnants of his army from Tripoli.[76]

It is small wonder, therefore, that the Papandreou government thought it necessary to assure Greek Jews in both 1982 and 1983 that it was not anti-Semitic.[77] At the same time, Papandreou's temporizing over control of terrorist activity in Greece must have resulted from his strong commitment to Palestinian rights in the Arab-Israel conflict.

More ominous for the prime minister, as far as American liberal support for his government was concerned, were comments in 1986 by New York City Mayor Edward Koch that Papandreou's government was anti-American and anti-Jewish. In Athens widespread anger greeted these remarks, condemned as American intervention against PASOK. No less an American personage than Archbishop Iakovos, Primate of the Greek-Orthodox Archdiocese of North and South America, pronounced himself unsatisfied by Koch's attempts to clarify his remarks, and Greece's interior minister said that Koch would not be welcome in Greece.[78]

Perhaps a certain parochialism in Greek political circles has prevented partisans of Greece's newly found "independence" under PASOK from grasping the true import of Koch's remarks: a foe of the Greek military dictatorship as a member of Congress, the mayor was now clearly troubled about the political values of the same Andreas Papandreou whose cause he championed in the 1960s and 1970s. This anxiety on the part of a powerful American liberal bodes ill not only for

Papandreou's support in the United States but for Greece as well: Turkey looks more and more like a constructive influence in both NATO and the Middle East when compared with its Aegean rival. It would not be in Greece's national interest for this invidious comparison to become a matter of bipartisan consensus in the United States.

VI. THE FUTURE

What will be the future of U.S.-Greek relations under PASOK? The future of PASOK? Of the Reagan Revolution? While the course of domestic politics in the United States and Greece are quite unclear, there was evidence in the 1985 Greek parliamentary and 1986 U.S. Congressional elections that PASOK and the Reagan Revolution had lost the vigor each enjoyed in 1981 when Papandreou and Reagan began their *pas de deux*. Yet it is apparent that foreign relations between the two alliance partners have been skewed since 1981 by tensions between ideological movement and practical government in both countries. It is doubtful that U.S.-Greek relations will ever quite return to the point at which they were when this decade opened. While Turkey has always been a problem between Athens and Washington, NATO has not; Greece and the United States shared, until 1981, a common view of the Soviet Union and agreed that the chief threat to their common security was northward and not in Ankara.

Since Papandreou's election as prime minister in 1981 there has been a notable shift in official Greek attitudes toward the East-West conflict, a shift that is likely to be even more noticeable with the maturing of Mikhail Gorbachev. While differences over Turkey will continue to play a role in Greece's perception of the Western alliance, other factors, such as socialist predispositions to see the U.S. as imperialist and the Soviet Union as progressive, have entered the picture, as have strong sympathies in PASOK for Third World national liberation struggles. Papandreou has been restlessly unhappy playing the role of junior alliance partner sharing police powers over NATO's "southern flank" with Turkey. He sees his own personal role, and perhaps his movement's, of world importance, as evidenced in his participation in the Group of Six. Presumably the Soviet Union is aware of his ambitious discontent.

It was noted (in section IV above) that with the ascendancy of Gorbachev as leader and Gromyko's removal as foreign minister the Soviet Union's interest in Greece's possible "independence" from the West became much less important than Moscow's interest in Reagan's ambitious disarmament deals with the Kremlin. Yet it was also argued that "the maturing of Mikhail Gorbachev" might still bring Greece and the U.S.S.R. into a closer relationship, reviving Gromyko's propensity for seeing NATO as a kind of Soviet hunting ground where lame and stray alliance members, perhaps disenchanted with their relations with the United States, might be fair game. For over two years after Gorbachev's election as general secretary, the Soviets seemed to avoid exploitation of obvious tensions between Athens and Washington, apparently ignoring Papandreou's alienation. Then in May and June 1987, letters were exchanged between Greece's prime minister and the Soviet leader. Their existence was-made public by a Greek government outraged by a protest made by U.S. Ambassador Robert Vossler Keeley about alleged Greek negotiations with Abu Nidal, through Syrian intermediaries, to avert terrorist attacks from Greek soil. Suddenly in mid-1987 all the tensions in U.S.-Greek relations under PASOK appeared to coalesce: the bases, NATO, the threat of Turkey, Greek relations with the Soviet Union and its allies, and the Middle East.

With the future of U.S. bases in Greece in the greatest jeopardy since the end of the war, Gorbachev seemed to sense an opportunity for probing further. He was anxious to express agreement, his letter said, with "the unanimous demand of the Greek people" that the four major American bases in Greece, dedicated to NATO's defense, "should be removed from the country." According to the *New York Times* account of this exchange of correspondence, "Mr. Papandreou was reported to have suggested that, whatever else happens to American bases in Greece after the current agreement on them expires next year, they would not be used for hostile acts against friendly third powers, presumably including the Russians and their allies."[79]

In light of the mid-1987 correspondence between Gorbachev and Papandreou, as well as all the other evidence analyzed in this essay, there has been a substantial confusion of motives and aims in the Papandreou government as far as relations with the United States are concerned. It is often impossible to locate Papandreou's policy priorities and preferences. As argued earlier, one suspects that this ambiguity may well be by design in Athens and not by chance, but this is hardly a sound basis for steady U.S.-Greek relations. The results of the Reagan-Papandreou *pas de deux* on alliance defense, which may find its parallel in a second such intricate relationship between Gorbachev and Papandreou on détente, have remained provisional rather than disastrous, but the U.S.-Greek accommodation under PASOK remains improvisation and, therefore, subject to reversal. It is not the stuff of stable alliances.

NOTES

1. *New York Times*, 19 June 1981.
2. *New York Times*, 22 November 1981.
3. *New York Times*, 16, 20 May 1982.
4. *New York Times*, 6 November 1982.
5. *New York Times*, 13 January 1983.
6. *New York Times*, 29 April 1983.
7. *New York Times*, 15 July 1982; 16 July 1983.
8. *New York Times*, 31 March 1983; 1 April 1984.
9. *New York Times*, 22 February 1987.
10. *New York Times*, 3, 6 June 1985.
11. *New York Times*, 3 November 1985.
12. *New York Times*, 24 January 1987.
13. See Section III.
14. *New York Times*, 25 April 1987.
15. *New York Times*, 16 October 1987. See also section VI.
16. *New York Times*, 10 December 1981.
17. *New York Times*, 12 June 1983.
18. *New York Times*, 14 December 1984.
19. *New York Times*, 7 June 1985.
20. *Dictatorships and Double Standards: Rationalism and Reason in Politics*, New York: Simon & Schuster, 1982.
21. *New York Times*, 23 January 1985.
22. The International Institute of Strategic Studies (IISS), *The Military Balance 1986-1987*, London: IISS, 1986, p.55.
23. *Ibid.*, pp. 55-56.
24. *New York Times*, 21 August 1984.
25. *New York Times*, 17 May 1985.
26. *New York Times*, 20 December 1986.
27. *New York Times*, 28 March 1987.
28. *New York Times*, 29 March 1987; see also *New York Times*, 1 February 1988 on Papandreou-Ozal summit at Davos, Switzerland.
29. *New York Times*, 18, 21 January 1982.
30. *New York Times*, 13 January 1982.
31. *New York Times*, 6 November 1982.
32. *New York Times*, 16, 22, 25 February 1983.
33. *New York Times*, 18 May 1983.
34. *New York Times*, 9 September 1983.

35. *New York Times*, 12, 13 January 1984.
36. *New York Times*, 1 May 1984.
37. *New York Times*, 11 July 1984.
38. *New York Times*, 13 July 1984.
39. *New York Times*, 26, 27 October 1984.
40. *New York Times*, 25 November 1984.
41. *New York Times*, 22, 23 May 1984.
42. *New York Times*, 6, 7 August 1986.
43. *New York Times*, 11, 14 April 1986.
44. *New York Times*, 31 December 1986.
45. *New York Times*, 26 September 1986.
46. *New York Times*, 16 November 1986.
47. *New York Times*, 3 June 1985; 14, 20 October 1986.
48. *New York Times*, 10, 11, 12 March 1985.
49. *New York Times*, 21 November 1985; 20 October 1986.
50. *New York Times*, 12, 13 February 1985.
51. *New York Times*, 17, 27 March 1986.
52. *New York Times*, 24 January 1987; see also section VI.
53. *New York Times*, 29 January 1987; 29 March 1987.
54. *New York Times*, 25, 28 April 1987.
55. *New York Times*, 10 August 1987.
56. *New York Times*, 26 September 1984.
57. *New York Times*, 20 January 1986.
58. *New York Times*, 28 January 1986.
59. *New York Times*, 21-26 April 1986.
60. *New York Times*, 29 May 1986.
61. *New York Times*, 4 June 1986.
62. *New York Times*, 12 July 1984.
63. *New York Times*, 16 April 1984; 28 June 1984.
64. *New York Times*, 9 July 1984.
65. *New York Times*, 14 June 1985.
66. *New York Times*, 19 July 1985.
67. *New York Times*, 4 September 1985.
68. *New York Times*, 23 November 1985; 27 December 1985.
69. *New York Times*, 27 March 1986.
70. *New York Times*, 30 May 1986.
71. *New York Times*, 10 December 1986.
72. *New York Times*, 23 October 1981; 10 December 1981.
73. *New York Times*, 21, 26 June 1982.
74. *New York Times*, 29 June 1982.
75. *New York Times*, 1 September 1982.
76. *New York Times*, 16, 20, 21 December 1983.
77. *New York Times*, 14 August 1982; 14 January 1983.
78. *New York Times*, 17 September 1986; 6, 13 October 1986; 8 November 1986.
79. *New York Times* , 15 July 1987.

Greece and European Political Cooperation: The Intractable Partner

Theodore Christodoulides

THE DIVERGENCE OF THE NATIONAL INTERESTS OF GREECE FROM THE INTERESTS OF ITS FELLOW MEMBERS IN THE EEC AND ITS IMPLICATIONS FOR EUROPEAN POLITICAL COOPERATION

PASOK's accession to power in October 1981 resulted in a radical change of Greece's policy within the framework of the European Political Cooperation (EPC) system, the institutionalized process for the coordination of the EEC member states' foreign policy. These changes intruded on the national decision making process on an almost daily basis.[1]

As soon as the Greek Socialist government made its political debut in the European Community, it showed its intention to drop its predecessor's pro-European stance in favor of a new, high-sounding policy. This policy consisted of an eclectic blend of national pride, distrust of Brussels, a preference for privileged links with the nonaligned countries, upgraded relations with Moscow, and a willingness to quarrel with Washington. These vital ingredients in the political chemistry of Papandreou's foreign policy gave Greece a holiday from the constraints of the EPC system, at least during the first term of the Socialist government, disrupting the consensus basis of EPC and consequently undermining its effectiveness.

However, any attempt to evaluate PASOK's policy in the field of EPC would fall short of its target without first discussing the systemic variables that influence, in a very decisive way, the shaping of Greek foreign policy and limit its choices. In addition to these systemic variables, since October 1981 certain variables that arise from the personality and psychological makeup of PASOK's leader have had a strong bearing on the formulation of Greek foreign policy and have resulted in an increase in its fluidity.

The systemic variables that impose constraints on the

foreign policy of Greece occasionally act to impede the convergence of the national interests of Greece and those of its EEC fellow members in the EPC process. This political reality, however, was allowed for when EPC was conceived. Though the effectiveness of the EPC system depends on the increasing convergence or homogenization of the national interests of the twelve EEC member states, such a homogenization has not yet been achieved. The EPC machinery, however, attempts to smooth the edges of diverging or conflicting national attitudes in order to make common action possible. The feasibility of this attempt is minimized whenever the divergence from the common position shaped by the EPC process is not due to the pursuit of the fundamental goals of a nation's foreign policy but is instead either dictated by parochial and short-term domestic political interests or serves the purpose of exalting the image and personality cult of a national leader. This point has to be kept in mind for the proper understanding of PASOK's policy in the field of EPC.

The systemic variables are, in general terms, such matters as dependence and interdependence, alliances, actions and intentions of third states, and disputes with neighboring countries. The goals and priorities of Greek foreign policy that might make Greece's interests divergent from those of its fellow members in the EEC are the Greek-Turkish dispute, the Cyprus issue, Greece's relations with the United States, the Arab countries and the Balkan states, its crucial geographical location, and a worrisome and worsening hard-currency debt that makes the country increasingly more dependent on the international credit system.

The Greek-Turkish dispute concerning the division of the continental shelf in the Aegean and the obvious expansionist policy of Ankara create security priorities for Greece that are substantially different from those of the other EEC countries. Admittedly, the participation of the latter—with the exception of Ireland—in NATO evidences their perception that their security is being threatened only by the Warsaw Pact.[2] For Greece, the direct threat to its security and territorial integrity comes from Turkey. This is a strong conviction shared alike by the Greek people and their political leadership.[3] The official confirmation of the divergence of Greek security priorities from those of Greece's EEC partners was the promulgation of a new defense doctrine by the PASOK government in January 1985. This doctrine addresses the military threat from the east (i.e.,

Turkey) rather than that from the north (the Warsaw Pact).[4] Certainly, Greece remains in NATO not only for the reason that dictated its accession to the alliance—viz., its need for the protection from an attack by the Warsaw Pact powers—but also to avert the expansion of Turkey's operational role in the Aegean in the event of a Greek withdrawal from the alliance.[5] Such an act would have enhanced Ankara's role as the only credible defensive support of Western interests in the Eastern Mediterranean.

The Cyprus issue also compels Greece to pursue a policy that will secure the support of the nonaligned countries in the United Nations that could provide the institutional framework and the mechanisms whereby a solution to the problem might be devised. In trying to obtain the backing of Third World countries, Greece has to align itself with them, often resulting in the disruption of community cohesion in the U.N. General Assembly.

The Greek-Turkish dispute and the Cyprus issue strengthen Greece's dependence on the United States. The maintenance of a 10:7 ratio in military aid granted respectively to Turkey and Greece seems to secure the balance of power in the Aegean, but only if the United States continues its funding in these proportions. Washington might also play a significant role in the solution of the Cyprus problem by either actively espousing the initiative of the U.N. secretary-general or by pressuring Turkey to limit its intransigence; although the effectiveness of such an action—even if it is in fact among the responses planned by the American administration—should not be overestimated. Greek dependence on the United States interposes another factor that differentiates or particularizes Greece's interests with regard to those of the other EEC member states. The latter, even though they may have a "special relationship" with the United States (as does Great Britain), or even though their security may depend directly upon the presence of American troops on their soil (as in the case of West Germany), nevertheless maintain a greater margin of choice than does Greece in the field of foreign policy.

The long-standing and warm relations of Greece with the Arab countries rest on historical, economic, and political grounds. After 1974 the Greek government's pro-Arab policy gained new momentum. The policy was designed firstly to advance Greece's economic interests in Arab markets (by increasing the market for Greek exports and for overseas construction of public works by Greek companies) and to help Greece meet its oil needs with imports from Arab oil-exporting states; and, secondly, to counterbalance the growing Turkish influence in the Moslem world and to avert the recognition of the Turk-Cypriot "pseudo-state" by the Islamic countries.[6] Thus Greece is not only the sole EEC member state that has not yet recognized Israel *de jure* but also the only country of the European Community that conferred diplomatic status on representatives of the PLO and bestowed a warm welcome on its leader. Greece's pro-Arab stance might strengthen the credibility of the European Community in the Arab world, but at the same time it restrains the formulation of the European Community's Middle East policy whenever this rests on the rule of equidistance (i.e., on the determination to avoid favoring either side). Apart from that, Greece's refusal to recognize Israel *de jure* is a considerable constraint on the undertaking of any initiative by the PASOK government for the settlement of the Middle East issue during periods when Greece presides over the European Community.

Included among the priorities of Greek foreign policy are the maintenance of smooth relations with the Balkan countries and the development of a multidimensional cooperation with them in economic, technical, and cultural fields. The *Nordpolitik* that Constantine Karamanlis embarked on after the restoration of the democratic regime in Greece is being pursued by Papandreou's government, though the venture of Balkan cooperation has degenerated into a flabby and often retrograde process. Papandreou's initiative for a nuclear-free Balkans, which has been the main ideological component of the Greek government's Balkan policy since 1983, has fallen through mainly because of Turkey's opposition.[7] Turkey opposes denuclearization of the Balkans without an agreement with the Soviet Union on the reduction of conventional forces. The plexus of Greece's relations with the Balkan countries is another cause of the divergence of interests within the EPC framework, as Greece's fellow members in the EEC have a very limited interest in Balkan affairs and are unlikely to become deeply involved in them.[8]

Greece's geographic location, considered in relation to the spread of the armed conflicts in the Mediterranean and the Middle East, might also lead to the divergence of Greek positions from those of other member states within the EPC system. In this context the proximity of Greece to regions of temporary or prolonged crises results in a circumstantial redefinition of the country's security priorities that limits its political choices.

Last, but hardly least, Greece's ever-increasing dependence on the international credit system acts as a restrictive factor on its foreign policy. This dependence is due to the great deficit in its balance of payments and a still-growing public debt that is reaching unsustainable levels. However, it may also contribute to the convergence of Greek positions and those of the other community members in the foreign-policy coordination process. For example, an EEC loan to Greece of 1.75 billion Eurocurrency units (ECU) in November 1985, which enabled the Greek government to avoid the politically humiliating rescheduling of its external debt and the necessity of resorting to the International Monetary Fund (IMF), has put a temporary brake on the tendency of Greek foreign policy to diverge from the common positions adopted within the EPC system. Such an effect is likelier to occur whenever the need for such a loan, or the payment of an installment of one, coincides with the making of significant decisions by the twelve member states in the sphere of foreign policy.

PASOK'S ATTITUDE TOWARD THE EPC SYSTEM

Since its establishment in 1974, PASOK has adopted radical positions in the realm of foreign policy. The protection of national independence that would be secured by Greece's withdrawal from, or nonaccession to, military alliances and economic organizations had been the focal point of PASOK's foreign policy. In relation to the entry of Greece into the EEC, the founder and president of PASOK, Andreas Papandreou, had pointed out, "The safeguarding of our national independence implies that Greece will remain out of the EEC, as its accession to the Community will complete the dependence of our country on the Brussels Directoire."[9] According to the assessment of PASOK's leader, "the EEC is essentially the economic aspect of the same coalition of powers which in the political-military field is being manifested through the North-Atlantic Pact. Therefore the view of some romantics who believe that the accession of Greece to the EEC implies the relieving of our country from the dominant influence of the USA is logically unacceptable. The time has come to realize that the parallel developments in the EEC and NATO express after all the strategy of one and the same decision-making center, in which the USA plays a leading role."[10] PASOK's strong opposition to the accession of Greece to the EEC, and its view of the EEC as an instrument for the advancement of Atlantic interests responding to the directives of Washington, shape the Socialist party's negative attitude towards EPC. Besides, in accordance with PASOK's ideological pronouncements, "the European policy cannot aim for the establishment of a new superpower [a new political entity with its own foreign and defense policy] but for a general transformation that will result in the creation of a confederated Europe...with the inclusion of Western and Eastern countries...."[11]

After its accession to power, PASOK—and especially its leader—moved with an uncommon political flexibility towards moderate positions with regard to European policy. This quasi-Damascene conversion was due in part to the pressure of the harsh realities of the international environment, but its more important cause was the dire necessity caused by the state of the Greek economy. After two years in office, the Greek prime minister realized that although the cost of Greece's entry into the EEC was high, the cost of withdrawal might be even higher.[12] But PASOK's attitude towards EPC did not change significantly until 1985, for three reasons.

The first is the Socialist party's political obsession with its "independent Greek foreign policy that would contribute by all means to the breaking up of the coalitions which divide the world and Europe" and manifest Greece's "active solidarity with all the peoples who struggle for their national independence and fight against imperialism."[13] The objective of an "independent Greek foreign policy," with all that that objective implies, prevented Greece from complying with the rules that govern the political cooperation of its fellow members in the EEC. This is mainly due to the fact that those rules are meant for a group of states that, despite differences and divergence in their own foreign policies, belong ideologically and politically to a coalition of powers that includes the United States.[14]

The importance that PASOK's government attributed to the pursuit of an "independent Greek foreign policy," even though it ran counter to the logic of the EPC system and undermined its effectiveness, had been made clear through Greece's meaningless reservation to the Solemn Declaration of European Union signed by the ten member states in Stuttgart on 13 June 1983. With regard to EPC the declaration provided that in order "to promote the objective of a Europe speaking with a single voice and acting in common in the field of foreign policy, the Governments of the Member States will make a constant effort to increase the effectiveness of Political Cooperation and will seek in particular to facilitate the decision making process, in order to reach common positions more rapidly...."[15] Despite the politically watered-down and legally platonic character of this provision, the Greek government considered it necessary to make the following declaration, which was recorded in the minutes of the Stuttgart conference: "By signing this Declaration Greece declares that nothing can limit its right to formulate its foreign policy according to its national interests."

This reservation was particularly astonishing, as the Stuttgart Declaration has no legal binding force and therefore can in no way limit the rights of the signatory states. Apart from that, since EPC is based on consensus, it can under no circumstances compel a member state to act in opposition to its national interests. By making this reservation to an instrument that aims to strengthen the European cooperation, Papandreou's government proved that it did not realize or accept the fundamental principle that inspired the establishment of the EPC system. It is self-evident that all the EEC countries seek to shape their foreign policy in conformity with their national interests. But they rightly consider that their national interests are served more effectively by formulating common positions and pursuing common actions, the *raison d'être* of the EPC process. However, the Greek reservation to the Stuttgart Declaration made clear that PASOK's government does not share this view.[16] Through this reservation, devoid of any real significance but implying an indirect political cost at the community level, Papandreou's government seized the chance to reaffirm the doctrine of an "independent Greek foreign policy" at a time when the latter had lost its ideological brightness because of Greece's decision not to withdraw from the EEC and NATO. Simultaneously PASOK tried to blunt the reactions of the Greek Communist party, which was watching the overtures of the Socialist government towards Europe with ever-growing distrust and disappointment.

One may find a confirmation of the motives behind the PASOK government's attitude in a statement by the then foreign minister, Giannes Charalambopoulos. A few days after the signing of the Stuttgart Declaration, Foreign Minister Charalambopoulos, addressing the European Parliament in his capacity as president of the Council of Ministers, pointed out, with regard to EPC, that "the acceptance of the overall acquis politique' of the Community implies for us a higher cost; a cost that we cannot bear in certain cases. This is due not only to the fact that, as you may realize, we cannot abandon some of our traditional positions but also because it would not be suitable for us to give the world the impression that after our entry to the Community we are obliged to adopt views that are diametrically opposed to those we upheld until now."[17] Four months later, from the same forum and in the same capacity, the Greek foreign minister answered oral questions from members of the European Parliament; he stressed that "it's becoming obvious...from the recent Stuttgart Declaration that certain countries have reserved for themselves the right to carry out their foreign policy without any constraint."[18] In a similar vein the Greek prime minister, pointing out the ideological importance of an "independent Greek foreign policy" doctrine for his government, asserted: "Our national independence poses a problem for us that either does not exist for the other [community] countries or, if it does exist, is different and on a much smaller scale. The acquisition of Greek voice, namely to enable our people through their government to determine the course of the country, is something new for us."[19]

We should also note that the fact that PASOK's government hastened to represent the signing of the Stuttgart Declaration as a tactical maneuver and not as an act of commitment to European Community ideals lays bare its political mentality and intentions. Signing the Declaration not only did not constrain, but on the contrary extended, Greece's ability to implement a national foreign policy, considering that the Stuttgart Declaration was represented by the Greek government as a step in the process of disengagement from the United States. This was the position held by the Greek foreign undersecretary, Theodoros Pangalos, in his answer to a question put to him in the Parliament by a deputy of the Greek Communist party. This governmental official, having emphasized the significance of the reservation made by the Greek prime minister to the Stuttgart declaration, stated in Parliament: "We deeply believe in the idea that the disengagement of Europe from the influence of the United States will not only increase the ability of European countries to develop their national identities but will also contribute positively to the pursuance of detente and international peace."[20]

The second ground that inspired PASOK's negative attitude towards the EPC system until 1985 was PASOK's anti-European—or more correctly its anticommunity—ideology. The influence of the Socialists' ideological stance towards Europe was much stronger in the field of EPC than in the European Economic Community itself. This was due to the nature of the topics discussed within the context of EPC as well as to the government's inability to invoke the same alibi in EPC discussions that it cites within the EEC framework, a given measure's economic cost to Greek interests. PASOK considers the EEC to be an economic venture, a "common market" that does not impose obligations in the realm of political integration, rather than a "community" whose definition includes an ideological dimension. This dimension rests on an established belief in certain political, economic, social, and cultural values that differentiate the EEC from traditional intergovernmental organizations. Moreover, according to PASOK's view, the success of this economic venture and especially the development of community solidarity depend on the intensity of financing flows from the Brussels funds. This economic conception of the community undertaking has been portrayed by Charalambopoulos in his capacity as president of the Council of Ministers, addressing the European Parliament. Having initially stressed that the direct targets of the Greek presidency were "the convergence of the economies of the Member States and the blunting of structural or other disparities, as well as the future financing of the Community," the Greek foreign minister pointed out, with regard to EPC, that "it is neither possible nor advisable for the Ten to adopt a monolithic attitude in the world affairs."[21] What is more surprising is the fact that the above position was advanced only sixteen days after the signing of the Stuttgart Declaration. Speaking from the same forum, Prime Minister Papandreou, being less blunt but equally revealing, made no mention of the EPC system but referred to a Europe "with a more *cohesive external trade policy* presenting a more powerful identity to the rest of the world." (emphasis added)[22] Even while underscoring the need for "a new Messina," the Greek prime minister made his position clear by stating that "*without abolishing the spirit of the Treaty of Rome* we shall attempt to redefine our positions on the more important problems of our times."(emphasis added)[23]

The third reason for PASOK's negative stance towards European cooperation, until the formation of its second government, must be sought in the nature of the EPC system itself. More specifically, what made possible the negative attitude of the Socialist government was the absence of a legally constituted institutional framework with procedures of binding character that would, despite the existence of escape clauses, justify deviations from common positions only on certain conditions or under special circumstances. On the contrary, the required consensus for the EPC system and the loosely articulated mechanisms by which it functioned could rarely avert the failure of member states to follow the foreign-policy convergence process. That was particularly evident in the case of those EEC countries that had not yet developed the concert reflex because of their relatively recent entry into the European Community.

PASOK's position towards EPC began to change after its victory in the 1985 parliamentary elections and the formation of the second, or "new," Socialist government. It is not certain whether this change was due "to an attempt of the government to exploit the EPC mechanisms and processes" or whether it was related to the faltering Greek economy.[24] Greece's patent inability to service a constantly increasing external debt forced the Papandreou government to resort to the EEC in order to secure a loan. It is self-evident that the EEC's upgraded importance to the Greek economy did not allow the PASOK government to play the part of the "terrible child" within the EPC system any longer without bearing the consequences. However, it seems that both factors had contributed equally to making Papandreou's government veer towards EPC: namely, the government's attempt to exploit the mechanisms and processes of European cooperation in order to reinforce its politico-diplomatic supports in view of the intensifying Turkish threat in the Aegean and Greece's growing dependence on the EEC to meet the dire needs of its wretched economy.

The enhancement of political cooperation by the conclusion of a treaty on the formulation and implementation of a common foreign and security policy had been discussed in the European Council during its Milan session in June 1985. Although the Greek prime minister accepted the necessity of a European identity in the external relations and combined it with the maintenance of international peace, detente and good relations with the Third World, he eventually opposed the proposal of convening an international conference that would draw up such a treaty. Any progress towards the goal of common foreign policy through EPC would imply a shrinking of the discretionary power of EEC member states, either to undertake initiatives or to diverge from the common foreign policy positions. However, such a development could not be accepted by a government that had made an "independent Greek foreign policy" doctrine the frontispiece of its programmatic pronouncements. The Greek prime minister did not agree to the proposed creation of a secretariat for political cooperation, an organ that "would tend to progressively limit the role of the Council and become a new centre of power." Nevertheless, during the same summit meeting Papandreou's consent to the extension of EPC into the sphere of security had exhibited a definite change from PASOK's previous positions. The Greek premier agreed to such an extension since "it aims to seek a European identity in this field on the condition that the special security problems confronted by certain Member States, such as Greece, would be duly taken into consideration."[25]

In spite of the prime minister's negative attitude in the Milan meeting of the European Council, a month later Greece agreed to an intergovernmental conference, to be convened on 9 September. This conference would draw up the treaty on the European Political Cooperation policy and revise the EEC Treaty according to its article 236.[26] During the intergovernmental conference Greece did not hold considerably different positions with regard to EPC from those of its fellow members in the European Community. On the contrary, it adopted a low profile, without stating any reservations about the treaty, as it had in the case of the Stuttgart Declaration; even though this time it was a question of a legally binding text with precise engagements and not a proclamation of abstract political views. According to the communiqué that followed the end of the conference, "unlike the other issues dealt with by the Conference endorsement of the Treaty on political cooperation did not raise any special problems."[27] Moreover, in the European Council that met in Luxembourg on 2 December 1985, the Greek prime minister took a fairly positive view of the work of the intergovernmental conference.[28]

THE INTERACTION BETWEEN THE EPC SYSTEM AND GREEK FOREIGN POLICY: GREEK DIVERGENCES FROM EUROPEAN COMMUNITY POLICY

Greece was the first country to join the European Community after the mechanisms of EPC had been articulated and a set of principles, rules, and practices that secured the functioning of EPC had nearly been completed. The first enlargement of the European Community had coincided with the initial stage of the EPC venture and consequently the three new EEC members—Great Britain, Ireland, and Denmark—were not confronted with problems of adaptation. Greece was certainly under no legal obligation to endorse all the decisions taken in the EPC context and adapt its foreign policy accordingly, since these decisions do not have the character of "acquis communautaire" like the law-enacting acts of the EEC. However, the Greek government, in order to facilitate the smooth functioning of the EPC mechanisms, was obliged to comply with the basic rules of the game, viz., all the regulations instituted up to that time.

Greece's first year in the EPC system coincided with the change in government and PASOK's accession to power. During the adaptation period, the New Democracy government had manifested no intention to diverge from the common positions or to undertake initiatives for the advancement of Greek interests through the EPC process. Besides, there was no significant development in the crucial questions of Greek foreign policy, and the forthcoming elections had shifted the emphasis of the governmental activity into the domestic field. The vigorous attempt of the government to meet the challenge and respond to the obligations and requirements of accession to the EEC had considerably narrowed the margin for any action or initiative that would justify the introduction of divergence into the EPC system. The acceptance of the London Report (13 October 1981) by the government of the New Democracy clearly, though indirectly, evidenced its intention to contribute to the enhancement of EPC by making the system more functional and effective, even though the report implied additional obligations in certain cases.[29]

What followed PASOK's accession to power was a dramatic change of the diplomatic scenery. In a paradoxical way, the EPC was considered by the Greek prime minister to be the politically appropriate framework for the direct application of the "Greco-centric" foreign policy doctrine that would allow Greece to shake off the master-client relationship that in his view had decisively influenced the policy of his predecessors. In addition, Papandreou seized the opportunity to demonstrate his anti-European ideology, aiming, *inter alia*, at dissipating the impressions created by his backing down on the issue of Greece's withdrawal from the EEC. At the same time the EPC system provided the forum for the prime minister to send out "confused signals" that would keep open or even enlarge the political approaches to the socialist states and the Third World countries. However, it was to be expected that the Papandreou government's intentions would be irreconcilable with the rigid pro-Western stance of the EPC system, and that consequently Greece's participation would disrupt its cohesion. Under these conditions the interaction between EPC and Greece's foreign policy was brought down to a very low level.

As becomes clear from the account of Greece's participation in the EPC system, the divergence of PASOK government policy from the policy and process of other governments within the EPC framework has been dictated by other goals as well as those mentioned above. This policy divergence was also intended to provide immediate advantages in the field of domestic politics either by holding the sympathy of the Left or by allowing the government to make certain politically painful but unavoidable choices at the least possible cost. Thus it is not merely coincidental that in the Athens EPC meeting on 12 September 1983, during the Greek presidency of the European Community, the PASOK government, having just signed an agreement with the Americans to allow them to keep their military bases in Greece, vetoed an EEC attempt to condemn the Soviet Union for shooting down Korean Airlines Flight 007. This was an act of brassy political theater that aimed at distracting attention from the American bases deal, appeasing PASOK's left wing, which had been disappointed at seeing their leader back down, and satisfying the powerful pro-Moscow Greek Communist party. At the same meeting Foreign Minister Charalambopoulos, who held the chair, restated a Greek proposal to put off deployment of American missiles in Europe for six months, as this would have taken the pressure off the Russians and made a compromise in the Geneva arms-control talks easier. He also suggested an easing of the EEC's sanctions against the Soviet Union, which had been introduced after the imposition of martial law in Poland.[30]

However, Greek policy divergence in the EPC system had started much earlier—only a week after the formation of the PASOK government. The Greek foreign minister, attending his first EEC meeting in Luxembourg, on 28 October 1981, opposed the European Community's plan to take part in an international peacekeeping operation by contributing troops from four of its members—Great Britain, Italy, France, and Holland.[31] Army units from these countries would join the Sinai peacekeeping force that had been provided by the Camp David Accord for policing Sinai until the Israeli withdrawal. This suggestion of linking the EPC system with the Camp David Accord which did not provide for the participation of the Palestinians in the settlement of the Middle East issue, ignited the opposition of the Greek government, which had just decided to recognize the PLO and intended to "cozy up to the Arabs."

A month later, the Greek government's pro-Arab stance gave rise to a new divergence of attitude in the EPC context. In the foreign ministers meeting on 17 November, the defense of Libya's regime by the Greek delegate resulted in a watered-down community statement on Chad that made no mention of Colonel Qaddafi's intervention in that country.[32]

The PASOK government's divergence in the EPC grew on a considerable scale with regard to the Polish question. After the Brussels meeting on 4 January 1982, the foreign ministers of the ten European Community countries condemned the repression in Poland, called for an early end to martial law and extended their censure to the Soviet Union.[33] This mildly formulated communiqué represented the least possible reaction of the EEC members, whose differing interests and diverging views precluded their taking a stronger stance and imposing sanctions against the Soviet Union over Poland. Even so, the Greek government hastened to break rank immediately. Within hours after the end of the meeting, Prime Minister Papandreou peremptorily dismissed Deputy Foreign Minister Asimakis Fotilas, who had signed the communiqué, even though the latter had worked hard to smooth its edges. This dramatic disassociation of the Greek government from the common position adopted by the other nine EEC countries conveyed a clear message: Papandreou was determined to avoid any anti-Soviet move that would cost him the sympathy of the socialist states and might terminate the support or even possibly the tolerance of the Greek Communist party.

On 23 February the EEC members agreed to impose mild sanctions against the Soviet Union over Poland. Half of the Soviet exports of luxury and manufactured goods to the EEC, not exceeding 8 percent of the total Soviet exports to the European Community countries, would be blocked by import quotas.[34] This decision had been taken in the context of the trade policy of the EEC on the basis of Article 113 of its founding treaty. By not voting on the decision to impose sanctions against the Soviet Union, Greece distanced itself once more from the common attitude of its EEC partners.

Greece's next divergence within the EPC framework—which resulted in the use of the veto by the Greek presidency in order to avert the condemnation of the Soviet Union for shooting down the Korean airliner—has already been mentioned. However, the fact that during the Athens meeting of 12 September the presiding Greek foreign minister violated the confidential character of the EPC system is not devoid of political significance. This Greek official's noncompliance with EPC rules lends support to the view that the government's attitude was mainly aimed at creating a favorable impression on a certain part of Greek public opinion. The confidential character of the EPC process is safeguarded by the prohibition of any unauthorized leak to the press. After the EPC ministerial meetings, during a press conference the foreign minister who holds the chair is supposed to make a general reference to the discussed topics according to the commonly defined directives. The briefing of the press concerns the points of agreement exclusively, and the interviewee is not to refer to points of divergence or disagreement.[35] However, the Greek foreign minister openly violated this rule when, after the Athens EPC ministerial meeting, he announced to the press that Greece was the only country that struggled to prevent its partners from formally condemning the Soviets.[36] Finally, with regard to the Korean airliner incident, it is noteworthy that after a few tense hours, Greece and its EEC partners reached agreement in New York on 26 September on the European Community's statement of its policy to the U.N. General Assembly. After lengthy discussions, the Greek foreign minister agreed to be tougher, and he straightforwardly condemned the downing of the Korean airliner by the Soviets.[37]

In the Luxembourg EPC meeting on 21 April 1986, a week after the American bombing of Tripoli and Benghazi, the EEC countries agreed to impose certain mild diplomatic sanctions on Colonel Qaddafi. They decided to cut the size of Libyan diplomatic and trade missions down to a minimum, limit the freedom of movement of Libyan diplomats, and tighten controls on other Libyans.[38] Greece not only wanted milder sanctions but refused to apply the measures against the Libyan regime, even though it had voted for them, unless it had "tangible proof" that Libya fostered terrorism.[39] The PASOK government's attitude in this incident must be viewed in the light of the then forthcoming municipal elections and the austerity program that had alienated the government from a considerable portion of leftist sympathy. The prime minister had not the least hesitation in seizing his chance in the EPC meeting and mounting an anti-American diversion in order to enhance his tarnished political image and recapture the alienated leftist vote.

Last in the series of Greek deviations from EPC policy-making, but possibly bearing more serious implications, was Greece's refusal to align itself with its partners in the condemnation of Syria for the latter's role in the attempt to blow up an EL-AL airliner. During the EPC ministerial meeting on 27 October 1986 the EEC members, irked by Greece's attitude, announced their readiness, through the presiding foreign minister Sir Geoffrey Howe, to take measures against Syria even without Greece's concurrence.[40] Eventually, in the London EPC meeting of the foreign ministers on 10 November 1986, the European Community states took the threatened measures—a ban on arms sales to Syria, a limitation of high-level contacts with Syrian officials, control of the activities of the diplomatic and consular missions of Syria in the EEC countries, intensification of the preventive security measures taken with respect to the movement of Syrian airliners—but Greece refused to sign the common communiqué. The Greek attitude, which may be attributed to PASOK's close and helpful relations with the ruling party of Syria, has been justified by Foreign Undersecretary Pangalos with the contention that Greece was not ready to accept the Syrian government's involvement in the Hindawi affair.[41] According to the statement of the Greek undersecretary during a press conference, "Syria is a serious country," and consequently its claims should be taken duly into consideration. On the other hand, he stated, the sanctions against Syria "cannot be practically applied by Greece as our country does not sell arms to Syria, has no regular high level official contacts with this country and already exerts strict control on the embassies and the air companies of the States involved in the Middle East issue."[42]

The eleven EEC members' decision to impose sanctions against Syria was the first to be taken through the EPC process without the consent of a member state. It was undoubtedly due to Greece's frequent divergence from the EPC policy making process in the past and set a precedent that limits the effectiveness and consequently the significance of such divergence in the future. In other words, from now on it is likely that the eleven community partners will proceed to the decision taken within the EPC context even without Greece's consent. Such a development may take place despite the fact that the Single European Act enhances the importance of consensus in the EPC process, providing, however, that "the High Contracting Parties shall, as far as possible, refrain from impeding the formation of a consensus and the joint action which this could produce." (art. 30, par. 3, c)

The diplomatic handling of the Greek-Turkish crisis of March 1987 by the PASOK government has confirmed the reduction in importance of the EPC process in the context of Greek foreign policy. In the Hague session of the European Council on 26 June 1986, Prime Minister Papandreou had entreated the solidarity of Greece's community partners in order to enlist their support in the Greek-Turkish dispute. Although just after the council's session the Greek prime minister seemed fully convinced that "Greece would have Western Europe's support," during the March 1987 crisis he did not request community assistance through the EPC mechanisms.[43] On the contrary, the Greek government gave an intentional and blatant snub to the EPC system and ignored its possible use in backing the Greek position. Instead of requesting, along with two other EEC member states, the urgent convening of an EPC ministerial meeting, the Greek government hastened, through Foreign Minister Karolos Papoulias, to keep the ambassadors of Warsaw Pact countries informed; whereas at the same time, the foreign undersecretary, Yannis Kapsis, was briefing the NATO and EEC ambassadors accredited to Athens on the Greek-Turkish crisis.[44] That is to say, there was no particular briefing of the EPC members as a distinct group of states on the developments of the Greek-Turkish dispute, but instead they were kept informed within the NATO framework. Moreover, their briefing was not made by the foreign minister, as in the case of the Warsaw Pact members, but by his subordinate, Foreign Undersecretary Kapsis. The significance of such a hierarchical deviation in the official contacts of a government with the ambassadors accredited to it is more than obvious, and in no case could it have been ignored by the head of the Greek diplomatic service. This intentional slight to the EPC process gains even more significance in light of the mission of Foreign Minister Papoulias to Sofia, which began even before the briefings in Athens. Papoulias was charged with informing President Todor Zhivkov of Bulgaria of the escalation of the Greek-Turkish dispute, even though the Greek government did not brief the Belgian foreign minister, Leo Tindemans, who was the acting president of the European Community at that time. The requirement to do so was implied, if not by the letter, then by the spirit of the EPC regulations.[45]

The limited extent of the coordination between Greek foreign policy and the policy set by the EPC process has serious implications also in the U.N. Though EPC system members must endeavor to avoid any action or position that impairs their common attitude in international organizations, Greece has broken the community cohesion in more cases than any other EEC state. During the first year of its accession to the European Community, Greece's voting record in the U.N. General Assembly had been divergent in twenty-eight cases, whereas the second most divergent among the EEC countries had voted differently in only four cases.[46] In 1984 the voting record of the EEC member states in the U.N. General Assembly showed twenty-one cases in which only one country's vote prevented uniformity. In seventeen cases of those twenty-one, Greece was the country that broke the community cohesion.[47]

Divergence of Greek policy in the U.N. General Assembly takes place mainly with regard to Middle East issues and is dictated by Greece's political investments and interests in the Arab world. Therefore, in this case, divergence is in accordance with a firm policy implemented not only by PASOK's government but even by its predecessors.

The PASOK government has failed to use the EPC mechanisms to advance Greek positions on issues of national importance or to enlist support for its political initiatives. Greece has not activated the EPC mechanisms to procure a settlement of the Cyprus issue, but only to obtain a response to the proclamation of a Turk-Cypriot "pseudo-state," which has been condemned by the EEC member states.[48] Apart from that, the Greek government has not succeeded in securing the support of its community partners in the General Assembly. With the exception of France and Ireland, the EEC countries abstain from voting on resolutions relating to the Cyprus issue. The PASOK government's three initiatives, directly related to its ideological choices, shape the angle of divergence of Greek foreign policy from the policy of nations adhering to the EPC system.

The first of these initiatives aimed for the creation of a nuclear-free zone in the Balkans. It constituted the "main objective of the Papandreou government's foreign policy" and was put forward by the Greek premier in his proposal of 22 November 1981.[49] However, the Greek government's initiative would have indirect implications on the security of the other EEC countries, which, except for Ireland, are all members of NATO. The latter had officially rejected the nuclear-free Balkan zone with the reasoning that its realization would entail the nuclear disarmament of the NATO countries in the region. The Warsaw Pact member states in the Balkans (Bulgaria, Rumania) would not make any similar concessions, since no nuclear arms are stored or deployed on their territory.[50] According to EPC system rules, Greece was obligated to consult its EEC partners before undertaking its initiative.[51] But it seems that such consultations did not take place, and therefore whatever negative reaction—though it is not quite certain there was any—the EEC countries had to the Greek initiative would be justified, as the plan would constitute a threat to their security in the event of its fruition.

By contrast, the Greek government's proposal to put off deployment of American missiles in Europe for six months was submitted for consideration through the EPC process. The Greek foreign minister pointed out in his letter of 13 August 1983 to his counterparts in the European Community that it would be of great interest to him to hear their responses to his government's proposal.[52] Consultations with regard to the Greek proposal had not taken place because of the objections of the other EEC member states. The question of the deployment of American missiles in Europe was a matter of defense policy and as such it lay within NATO's jurisdiction; it was not a matter for the EPC. Thus when Foreign Minister Charalambopoulos restated the Greek proposal at the Athens EPC meeting of 12 September 1983, his British counterpart, Sir Geoffrey Howe, dismissed the Greek idea as "the wrong proposal, in the wrong forum at the wrong time."[53]

Last in the series of instances of Greek foreign policy divergence may be considered the initiative for peace and disarmament—officially known as the Five Continents' Peace Initiative—whereby the Greek premier, along with another five equally poorly placed leaders, champions the frail dream of international peace. This initiative has neither been discussed within the EPC framework nor been mentioned in the annual speech of the presiding foreign minister before the U.N. General Assembly.[54]

The "lost opportunity" in the Falklands crisis has to be mentioned in order to round out the survey of the limited interaction between the foreign policy of Greece and that formulated in the EPC system. The exploitation of this opportunity might have added a new dimension to the EPC system with the initiation of a process that would lead to the establishment of a "security community" having as its main objective the protection of the independence and territorial integrity of its members in the event of a threat from a third state. The case of the Falklands was the first in which an EEC member state was attacked by a third country. This occurred during a time when certain developments, which later would be shaped into a more concrete though less ambitious form in the Single European Act, had advanced security issues to the forefront of EPC policy considerations. The London Report of 1981 had already made an explicit mention of the important problems relevant to the political aspects of security; the EPC process had been utilized to approve the dispatching of troops from four EEC countries to join the Sinai peacekeeping force; and the European Parliament had adopted a resolution that provided that the European Community should undertake a more active role in the defense of its security.[55] With these developments in mind, and taking into account the similarity between the Argentinian invasion of the Falklands and a Turkish attack in the Aegean, the Greek government should have attempted to enhance the principle of community solidarity in order to create a precedent that could be invoked in case of a Turkish armed threat against Greece.[56] Such an attempt would have been facilitated by the attitude of certain EEC member states—France in particular—that evinced their readiness to back Great Britain during the Falklands crisis. It is time that Greece cosigned the common declarations (2, 10, and 20 April 1982) whereby the ten member states condemned Argentina's armed attack on the Falklands and imposed sanctions against the invader.[57] However, even in this case, the Greek government stood wavering on EPC's threshold, having fixed its gaze at the Latin American countries, whose vote in the U.N. was of vital significance for the Cyprus issue. The Greek government's indecisiveness was made clear when its initially pro-British attitude later changed to a pro-Argentinian stance when Greece diverged from its EEC partners in the U.N. General Assembly and sided with Argentina, voting in favor of Resolution 37/9 (4 November 1982).[58]

The positive aspects of the interaction between the community's foreign policy coordination process and Greek foreign policy, mainly the advancement of Greek positions through the EPC channels, can hardly be traced and defined because of the confidential character of the EPC system. PASOK's government either did not attempt or possibly failed to secure support for the great issues of Greek foreign policy in the EPC system. The periodic briefing of EPC system members on Turkish expansionist policy in the Aegean and on the Greek positions with regard to the Cyprus issue, and the elimination of a phrase from a community communiqué relating to the satisfaction of the ten members of the European Community with the democratization process of the Turkish regime do not suffice to evidence a proper use of the EPC mechanisms by the PASOK government in achieving the basic goals of its foreign policy. Greece failed to exploit the opportunity of the Single European Act in order to give concrete content to community solidarity. That would have been made possible by a provision specifying the obligation of EPC system members to take certain economic and diplomatic measures against a third country that threatens the security or territorial integrity of an EEC member state.

On the other hand, Greece's influence in shaping the positions and directives of the EPC councils has been limited to the temporary revival of the Euro-Arab dialogue during the Greek presidency and its contribution to the rejection of the Reagan plan for the settlement of the Middle-East issue. The Greek premier's proposal for the settlement of this issue through an *ad hoc* committee of high-level European personalities, made in the Dublin meeting of the European Council in November 1984, was shelved without any further discussion.

In summary, it has become apparent that the PASOK government has paid lip service to the concept of European cooperation. The Papandreou government has not only been inattentive to the requirements of the EPC system but by accentuating differences and playing down longstanding ties, it has drawn upon itself charges of duplicity. At the risk of repetition it must be pointed out that this policy has not served lasting Greek interests. It has specifically aimed at lending credibility to the overtures of the PASOK government to the socialist countries and, even more often, at burnishing the dimmed ideological appeal of Andreas Papandreou to the Greek

Left; but it has ultimately resulted in estranging Greece from its community partners. In the case of the EPC system the Greek prime minister has not realized that "implementing two foreign policies does not mean that you have one more; it means that you have none."

NOTES

1. The origins, development, and structure of the EPC system are described in Philippe de Schoutheete, *La Coopération politique européenne*, 2nd ed. (Brussels: Labor, 1986). See also William Wallace and David Allen, "Political Cooperation: Procedure as a Substitute for Policy" in H. Wallace, W. Wallace, and C. Webb, eds., *Policy-making in the European Communities* (London: Wiley, 1977); Beate Lindeman, *EG-Staaten und Vereinte Nationen* (Munich: Olenbourg, 1978); David Allen, "Foreign Policy at the European Level: Beyond the Nation State?" in W. Wallace and W. Paterson, eds., *Foreign Policy Making in Western Europe: A Comparative Approach* (Farnborough: Saxon House, 1979); Werner Feld, ed., *Europe's Global Reach: Regional Cooperation and Worldwide Aspirations* (New York, 1980); Gianni Bonvicini, ed., *La Politica Estera dell'Europa, Autonomie o Dipendenza?* (Bologna: Il Mulino, 1980); Fonseca-Wollheim, *Ten Years of Political Cooperation* (Brussels, 1981); David Allen, Reinhard Rummel, and Wolfgang Wessels, eds., *European Political Cooperation: Towards a Foreign Policy for Western Europe* (London: Butterworth, 1982); Christopher Hill, ed., *National Foreign Policies and European Political Cooperation* (London: Allen and Unwin, 1983); Theodore Christodoulides, *The International Dimension of the EEC* (in Greek) (Athens: A. Sakkoulas, 1984); Panayotis Ifestos, *European Political Cooperation. Towards a Framework of Supranational Diplomacy?* (London: Grover, 1987).

2. See Trevor Salmon, "Ireland, a Neutral in the Community," *Journal of Common Market Studies* 20 (1982): 205-227.

3. According to a poll, 91 percent of the Greek people believe that the most serious threat to their security comes from Turkey. See *Foreign Assistance Legislation Hearings*, March-April 1985, pt. 3: 316.

4. See Richard Haas, "Managing NATO's Weakest Flank: The United States, Greece and Turkey," *Orbis* (Fall, 1985): 462.

5. For this Turkish goal see Paris Kitsos, "Roles and Aspirations of Turkey in the Atlantic System," in Giannes Valinakis and Paris Kitsos, eds., *Greek Defensive Problems* (in Greek) (Athens: Papazisis, 1986): 157-158.

6. See Hélène da Costa, "La Turquie: Pont entre l'orient et l'occident," *Défense Nationale* (April 1986): 90.

7. Nikos Andrikos, "Free nuclear arms zone in Balkans" in Valinakis and Kitsos, 170.

8. François Duchêne, "The Foreign Policies of an Enlarged

European Community and the Member States," in J.W. Schneider, ed., *From Nine to Twelve: Europe's Destiny* (Alphenaan den Rijn: Sijthoff and Noordhoff, 1980): 207.

9. Andreas Papandreou, address to PASOK's Youth Organization Festival, *To Vema* , 9 September 1979.

10. Andreas Papandreou, statement on the occasion of Greece's entry into the EEC, 26 May 1979. *About the EEC,* PASOK's Publication, A 36/1981, 56-57.

11. PASOK, Declaration of Governmental Policy, PASOK's Publication (undated): 36.

12. Interview of the Greek Prime Minister to *Times* , 1 December 1983.

13. PASOK, Declaration of Governmental Policy, 35, 36.

14. de Schoutheete, 205.

15. *Bulletin EC* (June 1983): 2.2.3.

16. de Schoutheete, 206.

17.Giannes Charalambopoulos, speech to the European Parliament, 5 July 1983. *The First Greek Presidency of the European Community* (July-December 1983). Texts edited by the Greek Foreign Ministry (in Greek), 1986, 8.

18. *Ibid.*, 137.

19. Andreas Papandreou, speech to the President and the Vice-Presidents of the Socialist Group of the European Parliament, *Kathemerine,* 9 November 1983.

20. *Parliamentary Minutes* , 30 March 1984, 5562.

21. Charalambopoulos, speech. *The First Greek Presidency of the European Community,* 8.

22. Andreas Papandreou, speech to the European Parliament, 13 December 1983. *Ibid.,* 111.

23. *Ibid.*, 114.

24. Giannes Valinakis, "The Greek participation in the European Political Cooperation, 1981-1985" in Panos Kazakos and Konstantinos Stephanou, eds., *Greece in the European Community. The First Five Years* (in Greek) (Athens: A. Sakkoulas, 1987): 324.

25. Valinakis, 325, n. 52.

26. *Bulletin EC,* (July 1985): 1.1.1.

27. *Ibid.* (November 1985): 1.1.4.

28. *Ibid.*: 1.1.2.

29. Under certain conditions the London Report made absolutely strict the EEC countries' obligation to adopt foreign policy positions only after having previous consultations with their fellow members in the EPC system.

30. *Economist,* 17 September 1983.

31. *Economist,* 31 October 1981.

32. *Eleutherotypia,* 24 November 1981, and *Economist,* 24 November 1981.

33. *Bulletin EC* (December 1981): 1.4.2.

34. *Bulletin EC* (February 1982): 2.2.45.

35. de Schoutheete, 55.

36. *Kathemerine*, 13 September 1983.

37. *Bulletin EC* (September 1983): 3.4.1.

38. *Ibid.* (April 1986): 2.4.4.

39. *Economist*, 10 May 1986.

40. *Bulletin EC* (October 1986): 2.4.4.

41. Nezaz Hindawi was the Jordanian holder of a Syrian service passport who attempted to blow up the EL-AL jumbo jet. *Economist* , 25 October 1986.

42. *Europe*, 4427, 10 and 11 November 1986.

43. *Kathemerine*, 29 and 30 June 1986.

44. *To Vema*, 29 March 1987.

45. For the reactions to Papoulias's visit to Sofia see *Wall Street Journal*, 31 March 1987, and *Economist*, 4 April 1987.

46. *Economist*, 4 December 1982.

47. See de Schoutheete, 210.

48. *Bulletin EC* (November 1983): 2.4.1.

49. Andrikos, 167.

50. *Ibid.*, 174.

51. See London Report, 13 October 1981. *Bulletin EC*, Supplement 3/81, 14.

52. *The First Greek Presidency of the European Community*, 167.

53. *Economist*, 17 September 1983.

54. For the peace initiative, see Raoul Alfonsin, Indira Gandhi, Miguel de la Madrid, Julius Nyerere, Olof Palme, Andreas Papandreou, joint declaration, 22 May 1984. On the role of the acting president, see Perrakes, "Greek Foreign Policy Through the Intervention of the Presidents of the European Community" in the U.N. General Assembly, 1981-1985," in Kazakos and Stephanou, eds., 336.

55. de Schoutheete, 226-27.

56. See Valinakis, 324, who is credited with comparing the two situations and originating the idea.

57. *Bulletin EC* (April 1982): 1.1.1.-1.1.6.

58. See Irene Cheila, *The EPC in the U.N. General Assembly and Greece's Votes in International Crisis Issues*, 1981-1985, in Kazakos and Stephanou, eds., 358.

PASOK's Third World/Nonaligned Relations

Charles W. McCaskill

Author's note: While the title of this chapter is "PASOK's Third World/Nonaligned Relations," it should be noted that "Papandreou" and "PASOK" are used interchangeably throughout. This was done knowingly since, in my opinion, it is impossible to separate the two. As noted in the body of the essay, Prime Minister Andreas Papandreou is PASOK, and party doctrine comes directly from him or is subject to his approval.

PASOK'S PREDISPOSITION TOWARD THE NONALIGNED AND THE THIRD WORLD

The overwhelming victory of Andreas Papandreou and his Panhellenic Socialist Movement (PASOK) in the national elections of October 1981 meant that Greece's foreign policy would probably undergo some radical changes and might never be the same again. Papandreou had played an increasingly important role in Greek domestic politics since the founding of his "movement" in September 1974, as his share of the vote grew from 13.6% (and 13 of the 300 seats in Parliament) in the elections of 1974 to 25.3% (and 93 seats) in 1977; the 1977 elections made him the leader of the opposition in Parliament—since his was the largest party after the governing New Democracy party (ND)—and gave him an official position from which to speak. His views on all important domestic and foreign policy questions had become quite well-known to the Greek electorate by 1981. On the so-called "core issues," his threats to take Greece out of NATO, to close U.S. bases in Greece, and to call a referendum on Greek membership in the European Economic Community (hereafter referred to as the EC or "the Community")[1] provoked considerable uneasiness among many Greeks—and Greece's western allies as well—who took PASOK at its word when it promised that it would bring "big change" to the country.[2]

Papandreou's reputation as a radical had in fact been

growing steadily among more conservative Greeks since 1974. Even in the sixties after his return to Greece and before his arrest by the colonels, he had been considered "leftist" or "radical," an image greatly enhanced since the return of democracy to Greece in 1974 by his known reputation as a Marxist, his consistent and public anti-Americanism, his intemperate oratory, his support for radical causes, and his deliberate and studied nonconformity. A classic demagogue, he constantly exhorted the people to throw off their bonds of dependency and be free. With all of this he was soft-spoken and professorial in private, leading to speculation around Athens that he was a "split personality."[3]

PASOK's founding proclamation had given Greeks a good insight into Papandreou's philosophy and his party's goals. A few excerpts will give some flavor. Couched in Third World/national liberation movement jargon, the *Proclamation of Basic Principles and Goals* blamed the "continuing expansionist policy of the Pentagon within the framework of NATO" and "the American-controlled junta" for the "tragedy of Cyprus" and the resultant situation facing Greece. The "root" of Greece's "holocaust" lay in the dependence of Greece "on the imperialist establishment of the U.S. and NATO." The military government of Greece had been imposed in 1967 "so that the people's march towards sovereignty and national independence would be blocked." The proclamation stated, as the party's basic aim, "the creation of a polity free from control or intervention, a polity free from the control or influence of an economic oligarchy.... National independence... inseparably bound to popular sovereignty." All power came directly from the people. Greece should withdraw completely from NATO and all bilateral agreements contributing to Greece's "subjugation" would be nullified. "An actively independent foreign policy" would reflect that Greece at the same time belongs to Europe, the Balkans and the Mediterranean and should make its presence felt in all three. The elimination of nuclear weapons from the Mediterranean and a Balkans free of military alliances were goals, and the annulment of "international contracts and agreements which have led Greece to an economic, political and military dependence on the monopolistic establishment of the West and particularly of American imperialism" was among the measures designed to free Greece.[4]

The majority of Greeks, preoccupied with the overthrow of the military dictatorship, the return of democratic government to the country, and the Turkish invasion of Cyprus, probably paid little attention to the PASOK document in 1974. Indeed, the chances of a PASOK electoral victory must have seemed remote to the average Greek voter in 1974. As a PASOK victory in 1981 became increasingly likely, re-reading it could only have caused some concern among those who supported Prime Minister Constantine Karamanlis's efforts to keep Greece firmly in the West as they realized that a PASOK government headed by Papandreou would probably mean prolonged uncertainty for the country.

Other Papandreou/PASOK statements and activities provided Greeks a further basis on which to judge the man and his party. Soon after its formation, PASOK began developing ties with "progressive parties" and movements considered progressive in Europe, while maintaining close relations with certain North African and Middle Eastern governments. Both the man and the party showed considerable sympathy for "the genuine anti-imperialist forces of the Arab countries," especially Libya, Iran, Syria, Algeria and the Palestine Liberation Organization (PLO) with which PASOK maintained close relations.[5] (Support for the Palestinians was one of PASOK's cornerstones and from its very inception the party maintained that no peace in the Middle East could come about without the participation of the Palestinians.) A PASOK paper submitted to the conference of Socialist and Progressive parties of the Mediterranean in Malta, 22-25 July 1977, contained what had by then come to be regarded as the very center of PASOK's creed: "the dominant form of class struggle is the struggle between the capitalist metropolis and periphery, i.e., the struggle for national liberation."[6] And, of course, the U.S. was—and has continued to be—the "capitalist metropolis." Papandreou's policy toward NATO was taking shape during this time. In an address to his party early in 1981 he gave what had come to be the accepted PASOK line: NATO, led by the U.S., was turning Turkey into a truly great military power, Greece was the only NATO member that had suffered such humiliation, Greece's forces were aligned against the North and not against the real enemy, etc.

In his book, *Democracy at Gunpoint*, Papandreou placed Greece in the Third World, "even though it is part of the European continent and the Western European community."[7] In a lecture in the U.S. in 1969, he described Greece as "partaking of the characteristics of the Third World" while belonging to

Europe.[8] Over the years, Papandreou had shown a preoccupation with Third World/nonaligned matters not found among any except the most leftist or communist Greek politicians, and the Third Worldism adopted by him and PASOK as they ascended to power sounded strange in the Greek political context. Personally Papandreou's rhetoric during those years was decidedly Third World or nonaligned, certainly not what one would have expected from the leader of the opposition of a NATO country. In practical terms, Greece might have qualified for Third World status under the "elaborate criteria" devised to define the Third World since those relate "more to development than to group dynamics."[9] But more worrisome was the fact that the Papandreou/PASOK foreign policy seemed more characteristic of a nonaligned nation than of a NATO and EC member. Political scientist Theodore Couloumbis, who once described PASOK as a party "whose mind is in the West but whose heart is in the Third World," explained further that "Papandreou has felt that the country would be served best by adopting a model of self-reliance in solidarity with other member states of the Third World."[10] Still another observer concluded that Papandreou believed that a truly national policy, separate from the superpower blocs, was essential for the protection of Greek national concerns and would appeal to Greek nationalism.[11] Whatever the basis of his anti-American Third Worldism, Papandreou during his rise to power appeared intent on leading Greece out of the Western camp if he should ever come to power.

The PASOK Policy Declaration published in Athens in the summer of 1981, a kind of election statement, was a detailed catalog of PASOK's program as it entered the homestretch leading up to national elections in the fall. Much of the Policy Declaration had been said by PASOK before one way or another, but it was an excellent, if long, compilation of the party's principles, both domestic and foreign, far more complete than the earlier founding document. It left the voter with little question about PASOK's positions on most issues of importance to Greece. Pertinent to this paper was PASOK's pledge to work actively for "a genuine, proud, nonaligned and multifaceted foreign policy" to strengthen Greece's national independence. PASOK's aspiration "to make Greece the crossroads of cooperation and friendship among the peoples of the Balkans, the Mediterranean and Europe without intervention and dependency" was set forth early in the paper. Great stress was placed on the development of good relations with the Balkans and "with the Arabic nation, which constitutes a dynamic factor in the world's progress." In its quest for a new "independent" foreign policy, PASOK was clearly not looking to its old friends and allies; for example, the only mentions of NATO, in which Greece had been a member since 1952, were negative. The PASOK policy looked ahead to "the defensive arming of the country and ... a genuine multifaceted foreign policy." With a PASOK victory increasingly certain, Papandreou had begun to equivocate on Greece's membership in the EC, another tactic that continued for some years, until he finally put that particular question to rest by declaring categorically that Greece would not leave.[12] The PASOK Policy Declaration made it clear that a PASOK victory would not only mean change in Greece, but would in fact bring a sea change in both domestic and foreign affairs.

Outside the NATO, the EC, and the bases issues, much of what Papandreou and his party were advocating was in fact not new. Before he left the prime ministry for the presidency in 1980, Constantine Karamanlis had begun what he considered a more independent foreign policy, though he made no bones of the fact that he and his New Democracy party were firmly committed to NATO and the West. Karamanlis's own "multifaceted" policy included a new opening to the East, with official trips to the Soviet Union, Hungary and Czechoslovakia, and better relations with the Balkans, which had already resulted in new understandings with Bulgaria and Romania. And Greece, ever mindful of Greek communities throughout the Middle East, traditionally had had good relations with the Arab World and had long considered itself the Arabs' bridge to Europe.

Moreover, since the fall of the colonels, Greece under New Democracy governments had not always been an easy NATO partner nor as cooperative as some of the allies—including the U.S.—might have hoped. Karamanlis had taken Greece out of the military wing of NATO in 1974 in protest over the alliance's failure to take action when Turkey invaded Cyprus, and a formula for her return had become a major problem for the alliance. (SACEUR Bernard Rogers finally found an arrangement acceptable to both Greeks and Turks in late 1980 only to have the new Papandreou government in effect suspend it.) On a matter of considerable interest to the Carter administration, Greece participated in the Moscow Olympics of

1980 despite our requests that it not do so. (The reasons had to do with Greece's effort to have the Olympic Games permanently based in Greece and the fact that the Greek contingent always led the opening parade and carried the Olympic flag into the stadium.) And while PASOK seemed to regard Greek interest in the PLO as uniquely its own, the PLO had actually received permission from the New Democracy government to open an office in Athens in 1980.

PAPANDREOU COMES TO POWER: A NEW KIND OF FOREIGN POLICY FOR GREECE

Papandreou rode into office on a wave of populist support with a clear mandate to implement the "change" he had promised. (PASOK received 48.1% of the vote and obtained 172 of the 300 parliamentary seats.) The question in the minds of many Greeks and their friends was how much change he would bring about. If, in politics, a man is known by the company he keeps, it was not reassuring to note that his closest friends in Europe appeared to be Olof Palme of Sweden and Bruno Kreisky of Austria. He invoked the names of others—Francois Mitterrand and other socialist leaders whom he had attempted to cultivate over the years—but Palme and Kreisky were the two who appeared closest to him philosophically and personally. However, Papandreou seemed to be sobered, at least temporarily, by his election and he admitted that the conservative Karamanlis's presence in the presidency, where he could presumably act as a brake on Papandreou and PASOK, had probably made PASOK's victory possible. Moreover, Papandreou moved immediately to assure the U.S. and the allies that he would do nothing rash. Appearing on ABC's "Issues and Answers" one week after his victory, he seemed the voice of moderation as he pledged that Greece would not act unilaterally toward NATO or the U.S. bases in Greece. He repeated his well-known position regarding NATO and Turkey but said that Greece desired no confrontation with the U.S.[13] In other interviews and statements, he reflected the same themes, saying he did not want "to send the Greek people into adventures." In an obvious reference to his hope for special status for Greece within the EC, he told *Le Monde* on 29 October that Greece did not want to break its ties with Europe since it is, "above all," European.[14] The "special relationship" with the EC was the latest gimmick in his search for a way to keep Greece in the EC and to prepare the way for backing off entirely from his threat made long ago to take Greece out.

Papandreou established himself as Greece's new media star with his ABC interview, proving to be charismatic, convincing and sure of himself. Newspapers across the political spectrum hailed his performance as a "Greek prime minister speaking Greek," indicating not only pride in how he had handled himself but also general agreement with what he had said. Shortly thereafter, he left for an EC meeting in London, with a stop in Paris along the way. The departure of the Marxist/socialist, Third World-leaning Greek prime minister for a meeting of the most exclusive club in Western Europe might have struck some as contradictory, but any doubts about how he would behave were soon put to rest. Television coverage of his meeting with Mitterrand in Paris and with his Community partners in London added to the impression at home that, whether or not you agreed with Papandreou, he cut a mean figure in the international arena and would probably be a man to be reckoned with one way or the other.

At the same time that Papandreou was reassuring his friends and allies of his good intentions, he was putting into practice some of what he had been preaching. In the first week following his election, it was announced that Greece would recognize the PLO by giving its office in Athens full diplomatic status and that Papandreou would invite Yasir Arafat to pay an official visit to Greece at his earliest convenience.[15] The recognition marked the beginning of a real Papandreou/Arafat love feast and triggered a statement from Arafat that, among other things, (1) stressed that as a result of the action, Greece now had "a front of allies in the Arab World extending from the Atlantic Ocean to the Indian Ocean," and (2) promised that "now the Arabs will prove their friendship toward Greece with deeds."[16]

The pro-PASOK Athens daily, *Eleutherotypia*, interpreted Arafat's statement as assurance that Papandreou's government could rely on financial support from the Arabs.[17] It was open gossip in Athens at the time that the new government's recognition of the PLO and its promised stress on relations with the Arab states were designed to induce wealthy Arab states to assist the new government by depositing capital in Greek banks or otherwise making surplus Arab money available to the Greek economy. So far as was ever known, this appears to have been wishful thinking by PASOK, as no significant amounts of Arab money were known to have reached Greece. Numerous economic agreements would be signed with Arab states over the next several years, but the Arabs' economic contribution to the PASOK government was not particularly noteworthy. It had also been widely rumored in Athens that Libya had financed the PASOK campaign with generous amounts of money and the new government's obvious willingness to increase the tempo of Greek/Arab relations was interpreted simply as payment of its IOUs. Even in the atmosphere of closer relations with the Arabs, Libya would clearly occupy a special spot in the new PASOK scheme of things.

The pattern to be followed by the Papandreou government was fairly well set in the first three months after his government took office. In addition to the Arafat visit, an unusual number of contacts between Greece and various Arab states and groups were taking place, with comings and goings on both sides. The Libyan representative in Athens, perhaps wanting to put down his government's marker in the Greek capital or maybe even unaware of diplomatic requirements, "demanded" the expulsion of the Israeli diplomatic mission from Athens as part of Libya's "demand for full neutrality of Greece," and was taken to task by the Greek government.[18] A few months later the Libyan representative in Athens involved himself in a quarrel between ND leader Evangelos Averoff and the government over PASOK's PLO policy by sending a statement critical of Averoff to the press for publication. This "interference in domestic affairs" was "unacceptable" and strong protests were delivered to the Libyans in Athens and in Tripoli.[19] The Arafat visit, when it finally occurred on 14 December, was not anticlimactic as might have been expected, but it was an exercise in excess, as the PASOK government left no stone unturned to demonstrate beyond question its support for the Palestinians' cause. Papandreou's television image, which had emerged from his ABC interview and his trip to France and England, was undone to some degree as Greek television, for the duration of the visit, was full of Arafat and Papandreou meeting, embracing, and pledging mutual support for all time. For many Greeks, the Arafat visit gave substance to PASOK's pledge of a new kind of foreign policy for Greece.

In late November, barely a month after taking office, the PASOK government disagreed with its EC partners over the question of a Sinai Peace Force, serving notice that it would henceforward plead the Arab cause in the Community, a policy it has continued to the detriment of its credibility in that organization. In December, Papandreou, who attended the NATO defense ministers' meeting in Brussels as defense minister (he had retained the defense portfolio in his first government), vetoed the final communiqué by insisting on language unacceptable to the other partners, the first time a communiqué had not been issued following such a meeting. This was followed fairly soon by Greek government disagreement with its EC partners on the question of sanctions against Poland: the Greek representative attending the meeting to discuss the question apparently misunderstood—or disregarded—his instructions and was fired for his transgression. The government of Greece then announced that it would not be bound by the EC communiqué issued after the meeting.

The new government's apparent readiness to make its differences with its allies known was a portent of things to come and caused considerable concern in both NATO and the EC. Despite Papandreou's earlier efforts to reassure the allies that he could be trusted, it was to become increasingly clear that Greece under PASOK was another Greece, an unpredictable, sometimes unreliable ally with little apparent sense of responsibility to its longtime partners. Personally, Papandreou would prove to be an enigma: after threatening to take Greece out of NATO and the EC and to close the U.S. bases, he would do none of these. Greek membership in NATO may best be described as "restricted" since Greek participation in military exercises is increasingly selective, but Papandreou has not taken Greece out of the alliance; and while its membership in the EC presumably rests more on economic rather than ideological grounds, the question of Greek membership in the Community no longer arises.[20] The renegotiation of the bases agreement in 1983 was based in large part on practical considerations, some economic and some tactical, but certainly not on any desire to be so openly allied with the U.S. Papandreou did an excellent job of selling that agreement to his followers, proving that the pragmatist in him had prevailed over the ideologue. He has obviously paved the way for party approval of the new agreement to be negotiated soon.[21]

PAPANDREOU IN POWER: A THIRD WORLDER IN NATO AND THE EC

As contradictory as it might seem for a NATO and EC member to be less than completely Western-oriented,

Papandreou in power had taken Greece one step out of the Western camp in the direction of the nonaligned world and in that regard has fulfilled his pledge to his party to make Greece more independent. He is pragmatist enough to appreciate the advantage of Greece's attachment to the West, as this essay indicates throughout, but he seems more at home in a Third World or nonaligned context and in espousing Third World-type initiatives not associated with membership in the Western alliance. His intemperate, almost reckless, reactions to developments and his constant sniping at the U.S. remind one more of Indira Gandhi, Bhutto, Palme or Dom Mintoff than of a Western leader; his invidious comparisons of the U.S. and the Soviet Union stretch the imagination and provoke comments like that of one pundit who observed that Greece often sounds like an Eastern member of NATO.

Papandreou's defenders say that much of what he says and does is meant to placate the left wing of his party, and certainly his most outrageous statements over the past few years have been made to party gatherings. However, his constant repetition that Greece belongs to both Western and Eastern Europe, that neither he nor his party recognizes the division of Europe by the Yalta and Potsdam Agreements, that he and his party prefer a bloc-free Europe, that Greece "logically" should not be in NATO, etc., have come to be accepted as reflecting the real Papandreou, and his more moderate statements have begun to be looked upon with suspicion. He has insisted on taking issue with NATO and EC policies and on involving himself in activities inconsistent with membership in those organizations, often upsetting unity on an important policy issue. In these circumstances, it is not surprising that Greece would come to be the odd man out when NATO, EC or other Western groups convene, but too much a part of the family to be excluded. Papandreou's admission, finally, that Greece has no intention of leaving the EC, and that it is not in Greece's interest to leave NATO, has merely confirmed what many observers have thought for some time, i.e., that Greece will not leave either organization as long as it is able to continue its membership on its own terms. This brinkmanship might catch up with Papandreou some day, if, under other circumstances, his partners run out of patience.

As with Palme, it is not always so much what Papandreou does as the way he does it. Like his friend, Papandreou seems to go out of his way sometimes to irritate the allies with ill-timed, intemperate reactions or statements. He has apparently not learned from his friend's experience with the Soviets, however, and all too often Papandreou's criticism of the U.S. has been implicitly or explicitly pro-Soviet. Moreover, Papandreou has consistently refused to tailor Greek national interests to the needs of the Western alliance. It is axiomatic that national interests of one member or ally sometimes come into conflict with the will of the alliance, and in such cases national interests are usually overriding. But like most Third World and nonaligned countries, Greece under PASOK has been unwilling to adapt its national interests to the needs of NATO or the EC. It is therefore small wonder that Greece has come more and more to be regarded as the weak link in the Western alliance.

Papandreou's first term, which ended in June 1985 when he called new elections, continued the tone set in the first few months in office, with growing emphasis on Greece's ties with the Arab states and the Balkans and his increasing involvement in disarmament activities. Arabs and Arab affairs were more and more a part of the Athens scene: the state-owned Athens Domestic Radio announced on 12 December 1981 that it would broadcast the news in Arabic "in view of the spectacular increase in the number of Arab visitors, businessmen and tourists" and after all, Arabic is one of the five official languages of the U.N.[22]

Greece was very cooperative in the evacuation of the Palestinians from Beirut, not only offering merchant ships to transport them but furnishing army officers from its contingent in Cyprus to act as escorts/observers when the Palestinians refused to accept the Red Cross in that capacity. Greece agreed to treat 200-300 wounded Palestinians in Greek hospitals and help trans-ship others (60 finally remained in Greek hospitals). Arafat stopped in Athens 1 September 1982—his first stop after leaving Beirut—on his way to Tunis, provoking another outpouring of sympathy and friendship (and creating a protocol problem since Francois Mitterrand arrived the same day on an official visit to Greece). Reports that the PLO would set up headquarters in Athens recurred regularly and were always denied. However, Palestinians were always welcome in Athens and Papandreou's support for the Palestinians' cause has never wavered. He has balanced his support with a statement on Israel's right to secure borders, but both Papandreou and PASOK appear genuinely committed to the Palestinians.

Greece's courtship of other Arabs continued with regular

exchanges between Athens and various Arab capitals. Not one of these initiatives caused more heartburn at home and abroad than did Greece's effort to solidify its relations with Libya. Rumors that Qaddafi would visit Athens persisted over several months and an official visit seemed imminent in the spring of 1982, only to be cancelled at the last minute when President Karamanlis reportedly refused to meet him at the airport on his arrival.[23] Various agreements—oil and/or improved trade at the root of many of them—were signed with Libya and other Arab states, most of them of little real significance despite the fanfare accompanying the signings. One such agreement with Libya was said to be worth one billion dollars over three years, described at the time as one of the most important economic cooperation agreements that Greece had with any country. This appears to have been much ado about nothing since it seems merely to have formalized the $250-300 million trade both ways already in the books. Still another one billion dollar deal involving arms was signed with Libya in early 1985 and finally cancelled in 1987 because it had never been activated.[24] The PASOK government's support for the "Arab nation," as Papandreou referred to the Arab states, may have been intended to insure continued support on the Cyprus question or even to offset increasing Turkish activity among the Muslim states, but neither of these would seem to justify the effort Papandreou and his government put into improving Greece's Arab ties. As noted elsewhere in this paper, Greece has always had relatively good relations with the Arabs, as Athens has made a special effort not to jeopardize the Greek communities in the Middle East. PASOK's exaggerated emphasis on the Arab world was, it appears, part of its stated policy to be more independent and to seek partners outside NATO and the EC, another move, if you will, in the direction of the nonaligned.

Closer relations with Greece's northern neighbors also became a focus of Papandreou in power as he moved to implement his pledge to make Greece's influence in the Balkans a reality. Seizing an old Romanian plan for a Balkan nuclear-free zone as a vehicle for asserting his aspirations in disarmament, he joined with Ceaucescu to become one of the chief advocates of a proposal which undoubtedly had full Soviet blessing and might even have been Soviet sponsored at an earlier time. Support for the Balkan nuclear-free zone became another of the constants in PASOK's foreign policy, and no government policy paper fails to include it as one of Greece's primary policy goals. Only Turkey's refusal to participate has prevented the proposal from becoming anything other than an outlet for Papandreou and his leftist followers who seemingly thrive on Greece's independence from its Western partners. In August 1983, one month after Greece had assumed the presidency of the EC, the Greek foreign minister proposed a six-month postponement of the deployment of Pershing II and Cruise missiles in Europe. Shortly thereafter, Papandreou and Ceaucescu sent a joint letter to President Reagan and Soviet leader Yuri Andropov, calling for a simultaneous halt to the NATO deployment and Soviet retaliatory action. The first of these reportedly brought a sharp protest from Washington while the second apparently drew a "strong rebuke" from the British government, which could "not understand how Greece could sign joint letters with non-Western countries on issues that directly concern the British government and people."[25] An Athens newspaper reported that the British Foreign Office told the Greek ambassador that Greece's behavior was "detrimental to the Atlantic alliance and that in fact the joint Papandreou/Ceaucescu proposal did not help anyone but the Soviet Union."[26] The proposal would in fact have benefited the Soviet Union by stopping the deployment of the American missiles and leaving the Soviet SS-20s in place, thereby freezing a strategic imbalance in the Soviets' favor. The Greek government spokesman, quoted on Athens Radio, said only that "a counselor" at the Greek embassy in London had been called to the Foreign Office to furnish more information on the letter, but in what appears to have been confirmation of a British protest, said that it was only natural that "governments of various countries expressed their views on the matter."[27]

Papandreou found the perfect outlet for his disarmament and neutralist activities when in May, 1984 he joined with Palme, Miguel de la Madrid of Mexico, Julius Nyerere of Tanzania, Raoul Alfonsin of Argentina and Indira Gandhi of India in forming a group for nuclear disarmament, which called for a worldwide halt to testing and production of nuclear weapons. While his membership in a group such as this is another irritant to his NATO and EC partners, the "Six" have been relatively ineffective thus far. However, no one takes them seriously and it does have the effect of further distancing Greece from its allies. Papandreou would probably contend that disarmament transcends allied unity and discipline, though the argument could be made that a strong and united Western

Europe could play a much stronger role in the disarmament process than this group of six countries. This proved to be the case with the signing of the INF treaty.

It has been argued by some that if Papandreou keeps Greece in NATO and the EC and agrees to the maintenance of the U.S. bases, what he does on other "marginal" issues is unimportant since only the "core" issues matter. This does not bear close scrutiny, however, as the PASOK government's policies often have been uneven, characteristic more of a Third World or nonaligned country, to such an extent that, as noted previously, they have undermined allied and EC unity. When the KAL plane was shot down by the Soviets in 1983, the Greek government issued a statement entirely without teeth, regretting the loss of life and calling for an investigation "to establish the circumstances under which this tragic accident occurred."[28] Greece, then occupying the presidency of the EC, opposed the issuance of a statement by the EC, despite the fact that nine other members reportedly were prepared to adopt a declaration that condemned the attack.[29] Papandreou later declared that the plane was on a spy mission for the CIA and that it had actually violated USSR airspace for the purpose of spying. Others in his government said the same thing publicly. In what was described as a "stormy" EC ministerial session, Greece was also at odds with its partners on Poland, the Euromissiles question, and the Middle East, and was said to have annoyed the other nine ministers by what they considered "a conciliatory attitude on the part of Greece toward Syria."[30] On Grenada, a matter of considerable interest to the U.S., Athens Radio on 26 October 1983 carried a Greek government condemnation of "any kind of intervention in the internal affairs of independent U.N. member states"; the official spokesman continued that "the Greek government is deeply concerned because of yesterday's developments in Grenada, which aggravate the already tense situation in that sensitive area."[31] Gratuitous official statements which exceed the bounds of normal requirements have become the rule rather than the exception with Greece, and they make no friends for Greece in the U.S. or in Western Europe.

In particularly scathing remarks directed at the U.S. and delivered to a PASOK party congress on 10 May 1984, Papandreou stated that the Soviet Union is not a capitalist country and "not an imperialist power."[32] In the following breath he referred to the United States as "the metropolis of imperialism" and went on to describe the Soviets as "a restraining factor in the propagation of capitalism and of its imperialist aims." Still further, he accused the U.S. of "undermining UNESCO's universality and economic potential."[33] In the same speech, he placed the blame for the Cold War on the U.S. and the West, saying that NATO was the first political-military bloc formed immediately after World War II, "and as an inevitable consequence the Warsaw Pact followed 6 years later."[34]

Greece under Papandreou involved itself to a much greater extent in Latin America, using an area where it had traditionally had little interest as an outlet for PASOK's desire to involve itself in leftist causes and national liberation movements. Representatives of various leftist Latin American organizations visited Athens to seek and get assurances of Greek support. Cuban Foreign Minister Isidoro Malmierca visited Athens officially in the summer of 1982 and Papandreou met Fidel Castro in Moscow at Brezhnev's funeral and discussed "the fate of the Third World" with him.[35] Relations between the two countries continued to improve, with periodic exchanges of visits usually at the ministerial or alternate ministerial level. Greece recently opened an embassy in Havana, and in May of 1987, Castro invited Papandreou to visit Cuba.[36] As an interesting footnote, the invitation was delivered by a member of the Cuban Communist party political bureau, who reportedly called on Papandreou and "had an exchange of views based on bilateral and international issues."[37] As with the Greek statement on Grenada, it is difficult to see what Greece gets out of involving itself in Latin America except that such involvement provides one more example of support for leftist causes and national liberation movements that PASOK can hold out to the party leftists.

Greece continued to distance herself from her Western partners on other issues, most notably on terrorism and terrorism-related matters, and Greece's refusal to comply with U.S. and other suggestions for tightening security at Athens airport led to the charge that it was "soft" on terrorism. Over the past several years, Athens has in fact become the scene of continuing terrorist incidents: since PASOK came to power in October 1981, the publishers of two of Athens' well-known conservative newspapers, a public prosecutor, and a well-known conservative businessman have been gunned down in what appear to have been political killings. Other killings, including that of American Navy Captain George Tsantes, have occurred regularly, many of them involving the PLO or other Arab organizations. The opposition has charged that terrorists enter Greece freely, without any control, and that terrorism has gone unchecked in the country. Bombings occur on a regular basis, many of them directed at Americans or American facilities. The most serious incident involved the TWA hijacking in 1985, which provoked the issuance of a U.S. travel advisory and resulted in a major drop in tourism, Greece's major foreign exchange earner. U.S. travel to Greece reportedly dropped 60% in 1986 and the country lost an estimated $700 million in tourist revenues.[38] Greece responded by tightening up security at Athens airport but it remained acutely sensitive to criticism that it did less than it should to curb terrorism. Greece also developed some ideas of its own regarding the involvement of some of its Arab friends in terrorism, refusing to recognize or admit its friends' participation in terrorist activity.

With regard to the question of Libyan involvement in terrorism, Papandreou and his government took a decidedly pro-Libya stand, publicly condemning U.S. action against Libya and refusing to go along with sanctions. Speaking in Parliament on 30 May 1986 on the subject of violence and terrorism, Papandreou said that Greece had endorsed the EC resolution on Libya "but the measures Greece took were decided in Athens and not suggested or dictated by foreign capitals despite the great efforts" of others to pressure Greece in that direction.[39] In an earlier reference to "external state violence" where the goal is the destabilization of a political regime in another country, Papandreou listed "Libya, Nicaragua and Afghanistan."[40] When the EC, meeting on Syria, condemned state terrorism and adopted a package of limited sanctions against Syria, as stated earlier, Greece refused to go along with its partners.

At the time when speculation concerning new base negotiations had begun to be bandied about—the present agreement ends in 1988—Papandreou unloaded another surprise by announcing that he would submit the final agreement to a referendum before it is initialed or signed.[41] There had been no indication that this was in his thinking, and it could only be assumed that it was a way of putting pressure on us to make concessions he considers necessary, throwing a sop to the leftists in PASOK, and giving himself a peg on which to hang the agreement, which he presumably wants. If no agreement is reached, the terms of the old agreement will obtain and the bases will be closed as that agreement provides. While the referendum might not show the 85% approval *The Economist* thinks it might get, it could go as high as 75-80% with only the Greek communists and disgruntled leftists voting against it.

More worrisome was Papandreou's reaction to an approach by Ambassador Robert Keeley, obviously on instructions, with information alleging that Papandreou's government had been in contact with terrorist Abu Nidal to insure that there would be no terrorist activities on Greek soil, thus protecting Greece's tourist industry from further strains. At issue, apparently, was inclusion of this information in a forthcoming State Department White Paper which would list three European countries—Greece, Yugoslavia, and Bulgaria—as "weak-kneed in their dealings with guerrilla or terrorist groups."[42] The publication of such material could have had a severe reaction on the tourist trade by rekindling the fears of 1985, something Greece obviously wants to avoid at all costs. To that end, Papandreou reportedly exploded on hearing of Keeley's demarche. Terming the allegations "a hostile act against Greece," Papandreou threatened that there would be no new base negotiations and that the present bases would go at the end of 1988 unless the U.S. publicly retracted its "false assertions." It was also indicated that Undersecretary of State Michael Armacost, who was scheduled to stop in Greece in late July, would not be welcome unless Washington retracted. The crisis receded when a letter from Armacost to Minister of Foreign Affairs Karolos Papoulias declared that there was no intention of accusing Greece of cooperating with terrorists. The White Paper apparently was put on hold and subjected to further editing.

PAPANDREOU AND PASOK: BOTH MULTIFACETED

Over the years, Papandreou had gained the reputation of being anti-American, a reputation strengthened as he moved toward the Balkans, flirted with the nonaligned and Third World, and tilted toward the Soviet Union. He denies being anti-American, explaining that he disagrees with the foreign policy of the Reagan administration and wants to make his disagreement known. However, it is one thing to register disagreement privately and officially on a government-to-government level, and another to do it publicly in a way seemingly designed to undermine Western solidarity. Papandreou almost inevitably chooses the latter. An American who has known him since he taught at Berkeley theorized a few years ago that he is torn between the two cultures and that his anti-Americanism is partly tactical and also perhaps a kind of psychological means of balancing off his years away from his native land in relative comfort while Greece was undergoing the trauma of invasion, occupation, civil war and reconstruction.[43] Papandreou was in Greece for the military coup in 1967 and was imprisoned for several months before being released as a result, at least in part, of U.S. overtures, but the twenty years he was away were extremely difficult years for Greece and his opponents have criticized him for not going home until things had begun to improve. In any case, while part of his anti-Americanism may be tactical, as his apologists contend, part of it also seems to be personal, as he has what appears to be an almost visceral, automatic reaction against things American, or more precisely, against the United States. Despite the fact that he professes to have been very happy during his long residence here, he almost seems to have been scarred in some way during those twenty years. His attitude toward the U.S. could be attributable to his disillusionment with U.S. policy following the coup, but it predates the coup.

As noted elsewhere in this analysis, his anti-Americanism, his predisposition toward the nonaligned and Third World, and his tilt toward the Soviet Union have not taken him out of the Western partnership, though Greece's participation in NATO can be considered "restricted" and in the EC less than completely cooperative. He has more often than not been a difficult partner, usually more critical of his partners than of his partners' adversary, the Soviet Union. He has never seemed to understand that partnership means responsibility to the organization and the partners alike, and staying in both NATO and the EC on his own terms has enabled him to have his cake and eat it too. Like all Greeks, he is preoccupied with Turkey and probably is genuinely convinced that the real threat to Greece is from the East rather than from the North, but he has made this point repeatedly for the last six years, and for the sake of the alliance could have softpedalled his relations with his Balkan neighbors. His insistence on stressing the excellence of his relations with Bulgaria and Romania only reinforces the perception that Greece has moved away from its long-time partners and tilted toward the other side. Similarly, his repetition of his belief in a Europe undivided by Yalta and Potsdam, without military blocs, and a Mediterranean without foreign fleets is impractical Third Worldism. Coming from the leader of a country that, except for U.S. assistance, could by his own admission be a member of the Soviet bloc, it sounds unreal. That it is the philosophy of the leader of a NATO/EC country makes it all the more incomprehensible.

The U.S. has had what it considers a special relationship with Greece founded on a romantic attachment for the "cradle of democracy," the considerable contribution to our society made by the large Greek-American community, and our involvement in Greece beginning in 1947 with the enunciation of the Truman Doctrine. Americans have looked with pride on Greece as one of the most successful examples of what U.S. assistance can do, as a country devastated by eight years of war fought its way back to become a respected member of the Western world. But most Americans do not realize how deeply the U.S. was involved in the daily affairs of Greece, as even the simplest of decisions had to be referred to American officials for approval before they could be implemented. With the benefit of hindsight, it is hardly surprising that this "patron/client" relationship, as it has come to be called, created deep resentment in Greece, particularly among the young people. Over the past several years, Papandreou himself has often told how his father, George Papandreou, as deputy prime minister and minister of coordination in the 1950s could not make important decisions without approval of the director of the U.S. aid mission.

In this context, it is understandable that thousands and thousands of young Greeks believe that, despite repeated denials, Washington must have been behind the coup of 1967 since, in their minds, it could not have happened without U.S. approval. If we did not initiate the coup, their reasoning goes, at least our support enabled the dictatorship to last for seven years. They cite a flow of high-ranking American visitors, including Vice President Spiro Agnew, as evidence that Washington was fully behind the military government, not to mention, of course, military assistance. We are also suspected of involvement in the Athens-inspired coup against Archbishop Makarios in 1974 since, they say, that was a coup to depose Makarios and bring Cyprus into NATO. Papandreou himself refers to this particular point from time to time, though he has been assured that this was not the case. Even if we were not involved in the coup, they stress, U.S. and NATO failure to stop Turkey led to the Turkish invasion of Cyprus and the occupation of 36% of the island by the Turkish Army. The continuing presence of over 30,000 Turkish troops is a bitter pill for all Greeks, a reminder of NATO and Western inability or unwillingness to prevent the Turkish invasion and occupation and clear proof of Washington's pro-Turkey tilt. Since it is widely believed that only we can move the Turks to make meaningful concessions, the inexorable march toward a settlement antithetical to Greek and Greek Cypriot interests is, in their minds, at least partly our responsibility. Papandreou involved himself personally in the Cyprus problem from the first days after his election and his inability to move the problem may well increase his antipathy toward the U.S.

In using party platforms to deliver some of his vilest criticism of the U.S., Papandreou once again has his cake and eats it too, since he would explain that he speaks in party meetings as party president and not as prime minister. This is a weak argument, of course, and will not hold up, since his position as prime minister derives directly from his position as party president and since he can not, in any case, put aside his prime ministerial hat any time he likes. Similarly, his desire to divorce himself from party statements critical of the U.S. does not hold up since Papandreou is PASOK. Two such party statements deserve mention: Athens Radio on 25 March 1986 carried a statement of PASOK's International Relations Committee which denounced "the latest super power action being attempted by the *stratocracy of the United States* (emphasis supplied) in the Gulf of Sidra."[44] The people of the region will not accept "the imposition of a new pax Americana through the use of arms," the statement said, continuing that it expressed the "feelings of the Greek people who unequivocally condemn this attempt to initiate a holocaust in the Mediterranean." After the U.S. bombing of Libya in April 1986, a PASOK statement condemned the action in strong, intemperate language, stating that "the U.S. has dynamited peace and at the same time destroyed the independence of a nation in the name of imposing its hegemonistic presence in the area."[45] This is pretty strong stuff from the ruling party of an allied country. These statements probably would not have been issued by the governing party, and surely not carried on stated radio, if PASOK and government functionaries had not thought they had blanket approval from Papandreou for such actions.

Is Papandreou really pro-Soviet? Certainly, like many nonaligned and Third World leaders, he reinforces his anti-Americanism with what appears to be a pro-Soviet bias for tactical or other reasons. On CBS's "60 Minutes" on 6 January 1985, for example, Papandreou equivocated when pressed by Diane Sawyer on the question of Soviet adventurism, saying that he "can have a very long list ... for America" if she wished. He admitted believing that Greece would be in the Soviet bloc today if it had not been for U.S. assistance in the late 1940s and stated that "very clearly" he would not want that.[46] But he has had no compunction about cozying up to members of that bloc or participating in activities favorable to or promoted by the Soviets, such as his promotion of the Balkan nuclear-free zone concept, the letter he and Ceaucescu sent to Reagan and Gorbachev, and his participation in the Group of Six. His exchange of letters with Gorbachev in May and June 1987, with not-altogether happy results for either, may be viewed as part of the Soviets' continuing efforts to woo him. With all of this, however, it is worth noting that his official visit to Moscow in 1985 accomplished little more than did the visit of Karamanlis some years earlier. A good example of his cozying up was a "new and upgraded" declaration of friendship and good neighborliness signed in 1986 with Bulgaria, the most solid of the Soviet satellites.

Papandreou's foreign policy has been a matter of satisfaction to the Soviets, who have expressed their appreciation a number of times. In 1983, a Soviet vice admiral expressed Soviet satisfaction "for the similar positions and the identity of views of the Greek and Soviet governments on the major issues of international policy."[47] *Pravda*, too, has commented favorably on the Greek foreign policy since Papandreou and PASOK came to power.[48] In December 1986, at a Greek-Soviet symposium in Athens marking the 170th anniversary of the founding of the "Philike Hetaireia," the Greek patriotic organization that played a big part in Greece's struggle for independence, the Soviet ambassador to Athens said that the Soviet Union appreciated Greece's "constructive stance in international relations and the prime minister's foreign policy." The ambassador commented that while Greece and the Soviet Union belong to different political and military alliances, "their views on a series of very acute problems in the world are very close and sometimes identical."[49] More recently, a CPSU delegation visiting Athens in April 1987 for talks with the PASOK party organization, "stressed its great appreciation for the initiative of the Group of Six."[50] When a flap with Turkey over drilling in the Aegean occurred in March 1987, Foreign Minister Papoulias hurried off to Sofia to brief Bulgarian leader Todor Zhivkov and another foreign ministry official went to Belgrade to fill in the Yugoslavs. Briefings in Athens for the Warsaw Pact and Islamic ambassadors all were part of the effort to drum up support for the Greek position and at the same time send a message to the allies. The announcement of the Gorbachev/Papandreou exchange of letters, which came shortly after the dispute over the Abu Nidal information broke out, was also a thinly-disguised message to the U.S. and other allies.

All of the above, suggestive rather than definitive, lead to a conclusion that Papandreou is at least tactically pro-Soviet. While he probably does not in fact want to be part of the Soviet bloc, he apparently feels that his pro-Soviet tilt is a double-edged sword for him, reasserting his independence from his allies and partners and keeping the Greek Left happy. The last is particularly important to him since the communist-controlled Greek labor unions could paralyze Greece if they chose to do so. Some accuse Papandreou of leaning over backwards to keep the communists and leftists happy but nobody would argue that they have not been a factor in his foreign policy. The danger is that Papandreou could become prisoner of his own rhetoric. He has managed to wiggle out of most of the crises he has faced—many of them self-inflicted—but as he faces new elections in 1989 (or even sooner) he may become dependent on the communists to remain in power and they could exact a heavy price for cooperation.

Is Papandreou a Third Worlder who would like to see Greece in the nonaligned movement rather than in NATO and the EC? The answer again is a qualified yes. As noted throughout this essay, some of his neutralist/pro-Soviet activity has been designed for effect at home or abroad; the latter concerned support for Greece against Turkey and/or eastern, nonaligned and Arab support on the Cyprus question. In that regard, it could be said to involve Greece's national interests as seen by PASOK. But it also involves political dogma, and probably reflects to some extent a genuine desire by the PASOK faithful for neutrality/nonalignment like that advocated by most radical, progressive parties. From its very inception, PASOK has seemed philosophically committed to a many-sided Greece, a country not Western or Eastern, a country not European, Balkan or Mediterranean but a bit of all, a country with no business in NATO or the EC. This would seem to leave nothing for Greece but nonalignment or neutrality, neither very good choices. Papandreou himself sometimes expresses what seems to be a real desire for neutrality. For example, his "60 Minutes" interview concluded with his saying "I want a Mediterranean without the Soviet fleet, without the American fleet. I don't want American bases; I don't want Soviet bases. I want to be left alone." While this may have been designed to keep pressure on us on the bases or other questions, or with an eye on the elections coming up in June 1985, it might have reflected a real desire for neutrality or nonalignment. On the pragmatic side, Papandreou and PASOK must realize that membership in the nonaligned movement has done nothing for Cyprus; indeed, joining the movement in 1961 may have been one of Archbishop Makarios's biggest political mistakes. And they must know that membership in, or some kind of association with, the NAM and/or Third World would be almost purely cosmetic and would do little for Greece. But even PASOK's affinity for the nonaligned and Third World countries is tempered by pragmatism. Greece was discouraged from seeking guest status at the New Delhi summit of 1983 by the prospect that if its efforts proved successful, Turkey would follow suit.[51] It has attended other NAM meetings as an observer or a guest, however.

How much of this is Papandreou posturing for political consumption at home is open to question, since even Papandreou himself probably could not say where the play acting stops and reality begins. But it seems naive to say that Papandreou draws his inspiration from the party when the reverse is probably closer to the truth. If he keeps the most radical elements of PASOK in check, it is equally true that he rekindles the ardor of the party faithful periodically. Certainly his addresses to the party over the past six years disclose rhetorical excesses unknown anywhere in the Western partnership as he repeats the party platform over and over and attacks the U.S. repeatedly. To return to an earlier point, his criticisms of the U.S. and its policies have been equalled in Western Europe only by some of those of Olof Palme.

One individual who appears to have played an active and important role in PASOK's tilt toward the NAM and the Third World is Minister of Foreign Affairs Karolos Papoulias, the party's foreign affairs specialist before it came to power and a key member of the PASOK foreign affairs team since. Chairman of the party's foreign relations committee before 1981, Papoulias was successively deputy minister of foreign affairs, alternate minister of foreign affairs, and finally minister of foreign affairs. His steady progress reflects the confidence Papandreou places in him on foreign affairs matters. A doctrinaire socialist and convinced nonaligned/Third World supporter, Papoulias appears to have been given some latitude in the areas marginal to Papandreou's immediate interests, such as Latin America. He appeared to be the force behind the Libyan love match and has been considered the party's—and of course the government's—point man on questions of relations with other Arabs, the Third World and the NAM, Africa, and various national liberation and revolutionary organizations. Even after 1981, when he became a member of the government, Papoulias would revert to his position as chairman of the PASOK foreign relations committee to receive delegations visiting Athens unofficially, according the visitors a measure of official reception they could not otherwise expect. Papandreou himself received many of these visitors, presumably on Papoulias's advice. While Papandreou makes all final decisions, Papoulias's role in the PASOK foreign affairs apparatus and his influence on Papandreou should not be underestimated, particularly in those areas mentioned previously on which he seems to have focused.

If Papandreou is an anti-American, pro-Soviet closet Third Worlder who would prefer a nonaligned, independent Balkan Greece, why then does he not take Greece out of NATO and the EC? Regarding the first, despite NATO's failure to move against Turkey in 1974, Papandreou probably feels that Greece is more secure in NATO than it would be outside NATO. Greece's withdrawal would solidify Turkey's position as Washington's favored ally in the Eastern Mediterranean and would run the danger, for Greece, of further improving Turkey's military position in the Aegean. Moreover, Greece's military establishment is irrevocably tied to the West; cutting supply lines with the West would be costly, for obvious reasons. These were presumably among the considerations which led Papandreou to declare on the floor of the Greek Parliament on 24 May 1987 that Greece "shall not withdraw from NATO because our country's security dangers within the Washington-Ankara-Athens triangle will be deadly." Indicating, unfortunately, that Greece will continue to be a difficult partner, he added that "However, this will not stop us from stating the truth and charting a policy of realism and independence."[52] In the same speech, Papandreou declared that "the (U.S.) bases for us are inseparably linked to the issue of our country's security." He prepared the country for new agreements to be negotiated *ab initio*, seemingly putting to rest the question whether there would in fact be new base agreements. Parenthetically, this would appear to confirm that his outburst following Ambassador Keeley's demarche was tactical. Papandreou ended any lingering speculation about Greek membership in the EC by saying that "withdrawal from the EEC is not an issue for this Government. We are in the EEC."

Papandreou's refusal to take Greece out of the EC has generally been attributed to the fact that financial benefits deriving from membership override any political drawbacks involved in belonging to the Community. But there is a political side as well. Papandreou would be highly unlikely to take Greece out of the world's most sophisticated union when others, most notably Turkey, are trying to get in. Greece likely will hang tough on Turkey's application, and Turkish concessions on Cyprus and in the Aegean could be the price Turkey has to pay for admission. In fact, Western Europe may be faced with a golden opportunity to do something about the long-standing Cyprus problem. Despite its own membership in the NAM, the government of Cyprus would probably not be averse to an EC effort; it has recently signed an agreement of association with the Community. The desire for EC membership—carrying with it full acceptance in Western Europe and full EC benefits—would be a powerful incentive to Turkey and might push it toward concessions it is unlikely to make otherwise.

Is Papandreou, for all of his posturing, really a Western man? Maybe yes and maybe no. Athens journalist Andriana Ierodiaconou was quoted some years ago as saying that "Papandreou has made his bed in the West but refuses to lie in it."[53] Certainly one would have hoped that his long ties with the West—political refuge, wife, children, education, successful teaching career—would be more evident in his official life and that he would not turn, à la Bhutto, toward neutralism. He has not visited the United States in some years and his misreading of us may stem from the fact that he still sees the U.S. as it was in the 1960s. He presumably has wanted to come to Washington on an official visit and his failure to receive an invitation has probably not only rankled him, but may have given him some impetus to turn away from the U.S. Perceived or real slights have shaped leaders' attitudes towards us before and it might be unwise to continue to deny him the invitation he would like to have. One of the interesting things about Papandreou is that he gets along very well with U.S. leaders when he meets them face to face. In what seems an unlikely match, he hit it off beautifully with Secretary of State Alexander Haig, whom he met at NATO and when Haig visited Athens, and seemed genuinely upset when Haig resigned. When Secretary of State George Shultz visited Athens in March of 1986, Papandreou was quoted as saying that his meeting with the secretary was "one of the most important meetings" he had ever had with a foreign visitor and he stressed that "the talks had been extremely positive and constructive for Greece."[54]

A good example of Papandreou hyperbole, this reaction demonstrates how Papandreou is very often influenced by the last person he sees, a failing that has bothered his allies in the past. Equally troublesome is his inclination to tell his audience what they want to hear. This explains to some extent—but only to some extent, it should be stressed—the strident anti-American tone of his speeches to party audiences. It cannot be discounted that Papandreou, like many Third World and NAM politicians, gets carried away by the passion of his own rhetoric.

Papandreou has shown some signs of mellowing as his government seems to be moving in the direction of de jure recognition of Israel. Speculation concerning recognition is not new, however, and it must be considered just that until it happens. Still, the visit of Foreign Minister Papoulias to Tel Aviv is of special significance, particularly in light of his past advocacy of Greek ties with Libya and other states and organizations antithetical to Israel. The PASOK government, like its conservative predecessors, maintains full relations with South Africa, though it consistently calls for abolition of apartheid, the unconditional independence of Namibia, and sanctions against South Africa. The presence in South Africa of a relatively affluent Greek community—what Papandreou would call "South African Hellenism"—inhibits Greek activity regarding South Africa to some extent and forces the PASOK government to temper its radicalism with pragmatism. In early 1986, in what was dubbed an "Opening Towards Africa," Foreign Minister Papoulias made a lengthy trip to Africa, with stops in Zimbabwe, Zambia, Kenya, and Ethiopia. In Lusaka, at a meeting of the EC delegation with the front-line states, he met with the foreign ministers of Tanzania, Botswana, and Mozambique. The purpose of his trip seems to have been drumming up support for Cyprus as well as support for "initiatives towards peace and disarmament." As a footnote, his meeting with Mengistu was described as "cordial and friendly," and agreement was reached to look for ways to cooperate, and sectors in which cooperation might be possible.[55]

While Papandreou's government can be an irritant at the United Nations, statistically it comes out much better than Turkey and far better than the NAM. For example, on all UNGA plenary votes in 1986, Greece voted with us 42.7% of the time compared with 37.1% for Turkey, both well below the 68.6% average for NATO and 71.3% for EC countries, but well above the NAM average of 16.7%. On the so-called ten most important issues, Greece voted with us on 7, opposed us on 2, and abstained on 1; Turkey voted with us on only 5, opposed on 1, and abstained on 4. (Both Greece and Turkey abstained on the resolution condemning our military action against Libya.) The statistics are inconclusive for highly analytical purposes but the U.S. Mission to the U.N. believes that using as a criterion the votes on issues of particular importance and on which we extensively lobbied other governments, "we can measure with some accuracy a country's level of support for the United States in the U.N."[56] If indeed the voting pattern of a country provides one criterion for judgment, Greece is not as close to the NAM and Third World as other factors would lead us to believe.

CONCLUSION

On the basis of empirical evidence assembled, the author has described a Papandreou as contradictory as his government's multifaceted foreign policy; a leader of a Western nation who frequently looks to the East and the Third World/nonaligned movement for support, an unpredictable, independent-minded Western partner who not only flaunts the rules but plays footsie with the other side and seems more at home with them than with his partners. The inevitable question is, What can the West expect from him and his party in the future? The answer, in brief, is probably more of the same. Ostensibly, the major irritants in Greek-U.S. relations will be out of the way: the three "core" issues have been, or soon will be, put to rest, if we can take Papandreou at his word as indicated in his speech to Parliament on 24 May 1987. Indeed, if a new agreement is signed within the next several months, U.S. bases should not be a factor in Greek-U.S. relations for the remainder of Papandreou's present term or in the next elections. On the surface, then, Greece's relations with the U.S., likened by some to a roller-coaster, should soon be on the upswing.

But like many Third World or NAM leaders, Papandreou seems to make a fetish of his unpredictability and things may not always be what they ought to be. He actually told Diane Sawyer in the "60 Minutes" interview that "in foreign policy one should give confusing signals" since "this is the best policy for a small nation. It is a good strategy." A case in point to be remembered is that only two months after he had seemingly opened the way for a new bases agreement with his speech in Parliament, he reacted irrationally to Ambassador Keeley's demarche over Abu Nidal, threatening to end base talks before they began if Washington did not retract the information. Without a shift in U.S. policy away from what Greeks perceive as a tilt toward Turkey, Greek-U.S. relations are almost sure to continue to be subjected to sudden ups and downs. What the Greeks really want—some plain talk from Washington and other NATO capitals with Turkey about Cyprus and the Aegean—is probably not in the cards for some time to come and the volatile Papandreou may well choose other, perhaps peripheral, issues for making his displeasure with Washington known. A democratic administration that emphasizes defense policy less might be more sympathetic to Greek problems, but Turkey's strategic location is likely to be the overriding consideration in the formulation of U.S. policy in the Eastern Mediterranean for some years to come, despite Greek protestations that historically it has been the more reliable ally and should be Washington's favorite in the area.

The U.S. and its allies have never seemed to understand that Papandreou reflects the feelings of the majority of Greeks when he says that Greece is the only member of NATO which feels threatened by another member of the alliance, that Greece is the only member to suffer humiliation at the hand of another member. The Turks' assurances that they have no designs on Greek Islands in the Aegean or other Greek territory may be accepted at face value by the U.S. and others, but in fact the Greeks do feel threatened. Irrational it may be, but this fear of Turkish intentions is part of the Greek psyche, a reminder that

Greeks have not forgotten that Turkey occupied Greece for four hundred years before Greece "threw off the Turkish yoke" in the early nineteenth century. The Greeks point to Cyprus as proof of Turkey's real intentions in the area, as proof that Turkey can not be trusted. Not surprisingly, the Greeks see themselves as the wronged party in the Cyprus dispute, since despite its rationale for the action it took in 1974, Turkey did invade Cyprus and continues to occupy a large part of the country after thirteen years, disregarding world opinion and numerous United Nations resolutions, as it has continued to refuse to withdraw its troops.

Actually, Turkey has expanded its occupation forces within the past few years, giving what many take as proof that it is on the island to stay. Subtle pressures on Turkey from Washington and the allies to begin drawing down its troops would do much to assuage the bruised feelings of Greeks, who perceive U.S. reluctance to pressure Turkey even slightly as proof of Turkey's favored position in Washington. More support for Papandreou and Greece on these questions from his partners might make him less inclined to seek support from the Third World, the NAM, and the East. Papandreou for his part must recognize that nonaligned support for Cyprus over the years has in fact had little effect on the Cyprus problem, but he is presumably willing to accept help from whatever quarter in his efforts to drive Turkey out of the island. For a long time Greeks have felt—some say not without justification—that they are victims of a double standard in the Eastern Mediterranean and are judged more critically than are the Turks. Cyprus is only one area in which they feel that more balanced treatment by Washington would contribute to a resolution of some of the problems in the area.

While not many of its ambassadorial appointments have been particularly noteworthy, the Reagan administration has used uncommonly good judgment in its selection of ambassadors to Greece. Monteagle Stearns, a career foreign service officer fluent in modern Greek and extremely knowledgeable on Greek affairs, did an outstanding job as U.S. ambassador from 1981 to 1985. He was succeeded by Robert Keeley, another career man with language and country expertise. Both had known Papandreou previously and were known to be favorably disposed toward Greece. Both were able to calm the waters in Athens and in Washington when differences arose between the two capitals and presumably helped to moderate some of

Papandreou's more radical and pro-Third World tendencies. Staffing of other key positions in the embassy in Athens with language officers has also been helpful, taken by the Greeks as a manifestation of U.S. interest in improving the situation. Washington has been a problem over the years, however, as the Pentagon, put off by Papandreou's radicalism and uncooperativeness, has tilted more toward Turkey. The U.S. military, obviously influenced by strategic considerations and the perception that Turkey is the more reliable ally, traditionally has been pro-Turkish, and Papandreou's election merely pushed them further in that direction. In general, senior State Department officers have not been noted for their Greek expertise or predisposition toward Greece. Greek reliance on the Greek-American lobby to support military assistance legislation is not viewed favorably in the State Department or the Pentagon, but all Greek governments, conservative as well as the present PASOK government, depend on the lobby to pressure Congress to maintain a level of military assistance favorable to Greece. The entire question of military assistance is a vital one for Greece, and adherence to the "seven to ten" ratio will be a factor in Greek-U.S. relations for some time to come.[57]

The limited options for the NATO and EC partners—which amount to little more than a measure of understanding of the Greek position in the Eastern Mediterranean—may in turn elicit more understanding and cooperation from Athens and hopefully head off further Greek flirtations with the East, the NAM, and the Third World. Papandreou has never seemed to recognize—or admit that he recognizes—the obligations devolving upon the U.S. as a superpower or on NATO as the Western alliance. As long as his heart remains in the Third World and he continues to be personally anti-American, the confusing signals out of Athens are likely to continue. The danger in this is the possibility that NATO and EC capitals might tire of Papandreou's obstructionist, opportunist ways some day and decide that Greece must play by the rules or withdraw. Papandreou and PASOK have played a high stakes game for six years, gambling that this would not happen. It is highly unlikely that it ever will, since many NATO and EC leaders admit that they cannot envision a united Europe without Greece. But it is always a possibility—even if a remote one—and it should not be disregarded entirely in any assessment of PASOK's relations with its partners.

In conclusion, it is difficult to imagine Papandreou and PASOK moving substantively closer to the Third World and the NAM than they did in PASOK's first six years in power. Greece's policies with regard to the Balkans, Eastern Europe, the Middle East, Latin America, the Third World, and the nonaligned countries, are almost certain to be at variance with those of its allies and partners at times. But if Papandreou had really wanted to take Greece out of the West and into the nonaligned camp, he has had ample opportunity to do so before now, and for all his posturing, he is probably as close right now to the Third World and nonaligned as he wants to be.

NOTES

1. Papandreou had earlier threatened to take Greece out of the EC but began to modify his stand as elections came closer. His final ploy was to call a referendum on the question—thereby giving the people a chance to decide—all the while reminding the people that the question of a referendum fell within the powers of the president and knowing full well that President Karamanlis, who had worked many years to get Greece into the EC, was not likely to call a referendum. Papandreou was obviously having it both ways.

2. Papandreou ran in 1981 on a slogan of "change" ("allage" in Greek). The theme that the time for a change had arrived was used very effectively throughout the entire campaign. The PASOK Policy Declaration published in the Athens newspaper *To Vema* on 5 July 1981, noted that "The time for *big change* has come to our country." (underscoring supplied.) The Policy Declaration will be referred to further on in this paper.

3. A member of the New Democracy party, told by an American visitor in 1980 that the visitor would be calling on Papandreou during an official visit to Athens, warned the visitor not "to be taken in" by Papandreou. "He can be very charming," the ND member said, "but you should never trust him since he is entirely unpredictable." Visitors calling on Papandreou were usually surprised and disarmed to find him so soft-spoken and professorial in private meetings, reflecting none of the demagogic behavior attributed to him by press and other reporting.

4. *Proclamation of Basic Principles and Goals of the Panhellenic Socialist Movement*, (Athens 3 September 1974).

5. Angelos Elephantis, "PASOK and the Elections of 1977" in Howard R. Penniman, ed., *Greece at the Polls, the National Elections of 1974 and 1977*. (Washington and London: American Enterprise Institute for Public Policy Research, 1981): 113-4.

6. *Ibid.*

7. Andreas Papandreou, *Democracy at Gunpoint: The Greek Front*. (London: Andre Deutsch, Limited, 1971): 318. Papandreou seemed to be placing Greece in the Third World in a political, rather than an economic context, when he spoke of "the struggle of the Third World for emancipation and national sovereignty." He was, of course, speaking of a Greece governed by a military junta. He continued that Greece's "political development will be deeply affected by the overall pattern of changing relations between Third World countries and the two blocs. Despite the overwhelming power of the two superpowers and their determination to maintain and intensify the division of the world into two blocs, to snuff out neutralism and to satellitize the emerging new nations, the outcome of the struggle is far from predictable."

8. Andreas Papandreou, *Man's Freedom*. (New York: The Columbia University Press, 1970): 56. In this compilation of three lectures delivered as part of the Benjamin F. Fairless Memorial Lectures, Papandreou likens Greece after the 1967 coup to Czechoslovakia, saying that "superpower intervention in both cases has all the characteristics of bloc-internal police action. The official United States (sic) let it be understood in European government circles that the assumption of power by the Greek military junta was intended to prevent a communist takeover which would have corroded the strategic position of NATO in the Eastern Mediterranean basin, and Moscow lost no opportunity in telling its people and the people of its satellites that the invasion of Czechoslovakia became necessary in order to thwart capitalist imperialism and West German revanchism." Papandreou said that, "Despite their superficial differences, the events in Czechoslovakia are in broad perspective a replica of and a response to the events in Greece."

9. Richard Jackson, *The Non-aligned, the U.N. and the Superpowers* . (New York: Praeger Publishers, 1983): 5.

10. Theodore A. Couloumbis, "The Structures of Greek Foreign Policy" in Richard Clogg, ed., *Greece in the 1980s* . (New York: St. Martin's Press, 1983): 95-96.

11. Victor Papacosma, "The Historical Context" in Clogg, *op. cit.*, 35.

12. No question shows Papandreou's ability to tack with the wind better than the one of Greek membership in the EC. After first preaching withdrawal, he began to advocate a referendum, knowing full well that would never come about. Unwilling to admit, presumably for political reasons, that Greece would stay in the Community, he then began to demand "a special arrangement" for Greece. He did get a good hearing in the EC, which proved sympathetic to Greece's "special problems," which he could label "special arrangement" for home consumption. At the end of his first term, he finally declared that there was no further doubt about Greece's membership in the EC, i.e., Greece is in to stay.

13. ABC interview, "Issues and Answers," 25 October 1981, carried

on Athens Radio and in the *FBIS Daily Report* for Western Europe, 26 October 1981. (The FBIS Daily Report will hereafter be referred to simply as "FBIS" with the appropriate date.

14. Interview with Paris *Le Monde*, 29 October 1981, reprinted in *FBIS*, 2 November 1981.

15. Paris *AFP* in English, 23 October 1981, reprinted in *FBIS*, 26 October 1981.

16. *Eleutherotypia*, (Athens), 5 November 1981, reprinted in *FBIS*, 6 November 1981.

17. *Ibid.*

18. *Athens News*, 18 November 1981, carried in *FBIS*, 19 November 1981.

19. *Athens Radio*, 9 August 1982, carried in *FBIS*, 10 August 1982.

20.*The Economist* of 27 June 1987, reports that since the establishment of the EC's regional development fund in 1975, Greece has been second only to Ireland among recipients of EC assistance by head of population. *The Economist* notes that "With the entry of Spain and Portugal last year, more than a fifth of the Community's population now lives in regions where income per head is 80% or less of the ECC average. These include the whole of Greece, Portugal and Ireland, most of Spain and the south of Italy." For an idea of what membership has meant to Greece in economic terms, *The Economist* of 23 May 1987 reports that in 1984 the French got a net of 6 pounds each, the British got 18 pounds, and the Greeks got 75 pounds.

21. See Section III for further elaboration on this point.

22. *Athens Radio*, 12 December 1981, carried in *FBIS*, 14 December 1981.

23. Qaddafi reportedly made numerous demands on the government of Greece concerning his visit, including that he be met at the airport by President Constantine Karamanlis. Karamanlis, a very proud man, allegedly declined to dignify Qaddafi's visit by meeting him on his arrival. Political observers in Athens at the time were of the opinion that the PASOK government was in fact relieved when the visit was cancelled.

24. *The Washington Post*, 12 June 1987: 5.

25. *Mesemvrine*, (Athens), 18 January 1984, reprinted in *FBIS* 19 January 1984.

26. *Ibid.*

27. *Athens Radio*, 19 January 1984, carried in *FBIS*, 20 January 1984.

28. *Athens Radio*, 2 September 1983, text carried in *FBIS*, 2 September 1983.

29. Paris *AFP* in English, 12 September 1983, reprinted in *FBIS*, 13 September 1983.

30. *Ibid.*

31. *Athens Radio*, 26 October 1983, carried in *FBIS*, 27 October 1983.

32. Papandreou's speech opening the First PASOK Congress in Athens, 10 May 1984, reported in *Eleutherotypia*, 11 May 1984, reprinted in *FBIS*, 15 May 1984.

33. *Ibid.*

34. *Ibid.*

35. *Athens Radio*, 15 November 1982, carried in *FBIS*, 16 November 1982.

36. *Athens Radio*, 18 May 1987, carried in *FBIS*, 19 May 1987.

37. *Ibid.*

38. *The Washington Post*, 12 July 1987.

39. *Athens Radio*, 30 May 1986, carried in *FBIS*, 2 June 1986.

40. *Ibid.*

41. *The Economist*, 30 May 1987: 50.

42. *The Economist*, 4 July 1987: 48.

43. "Papandreou Fares Well Politically in Poor Economy," *The Los Angeles Times*, 27 November 1983: 1.

44. *Athens Radio*, 25 March 1986, carried in *FBIS*, 26 March 1986. The *Webster's New Unabridged Dictionary* defines "stratocracy" simply as "a military government." It is a direct transliteration from the Greek word which means the same thing.

45. *Athens Radio*, 15 April 1986, carried in *FBIS*, 17 April 1987.

46. "60 Minutes," Vol. XVII, Number 17, broadcast by the CBS Television Network, Sunday, 6 January 1985.

47. John C. Loulis, "Papandreou's Foreign Policy," *Foreign Affairs*, 63:375-91, Winter 1984-85.

48. *Ibid.*

49. *Athens News*, 11 December 1986, reprinted in *FBIS*, 15 December 1986.

50. *Athens Radio*, 11 April 1987, carried in *FBIS*, 14 April 1987.

51. Jackson, *op. cit.*, p. 83.

52. *Athens Radio*, 24 May 1987, carried in *FBIS*, 26 May 1987.

53. *The Los Angeles Times*, *op. cit.*

54. *Athens Radio*, 28 March 1986, carried in *FBIS* of the same date.

55. *Spotlight, A Fortnightly Publication of the Institute for Political Studies*, Athens, Greece, No. 37, 1 March 1986.

56. *Report to Congress on Voting Practices in the United Nations, Submitted Pursuant to Public Law 99-500 and Public Law 98-164*, 23 April 1987: 1-5.

57. The seven-to-ten ration in military assistance came into being in 1976 when the draft agreement with Turkey provided for $1 billion in assistance over four years; the Greek draft agreement called for $700 million over the same period. The agreements were initialed but never signed and hence never came into effect. The ratio has come to be accepted, particularly by the Greeks, as binding though it has never been incorporated into law and any deviation or prospective provokes loud protests from Athens.

PASOK and the Eastern Bloc: A Growing Relationship

Demetres Michalopoulos

The foreign policy of the Panhellenic Socialist Movement (PASOK), which assumed power in 1981, is a complex problem, directly linked to the internal policies and economic issues affecting Greece. In particular, relations between Greece and Eastern European countries, both Balkan and others, are important indicators of political trends.

A systematic evaluation is difficult, for the time being, because of the increasing secrecy that surrounds the Socialist government's handling of foreign affairs. Another problem in analyzing PASOK's policy towards Eastern Europe and the Soviet Union is inherent in the changing self-image of the Panhellenic Socialist Movement. No longer is it presented as a "radical" structure, but as a political party with social democratic tendencies which is supposedly moving towards the mainstream of social democracy. Pro-PASOK Socialists and government image-makers are hard at work to redefine the party and its leader. Its third world policies are deemphasized and its anti-Americanism "explained" in an historical context. PASOK's reversals are interpreted as ingenious ways to attract the left-wing voters without losing its conservative clientele and, most important, without alienating the country's traditional allies.[1] Nevertheless, sufficient information is available in the public domain, which, carefully analyzed, can provide the framework of Greek foreign policy towards Eastern Europe. An analysis of the entire spectrum of Greek foreign policy under PASOK reveals a reality different from that created by the party. PASOK is attempting, with undeniable consistency, to achieve the goals it set for itself while in opposition, namely, socialist transformation of Greek society, national liberation, social justice, and so on. Foreign policy has been systematically linked to vital issues of domestic life or, to put it differently, foreign policy has become a vehicle for achieving internal ideological predominance and retaining power. The subordination of foreign policy to domestic partisan objectives is evident.

HISTORICAL FOUNDATIONS OF GREEK-EAST EUROPEAN RELATIONS

With the Balkan countries Greece has necessarily had constant relations, both of friendship and adversity, from very old times. Albania, the newest of the Balkan states (international recognition occurred only in 1913), has been treated with favor by the Greek government and the Greek people, despite unsettled territorial issues. The existence in the very heart of Greece of Albanian-speaking enclaves (Attica, Argolis, and some islands in the Saronic Bay) creates a bond between the two countries. Christian Albanians who fled from the Ottomans sought refuge in Greek lands. These people adapted to the Greek environment, acquired a Greek way of thinking and their descendants contributed considerably to Greece's War of Independence. A dialect of Albanian has survived in some parts of Greece, as a reminder of their ancestry.[2] On the other hand, the presence in Northern Epirus (southern region of Albania) of a Greek minority, whose linguistic, religious and human rights were recognized by the League of Nations and by the Albanian government in 1921[3] but hardly respected after World War II, was often a cause of bitter friction between Athens and Tirana.[4]

Relations with the Serbs have been friendly and cordial for most of their history as independent nations. Early in the nineteenth century Serbia shook off Ottoman rule, and on this common ground was the first country with which Athens developed close relations from the second half of the nineteenth century. Greeks and Serbs were allies in the First and Second Balkan Wars. The Kingdom of Serbs, Croats and Slovenes was formed in 1919 and renamed Yugoslavia ten years later. Allies in the First and Second World Wars, the two neighbors continued their traditional friendly policy toward each other in the twentieth century, with only minor frictions in the 1920s over exit rights to Salonica.

Belgrade sought a zone in the port of Salonica over which it would have sovereign rights and which would be connected to the Greek-Yugoslav border by a railroad under the supervision of both governments. In the summer of 1926, General Theodoros Pangalos, then president of the Hellenic Republic with dictatorial powers, signed an agreement granting the zone to Belgrade. However, in August of the same year Pangalos was overthrown and the Parliament refused to ratify the conventions already signed. The Yugoslav government let it be understood that this was grounds for war. This war threat persisted until September 1928, but abated when, upon signing a Greek-Italian treaty in Rome, Benito Mussolini, then leader of the fascist government, told Eleutherios Venizelos, the Greek prime minister, that in case of a Yugoslav attack, Greece would not fight alone.[5]

In contrast of the relations between Greeks and Serbs/Yugoslavs, those between Greeks and Bulgarians were marked by intense hostility from the end of the 19th century. This was not something new: Bulgarians, although Orthodox Christians, had many times during the middle ages, disputed Byzantine authority and sovereignty over their lands. The conflicts between Byzantine emperors and Bulgarian kings and chiefs were brutal during the tenth and eleventh centuries.

When the domination of the Ottoman sultans was established in the Balkan Peninsula, the two neighbors met each other under a common ruler. Many Bulgarians fought on the side of the Greeks in the War of Independence; later many of them settled in liberated Greece.

In the second half of the 19th century, the Bulgarian church and national leaders rejected the Ecumenical Patriarchate's spiritual primacy. As a consequence, other disputes arose. For example, during the first decade of the twentieth century, Greek and Bulgarians fought bitterly among themselves for the "Ottoman heritage": both wanted control over Macedonia. In fact, it was then clear that the Turks would sooner or later yield territory in Europe, which would be taken over by the more powerful of their neighbors. In this contest, it was the Greeks who won. Their victory was confirmed during the First Balkan War: Thessalonike, Macedonian capital and the apple of discord between many powers, was liberated by Prince Constantine, commander-in-chief of the Greek troops and heir to the Greek throne. Sofia, however, did not accept the outcome and during the Second Balkan War the Bulgarians fought not only the Greeks but also the Serbs and the Rumanians. Their defeat resulted in Eastern Macedonia's being annexed by Greece. Their participation in the First World War on the losing side cost them Western Thrace. Again, Greece was the beneficiary. In an attempt to recover these regions, the Bulgarians, in a peculiar manner, entered the Second World War on the side of Hitler, but not against all of his enemies. Sofia never declared war on the Soviet Union, and its troops practically did not participate in operations against the British or the Americans. Bulgaria, a formal ally of the German Reich, aimed only in a vast revanchist dream to occupy the Greek territories of Western Thrace and Eastern Macedonia. Bulgarian troops occupied much of Greek Macedonia and Thrace, until they were forced to withdraw at the end of 1944.

Finally, with Rumania, unlike the above countries, Greece has no common frontier. During the 20th century, a cause of a rather subtle conflict between Athens and Bucharest was the latter's propensity to appear as "protector" of an ethnic group living in Greece, speaking a Romance language, and considered racially related to the Rumanians. These people were treated better by the Greek government after 1913, when Athens, in need of Rumania's support against Bulgaria, granted rights previously denied.[6]

Small Greek colonies established in the major cities of Hungary and Czechoslovakia have created common ground for relations between Greece and those countries.

A bond between Greece and Poland was the Ecumenical Patriarchate's attempt, during the first centuries of Ottoman rule (1450-1600) in Greece, to prevent domination of the Orthodox church in Poland by the Vatican and to restrain the expansion of Catholicism.[7] Moreover, many *philhellenes* from Poland took part in the Greek War of Independence and later, up to the beginning of the 20th century, a significant number of Poles settled in Greece. (It is characteristic that Andreas Papandreou's mother is of Polish origin.) On the other hand, from the end of the 19th century up to the outbreak of World War II a number of poor Greeks sought their fortune in Poland. The bonds between the two countries may be stronger than they seem.

Even a brief analysis of Russia's relations with Greece would be beyond the scope of this essay. However, some main points should be noted. The Russians were converted to Christian Orthodoxy, which was to become the most important factor of their cultural life, thanks to the action of Byzantine emperors. After Constantinople fell to the Ottomans, Moscow was viewed as the Third Rome. As a result, subjugated Greeks gradually began to look on the czar as their future savior. From the time of Peter the Great, this impression became a strong belief. Often the population of southern Greece took up arms to help the Russians in their wars against the Turks.

In a more concrete way, the right to raise the Russian flag, granted to Greek ships before the outbreak of the Greek War of Independence, helped Greece to become a naval power. The *Philike Hetaireia* , a secret organization consisting of prominent Greek intellectuals and merchants, which masterminded Greek strategy in the War of Independence, was founded in Odessa. The Russian victories of 1829 against the Sublime Porte contributed significantly to ending Ottoman domination in southern Greece.

The eventual appearance and activity in Greece of a strong "Russian" political party in the 1840s was not surprising. One of the heroes of the Greek revolution, Theodoros Kolokotronis, was a pro-Russian leader whose policy was to coordinate Greek tactics with those of imperial Russia.

The overthrow of King Otto in 1862 put an end to Russophile tendencies. Greece came under British influence, which lasted until 1946. The pro-British orientation was the choice of Greece's ruling classes and of the economically powerful Greek colonies in Western Europe and the Near East. But many Greek peasants continued to feel close to Russia because of the common religion and their belief that poor Greeks seeking their fortunes were welcome in Russia. The czar remained to Greek lower classes the powerful protector of Christian Orthodoxy, the Ecumenical Patriarchate and even the Greek crown against the Moslem East and Catholic or Protestant West.

The events of 1917 put an end to this situation. The aid given by the Soviets to Kemal Atatürk's army during the Greek-Turkish conflict of 1919-1922 created bitterness among Greeks. The activities of Greek Socialists, who strove to follow Lenin's example, were attributed to Moscow's instigation.[8] This also turned many Greeks against Russia.

The Greek governments of the 1918-1940 period faced with distrust the militant but isolated Soviet Union. The latter, however, persisted in its efforts to win the hearts of peasants whom the industrialization of the country was turning into proletarians.

THE LEGACY OF THE 40s

The events that took place in the 1940s altered relations between Greece, Eastern Europe, and the Soviet Union. Conditions were ripe for the establishment of a communist regime in Albania and Yugoslavia and in the former Axis allies, Bulgaria and Rumania. In Greece, however, the armed attempt of the communists in December 1944 to seize power failed. The northern boundary of Greece became the boundary of the two blocs already formed in the Balkans.

In 1946, the Greek Communists initiated a new attempt to overthrow the regime. More systematic than the first, it led to a bloody civil war, which lasted until 1949. The Communist Democratic Army was supplied (and trained) by Albania and Bulgaria; other "Peoples Republics" assisted in indirect ways. As it turned out, this support was not given only for ideological reasons: in fact, it was common knowledge to both the government of Greece and to the peasants of the provinces that a communist victory would mean the loss of a large part of the country's northern territory. This impression was reinforced by the aid that Macedonia's slavic minorities were giving to the Democratic Army, and by the efforts the Communists made to win over these minorities. The government troops fought during the Civil War not only for the preservation of democratic pluralism but also for the defense of the country's territorial integrity. It was the latter that mainly mobilized the nation and led to victory in August 1949.

The dispute between Tito and Stalin resulted in the sealing off of the Yugoslav border to the Democratic Army, and an end to supplies from Yugoslavia and the training of Democratic Army troops in Yugoslavia. Belgrade thus contributed decisively to the defeat of the Communists in Greece, which is the main reason that Yugoslavia was the only communist state with which Athens had good relations after 1949.[9] Relations with the other countries of Eastern Europe remained strained for decades. Greece emerged from the Civil War strongly anti-communist. The Communist party was declared illegal. The psychology dominating political elites and the people in general was that of a garrison state guarding an advanced check point of the West in the midst of the Eastern camp. This situation was aggravated by the thousands of soldiers of the Democratic Army who had settled in the People's Democracies and continued their propaganda warfare against the legitimate Greek governments, and by the traditional distrust towards Albania and Bulgaria—two countries which exploited their wartime alliances with Mussolini and Hitler to satisfy territorial claims and which provided critical support to the Greek Communist party in its quest for power.

Relations with the Soviet Union were at their lowest in the 40's. Although Stalin had agreed with Churchill in Moscow, in October 1944, that Greece would remain under British influence[10] and during the Yalta conference had displayed indifference towards the defeat of the Greek Communists,[11] the USSR was nevertheless the leader of the socialist camp, which had openly supported the Democratic Army and threatened the integrity of the country. As late as 1961 Nikita Khrushchev warned the Greek public opinion that, in case of a new world war, he would not hesitate to attack the American bases in Greece with missiles, "which would spare neither olive-groves nor the Acropolis."[12] These blatant threats reminded the Greeks that the threat from the north had not faded.

Indeed, from the end of the Civil War to 1974, nearly the entire Greek defense doctrine was geared to defending the northern border from attack by Warsaw Pact countries. The elite units were stationed in the northern territories, especially in Macedonia, where military authorities had broad powers in civilian matters as well. During the same period, Greece and Turkey were in theory friends, since both countries belonged to the same camp, but relations deteriorated because of the Cyprus issue.

The Cyprus issue is traceable to promises made by Great Britain to return the island to Greece, but it entered a new phase in 1950. In that year, the Autocephalus Church of Cyprus, without consulting Athens, held a plebiscite on the future of the island. This action satisfied a demand of Cyprus's Progressive Party of the Working People (AKEL, the Cypriot Communist party), which had adopted the anti-colonial rhetoric emanating from Moscow; it was sure to cause friction between Greece and Great Britain. The results of the plebiscite showed that the vast majority of the Greek-Cypriots wished to end the colonial rule and unite with Greece.[13] The Greek government at first ignored the Cypriot action. Bonds between Athens and London were then strong and the British were given credit for preventing the Communists in 1944 from seizing power. For several reasons, chief of which was the strategic importance of the island, the British government could not accept the Cypriot demands.[14]

However, public opinion favored *enosis* (union of Cyprus with Greece) and the Greek government was forced to support it. The unsettled situation in Cyprus brought Turkey into the picture under the pretext of protecting the Turkish minority there (17.9% of the island's population in 1950). After prolonged negotiations of the United Kingdom, Greece, Turkey, the Greek-Cypriots and the Turkish-Cypriots, the Republic of Cyprus was established as an independent country in 1960.

The life of this Republic proved to be very difficult, but in retrospect it became a catalyst in the reorientation of Greek foreign policies. In early summer, 1974, the military regime of Greece overthrew the government of Makarios. Turkey feared that the new government formed in Cyprus after the overthrow of Makarios would threaten the welfare of the Turkish-Cypriots and sent in troops, occupying nearly 40% of the Republic's territory. Meantime, under the force of these events, the military regime in Greece collapsed and Constantine Karamanlis returned to Greece as prime minister in July 1974.

Following events in Cyprus, a majority of Greeks adopted the notion promoted by the Left that the ruling circles of the United States were responsible for the seven-year military regime in Greece (1967-1974) and for the Turkish invasion of Cyprus. Karamanlis, whose government reflected a broad popular consensus, could not afford to come out against this view.[15] Encouraged by its "easy victory" in Cyprus, Turkey exploited the weaknesses of Greece and sought to "resolve" other problems with Greece from a position of strength. The Turkish threat, following the Cyprus invasion, was seen as real by all political parties.

Under the circumstances, the Greek government began to reconsider relations with Greece's northern neighbors and the Eastern bloc. A friendly disposition of northern Balkan countries, Eastern Europe and the Soviet Union would be of vital importance for Greece in case of hostilities with Turkey, which in 1974 seemed quite real. Thus, a new chapter in Greek-East European relations opened. The first phase of the new policy commenced with the fall of the dictatorship in 1974 and ended with the assumption of power by PASOK. A sensible improvement of relations took place with Albania.

In 1939, when Italian troops landed in Albania, the Albanian crown was offered to King Victor Emmanuel of Italy, and Albania became a springboard for the Italian attack against Greece in October 1940. One of the reasons given by Rome for the declaration of war against Greece was the "liberation" of the 16,661 Chams (i.e., Albanian speaking Moslems), who lived along the coast in the Greek part of Epirus.[16] Albania joined Italy in the war against Greece. As a consequence, in November

1940, the Greek government declared Albania a belligerent country[17] and with law No. 2636 placed under sequestration all the properties of Albanian citizens in Greece.[18] The status of "belligerence" was maintained even after World War II ended. Every Greek government since then has taken the position that a peace treaty with Tirana had to be signed only if it confirmed the basic rights of the Greek minority in Albania. Law 2636 remained in effect since, mostly, it concerned the properties of Greek nationals. Termination of the state of war was linked to improvements of conditions for the Greek minority in Albania.[19]

In 1971, although still technically in a state of war, the two countries established diplomatic relations.[20] After the downfall of the military regime, the Karamanlis government sought to improve relations, even in military matters.[21] He believed that harmony between Athens and Tirana was the most effective way for the preservation of the identity of the Greek minority, which the Albanian government places at less than 60,000, but the Greek Ministry of Foreign Affairs places at about 400,000.[22] To achieve meaningful rapprochement, the Tirana government requested an end to the status of belligerency, but New Democracy governments had refused to satisfy that demand.[23] Commercial exchanges between the two countries, however, increased considerably[24] and in scientific, cultural and educational spheres relations also improved.[25] But these improvements gave Tirana the opportunity for a new propaganda campaign aimed at the assimilation of the Greek minority in Albania and the revival of "Albanian conscience" among the Albanian-speaking residents of Attica.[26] At the same time, a branch of the Greek Communist movement, which considers Albania a valid socialist model, started its own pro-Albanian campaign.[27]

Diplomatic relations between Athens and Belgrade had been reestablished in 1949, after the end of the Civil War in Greece. In the 1950s the two countries together with Turkey signed an agreement known as the Balkan Pact, which linked Yugoslavia to NATO in an indirect manner.[28] After 1974 Karamanlis visited Belgrade three times, and Tito visited Greece once.[29] Bilateral commercial exchanges grew spectacularly, and a close cooperation began, based on common long-term plans of economic development. A beneficial coordination in foreign policy and military matters was also developed, aiming at making Yugoslav-Greek borders secure.[30] Indeed, Athens considered Yugoslavia a "barrier" to encroachments of the Warsaw Pact powers in the area of the Mediterranean and the Adriatic.[31]

As in earlier times, the so-called "Macedonian question" was a problem in relations between Greece and Yugoslavia. Since 1950, Belgrade had been asking the Greek government persistently (but without exerting strong pressure) for the cultural rights of the slavophone groups of Macedonia.[32] The slavophones, numbering only 40,000 at the end of the war and even fewer today,[33] have a Greek national consciousness, and most of them speak Greek. As a result, it is neither practical nor acceptable to them to be defined as a minority.[34] In fact, it is a deeply held new impression in the Greek Ministry of Foreign Affairs that the Yugoslavian demands constitute "irredentist revisions" against Greek Macedonia.[35]

The country towards which dramatic changes have occurred since 1974 is Bulgaria, Greece's traditional enemy. Even when the two nations were not at war against each other, constant tensions did not ease, owing to Sofia's propensity to form alliances with Greece's enemies in all major international conflicts. Two strange bedfellows, Constantine Karamanlis and Todor Zhivkov, played an important role in the transformation of Greek-Bulgarian relations.

It is argued that the key ingredient in this change was the personality of the two statesmen who felt respect for each other.[36] The abandonment of political dogmatism by Karamanlis and his pragmatic approach to East-West relations contributed significantly in the improvement of relations with Sofia. Bulgaria, for reasons of its own, supported Greece in the latter's dispute with Turkey. Bulgaria's support enabled Greece to withdraw large military units stationed near the Greek-Bulgarian border to the interior of the country, permitting Greece to redeploy its forces in Thrace and the Aegean islands to face threats from Turkey.[37] Furthermore, from the summer of 1974 to 1981, 34 bilateral agreements were signed, which form the framework of a close cooperation between Athens and Sofia in all fields.[38] In the important matter of the exploitation of the Nestos River, however, the Bulgarians attempted as early as 1975 to circumvent agreements reached with Greece.[39] This issue remained unresolved at the end of Karamanlis's stay in power, and has become even more complex today.[40]

The rapprochement with Rumania was equally impressive. In May 1975, Karamanlis visited Bucharest, where he signed the Common Declaration of Principles, which was to be the basis of their relations towards each other and towards other countries.[41] One point of disagreement, however, was the establishment in Greece of joint Greek-Rumanian industrial units: Rumania wanted them, but Greece rejected them.[42] Greece did wish to cooperate in another area: Rumanian technical aid was sought by Athens to search for oil in northern Greece and the Aegean.[43]

The main purpose of the new policy of Greek governments after 1974, characterized as multifaceted, was to sensitize Eastern European countries to Greece's problems with Turkey and to secure their support in the U.N.[44] The results of these efforts have been poor. Although all these countries remained faithful to the general line of the Soviet Union regarding the Cyprus issue, which called for support of U.N. decisions on matters concerning the independence and integrity of the Republic of Cyprus, they maintained, in general, a pro-Turkish stance on other Greek-Turkish disputes. Only Bulgaria tended to side with Greece; while Hungary supported Turkey.[45]

Despite difficulties and Greek disappointments, Poland has sought successfully to increase its economic relations with Greece.[46]

On the other hand, Greek demands for war indemnities have caused friction in relations with East Germany.[47]

Karamanlis visited Czechoslovakia in October 1979 and signed the Declaration of Common Principles, similar to the one signed with Rumania. It has become the basis of rapprochement .[48] He also visited Hungary in October 1979 for the same purpose.[49] After Karamanlis's visit, Hungary expressed a wish to be considered a Balkan country. It declared that it was willing to cooperate with other Balkan countries. Greece had increased efforts to achieve cooperation among the Balkan countries after the Helsinki accords; the initiative led to the First Inter-Balkan Conference in Athens in January 1976.[50] According to Hungarian spokesmen, their wish to enter into Balkan cooperation stemmed from concerns about the formation of a "private club" close to their country.[51]

In reality Hungary made this unexpected request on the advice of Moscow. The Soviets were watching with increasing interest the changes in Greece and wished to encourage, through allies like Hungary, Greece's efforts in the Balkan Peninsula. Bulgaria was not enough.[52] Moscow's interest in Greek affairs had always been strong. The USSR had established broad economic ties with the military regime.[53] The restoration of democracy was not considered by Moscow particularly decisive, except that it secured the legalization of the Greek Communist party (KKE), traditionally a docile pro-Moscow organization.[54] Almost immediately upon his return to Greece from Paris in 1974, Karamanlis tried to give signs of good will towards the Soviets in the hope that they would support Greece in its disputes with Turkey. As it turned out, Moscow refused to take sides. It wanted additional proof that Greece was loosening its ties to the West.[55]

Leonid Brezhnev declined Karamanlis's proposals for a meeting with him[56] until the Soviet leadership was convinced that the anti-American and, generally, anti-West climate that dominated in Greece after July 1974 provided opportunities for political penetration. Only then did the Soviets declare a new era in Greek-Soviet relations. After an exchange of visits of Soviet and Greek officials in Athens and Moscow to pave the way,[57] Karamanlis was invited to Moscow in October 1979.[58]

Relations between the two countries in all fields—even in the military—had improved significantly by 1981,[59] but the main goals pursued by the Greek side were not achieved. The Soviets continued to support U.N. resolutions on Cyprus and the independence, non-alignment and territorial integrity of the Republic. But this position was hardly novel. In reality, the sole aim of the USSR was to prevent the NATO countries from gaining credit by solving the problem; it hoped to play an important role itself, preferably in an international conference.[60] It is characteristic of Soviet pragmatism that Soviet diplomacy avoids using the term "invasion" to characterize the Turkish operation against Cyprus in the summer of 1974, so as not to displease Ankara.[61] Indeed, in all the other matters concerning Greece and Turkey, the Soviet Union studiously pursues a policy of equidistance. It counts on the Greek Communist party to promote its goals in Greece by blaming the Americans for Turkish aggressiveness against Greece.[62]

The rapprochement policy with the countries of Eastern Europe, initiated by Karamanlis and continued by his successor George Rallis, was the result of necessity, not of ideological affinity. Turkey's threat to Greece and the Greek population in Cyprus, and the perception that the United States had bolstered the military dictatorship influenced Greek public opinion and forced Karamanlis to seek ways to avoid losing support by taking pro-Western positions. He acted rashly at times; for example, he withdrew Greece from the military wing of NATO in August 1974, setting in motion intense pressure by the revitalized Greek Left to permanently separate Greece from the West and to prevent its reintegration into NATO.

The results of this policy are debatable. However, it is undeniable that Karamanlis remained in the Western camp, though he sought improved relations with the Eastern bloc.[63] Indeed the former Greek prime minister and president showed no signs of ever betraying Western interests. The opening to the East secured his country's interests. It was viewed as a belated attempt by Greece to catch up with other NATO countries, all of which had broadened their relations with the Warsaw Pact countries in the 1960s and 1970s.

PASOK AND THE EASTERN BLOC

The PASOK approach to relations with Eastern Europe is qualitatively different. In preparation for the October 1981 elections PASOK published its ideological manifesto, "Contract with the People."[64] It defined the course the party would follow if elected. Foreign policy issues occupied a central position in PASOK's ideology, since its founder had, over two decades, linked the domestic problems of the country to the pervasive influence of foreign powers, most notably the United States.

The Contract began by pointing out that the precondition of PASOK's vision of change is "national independence,"[65] which is necessary for the securing of sovereignty, democracy and social liberation."[66]

The emphasis on independence implied that Greece was subject to the whims of the Atlantic alliance.[67] NATO was responsible for the 1965 "coup d'état," for the dictatorship imposed in 1967 and for the 1974 Turkish invasion in Cyprus.[68] An unrestrained press tends to repeat the PASOK and communist arguments about NATO and American complicity in the military dictatorship and the Cyprus invasion. As yet no credible evidence has linked NATO or the Americans to the establishment of the Greek dictatorship or to the Cyprus invasion; propaganda continues to confuse myth and reality. Over the years, the PASOK-KKE mythology has had its impact on public opinion.[69] Thus, few people suspect the falseness of the view attributing all ills that have affected Greece since World War II to foreign intervention. The deeper meaning of that view few care to investigate. What explains such wholesale acceptance of PASOK's position?

The study of PASOK's "Contract with the People" offers

some answers to this fundamental question. The left wing of the party formulated this document and its primary goal was getting Greece out of NATO.[70] NATO was thought to be responsible for the country's misfortunes. Moreover, Greece had no need to belong to the alliance because there was no danger coming from the northern neighbors of Greece.[71] To make its rhetoric appear balanced, PASOK also supported the dissolution of the Warsaw Pact.[72] PASOK thought that it would succeed in withdrawing Greece from NATO because attitudes in Greek society had changed and PASOK's vision of a new Greek foreign policy had gained credence. In broad generalities, PASOK promised an alternative foreign policy, free of NATO and Western interference. It would bring about "development of friendly relations all over the world and mainly with the Balkan countries, the peoples of the Mediterranean Sea ... and the Arab nation."[73] It would mean "solidarity with every people that struggles for independence and with those who fight against imperialism,"[74] "support for the Palestinians and all liberation movements against colonial and racist regimes."[75] The Cyprus issue was called the "primordial national question,"[76] and it was claimed that American military bases had no reason to be in Greece—they did not serve Greek interests, and their very existence could subject Greeks to a "holocaust" if war were to break out.[77] These goals would take time to be achieved, but they were possible.[78]

It was obvious that if the positions in the Contract materialized, the country would drift away from the West and could slide towards the Third World or the Warsaw Pact. Thus, when PASOK's victory in the October 1981 elections was announced, the chiefs of the armed forces decided to resign immediately, creating uncertainty and leaving the way open for the military to intervene again in politics.[79] The danger was averted by Karamanlis, then president of the Republic, who was anxious to put an end to military interventions and thus stabilize the civilian democratic government.[80] Although Karamanlis feared that the PASOK government could destroy "in a few months the achievements of decades,"[81] he defused the crisis by asserting the common belief that PASOK's declarations before the elections were part of its tactics to gain power and that it would moderate its views once it achieved that goal.[82]

This impression was reinforced in the months after the 1981 elections: the first statements after the election victory were moderate indeed.[83] Papandreou met with the president, who stressed in his discussion with the new prime minister critical foreign affairs and defense issues, which were closely connected. The president pointed out that in these matters they had completely different opinions and warned the prime minister that if he insisted on carrying out plans announced during the election campaign, there would be an open clash between them. Papandreou assured him he would not undertake any major foreign policy or defense initiatives without consulting the president.[84] Until February 1982 Papandreou made no attempts to put distance between Greece and its Western allies. Karamanlis was pleased with Papandreou's moderation and facilitated his requests for meaningful contacts with NATO leaders and leaders of the European Communities.[85] The government's rhetorical attacks against NATO and EEC were explained, even by Karamanlis, as attempts by Papandreou to "appease" the left wing of his party.[86]

OPENING TO THE NORTH

In May 1982, Papandreou visited Yugoslavia. It was his first visit to a Balkan country since he became prime minister. During talks with the president of the Federal Executive Council, Milka Planinc, and the president of the Republic, Petar Stambolic, he had the opportunity to unfold his views on foreign and domestic policy in a "close and sincere manner."[87]

Papandreou started the talks by praising the "eternal brilliance of the great leader Tito" and pointing out Yugoslavia's very important role "in the region"—a role that should be maintained for the benefit of the people... and the balance of power in the Balkans." Following this praise of Tito, he broached to the subject of East-West relations, regretting the failure of détente, which he attributed to the American government's belief that they were losing the arms race. He concluded that it was impossible to find common ground between Ronald Reagan and Leonid Brezhnev. Thus, promoting peace was the responsibility of other countries.[88]

Papandreou then offered his analysis of the situation in Poland. His views on the latter were at variance with those of the rest of NATO and the European Communities. He absolutely refused to impose sanctions which, he claimed, would worsen relations between the two blocs, and, more important, he thought the West "had no right to criticize the political systems of the East."[89] He implied that the policy of sanctions was aimed not only at Poland but at other Eastern European countries and was the product of "deeper calculations" on the part of the United States, which aimed to undermine the economic development of the Warsaw Pact countries. Greece would not contribute in this "American effort."[90] Parallel to his pro-Soviet policy, a new emphasis of the Greek foreign policy became apparent. Greece was inching closer to the nonaligned camp. Its historical closeness to Western Europe did not permit Athens to withdraw from the European Community and NATO, but the Greek government chose to disagree systematically with its allies on matters of principle. These disagreements were then expressed by Giannes Charalombopoulos, minister of foreign affairs.[91] As it relates to NATO, it appeared that the immediate goal of the Greek foreign policy was to object to any "dangerous remarks" against the USSR.[92]

These revelations about the inner workings of PASOK's policy surprised the Yugoslavs. The discussion went on to other subjects such as the situation in the Middle East, the conflict between Great Britain and Argentina, Greek-Turkish relations, and the Cyprus issue.[93] During the last phase of the talks, on 27 May 1982, Papandreou volunteered another important statement. This time he pointed out that the principles of PASOK were the same as those of the Yugoslav government and asked for understanding on the part of Belgrade for the different way that the Greek government was following Yugoslavia's transition to socialism. The difference, Papandreou stated, was simply that the Yugoslavs "had started several decades ago, while Greece [began the transition] only recently."[94]

Papandreou talked frankly in Belgrade, and what he said there, in retrospect, sounds like a sincere description of his goals, which clearly differed from his pre-electoral pronouncements—nowhere in the Contract with the People, for example, is the Yugoslav model mentioned. The party manifesto, however, underscores that "Poland has the right to face itself any problem it has and to move on the way its responsible government and the will of its People have planned."[95] It must be noted that Papandreou systematically avoided, up to his Belgrade trip, discussing with Karamanlis his long-term intentions. Karamanlis continued to believe that the declarations concerning socialist transformation and the anti-

Western, anti-American rhetoric were still for domestic consumption.[96]

The Yugoslavs were surprised by the Greek prime minister's visions and goals. Yugoslavia had the same general position on the Polish problem, but Papandreou was more pro-Soviet. Yugoslavia's view, as expressed by Planinc, was that "it is the right of every nation to determine for itself its political system and to find for itself necessary solutions [to its problems]."[97] Lazar Mojsov, a Yugoslav foreign policy specialist, emphasized—with undisguised irony—to Papandreou that he fully agreed with his opinion on the sanctions question because sanctions were merely symbolical—the only thing the Westerners had done was to reduce the fur and caviar imports from the USSR.[98]

As far as Papandreou's plan for a nuclear-free Balkan zone was concerned, the Yugoslavs agreed with the principle, but explained that it was not a realistic goal because it would require an agreement between the two blocs. The Balkan Peninsula, unlike Scandinavia, was not a homogeneous political region. Moreover, they saw that much of what Papandreou said was only propaganda.[99] Finally, Papandreou's assurances that Greece intended to behave as a nonaligned country and that he was seeking to influence NATO to adopt a more moderate attitude vis-à-vis the Soviet Union were not welcome by the Yugoslav side, which was more interested in reminding him that the situation in Kosovo was critical, that the Albanian government was undoubtedly behind the riots taking place there, the aim of which was the breaking up of the Yugoslav federation, and that the whole matter could lead to a broader conflict.[100] This was an indirect way of warning Papandreou not to get too close to Enver Hoxha's Albania.

A few additional remarks on Kosovo are called for. In the spring of the 1980s, riots broke out in that autonomous region, where approximately 1.5 million Albanians live.[101] The Yugoslav government believed that these riots were incited to destabilize the Federation and to bring about the union of Kosovo with Albania. Belgrade viewed the riots as part of an "irredentist movement," that could result in the dissolution of the federation.[102] Moreover, the Yugoslav government believed that the Albanian intelligence service had infiltrated Kosovo's intellectuals and disseminated "irredentist propaganda" among

Albanian workers (with Yugoslav citizenship) in Western Europe, often in cooperation with Albanian royalist organizations.[103]

When the riots broke out, the position formulated by Athens went as follows: 1) the riots in Kosovo could easily lead to a conflict between Albania and Yugoslavia; 2) that this conflict would eventually become a worldwide one; 3) in such an eventuality the West, including Greece, would support Belgrade, while Eastern European countries would side with Tirana.[104] This was the traditional Greek policy toward Belgrade and created a feeling of security in Yugoslavia. It was clear that Yugoslavia wished Greece to stay in NATO. In this context, it was natural for the Yugoslav officials to hear with concern Papandreou's determination to undermine the unity of NATO and to support Moscow. In the same vein, they dismissed the nuclear-free Balkan zone as having only propaganda value.

On the nonalignment question, Yugoslavia, even though a founding member, found itself in deep disagreement with pro-Soviet states like Vietnam and Cuba, which unreservedly adopt the Soviet line.[105] As a result, the initial satisfaction with which the Yugoslavs heard that Greece wanted to become one of the nonaligned countries was dampened when it became clear that Athens, too, was willing to give wholesale support to Soviet policies.

So in a strange way the Yugoslavs immediately understood, in May 1982, what Greek politicians could not foresee, namely, that the main goals of PASOK's foreign policy were to alienate Greece from the Western alliance, convert it into a nonaligned state, and promote basic Soviet policies. After 1982, the Yugoslavs cooled towards Papandreou, if one is to judge from the tone of démarches made by them to the Greek embassy.[106]

By the summer of 1983, the pro-Soviet inclinations of the Greek government's foreign policy started to worry Karamanlis, who until then wanted to believe that PASOK would gradually become a western style social-democratic party. The secretary-general of the Presidency of the Republic, Petros Molyviates, met with the prime minister on 31 August 1983 to express Karamanlis's displeasure about the initiatives the prime minister had taken against the U.S. government's decision to deploy Pershing and Cruise missiles in Europe. On that occasion, Molyviates, speaking on behalf of Karamanlis, pointed out that in the "psychological war" that was going on between the East and the West, it was important that NATO allies take one position. The actions of the Greek government were divisive. Papandreou expressed his regret, but stressed that he agonized over nuclear arms and the threat they posed to peace in Europe. His "agony" motivated him to oppose the deployment of American missiles in Western Europe. Immediately after his discussion with Molyviates, he confessed that the foreign policy he was following was "acrobatic" and therefore entailed certain dangers. He was convinced, however, that thanks to his "acrobatics," Greece had finally begun to play an active role on the international stage.[107]

Papandreou was being sincere only in admitting the dangers of his foreign policy. If one studies systematically the facts, one realizes that his policy was not at all "acrobatic"—it was consistently that of a pro-Soviet Third World country. It is probable that Karamanlis's realization of the true nature of PASOK's foreign policy led to his "dismissal" from the Presidency of the Republic in March 1985.

PASOK's policy towards Eastern Europe and the Soviet Union since 1981 has had a deep impact on domestic affairs. PASOK's approach to East European states has been consistent; it reflects Papandreou's vision of Europe. It should be pointed out that foreign policy is handled personally by the prime minister, who is advised by a small group of Marxist collaborators, whose precise roles are difficult to discern. The minister of foreign affairs only carries out policy; he does not originate it. This was especially true when Giannes Charalombopoulos occupied that office. He obeyed without comments his chief's orders.[108] His successor, Karolos Papoulias, a hardcore left-winger, also toes the line of the prime minister.

Given the direct connection between foreign policy and domestic affairs,[109] the entire process became mired in "sensitivity" and "partisan calculations." To free itself from parliamentary scrutiny, the government has invented "legal" interpretations that justify its acting on its own.[110] It is characteristic that only on 23 April 1986 did the prime minister brief Parliament on foreign policy matters—for the first time since the 1981 elections![111] But in a peculiar and conspiratorial way, occasional leaks of classified matters and documents from the Foreign Ministry or even from the prime minister's diplomatic office, reach the press and provide telling glimpses of Greece's international relations. Our examination of Greece's relations with Eastern Europe and the Soviet Union is by necessity tentative because of the chaotic manner by which the government informs the public on these matters. Nevertheless, the main lines and directions are clear.

Any evaluation of Greece's relations with Eastern Europe and the Soviet Union must consider the diversity of that region, even though PASOK insists on ignoring that diversity. For purposes of our analysis, we shall group the Eastern European states into two categories: first, there are the countries that border Greece (Albania, Yugoslavia, Bulgaria), whose proximity influences their relations; second, there are the central core states of the Warsaw Pact (Hungary, Rumania, Czechoslovakia, Poland and East Germany), whose relations with PASOK reflect ideological affinity.

Greece's relations with the countries of the first group improved impressively during the past six years. Six commercial protocols have been signed with Albania since 1981,[112] as well as agreements on linking the electric systems of the two countries,[113] on overland transportation,[114] on educational exchanges,[115] on a joint postal system,[116] and on telecommunications.[117] Furthermore, negotiations on the distribution and utilization of the waters of the Aoos River, which runs through both countries, and of other rivers that run on both sides of the border have been undertaken. Joint committees of Greek and Albanian specialists met on this issue in Tirana in April of 1984 and in Argyrokastro in November of 1985. Protocols were signed, but their texts were, for some reason, kept secret.[118] Secrecy characterized another meeting of specialists that took place in Athens in July of 1985.[119] Indicative of warming relations was the signing in Athens in 1987 of a protocol on cooperation in the tourist industry.[120]

However, as stated earlier, the state of belligerency in effect since 1940 has been a big obstacle to further improvement of Greek-Albanian relations. On 23 April 1986 Papandreou declared in Parliament his intention of putting an end to this situation.[121] But he was opposed by Constantine Mitsotakis, leader of the opposition. Mitsotakis pointed out that abolishing belligerency without gaining concessions from the Albanian side on the welfare and human rights of the Greek minority in Albania would be tantamount to abandoning the minority and releasing Albania from its pre-war treaties and obligations vis-à-vis Greece.[122]

Backing Papandreou's position was Foreign Minister Karolos Papoulias. He vehemently pursued the ending of belligerency between Greece and Albania. He was motivated in part by his being from Pogoniane Epirus (though some believe he is actually from Northern Epirus). He believes that once the state of belligerency is ended, the financial benefits to Albania of selling Albanian properties under sequestration since 1940 will induce the Tirana authorities to improve the living conditions for the Greek minority.[123] Concrete concessions would be reciprocated by Albanian good will. On 28 August 1987 the government announced unilaterally and without parliamentary (or presidential approval) the end of the state of war. The foreign minister justified his recommendation by referring to general improvement in Greek-Albanian relations. For example, in the first eight months of 1987 a total of 502 Greeks from Albania were allowed to visit Greece. Other officials of the Greek Ministry of Foreign Affairs shared Papoulias's view that the end of belligerency and the return of property to Albania would benefit the Greeks in Northern Epirus. They thought the Albanian government would perhaps give part of the repatriated properties to Greeks from Northern Epirus who actually live in Greece or abroad and who adopt a friendly attitude towards the Albanian regime.[124]

The termination of the state of war with Albania caused massive reaction in Greece and among Greeks outside the country. The leader of the opposition declared he was not bound by it, and the Archbishop of Athens and All Greece Seraphim issued a cyclical letter opposing it. President Christos Sartzetakis expressed serious doubts about the government's method of resolving the issue of belligerency.

The PASOK government, besides its ideological affinity for Titoism, did not break any new ground in Greek-Yugoslav relations. A Greek-Yugoslav committee for economic, scientific and technical cooperation (formed before PASOK came to power) had four routine meetings in Athens and Belgrade.[125] A joint committee for scientific and technological cooperation has met in Belgrade and in Athens.[126] Again, the secretiveness characterizes PASOK's foreign policy in Greek-Yugoslav relations: neither the issues discussed in these meetings nor the content of a technical cooperation agreement signed in Belgrade in May 1987 have ever been disclosed.[127] Similarly, a Greek-Yugoslav committee on industrial cooperation, which met for the last time in Belgrade in 1986, never disclosed its work, nor did the government inform the Parliament about it.[128] Yugoslav-

Greek cooperation has not yet extended to defense matters. The government's efforts to keep Bulgaria informed about issues affecting Greek security[129] is thus surprising.

In fact, Greek-Bulgarian relations under PASOK expanded dramatically in all critical areas. As already noted, Karamanlis should be credited with initiating the improvement, but the Socialist government broadened cooperation. Like other Eastern European countries, Bulgaria has been primarily interested in high technology. A joint committee on technological cooperation formed before October 1981 has met four times.[130] The proceedings of these talks, again, were not brought before the Parliament, nor was the public informed about their objectives, other than through the perfunctory communiqués at the conclusion of each meeting. A parallel joint committee at the ministerial level, also on scientific and technical cooperation, has met three times.[131] The emphasis on science and technology in Greek-Bulgarian relations is obvious by the level and number of exchanges. In 1983 the Greek minister of research and technology visited Sofia and signed a protocol.[132] A few months later the same ministry concluded another, as yet unexplained, protocol with the Bulgarian State Committee for Science. Its subject was described vaguely as "common programs of research and development."[133] The exact content of the two protocols was not made public, but cooperation between the two countries in the microelectronics field was put into effect by an agreement signed in July 1984.[134] The point of this cooperation is hard to grasp, as neither Greece nor Bulgaria is known for its high technology achievements. Most think that Bulgaria is merely looking to channels for the acquisition of Western technology.[135]

Bulgaria has officially abandoned all territorial claims it had against Greece[136] and currently offers its support—thus far rather moral—to Athens in Greek-Turkish disputes. It sides with Greece on the so-called "Macedonian question." This attitude stems less from a recognition of Greek rights, than from Bulgaria's pursuit of its own interests. The Bulgarians are concerned about Turkish involvement in the affairs of the Moslems who live in Bulgaria.[137] Similarly, the "Macedonian question" is of great interest to Sofia, since Yugoslavia demands recognition of a "Macedonian minority" in Bulgaria as well as in Greece.[138] In other matters, such as the exploitation of the waters of Nestos River, Bulgaria continues to insist on positions seen in Athens as "undermining [Greek] legal interests."[139]

Greek relations with the core group of the Warsaw Pact (Rumania, Hungary, East Germany, Czechoslovakia and Poland) on the face of it, follow the same patterns as those it maintains with neighboring countries. Agreements of industrial, economic and technical cooperation have been signed with all of them[140] and long-term plans for the development of this cooperation are in place.[141] The rapprochement with Eastern Europe has raised some serious concerns in the European Community. As yet, the overall nature, extent and objectives of the PASOK government with the Eastern European countries (apart from concrete agreements) are difficult to define or explain, so it is uncertain whether there are grounds for alarm. Even specific actions by the prime minister have been subjected to multiple interpretations. Secrecy prevails. For example, although Papandreou's views on the Polish problem are known, the content of a letter he sent to Wojcieck Jaruzelski, at the beginning of 1983, was never published.[142]

Technical and economic cooperation benefits Eastern European countries, since Greece has been the only Western nation willing to buy their products and technology rather than Western products. East German, Hungarian and Czechoslovakian companies have virtually dominated the sale of equipment to the "Telecommunications Organization of Greece" (OTE), the "Public Utility Enterprise" (DEI), "Public Oil Enterprise" (DEP) and the "Rail Organization of Greece" (OSE). In fairness, we should note that the process of penetration by Eastern European companies, such as the Hungarian company known as Nimex, the Czech companies Stojexport and Vitcovice Steelworks, and the East German companies Elektrotechnik Export-Import and WMV Export-Import, had started prior to the 1981 elections;[143] but today their share of the Greek market far exceeds that of Greece's traditional partners in these areas.

Another factor shaping relations between Greece and these countries has been the return of Greek political refugees, who had escaped or been abducted to East Europe following the defeat of the Greek Communist insurrection in 1949. After the collapse of the Greek military regime in 1974, there was more latitude for political dissent in Greece, and Greeks who had lived in Eastern Europe for political reasons began to return. The process was slow because of technical reasons such as pensions and insurance earned by Greek refugees in Eastern Europe. But there were also political impediments. Left-wing parties feared that these individuals would expose the seamy side of communist regimes and even declare themselves outright enemies of communism. An agreement with Bulgaria on the status of Greek political refugees in Bulgaria was signed in Sofia in February 1986,[144] but the largest part of those who settled in Yugoslavia have been listed by the authorities there as Macedonians and been given Yugoslavian citizenship.[145] Their mass return could have been adversely affected if they chose to identify themselves as "Macedonians." As regards those who had settled in the other Eastern European countries and in the USSR, the relevant procedures for their repatriation have been discreetly shifted from the Ministry of Foreign Affairs to other ministries or even to party organizations.[146]

Though Eastern European countries have worked more with Greece in the economic and technical spheres, their positions on the critical issue of Greek-Turkish relations have not changed to the benefit of Greece.[147] In some cases, like Rumania and Yugoslavia, they even raise their own ethnic issues.[148]

Six years of PASOK rule have had an impact in another area: there has been significant ideological convergence between PASOK and the communist parties of Eastern Europe. Cultural exchanges and massive distribution of Eastern European literature have been conducive to this convergence.

Undoubtedly, the key to understanding Greece's current relations with the countries of Eastern Europe is to be found in Athens's relations with Moscow. Most of the countries, including Rumania, follow the Soviet line in critical issues of international relations, even though their approach and level of solidarity differ.[149] The exceptions of course, are Albania and Yugoslavia.[150]

But the study of the development of Greek-Soviet relations after PASOK's rise to power is important in itself: it offers clear clues to PASOK's probable stand on international issues of importance to the West. Greek-Soviet relations also help us to understand the nature of the Panhellenic Socialist party.

The strictly bilateral Greek-Soviet relations have been defined by the Agreement on Economic and Industrial Cooperation, which was signed in Athens before the 1981 elections but came into force only on 4 March 1982.[151] In February 1983, a long-term plan for industrial, scientific and technological cooperation was also drawn up in Athens.[152] These acts tighten and broaden the economic relations of the two countries, which had started when the New Democracy party was still in government, but progressed rapidly after 1981.[153] The commercial exchanges have been, in general, more to Moscow's benefit than to Greece's, which has been attributed by the Greek Foreign Ministry to the unwillingness of the Soviet Union to buy from Greece as many products as it could.[154] During the first years after PASOK's assumption of power Greece was in dire need of energy (electricity and oil). In return for energy, Greece would export such products as tobacco, citrus fruits and bauxite.[155]

This beneficial exchange did not materialize as planned. Soviet companies (Energomachexport, Sojuzpromexport, Machinoexport, Teploenergo, etc.) have become permanent and aggressive participants in the Greek market,[156] but Greek companies have made few gains in the Soviet market. Soviet industrial plants may soon be built in Greece, and an agreement has been signed permitting Greek trucks to drive through Soviet territory to reach Iran.[157]

Along with the growth in economic relations, the Soviets have sought to increase the number of personnel involved in business or diplomacy, stationed in Greece.[158] The Foreign Ministry has been suspicious of such requests and refused to satisfy many of them.[159] It seems, however, that recently at least some requests for enlarging the Soviet presence in Greece have been quietly granted.[160]

A significant change in the two countries' relations began with the visit of Papandreou to Moscow in December 1982 to represent Greece at Brezhnev's funeral. He used the opportunity to meet with Yuri Andropov, the new general-secretary of the Communist party, and had his "first useful exchange of opinions [with the Soviet Union] on international matters."[161] What is significant about this meeting was that Papandreou was willing to give the appearance that Greek positions were identical to Soviet ones on critical issues and that he emphasized his independence from the West.

PASOK's tendency to go against the positions of NATO countries was evident on the Afghanistan question. Although the Soviet invasion was condemned by PASOK before the 1981 elections,[162] after PASOK took power, it ceased to criticize the Soviet actions.[163] PASOK's views on disarmament also favor the Soviet Union,[164] as does the stance it has taken on the shooting down of the South Korean jet in August 1983,[165] the Berlin Wall (Giannes Charalombopoulos, minister of foreign affairs had refused to admit its existence),[166] and the Sandinistas regime in Nicaragua.[167]

Soviet leaders have become convinced that PASOK's divergence from the West is more than a temporary phenomenon: it offers them an opportunity to Findlandize Greece. The Greek initiative for the creation of a nuclear-free zone in the Balkans is seen as a "positive" development in that direction. The idea was initially proposed by Rumania in 1957,[168] adopted by the Soviet Union in 1959, and promoted by Adam Rapacki (Poland's foreign minister) in the 1960s.[169] In 1981, Zhivkov again urged the creation of a nuclear-free zone two days after PASOK's victory, and Papandreou's assumption of power.[170] Papandreou endorsed enthusiastically Zhivkov's proposal and, in a July 1983 letter to all the Balkan leaders, invited them to support it.[171] In March of 1982 a meeting took place in the Ministry of Foreign Affairs in which several career diplomats, Papandreou's most important advisers (including Christos Machairitsas) and Nikos Koures, then chief of the General Staff of the Greek Air Force, participated.[172] The diplomats took the position that, given today's development of weapon systems, the removal of nuclear missiles from the Balkans would be "a contribution of minimal value" to world peace. Koures and Machairitsas argued that the Greek government would gain politically if it sided with Bulgaria and that a nuclear-free zone would lessen the risk of war in the Balkan Peninsula.[173] One must admit that their answer was sincere. But some questions beg to be raised: Was there some ulterior motive to the Bulgarian proposal, made as it was immediately after Papandreou's victory and openly supported by the Soviet Union? Was it a test of the new Greek government's intentions? There is no easy or verifiable answer to this question. At any rate, the adoption of the Bulgarian proposal by Athens coincided with new Soviet attempts to loosen Greece's bonds with the West.

Indeed, since the summer of 1974 the Greek people have felt threatened by Turkey. Turkey's invasion of Cyprus and its tendency to impinge on Greek sovereignty have brought about this perception. PASOK exploits this threat in order to stay in power and to justify radical changes in the country's orientation. Thus, the Socialist government has never explained to the Greek people the specific demands of the Turks. Instead, the government makes vague statements about the Turkish danger and uses such a popular issue to achieve widespread support. Turkey's membership in NATO is emphasized, which associates the alliance with Ankara's aggressive policies. In this general scheme, it is incongruous that moral support should be given by pro-government groups to such Turkish politicians as Bülent Ecevit, who, though opposed to the present Turkish military regime, do bear responsibility for the 1974 invasion of Cyprus. In short, the present regime in Turkey is portrayed as the only real enemy, and PASOK can thus justify the realignment of Greek foreign policy.

The corollary is that Greece must find allies in the East. This explains PASOK's adoption of positions similar to those of Moscow in nearly all international matters. Those who question this reasoning are accused of "breaking national unity," and it is implied that they are unpatriotic. One consequence is that the ideas and views of the Left dominate in education, intellectual life, and much of the mass media. Honest debate on critical foreign policy issues is stifled.

This state of affairs contradicts even Marxist analyses of society. According to Antonio Gramsci's classic study, Marxist doctrine should prevail initially only in the handling of big theoretical problems and only afterwards is it inculcated in the thinking of the average man. In Greece the opposite has been successfully attempted: because of the Turkish threat, everybody, regardless of political preference, is expected to adopt pro-Soviet, anti-Western ideas, even though Marxism has not yet become the predominant ideology. No serious dialogue on critical issues is possible when Marxism parades as fervent nationalism. Statements, like, "our position against Turkey is supported by all political parties" or "the relations with the East were started by Karamanlis" or even "EEC and NATO are mostly criticized by newspapers which are anything but communist," are standard responses by followers and spokesmen of the government when criticized by the opposition or the Western press. These answers reflect the surface of matters, but they obscure their essence. Indeed, PASOK appeals very cleverly to Greek sentiment: it reawakens the fear of the Turks, a fear nearly six hundred years old, to which the only efficient antidote has appeared to be friendship with the Russians.[174]

As might be expected, the Athens-Moscow "partnership" has not induced the Soviet Union to provide any significant help in dealing with Turkey. Indeed, up to now, there has not been any sign of change in Moscow's policy of treating in one way Athens and Ankara.[175] Turkey has developed good relations with the Soviet Union, but it does not belittle the dangers in certain Soviet policies.[176] Ankara thus impresses the international community as a country friendly to all but always loyal to its allies. In contrast, Greece's reliability as an ally has become questionable.

The chances of resolving the problems between Athens and Ankara in a way favorable to Greece have never been as slim as they are today. Owing to PASOK's dramatic changes in Greek foreign policy, the Turks can argue that Papandreou has caused the relations between the two countries to deteriorate.[177] Whether this is true or not, the impression has been created that the Socialist government of Greece will cross with the NATO alliance and oppose its pro-Western neighbors.

What are the Soviet objectives as far as Greece is concerned? Moscow's policy towards Greece has been constant and stable: the long-term, principal goal is the breaking up of the bonds between Greece and the West—something that can be achieved if Greece ceases to be a cooperative member of the European Community and NATO.[178] One may wonder why the Socialist government has not taken Greece out of NATO. According to PASOK's doctrine, NATO is harmful to the Greek interests, and the European Community is viewed as a prop to stave off the collapse of capitalism. Yet Greece has remained part of NATO and the European Community because they offer tactical advantages to the ruling party. Greece's membership in them is meant to suggest that the present Greek government is more careful in action than it is in speech and, therefore, it does not threaten either the United States or Western interests, as it is accused of doing by its so-called enemies. The truth is that the present government remains a member of the European Community and NATO because it cannot afford to do otherwise. The subsidies of the EEC are what averts the collapse of Greek economy.[179] On the other hand, it seems that Prime Minister Papandreou does not withdraw Greece from NATO because he understands that, contrary to what he declares, the very fact that Greece and Turkey are allies is a decisive obstacle to war between the two countries. Papandreou's position is easily understood if one considers that in 1964 only President Lyndon Johnson's intervention prevented a Greek-Turkish conflict. But such prudence may not last. The Greek prime minister may believe that the time is simply not ripe for Greece's withdrawal from the West, and he has thus paced his drift to the East until a break with the West becomes opportune.[180]

Besides its overall goal of pulling Greece away from NATO, what matters to Moscow at this stage is the future of the American military bases in Greece. Before coming to power Papandreou had declared his intention of removing them from the territory of Greece. This has not yet happened because the bases are perceived as leverage to blackmail the U.S. and force a change of policy toward Turkey.[181] The issue of the bases is handled by the prime minister personally and his most trusted advisers, Yannis Kapsis, Nikos Koures and Giannes Roubatis.[182] According to these advisers of Papandreou, U.S. bases in Greece "neither serve Greek military interests nor contribute to [Greece's] national defense": Moreover they do not even serve NATO's requirements, but only those of the U.S.[183] Since they are considered irreplaceable by the U.S. government, they are useful to extract concessions from Washington on a variety of issues, especially those relating to Greek-Turkish relations.[184]

Thus, the Greek government uses the U.S. bases to check any inclination on the part of the U.S. to lean toward Turkey. If the Turkish threat disappeared or if Moscow had the will and the power necessary to hold Ankara back, the U.S. bases could be closed. Neither has happened thus far, and so the bases remain. Furthermore, Mikhail Gorbachev made clear his views about these bases in an unusual letter to the Greek prime minister.

On 3 July 1987, the Greek people were surprised by the publication in the leftist weekly *Pontiki* (The Mouse) of the text of a letter sent by Mikhail Gorbachev to Papandreou in mid-May of the same year and the text of the prime minister's answer. In his letter the Soviet leader asked the Greek prime minister to remove the U.S. bases or, at least, to insist on periodic inspections so that the activities taking place there could be controlled.[185] Papandreou was more explicit in his response to Gorbachev than in his statements to the press and his declarations to the people. Papandreou's letter assured Mikhail Gorbachev that if the bases were to remain in Greece because of the Turkish threat, a clause would be included in the new agreement being negotiated that would "prohibit [on the bases] any activity against countries with which Greece is in good relations."[186] Among these countries are, of course, those of the Warsaw Pact. Such a promise neatly undermines the purpose of the bases and Greece's continued participation in purpose of the bases and Greece's continued participation in NATO.

NOTES

1. "PASOK is probably the only political party in Europe that won the elections because everyone knew that it was not going to implement its pre-election declarations." This was an opinion expressed by Constantine Karamanlis, then president of the Hellenic Republic, shorty after the elections of 18 October 1981, as it was registered by the author.

2. This bond became especially evident during the years 1925-1926, i.e., when Greece was governed by general Theodoros Pangalos, who was himself a member of an Albanian-speaking family. See Pangalos's article "The Albanian Question" (in Greek), *Akropolis* , Athens, 29 July 1949, 3, 5.

3. Société des Nations, *Recueil des traités et des engagements internationaux enregistrés par le secrétariat de la Société des Nations* , Volume IX, 1922, numéros 1, 2, 3 et 4, "Albanie. Déclaration concernant la protection des minorités en Albanie," Geneva, 2 October 1921, especially article 6, p. 176.

4. Friction lasted during practically the whole period between the two world wars. Moreover, Italian influence on Albania complicated the situation: the fascist government considered the Greek minority "hostile" to Italy. The documents of the Italian Foreign Ministry archives (*Archivio storico del ministero degli Affari Esteri*, Rome) are very explicit on this matter.

5. This statement of Mussolini was of great importance not only for Greece but for all the Balkan countries in general. See the relevant article entitled "The relations between Greece and Albania" in the Tirana newspaper *Gazeta e Re* , 13 November 1928, 1.

6. Interesting information on this matter in Spyros Melas's book, *The 1912-1913 Wars* (in Greek) (Athens: Biris, 1958): 521.

7. Before the outbreak of World War II there were 5,000,000 Orthodox Christians in Poland. Today there are only 600,000. (Ministry of Foreign Affairs. First Department. A1 sub-section of political affairs, *Brief memorandum on the Greek-Polish Relations* [in Greek], Athens, 19 October 1981.)

8. During the period between the two world wars prominent communist prisoners who managed to escape flew immediately to the Soviet Union.

9. This was also due to the new diplomatic orientation of the country, which was practically the same as that of Greece during a certain period.

10. A.I. Korantes, *A Diplomatic History of Europe, 1919-1956, vol. IV* (in Greek) (Athens 1981): 226-227.

11. *Ibid.*, 465.

12. C.M. Woodhouse, *Karamanlis: The Restorer of Greek Democracy* (Oxford: Clarendon Press, 1982): 110.

13. Demetres Michalopoulos, "The 1950 Plebiscite in Cyprus," *Hellenic Review of International Relations* (Thessalonike), Volume 2, No. II (1981-1982): 569-579.

14. National Archives, Washington, D.C., Record Group 59, Decimal File 1945-1949, DS 849C.0I/8-348 (Memorandum of Conversation: British Views on Cyprus, Washington, D.C., 3 August 1948).

15. Statements of Constantine Karamanlis during private talks, registered by the author.

16. About the Chams see Demetres Michalopoulos, *Relations between Greece and Albania, 1923-1928* (in Greek) (Thessalonike: Paraterites, 1986).

17. Kingdom of Greece, *Official Gazette* , I, 10 November 1940.

18. *Ibid.*

19. Author's talks with officials of the Greek Ministry of Foreign Affairs.

20. Ministry of Foreign Affairs. First Department. A1 sub-section of political affairs, *Evolution of Greek-Albanian Relations* (memorandum for internal circulation, in Greek), Athens, 17 December 1980.

21. *Ibid.*, *Defensive Co-operation between Greece and Albania,* (memorandum for internal circulation, in Greek), 17 December 1980.

22. *Ibid.*, *The Greek Minority in Albania* (memorandum for internal circulation, in Greek), Athens, 17 December 1980.

23. *Ibid.*, *Possibilities of Ending the Belligerency between Greece and Albania* (memorandum for internal circulation, in Greek), Athens, 17 December 1980.

24.*Ibid.*, *Commercial Relations between Greece and Albania* (memorandum for internal circulation, in Greek), Athens, 17 December 1980.

25. *Ibid.*, *Educational Relations Between Greece and Albania* (memorandum for internal circulation, in Greek), Athens, 17 December 1980.

26. *Ibid.*, *Pro-Albanian Propaganda in Greece* (memorandum for internal circulation, in Greek), Athens, 17 December 1980.

27. *Ibid.*

28. On this pact, see among other books, and John Demetriades, *Soviet Infiltration of Greece* (in Greek) (Athens: Roes, 1984): 45-46, 50, 51.

29. Ministry of Foreign Affairs. First Department. A1 sub-section

of political affairs, *Greek-Yugoslavian Relations* (memorandum for internal circulation, in Greek), Athens, 19 October 1981.

30. *Ibid.*

31. *Ibid.*

32. Ministry of Foreign Affairs, *Yugoslavian Policy Towards Greek Macedonia* (memorandum for internal circulation, in Greek), Athens, 19 October 1981.

33. Ministry of Foreign Affairs. First Department. Al sub-section of political affairs, *Bilingualism in Macedonia* (memorandum for internal circulation, in Greek), Athens, 20 October 1980.

34. Ministry of Foreign Affairs, *The Macedonian Question* (memorandum for internal circulation), Athens, 19 October 1981.

35. *Ibid.*

36. Presidency of the Hellenic Republic, *Minutes of the talks between the President of the Hellenic Republic Mr. Constantine Karamanlis and the President of the State Council of Bulgaria Mr. Todor Zhivkov in the Euxinograd Palace* (in Greek), Varna, 25 April 1983; also opinions and recollections expressed by Karamanlis in private talks with the author.

37. Presidency of the Hellenic Republic, *Minutes of the talks between the President of the Hellenic Republic Mr. Constantine Karamanlis and the President of the State Council of Bulgaria Mr. Todor Zhivkov in Euxinograd, on 26 April 1983* (in Greek), undated.

38. Ministry of Foreign Affairs. First Department. A1 sub-section of political affairs, *Greek-Bulgarian Relations* (memorandum for internal circulation, in Greek), Athens, 19 October 1981.

39. *Ibid.*

40. Presidency of the Hellenic Republic, *Minutes of the talks between the President of the Hellenic Republic Mr. Constantine Karamanlis and the President of the State Council of Bulgaria Mr. Todor Zhivkov in the Euxinograd Palace* (in Greek), Varna, 25 April 1983.

41. Ministry of Foreign Affairs. First Department. A1 sub-section of political affairs, *Greek-Rumanian Relations* (memorandum for internal circulation, in Greek), Athens, 19 October 1981.

42. *Ibid.*

43. *Ibid.*

44. Private talks between Karamanlis and the author.

45. Author's talks with officials of the Greek Ministry of Foreign Affairs.

46. Ministry of Foreign Affairs. First Department. A1 sub-section of political affairs, *Greek-Polish Relations* (brief memorandum for internal circulation in Greek), Athens, 19 October 1981.

47. *Ibid.*, *Relations between Greece and East Germany* (brief

memorandum for internal circulation, in Greek), Athens, 19 October 1981.

48. *Ibid.*, *Relations between Greece and Czechoslovakia* (brief memorandum for internal circulation, in Greek), Athens, 19 October 1981.

49.*Ibid.*, *Relations Between Greece and Hungary* (brief memorandum for internal circulation, in Greek), Athens, 19 October 1981.

50. *Ibid.*

51. *Ibid.*

52. *Ibid.*, *Relations between Greece and Soviet Union* (brief memorandum for internal circulation, in Greek), Athens, 20 October 1981.

53. Author's talks with officials of the Greek Ministry of Foreign Affairs.

54. Author's talks with officials of the Greek Ministry of Foreign Affairs.

55. See Demetriades, *op. cit.*, 127.

56. Ministry of Foreign Affairs. First Department. A1 sub-section of political affairs, *Relations between Greece and Soviet Union* (brief memorandum for internal circulation, in Greek), Athens, 20 October 1981.

57. *Ibid.*

58. *Ibid.*

59. *Ibid.*

60. Author's talks with officials of the Greek Ministry of Foreign Affairs.

61. Ministry of Foreign Affairs. First Department. A1 sub-section of political affairs, *Relations between Greece and Soviet Union* (brief memorandum for internal circulation, in Greek), Athens, 20 October 1981.

62. *Ibid.*

63. It seems, indeed, that Karamanlis and Zhivkov believed that direct contact between them could avert tensions and crises between NATO and the Warsaw Pact. Presidency of the Hellenic Republic; *Minutes of the talks between the President of the Hellenic Republic Mr. Constantine Karamanlis and the President of the State Council of Bulgaria Mr. Todor Zhivkov in Euxinograd, on 26 April 1983* (in Greek), undated.

64. *Declaration of Government Policy. A Contract with the People. Panhellenic Socialist Movement* (in Greek), Athens 1981.

65. *Ibid.*, 13.

66. *Ibid.*, 15.

67. *Ibid.*, 16.

68. *Ibid.*, 31.

69. It is characteristic that PASOK, already in 1981, was asking for the "opening" of the "Cyprus file"; this "file" was opened recently, but up to now neither "American responsibility" nor the treason of prominent Greek conservatives has been proved.

70. *Declaration of Government Policy ..., op cit.*, 31.

71. *Ibid.*, 31, 32.

72. *Ibid.*, 31.

73. *Ibid.*, 16.

74. *Ibid.*, 36.

75. *Ibid.*

76. *Ibid.*, 33.

77. *Ibid.*, 32.

78. *Ibid.*, 37.

79. Memorandum concerning the events before and after the 1981 elections, written in February 1982 by Karamanlis.

80. *Ibid.*

81. *Ibid.*

82. *Ibid.*

83. *Ibid.*

84. *Ibid.*

85. *Ibid.*

86. *Ibid.*

87. Ministry of Foreign Affairs, *Minutes of the talks between the Greek Prime Minister Mr. Andreas Papandreou and the President of the Federal Executive Council of the Federal Socialist Republic of Yugoslavia Mrs. Milka Planinc* (in Greek), Belgrade, 26 May 1982.

88. *Ibid.*

89. *Ibid.*

90. *Ibid.*

91. *Ibid.*

92. Ministry of Foreign Affairs, *Minutes of the talks between the* [Greek] *Prime Minister and the President of the Presidency of the Federal Socialist Republic of Yugoslavia Mr. Petar Stambolic* (in Greek), 27 May 1982.

93. *Ibid., Minutes of the talks between the Greek Prime Minister Mr. Andreas Papandreou and the President of the Federal Executive Council of the Federal Socialist Republic of Yugoslavia Mrs. Milka Planinc* (in Greek), Belgrade, 26 May 1982.

94. *Ibid., Minutes of the talks between the* [Greek] *Prime Minister and the President of the Presidency of the Federal Socialist Republic of Yugoslavia Mr. Peter Stambolic* (in Greek), 27 May 1982.

95. *Declaration of Government Policy ..., op. cit.* , 36.

96. Author's impressions from private talks with Karamanlis.

97. Ministry of Foreign Affairs, *Minutes of the talks between the* [Greek] *Prime Minister Mr. Andreas Papandreou and the President of the Federal Executive Council of the Federal Socialist Republic of Yugoslavia Mrs. Milka Planinc* (in Greek), Belgrade, 26 May 1982.

98. *Ibid.*

99. *Ibid.*

100. *Ibid., Continuation of the talks* (minutes, in Greek), 27 May 1982.

101. Information given to Karamanlis by the Yugoslav minister of Foreign Affairs, on 3 April 1982. Presidency of the Hellenic Republic, *Minutes of the talks between the President of the Hellenic Republic Mr. K. Karamanlis and the Yugoslav minister of Foreign Affairs Mr. Vrhove on 3 April 1982* (in Greek).

102. *Ibid.*

103. *Ibid.*

104. Author's talks with officials of the Greek Ministry of Foreign Affairs.

105. Ministry of Foreign Affairs. A1 sub-section of political affairs, *Foreign policy of the Soviet Union* (memorandum for internal circulation, in Greek), Athens, 15 February 1983.

106. Author's talks with members of the Greek embassy in Belgrade.

107. Presidency of the Hellenic Republic. Secretary General, *Memorandum* (on Petros Molyviates's meeting with the prime minister), Athens, 31 August 1983.

108. He had become famous in Greece for never talking about anything. In forums elsewhere, on the other hand, he expressed with apathy Greece's constant disagreement with its allies, starting his speech by saying: "I'm sorry, but ...." For this reason, he was nicknamed "Mr. Sorry" by his Western European colleagues. (Author's talks with officials of the Greek Ministry of Foreign Affairs.)

109. *Declaration of Government Policy ..., op. cit.*, 34.

110. From author's personal experience of searching in the "International Agreement Catalog," which exists in the Greek Ministry of Foreign Affairs. Next to the title of many agreements, protocols etc., concluded between Greece and Eastern European countries there is very often the remark: "No ratification needed." Obviously, the necessary dispositions for not ratifying some international agreements existed in previous years, too; after PASOK came to power, however, this use became extensive. It is worth noting, furthermore, that although theoretically any scholar may see this catalog, it was difficult for the author to obtain permission to have a look at even a part of it.

111. *Records of Parliamentary Debates* (in Greek). 1st parliamentary term, 1st session, sitting of 23 April 1986 (Athens, 1986). See mainly p. 6374.

112. Hellenic Republic, *Official Gazette* , I, 16 February 1982; 12 January 1983; 21 February 1984; 5 April 1985; 24 April 1985 and 26 March 1987.

113. *Ibid.,* I, 23 December 1982.

114. *Ibid.,* I, 4 December 1984.

115. *Ibid.,* I, 12 July 1986.

116. *Ibid.,* I, 18 July 1986.

117. *Ibid.*

118. Information given to the author by officials of the Greek Ministry of Foreign Affairs.

119. Information given to the author by officials of the Greek Ministry of Foreign Affairs.

120. Information given to the author by officials of the Greek Ministry of Foreign Affairs.

121. *Records of Parliamentary Debates* (in Greek). 1st parliamentary term, 1st session, sitting of 23 April 1986, (Athens, 1986), 6370.

122. *Ibid.*, 6377-6378.

123. Author's talks with officials of the Greek Ministry of Foreign Affairs. A minister's portrait, containing, however, very few biographical details, was published in *Epikaira* (Athens), 30 July-12 August 1987.

124. Author's talks with officials of the Ministry of Foreign Affairs.

125. The minutes published in: Hellenic Republic, *Official Gazette*, I, 12 January 1983; 21 May 1984; 21 April 1986. The minutes of the 1987 meeting have not been published yet.

126. Information given to the author by officials of the Greek Ministry of Foreign Affairs.

127. Information given to the author by officials of the Greek Ministry of Foreign Affairs.

128. Information given to the author by officials of the Greek Ministry of Foreign Affairs.

129. During the March 1987 Greek-Turkish crisis Karolos Papoulias visited Sofia to brief Zhivkov. No such high level visit to Yugoslavia took place, even though in the 1950s the two countries had signed the Balkan Pact.

130. Information given to the author by officials of the Greek Ministry of Foreign Affairs.

131. The protocols then signed are published in Hellenic Republic, *Official Gazette* , I, 22 July 1983; 8 March 1984; 29 March 1985.

132. Information given to the author by officials of the Greek Ministry of Foreign Affairs.

133. Information given to the author by officials of the Greek Ministry of Foreign Affairs.

134. Information given to the author by officials of the Greek Ministry of Foreign Affairs.

135. Author's impression after talks with officials of the Greek Ministry of Foreign Affairs.

136. Presidency of the Hellenic Republic, *Minutes of the talks between the President of the Hellenic Republic Mr. Constantine Karamanlis and the President of the State Council of Bulgaria Mr.*

Todor Zhivkov in the Euxinograd Palace (in Greek), Varna, 25 April 1983.

137. *Ibid.*; also talks of the author with officials of the Greek Ministry of Foreign Affairs.

138. *Ibid.*; see also Ministry of Foreign Affairs, *The Macedonian Question* (a study for internal circulation, in Greek), Athens, September 1978.

139. The Assistant Minister of National Economy to the President of the Hellenic Republic, Memorandum: *Evolution of the Nestos River Issue* (in Greek), undated. Also author's talks with officials of the Greek Ministry of Foreign Affairs.

140. Hellenic Republic, *Official Gazette* , I, 22 June 1983; 16 June 1984 and 12 March 1985.

141. Hellenic Republic, *Official Gazette* , I, 28 November 1984; 12 March 1985 and 18 July 1986. The plan with Poland, signed in Warsaw on 23 October 1984, has not come to Parliament for ratification. (Information given to the author by officials of the Ministry of Foreign Affairs.)

142. Demetriades, *op. cit.*, 122.

143. *Ibid.*, 223.

144. Hellenic Republic, *Official Gazette* , I, 22 April 1986.

145. Ministry of Foreign Affairs. First Department. A1 sub-section of political affairs, *Greek-Yugoslavian Relations* (memorandum for internal circulation, in Greek), Athens, 19 October 1981.

146. Author's talks with officials of the Greek Ministry of Foreign Affairs.

147. Author's talks with officials of the Ministry of Foreign Affairs.

148. Ministry of Foreign Affairs. First Department. A1 sub-section of political affairs, *Greek-Rumanian Relations* (memorandum for internal circulation, in Greek), Athens, 19 October 1981. Also author's talks with officials of the Greek ministry of Foreign Affairs.

149. *Ibid.*, *Foreign Policy of the Soviet Union* (memorandum for internal circulation, in Greek), Athens, 15 February 1983.

150. *Ibid.*, *Soviet policy in the Balkans. Albania, Bulgaria, Yugoslavia, Rumania* (memorandum for internal circulation, in Greek), undated.

151. Hellenic Republic, *Official Gazette,* I, 17 February 1982.

152. Hellenic Republic, *Official Gazette,* I, 24 May 1985.

153. Ministry of Foreign Affairs. B2 sub-section of economic relations, *Economic Relations Between Greece and USSR* (memorandum for internal circulation, in Greek), Athens, 18 January 1983.

154. *Ibid.*

155. *Ibid.*

156. *Ibid.*; see also Demetriades, *op. cit.*, 223.

157. Hellenic Republic, *Official Gazette* , I, 7 July 1986.

158. Ministry of Foreign Affairs. B2 sub-section of economic relations, *Economic Relations Between Greece and USSR* (memorandum for internal circulation, in Greek), Athens, 18 January 1983.

159. *Ibid.*

160. Author's talks with officials of the Greek Ministry of Foreign Affairs.

161. Ministry of Foreign Affairs. A1 sub-section of political affairs, *Relations Between Greece and Soviet Union* (brief memorandum for internal circulation, in Greek), Athens, 15 February 1983.

162. *Declaration of Government Policy ..., op. cit.,* 36.

163. Ministry of Foreign Affairs. A1 sub-section of political affairs, *Relations Between Greece and Soviet Union* (brief memorandum for internal circulation, in Greek), Athens, 15 February 1983.

164. *Ibid.*

165. Author's talks with officials of the Greek Ministry of Foreign Affairs.

166. Author's talks with officials of the Ministry of Foreign Affairs.

167. Demetriades, *op. cit.,* 124.

168. Ministry of Foreign Affairs, *A Balkan Zone without Nuclear Weapons* (memorandum, in Greek), undated.

169. *Ibid.*

170. *Ibid.*

171. *Ibid.*

172. Ministry of Foreign Affairs, *Memorandum* (of this meeting), Athens, 1 April 1982.

173. *Ibid.*

174. It is characteristic that in the revival of this pattern, even the Orthodox Church is used by the Soviet Union; some see an attempt on the part of the Soviet Union to promote Moscow's position as the "Third Rome." Ministry of Foreign Affairs. A1 sub-section of political affairs, *Relations Between Greece and the Soviet Union* (brief memorandum for internal circulation, in Greek), Athens, 15 February 1983.)

175. Ministry of Foreign Affairs. A2 sub-section of political affairs, *Relations Between Turkey and Soviet Union* (memorandum for internal circulation, in Greek), 13 December 1982.

176. The Turkish government suspects that the USSR gives clandestine help to the Armenian Liberation Movement "Asala" and that the Soviets still wish to gain territory in the Kars and Ardahan regions.

177. Giannes Synodinos, "In the Greek schools of Constantinople," *Tachydromos* (an Athens pro-government magazine), 11 June 1987, p. 112; also talks between the author and officials of the Turkish embassy in Washington, D.C., in August 1984.

178. Ministry of Foreign Affairs. A1 sub-section of political affairs,

Relations Between Greece and Soviet Union (brief memorandum for internal circulation, in Greek), Athens, 15 February 1983.

179. As emphasized by a high-ranking PASOK official to the author: "The EEC keeps Papandreou in power with the money it gives him!"

180. Before the 1981 elections he had underlined that the "materialization" of his "vision" would require time and it would take place only when time would be ripe. (*Declaration of government policy..., op. cit.,* 37.)

181. *Prime minister's file on the bases* . A brief memorandum with summaries of all the opinions and views expressed. (In Greek), undated.

182. *Ibid.*

183. *Ibid.*

184. *Ibid.*

185. *Pontiki* (Athens), 3 July 1987.

186. *Ibid.*

The Cyprus Issue: Waiting for Sadat

William S. Shepard

During the period since Andreas Papandreou's electoral victory, with the slogan *Allage* (change) and assumption of national office on 21 October 1981, the Cyprus question has become further mired in the inflexibility of the immediate parties and their off-shore guarantors. For one who has followed the Cyprus issue for a number of years,[1] the lack of real progress is disheartening.

In the past six years, the Turkish Cypriot UDI in November 1983, and the failure of the parties to reach agreement following years of painstaking intercommunal talks under United Nations sponsorship in January 1985, have been succeeded by the consolidation, step by step, of *de facto* partition on the island, as the 133-mile green line separating the Greek and Turkish Cypriots is patrolled by a 2300-man United Nations force.

With this downward spiral of settlement prospects, one is even tempted to conclude with a recent assessment, that the Cyprus question may really be "moving beyond a solution."[2] If so, then we must assess the record for this period, find out what has gone so seriously amiss, and ask what American national interests may require. Is it really a matter of national indifference to the United States to let the issue proceed at its own dynamic? And how do we perceive that dynamic?[3]

As a democracy, we must respect the strong desires of the people most directly suffering for an overall lack settlement of their national issue. During the past few years, several incidents have testified to this continuing desire for a settlement, and for real intercommunal security. Rather surprisingly, on 29 December 1984, prominent Greek and Turkish Cypriots (including both President Spyros Kyprianou and Rauf Denktash, chairman of the Turkish Cypriot Socialist party and the son of Kyprianou's main antagonist, Rauf Denktash), attended a social function together and publicly called for reconciliation. And on 14 June 1987, some 400 Greek Cypriot women staged a protest against the forced partition of their country, and sweeping aside U.N. peace-keeping troops, entered the buffer zone between the Greek and Turkish portions of the island. If there is, indeed, still hope on the part of Cypriots for a solution to their national tragedy, that hope is a hardy plant worth nurturing.

The Cyprus problem is rooted in the failed policies that gave birth to the new nation, for national self-determination was only achieved following a prolonged and bloody armed struggle that ended with Great Britain working out terms of independence for Cyprus in connection with the Turkish and Greek governments. Greek Cypriot leader Archbishop Makarios III and Turkish Cypriot leader Fazil Kutchuk ratified that agreement in London on 19 February 1959, having played no role in the terms of their own independence.[4]

The Cypriot constitution was thus not a well-tempered document in the minds and experience of those who were to abide by its provisions in governing the new nation. After only a few years, the agreements became unmanageable. They had become starting points for intercommunal demands, not mandatory provisions for governing. Archbishop Makarios, now president of Cyprus, presented a list of constitutional changes in late 1963 that would have undone the carefully worked out (and unworkable) series of checks and balances, including veto power for both the Greek Cypriot president and the Turkish Cypriot vice president in matters affecting national and internal security, and weighted representation for the two communities in the Cypriot House of Representatives.[5] Violence broke out at Christmas, 1963, and the Turkish Cypriot community was forced by its leadership to move into enclaves. As the situation deteriorated, President Lyndon Johnson frankly warned the Turkish government that the United States would not come to Turkey's assistance should the Soviet Union come to Makarios's rescue in the event of a Turkish military intervention. The Turks—this time—backed off.

The situation stagnated, its diplomacy punctuated by yet another high-handed attempt by outsiders to settle the issue. After Under Secretary of State George Ball proposed (for independent Cyprus) a peace keeping NATO military force, Dean Acheson proposed a form of *enosis* (union) of Cyprus with Greece, compensation for Turkey consisting of the creation of a Turkish sovereign military base area on Cyprus, secure Turkish enclaves, compensation for those Turkish Cypriots who wished to emigrate, and the awarding of an offshore island, Kastelorizo, to Turkey. However, following the familiar pattern, "there was no Cypriot present at the meeting (between Dean Acheson and the Greek and Turkish representatives held in Geneva that determined these arrangements), and, esoecially since the concept called for a form of partition, President Makarios rejected it."[6] In lieu of the ill-fated NATO troops proposal, a peace-keeping force was authorized by the U.N. Security Council together with a U.N. special representative as a mediator of sorts.[7]

More violence on the island followed in November 1967, after pro-*enosis* groups on Cyprus allied with the new military junta that had seized power in Greece on 21 April 1967, opened fire on Turkish Cypriots. Following the failure of efforts by the U.N. to defuse the situation, President Johnson sent former Deputy Secretary of Defense (and future Secretary of State) Cyrus Vance into the region.[8] Vance did arrange for the withdrawal of some of the forces introduced into Cyprus by both the Greeks and Turks in violation of levels established by the framework agreements.

In 1974, the Greek military junta launched an attempt to force *enosis*, murder Archbishop Makarios, and install the possible psychopath, Nikos Sampson, in his place. This time, unlike Lyndon Johnson's decisive actions in 1964 and 1967, the dying Nixon administration took no action to restrain the Turkish military reaction. Two military incursions followed. In July 1974, the Turks established a military base area in the Kyrenia area in northwestern Cyprus, an extensive, but exposed salient. Then they agreed to a cease-fire. What followed in August has defined the present political geography of Cyprus. Responding to dubious "reports" of impending killings of Turkish Cypriots, what they considered an untenable position from the military point of view, and the probable collapse of talks in Geneva, the Turks expanded their military foothold with a second invasion that expanded their holdings to 37% of the island. The United States—in seeming contrast to its representations in earlier stages of the continuing Cyprus crisis—had not played an efficacious role.

The Turks now controlled an area greatly disproportionate to their 18% share of the island's population. A U.N.-patrolled "green line" now physically separated the two communities. Turkish troops (and later, Turkish settlers) gave the division an air of permanence, as population shifts between the two portions of the island isolated the communities in their respective zones. And following the downfall of the junta in Greece shortly thereafter, American diplomatic credibility with our longtime friends in the Eastern Aegean fell to a sorry low, punctuated only by the American initiative of State Department Counselor Matthew Nimetz four years later to nudge along the sporadic intercommunal talks, now with President Spyros Kyprianou and Turkish Cypriot leader Rauf Denktash as the principals of their respective communities. By 1981, however, the attempts to get the supporting intercommunal talks on track once again were in the hands of the United Nations, following landmark elections held that year in both Cyprus and Greece.[9]

On the island, in May, elections were held for the 35 Greek Cypriot seats in Parliament, according to a system of proportional representation. Conservatives in the Democratic Rally (led by Glafcos Clerides, himself a former intercommunal negotiator) had been unrepresented in the former Parliament but won 12 seats in the new Parliament. AKEL (the Greek Communist party led by 73-year-old Ezekias Papaioannou) also won 12 seats in the new Parliament. With renewed AKEL support (following a debate over Kyprianou's handling of the national issue[10]), President Kyprianou's Democratic party retained power, despite its dismal showing of just 8 seats in the new Parliament. Socialist EDEK took the remaining 3 seats.

By contrast, the stunning victory of Andreas Papandreou's PASOK (with 170 seats in the 300-member Parliament, while formerly ruling conservative New Democracy took just 113 seats, and the pro-Moscow Communist party held 13 seats) in October brought in a new era in postwar Greek national politics. The election of Papandreou seemed also to herald a new concentration by Athens on the Cyprus issue, an activism that was symbolized by President Kyprianou's visit to Greece just the day after the new Greek government was sworn into office!

For PASOK had pledged that they would make the Cyprus issue their primary foreign policy concern, in alleged contrast to New Democracy's "abandonment of the sacred issue of Cyprus." Further, according to the PASOK platform, Greece "has both the legal right and duty to actively support the struggle of the Cypriot people for the withdrawal of foreign troops *and bases* " (emphasis supplied). Commenting on the election results and their implications for the Cyprus issue, a former official in the Carter NSC noted with some prescience that Papandreou would take "a hard line, arguing that intercommunal talks under U.N. auspices can succeed only once Turkish troops have left the island. Given his suspicion of American interests and policy regarding Cyprus, he will probably favor internationalization of the issue rather than seeing it resolved within NATO. Thus, progress toward resolution of the Cyprus issue will be neither quick nor smooth."[11]

And so it has proved. The constituent parts of a diplomatic problem that defied solution already included an agonizing history of mistrust on the island between communities whose offshore national protectors bear fierce enmity towards each other. Military interventions in 1974 brought untold suffering in their wake, and attendant misery to refugees and survivors. The related issues of missing persons (including five American citizens said to be in Turkish hands) and the stated security needs of the fearful Turkish Cypriot minority hardly exhaust the list. And the personal expressions of misery by members of both communities must touch any student of the issue.[12] Indeed, they belie the notion that the issue is too complex for solution, by putting it in terms of human, understandable immediacy.

The new elements of the issue included now a weak central authority on Cyprus that relied on Communist support for its survival. By contrast, an assertive new government had been elected in Athens that remained deeply suspicious of the United States and was on record as dedicated to the primacy of the Cyprus issue. Should, as Larrabee predicted, PASOK's election program become government policy and Turkish troop withdrawal from Cyprus become a precondition for intercommunal talks (a total and known non-starter for the Turkish Cypriot side), with parallel insistence on the internationalization of the issue itself and an eventual game plan including the withdrawal of British sovereign base areas, then a solution to the Cyprus issue would, indeed, be "neither quick nor smooth." What was apparently not foreseen was the Turkish reaction to these policy elements.

Meanwhile, United Nations efforts to revive intercommunal talks were pursued doggedly by the special representative of the secretary-general, Ambassador Hugo Gobbi of Argentina, who presented an "evaluation" of the status of the intercommunal talks of 18 November 1981. This document was characterized as "not a formal proposal, (but it) embodies ideas and concepts which may prove useful for the parties in their decision of outstanding issues."[13] Detailed and often weekly working level intercommunal talks were held, beginning 2 December 1981, on the basis of this "evaluation," under the aegis of Ambassador Gobbi's mission, at the Ledra Palace in Nicosia, which straddles the green line separating the two communities. The talks, said to be "serious and businesslike," focused on both "points of coincidence" and "points of equidistance" in the positions of the two sides, as appreciated by the "evaluation."

Thorough reviews were also held in separate meetings that the new United Nations Secretary-General Perez de Cuellar (himself a former special representative of the secretary-general for the Cyprus issue) held in April 1982 with President Kyprianou and Turkish Cypriot leader Denktash. At that time, the two sides agreed to accelerate their contacts and meet twice a week. With various recesses, those talks continued throughout 1982. On 1 December 1982, the secretary-general's report noted that the two sides had essentially finished their consideration of constitutional issues, and would turn next to the territorial issue. He anticipated that next, an "overall package deal" should be undertaken, setting the stage for an agreement, should the requisite political will exist for one.[14]

Prime Minister Papandreou paid a three-day official visit to Cyprus 27 February—1 March 1982, the first visit by a Greek prime minister to Cyprus. Interviewed just prior to the trip by the *New York Times* correspondent Marvin Howe, Papandreou stressed the key importance of troop withdrawals in settling the Cyprus question. He said that "if Turkey would withdraw the nearly 30,000 troops he estimated it had in northern Cyprus, his government would pull out Greece's 1,000 soldiers and agree to the presence of a strong United Nations force."[15] He said that the function of this force would be "to protect the interests of the Turkish minority until such time as an agreement" could be worked out between the two sides. The Greek prime minister also offered that Greece would help pay for these troops.

Papandreou received a tumultuous welcome from the Greek Cypriots. Although largely taken up by ceremonial events, still he pressed for "internationalization" of the Cyprus issue. While diplomatic observers reportedly wondered about the effects that "internationalization" would have on the intercommunal talks under Ambassador Gobbi's mission, Papandreou said that those talks could only deal with internal matters. An "internationalization" of the issue, on the other hand, would deal with "the main international question—'the occupation' by

Turkish forces and their 'continuous threat.' " Papandreou said that the "internationalization" he had in mind included multilateral diplomacy, taking the issue before the General Assembly and the Security Council, as well as convening an international conference. He reportedly took some pains to rebut the notion that *enosis* was the policy of Greece, and he said that Turkish Cypriots were also harmed by the presence of Turkish mainland troops in their midst. He did, however, put the case of Cyprus in an overall Aegean context of Turkish expansionism. As the visit ended, Papandreou announced that he and President Kyprianou did "agree on the idea of a move toward an international conference."

Turkish Cypriot leaders viewed Papandreou's purpose as undermining the intercommunal talks. Predictably, on 20 May 1982, Turkish Prime Minister Bulent Usulu flew to northern Cyprus for the first such visit by a Turkish prime minister. Although Athens protested that Usulu was visiting sovereign Cyprus without the approval of the government of Cyprus, the Turkish foreign ministry in Ankara replied that "there are two internationally accepted communities under separate governments in Cyprus. Therefore it is out ot the question for the prime minister of the Republic of Turkey tc get permission from the Greeks to visit the northern part which is under the rule of the Turkish Cypriots."[16]

The next developments concerned the Cyprus presidential elections. President Spyros Kyprianou announced on 20 April that he would seek re-election, and that he would receive the support of AKEL in doing so. He said that he and the communists had put aside their ideological differences, and had reached an agreement for "cooperation on a minimum program" on the national issue. It is interesting to note that Greece's pro-Moscow Communist party then criticized Prime Minister Papandreou following the latter's objections to the AKEL-Kyprianou alliance. The purported grounds for Papandreou's objections were that the alliance would undermine Papandreou's initiatives on the Cyprus issue!

Speaking before the United Nations General Assembly on 7 October 1982, Kyprianou then proceeded towards "internationalization" of the Cyprus issue by calling for a new debate on the question. At a news conference following his speech, however, Kyprianou said that any new Cyprus debate should follow the scheduled presidential elections on Cyprus, and be held in March 1983.

The following year, 1983, was a vintage year for disastrous development of the Cyprus issue. Unlike the missed opportunities that have characterized other stages of the evolution of the Cyprus question (a pattern that would recur in 1985), 1983 was a year that created fresh impediments to progress on the issue on both sides. And yet it need not have been so. As usual, the warning signs were in place.

The presidential elections were sharply contested, with the position of Kyprianou's Democratic party-AKEL alliance on the national issue sharply contested by Glafcos Clerides. (The third candidate, Vassos Lyssarides of socialist EDEK, hoped to provoke a run-off election by denying Kyprianou the majority that would provide a first-round victory.) The Kyprianou-AKEL alliance supported the intercommunal talks held under United Nations sponsorship, while at the same time favoring internationalization." By this was intended the intensified presentation of the national issue before the United Nations, and such other groupings as the Council of Europe, the non-aligned movement, and the British Commonwealth. Clerides stressed the dangers of Kyprianou's alliance with the communists (for which, Kyprianou insisted, no political price had been paid), and emphasized that Western "backstage" influence with Turkey was the key to a solution of the national issue. Prime Minister Papandreou continued to oppose the communist AKEL influence, while stressing "internationalization" of the issue as a means of putting pressure on the Turks to withdraw their military forces *as a prerequisite for negotiations* (emphasis supplied). The Kyprianou-AKEL alliance emphasized as well the continuation of the intercommunal talks. Kyprianou stated that he favored dismantling of the two British sovereign base areas, but also said that this was a matter to be addressed over the longer term.

President Kyprianou was re-elected with 56 percent of the vote. Glafcos Clerides won 34 percent, while the socialist candidate, Vassos Lyssarides, took 9.53 percent of the vote. The Turkish Cypriots had not participated in the election on the grounds that the 1960 constitution required a Turkish Cypriot vice president, to be elected by the Turkish Cypriots. The Turkish Cypriots instead marked what they termed the eighth anniversary of their "Turkish Federated State of Cyprus," supposedly formed after the 1974 invasion. The speaker of the Turkish Consultative Assembly, Sadi Irmak, who was in attendance, called for a solution to the Cyprus issue based on "the equality of the two communities."

Following the election, President Kyprianou, disheartened, he said, by the reduction of the intercommunal talks to "two monologues" which could not produce results "because cf the presence of Turkish soldiers on the island," urged that the United States use its influence with Turkey on the troop withdrawal issue. He also announced public "internationalization" of the issue that would be "parallel to but separate from" the intercommunal talks. He scheduled talks in Athens to occur shortly after his 28 February inauguration. After that, he would raise the issue personally at the March nonaligned summit in New Delhi, then in April, talks with United Nations Secretary-General Perez de Cuellar, followed by a General Assembly debate on the Cyprus issue in May.[17]

In May, pressures on the Turks were intensified. In Washington, the House Foreign Affairs Committee voted 14-13 to cut off all aid to Turkey in 1987 if there were still Turkish soldiers occupying Cyprus then. On the same day, 10 May, Cypriot Foreign Minister Nikos Rolandis told the General Assembly that the "Turkish occupation is the cardinal factor for the lack of progress" on the Cyprus issue. On 13 May, following a four-day debate, the United Nations General Assembly passed a resolution demanding the immediate withdrawal of occupation troops from Cyprus and stating that this withdrawal was the basis for a solution to the problem. The resolution passed 103-5 (the nonaligned Contact Group plus 12 others voted in favor of the resolution). The United States was one of 20 nations that abstained, and Deputy Delegate William C. Sherman "deplored the fact that the issue had been brought to the Assembly."[18]

A week later, Turkish Cypriot leader Rauf Denktash threatened to create an independent state in northern Cyprus. In Athens, concern was officially expressed to the five permanent members of the United Nations Security Council, as the ambassadors of the United States, France, Great Britain, China and the Soviet Union were summoned to the Greek foreign office. According to officials in Athens, the Denktash threat was a reaction to the General Assembly resolution voted the previous week. And on 17 June 1983, the Turkish Cypriot "Legislative Assembly" voted in favor of a resolution to hold a referendum on the declaration of a separate state, or UDI, for northern Cyprus. And throughout the summer and early fall,

U.N. Secretary-General Perez de Cuellar attempted to revive the sputtering intercommunal talks, which had been suspended in May.

On 15 November, Cyprus again held center stage in the world's press, as Turkish Cypriot leader Rauf Denktash carried out his threat to declare the "Turkish Republic of Northern Cyprus" as an independent state, following a vote of approval by the Turkish Cypriot "Legislative Assembly."

The Turkish Cypriot UDI was roundly and virtually universally condemned, and in the end, only Turkey recognized the new "state." The United States condemned the move forcefully and immediately, and took swift and effective diplomatic action to forestall recognition of the "Turkish Republic of Northern Cyprus" by other nations.[19] The United Nations Security Council, voting 13-1 (Pakistan, with Jordan abstaining) on a resolution offered by Great Britain, condemned UDI as illegal and urged all nations not to recognize it. The *New York Times* noted editorially on the day after UDI that "Incredibly, Turkey claimed to be surprised by its compatriots' action yesterday. But the timing was too obviously deliberate: only days after the election of a partly civilian Turkish government and only *hours* after President Reagan signed an aid bill earmarking nearly $1 billion for Turkey...."[20]

For those accustomed to silver linings, it could be noted that the UDI proclamation itself precluded the uniting of the new "state" with any state (meaning Turkey), and it stated that "The proclamation of the new state will not hinder, but facilitate the establishment of a genuine federation." The reactions of other nations came swiftly. Greece said that unless Turkey withdrew its recognition of UDI, Greece would break off all talks with Turkey. The Soviet Union, through a Soviet press agency Tass commentary, repeated its call for an international conference on Cyprus and for the withdrawal of foreign troops and bases. And President Kyprianou, following talks in late November with President Ronald Reagan, expressed his appreciation for official and forceful American support during the crisis. As the year concluded, Turkish Cypriot leader Rauf Denktash told 10,000 cheering Turkish Cypriots upon his return from a visit to the United Nations and to London that Turkish troops would stay until a lasting peace was achieved on the island. He refused to consider withdrawing UDI, stating that "the Northern Cyprus Turkish Republic was created by the blind, erroneous policies of Papandreou, which are based on enmity toward the Turks." He added that the Greek prime minister was to be criticized "for not allowing the Greek Cypriot leaders to return to the road of common sense for a negotiated, federal settlement with the Turkish Cypriots."[21] And the Turkish Cypriots then established a new 70-member Constituent Assembly to draft a constitution for their new "state" and also legislation for presidential and parliamentary elections.

The stage then turned once again to efforts to get the intercommunal talks underway and then to keep them moving as a series of nimble backstage American and United Nations diplomatic proddings (including, on the American side, U.N. Representative Jeane Kirkpatrick) sought to prevent total stagnation of the process. In April, the Turkish Cypriot "state" exchanged ambassadors with Turkey, a move that again met widespread condemnation as unhelpful to the settlement process.[22]

Meanwhile, in the United States House of Representatives, a 9 May vote showed House action on what Representative Lee Hamilton (D-Indiana) termed a "new approach" to the Cyprus issue. The floor vote trimmed 1985 aid to Turkey to $670 million (down from the $755 million requested by the administration), provided half of Greece's $500 million military aid at "vastly reduced interest rates," and provided, as the administration had requested, a $250 million Cyprus reconstruction special fund, to be released by the White House when "real progress" had been achieved by the opposing parties towards solution of the Cyprus issue. The notion seemed to be to display evenhandedness towards the parties, while providing a financial incentive towards solution of the Cyprus issue.

On 1 September 1984, U.N. Secretary-General Perez de Cuellar announced that both the Greek Cypriots and the Turkish Cypriot side had accepted his patient diplomatic initiative for high-level proximity talks involving the parties, a development which, it was hoped, would then result in the first face-to-face Kyprianou-Denktash meeting since 1979. The proximity talks began in New York on 10 September 1984, lasting for 10 days. Two more rounds of talks were held that fall, also in New York, first from 15-26 October and then from 26 November-12 December. At length, U.N. Secretary-General Perez de Cuellar announced that sufficient progress had been made to warrant convening a direct meeting between President Kyprianou and Turkish Cypriot leader Rauf Denktash. That summit of the principal disputants would begin in New York on 17 January 1985.

During the "proximity talks," the Greek Cypriots and

Turkish Cypriots had met separately each day with the secretary-general, while "technical teams" also held talks with United Nations officials. In effect, the two sides talked with each other through the United Nations. And this time, the approach differed from the earlier round of intercommunal talks that had been suspended eighteen months earlier, although the positive results of those talks were built upon. Instead of a step-by-step approach, however, the central premise was to negotiate an overall draft framework agreement on the most intractable issues. Furthermore, it was repeatedly made clear to the participants that none of the more difficult issues would be implemented piecemeal (although phased implementation of an overall accord was possible). In an atmosphere where mutual trust was nonexistent, this seemed a clearly sensible approach.

Positions obviously evolved over the course of the three series of proximity talks. But there was an imperative now, the spreading impression that Turkish Cypriot UDI had altered realities on the island, and that to prevent any further Turkish Cypriot steps towards the trappings of nationhood, each of which would through a separate dynamic have to be undone in any further negotiations, adding further to the difficulty of an overall solution to the Cyprus issue, this opportunity must not be lost. Youngsters were growing up on both sides of the green line who did not even possess the illusion of understanding people from the other side. And perhaps the feeling would become settled on the Turkish Cypriot side that unsatisfactory as conditions might be (with an influx of settlers from mainland Turkey and inflation, unemployment and median earned income statistics considerably inferior to those enjoyed by Greek Cypriots), at least now there was security, and that security was not worth jeopardizing lightly, merely for the sake of an agreement.[23]

Negotiations proceeded on the thorny issues of guarantors to the agreement (with the Turkish Cypriots insisting on Turkey's continuation as a guarantor), the withdrawal of Turkish military forces, the "three freedoms" of settlement, movement, and property rights, and constitutional issues. The initial Turkish Cypriot position contemplated resettlement of Greek Cypriot refugees in seven zones, under United Nations administration. As the series of proximity talks continued, a clear breakthrough on the difficult territorial issue occurred, reportedly as a result of a direct appeal to the government of

Turkey from President Ronald Reagan. The Turkish Cypriot position was revised, and for the first time, they went beyond their 32% territorial offer, and tabled 29% as their territorial position. It was with this breakthrough achieved, thanks in part to adroit American backstage diplomacy, that U.N. Secretary-General Perez de Cuellar was able to announce the 17 January 1985 Kyprianou-Denktash meeting. And it was in this heady atmosphere of possible agreement that the impromptu holiday meeting between President Kyprianou and Rauf Denktash, noted earlier, took place. For if issues of this magnitude could be positively addressed, then possibly the remaining thorny issues of power-sharing in a new governmental structure might also be solved.

There had long been agreement on a bicameral legislature, with equal representation in the upper house and 70%-30% representation in the lower house. A Turkish Cypriot demand for a rotating presidency had been dropped in favor of the 1960 formula (a Greek Cypriot president and a Turkish Cypriot vice president). But key constitutional issues remained to be discussed, including the composition of the cabinet, and veto rights for the Turkish Cypriot minority—the very issues that had set off communal violence twenty years earlier.

On the very day that the long-awaited talks were beginning in New York, a disturbing analysis by Henry Kamm appeared in the *New York Times* . Filing from Athens, Mr. Kamm reported Greek concerns that in the event of a settlement of the Cyprus issue, the lid would be off for American military assistance to Turkey. They feared that the Congress would no longer feel an imperative to reduce such aid to a proportion of 7 to 10 between Greece and Turkey, respectively, the level traditionally sought by Greece, which permits sufficient modernization by Greece through more sophisticated arms supplies while reducing the danger of creating a Turkish military advantage over Greece through the aid process. Greek officials were reportedly apprehensive that the United States had used this carrot with the Turkish government in order to induce the reduction of the Turkish Cypriot territorial proposal below the 30% psychological barrier. And they cited underlying, pervasive security fears that would persist despite settlement of the Cyprus issue.[24]

The long-awaited New York summit fell apart. Both sides should take a share of the blame. Greek Cypriot sources insist that negotiations were planned over the four-day period, and that President Kyprianou had not intended to sign the draft agreement, treating it as merely an agenda for the talks. The Turkish Cypriots, by contrast, stated that they had come prepared to sign the draft agreement and then negotiate further details.[25] The fact of the matter is that neither side had the willingness of a Sadat to transcend differences and exercise the political will required to come to an agreement that would settle the Cyprus issue. When asked the reason for this breakdown, U.N. Secretary-General Perez de Cuellar finally yielded to frustration and candidly admitted in reply: "The tremendous imagination of the parties."

The failure of the talks led to several unpleasant consequences involving the main parties in interest. A tentatively scheduled visit to Washington by the Turkish prime minister (the first since 1974) was shelved. Greece received press criticism for allegedly discouraging an agreement on Cyprus for reasons of her own national security involving Turkey. (Predictably, Turkish Cypriot leader Denktash stated that "Greece doesn't need a settlement because they use Cyprus to punish Turkey in the U.S. Congress with the help of the Greek lobby here in the U.S.") The general perception was that both sides had badly overplayed their hands, losing the best chance in years for a settlement of the problem, and giving fresh evidence to those who argue that the seemingly intractable Cyprus issue—not its solution—has become a profession. President Kyprianou ran into an unexpected and severe firestorm of domestic political criticism from both right and left upon his return to Cyprus for the summit's failure. And the Turkish Cypriot side now proceeded to take further steps to give their region something of the panoply of statehood.

In Nicosia, the Democratic Rally of Clerides combined with AKEL to censure President Kyprianou by a 23-12 vote in the Cypriot Parliament. Together they demanded that Kyprianou accept the draft agreement prepared by U.N. Secretary-General Perez de Cuellar that he had refused to sign in January. Kyprianou then rejected calls from both parties for his resignation, or that the legislature be given future control of talks with the Turkish Cypriots! Under this considerable domestic pressure, the government of Cyprus renewed contacts with the United Nations in the apparent attempt to have the January draft agreement altered sufficiently so that it could be accepted. In April this process was complete, but the second version had unaccountably not been cleared with the Turkish Cypriot side, which then rejected it. The Turks were still miffed by United Nations handling of the matter and to this day refuse to accept it as even a valid proposal.

Throughout the remainder of 1985, both Greek Cypriots and Turkish Cypriots were preoccupied with elections. Little noticed at the time, however, one key element in the larger Greek-Turkish controversy hardened. On 15 March, Athens rejected a proposal by the Turkish prime minister for bilateral substantive talks. The Greek government spokesman, Demetres Maroudas, said that no such talks could be held while Turkish troops occupied northern Cyprus and challenged Greek control of the Aegean. These conditions were, therefore, added to the prior condition that the UDI of the Turkish Cypriot "state" be undone prior to the holding of any official talks between Greece and Turkey.

On 9 May, the Turkish Cypriots voted for a new constitution for their "state." Predictably, the document was approved by 72.8% of the voters. On 9 June, Rauf Denktash was re-elected president of the "Turkish Republic of Northern Cyprus." He received 70.5%, with the remainder of the vote split amongst five other candidates. And in a third vote on 23 June, Turkish Cypriots chose a new Parliament. Following that vote, Denktash stated that "this election completes the final circle in the establishing of this republic." Denktash's center-right National Unity party won 37% of the vote, or 24 of the 50 seats. An alliance with New Dawn, representing settlers from mainland Turkey, which won 4 seats, would ensure narrow control over two left-wing parties that made strong parliamentary showings.

Parliamentary elections in the truncated Republic of Cyprus were set for 8 December. The stakes were unusually high, for if AKEL and the Democratic Rally party of Clerides succeeded in obtaining a two-thirds majority, they vowed to amend the Cypriot constitutional procedures to force the president to resign if a majority of Parliament so voted—in effect, making Cyprus more nearly a parliamentary system than a mixed parliamentary-presidential one.

As the election neared, Greece intervened dramatically. Two days before the voting, Greek Prime Minister Andreas Papandreou, in a major address to the Greek Parliament, said that "We must state clearly to the Cypriot people that if they accept a timetable of withdrawal—which would mean that the Turkish troops would never withdraw—we would consider that damaging to the Greek national interest. If the Turkish occupation of Cyprus is legalized, the threat to the Aegean will become more immediate and menacing. A decision to reach a solution while Turkish troops remain is nationally unacceptable to us. We, for our part, will not agree that there is a solution until the last Turkish occupation soldier leaves."[26] As *New York Times* correspondent Henry Kamm noted, this position amounted to a direct endorsement of President Kyprianou's position in the United Nations initiative.[27]

President Kyprianou's Democratic party, thus bolstered by Athens, increased its percentage of the overall vote to 27.5% from the 19.5% won in the 1981 legislative elections. They won 16 seats in the Parliament, which had been enlarged through legislation since the 1981 elections to 80 seats (from 50), with 56 seats (from 35) allocated to Greek Cypriots (the Turkish Cypriots again not participating). The Democratic Rally party of Clerides advanced its percentage total of the vote marginally (to 33.6% from 31.9%) and with 19 seats, became the largest parliamentary party. Communist AKEL was the main loser, with a total of 15 seats, but a reduced percentage of the vote (from 32.7% to 27.4%). Socialist EDEK under Lyssarides advanced somewhat (to 11% from 8.1%) and took 6 seats. And both President Kyprianou and the Turkish Cypriot leader Rauf Denktash, their positions bolstered by the authority of elections, expressed hard positions publicly. Kyprianou advanced the position (taken publicly before the elections by Greek Prime Minister Papandreou) that Turkey could not be a guarantor of a newly reunited Cyprus, and he ruled out the formation of a transitional Cyprus government pursuant to United Nations agreement prior to the withdrawal of all Turkish armed forces... an agreed "timetable" would be insufficient. He also said that all Greek Cypriot refugees should have the right of return to their previous homes Denktash, on the other hand, insisted upon Turkey as a continued guarantor, maintained that Turkish troops should leave the island gradually, and wanted to negotiate the issue of return.

On 29 March 1986, the U.N. secretary-general presented his third draft agreement (the second, according to the Turkish Cypriot leader) for the settlement of the Cyprus issue to the parties. Following lengthy consultations with Greek Prime Minister Papandreou, President Kyprianou rejected the draft. The Greek Cypriots insisted upon total withdrawal of Turkish armed forces prior to establishment of the new government, raised the settler issue, and rejected Turkey as a guarantor.

Objections were also raised to the system of veto powers designed to offer minority protection to the Turkish Cypriots in the constitution, and to provisions concerning the return of refugees. The Turkish Cypriots accepted the draft proposal. Both Turkish Cypriot leader Denktash and Greek Cypriot opposition leader Clerides expressed pessimism that a negotiated solution to the Cyprus issue would be found while President Kyprianou remained in office. Clerides said that Cyprus suffered from "two irrational anguishes: the Greek Cypriot conviction that Turkey intends to take over the whole island, and the Turkish Cypriot fear that the Greek Cypriots still want *enosis* ."[28]

The visit of Turkish Prime Minister Turgut Ozal to the Turkish Cypriot area in July 1986 prompted a closing of border crossing points by demonstrators from Greek Cypriot Socialist party EDEK. In retaliation, Turkish Cypriot leader Denktash closed the border, splitting United Nations forces. The blockade lasted one week before Denktash ordered it lifted, having demonstrated, he said, the equality of his community. Although Nicosia offered verbal support for U.N.-sponsored "parallel talks" on the Cyprus issue, the series of initiatives brought forth by U.N. Secretary-General Perez de Cuellar and concluding in his 29 March 1986 proposal now seemed at an impasse. The government of Cyprus has instead proposed either an international conference or a meeting between President Kyprianou and Rauf Denktash.[29]

The international conference, in the Greek Cypriot view, would concern only the "international aspects of the Cyprus problem, namely, 1. withdrawal of the Turkish forces of occupation and settlers; and 2. effective international guarantees." The alternative, a face-to-face meeting between Kyprianou and Denktash, would add as a third agenda item "Application of the three freedoms (movement, settlement, and the ownership of property)."[30] Letters to the secretary-general from President Kyprianou dated 10 March 1987 and 19 May 1987 tend to illustrate the secretary-general's reluctance to use his office for the convening of the requested international conference, a probable nonstarter given objections from Turkey.

Pending new presidential elections to be held on Cyprus in February 1988, that is where the Cyprus issue now stands, seemingly further mired than ever, following six years of the issue having become the stated primary foreign policy issue of Papandreou's Greece. Positions between the two communities on the island have hardened considerably, and the Turkish Cypriot UDI and subsequent series of elections and visits, while not capturing any support beyond that of Turkey, still have manufactured fresh obstacles to a solution to the issue. The "internationalization" of the issue on terms totally unacceptable to the Turkish Cypriots, and the concomitant withdrawal of the Greek Cypriots from the intercommunal process under the sponsorship of the United Nations, although they mirror attitudes held in Athens, still all constitute further steps away from a solution to the problem.

The viable battleground of these issues has shifted almost entirely now to the United States Congress, and to the annual hearings held to determine relative aid levels to our two NATO allies, Greece and Turkey. One must question seriously whether, at this point, such a continued emphasis suits either the national security interests of the United States, or the aspirations of both Greek Cypriots and Turkish Cypriots for a resolution of their national issue. For the current forum is a sharply partisan and divisive one, and those who seek to maintain high aid levels for Greece (which, in the author's view, are justified on their own merits by both common values and our national security interests) do not pursue this interest in a manner furthering the resolution of the Cyprus issue.

Furthermore, the "internationalization" of the Cyprus issue, as it is currently formulated, simply lends a legitimizing role to the Soviet Union, which has actively sought such a role since 1974, without doing anything worthwhile to solve the underlying Cyprus issue. Should a solution, now unforeseen, be found that somehow validated Soviet participation in the process, their exacted price would not be difficult to imagine. For strategic Cyprus, once a keystone to Great Britain's naval authority east of Suez, is still a location of potentially great strategic value, particularly in terms of the Soviet Union's long-cherished ambitions for a permanent presence in the Eastern Mediterranean.

A responsible solution to the Cyprus problem on its own merits would therefore accomplish three main purposes. First, it would remove a thorny issue that threatens to explode periodically, and permit residents of this small island nation—with whom we have no quarrel whatsoever—to resolve their differences in a way that serves their own interests. Second, it would remove a highly inflammatory issue from our own foreign relations with two NATO allies and have a positive effect on the Congressional theater. Third, it would, over the longer run, tend to deny to the Soviet Union the possibility of a prime strategic foothold in the Eastern Mediterranean.

As these comments are noted in early 1988, some movement of the issue seems possible. Previously Greece herself—by stating the hardest imaginable line for the resumption of any sustained dialogue between Greece and Turkey (Turkish troop withdrawal, revocation of UDI, and Turkish acceptance of the *status quo* in the Aegean)—had ensured that no such talks could be held. At the end of January, however, following several meetings between Papandreou and Prime Minister Ozal, contacts between Greece and Turkey were reestablished. The projected exchange of official visits, and the mutually stated intention to avoid a further Aegean crisis and proceed towards "a thaw and a rapprochement between the two countries" were hopeful signs.[31]

On the United Nations scene, attempts to have another debate on the Cyprus issue would surely be followed by further moves on the part of the Turkish Cypriots to consolidate their position. A further problem became the replacement of Sweden, which has participated in the U.N. peace-keeping force on Cyprus since the outset and which will not renew its contingent, the third largest troop contribution (after Great Britain and Canada) to the peace-keeping force. And meantime—although at present seemingly blocked by both Turkey and the United States—a campaign may yet be mounted for the "internationalization" of the Cyprus issue, which would involve, should the campaign succeed, in the seeming legitimization of a role by the Soviet Union in the Eastern Mediterranean, an area where the Russians have coveted a strategic role since Czarist times.

The United States is not a principal actor in the Cyprus issue, nor, in the author's view, should it be. However, the prospect for "internationalization" along the terms specified, together with the unseemly military assistance debates held annually before the Congress, and the undeniable American national interest in the security of the Eastern Mediterranean seem to indicate that a new approach may be needed. In February 1988, new presidential elections will be held on Cyprus. The lineup of parties behind candidates in that election remains to be seen. In December 1988, following the American presidential elections, the current American bases agreement with Greece is scheduled to expire, and over the next year, negotiations over the terms of a successor agreement will occupy both parties. The next general elections will be held in Greece, according to an announcement by Prime Minister Papandreou, in July 1989.

Although given this election and negotiating schedule a Cyprus initiative would be ill-timed, it is perhaps not too early for serious thought to be given by the American government to the possibility of a new and constructive American role in solving the Cyprus issue. Such a role could not substitute for a lack of resolution on the part of the parties directly concerned, nor could any American "plan" be surfaced that would have the least chance of success. The recent history of the island, after all, is replete with missed opportunities that involved precisely such third-party intervention. But the interests of the United States in an overall solution are not coextensive with the interests of any single party to the dispute.

A solution to the issue, while hardly the key to the virtually automatic settling of other Aegean problems between Greece and Turkey that some have alleged to exist, still would constitute a major step forward to stability in the region. In view of the continued human misery that the Cyprus issue causes, and our own national interest in its solution, we should undertake a serious national assessment, on a priority basis, of the timing, role and substance of an American initiative.

Such an initiative, if warranted by the assessment, would far better suit our national interests than does the current deterioration of the issue as we attempt to "manage" from the sidelines. It would end, from our standpoint, any suggestion of manipulation of the Cyprus national tragedy for other purposes. And it would put the initiative for a national policy on the Cyprus issue into official American governmental hands—where it rightfully belongs. Should my proposal be adopted—and then, a carefully considered American initiative be undertaken—there would be risks of failure. But such possible future risks clearly seem worth taking in view of the present certain deterioration of the prospects for settlement of the Cyprus issue.

According to PASOK's 1981 electoral platform—and in stated contrast to the policies of the conservative New Democracy government that PASOK then aimed to succeed—there was to be a new activism and emphasis on the Cyprus issue. Now, PASOK has been in power for over six years, and by any standard, the Cyprus problem has grown more difficult to solve.

Two considerable steps backward have marked the evolution of the Cyprus issue since the Papandreou government assumed office in October 1981. First—following an earlier "internationalization" of the issue at the United Nations and elsewhere—the Turkish Cypriots responded with UDI in November 1983 and then successive steps towards its implementation. And then in January 1985, following lengthy preliminary talks monitored by United Nations officials, the last serious effort for direct Kyprianou-Denktash talks fell apart.

During this period, Athens first upped the Cyprus stakes for bilateral discussions of matters of fundamental importance to the Greek nation with the ancient enemy, Turkey. The position was taken that the Cyprus issue and other contentious matters must be resolved in favor of Athens prior to the discussion of other fundamental differences between Greece and Turkey. Although some of this might be dismissed as posturing for the domestic audience, it is hard to see how such hard and publicly expressed attitudes did anything but make prospects more difficult for an overall settlement of the Cyprus issue. With the Davos, Switzerland Papandreou-Ozal meetings, however, an opportunity may exist to explore ways to relieve tensions in the region, setting the stage for a fresh look at the Cyprus issue.

It is not acceptable for the United States to let the situation drift "beyond solution," and adopt a posture of managing from the sidelines. For one thing, absent a cohesive national posture, the Cyprus issue will continue to be played out each year in the halls of Congress, and the continuation of the problem itself will suit those who wish to cite it rather than solve it.

The Cyprus issue, in the stated view of the secretary-general of the United Nations, is now at an impasse. But the possibility for movement is there. The challenge is posed how to move from that impasse towards a possible easing of tensions and in the direction of a solution to the problem. As a first step, the national reassessment that I have proposed of the Cyprus issue and its implications for American national security, in the light of growing Soviet activism in the region, should be undertaken on a priority basis.

But in the final analysis, it must be those directly concerned and their respective off-shore parties in interest who must take the necessary steps towards a settlement of the issue. But first, the same parties must make the essential judgment that the problem should be solved. It is the task of American political diplomacy to find ways for this necessary judgment to be more likely. And then—one must see whether there really are statesmen of the first rank in the region. It would be a nice and fitting irony, in view of the tangled recent past history of U.S.-Greek relations, if the political leader willing to assume the stature of Sadat in the Cyprus issue were Andreas Papandreou.

NOTES

1. The author would like to acknowledge the generous assistance of officials at the embassy of Greece, the embassy of Turkey, the Department of State, the embassy of Cyprus, and the Washington, D.C. Information Office of the United Nations in the preparation of this article.

2. Richard N. Haass, "Cyprus: Moving Beyond Solution?," *The Washington Quarterly*, Spring 1987, 183-190.

3. When the author served as staff aide to Ambassador Henry Cabot Lodge in Vietnam, Ambassador Lodge used to observe that the American experience there had three different realities, and he would cite the Saigon, Washington and New York (meaning the United Nations) realities. As applied to the Cyprus issue, the realities of New York, London, Ankara, Athens, Nicosia and the Turkish Cypriot area coalesce in two quite different Washington realities, an official administration view, and the problem as seen from Capitol Hill.

4. Leigh H. Bruce, "Cyprus: A Last Chance," *Foreign Policy*, Spring 1985, 115-133. As Bruce notes, the "straitjacket" created by the new republic's constitution was the more unpalatable because the communities had not participated in its formulation. Greek Cypriot authorities lament this lost initial opportunity, and it is ironic that some more recent proposals made by the parties themselves now parallel some of its provisions. See Durrell's *Bitter Lemons* for the 1953-56 period.

5. Elections for the Cypriot House of Representatives in 1981 were held for only the 35 seats allocated to the Greek Cypriot community, as the constitution required, while the 15 Turkish Cypriot seats remain unfilled.

6. *Area Handbook for Cyprus* (1971 edition), The American University, 50.

7. The semiannual U.N. troop reauthorizations, like the 60-day "progress" reports required of an American president by Public Law 95-384, now provide some continuing coverage of the issue periodically. Sometimes these U.N. debates and 60-day reports are the only focus at all that the Cyprus issue will receive during a semiannual period.

8. The special illumination of the Acropolis for the night flight carrying Cyrus Vance back to Athens during one of his shuttle flights

in this frenzied 10-day period in 1967 reminded all of us how close hostilities seemed.

9. In a May 1981 "farewell briefing," U.S. Ambassador Galen Stone stated that "there was no United States initiative on the Cyprus issue, and that all (American) efforts will be directed toward supporting the United Nations-sponsored talks." During the same press briefing, Ambassador Stone is reported to have "caused a furor" by asserting that not all refugees could return home (a suggestion that is anathema to Greek Cypriot politicians), and conversely, that some Turkish Cypriots might have to return their current homes to the original Greek Cypriot owners (a suggestion equally repellent to Turkish Cypriot politicians). *New York Times*, 24 May 1981, 3:1.

10. The sometime alliance of AKEL and the Democratic Rally on the national issue is curious, and worth more public examination than it has received. Based on conversations with ranking officials of both parties on the island in 1979, the author gathered the impression that the Democratic Rally looked towards a solution of the problem based less upon *a priori* positions than upon a series of pragmatic steps, in order to salvage what might be, in the American idiom, "do-able." AKEL, on the other hand, sought progress towards settlement in order to introduce, if possible, a Soviet hand into the proceedings themselves—with the further agenda of subsequently eliminating the British sovereign base areas.

11. Larrabee, "Dateline Athens: Greece for The Greeks," *Foreign Policy*, December 1981, 158, 171.

12. An elderly Greek Cypriot told the author that he had lost everything simply because, believing that personal debt was shameful, he had put all of his personal savings into the construction of an investment luxury hotel in Varosha, on Cyprus's east coast, rather than use a mortgage. Six months later the Turkish incursions came and his hotel now stands empty like so many others there. An elderly Turkish Cypriot in neighboring Famagusta told the author that during the enclave period prior to 1974, Turkish Cypriots were forbidden, despite often sweltering heat, to bathe in the ocean there. The author was reminded that as a teenager in 1951 he once asked a native Floridian why there were no blacks on the beach at Daytona Beach. The answer came that "this is a white beach."

13. Fifth Report on Cyprus, Message to the Congress from President Ronald Reagan, 3 December 1981, 82 *Department of State Bulletin* 45, February 1982.

14. Twelfth Report on Cyprus, Message to the Congress from President Ronald Reagan, 27 January 1983, 83 *Department of State Bulletin* 67, April 1983.

15. *New York Times*, 27 February 1982, 4:1.

16. *New York Times*, 21 May 1982.

17. According to the Cyprus government's official publication, in view of the lack of progress in the talks and the serious threat to the

security of the Greek Cypriots, the government felt it had no option but to internationalize the Cyprus problem by taking its case to the United Nations once again.

The United Nations itself also gave signs that it was concerned about the stalemate and deteriorating situation, and finally, following a meeting between President Kyprianou and the new U.N. secretary-general, Mr. Perez de Cuellar, in Paris on 24 April 1983, the latter disclosed that he intended to strengthen his personal involvement in the efforts to achieve a settlement. He said he planned to sound out all the interested parties about the new ideas and initiatives that might help the search for a solution.

The Cyprus Problem, Press and Information Office, Ministry of Interior, Republic of Cyprus, 36 (Nicosia, June 1986).

18. *New York Times,* 14 May 1983, 5:4.

19. The American announcement contained the astonishing statement, in view of the earlier diplomatic *démarche* in Athens, that "This move by the Turkish Cypriots comes as a complete surprise to us." Neither was the prospect raised in the statement made before the Subcommittee on Europe and the Middle East of the House Foreign Affairs Committee on 2 November by Richard N. Haass, special Cyprus coordinator for the Department of State. Haass, "Developments in Cyprus," 84 *Department of State Bulletin* 52 January 1984. (The State Department's 15 November official statement on the Turkish Cypriot UDI is also to be found there.)

20. *New York Times,* 16 November 1983.

21. *New York Times,* 26 November 1983, 4:3.

22. Aside from this predictable minimum, and the customary Security Council debate on the issue, both sides seem to have avoided exacerbating the issue publicly while the intercommunal talks went through a new developmental phase.

23. Both Christopher Hitchens, Washington correspondent for *The Nation*, and Clifford P. Hackett, former staff director of the House Foreign Affairs Committee subcommittee on Europe, appear principally attracted to the simplicities of an approach that assigns to the United States a disproportionate share of blame for the woes of the Aegean. Nevertheless, some sense of reality is preserved as each also recognizes the essential problem of dealing with the legitimate security concerns of the Turkish Cypriots. See Hackett, "Betting on All the Wrong Horses," *Washington Post,* 9 September 1984, D 5:4, and Hitchens, "The Island Pawn That Won't Go Away," *The Nation,* 19 June 1982, 741-742.

24. Kamm, "Athens Fears Rise in Arms for Turks," *New York Times,* 18 January 1985, 3:1.

25. A fascinating new official document published by the government of Cyprus now blames the United Nations for the collapse of the January 1985 summit. The pamphlet alleges "paternalism" on the part of United Nations officials in substituting views of what the

parties might ("should" seems to convey the meaning better: author's note) have agreed to, in urging direct talks between the parties rather than proximity talks. Further, the document states flatly that "In January 1985 the two sides were summoned to a high level meeting in New York, with the Turkish Cypriot side being told it was merely to sign an agreed document, while the Greek Cypriot side was *induced to attend* (emphasis supplied) by being told that the documentation was to be negotiated. That is why the January 1985 meeting collapsed, as the documenation presented largely reproduced the Turkish Cypriot side's views of what was acceptable." "The March 1986 'Draft Framework Agreement and the Greek Cypriot side's attitude towards it," *Cyprus Problem*, Press and Information Office, Ministry of Interior, Republic of Cyprus (undated): 11-12.

26. Kamm: "Papandreou Says the Voting in Cyprus Concerns Greece," *New York Times,* 7 December 1988, 4:3. Papandreou at the same time rejected Turkey as a guarantor of the independence of a reunited Cyprus.

27. *Ibid.*

28. Randal, "Greek Cypriot Leader Resisting Latest U.N. Plan for Reunification," *Washington Post.* 25 June 1986, A19:1. Clerides added the pungent note that in his opinion the Cyprus issue would be solved in 24 hours if a way could be found to "attach (the island) to a tugboat and tow it into the Atlantic!"

29. Twenty-Seventh Report on Cyprus, Message to the Congress from President Ronald Reagan, 1 July 1986, 86 *Department of State Bulletin* 34, October 1986. The stated view that the secretary-general "under the circumstances (believed that) the way forward will require careful reflection by all concerned" is a small masterpiece of diplomatic understatement.

30. See footnote 24.

31. Hoagland, "Greece and Turkey Set Up Means to Resolve Differences," *Washington Post* , 1 February 1988, A17:1.

Appendix

*Defense Policies of PASOK**

TABLE: BALANCE OF POWER

ELEMENTS OF COMBAT POWER	GREECE		TURKEY		NOTES
Population	10,372,000		51,421,000		1 to 5 ratio
Defense spending	$2.04 Billion		$1.895 Billion		
NATO "	$2.320 "		$2.295 "		
FMS "	$550 Million		$750 Million		about equal
Manpower	209,000		654,000		1 to 3 ratio
Reserve manpower	404,000		951,000		1 to 2.4 ratio
ARMY					
Manpower	165,000		542,000		
Medium Tanks	**tot.:**	**1,776**	**tot.:**	**3,700**	
M 47		320		900	
M 48A1		585		1,085	
M 48A3		250		—	
M 48A5		265		1,615	
AMX		250		—	Ordered by New Democracy
Leopard		106		77	
Light Tanks	186 M24		100 M41		
APC	**tot.:**	**2,190**	**tot.:**	**3,750**	
M2.M3		120		800	
M59		430		700	
M113		1,000		2,250	
AMX APC		240		—	Ordered by New Democracy
Leonidas		300		—	

*The table and map that follow supplement the article "Defense Policies of PASOK" by George J. Tsoumis, pp. 91-114.

TABLE: BALANCE OF POWER (cont.)

Ground to Air Missiles	36 Hawk	—	
	Chaparal	4 Rapier	
	Red Eye	Red Eye	
Antitank Missiles	Cobra	Cobra	about equal
	Milan	Milan	
	TOW	TOW	
	SS11	SS11	
Field Artillery			
M-101 105mm	180	360	a 1 to 2 ratio plus a large number of World War II artillery
M-101 155mm	270	500	
M-115	72	150	
Self-Propelled Artillery			
M-109 155 mm	100	200	
M-107 175mm	36	72	
M-110 203mm	20	36	
Helicopters			
Bell with TOW	8	—	
Bell 47G	5	20	
Bell UH-ID	22	30	
Augusta Bell	90	65	
Boeing	10	30 (Hughes)	
On Order			
Medium Tanks	300 M48 A5	M60?	All for the next 5-year plan
	106 Leopard	—	
Antitank Missiles	36 TOW	—	
	300 Milan	1,040 Milan	
Strike Helicopters	20 AH-IS	26 Cobra	
		25 UH-1H	
Antiaircraft system	Artemis	Oerlicon Rapier	

TABLE: BALANCE OF POWER (cont.)

NAVY		
Manpower	19,500	50,000
Submarines		
209 Class	8	6
US Guppy	2	9
TANG	—	2
Destroyers		
Gearing	7	9
Sumner	1	1
Fletcher	4	—
Carpenter	—	2
Smith	1	1
Missile Boats		
Combattand		
with Exocet	8	—
with Penguin	6	—
L'Esterel	2	—
Dogan with Harpoon	—	6
ATA with Penguin	—	9
Frigates		
Kontanaer	2	—
US Cannon	4	—
Rhein	1	—
Berg	—	2
Koln	—	2
Torpedo Boats		
Type 143	6	—
S. 141 Jaguar	—	5
Zobel	—	2
Helicopters		
Antisubmarine	14	6
Landing ships	10	For two brigades
On Order		
Submarines 1200	2	1
Strike Ships OL	10	—
Frigates MEKO 200	—	4
Light "	6?	

TABLE: BALANCE OF POWER (cont.)

AIR FORCE		
Manpower	24,000	57,300
Bombers, A-7	50	—
Fighters F-104	66	220
F-5	**tot.: 76**	**tot.: 91**
F-5A	54	30
F-5B	8	16
F-5ERF	14	21
5-5A-B	—	24
F-4E	54	90
F-4ERF	7	7
Mirage	33	—
F-100 O/F	—	40
Cargo C-130 HE	12	7
YS-11-200	6	—
Trans Vall C -160	—	20
C-47	12	40
Noratlas	20	—
AT-11	—	18
Helicopters		
Augusta Bell	12	—
UH-1H	—	15
CH-47C	6	—
On Order		
F-16	40	160
Mirage 2000	40	—
F-4 Phantoms	—	40
War Doctrine	Defense (With Total Popular Defense)	Offensive (Air-Land Battle)

SOURCE: International Institute of Strategic Studies, Great Britain

Map: The Buffer Zone between NATO and the Warsaw Pact

About the Authors

PAUL ANASTASI was born in Cyprus in 1950; he received his bachelor's degree from Southampton University, England, in modern history, politics and sociology, and an M.A. with honors from London University in modern history and current affairs. He is foreign correspondent in Greece for the *New York Times* and the *London Daily Telegraph*. He recently established the Greek Center for the Study of Disinformation and launched a monthly political magazine called *Prote Gramme* (Front Line). Earlier he launched and was the managing editor of the English-language daily newspaper *Athens Star*. Mr. Anastasi is the author of two books in Greek, one dealing with Soviet manipulation of Greece's largest circulation daily, *Ethnos*, and the other with that newspaper's recent legal confrontation in London with *The Economist* magazine. He is currently writing a book in English titled *The Mindbenders: Soviet Manipulation of the Greek Press and Public Opinion.*

THEODORE CHRISTODOULIDES received a Ph.D. from the University of Thessalonike, an LL.M. from the University College, London and did post-graduate studies at the Institute of International Studies in Geneva. He is Professor of International Relations in the Panteios School of Political Science and has specialized in international organizations. His most important publications include *Introduction to the Theory of International Organization* (1979), *International Dimension of the European Economic Community* (2nd Edition, 1984), *International Personality and the Treaty-Making Power of the European Communities* (1986), and *Individual Liberties in the Law of the European Community* (1965).

YANNIS KAPSIS was born in Athens in 1929 and graduated from the Law School of Athens University. He worked as a journalist on Greek and foreign newspapers and magazines. As a young student, Mr. Kapsis was a member, and later secretary general, of the Liberal Youth Organization. In 1970, when he was editor of the newspaper *Ethnos,* he was sentenced to five years of imprisonment by a court martial of the military dictatorship of that time. He served 18 months of that term. Sought by the military police for his part in the events surrounding the uprising of the students of the National Technical University of Athens in 1973, he escaped to England. Following the restoration of democratic government in 1974, he became executive editor of the afternoon newspaper*Ta Nea,* a post which he retained up to the time of his appointment as undersecretary of foreign affairs in April 1982. He has been an active member of the political movement led by Mr. Andreas Papandreou from its beginning, and has actively pursued its objectives for change, especially during the seven years of the dictatorship.

Mr. Kapsis was appointed alternate minister of foreign affairs on September 22, 1987. From April 1982 until September 1987 he served as undersecretary of foreign affairs. Between February and September 1987 he served also as undersecretary of press. One of his primary areas of responsibility at the Foreign Ministry has been Greek-American relations. He was chief Greek negotiator of the Defense and Economic Cooperation Agreement signed between Greece and the United States in 1983. He is a member of the Athens Union of Journalists, the Greek Literary Society, the International Press Institute, the Political Science Society, and the International Federation of Journalists. His publications include *Lost Homelands* (1960), *Liberated Oceans* (1968), *Let Democracy Be Born* (1972), *Press Law and Censorship* (1979), ""Kremlin Conversations" (1981), "Polish Conversations" (1982).

JUDITH KLEINMAN received a B.A. degree in public policy studies from Duke University and an M.A. degree from the University of New South Wales, Sidney (Australia). She served as analyst of the Greek economy for the Board of Directors of the Federal Reserve System. Currently Ms. Kleinman is pursuing post-graduate studies at the London School of Economics.

CHARLES W. McCASKILL was born in South Carolina, and received an B.A. degree in political science from the Citadel and an M.A. in history and political science from the University of South Carolina. He spent one year in Greek area studies at Princeton University. He retired from the Foreign Service of the Department of State in 1985 after 35 years of service. He served in Greece twice: in the American Consulate General in Thessalonike from 1957 to 1960, and in the American Embassy in Athens as counselor of embassy in Nicosia from 1960 to 1964, and later served as Cyprus desk officer in the Department of State for two years.

DEMETRES MICHALOPOULOS was born in Athens in 1952. He studied history in the University of Athens on an honor scholarship of the Greek state (1970-1974). In 1975, he went to Paris, on a French Government scholarship, to pursue post-graduate studies in the École des Hautes Études en Sciences Sociales, where he obtained his doctorate in 1978. During the years 1979-1981 he served in the Navy. One of his tasks was to catalogue all documents held in the Naval Archives. In 1981 he served in the office of Constantine Karamanlis, then president of the Hellenic Republic. In that capacity he was occupied with matters concerning modern Greek political history and relations between Greece and other Balkan States. Since 1982 he has been lecturer in diplomatic history and Greek foreign policy at the University of Thessalonike (Law School). In 1984 he visited the United States as a Fulbright scholar and conducted research on Greek-Albanian relations during the period 1919-1944 in the National Archives, the Library of Congress and the Dag Hammarskjold Library (United Nations). He has written two books: *Vie politique en Grèce pendant les années 1862-1869* (in French) (Athens: published by the University, 1981), and *Relations between Greece and Albania, 1923-1928* (in Greek) (Thessalonike, 1985), and numerous articles in Greek, French and American reviews.

MATTHEW NIMETZ was born in New York City on June 17, 1939, and received degrees from Williams College and the Harvard Law School, where he was president of the Harvard Law Review. He also holds an M.A. from Balliol College, Oxford University, where he was a Rhodes Scholar. Mr. Nimetz served as undersecretary of state for security assistance, science and technology from February through December 1980. In that capacity he supervised the United States security assistance programs, military sales and related security activities of the

Department of State. He also supervised the Department's international scientific and technological programs, including nuclear non-proliferation issues, environmental matters and communications activities. Prior to his appointment as undersecretary he was counselor of the Department of State (1977-1980) serving as senior advisor to the secretary of state, with special responsibilities for Cyprus, the Eastern Mediterranean, Eastern European relations, SALT, and Mexican affairs. Mr. Nimetz is a partner of the law firm of Paul, Weiss, Rifkind, Wharton & Garrison, in New York City, where he specializes in corporate, securities and international law; he is also a trustee of Williams College, chairman of the United Nations Development Corporation, chairman of World Resources Institute, and a member of the Council on Foreign Relations.

ROBERT JOHN PRANGER received a Ph.D. from the University of California at Berkeley in Political Science/Political Theory. At present he is a fellow at the Center for International Development and Conflict Management, University of Maryland. He served as deputy assistant secretary of defense for Near East and South Asian affairs (1969-1970), and as deputy assistant secretary of defense, policy planning and national security council affairs (Office of International Security Affairs). Among his numerous publications are *Nuclear Strategy and National Security* (edited with Roger P. Labrie) (Washington, D.C.: American Enterprise Institute, 1977); *Détente and Defense* (edited volume) (Washington, D.C.: American Enterprise Institute, 1976); *Action, Symbolism and Order: The Existential Dimension of Modern Citizenship* (Nashville: Vanderbilt University Press, 1968); *The Eclipse of Citizenship: Power and Participation in Contemporary Politics* (New York: Holt, Rinehart and Winston, 1968; in Japanese, Tokyo: Keiso Shobo, 1972). Dr. Pranger was resident scholar in international studies at the American Enterprise Institute (1971-1986), where he also served as vice president for external affairs.

JAMES G. PYRROS was administrative assistant to Congressman Lucien Nedzi (D.-Mich) for 19 years (1961-1980) in Washington. He was a board member of the U.S. Committee for Democracy in Greece. Formerly an assistant attorney general, Michigan, he is now an attorney with the Detroit Edison company.

"JEFFREY SCHAFFER" is a pseudonym for a long-time observer of the Greek political scene, who has followed Andreas Papandreou's career closely since Papandreou entered Greek politics in 1964. He has lived in Greece for more than six years and has visited the country numerous times during the past 25 years.

WILLIAM S. SHEPARD served in the Political Section of the U.S. Embassy Athens, Greece. He had responsibility for monitoring the Cyprus issue from 1978 to 1980, the period beginning with the American initiative associated with State Department Counselor Nimetz. During that period, the author discussed the issue with the relevant authorities in Athens, Ankara and Nicosia, as well as with representatives of the Turkish Cypriot community north of the UN-guarded green line. Information was also received from officials at the Embassy of Greece, the Embassy of Turkey, the Department of State, the Embassy of Cyprus, and the unrecognized office of the Turkish Cypriots in Washington, all of whom shared their experiences generously with the author.

SPELIOS SPELIOTOPOULOS was born in Pyrgos (Peloponnese) in 1946. He entered the [Greek] Air Force Academy from which he graduated with honors in Flying and academic subjects in 1968. He attended the Staff Officers School, the Tactical Weapons School and Instructor-Pilot School both in Greece and abroad. He also attended the Institute of South Florida, the Law School of the University of Athens (1974), the Philosophy School of the University of Athens (1978), and Seminar on Air and Space Law, King's College, University of London (1979). He holds a doctorate from the School of Law, Economics and Political Science, University of Athens, where he specialized in Air and Space Law (1981). He served as aide-de-camp to the president of the Greek Republic (Constantine Karamanlis) from 1980-1985 He is a member of the Committee for the Codification of Air Law (Ministry of Communications and Transportation) and associate of the annual law publication, *Litigation Review*. Among his publications are *Air Carrier's Liability for Passenger's Death,*

Injury of Bodily Harm (in Greek) (Athens, 1985) and numerous articles in periodicals and daily newspapers.

NIKOLAOS A. STAVROU received his M.A. in international affairs and his Ph.D. in political science from George Washington University. He is professor of political science/international affairs, Howard University; he has specialized in Eastern Europe and the Balkans. He has also been visiting professorial lecturer on East European affairs at George Washington University. He is the author of *Allied Politics and Military Interventions: The Political Role of the Greek Military* (1978) and editor of *Edvard Kardelj: The Historical Roots of Non-Alignment* (2nd Edition, 1985). He has contributed to numerous scholarly volumes dealing with such subjects as ethnicity, political parties, pressure groups and Albanian affairs. He is a member of the International Studies Association and the International Advisory Board on *Terrorism: An International Resource File.*

LIEUT. GENERAL (RETIRED) GEORGE J. TSOUMIS was born 1930 in Kozani, Macedonia; he graduated from the Greek Military Academy in 1952, from Infantry School in 1956, from the War College in 1966 and from Special Warfare School Fort Bragg USA in 1968 (Honors Graduate). He studied political science and economics in the Aristoteleion University of Thessalonike. He also studied business administration in the Supreme Commercial School of Athens. He served 35 years continuously in the Army as company commander of the 525 Mechanized Infantry Battalion of 575 Marines Battalion and in the National Guard of Cyprus in 1964-65. He has also been commander of 4301 Intelligence Unit in Evros (1960-61), of 5551 Intelligence Unit in Cyprus (1974-76), of 568 Infantry Battalion in Roupel Gap, of 30th Infantry Regiment in Didimotion and of the 2nd Mechanized Infantry Division. As staff officer his service includes AssG3 in A Corps, deputy chief of staff in B Corps, staff officer in Section of National Issues of Hellenic Central Intelligence Agency and defense attaché of the Embassy of Greece in Ankara, Turkey 1981-83. He is also accredited in Iran and Pakistan. He is the honorary commander of 2nd Mechanized Infantry Division, a collaborator of the Foundation of Political Studies and Education, and a member of the Commandos Club of Athens. He has published articles in military and defense journals, in the magazine *Politika Themata* and in the daily *Eleutheros Typos.*

Index

Quantum Waveguide in Microcircuits

Quantum Waveguide in Microcircuits

Jian-Bai Xia | Duan-Yang Liu | Wei-Dong Sheng

Pan Stanford Publishing

Published by

Pan Stanford Publishing Pte. Ltd.
Penthouse Level, Suntec Tower 3
8 Temasek Boulevard
Singapore 038988

Email: editorial@panstanford.com
Web: www.panstanford.com

British Library Cataloguing-in-Publication Data
A catalogue record for this book is available from the British Library.

Quantum Waveguide in Microcircuits

ISBN 978-981-4669-85-6 (Hardback)
ISBN 978-1-315-36477-3 (eBook)

Printed in the USA

Contents

Introduction

Last century, the development of semiconductor microelectronic technology changed the whole world. The world entered the information society from the industrial society. The productive forces rose greatly, which promoted the development of human material and the spirit of civilization. Just because of the importance of semiconductor microelectronic technology, many governments and international companies invested heavily in developing the technology, hoping to make a break through and occupy an advanced position in the development of the whole information technology.

Integrated circuits were invented in 1958, and in subsequent years, development and progress in the degree of integration have largely followed Moore's law. Moore's law is a rule that combines technology development and economics to predict the degree of advancement in microelectronic circuit integration within a specified period. It predicts that the degree of microprocessor integration would double every 18 months in DRAM. Moore's law is still proving accurate today. However, as the sizes of circuit elements approach their physical limits, the optical method used in manufacturing 16-nm-node chips is also approaching a limit. Although the scaling of microelectronic circuit elements still follows Moore's law, the unit density of power consumption will become unacceptable. Therefore, on the one hand, people continuously develop microelectronic technology, while on the other hand, they consider the developing road after Moore's law is broken, that is, more Moore's law or more than Moore's law.

Physically, when the scale of the circuit element decreases to 10 nm or even less, the quantum effect will appear and play an increasingly important role. The electron transport becomes non-classical and non-linear, and even the electron motion likes the waveguide motion. This book consists of two parts: (i) non-classical, non-linear transport, and (ii) quantum waveguide theory.

The first part discusses the quantum correction effect in ultrasmall devices, including strong field transport and transport related to space (Chapter 2). The quantum mechanics effect is most obvious in the longitudinal transport of superlattices because the longitudinal length of the superlattice is about 10 nm, smaller than the electron mean free path. Quantum transport includes resonant tunneling (Chapter 3) and longitudinal transport of a superlattice (Chapter 4), which were observed early in the last century eighties. Due to the development of electron beam lithography in the last century nineties, people can fabricate an ultrathin metallic wire on a two-dimensional electron gas (2DEG). Applying a bias voltage on a metallic contact can form a small quantum dot in the 2DEG underneath the contact. In studying the transport of quantum dots and thin circuits, Landauer and Büttiker proposed their famous formulas named after them. This kind of transport is named mesoscopic transport (Chapter 5). People fabricated 3D quantum dots in the longitudinal direction of a quantum well by using lithography. The quantum dot is confined in the upper and lower directions by the barriers in the original quantum well, and its lateral direction is confined by vacuum due to the lithography. These kinds of quantum dots are similar to an artificial atom, in which the electrons are filled according to the shell. This characteristic is reflected in the quantum transport, for example, the Coulomb blockade (Chapter 6). Last, we introduce the applications of single-electron transport: single-electron transistor (Chapter 7) and single-electron memory (Chapter 8).

The second part studies quantum waveguide theory, mainly our own works. Since the Aharonov–Bohm effect (AB effect) was experimentally discovered by Webb et al., there have been many advances in the transport of mesoscopic systems. Electron transport in mesoscopic systems is not of the diffusing type but of the waveguide type because there are no electron collisions in such small systems. Transport of the waveguide type has many characteristics different from those of the diffusing type, and the theoretical research methods of these two types are also different. The former is based on quantum mechanics, while the latter is based on the classical statistical physics: Boltzmann equation. In application, mesoscopic systems, especially semiconductor mesoscopic systems, will be the basis of next-generation microelectronics.

This part summarizes the research results of our group in this field in the past 20 years. Chapter 9 covers the general concept of quantum transport. Chapter 10 discusses 1D quantum waveguide theory, which proposes two basic equations similar to Kirchhoff equations in electric circuits. Then the two basic equations are applied to many cases: AB rings, quantum interference devices, etc. Last, the theory is extended to the hole case, whose wave function has two components. Chapter 11 describes 2D quantum waveguide theory. When the width of the circuit is so large that the energy level spacing between the transverse modes in the circuit is comparable to the electron kinetic energy, we should consider the transport of multiple transverse modes, that is, 2D waveguide theory. In this chapter, the transfer matrix method, the scattering matrix method, and the theory of a waveguide with multiple terminals are developed. Chapter 12 discusses the 1D quantum waveguide theory of Rashba electrons. In recent years, much attention has been paid to the field of Rashba spin–orbit interaction (RSOI) in low-dimensional semiconductor structures because of its potential application in spintronic devices, which is based on the idea of the possible manipulation of electron spin by a magnetic or an electric field. Chapter 12 extends the 1D quantum waveguide theory of electrons without considering spin to the case of electrons with spin and RSOI, deriving the boundary conditions of the Rashba current. The theory is applied to study the transport of Rashba electrons in turning structures, spin-polarized devices, etc. Chapters 13 and 14 extend the 1D quantum waveguide theory of a Rashba electron in straight-line structures to curved-line structures. For this objective, the transfer matrix method is developed. With this method, the Rashba electron transport in the AB circular ring and square ring and related spin polarization modulation are studied. In Chapter 15, the 1D quantum waveguide theory of a Rashba electron is extended to the 2D case and some basic results are obtained.

In summary, the transport theories and experiments beyond classical transport quantum waveguide are introduced, which are prepared for future semiconductor micro- and nanoelectronics. They will be the basis of next-generation semiconductor electronics and industry. We believe that these theories will have more and more applications, popularization, and developments.

In January 3–8, 2011, I (J.-B. Xia) gave a talk in the IEEE INEC 2010 (HK) titled "Rashba Electron Transport in Quantum Waveguide." Afterward, the director and publisher of Pan Stanford Publishing, Dr. Stanford Chong, wrote to me on February 7, 2011: "You have given an interesting talk on the above topic at the recent IEEE INEC 2010 (HK, 3–8 Jan 2011) and I am wondering if you would be keen to develop this idea into a book.... The scope could be further expanded and the primary aim would be to inspire students and new scientists into the field." Under his kind urge and help, I and my undergraduate colleagues Dr. Duan-Yang Liu and Dr. Wei-Dong Sheng finished this book. Here we would express our sincere thanks to Dr. Chong and the editor Sarabjeet Garcha. We also thank Dr. Hai-Bin Wu and Dr. Yi-Xin Zong for helping to prepare the manuscript.

Jian-Bai Xia
Duan-Yang Liu
Wei-Dong Sheng

Part I

Non-classical, Non-linear Transport

Chapter 1

Properties of Quantum Transport

1.1 Characteristic Length [1]

In traditional transistors, whose length is larger than the average free path of electrons, the electron's movement is classical, which can be described by the Boltzmann equation. But when the scale of a device is so small that its scale is about or smaller than some characteristic lengths, there will be distinct quantum effects of current.

Electrons in two-dimensional electron gas (2DEG) are degenerate at low temperature, so their Fermi wave vector can be written as

$$k_F = \sqrt{2\pi n_s}, \tag{1.1}$$

where n_s is the area density of 2DEG. The electrons' Fermi wavelength is

$$\lambda_F = \frac{2\pi}{k_F} = \sqrt{\frac{2\pi}{n_s}}. \tag{1.2}$$

For electrons with area density $n_s = 5 \times 10^{11}$ cm^{-2}, the Fermi wavelength is about 35 nm, so it is obviously comparable to the scale of mesoscopic devices. At low temperature, electric current

Quantum Waveguide in Microcircuits
Jian-Bai Xia, Duan-Yang Liu, and Wei-Dong Sheng

ISBN 978-981-4669-85-6 (Hardcover), 978-1-315-36477-3 (eBook)
www.panstanford.com

is contributed mostly by electrons near the Fermi energy, and other electrons with energy less than the Fermi energy have no contribution to the conductance. Therefore, the Fermi wavelength is associated with the quantum effect of current.

Electrons which move in a semiconductor are scattered by impurities, defects, or phonons, and their momentum relaxation time τ_{m} and scattering time τ_{s} have the following relationship:

$$\frac{1}{\tau_{\mathrm{m}}}=\frac{1}{\tau_{\mathrm{s}}}\alpha_{\mathrm{m}}, \tag{1.3}$$

where α_{m} is a constant between 0 and 1, and it denotes the effectiveness of different scatterings for the momentum relaxation.

The mean free path L_{m} is defined as the average distance travelled by an electron before it loses its momentum, so it can be written as

$$L_{\mathrm{m}}=v_{\mathrm{F}}\tau_{\mathrm{m}}, \tag{1.4}$$

where v_{F} is the Fermi velocity, and for electrons with area density $n_{\mathrm{s}}=5\times10^{11}\ \mathrm{cm}^{-2}$. On the basis of Eq. 1.1, we obtain

$$v_{\mathrm{F}}=\frac{\hbar k_{\mathrm{F}}}{m^*}=\frac{\hbar}{m^*}\sqrt{2\pi n_{\mathrm{s}}}=3\times10^{7}\ \mathrm{cm/s}, \tag{1.5}$$

where m^* is the electron's effective mass, m_0 is the static mass of an electron. If $m^*=0.067m_0$, $\tau_{\mathrm{m}}\cong100$ ps, then it can be obtained from Eq. 1.4 that $L_{\mathrm{m}}=30$ μm.

The phase relaxation length is defined as the average distance travelled by an electron before the electron wave loses its phase. Similar to the momentum relaxation time τ_{m}, the phase relaxation time τ_{φ} has the following relationship with the scattering time τ_{s}:

$$\frac{1}{\tau_{\varphi}}=\frac{1}{\tau_{c}}\alpha_{\varphi}, \tag{1.6}$$

where α_{φ} is a constant between 0 and 1, and it denotes the effectiveness of different scatterings for the phase destruction.

To understand the concept of phase destruction, we imagine an experiment of AB ring. The incident electron beam splits in two at one end of the ring, then moves along up and down the two arms, then meets at the other end of the ring. If the lengths of each arm are the same, the phases of two waves at the meeting point are equal, and the amplitude increases. Assume that there is an impurity or defect (named scatterer) in one arm. Then it will scatter the electron wave passed. Because the scattering is elastic, it does not change the electron's energy, just its phase. When the two electron waves meet, their phases are unequal, so interference makes the amplitude reduced. Because the scatterer is fixed, the phase relationship between the two paths is definite.

If we apply a magnetic field perpendicular to the ring, the electron wave moving up or down the arm is added or reduced a phase factor, which is in proportion to the magnetic flux Φ through the ring (magnetic field strength multiplied by the area of the ring). Therefore the amplitude of the output electron wave oscillates with Φ, and it is the AB effect. In case there are scatterings in the arms, although the amplitude reduces when $\Phi = 0$ (the magnetic field is zero), when the strength of the field increases, the amplitude's oscillation with Φ doesn't change. When Φ reaches a certain value, the amplitude reaches its maximum. We can say that the loss of the phase at the scatterings has been compensated by the magnetic field. In this condition, we can consider

$$\alpha_\varphi = 0, \ \tau_\varphi \to \infty. \tag{1.7}$$

That is, the elastic scattering of static scatterers does not affect the phase relaxation time. This fact has been proved by the experiment. Experiments found that the length of the two arms of the AB ring is much larger than the mean free path L_m in general—i.e., an electron has experienced repeatedly the momentum elastic scattering, but experiments still observe the AB oscillation.

A major factor which affects the phase relaxation is the inelastic scattering of the electron-phonon. A phonon is a quantum mode of lattice vibrations, and it is not a fixed point as an impurity or a defect, so its scattering on electrons is random. As it is inelastic scattering, in every scattering the electron's energy will increase or decrease the energy of a phonon. When two electron waves scattered by phonons meet, the relationship of their phases is irregular, so the average amplitude of the electron wave reduces. In other words, fixed scatterers do not contribute to phase relaxation; only fluctuating scatterers do.

Assume that after time τ_φ, the mean square energy that the electron gains during phonon scattering is equal to the square of energy that the electron gains each time multiplied by the number of scatterings:

$$(\Delta\varepsilon)^2 = (\hbar\omega)^2 (\tau_\phi/\tau_s), \tag{1.8}$$

where $\hbar\omega$ is the energy of a phonon. The phase relaxation time is defined as that after time τ_φ when the mean square value of an electron's phase change is of orders one:

$$\Delta\varphi \approx (\Delta\varepsilon)\,\tau_\varphi/\hbar \approx 1. \tag{1.9}$$

From Eqs. 1.8 and 1.9 we have

$$\tau_\varphi = \left(\frac{\tau_s}{\omega^2}\right)^{1/3}. \tag{1.10}$$

Therefore the influence of a low-frequency phonon (acoustic phonon) on the phase relaxation is small. A major factor of phase relaxation is the optical phonon.

At low temperature, a major factor of the phase relaxation is electron–electron scattering. The frequency of electron–electron scattering is determined by the difference in electron energy E and Fermi energy E_F: $\Delta = E - E_F$. Because Δ is small, the states which can be scattered are very few according to the Pauli exclusion principle. So the probability of scattering goes to zero. In 2DEG, it has been proved that

$$\frac{\hbar}{\tau_\varphi} \approx \frac{\Delta^2}{E_F}\left[\ln\left(\frac{E_F}{\Delta}\right) + \text{const}\right]. \tag{1.11}$$

Because the hot electron's average energy $\Delta \approx k_B T$, the relationship between τ_φ and T is the formula that Δ is replaced by $k_B T$ in Eq. 1.11.

In high-mobility semiconductors, $\tau_\varphi \le \tau_s$ in general. In low-mobility semiconductors, τ_φ changes less while τ_s decreases greatly, so $\tau_\varphi \gg \tau_s$.

1.2 Non-equilibrium Transport

When the scale of a device is smaller than 100 nm, a few volts in the applied voltage can lead to very high electric fields of the order of 10,000 V/cm. These high fields lead to values of the carrier drift velocity of the order of 10^7 cm/s. Because there is not enough time for these electrons to exchange energy with the surroundings, their average energy is higher than the thermal average value $k_B T$, so that they are called "hot electrons."

When the electric field strength is small, the drift velocity of electrons is proportional to the electron field strength,

$$v_d = \mu E, \tag{1.12}$$

where the proportional coefficient μ is called mobility. The regime where Eq. 1.12 is valid is called the linear-response regime. In this regime, the Einstein relation expresses the diffusion in terms of the mobility and thermal equilibrium temperature as

$$D = \frac{\mu k_B T}{e}, \tag{1.13}$$

where e is the electron charge taken with its sign. The Nyquist relation expresses the available noise power P_{av} of a two-terminal network for unit bandwidth of frequency Δf in terms of the thermal equilibrium temperature as

$$\frac{P_{av}}{\Delta f} = k_B T. \tag{1.14}$$

Therefore, under the thermal equilibrium we have

$$\frac{P_{av}}{\Delta f} = k_B T = \frac{eD}{\mu}. \tag{1.15}$$

Equation 1.15 is just a macroscopic expression of the fluctuation-dissipation theorem.

Under hot-electron conditions, the Einstein and Nyquist relations no longer hold in general. Figure 1.1 schematically shows the drift velocity, diffuse coefficient, and white noise as functions of the electric field in the linear-response and hot-electron regimes [2].

The experimental evidences of the main effects related to the hot-electron conditions are as follows [2], as shown in Fig. 1.1:

(1) Deviation from Ohm's law through a nonlinear dependence of the drift velocity upon electric field strength
(2) Deviation from the Einstein relation of the diffusion coefficient through a diffusivity which depends on the electric field strength

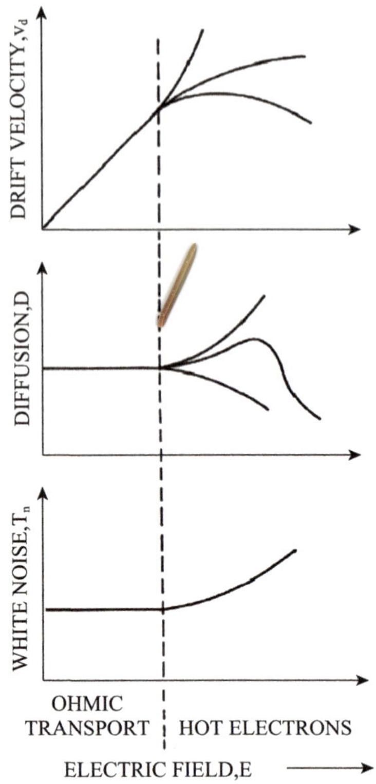

Figure 1.1 Schematic illustration of the drift velocity, diffusion coefficient, and white noise as functions of electric field strength.

(3) Deviation from the Nyquist relation of the noise power per unit bandwidth through an increase of the white-noise temperature T_n

(4) Anisotropy with respect to the direction of the applied electric field of the kinetic coefficients: differential mobility μ', diffusion coefficient D, white-noise temperature T_n

(5) Negative differential mobility for electric field strengths above a threshold value

In the linear-response regime, the transport behavior can be described by the Boltzmann equation, and it can be solved by the perturbation method. In the hot-electron regime, the transport is nonstatic, the distribution function deviates far from the balance distribution function, and its variation with the time is large. It is believed that if the concepts of the Boltzmann equation and the distribution function are still valid, three main assumptions will justify such an approach: (i) Carrier density should be sufficiently low so that only binary collisions occur. (ii) The time between successive collisions, τ, should be long enough when compared with the duration of a collision, τ_{coll}—i.e., $\tau_{\text{coll}}/\tau \ll 1$. (iii) Density gradients should be small over the range of the interparticle potential. In this case the perturbation method cannot be used to solve the Boltzmann equation, but the Monte Carlo method can be.

1.3 Quantum Effect

The hot-electron effect is a nonlinear transport behavior in ultrasmall devices, but the electron movement is still classical. If the scale of the devices becomes smaller and smaller, a series of quantum effects will appears [3].

1.3.1 Statistical Thermodynamics

Generally, modeling of quantum phenomena is more complicated than modeling of classical and/or semiclassical phenomena. For instance, one should consider the full nonlocal nature of the potential interactions in the dynamical variables. Consider a simple potential barrier system, where the potential distribution is

$$V(x) = V_0 u(-x),$$
$$u(x) = \begin{cases} 1, & x \geq 0 \\ 0, & x < 0 \end{cases} \tag{1.16}$$

where $u(x)$ is the Heavyside step function. For the case $V_0 \to \infty$, the Wigner distribution as a function of space coordinate x and momentum k obtained quantum mechanically is shown in Fig. 1.2 [4]. It may be seen that far from the barrier, the distribution approaches the classical Maxwellian form, but near the barrier it differs greatly. The repulsion from the barrier is required by the vanishing of the wave function at the barrier, but the first peak of

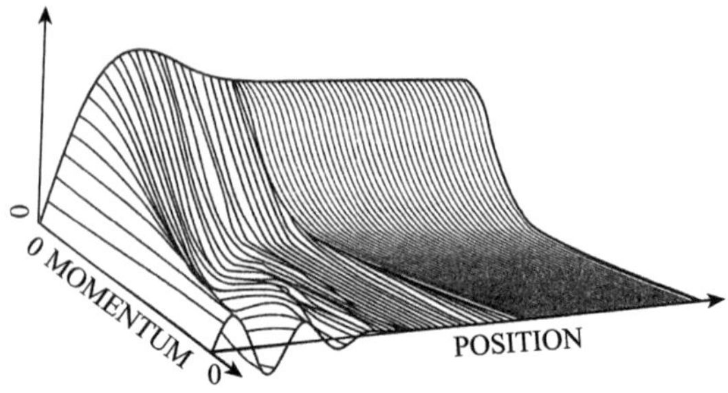

Figure 1.2 The Wigner distribution function as a function of space coordinate x and momentum k for a half infinite barrier.

the wave function, as one moves away from the barrier, occurs closer to the barrier for higher-momentum states. This variation exists for distances of the order of several thermal de Broglie wavelengths,

$$\lambda_{\mathrm{D}} = \left(\frac{\hbar^2}{2m^* k_{\mathrm{B}} T}\right)^{1/2}. \tag{1.17}$$

Thus, nonlocal variation can be expected over the range of 20–40 nm even at room temperature.

It is clear that the electron density no longer varies simply according to the Boltzmann distribution. The statistical mechanics should be modified with quantum mechanics, which is related to the electron momentum. One form introduces a quantum pressure term as a modification of the electron temperature,

$$\beta^{-1} = k_{\mathrm{B}} T_{\mathrm{e}} - \frac{\hbar^2}{8m^*} \nabla^2 \ln(n). \tag{1.18}$$

Although the results obtained using this model are in agreement with the intuitive expectations, the correction term does not have the momentum dependence expected from Fig. 1.2.

People attempt to more properly treat quantum effects without such hydrodynamic approximations. A problem with the use of quantum approaches to device modeling is that most quantum discussions, especially those of quantum transport, tend to revolve around closed systems, whereas most devices are open systems. In treating such open systems quantum mechanically, it is quite difficult to properly define the reservoir (thermal equilibrium contact) regions, as well as the interface regions between the reservoirs and the active device region. Because of the nonlocal nature of the quantum system, errors in defining the contact region will propagate throughout the device, often leading to spurious results.

The double-barrier resonant tunneling diode (DBRTD) is a typical device of quantum mechanical effect. The Wigner distribution function is calculated from the density matrix through the Fourier transform, often called a Weyl transform. The Wigner distribution has been used to model the DBRTD. It is found that the Wigner function shows a depletion region in the cathode area, which arises from a contact potential drop and the tendency to form a bound state in this area. Such contact potential drops are typical of most open systems, whether classical or quantum. Generally, the cathode "barrier" will develop when there is a mismatch between the injection characteristics of the cathode reservoir and the dissipative nature of the active device region. It is largely eliminated if a lightly doped region is introduced adjacent to the barrier layers.

1.3.2 Phase-Coherent Effect

When electrons pass through a device, if the size of the device is smaller than electrons' coherent length (inelastic mean free path), different waves will interfere. The coherent effect will result in additional scattering, then reduce the conductivity. In addition, the coherent effect also will result in the Aharonov–Bohm effect, universal conductance fluctuation, etc. All these are named mesoscopic effects.

One of important problems is the conductance fluctuation caused by quantum effects. Assume that the action area of the gate is $0.1 \times 0.05\ \mu m^2$, and carrier concentration in the inversion layer is $2 \times 10^{12}\ cm^{-2}$, then there are only 100 electrons under the gate. The conductance change caused by the phase coherence is on the order of e^2/h, about 40 μS. If the normal conductivity is 1000 mS/mm, then for a device with a gate width of 0.1 μm, the total conductance is 100 μS. Therefore, the conductance fluctuation caused by the phase coherence is 40% of total conductance, so it will limit the performance of the device greatly.

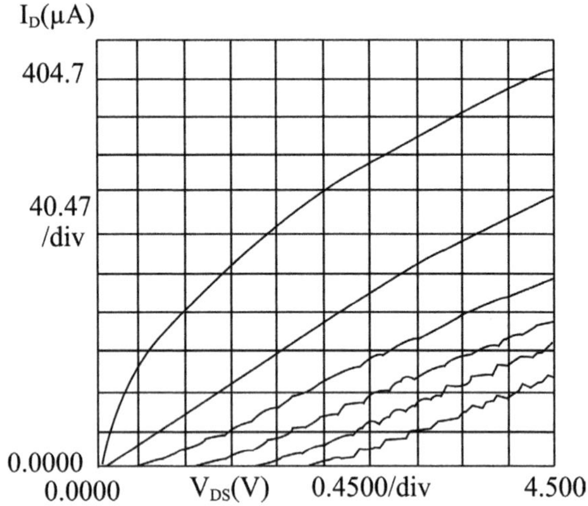

Figure 1.3 Current–voltage curves for a MESFET of 45 nm gate length and 20 μm gate width.

Figure 1.3 shows the current–voltage curves for a MESFET of 45 nm gate length and 20 μm gate width. Fluctuations, which are not time varying but d.c. fluctuations, are clearly evident in this figure, and these are estimated to have a rms (root-mean-square) amplitude of about 10 μS. In spite of the large gate width, it appears that the quantum fluctuations are clearly evident even at 300 K. Although the amplitudes of the conductance differ greatly, the fluctuations are of comparable rms amplitude. This strongly suggests a fundamental origin such as quantum interference.

A 0.1 μm gate width device is quite nearly a device formed on a quantum wire, which can be looked upon as a quantum wire device. The quantum wire has a series of the transverse bound states. When the gate potential increases, the number of the electron channels increases, resulting in a step-type jump in the conductance. The height of the step is $2e^2/h$. Figure 1.4 is the variation of the conductance of a wire with a rough boundary as the Fermi energy (gate potential) is varied. The upper curve is for $\Delta/\lambda_F = 0.1$, and the lower curve is for $\Delta/W = 0.1$, where Δ is the variation of the gate width, λ_F is the Fermi wavelength, W is the gate width, and L is the gate length. From Fig. 1.4 we see that the conductance curves

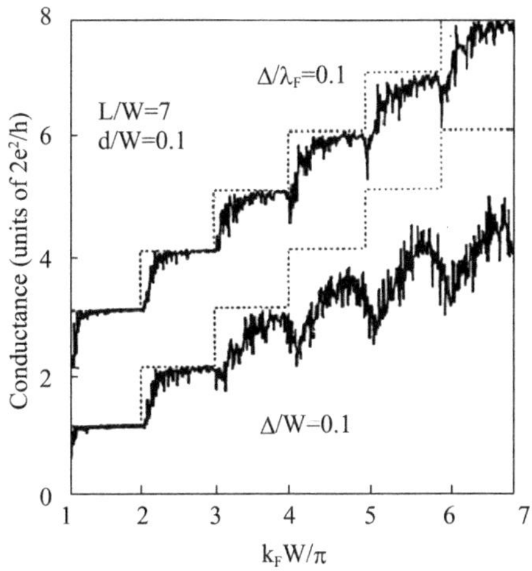

Figure 1.4 Variation of the conductance of a wire with the Fermi energy.

are basically of step form, and derivate from the step form due to the fluctuation of the gate width. Thus, the fluctuation of the gate width is also a reason behind the conductance fluctuation for narrow devices.

In addition, if the orbit of a ballistic electron surrounds an obstacle, such as an impurity atom, then interference between two orbits also will result in the phase-coherent effect. Especially when there is a perpendicular magnetic field in the area surrounded by two orbits, the Ahanorov–Bohm effect (AB effect) will occur. Here, the wave function in the closed loop can be expressed by the integral along the loop:

$$\Psi \approx \exp\left[\frac{e}{\hbar}\left(\int_1 \boldsymbol{A}\cdot d\boldsymbol{l} - \int_2 \boldsymbol{A}\cdot d\boldsymbol{l}\right)\right] = \exp\left[\frac{e}{\hbar}\oint \boldsymbol{B}\cdot d\boldsymbol{S}\right]$$
$$= \exp\left(\frac{\Phi}{\Phi_0}\right), \qquad (1.19)$$

where $\Phi_0 = h/e$ is the magnetic flux quantum. The electric current passing through the closed loop will oscillate periodically with the magnetic flux. When a current of 10 mA passes through the loop, if there is a magnetic field of 0.02 T, then the AB effect can result in distinct fluctuation.

1.3.3 Coulomb Blockade Effect

Experiments found that for a small quantum dot, only when the electric voltage is larger than a certain value, the electron can pass through the dot. The reason is that the Coulomb interaction between the electron in the quantum dot and electron in the circuit will reject the entry of the second electron to the quantum dot. Only when the energy of the electron exceeds the Coulomb interaction energy, the second electron can enter the quantum dot and the current can occur. This appearance is called Coulomb blockade effect, and the relationship curve between voltage and current has the shape of a step, which is called Coulomb staircase. The Coulomb blockade effects have been observed in 2DEG systems in Si-MOSFET and GaAs heterojunction.

From the point of view of large-scale integrated circuits, all the above effects are unfavorable, and we should avoid these in design. On the other hand, these mesoscopic effects may be utilized in the new generation of electronic devices. For example, in a device which has a size smaller than the inelastic scattering mean free path, electrons follow the motion law of quantum mechanics, so we can utilize properties of quantum interference and quantum waveguide to design a device and to control the movement of electrons. And we can design a single-electron transistor by using Coulomb blockade effects, which can greatly reduce the number of electrons stored in one bit, and can reduce power dissipation of memory devices. Because the spin of electron has a much longer scattering time and distance than that of the electric charge, we can utilize spin as the information carrier to design spintronics devices and so on.

1.4 Landauer–Büttiker Formula

Datta first proposed the concept of quantum device in 1989 [5], which can be understood only by considering the electron's wave property. Concepts which can describe the electron's movement are no longer the scattering probability, relaxation time, mobility, and so on. For a two-terminal device, assume that a^+, a^- and b^+, b^- are amplitudes of the electron wave in the input circuit and output

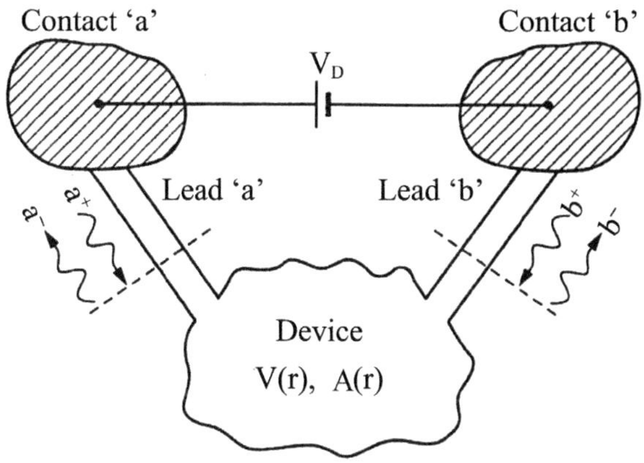

Figure 1.5 Two-terminal device, where a^+, a^- and b^+, b^- are amplitudes of the electron wave in the input circuit and output circuit, respectively.

circuit, respectively. Then, for a definite energy E, they can be related by a scattering matrix,

$$\begin{pmatrix} a^- \\ b^- \end{pmatrix} = \begin{pmatrix} r(E) & t'(E) \\ t(E) & r'(E) \end{pmatrix} \begin{pmatrix} a^+ \\ b^+ \end{pmatrix}, \tag{1.20}$$

where $r(E), r'(\mathrm{E})$ and $t(E), t'(E)$ denote reflection and transmission coefficients, respectively, which are determined by the internal potential and structure.

The circuit has a certain width, and there are transverse modes with different energy. In general, the transport in the longitudinal direction is of multimode, so the amplitudes a^+, a^- are column matrices with size $(M_a \times 1)$, b^+, b^- are column matrices with size $(M_b \times 1)$. Similarly, r is a matrix with size $(M_a \times M_b)$, t is a matrix with size $(M_b \times M_a)$, and so on. M_a and M_b are the number of transverse modes in the input circuit and output circuit, respectively.

In the Landauer–Büttiker formula, the conductance is expressed by the scattering matrix, so this theory is suitable for solving the conductance of a system which is made of different materials or conductors of different shapes that are put in contact with each other. This theory is the basic theory in the research on mescoscopic transport.

Suppose that an electron moves in an ideal conductor along the z axis, and neglect the positive ions in lattice points and scattering of positive electric charge on the electron. In the absence of a magnetic field (so take no account of spin), the Hamiltonian of the electron is

$$H = \frac{p^2}{2m} + V(x, y), \tag{1.21}$$

where $V(x)$ is the lateral confinement potential in the wire. On the basis of the Hamiltonian (1.21), we can obtain the system's eigenstate:

$$\Psi_{\alpha k}(x, y, z) = \frac{1}{\sqrt{2\pi}} e^{ikz} \phi_\alpha(x, y), \tag{1.22}$$

where k is the wave vector along the z direction of the wire, α denotes the α-th transverse eigenstate, and the eigenenergy corresponding to the α-th eigenstate is $E_{\alpha k} = E_\alpha + \hbar^2 k^2/2m$. The first term and the second term are lateral and longitudinal energy, respectively, and the lateral energy E_α is determined by the lateral confinement potential $V(x)$. We can use a square potential well to express the lateral confinement potential of an ideal wire. Suppose that the well in one direction is very narrow, and the width in another direction is W, then the lateral energy $E_\alpha = (n\hbar\pi)^2/2mW^2$ has discrete energy levels. Therefore, the energy spectrum of the system is made up of a series of parabolic and discrete energy subbands, and the minimum value of the corresponding curve is E_α.

When $T = 0$ K, the current in the α-th channel of the wire can be expressed as

$$\begin{aligned} I_\alpha &= \frac{2}{2\pi} \int_0^{k_{\max}} e v_{\alpha k} dk = \frac{2}{2\pi} \int_0^{k_{\max}} e v_{\alpha k} \frac{dk}{dE_{\alpha k}} dE_{\alpha k} \\ &= \frac{2e}{h} (\mu - E_\alpha), \end{aligned} \tag{1.23}$$

where $v_{\alpha k} = 1/\hbar \times dE_{\alpha k}/dk$ is the electron's group velocity, and μ is the chemical potential (Fermi energy level).

If the width of the ideal conductor is small enough, then the energy gap between two energy subbands will be large enough so that the electron can just occupy the lowest energy band, and then this energy band will become the one and only allowed channel. At present we can calculate the net current in the wires with the chemical potentials μ_1 and μ_2, respectively, connected to each other:

$$I = I_1 - I_2 = \left(\frac{2e}{h}\right)\mu_1 - \left(\frac{2e}{h}\right)\mu_2 = \left(\frac{2e^2}{h}\right)(V_1 - V_2). \tag{1.24}$$

Therefore, the conductance of the two-terminal and single-channel device is

$$G = \frac{I}{V_1 - V_2} = \frac{2e^2}{h}. \tag{1.25}$$

This is the Landauer formula of the two-terminal and single-channel system; $2e^2/h$ is called the quantum conductance.

If the wire has finite width, the electron may occupy several subbands. Assume that N subbands have been filled in, and $f(E)$ denotes the probability that the subbands have been occupied by the electron. At present the current can be written as

$$I = \frac{2e}{h}\int_0^{\infty} dE\left[f_1(E)\sum_i T_i(E) - f_2(E)\sum_j T_j(E)\right], \tag{1.26}$$

where $T_i = \sum_j T_{ij} = \sum_j |t_{ij}|^2$ denotes the total transmission probability that an electron transport from all channels of wire 1 to the i-th channel of wire 2. $f_1(E)$ and $f_2(E)$ are the Fermi–Dirac distribution function in the wire 1 and wire 2, respectively. Therefore the current of the system is

$$I = \frac{2e}{h}\int dE\,[f(E) - f(E + V_D)]T(E), \tag{1.27}$$

where $f(E)$ is the Fermi–Dirac distribution function, $V_D = V_1 - V_2$ is the bias voltage on the system, $T(E) = \Sigma_i T_i(E)$ is the total transmission probability. For a small bias, Eq. 1.27 can be simplified as

$$G = \frac{I}{V_D} = \frac{2e^2}{h}\int dE\left(-\frac{\partial f}{\partial E}\right)T(E). \tag{1.28}$$

At low temperature, $-\partial f/\partial E = \delta(E - E_F)$, then in the end we obtain

$$G = \frac{2e^2}{h}T(E_F) = \frac{2e^2}{h}\sum_{i=1}^{M_a}\sum_{j=1}^{M_b}\left|t_{ij}(E_F)\right|^2. \tag{1.29}$$

where $t_{ij}(E_F)$ is the transmission coefficient shown in Eq. 1.20, and Eq. 1.29 is the Landauer–Büttiker formula for the two-terminal and multichannel device. It follows that the key point of utilizing the Landauer–Büttiker formula is solving the transmission coefficient matrix t. Most research studies on mesoscopic transport focus on this problem.

The two-terminal Landaure formula can be extended to the multi-terminal device. Considering a three-terminal device, we can write its scattering matrix functions similar to Eq. 1.20:

$$\begin{pmatrix} a^- \\ b^- \\ c^- \end{pmatrix} = \begin{pmatrix} r_{aa} & t_{ab} & t_{ac} \\ t_{ba} & r_{bb} & t_{bc} \\ t_{ca} & t_{cb} & r_{cc} \end{pmatrix} \begin{pmatrix} a^+ \\ b^+ \\ c^+ \end{pmatrix}. \tag{1.30}$$

Büttiker has proved that current I_i $(i = a, b, c)$ has the following relationship with the chemical potential of every circuit μ_i:

$$I_i = \frac{2e^2}{h} \sum_{j=a,b,c} \left(T_{ij}\mu_j - T_{ji}\mu_i\right), \tag{1.31}$$

where

$$T_{ij} = \sum_{m,n=1}^{M} \left|\left(t_{ij}\right)_{mn}\right|^2. \tag{1.32}$$

When there is no external magnetic field, $T_{ij} = T_{ji}$, Eq. 1.31 can be written as

$$I_i = \frac{2e^2}{h} \sum_{j=a,b,c} T_{ij}\left(\mu_j - \mu_i\right), \tag{1.33}$$

where $\mu_j - \mu_i$ corresponds to the bias voltage between two circuits. The conductance between each pair of circuits can be defined as

$$G_{ij} = \tfrac{2e^2}{h} T_{ij},\ i,\ j = a,\ b,\ c\ (i \neq j). \tag{1.34}$$

Equations 1.29 and 1.31 are the fundamental formulas of quantum conductance. They form the theoretical basis of future quantum devices. For a certain device, we should obtain scattering matrices $r_{aa}(E)$, $t_{ab}(E)$, ... It is shown in Eq. 1.31 that the quantum device is nonlocal, and change of any terminal's chemical potential will influence currents in all circuits.

1.5 Quantum Interference Transistor

By using the interference effect of the electron wave, Datta [5] proposed the concept of "quantum interference transistor," as shown in Fig. 1.6a. The structure consists of a conducting channel with a barrier in the middle. The length L is small enough so that electrons

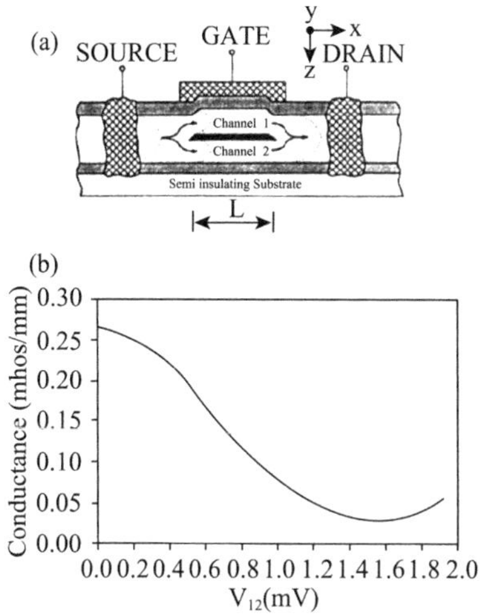

Figure 1.6 (a) A proposed quantum interference transistor, which consists of a conducting channel with a barrier in the middle. (b) Calculated conductance versus potential difference between the channels.

travel ballistically across it. The channels are narrow enough to be single-mode in the *z* direction. Without a gate voltage, the two channels have been assumed to be perfectly symmetric, so that the electrons passing channels 1 and 2 have the same phases when they meet at the drain of the device, the amplitude of the electron wave—i.e., the conductance will be maximum. But an applied gate voltage changes the average potential in channel 1 with respect to that in channel 2, resulting in the phase difference of electron waves traveling in channel 1 and channel 2, and the decrease in the conductance. Figure 1.6b shows the calculated conductance versus bias gate voltage, i.e., potential difference between the channels.

Figure 1.7a is another quantum interference transistor proposed by Datta [5]. It differs from the ordinary transistor in that the gate is not at the position between the source and the drain, but at the position beside the source and the drain. Thus it provides two primary paths from the source to the drain, with the gate controlling their interference, much like the Ahanonov–Bohm device. The length L can be controlled by the gate voltage, as shown in Fig. 1.7a. Figure 1.7b is the calculated conductance as a function of the

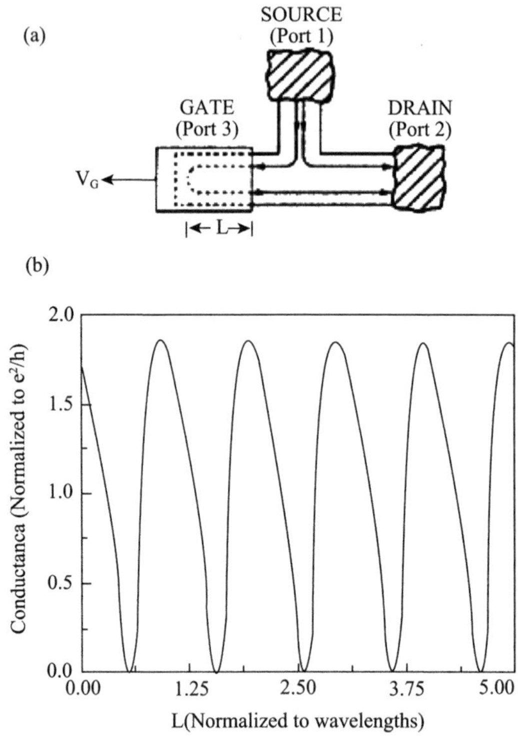

Figure 1.7 (a) Another proposed quantum interference transistor, which has the gate beside the source and the drain. (b) Calculated conductance versus the length *L*.

effective length *L*. From the figure we see that the conductance is modulated by 100% as the length *L* is changed. Therefore, the quantum interference transistor controls current not by changing the number of electrons, but by changing the phase.

In order to calculate the scattering matrix the authors proposed a one-dimensional quantum waveguide theory [6], which can be used to explain intuitively the above A-B devices and the quantum interference transistors, and which is also suitable for any shape and structure of one-dimensional quantum waveguide circuits. We also consider the quantum waveguide circuits with definite width. For details, see Chapter 9 and hereafter.

1.6 Spintronics Devices

Electron spin, or intrinsic electronic angular momentum, is another intrinsic property of electron besides electric charge. The electron spin has two discrete values $\pm\hbar/2$, which are generally named spin-up and spin-down states respectively. This is very similar to the high and low levels or switch off and switch on, which are used to realize logic 1 and 0 states. Thus, the 1/2 spin system is an ideal two-level system, and spin-up and spin-down states are an ideal choice to realize the quantum bit in quantum calculation. Recently, in traditional electronic industry, device integration has become higher and higher, and the size of devices smaller and smaller, which results in distinct quantum effects and too much energy consumption. Therefore, naturally, people think of utilizing spin-free degree, which was formerly always neglected, to replace or to combine the charge-free degree. The research on how to control spin-free degree effectively has attracted wide attention from scientists, and was named *spintronics* by S. A. Wolf et al. formally in 2001 [7]. Spintronics researches a particle's spin in a solid and applies it in devices, and it contains spin polarization's produce, control, transport, and exploitation. It is an interdiscipline field which involves electronics, magnetism, optics, and micro- and nanoprocessing technology. According to the materials researched, it can be grouped into two areas: metal spintronics and semiconductor spintronics.

Ideal spintronics devices realize functions by controlling spin orientation and spin, so they may not be restricted by the number of electric charges and energy dissipation. They have lower power dissipation and faster running speed. Moreover, electronic storage devices based on spin have the advantage of nonvolatility. These devices clearly show that spintronics will have wide prospects of development and application in areas of quantum calculation, communication, molecules, chemistry, and so on. Therefore, people expect spintronics to construct the physical foundation of a new generation of nanoelectronics, and spintronic devices to replace the current microelectronic devices.

The symbol of spintronics' birth is the discovery of the giant magnetoresistance (GMR) of the metallic multilayer structure in

1988 [8, 9]. The proposal of spin valves and room temperature magnetic sensor utilizing anisotropic magnetoresistance make GMRs a great success in commerce. Nowadays a new generation of the magnetic head of high-density disk is using the GMR principle. Thanks to the high sensitivity to the magnetic field of GMR, each GMR magnetic head has be reduced to 30–50 nm, and more than 4 T volume in desktops and more than 1 T volume in laptops have been realized.

Now spintronics devices that are practical are mostly made of metal magnetic materials, which belong to the first category of spintronics, i.e., magnetoelectronics. In 1995 scientists found a new phenomenon, tunneling magnetoresistance (TMR) [10]. When the moments of the above and underneath ferromagnetic layers change from parallel to antiparallel, the tunneling resistance changes 20–30%. The magnetic tunnel junction (MTJ) utilizing the TMR technology has been created, and new magnetoresistive random access memory (MRAM) is expected to replace nonvolatile memory based on CMOS. This new generation of memory has advantages such as no loss on data when power fails, rapid reading speed comparable to static random access memory (SRAM), and large memory space comparable to dynamic random access memory (DRAM), so it has wide application prospects.

The second category of spintronics mainly studies semiconductors, and it hopes to create an imbalance of spin number to realize spin transistor and spin valve, and then replace traditional electronic devices. These new spintronic devices have characteristics such as low energy consumption and rapid switching speed. Because ready-made mature semiconductor technology and equipment can be used to reduce developing cost, these devices have attracted wide attention. To utilize spin-free degree in semiconductors, we must produce, keep, control, and detect the spin polarization of carriers.

There are several methods which can produce spin current: ohmic injection, tunnel injection, ballistic electron injection, utilizing the giant Zeeman splitting of a dilute magnetic semiconductor (DMS) in a magnetic field, utilizing a ferromagnetic semicondutor (FMS) as spin calibrator, the optical method, and so on. Ohmic injection uses a ferromagnetic metal (FM) as electrode to inject spin-polarized electrons. If the ohmic contact is created in the junction between FM and semiconductor, then it can be expected that the spin-polarized current in the FM can be injected into the semiconductor. However, the ohmic contact by heavy doping produces scattering of spin flip, which reduces spin polarization. At $T < 10$ K, from FM-InAs ohmic contact, spin-polarized electrons of 4.5% have been obtained [11]. At room temperature, from the Fe-GaAs contact, spin-polarized electrons of 2% have been obtained [12].

As for how to control the spin polarization of carriers in a semiconductor, various semiconductor spintronic devices have been proposed. The spin field-effect transistor (SFET) proposed by Datta and Das in 1989 [13] is one such original device, and also the most famous one. Other important ones include the graphene spin field-effect transistor, metal-oxide-silicon spin field-effect transistor, Johnson spin switch, unipolar spin transistor, and so on. Despite making great efforts, people have not succeeded even with the original Datta–Das transistor yet, which shows that we have a long way to go, and there is much work to do.

The spin transistor first proposed by Datta and Das [13] is based on controlling the spin of an electron. The principle it works on is shown in Fig. 1.8a.

The principle of the electro-optic modulator shown in Fig. 1.8a should be introduced first. A polarizer at the input polarizes the light at 45° to the y axis (in the $y - z$ plane), which can be represented as combination of the z- and y-polarized light:

$$\begin{pmatrix} 1 \\ 1 \end{pmatrix}_{(45^\circ \text{ pol})} = \begin{pmatrix} 1 \\ 0 \end{pmatrix}_{(z \text{ pol})} + \begin{pmatrix} 0 \\ 1 \end{pmatrix}_{(y \text{ pol})}. \tag{1.35}$$

Because of the electro-optic material the dielectric constant ε_{zz} is slightly different from ε_{yy}. As this light passes through the electro-optic material, the two polarizations suffer different phase shifts $k_1 L$ and $k_2 L$, where L is the length of the crystal. The light emerging from the electro-optic material is represented as $((e^{ik_1^L})/(e^{ik_2^L}))$. The analyzer at the output lets the light with polarization (1/1) to pass through, so the output power P_0 is given by

$$P_0 \propto \left| \begin{pmatrix} 1 & 1 \end{pmatrix} \begin{pmatrix} e^{ik_1 L} \\ e^{ik_2 L} \end{pmatrix} \right|^2 = 4 \cos^2 \frac{(k_1 - k_2) L}{2}. \tag{1.36}$$

The light output is modulated by a gate voltage that controls the difference between the phase shifts $\Delta\theta = (k_1 - k_2)L$.

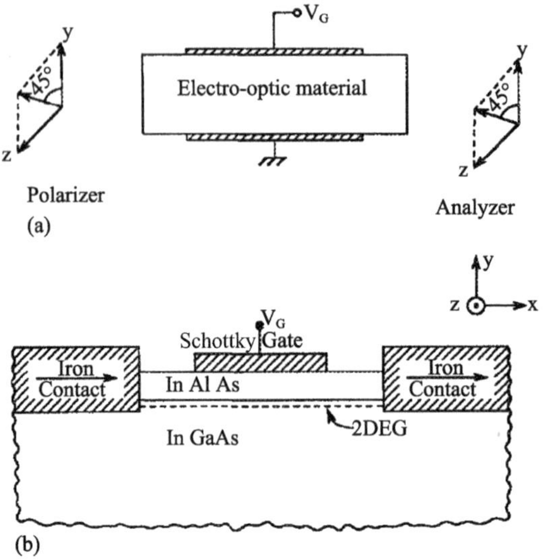

Figure 1.8 (a) Electro-optic modulator. (b) Spin transistor similar to electro-optic modulator.

The theorem of the spin transistor is based on the interaction of the electron orbit and spin, i.e., the Rashba interaction [14],

$$H_{\mathrm{R}} = \frac{\alpha}{\hbar}(\sigma \times p)_{y} = i\alpha\left(\sigma_{x}\frac{\partial}{\partial z} - \sigma_{z}\frac{\partial}{\partial x}\right), \tag{1.37}$$

where α is named the Rashba coefficient, generally being $1 - 10 \times 10^{-10}$ eV · cm, and σ_x and σ_z are the Pauli matrices. In the case of Fig. 1.8b the gate voltage produces a perpendicular electric field to the two-dimensional electron gas (2DES); i.e., it produces a nonsymmetric potential with respect to the $x - z$ plane, which produces a Rashba interaction between the orbit and spin of electrons, as shown in Eq. 1.37. The Rashba coefficient α is proportional to the electric field.

In the spin transistor shown in Fig. 1.8b, both ends are FM iron contacts, which are magnetized in the x direction and correspond to the polarizer and the analyzer in the electro-optic modulator of Fig. 1.8a. Electrons injected through the source electrode are spin-polarized along the x direction, which can be represented as a linear combination of positive z-polarized and negative z-polarized electrons:

$$\begin{pmatrix}1\\1\end{pmatrix}_{(+x\text{ pol})} = \begin{pmatrix}1\\0\end{pmatrix}_{(+z\text{ pol})} + \begin{pmatrix}0\\1\end{pmatrix}_{(-z\text{ pol})}. \quad (1.38)$$

Due to the Rashba term (1.30), in the absence of a magnetic field, the Rashba term causes the spin-up and spin-down states to split. If an electron is traveling in the x direction with $k_x \neq 0$ and $k_z = 0$, then considering the Rashba term, the energies of the electron can be written as

$$\begin{aligned} E\,(+z\text{ pol}) &= \frac{\hbar^2 k_{x1}^2}{2m^*} + \alpha k_{x1}, \\ E\,(-z\text{ pol}) &= \frac{\hbar^2 k_{x2}^2}{2m^*} - \alpha k_{x2}. \end{aligned} \quad (1.39)$$

Electrons with two kinds of spin polarization have the same energy, and it can be proved that they have different wave vectors. Their difference is

$$k_{x2} - k_{x1} = \frac{2m^*\alpha}{\hbar^2}. \quad (1.40)$$

Therefore there is a differential phase shift for spin-up and spin-down electrons after they pass through the junction area, and this shift is shown as

$$\Delta\theta = (k_{x2} - k_{x1})\,L = \frac{2m^*\alpha L}{\hbar^2}. \quad (1.41)$$

For InGaAs/InAlAs heterostructures, from the experimentally observed zero-field spin splitting, α was estimated to be $\sim 3.9^{-10}$ eV·cm. To make a phase difference of π, L is about 0.67 μm, which is less than the mean free path (≥ 1 μm) in high-mobility semiconductors at low temperatures. Therefore we can change the gate voltage, and then change the Rashba coefficient α to modulate the spin current just as the electric-optic modulator.

1.7 Carbon-Based Electronics [14]

In the last few decades, microelectronics has made dramatic advances, including the continuous miniaturization or "scaling" of electronic devices, particularly of the silicon-based large-scale integrated circuit (LSIC). However, this device scaling and performance enhancement cannot continue forever. A number of limitations in the fundamental scientific as well as technological nature of silicon devices place limits on their ultimate size and performance.

The approaches towards making a breakthrough in the limits are divided into two types. One is moving away from the traditional electron transport-based electronics: e.g., the development of spin-based devices. The other approach maintains the operating principles of the currently used devices, primarily those of the field-effect transistor, but replaces a key component of the device, the conducting channel, with carbon nanomaterials such as one-dimensional (1D) carbon nanotubes (CNTs) or two-dimensional (2D) graphene layers, which have superior electric properties. This book focuses mainly on the first kind of research and introduces only carbon-based devices in this section. The main problem with carbon-based devices is that it is difficult to integrate them into one large-scale circuit as silicon-based devices. Now the single carbon nanotube field-effect transistor (CNTFET) and graphene nano-ribbon field-effect transistor (GNRFET) have emerged.

Recently, graphene became the object of intense experimental study when it was realized that single layers, or a few layers, could be produced relatively easily by mechanical exfoliation of graphite [15], or by heating SiC [16]. Figure 1.9a shows the carbon atom structure in a honeycomb arrangement, and Fig. 1.9b shows the electronic band structure of this 2D material [14]. From Fig. 1.9b we see that the linear dispersion at low energies near the Γ point in the Brillouin

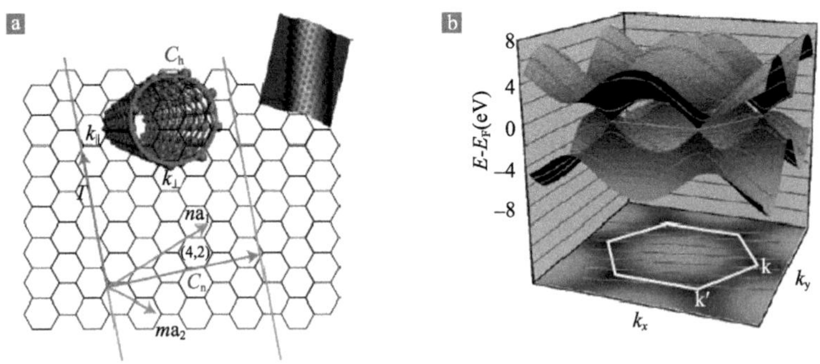

Figure 1.9 (a) Atomic structures of graphene and carbon nanotube. (b) Electronic structure of graphene.

zone makes the electrons and holes in graphene mimic relativistic particles that are described by the Dirac relativistic equation for particles with spin 1/2. Their dispersion,

$$E = \hbar v_F \sqrt{k_x^2 + k_y^2}, \quad (1.42)$$

where $v_F \approx 10^6$ m/s is the Fermi velocity. The linear dispersion means that quasi-particles in graphene display properties quite different from those of conventional semiconductor materials—e.g., the anomalous quantum Hall effect and half-integer quantization of the Hall conductivity. The quantum Hall effect in graphene can be observed even at room temperature.

1.7.1 Electronic Structure

As in Fig. 1.9a, the CNT is thought of as being formed by the rolling of a piece of a ribbon of graphene to form a seamless cylinder. The rolling process forming the nanotube and the resulting nanotube structure are specified by a pair of integers (n, m) defining the chiral vector,

$$\mathbf{C}_h = n\mathbf{a}_1 + m\mathbf{a}_2, \quad (1.43)$$

where $\mathbf{a}_1$ and $\mathbf{a}_2$ are the unit vectors of the graphene honeycomb lattice. The length of $\mathbf{C}_h$ describes the circumference of the nanotube $\mathbf{C}_h = \pi d_{CNT}$. The periodic boundary conditions around the circumference of a nanotube require that the component of the momentum along the circumference, $\mathbf{k}_\perp$, be quantized: $\mathbf{C}_h\mathbf{k}_\perp = 2\pi\nu$, where ν is a non-zero integer. This quantization leads to the formation of metallic and semiconducting nanotubes.

Whereas the infinite 2D graphene is a semi-metal, if the graphene is a narrow ribbon, there will be a gap in the energy band due to the quantization of k_x or k_y. The bandgap is inversely proportional to the width W of the GNR, and is approximately given by

$$E_g \approx 2\pi\hbar v_F/(3W). \quad (1.44)$$

The electronic states in GNRs are not degenerate, whereas those of CNTs are doubly degenerate. This is due to the difference in the boundary conditions: in a GNR the wavefunction has to vanish at the edges, whereas in a CNT the wavefunction is periodic in the direction of the circumference.

1.7.2 Electric Properties

The 1D nature of the electronic states of CNTs leads to a new type of quantized resistance related to its contacts with three-dimensional (3D) macroscopic objects such as metal electrodes. The confinement of the electrons in the CNT around its circumference produces a small number of discrete states (modes) that overlap the continuous states of the metal electrodes. This mismatch of the number of states that can transport the current in the CNTs and the electrodes leads to a quantized contact resistance, R_Q. The resistance is determined by the number of modes, M, in the CNT that have energies lying between the Fermi levels of the electrodes:

$$R_Q = \frac{h}{2e^2 M}. \tag{1.45}$$

For a metal CNT, $M = 2$, so that $R_Q = h/4e^2 = 6.45\ \text{k}\Omega$.

Excluding this quantized contact resistance and other contact resistances such as those caused by the Schottky barriers, the transport in the CNT is ballistic; i.e., no carrier scattering or energy dissipation takes place in the body of the CNT. The length over which a CNT behaves as a ballistic conductor depends on its structure perfection, temperature, and the size of the driving electric field. In general, ballistic transport can be achieved over lengths ≤ 100 nm. Even in long CNTs, or at high bias, many scattering collisions can take place. The mobility in CNTs can still be very high, as much as 1000 times higher than in bulk silicon.

Due to the 1D nature of the CNT, small-angle scattering is forbidden. There will only be backscattering, so that the elastic scattering in CNTs is weak, and the inelastic scattering determines their transport properties. At low temperature and low bias, only low-energy acoustic phonons can scatter the electrons, which results in an inverse temperature dependence of the carrier mobility in semiconducting CNTs, while in bulk materials the acoustic phonon scattering leads typically to a $\sim 1/T^5$ temperature dependence of mobility due to the small-angle scattering. Thus the CNT has very high mobility even at room temperature.

In addition to the low-energy acoustic phonons, electron scattering by the optical phonon of the radial breathing mode (RBM) is important in the low-bias regime. The RBM phonon energy is inversely proportional to the tube diameter, and its energy is comparable to the thermal energy at room temperature for tubes in the diameter range of 1.5–2.0 nm. For electrons to emit an optical phonon, their energy must be larger than the optical phonon energy. This can be achieved only under a very high bias of a few V cm^{-1}. Such scattering processes were first observed in metallic tubes, in which the current was found to saturate at about 25 μA.

As the carrier energy increases further, other inelastic process can take place, in particular impact excitation. The high-energy electron can excite an electron–hole pair and lose its energy. The electron–hole interaction is very strong in CNTs, which leads to the formation of excitons with large binding energy of a few tenths of an electronvolt. The calculations suggest that the impact excitation processes in CNTs are much more efficient than in conventional bulk semiconductors—about four orders of magnitudes higher.

Figure 1.10 shows the calculated scattering probabilities, $1/\tau$, for a (19,0) nanotube as a function of the energy higher than that of the first subband [14], where Δ_1, Δ_2, Δ_3, and Δ_4 denote the energies of subsequent subbands, respectively. The peaks labeled by A-Ph are the longitudinal acoustic ones; RBM, the radial breathing mode; O-Ph, the optical phonon; and I-Exc, the impact excitation exciton scatterings. The various curves represent angular momentum bands with different circumferences.

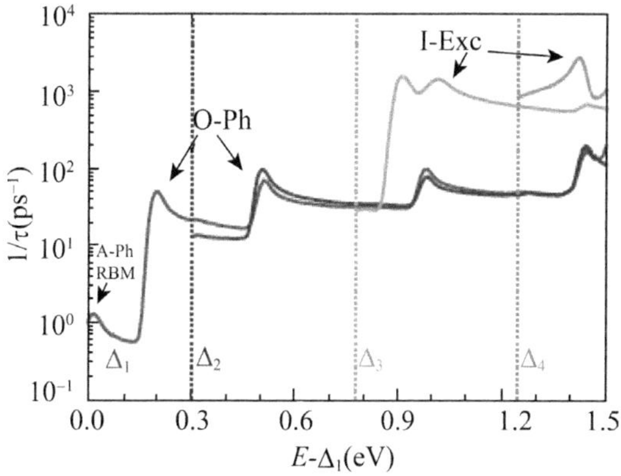

Figure 1.10 Calculated scattering probabilities, $1/\tau$, for a (19,0) nanotube as a function of the energy higher than that of the first subband.

1.7.3 Carbon Nanotube Field-Effect Transistor

The first carbon nanotube field-effect transistors (CNTFETs) were reported in 1998 [17, 18]. In a CNTFET one (or more) CNT plays the role of the channel. Figure 1.11 shows two different CNTFET structures: a top-gate CNTFET and an array of CNTFETs with wrap-around gates. The CNT as an FET channel has a number of advantages. Its small diameter allows optimum coupling between the gate and the channel. This strong coupling makes the CNT the ultimate thin-body semiconductor system and allows the device to be made shorter while avoiding the dreaded "short-channel effects." All bonds in the CNT are satisfied and the surface is smooth, so that the scattering by surface and roughness is absent. The key advantage is the low scattering in the CNT and the high mobility of the FET channel.

In MOSFETs, in addition to the channel, the source, drain, and gate are all made of heavily doped Si and the contacts are ohmic. This is not generally true for the CNT–metal contacts used in CNT

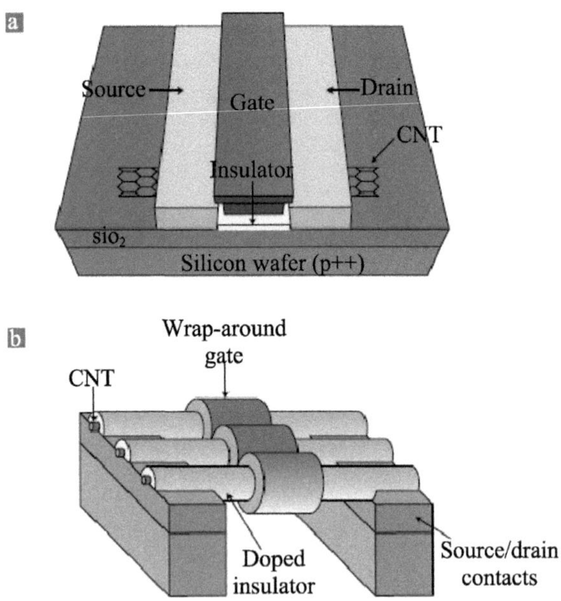

Figure 1.11 Schematic of two different CNTFET structures.

electronics. Metals like Au, Ti, Pd, and Al are used for the source and drain electrodes. The different work functions of the metal and the CNT lead to transfer of charge at their interface. The resulting interface dipole produces an energy barrier, the so-called Schottky barrier. The Schottky barrier height depends on their respective work function (Φ), the CNT bandgap, and the details of chemical bonding at the interface.

There are two Schottky barriers in an FET, one at the source and the other at the drain, as schematically shown in the insets of Fig. 1.12. Generally, it transports only one type of carrier: electrons or holes. From the left inset of Fig. 1.12 we see that if the electrode is a metal with high work function, such as Pd, and the valence band of the CNT is close to the metal Fermi level E_F, a nearly barrierless contact for holes will be formed. But electron injection at the other end would experience the maximum barrier of E_g, so that it is a unipolar device, a p-type CNTFET operation. If the electrode is a low work function metal such as Al, then it allows the electron transport and forbids the hole transport, as shown in the right inset of Fig. 1.12. Figure 1.12 shows the source–drain current as a function

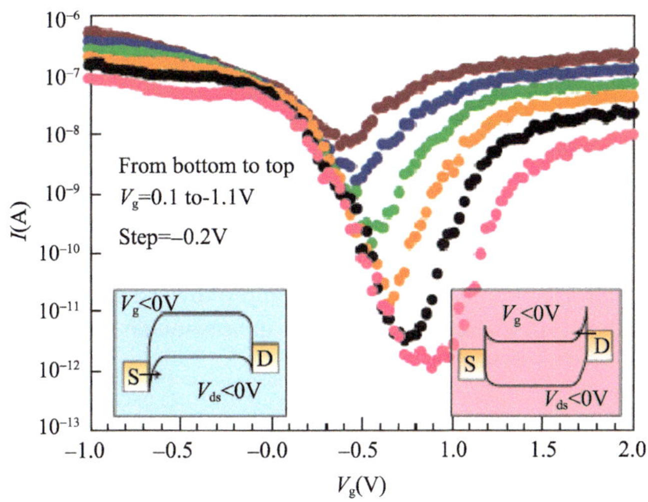

Figure 1.12 The source–drain current as a function of the gate voltage for different drain biases, increasing from 0.1 to −1.1 V in −0.2 V steps. The insets are the contact potential between the electrodes and the CNT.

of the gate voltage for different drain biases, increasing from 0.1 to 1.1 V in 0.2 V steps. From the figure we see that in the gate voltage variation range of 1 eV, the current can vary 5 $\sim$ 6 orders of magnitudes.

In general, the key advantage of CNTFETs over Si MOSFETs in logic applications is their much low capacitance of $\sim$10 aF (for a $d_{\text{CNT}} = 1$ nm, $L = 10$ nm, $t_{\text{ox}} = 5$ nm device) and their somewhat lower operating voltage. Thus, the CNTFETs have lower switching energy per logic transition. The dynamic switching energy of a device is given by $0.5(C_{\text{dev}} + C_{\text{wire}})V^2$, where C_{dev} and C_{wire} are the device and wire capacitance contributions, respectively. To minimize the switching energy, minimum-sized devices and interconnects should be used, as well as minimum supply voltage. The CNTFETs have the $I_{\text{on}}/I_{\text{out}}$ ratios in the range of $10^5 \sim 10^7$. Then the CNT can have a considerable advantage, of up to a factor of 6 over the convenient MOSFET.

More complex structures such as ring oscillators have been fabricated [19]. To build these circuits the complementary MOS architecture is preferred, which involves pairs of n- and p-type transistors. CNTs, in which the valence and conduction bands are mirror images of each other (equal effective masses for electrons and holes), are ideally suited for such application. The two types (p- and n-) of FETs can be made by doping the CNTs, but it is difficult to control doping in nanoscale devices. The ambipolar behavior of an undoped CNT can be successfully utilized to implement the CMOS architecture. For a given undoped CNTFET with a fixed energy gap and oxide thickness, tuning the work function of the gate metal is the only way. When the work functions are properly selected, the two characteristics can be relatively shifted toward each other, and this leads to a distinguishable on-state in one and an off-state in the other.

Figure 1.13 shows the scanning electron microscope image of a CNT ring oscillator circuit, and the frequency response in different supply voltages [14]. It is a ring oscillator using Pd gates for p-FETs and Al gates for n-FETs. The frequency response shows a strong dependence on the supply voltage. A 72 MHz frequency is measured for a supply voltage of about 1 V.

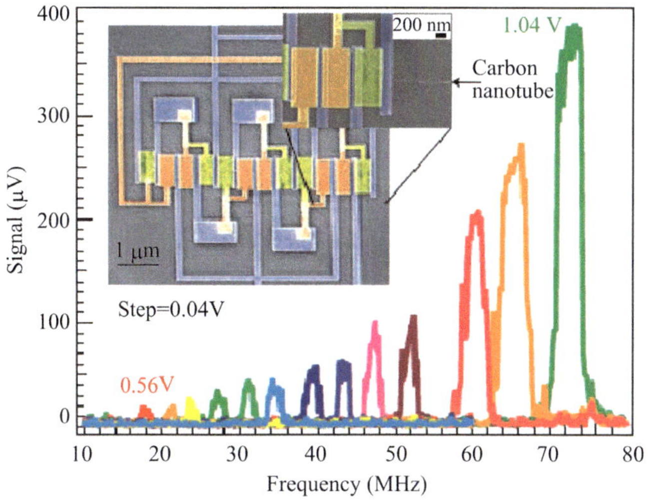

Figure 1.13 Scanning electron microscope image of a CNT ring oscillator circuit and the frequency response in different supply voltages.

1.7.4 Graphene Ribbon Transistor

The sub-10 nm width graphene ribbon field-effect transistor (GNRFET) has been fabricated [20]. The schematic structure of the GNRFET is shown in Fig. 1.14a, and the AFM images of two GNRs are shown in Fig. 1.14b,c. The height of the GNR is 1.5 nm, which is assigned as two-layer GNRs. The Ti-As is used as contact electrodes (source and drain) to minimize the Schottky barrier for holes in a p-type transistor. The GNRFET is placed on a 10 nm thick SiO_2 layer, and p^{++} Si is used as backgate. The widths of the GNRs in Figs. 1.13b and 1.14c are 5 and 60 nm, respectively.

Figure 1.15 shows the current–voltage characteristics for the $w \approx 2$ nm, $L = 236$ nm GNR device shown in Fig. 1.14b [20]. Figure 1.15a is current vs. gate voltage ($I_{ds} \sim V_{gs}$) under various V_{ds}, and the dashed lines are the turn-on and cut-off states of the current $I = 3.2$ μA and 10^{-12} A, respectively. Thus, at room temperature, when $V_{ds} = 0.5$ V, the ratio of the turn-on and cut-off currents $I_{on}/I_{off} > 10^6$. Figure 1.15b is ($I_{ds} \sim V_{ds}$) under various V_{gs}. From the figure, the subthreshold slope, ~210 mV/decade, and transconductance, ~1.8 μS, are obtained.

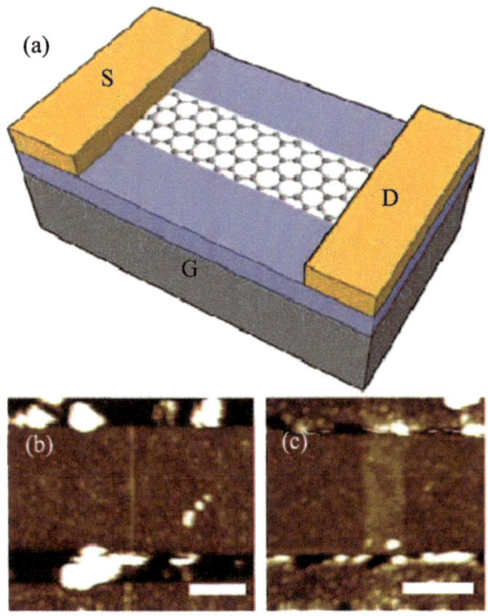

Figure 1.14 (a) Schematic structure of the GNRFET. (b, c) The AFM images of two GNRs.

Comparing experiments with theoretical modeling, it was found that the narrow device (Fig. 1.15) delivered about 21% of the ballistic current at $V_{ds} = 1$ V. The highest proportion that can be reached is 38%. The reason is that the optical phonon (OP) or zone

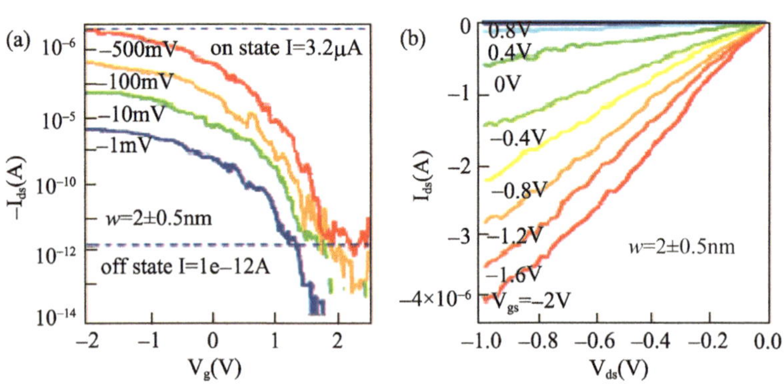

Figure 1.15 Transistor performance of the GNRFET shown in Fig. 1.14b. (a) (I_{ds}~ V_{gs}) under various V_{ds}. (b) (I_{ds}~ V_{ds}) under various V_{gs}.

boundary phonon (ZBP) emission needs higher energy (~0.2 eV). A carrier backscattered by emitting an OP/ZBP does not have enough energy to overcome the barrier near the source end of the channel, so that the OP/ZBP has a small effect on the current in GNRFETs. The wide GNRFETs (Fig. 1.14c) deliver higher current density of ~2000–3000 μA/μm.

1.7.5 Future of Carbon-Based Devices

Carbon nanotubes are ideal 1D model systems to study electrical and optical phenomena on the nanometre scale. Some new states of condensed matter such as the Luttinger–Tomonaga liquid can be studied. Graphene has exhibited a number of unique phenomena such as anomalous quantum Hall effect, Klein paradox, and so forth. New information on the physics of the nanoscale is expected to be found through the study of nanotubes and graphene. At the same time, the nanotechnology to handle and process nanomaterials has been developed. Besides electronic switching, emission/detection, and sensitive devices, nanotubes offer the potential of very fast (THz) transistors, ultimately scaled logic devices, and simpler and cheaper self-assembly-based fabrication. The excellent electrical conduction of metallic CNTs may eventually allow the development of electronic systems, where both active and interconnects are based on the same material: CNTs. Further integration to include optics could lead to a unified electronic-optoelectronic technology.

The large electronic and spin coherence lengths of both materials could lead to quantum interference and spintronic devices. Spin-polarized injection can be achieved using manganite electrodes. The weak spin-orbit coupling and short transit times of carriers in nanotubes tend to preserve the spin polarization. Spin transport and spin precession over micrometer-scale distances have been demonstrated in single graphene sheets at room temperature.

Single-wall carbon nanotubes (SWNTs) are potential candidates for application in electronic devices. The most severe bottleneck is to grow uniform, single type and scale of SWNTs, because the as-synthesized SWNTs are a mixture of semiconducting (SC) and metallic (M) tubes. Recently, the separation of SC and M tubes

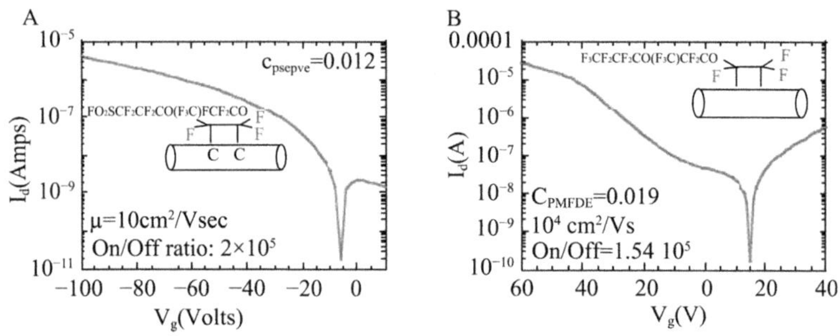

Figure 1.16 Source–drain current versus gate voltage for two functionalized SWNT FETs at $V_{ds} = -0.1$ V and -0.01 V, respectively.

has achieved some advances. The metallic M-SWNT cab be etched from the mixture through a controlled cycloaddition reaction with fluorinated polyolefins. The as-grown commercial nanotube mats are functionalized into a network of tubes that can then be dispersed in an organic solvent [21]. The resulting "denser" semiconducting inks, when coated as a percolating array, lead to high-mobility devices without requiring further nanotube separation.

Figure 1.16 shows the source–drain current versus gate voltage for two functionalized SWNT FETs [21]. The field-effect mobilities deduced from the linear regime are 10 $cm^2/V{\cdot}s$ and 104 $cm^2/V{\cdot}s$ with on/off ratio in excess of 10^5.

Along with the progressive improvement in the rapidly evolving technology of CNTs and graphene, the prospects of carbon-based devices are very bright.

References

1. Datta, S. (1995). *Electron Transport in Mesoscopic Systems* (Cambridge, London), p. 16.
2. Reggiani, L. (1985). *Hot-electron Transport in Semiconductors* (Spring-Verlag, Berlin), p. 7–11.
3. Ferry, D. K., Takagaki, Y., and Zhou, J. R. (1994). Future ultra-scale integration: transport physics in semiconductor nanostructures. *Jpn. J. Appl. Phys.* **33**, 873–878.

4. Kriman, A. M., Kluksdahl, N. C., and Ferry D. K. (1987). Scattering states and distribution functions for microstructures. *Phys. Rev. B* **36**, 5953–5959.
5. Datta, S. (1989). *Supperlatt. Microstruct.* **6**, 83.
6. Xia, J. B. (1992). *Phys. Rev. B* **45**, 3593.
7. Wolf, S. A., Awschalom, D. D., R. A. Buhrman, R. A., et al. (2001). *Science*, 294, pp. 1488.
8. Baibich, M. N., Broto, J. M., Fert, A., et al. (1988). *Phys. Rev. Lett.* **61**, 2472.
9. Binasch, G., Grunberg, P., Saurenbach, F., et al. (1989). *Phys. Rev. B* **39**, 4828.
10. Moodera, J. S., Kinder, L. R., Wong, T. M., et al. (1995). *Phys. Rev. Lett.* **74**, 3273.
11. Hu, C. M., Nitta, J., Jensen, A., et al. (2001). *Phys. Rev. Lett.* **63**, 125333.
12. Zhu, H. J., Ramsteiner, M., Kostial, H., et al. (2001). *Phys. Rev. Lett.* **87**, 016601.
13. S. Datta, S., and Das, B. (1990). Electron analog of the electro-optic modulator. *Appl. Phys. Lett.* **58**, 665.
14. Avouris, P., Chen, Z. H., and Perebeinos, V. (2007). Carbon-based electronics. *Nature Nanotechnol.* **2**, 605–615.
15. Novoselov, K. S., Geim, A. K., Morozov, S. V., et al. (2004). Electric field effect in atomically thin carbon films. *Science* **306**, 666–669.
16. Berger, C., Song, Z., Li, X., et al. (2006). Electronic confinement and coherence in patterned epitaxial graphene. *Science* **312**, 1191–1196.
17. Tans, S. J., Verscheuren, A. R. M., and Dekker, C. (1998). Room-temperature transistor based on a single carbon nanotube. *Nature* **393**, 49–52.
18. Martel, R., Schmidt, T., Shea, H. R., et al. (1998). Single- and multi-wall carbon nanotube field-effect transistors. *Appl. Phys. Lett.* **73**, 2447–2449.
19. Chen, Z., Appenzeller, J., et al. (2006). An integrated logic circuit assembled on a single carbon nanotube. *Science* **311**, 1735.
20. Wang, X. R., Ouyang, Y. J., Li, X. L., et al. (2008). Room-temperature all semiconducting sub-10-nm graphene nanoribbon field-effect transistors. *Phys. Rev. Lett.* **100**, 206803.
21. Kanungo, M., Lu, H., Malliars, G. G., and Blanchet, G. B. (2009). Suppression of metallic conductivity of single-walled carbon nanotubes by cycloaddition reactions. *Science* **323**, 234–237.

Chapter 2

Non-equilibrium Transport

In devices scaling larger than 100 nm the transport is described by the classical Boltzmann equation,

$$\frac{\partial f}{\partial t} + \mathbf{v} \cdot \frac{\partial f}{\partial \mathbf{r}} + \frac{e\mathbf{E}}{\hbar} \cdot \frac{\partial f}{\partial \mathbf{k}} = \int d\mathbf{k}' \left[f\left(\mathbf{k}'\right) W\left(\mathbf{k}', \mathbf{k}\right) - f\left(\mathbf{k}\right) W\left(\mathbf{k}, \mathbf{k}'\right) \right], \tag{2.1}$$

where $f(\mathbf{k}, \mathbf{r}, t)$ is the single-particle distribution function at time t, momentum space $\mathbf{k}$, and real space $\mathbf{r}$. For semiconductors, the group velocity of the carrier is given by

$$\mathbf{v} = \frac{1}{\hbar} \frac{\partial \varepsilon\left(\mathbf{k}\right)}{\partial \mathbf{k}}. \tag{2.2}$$

When the scale of the devices becomes smaller, the electron transport will be nonlinear and nonstatic, as shown in Fig. 1.1. The distribution function is a derivate of the equilibrium distribution farther and largely varies with space and time. In some cases, it is recognized that the concepts of the Boltzmann equation and the distribution function are still effective, whose three main assumptions, that is, effective mass, energy band model, and electron collisions at space and time are instantaneous, are all tenable. But the Boltzmann equation cannot be solved by the ordinary perturbation method, while it can be by other methods, for example, the Monte Carlo method.

Quantum Waveguide in Microcircuits
Jian-Bai Xia, Duan-Yang Liu, and Wei-Dong Sheng

ISBN 978-981-4669-85-6 (Hardcover), 978-1-315-36477-3 (eBook)
www.panstanford.com

2.1 Monte Carlo Method

The Monte Carlo method utilizes the numerical method to simulate the movement of one or many electrons in the applied fields and scattering processes [1]. The macrophysical quantities, for instance, drift velocity, diffusion coefficient, and energy, are the assemble averages of corresponding physical quantities. If the system is a steady, space homogeneous distributed system, it is enough to simulate the movement of an electron. The statistical distribution of a given subsystem does not depend on the initial state of any other small part of the same system, since over a sufficiently long time the effect of this initial state will be entirely outweighed by the effect of the much larger remaining parts of the system. It is also independent of the initial state of the particular small part considered, since in time this part passes through all possible states, any of which can be taken as the initial state. It means that the average of a variable ϕ over the assemble equals the average of that variable over a sufficiently long time,

$$\bar{\phi} = \frac{\int \phi(\mathbf{k}) f(\mathbf{k}) d\mathbf{k}}{\int f(\mathbf{k}) d\mathbf{k}} = \frac{\int_0^T \phi[\mathbf{k}(t)] dt}{T} + O\left(T^{-1/2}\right), \tag{2.3}$$

where $O(T^{-1/2})$ represents the fluctuation proportional to $T^{-1/2}$. When T is long enough, the statistical error can be neglected and the simulation reaches convergence.

If the system is not steady, or inhomogeneous, then the movement of many particles (assemble) should be studied. At any time the transport properties of the assemble can be obtained by the average of the simulation of these particles. This Monte Carlo simulation of many particles is generally used to simulate the various instantaneous properties of a homogeneous system in the varied electric field. In the simulation of many particles the initial distribution of particles should be given and the instantaneous characteristics of the transport property actually depend on the initial distribution. This method is called a many-particle Monte Carlo simulation.

The free flight of electrons at intervals of two collisions satisfies Eq. 2.2 and

$$\hbar\frac{d\mathbf{k}}{dt} = -e\mathbf{E}. \tag{2.4}$$

Assume that the scattering probability of electrons is $\lambda(t)$, there are N_0 particles have the same initial state and the number of particles that have not collided at time t is denoted by $N(t)$. Then the number of first collisions between the time t and $t+dt$ is $-dN(t)$, and

$$-dN(t) = N(t)\,\lambda(t)\,dt. \tag{2.5}$$

Solving Eq. 2.5 we obtain

$$\frac{N(t)}{N_0} = \exp\left[-\int_0^t \lambda(t')\,dt'\right]. \tag{2.6}$$

Equation 2.6 is the probability of particles that have not collided at time t. Hence the probability of particles that have collided at time t is

$$\begin{aligned} P(t) &= 1 - \exp\left[-\int_0^t \lambda(t')\,dt'\right] \\ &= \int_0^t \lambda(t')\exp\left[-\int_0^{t'} \lambda(t'')\,dt''\right] dt' \\ &= \int_0^t f(t')\,dt', \end{aligned} \tag{2.7}$$

where

$$f(t) = \lambda(t)\exp\left[-\int_0^t \lambda(t')\,dt'\right], \tag{2.8}$$

representing the collision distribution function at time t.

The Monte Carlo method is semi-classical, which simulates the random movement of a single or many particles. On this basis, the needed properties are obtained through a proper statistical average. In the semi-classical picture, the microscopic movement of charged particles can be looked as a series of free flight and stochastic scatterings. The Monte Carlo method deals with the stochastic events related to scattering by a series of stochastic numbers between 0 and 1. On the other hand, for a given electric field, initial state, and free flight time, the whole flight process is completely determined.

From Eq. 2.7 the free flight time t_f can be obtained with the stochastic number r_t through the integration equation

$$r_t = 1 - \exp\left[-\int_0^{t_f} \lambda(t')\,dt'\right]. \tag{2.9}$$

From Eq. 2.9 we obtain

$$\int_0^{t_f} \lambda(t)\,dt = -\ln(1 - r_t)\,. \tag{2.10}$$

Actually the solution of the integration equation (Eq. 2.10) for such a scattering event is difficult. Rees [2] introduced the concept of self-scattering, making the problem simpler. Assume that the total scattering probability Γ, including the self-scattering, is a constant, independent of energy,

$$\Gamma = \lambda(E) + \lambda_s(E)\,, \tag{2.11}$$

where $\lambda_s(E)$ is the self-scattering probability. Inserting Γ into Eq. 2.10 instead of $\lambda(t)$, we obtain

$$t_f = -\frac{1}{\Gamma}\ln(1 - r_t)\,. \tag{2.12}$$

The flight time t_f can be easily calculated from the stochastic number r_t.

Suppose that the initial state of each free flight is $\mathbf{k}_a$. Then from the movement Eqs. 2.2 and 2.4 we can determine the momentum $\mathbf{k}_b$ and energy of the final state. With this method the scattering probability of the final state by various scattering mechanisms $\lambda_i(\mathbf{k}_b)$ can be calculated. Given a stochastic number r, if

$$\sum_{i=1}^{j} \lambda_i(\mathbf{k}_b) < r\Gamma < \sum_{i=1}^{j+1} \lambda_i(\mathbf{k}_b), \tag{2.13}$$

then we think that the collision of electrons is caused by the j-th scattering mechanism, whose scattering probability is $\lambda_j(\mathbf{k}_b)$. From the momentum $\mathbf{k}_b$ and energy of the final state and $\lambda_j(\mathbf{k}_b)$, we can determine the electron energy and momentum of the initial state of the next free flight.

If the Eq. 2.13 is not satisfied and

$$\sum_{i=1}^{N} \lambda_i(\mathbf{k}_b) < r\Gamma < \Gamma, \tag{2.14}$$

then we think that the electron undergoes a self-scattering and the electron energy and momentum of the next flight's initial state is the same as those of the above flight's final state. Repeating the above described process, we can obtain the movement course of a single electron in the long period of time or the situations at various times and positions of assemble electrons.

The physical quantity in the static state is given by Eq. 2.3, in the Monte Carlo simulation,

$$\bar{\phi} = \frac{1}{T} \sum_i \int_0^{t_i} \phi \left[k \left(t' \right) \right] dt', \tag{2.15}$$

where t_i is the flight time of each flight.

The distribution function can be calculated by a similar method. At the beginning of the calculation, we prepare a **k**-space mesh and in the process of simulation record the duration of the electron in each mesh lattice. If the time is long enough, the normalized duration time represents the distribution function of electrons.

2.2 Time-Related Transport Behaviors in Homogeneous Semiconductors

2.2.1 Drift Diffusion Model

The Monte Carlo simulation needs the knowledge of the relaxation mechanisms, of energy band shapes, and of the coupling constants and requires rather long computation times. Moreover, the transient response is scarcely given. Nougier et al. [3] developed a simple model based on the relaxation time approximation to study the transient response in semiconductors and compared the results with the numerically computed curves.

The dynamical equations, in the relaxation approximation, are balanced equations related to the drift velocity $\bar{v}(t)$ and to the average energy $\bar{\varepsilon}(t)$ of the carriers. One then defines the momentum and energy relaxation time τ_p and τ_ε, which are the functions of energy. The balanced equations are

$$\frac{m\partial\bar{v}\left(t\right)}{\partial t} = qE - \frac{m\bar{v}\left(t\right)}{\tau_p\left(\bar{\varepsilon}\right)}$$

and

$$\frac{\partial\bar{\varepsilon}\left(t\right)}{\partial t} = qE\bar{v}\left(t\right) - \frac{\bar{\varepsilon}\left(t\right) - \varepsilon_0}{\tau_\varepsilon\left(\bar{\varepsilon}\right)}, \tag{2.16}$$

where E is the electric field, q is the electron charge, and ε_0 is the average energy in thermal equilibrium.

In the steady-state condition, equating $d\,(m\bar{v})/dt$ and $d\bar{\varepsilon}/dt$ to zero in Eq. 2.16 gives

$$\tau_{\rm p}\,(\varepsilon_{\rm s}) = \frac{m^* v_{\rm s}}{qE}, \quad \tau_{\varepsilon}\,(\varepsilon_{\rm s}) = \frac{\varepsilon_{\rm s} - \varepsilon_0}{qE v_{\rm s}} \tag{2.17}$$

where $v_{\rm s}$ and $\varepsilon_{\rm s}$ are the drift velocity and energy in the steady-state condition, which are all functions of the electric field or the energy $\bar{\varepsilon}$. Inserting Eq. 2.17 into Eq. 2.16 gives

$$\frac{d\,(m\bar{v})}{dt} = q\left[E - \frac{\bar{v}}{v_{\rm s}\,(\bar{\varepsilon})} E_{\rm s}\,(\bar{\varepsilon})\right] = q\left[E - \frac{\bar{v}}{\mu_{\rm s}\,(\bar{\varepsilon})}\right]$$

and

$$\frac{d\bar{\varepsilon}}{dt} = q\,[E\bar{v} - E_{\rm s}\,(\bar{\varepsilon})\,v_{\rm s}\,(\bar{\varepsilon})] = q\left[E\bar{v} - \mu_{\rm s}\,(\bar{\varepsilon})\,E_{\rm s}^2\,(\bar{\varepsilon})\right], \tag{2.18}$$

where $\mu_{\rm s}\,(\bar{\varepsilon}) = v_{\rm s}\,(\bar{\varepsilon})/E_{\rm s}\,(\bar{\varepsilon})$ is the steady-state mobility.

Figure 2.1 shows a comparison between the transient energy $\bar{\varepsilon}\,(t)$ in p-Ge deduced from the solution of the Boltzmann equation by an iterative method and from the relaxation time approximation. From the figure we see that the electron energies increase with time and the electric field, and approach saturation, but have no overshoot. The discrepancy between the results of the two methods is less than 10% until at least 20 kV/cm.

2.2.2 Transport in a Strong Electric Field

The calculated $\tau_{\rm p}$ and τ_{ε} as functions of the difference between the average and thermal energies for the case of electrons in Si and GaAs at 293 K are shown in Figs. 2.2 and 2.3, respectively [4]. From the figure we see that in the hot-electron regime the relaxation times are not constants, which depend on the electron energy. For GaAs, $\tau_{\rm p}$ and τ_{ε} increase first, then decrease with $\varepsilon - \varepsilon_0$ increasing, and for Si, $\tau_{\rm p}$ decreases and τ_{ε} increases with $\varepsilon - \varepsilon_0$. The momentum relaxation times are larger than the energy relaxation times by 1 order of magnitude.

The balanced equations Eq. 2.18 have already been used successfully to determine the dependence on time of the drift velocity and the average energy; when a given time configuration of the electric field is applied to the semiconductor, a good agreement with more exact calculations has been observed. Figure 2.4 shows

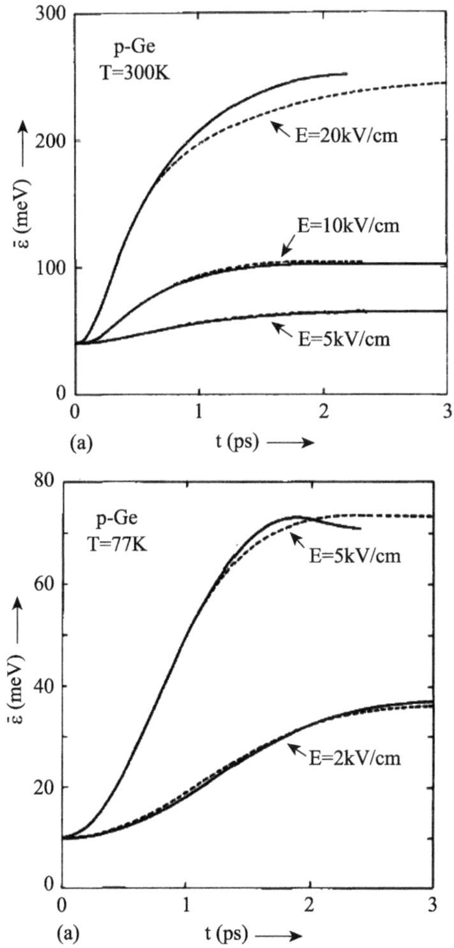

Figure 2.1 Comparison between the transient energy $\bar{\varepsilon}$ (t) in p-Ge deduced from the solution of the Boltzmann equation by an iterative method and from the relaxation time approximation: (a) at 300 K and (b) at 77 K.

a comparison of the draft velocities as functions of time when a step of the electric field is applied between the results obtained with the relaxation time description (dots) and Monte Carlo or the iterative method (curves) [4]. It can be seen that for the five semiconductors studied, the results obtained by both methods are in good agreement. Consequently, owing to its simplicity, the balance

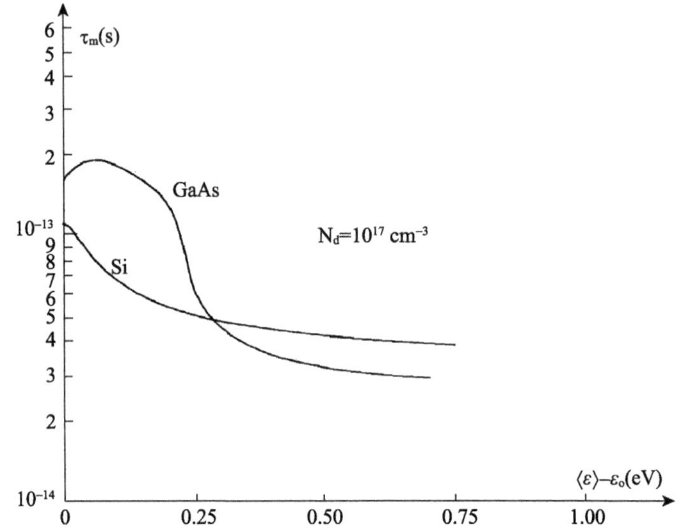

Figure 2.2 The momentum relaxation time as a function of the difference between the average and thermal energies for the case of electrons in Si and GaAs at 293 K.

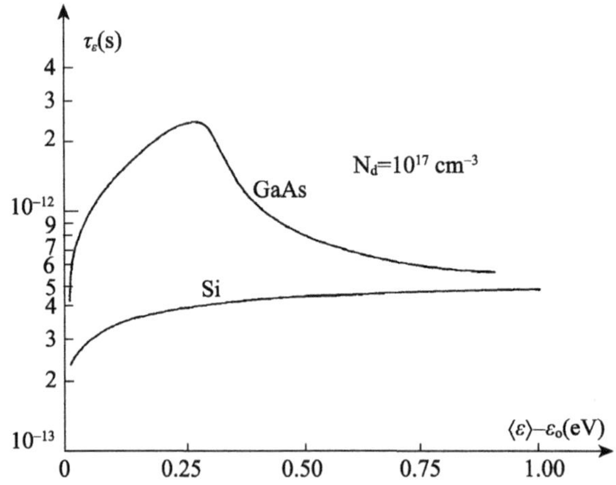

Figure 2.3 The energy relaxation time as a function of the difference between the average and thermal energies for the case of electrons in Si and GaAs at 293 K.

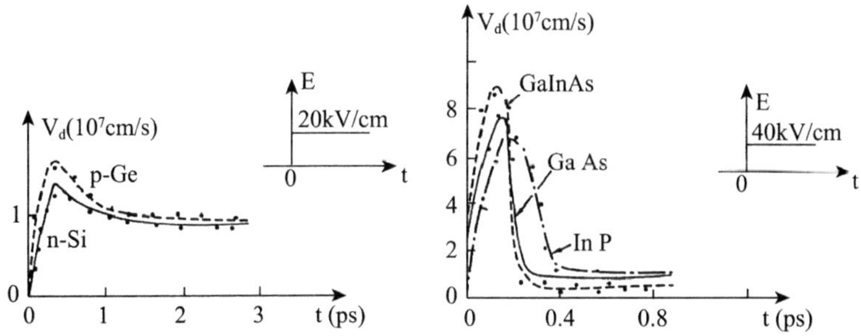

Figure 2.4 Comparison of the draft velocities as functions of time when a step of the electric field is applied between the results obtained with the relaxation time description (dots) and the Monte Carlo or the iterative method (curves).

equation method with the relaxation time approximation is very useful for the study of time-dependent phenomena.

From Fig. 2.4 we see that in a time of less than 1 ps the draft velocities rise rapidly, reaching $10^7 \approx 10^8$ cm/s. Then due to the momentum and energy relaxations, whose relaxation times are $0.1 \approx 1$ ps, the draft velocities decrease gradually and approach the steady-state values. The rapid increase of the draft velocity in a strong electric field is called a velocity overshoot. It is because at the initial stage of applying an electric field the electrons are accelerated suddenly by the strong electric field and do not have enough time to be scattered, so they can reach a very high draft velocity. Transport at this stage is called ballistic transport. The scattering plays a role with passage of time, which compensates the accelerating action of the electric field and makes the draft velocity approach a steady-state value.

In a transistor the size of the base region can be reduced to 100 nm or less without allowing the increase of the base resistance. In such a thin-base-region transistor the length of the electron-traveling region is very short, the transport of electrons could be near ballistic by a hot-electron injection structure, and then the working frequency will be very high. Hence such a transistor can be used to design a high-frequency transistor. Figure 2.5 shows a model of n-p-n heterojunction bipolar transistors of types (A), (B), and (C) [5]. The material in the n^+-emitter and p^+-base regions is

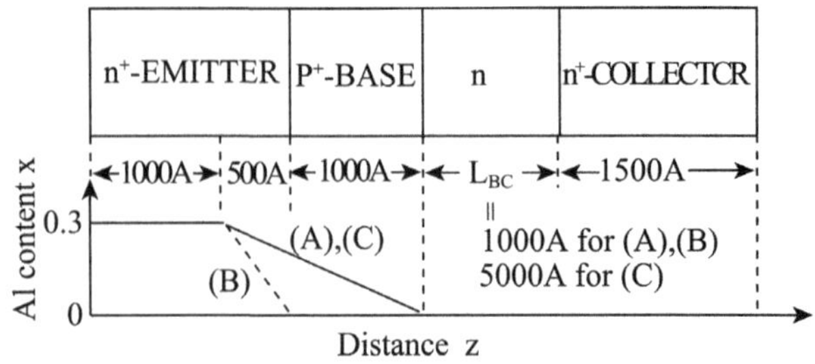

Figure 2.5 Model of n-p-n heterojunction bipolar transistors of types (A), (B), and (C).

$Al_xGa_{1-x}As$. The compositional grading x is linear and starts with $x = 0.3$ at 500 Å inside the emitter from the emitter-base junction and ends with $x = 0$ at the base-collector junction (types (A) and (C)) or at the emitter-base junction (type (B)). The grading for transistors of types (A) and (C) produces a quasi-electric field of about 20 kV/cm in the base region.

Figure 2.6 shows the profile of the mean electron velocity in a type (A) transistor (solid curve) and a type (B) transistor (dashed curve). The mean electron velocity in (A) reaches as high as 4.5×10^7 cm/s at base-collector junction. This is because electrons in the graded base region travel more or less ballistically as a result of the accelerating force of the quasi-electric field. The mean electron velocity in (B) is as low as 5×10^6 cm/s (notice that the ordinates in Fig. 2.6 are different for (A) and (B)) in the substantial part of the base region, suggesting that the electron motion in the nongraded base region is diffusion dominated.

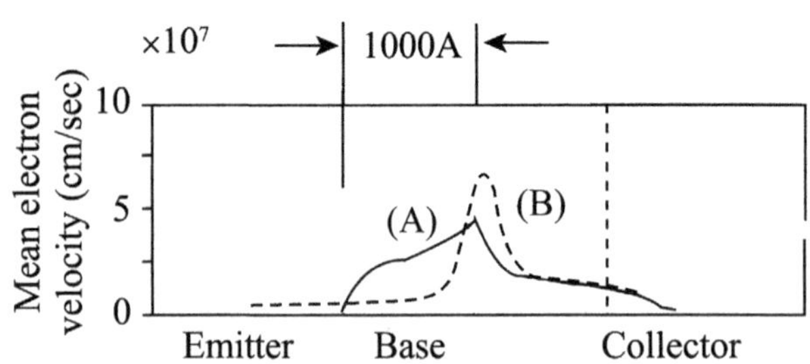

Figure 2.6 Profile of the mean electron velocity in a type (A) transistor (solid curve) and a type (B) transistor (dashed curve).

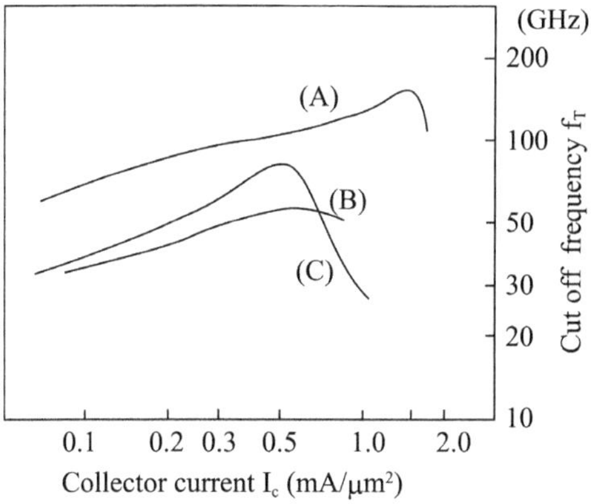

Figure 2.7 Current-gain cutoff frequencies f_T of transistors of types (A), (B), and (C).

Figure 2.7 shows the current-gain cutoff frequencies f_T of transistors of types (A), (B), and (C). It is seen in Fig. 2.7 that the f_T of a type (A) transistor shows an extremely high maximum value of about 150 GHz at $I_c = 1.4$ mA/μm^2. The maximum f_T of a type (B) transistor reaches only 58 GHz at $I_c = 0.6$ mA/μm^2. This is due to a large base capacitance caused by the diffusion-dominated electron transport in the base region. The maximum f_T of a type (C) transistor reaches only 80 GHz at $I_c = 0.5$ mA/μm^2, smaller than that of type (A). The decrease of f_T is due to the appearance of the base-push-out effect.

2.2.3 Application of a Balance Equation

From the above discussion we see that the results obtained by the relaxation time description (the balance equation) and the Monte Carlo or the iterative method are in good agreement. Due to its simplicity, the balance equation method with the relaxation time approximation is very useful for the study of time-dependent phenomena. The balance equation can be used to study the transport properties not only in the strong electric field case but also in the weak electric field case. In the weak electric field case, the momentum and energy relaxation times can be taken as constants; the calculation will be very simple. In the following we give an example: the terahertz (THz)-photocurrent resonances in miniband superlattices.

When a laser beam from the free electron laser (FEL) irradiates the GaAs/$Al_{0.3}Ga_{0.7}As$ superlattice in the differential conductance (DC) bias, giving pulses of intense THz radiation with a pulse length of several microseconds. The GaAs/$Al_{0.3}Ga_{0.7}As$ superlattice consists of 40 periods of an 8 nm wide GaAs well and 2 nm thick AlGaAs barrier. The width of the miniband is $\Delta = 22$ meV, and the electron density is 3×10^{15} cm^{-3}. The measured DC currents as functions of the DC bias for different laser powers are shown in Fig. 2.8 [6]. The FEL frequency was fixed to 0.6 THz (Fig. 2.8a) and 1.5 THz (Fig. 2.8b). The curves in the figure are shown for increasing FEL intensity from up to down. From Fig. 2.8 we see that at low intensities an additional peak emerges in the negative differential conductance (NDC) region. When the intensity is increased further, the first peak starts to decrease and a second peak at about twice the voltage of the first peak is observed due to a two-photon resonance.

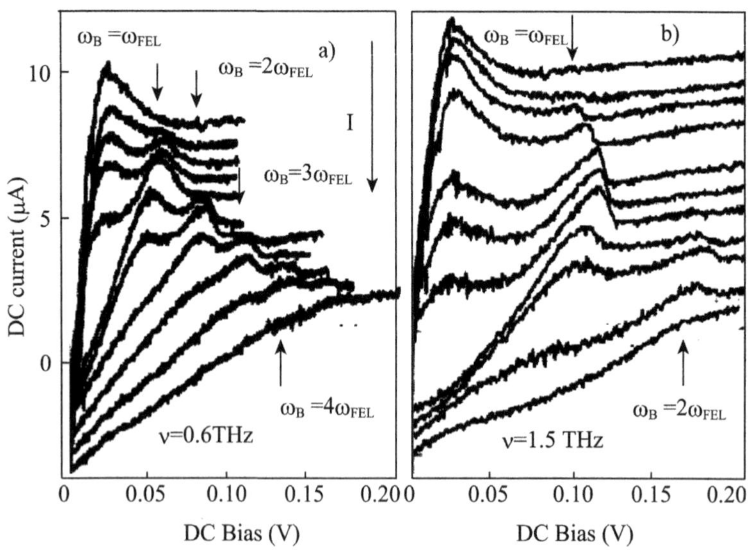

Figure 2.8 DC current-voltage for increasing the FEL intensity (the curves are shifted downward for an increasing laser intensity). The FEL frequency was fixed to 0.6 THz (a) and 1.5 THz (b).

The position of the peaks does not change with the intensity of the FEL. The authors attribute the first additional peak to a resonance of the external laser field where the Bloch frequency $\omega_B = \omega$. In Fig. 2.8b the laser frequency is 1.5 THz and the peaks are shifted to higher voltages and are much more pronounced. However, only the fundamental and the second harmonics are observed.

The Bloch oscillation is a special phenomenon in the longitudinal transport of the superlattice. In the intense electric field F the electron moves periodically in the one-dimensional (1D) Brillouin zone (BZ) of k space, $-\pi/L \leq k \leq \pi/L$, where L is the period of the superlattice. The oscillation is called the Bloch oscillation, whose oscillation frequency is $\omega_B = eFL/h$, proportional to the DC voltage and the superlattice period.

We use the balanced equations (Eq. 2.16) to study the miniband transport of superlattices under a direct bias and an alternating electric field and compare the theoretical results with the experimental results [7]. We take the relaxation time τ_v and τ_ε as constant, and the balanced equations are rewritten as

$$\frac{dv}{dt} = \frac{eF\,(t)}{m^*} - \frac{v}{\tau_v}$$

and

$$\frac{d\varepsilon}{dt} = eF\,(t)\,v - \frac{\varepsilon - \varepsilon_0}{\tau_\varepsilon}, \qquad (2.19)$$

where m^* is the effective mass along the electron draft direction (longitudinal direction), which depends on the energy ε, and

$$m^* = \frac{m_0^*}{1 - 2\varepsilon/\Delta} \quad \text{and} \quad m_0^* = \frac{2\hbar^2}{\Delta d^2}, \qquad (2.20)$$

where the origin of energy is at the conduction band bottom, Δ is the width of the miniband, and d is the period of the superlattice. In calculation we take the experimental parameters $\Delta = 23$ meV, $d = 10$ nm, $\varepsilon_0 = 0.05\,\Delta$, $\tau_v = 1.3$ ps, $\tau_\varepsilon = 6.5$ ps, and the frequency of the alternating field $\nu = 0.6$ THz. The electric field is applied to the superlattice from $t = 0$,

$$F\,(t) = F_0 + F_1 \cos \omega t. \qquad (2.21)$$

The balanced equations (2.19) are solved by a numerical method, and the velocity $v(t)$ and energy $\varepsilon(t)$ are obtained as functions of t.

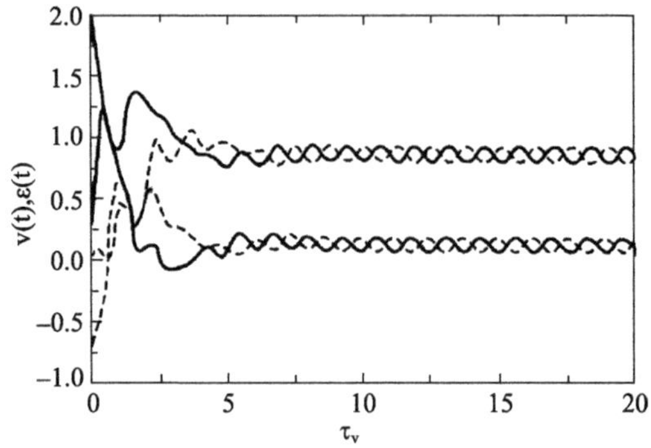

Figure 2.9 The $v(t)$ and $\varepsilon(t)$ for $F_0 = 0.5$ and $F_1 = 1$ (solid curve) and $F_0 = 0.5$ and $F_1 = -1$ (dashed curve).

Figure 2.9 shows the $v(t)$ and $\varepsilon(t)$ for $F_0 = 0.5$ and $F_1 = 1$ (solid curve) and $F_0 = 0.5$ and $F_1 = -1$ (dashed curve). The unit of the electric field is 1000 V/cm in the following. From Fig. 2.9 we see that after 10 periods of the external alternating field the $v(t)$ and $\varepsilon(t)$ reach steady states. At the initial stage the velocity and energy of electrons all reach very large values, which means there are "overshoot" and "overhot" behaviors, and the electrons do not have enough time to collide. The $v(t)$ and $\varepsilon(t)$ for $F_0 = 0.5$ and $F_1 = -1$ are similar to those for $F_0 = 0.5$ and $F_1 = 1$, only different from a phase π.

In the steady state the $v(t)$ is a periodic function with a period $T = 2\pi/\omega$, which consists of DC term and harmonic terms of ω,

$$v(t) = v_0 + \sum_{n=1} v_n \cos(n\omega t + \varphi_n). \tag{2.22}$$

Here for definition we assume that all v_n (except v_0) are positive. By Fourier transform, we obtained all v_n and $\cos\varphi_n$. If $\cos\varphi_1 < 0$, that means that the first harmonic current is in the opposite phase with the driven alternating field and the energy will be transferred to the alternating field, that is, the alternating field will be amplified.

The DC current is given by $j_0 = ev_0n$, where n is the electron concentration, which is taken as 10^{15} cm^{-3} in the following. The DC currents as functions of F_0 for different F_1 are shown in Fig. 2.10 [7]. From Fig. 2.10 we see that the global characteristic is in good agreement with the experimental results [7]: Fig. 2.8. The

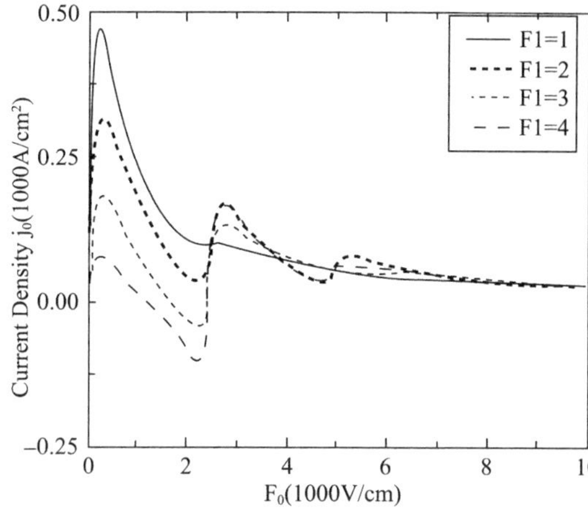

Figure 2.10 DC currents as functions of F_0 for different F_1.

DC currents show resonance peaks in the fields F_0 corresponding to the Bloch frequency $\omega_B = \omega, 2\omega, 3\omega, \ldots$. The resonance peaks in the DC current grow with increasing laser intensity (F_1), and simultaneously the current at the low bias side decreases.

The harmonic components of current j_0, j_1, j_2, and j_3 as functions of F_0 for $F_1 = 2$ are shown in Fig. 2.11 [7]. From Fig. 2.11

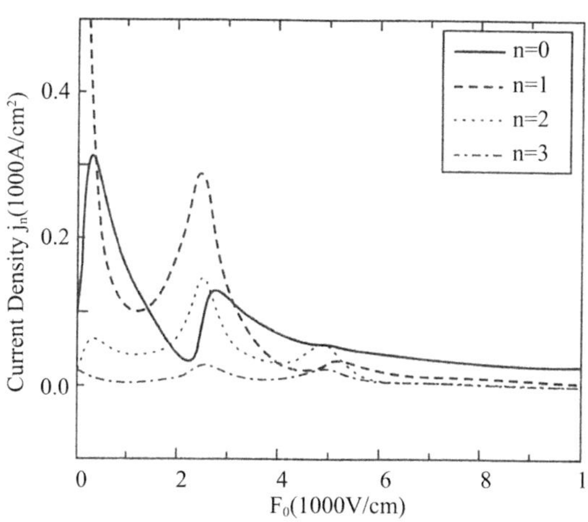

Figure 2.11 Harmonic components of current j_0, j_1, j_2, and j_3 as functions of F_0 for $F_1 = 2$.

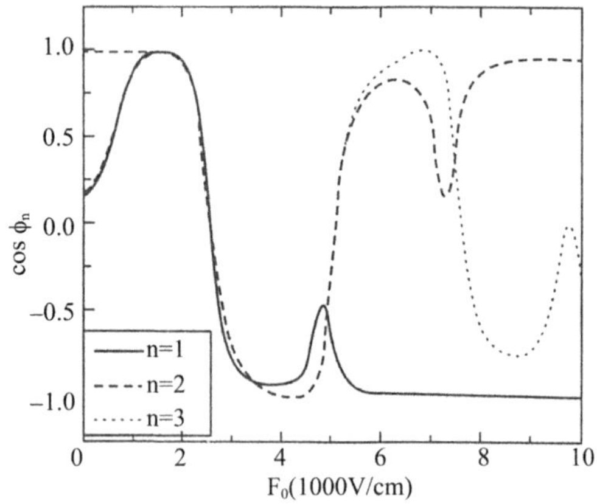

Figure 2.12 Cosines of the phase angle for each component $\cos\varphi_n$ as functions of F_0 for $F_1 = 2$.

we see that they also have resonance peaks at the resonance frequencies $\omega_B = \omega$, 2ω, and 3ω. At $\omega_B = \omega$, the values of j_1 and j_2 exceed that of j_0. The cosines of the phase angle for each component $\cos\phi_n$ as functions of F_0 for $F_1 = 2$ are shown in Fig. 2.12. From Fig. 2.12 we see that $\cos\phi_n$ oscillates with the DC field F_0 and becomes negative at the field range corresponding to the Bloch frequency ω_B between ω and 2ω. Cos ϕ_1 is negative for $\omega_B > \omega$, and with resonance peaks at $\omega_B = 2\omega, 3\omega, \ldots$.

2.2.4 Device Design Considering a Strong Field Transport

When we want to design high-speed devices, the main goal is to find the best way of making the electron go as fast as possible along the active region of submicron devices. Generally for a given active region of width d, the problem is to find the optimum electric field configuration and the doping concentration that should characterize the component.

The simplest way to solve this problem is to study the motion of an ensemble of electrons in a uniform bulk semiconductor to a time configuration of the electric field. From the variation of the average drift velocity $v(t)$, the average distance d traveled by the carrier over a time $t$and, consequently, the average velocity over a distance d can

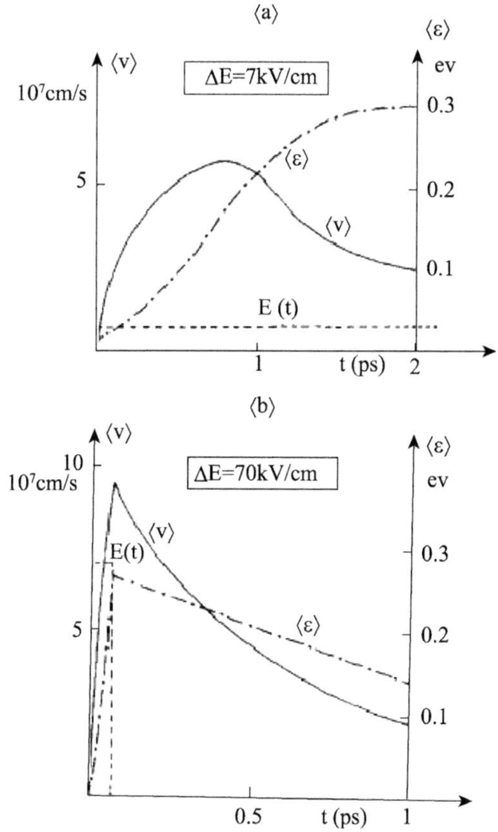

Figure 2.13 Average velocity and average energy of electron in GaAs. The impurity concentration $N_D = 0$ and $T = 77$ K subjected to a time-electric-field step as functions of time. (a) At $t = 0$ an electric-field step $\Delta E = 7$ kV/cm is applied; (b) an electric field pulse $\Delta E = 70$ kV/cm with the duration $\Delta t = 0.06$ ps is applied.

be obtained from the following equations:

$$d = \int_0^T v(t)\,dt, \quad v(d) = \frac{d}{T}. \tag{2.23}$$

Figure 2.13 shows the average velocity and average energy of electrons in GaAs. The impurity concentration $N_D = 0$ and $T = 77$ K are subjected to a time-electric-field step as functions of time [8]. The results are obtained by the Monte Carlo simulation. (a) At $t = 0$

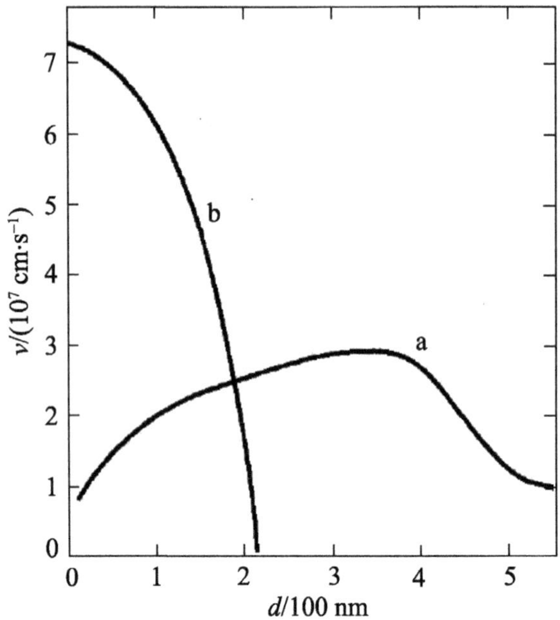

Figure 2.14 Electron average velocities v as functions of traveling distance d: (a) overshoot case and (b) ballistic case.

an electric-field step $\Delta E = 7$ kV/cm is applied; (b) an electric field pulse $\Delta E = 70$ kV/cm with the duration $\Delta t = 0.06$ ps is applied, shown by dashed curves in figures. The former case is called an overshoot, and the latter case is called ballistic by the authors.

When the electron energy is smaller than the polar optical phonon energy (case 1) or smaller than the intervalley energy of Γ and L valleys $\Delta\varepsilon_{\Gamma_L}$ (case 2), the scattering probability is small. Thus, it is possible to obtain very high instantaneous drift velocities 3.5×10^7 and 10^8 cm/s, respectively, in the two cases.

The distance and average velocity of electrons in the time period T can be calculated by Eq. 2.23. For the two cases the calculated $v(d)$ curves are shown in Fig. 2.14. From the figure we see that in the case of an overshoot the maximum average velocity is only half of that in the ballistic case, which occurs at $d = 375$ nm. At this distance the average energy reaches the polar optical phonon energy. In the ballistic case, the average velocity decreases monotonously with the distance, and at $d = 0$ it has the maximum value 7.3×10^7 cm/s. This is because after the electric field pulse the electron does not have energy supplement and the farthest distance is about 200 nm.

2.3 Transport Related to Space

Because the scale of the device becomes smaller and smaller, the role of the velocity overshoot in FET operation is still not entirely clear. The reason is multifold. For one, the overshoot, which may be important in FETs, arises not from the time dependence directly but from the fact that electrons travel across the device in small amounts of time. Transport at each point may, therefore, be time independent. It is the rapid variation (the gradients) of the electric field that results in a velocity overshoot and therefore in increased velocities in FETs even if the transistor is continuously on. Since the spatial gradients of the field are so important, the devices must be very short to exhibit such high gradients.

A high-electron-mobility transistor (HEMT) is shown in Fig. 2.15 [9]. The wider-gap AlGaAs is grown on top of GaAs and is highly doped. The electrons, however, leave their donors and transfer to the lower-gap GaAs, leaving the AlGaAs virtually depleted and creating a high-mobility channel in the GaAs, which is almost free of impurities (modulation doping effect). Electrons move in the high-mobility

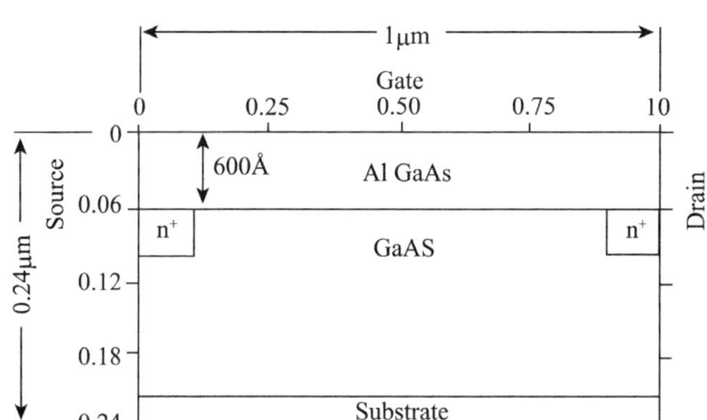

Figure 2.15 Schematic representation of the AlGaAs/GaAs HEMT.

channel, whose length is smaller than 1 μm; hence the electron transport is related to the space.

Here the Monte Carlo simulation needs simultaneously to study the electron motion orbits in the real and momentum spaces. And because the electric field at each point of space is not only decided by the applied electric field but also related to the charge density at that point, the complete self-consistent Monte Carlo simulation should include the solutions of Poisson's equation.

The average velocities of electrons in GaAs after injection in the ⟨100⟩ direction at *k* values are shown in Fig. 2.16 [9]. Figure 2.16a is for a given electric field in the base (10 kV/cm), and in Fig. 2.16b the electric field is varied and the injection energy (*k* value) is fixed. The injected electron is accelerated by a constant electric field and then decelerated due to scattering. Curves a–g in Fig. 2.16a are for injection energies below $\Delta E_{\Gamma L}$ and only curve h is for an energy slightly above $\Delta E_{\Gamma L}$. One can see that within the Γ valley average near-ballistic velocities of up to 8×10^7 cm/s are possible over distances close to 1000 Å. But if the electrons transfer to

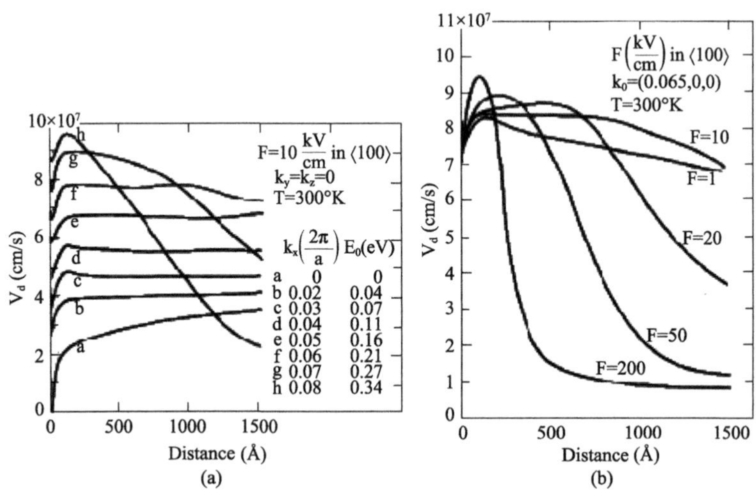

Figure 2.16 Average velocities of electrons in GaAs after injection in the ⟨100⟩ direction at *k* values. (a) Various injection energies for a given electric field in the base (10 kV/cm); (b) the electric field is varied and the injection energy (*k* value) is fixed.

the L valley, the velocity decreases quickly due to the intervalley scattering, as shown by curve h; the ballistic distance decreases to a few hundred angstroms. Figure 2.16b shows the field dependence of the velocity. The higher fields accelerate the electrons above ΔE_{Γ_L} and electron transfer, thus decreasing the velocity. When the electric field is 10 kV/cm, the scattering is compensated by the acceleration of the electric field. The ballistic velocity can be kept to a longer distance. Therefore, the near-ballistic range should extend from a few hundred to thousand angstrom distances depending on the injection energy and the electric field.

Generally, the range in which the electron velocity increases from 0 to the maximum in Fig. 2.16 is called the ballistic range and the range after the maximum to the point of reaching the steady-state velocity is called the overshoot range. In a moderate electric field the steady-state velocity is smaller than 10^7 cm/s. The separation of the ballistic range and the overshoot range is not always as clear as indicated above, and the ballistic range does not always extend to the point of velocity maximum. Especially when the electron injection energy is small (or zero) the velocity maximum is reached only after 4000 Å for an electric field of 10 kV/cm, while the ballistic range is much shorter ($\sim$1000 Å). The velocities as functions of distance for two different injection energies and electric fields are shown in Fig. 2.17 [9].

Figure 2.18 shows the velocity as a function of distance in the channel for a gate voltage of 0.4 eV and various drain voltages of the HEMT device shown in Fig. 2.15 [9], where the heavy horizontal bar marks source, gate, and drain regions. An overshoot is clearly present, particularly at the right side of the gate. There is, however, also a significant portion (close to the source) of the device in which the velocity is below the maximum steady-state value. In this region, the mobility is degraded by hot-electron effects and the field gradients are too small to produce an overshoot. As a consequence, figures of merit such as current switching time, cutoff frequency, and the average draft velocity in the channel, etc., are complicated averages over overshoot regions and regions of mobility degradation and may show no direct trace of overshoot effects.

An alternative method for studying space-dependent phenomena makes use of the balance equation as obtained by the integration

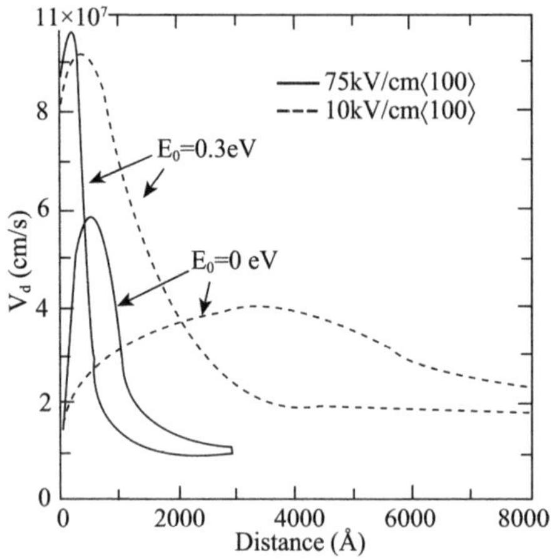

Figure 2.17 Velocities as functions of distance for two different injection energies and electric fields.

of the Boltzmann equation over k space [4]. In the single-valley case, by using a 1D treatment this integration leads to the three fundamental macroscopic equations similar to the balanced equations Eqs. 2.16, which express, respectively, the conversation of the number, momentum, and energy of the particle ensemble,

$$\frac{\partial n}{\partial t}+\frac{\partial\left(n\bar{v}\right)}{\partial x}=0,$$

$$\frac{\partial}{\partial t}\left(nm^{*}\bar{v}\right)=enE-\frac{\partial}{\partial x}\left(nk_{\mathrm{B}}T\right)-\frac{\partial}{\partial x}\left(nm^{*}\bar{v}^{2}\right)-\frac{nm^{*}\bar{v}}{\tau_{\mathrm{p}}\left(\bar{\varepsilon}\right)},$$

and

$$\frac{\partial}{\partial t}\left(n\bar{\varepsilon}\right)=enE\bar{v}-\frac{\partial}{\partial x}\left[n\bar{v}\left(\bar{\varepsilon}+k_{\mathrm{B}}T\right)\right]-n\frac{\bar{\varepsilon}-\varepsilon_{0}}{\tau_{\varepsilon}\left(\bar{\varepsilon}\right)}. \qquad (2.24)$$

Solving Eq. 2.24 and Poisson's equation, the spatial dependence of the drift velocity is obtained for a GaAs n^{+}-n-n^{+} structure under static conditions at 77 K and compared with that obtained with the Monte Carlo method. The results are shown in Fig. 2.19 [4]. It is seen that the agreement is good. The non-uniform velocity distribution in space is similar to that in Fig. 2.18.

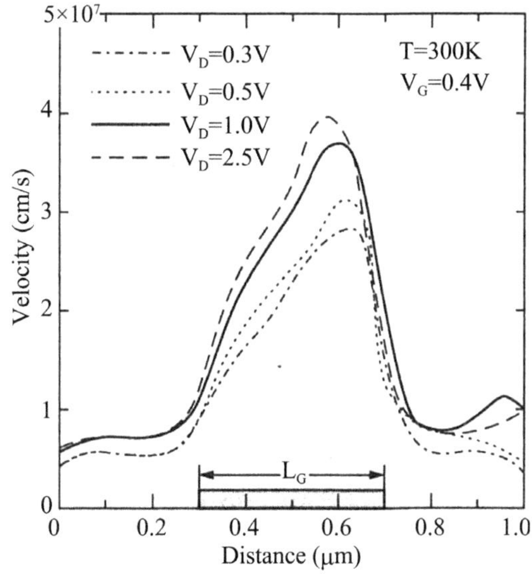

Figure 2.18 Velocity as a function of distance in the channel for a gate voltage of 0.4 eV and various drain voltages of the HEMT device shown in Fig. 2.15.

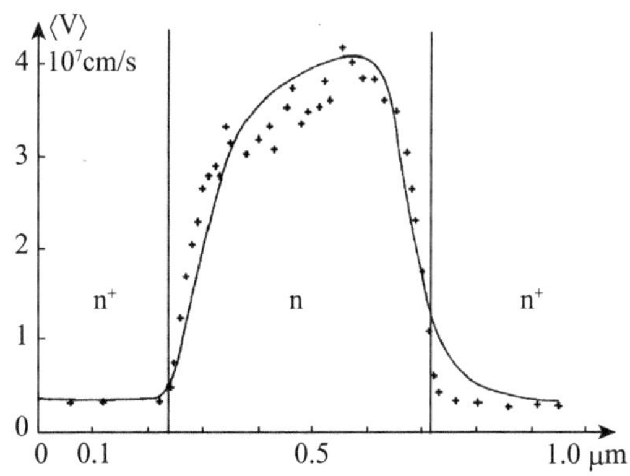

Figure 2.19 Spatial dependence of the drift velocity for a GaAs n^+-n-n^+ structure under static conditions at 77 K obtained from a Monte Carlo simulation (+ + +), and an analytical solution of Eq. 2.24 under static conditions (____).

2.4 Transport in a Si-MOSFET

Silicon metal-oxide semiconductor field-effect transistors (Si-MOSFETs) have been investigated using a large variety of physical models, from full-band Monte Carlo simulations to parabolic-band approximations coupled to Monte Carlo or simplified solutions to the transport equation, but relatively consistent results cannot be obtained. The reason is that the energy band structure of Si is more complicated. It is an indirect bandgap semiconductor, the conduction band bottom is not at Γ point but at X point in the BZ. Thus the various scattering and impact ionization mechanisms are highly anisotropic. Besides, the basic knowledge of transport of the high-energy (>1 eV) electrons in Si is still missed.

For example, due to the anisotropic band structure of Si and the anisotropic intrinsic in ionization processes the spread in the ionization rate is extended over about 1 order of magnitude. Taking into account the realistic joint density of states in Si, and the anisotropic ionization processes, Sano et al. [10] calculated the ionization rate at every point in the first BZ, as shown in Fig. 2.20 by points, with the electron energy measured from the conduction band edge. From the figure we see a large spread in the ionization

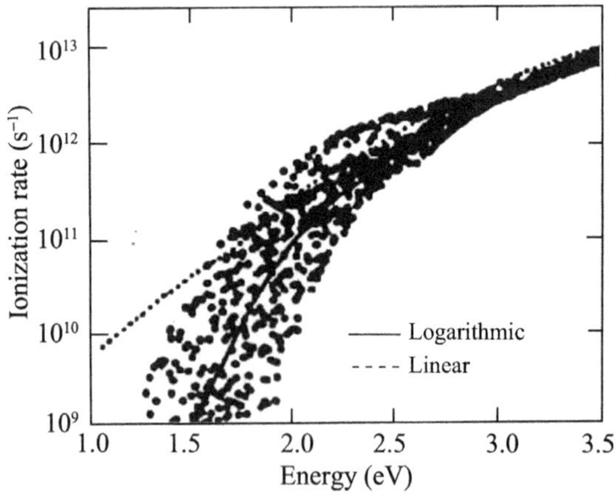

Figure 2.20 Calculated ionization rate as a function of electron energy marked by points, each point for a **k** point in the first Brillouin zone.

rates at low electron energies ($\leq$3 eV), which extends over 2 orders of magnitude. The anisotropy is greatly diminished above 3 eV, where the direct transition across the gap becomes possible. Therefore, a realistic model of the ionization process has to reflect this complexity at low electron energies associated with the realistic joint density of states.

The present anisotropic ionization rate $w_{ii}(\mathbf{k})$ can be transformed into the isotropic energy-dependent ionization rate $w_{ii}(\varepsilon)$ by integrating it over all directions,

$$w_{ii}(\varepsilon) = \frac{\int d\mathbf{k}\delta\left(\varepsilon - \varepsilon_{\mathbf{k}}\right) w_{ii}(\mathbf{k})}{\int d\mathbf{k}\delta\left(\varepsilon - \varepsilon_{\mathbf{k}}\right)}. \tag{2.25}$$

Here the wave-vector-dependent ionization rate $w_{ii}(\mathbf{k})$ is logarithmically interpolated with the eight nearest corners $(k^{(n)})$ $(n = 1, \ldots, 8)$ of each cubic mesh in the BZ,

$$\ln\left[w_{ii}(k)\right] = \sum_{n=1}^{8}\left[\prod_{m=x,y,z}\left(1 - \frac{\left|k_{\mathrm{m}} - k_{\mathrm{m}}^{(n)}\right|}{\Delta k_{\mathrm{m}}}\right)\right] \times \ln\left[w_{ii}\left(k^{(n)}\right)\right]. \tag{2.26}$$

The ionization rates interpolated logarithmically and linearly are shown in Fig. 2. 20 [10] by solid and dotted lines, respectively. From the figure we see that the linear interpolation yields a value larger than all values for the different **k**s, with a given energy near the threshold. This is because when the interpolation is done with a large mesh spacing, the energies at the eight corners in a cubic mesh could vary greatly so that some rates in a cubic mesh could be quite large. As a result, the ionization rate linearly interpolated from those values could be larger than the values for the different *k*s with a given energy.

The present energy-dependent ionization rate averaged over all directions (solid line) is compared in Fig. 2.21 [10] with Kane's ab initio theoretical result (dotted line), the rates extracted from recent experiments of the IBM group (dashed line), and the ab initio calculation result of the Osaka group (black points). The present results closely agree with those of both the IBM group and the Osaka group.

On the basis of the relative consistence of the ionization rates and electron-phonon scattering rates Sano et al. applied the full-band Monte Carlo method to simulate a typical MOSFET structure

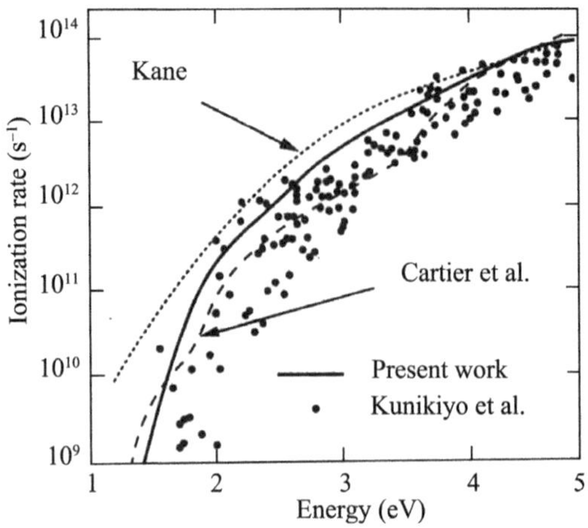

Figure 2.21 Present energy-dependent ionization rate averaged over all directions (solid line) is compared with Kane's ab initio theoretical result (dotted line), the rates extracted from recent experiments of the IBM group (dashed line), and the ab initio calculation result of the Osaka group (black points).

with two different gate lengths $L_g = 250$ nm and 40 nm to present, respectively, submicron and sub-0.1-micron devices. Figure 2.22 shows the electric field profiles as a function of distance along the channel under various applied source-drain voltages V_d [11]. From

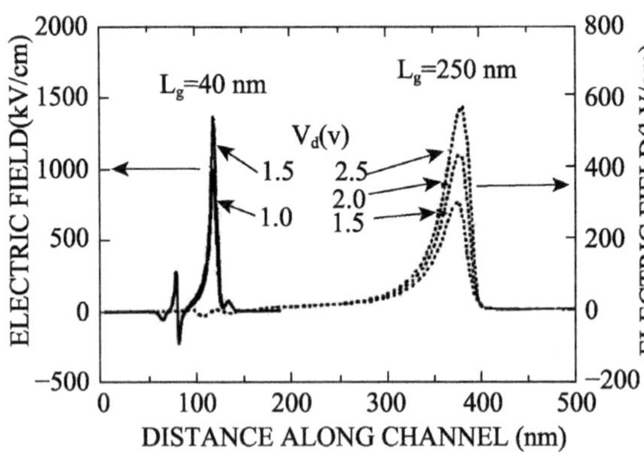

Figure 2.22 Electric field profiles as a function of distance along the channel under various applied source-drain voltages V_d. Notice that the scales of the electric fields of the two MOSFETs are different.

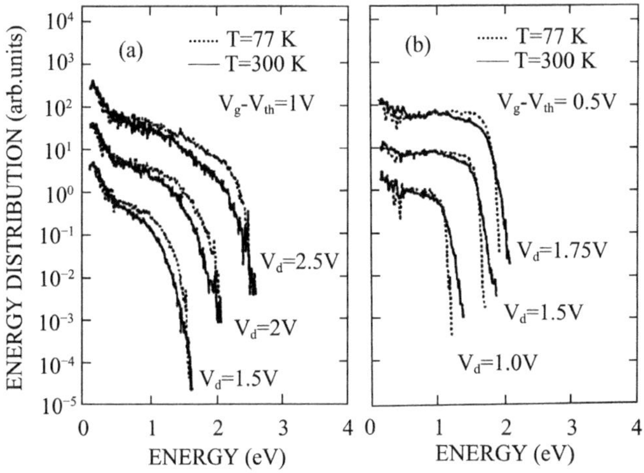

Figure 2.23 Electron energy distributions integrated over the drain regions at 300 K (solid lines) and 77 K (dotted lines) for (a) $L_g = 250$ nm and (b) 40 nm.

the figure we see that there is a very large electric field in the channel of the gate region. Especially in the small-scale device ($L_g = 40$ nm), the electric field can reach 1000 kV/cm.

Figure 2.23 shows the electron energy distributions integrated over the drain regions at 300 K and 77 K [11]. The shapes of the energy distribution are very different for the two devices: in the 250-nm-gate MOSFET, electrons suffer several energy-dissipating scatterings before they reach the drain and, thus, the energy distribution in the regions between several hundred millielectron volts and qV_d smoothly decreases. The number of electrons at 77 K in these energy regions is much larger because of the reduced phonon scattering. This fact demonstrates the diffusive transport property. On the other hand, in a 40-nm-gate MOSFET, the energy distribution does not show significant energy dissipation and the contribution of ballistic electrons is much more pronounced. The electron energy distribution shows a clear transition from a diffusion-energy-dissipating transport regime in a 250-nm-gate MOSFET to a quasi-ballistic transport regime in a 40-nm-gate MOSFET.

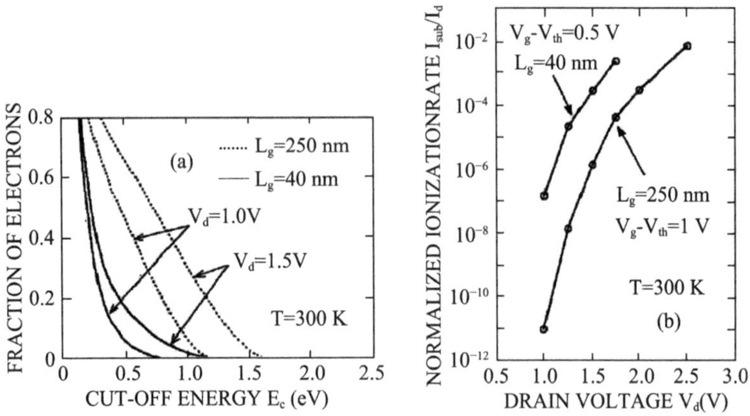

Figure 2.24 (a) Fractions of electrons with energy above the cutoff energy E_c (normalized by the total number of electrons) as a function of $(E - E_c)$ for $L_g = 250$ nm MOSFET (solid lines) and 40 nm MOSFET (dotted lines). (b) Normalized ionization rate for two MOSFETs at 300 K as a function of drain voltage.

Such transition of transport characteristics implies that the fraction of overshoot electrons with respect to the whole electrons in the drain becomes larger as the device size decreases. Figure 2.24a shows the number of electrons with energy above the cutoff energy E_c (normalized by the total number of electrons) as a function of $(E - E_c)$ [11]. The number of electrons with energy above E_c decreases rapidly in the 250-nm-gate MOSFET, whereas it occupies quite a large portion in the 40-nm-gate MOSFET. Therefore, as the device size shrinks, impact ionization tends to be more significant, as shown in Fig. 2.24b. In other words, even if the supply drain voltage is reduced, hot carrier effects could still exist in sub-0.1-micron devices and even more violent than in submicron devices.

2.5 Quantum Simulation Method: Quantum Moment Equations

The classical semiconductor transport theory is based on the Boltzmann transport equation (BTE). The Monte Carlo method provides the most accurate and detailed solution but is limited in practical engineering applications for its computational expenses. One improvement uses a set of quantum moment equations developed from a Wigner function prototype, which preserves explicit quantum corrections as well as the classical hydrodynamic model features [12]. Explicit quantum corrections are built into these equations by using the quantum-mechanical expression of the second moments of the Wigner function, which results in an average electron energy that consists of drift kinetic, thermal, and quantum-potential terms. These equations are then applied to the numerical simulation of ultra-submicron GaAs metal-semiconductor field-effect transistors (MESFETs), which demonstrates expected quantum effects in the devices.

To get explicit quantum corrections into the moment equations, several methods have been proposed. On the basis of the quantum representation of the second moments $\langle p^2 \rangle$, the quantum corrections through the energy representation are explicitly incorporated,

$$w = \frac{1}{2}m^* v^2 + \frac{3}{2}k_B T + U_q, \tag{2.27}$$

where T is the average electron effective temperature; U_q is the quantum correction,

$$U_q = -\frac{\hbar^2}{8m^*}\nabla^2 \ln(n); \tag{2.28}$$

and n is the electron density. The quantum correction involves the second-order space derivative of the log density. Thus the correction tends to smooth the electron distribution, especially where the electron density has a sharp change, for example, when approaching a large potential barrier.

A set of quantum moment equations with temperature representation is then written as

$$\frac{\partial n}{\partial t} + \nabla \cdot (n\mathbf{v}) = 0,$$

$$\frac{\partial \mathbf{v}}{\partial t} + \mathbf{v} \cdot \nabla \mathbf{v} = -\frac{q\mathbf{E}}{m^*} - \frac{1}{nm^*}\nabla\left(nk_B T_q\right) - \frac{\mathbf{v}}{\tau_m},$$

and

$$\frac{\partial T}{\partial t} + \frac{1}{3}\mathbf{v} \cdot \nabla\left(T_q\right) = -\frac{2}{3}\nabla \cdot \left(\mathbf{v}T_q\right) + \frac{m^* v^2}{3k_B}\left(\frac{2}{\tau_m} - \frac{1}{\tau_w}\right) - \frac{T - T_0}{\tau_w}, \tag{2.29}$$

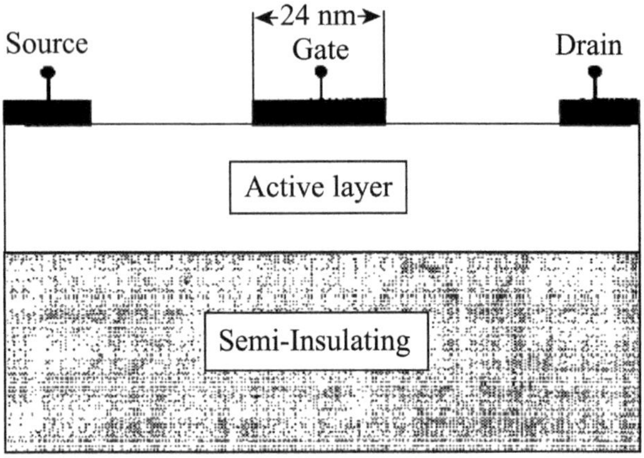

Figure 2.25 MESFET structure for simulation.

where **E** is the electric field, τ_m is the momentum relaxation time, τ_w is the energy relaxation time, T_0 is the lattice temperature, and

$$T_q = T + \frac{2}{3k_B}U_q. \tag{2.30}$$

This set of equations preserves all classical features and gives explicit quantum corrections. As $\hbar$ goes to zero, the equations return to full classical hydrodynamics equations. From Eq. 2.30 one observes that if the thermal energy of the electron is large, the quantum correction has less effect. But as the temperature is lowered, the quantum correction will become dominant. Allying with the Poison equation, Eq. 2.29 forms the basic equations for numerical simulation of ultra-small devices.

The MESFET for simulation is shown in Fig. 2.25 [12], which consists of semi-insulating substrate; an active layer; and three electrodes, source, gate, and drain. The source and drain electrodes are ohmic contact, and the gate electrode is a Schottky contact. The gate voltage V_g produces a depletion region in the channel, whose thickness depends on V_g, then decides the conduction channel between the source and drain.

The parameters of the simulated MESFET device are gate length 24 nm, doping in the channel 1.5×10^{18} cm^{-3}, and lattice temperature 300 K. Assume that the electron property is

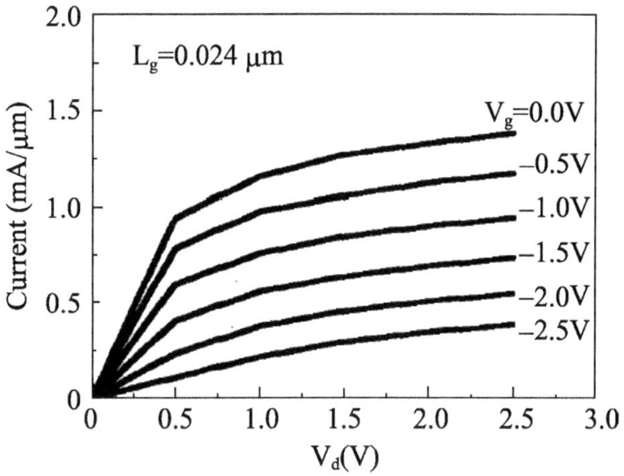

Figure 2.26 $I-V$ characteristics of the 24-nm-gate device.

independent along the transverse coordinate z, the current is along the x direction, and the perpendicular direction is y direction. The finite-difference method is used to discretize Eq. 2.29 and the Poison equation in the $x - y$ two-dimensional (2D) MESFET structure (Fig. 2.25).

The $I-V$ characteristics of the device are shown in Fig. 2.26 [12]. The gate voltage runs from 0 to −2.5 V. The characteristics suggest that the device has a normal working performance. Saturation of the current is observed. When $V_g = -2.5$ V, the electrons are completely depleted in the channel. The remaining current is due to the substrate current as the electrons are pushed into the substrate. Within the saturation region, the maximum transconductance occurs near $V_g = -0.5$ V.

The effect of the gate length on the transconductance is investigated at a drain voltage of 2.0 V, for a fixed active layer depth and doping concentration. Figure 2.27 shows the transconductance characteristics in the range of gate lengths from 24 to 96 nm, for two active layer depths ($a = 30$ nm and 39 nm) [12]. The transconductance for $a = 30$ nm has a maximum value of about 800 mS/mm at a gate length of 60 nm. The transconductance for $a =$ 39 nm decreases monotonically for the entire range as gate length

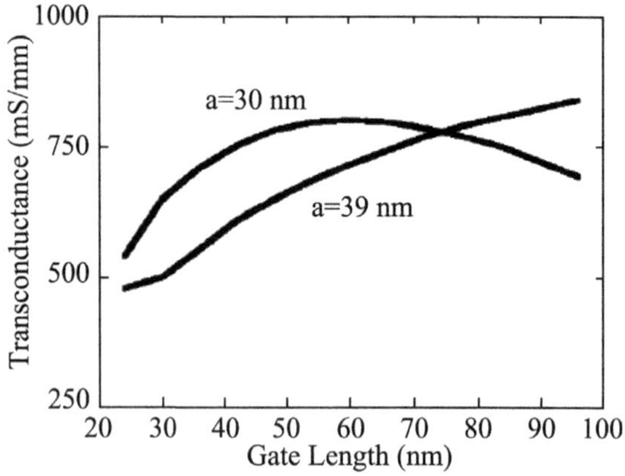

Figure 2.27 Transconductance versus gate length for two active layer depths ($a = 30$ nm and 39 nm).

decreases. The small aspect ratio effect begins at a larger gate length for thicker active devices.

2.6 Simulation of Ultra-Small HEMT Devices

The schematic structure of a HEMT is shown in Fig. 2.15. In a GaAs MESFET the impurity doping in the channel is high and ionized impurity scattering decreases the electron mobility at room temperature from the best value of $\sim$9000 $cm^2/(V{\cdot}s)$ to 2000 $\approx$ 3000 $cm^2/(V{\cdot}s)$. In the 1970s the modulation doping heterojunction was proposed. In a wide-gap semiconductor, for example AlGaAs, there is a δ doping layer. At room temperature the impurities are ionized and the electrons from the ionized impurities move into the neighboring GaAs layer. Due to the space charge effect of the ionized impurities a potential well of triangular shape is formed at the interface of AlGaAs and GaAs. The electrons gather in this quantum well and form a two-dimensional electron gas (2DEG) layer. Because the doping layer leaves from the interface a distance, the ionized impurities provide electrons and at the same time do not scatter the electrons in the 2DEG, thus greatly increasing electron mobility, which may even exceed the best value in bulk GaAs.

Zhou et al. [13] used the quantum moment equations (Eq. 2.29) to simulate the HEMT devices, including the carrier degeneracy effects. As the electron density increases to a high concentration level, the Pauli principle ensures that not all electrons can return to the lowest energy level, even at equilibrium. The effect leads to a higher value of the total average energy of the electrons. A direct effect of the degeneracy is on the electron mobility, which is determined by the scattering processes at a given energy level. The momentum and energy relaxation times are computed from Monte Carlo results. If one assumes that the increase of energy due to degeneracy is essentially the thermal energy $3/2\ \gamma k_B T$, then the use of scattering rates from the Monte Carlo results without degeneracy calculated at T instead of γT remains good approximation.

Modulation of the momentum equations (Eq. 2.29) can be made by assuming a drift Fermi–Dirac distribution function, which results in a degeneracy correction factor to the effective electron temperature. The total electron energy can be written as

$$w = \frac{1}{2} m^* v^2 + \frac{3}{2} \gamma k_B T + U_q, \tag{2.31}$$

where γ is the degeneracy factor,

$$\gamma = \gamma \left(\mu / k_B T \right) = \frac{F_{3/2} \left(\mu / k_B T \right)}{F_{1/2} \left(\mu / k_B T \right)}, \tag{2.32}$$

F_j is the Fermi–Dirac integral, and μ is the Fermi energy measured from the conduction band bottom. After modification of the equations, the T_q in Eq. 2.29 is changed to

$$T_q = \gamma T + \frac{2}{3k_B} U_q. \tag{2.33}$$

The degeneracy factor γ as a function of the factor $n/(k_B T)^{3/2}$ is shown in Fig. 2.28 for GaAs and AlGaAs [13]. The degeneracy factor γ rises significantly only after the ratio of density to thermal energy exceeds 10^{20} cm^{-3}·eV$^{-3/2}$, that is, the degeneracy effect occurs at a high density and low temperature.

The electron density profile of a 24-nm-gate-length device at the center of the gate as a function of the distance from the surface (see Fig. 2.25) into the bulk at a bias condition of $V_g = -1.5$ V and $V_d = 1.0$ V is shown in Fig. 2.29 [13], where the interface between GaAs and AlGaAs is at 40 nm. The solid line is the result including the

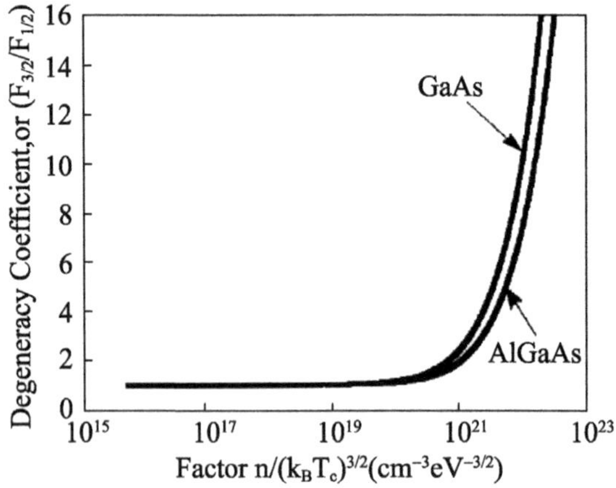

Figure 2.28 Degeneracy factor γ as a function of the factor $n/(k_B T)^{3/2}$ for GaAs and AlGaAs.

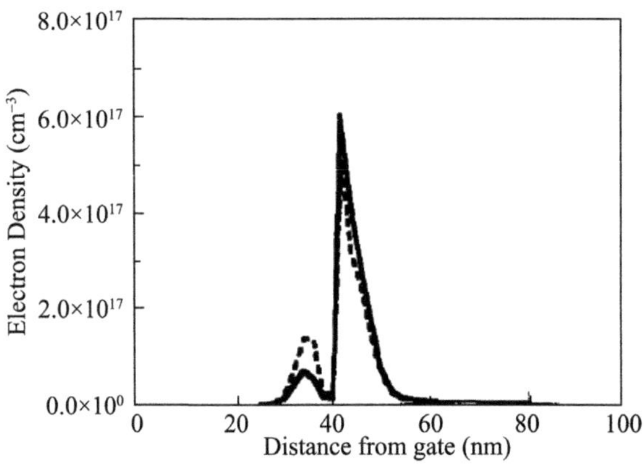

Figure 2.29 Electron density profile of a 24-nm-gate-length device at the center of the gate as a function of the distance from the surface (see Fig. 2.25) into the bulk.

quantum pressure effect, and the dashed line is that neglecting the quantum pressure effect. From the figure one sees that a parallel conduction channel in the AlGaAs is present but is reduced by the quantum effect. The conduction electrons are mostly confined within 10 nm of the interface in the GaAs. The tail of the density distribution in the GaAs (toward the bulk) shows evidence that more

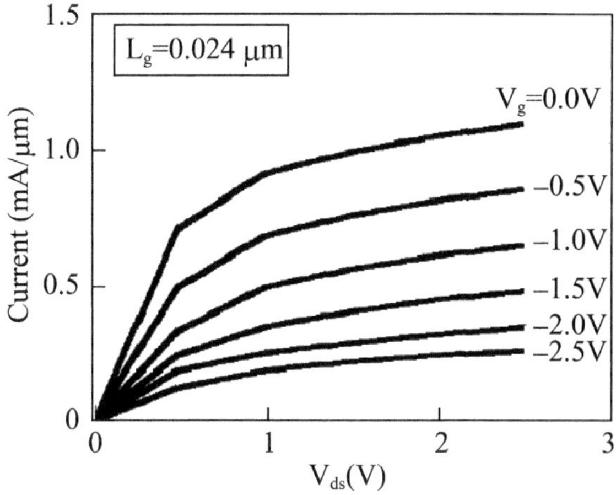

Figure 2.30 I–V characteristics for a 24-nm-gate-length device.

electrons are pushed into the substrate when the quantum pressure is included.

The computed I–V characteristics for a 24-nm-gate-length device are shown in Fig. 2.30 [13], where the gate bias runs from 0 to −2.5 V, in steps of −0.5 V. The transconductance decreases linearly from about 500 mS/mm to some 250 mS/mm as the gate bias becomes more negative.

References

1. Ye, L. X. (1969). Monte-Carlo Simulation of Small Scale Semiconductor Devices (Academic Press, Beijing) (in Chinese).
2. Rees, H. D. (1969). Calculation of distribution functions by exploiting the stability of the steady state. *J. Phys. Chem. Solids*, **30**, 643–655.
3. Nougier, J. P., Vaissiere, J. C., and Gasquet, D. (1981). Determination of transient regime of hot carriers in semiconductors, using the relaxation time approximations. *J. Appl. Phys.*, **52**, 825–832.
4. Constant, E. (1985). *Hot-Electron Transport in Semiconductors*, eds. Reggiani, L., Chapter 8 "Non-steady-state transport in semiconductors in perspective with submicrometer devices," (Springer-Verlag, Berlin), pp. 227–261.

5. Tomizawa, K., Awano, Y., and Hashizume, N. (1984). Monte Carlo simulation of AlGaAs/GaAs heterojunction bipolar transistors. *IEEE Electron Device Lett.*, **5**, 362–364.
6. Unterrainer, K., Keay, B. J., Wanke, M. C., et al. (1996). *Hot Carriers in Semiconductors*, eds. Hess, K., Leburton, J. P., Rivaioli, U., "Strong terahertz-photocurrent resonances in miniband superlattices at the Bloch frequency" (Plenum, New York), pp. 135–138.
7. Xia, J. B., (1998). Theory of terahertz-photocurrent resonances in miniband superlattices. *Phys. Rev. B*, **58**, 3565–3567.
8. Ghis, A., Constant, E., and Boittiaux, B. (1983). Ballistic and overshoot electron transport in bulk semiconductors and in submicronic devices. *J. Appl. Phys.*, **54**, 214–221.
9. Hess, K., and Iafrate, G. J. (1988). Theory and applications of near ballistic transport in semiconductors. *Proc. IEEE*, **76**, 519–532.
10. Sano, N., and Yoshii, A. (1994). Impact ionization rate near thresholds in Si. *J. Appl. Phys.*, **75**, 5102–5105.
11. Sano, N., Tomizawa, M., and Yoshii, A. (1996). *Hot Carriers in Semiconductors*, eds. Hess, K., Leburton, J. P., Rivaioli, U., "Impact ionization in submicro and sub-0.1 micro Si-MOSFETs" (Plenum, New York), pp. 337–342.
12. Zhou, J. R., and Ferry, D. K. (1992). Simulation of ultra-small GaAs MESFET using quantum moment equations. *IEEE Trans. Electron Devices*, **39**, 473–478.
13. Zhou, J. R., and Ferry, D. K. (1992). Modeling of quantum effects in ultrasmall HEMT devives. *IEEE Trans. Electron Devices*, **40**, 421–427.

Chapter 3

Resonant Tunneling

In 1970 Tsu and Esaki [1] proposed a one-dimensional superlattice. At the same time they proposed the concept of resonant tunneling. They indicated that in such a structure the period is smaller than the electron mean free path and intriguing transport properties such as negative differential conductivity and Bloch oscillation can be realized. Soon afterward Chang et al. [2] observed experimentally the resonant tunneling of electrons in double-barrier structures having a thin GaAs potential well sandwiched between two GaAlAs barriers. The current and conductance characteristics of this structure show the resonant singularities corresponding to the resonant states in the GaAs quantum well. The singularities actually exhibit a decrease in current, giving rise to a negative differential resistance (NDR). Due to the development of the molecular beam epitaxy technology, and the improving of the quality of the sample, the negative resistance can be observed not only at a low temperature but also at room temperature clearly [3–5]. The peak-to-valley ratio (PVR) representing the level of the resonant tunneling structure of 30 and 63 at 300 K and 77 K, respectively, has been reached for an AlAs/InAs/AlAs double potential barrier structure [5].

As for application, the advantage of the resonant tunneling diode (RTD) is that the basic time related to the tunneling process is very

Quantum Waveguide in Microcircuits
Jian-Bai Xia, Duan-Yang Liu, and Wei-Dong Sheng

ISBN 978-981-4669-85-6 (Hardcover), 978-1-315-36477-3 (eBook)
www.panstanford.com

short, generally taken as the reciprocal of the quasi-confined state in the quantum well (i.e., the reciprocal of the resonant width). For the high-frequency response of a RTD, it is decided by two time constants: one is the tunneling time through the barrier and the other is the RC time constant associated with the structure capacitance. Optimizing the device structure, these time constants can be minimized. The frequency of the mixed frequency device using the NDR effect has reached 1.8 THz (1.8×10^{12} Hz). When the NDR effect is used as an oscillator, the frequency reached is 0.42 THz [6]. When the NDR effect is used for a high-speed switch, the raising time is shorter than 2 ps [7].

3.1 Single-Barrier Structure

To explain some basic concepts of resonant tunneling (RT), we consider a single potential barrier as shown in Fig. 3.1. Assume that both sides are GaAs material and the middle potential barrier is $Al_xGa_{1-x}As$ material, whose width is $w = 2a$, and the barrier height is V_0 depending on x. The Schrödinger equation of electron motion is

$$\left(-\frac{\hbar^2}{2}\frac{\partial}{\partial z}\frac{1}{m^*(z)}\frac{\partial}{\partial z} + V_{\text{eff}}(z)\right)\varphi(z) = E\varphi(z), \tag{3.1}$$

where $m^*(z)$ is the effective mass, which is generally different for GaAs and $Al_xGa_{1-x}As$, and thus is a function of z.

An electron with energy E enters into the structure from the left 1 region and leaves from the right 3 region. The electron wave

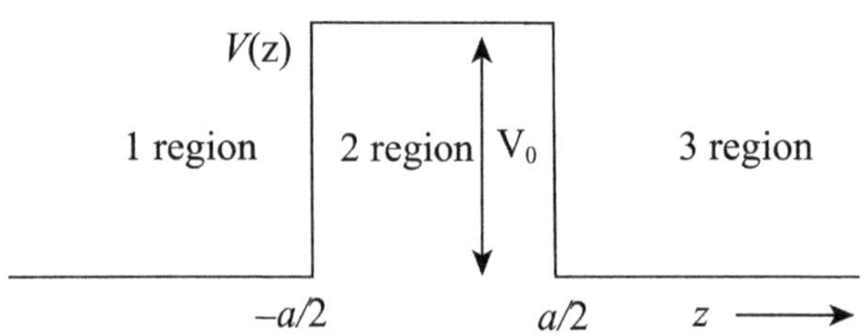

Figure 3.1 Energy band diagram of the single potential barrier.

function in the three regions in Fig. 3.1 are, respectively,

$$\varphi_1(z) = a_1 e^{ikz} + b_1 e^{-ikz}, \qquad z < -a;$$
$$\varphi_2(z) = a_2 e^{Kz} + b_2 e^{-Kz}, \qquad -a < z < a;$$

and

$$\varphi_3(z) = a_3 e^{ikz} + b_3 e^{-ikz}, \qquad z > a, \tag{3.2}$$

where

$$k = \sqrt{\frac{2m_1{}^*E}{\hbar^2}}, \qquad K = \sqrt{\frac{2m_2{}^*(V_0 - E)}{\hbar^2}}. \tag{3.3}$$

where $m_1{}^*$ and $m_2{}^*$ are the electron effective masses in the 1,3 and 2 regions, respectively. In the 1 and 3 regions, the electron energy $E > 0$. Hence the electron waves are plane waves. In the 2 region, $E < V_0$, and the electron wave is an evanescent wave.

By use of the boundary conditions at the interface of the 1 and 2 regions ($z = -a$),

$$\varphi_1(-a) = \varphi_2(-a),$$

and

$$\left.\frac{1}{m_1{}^*}\frac{\partial \varphi_1}{\partial z}\right|_{-a_-} = \left.\frac{1}{m_2{}^*}\frac{\partial \varphi_2}{\partial z}\right|_{-a_+}. \tag{3.4}$$

We obtain

$$a_1 + b_1 = a_2 + b_2,$$

and

$$\frac{ik}{m_1{}^*}(a_1 - b_1) = \frac{K}{m_2{}^*}(a_2 - b_2). \tag{3.5}$$

In calculating Eq. 3.5 we assumed that the coordinate origin is taken at $z = -a$. The choice of the coordinate origin can be as one pleases; the results are only different from a phase factor.

Introduce the concept of the transfer matrix, which connects the coefficients of the wave function at point A to those at point B. For example, the coefficients of the wave function at the 1 region $z = -a_-$ are a_1 and b_1 and those at the 2 region at $z = -a_+$ are a_2 and b_2. They are connected by the transfer matrix M_1,

$$\begin{pmatrix} a_1 \\ b_1 \end{pmatrix} = M_1 \begin{pmatrix} a_2 \\ b_2 \end{pmatrix}. \tag{3.6}$$

The M_1 can be calculated directly from Eq. 3.5,

$$M_1 = \frac{1}{2}\begin{vmatrix} (1-ir) & (1+ir) \\ (1+ir) & (1-ir) \end{vmatrix}, \tag{3.7}$$

where $r = m_1{}^*K/m_2{}^*k$.

In the 2 region, define the transfer matrix,

$$\begin{pmatrix} a_2 \\ b_2 \end{pmatrix} = M_2 \begin{pmatrix} a_2' \\ b_2' \end{pmatrix}, \tag{3.8}$$

where $a_2{}'$ and $b_2{}'$ are the coefficients of $\varphi_2(z)$ with the coordinate origin at $z = a$. Thus

$$M_2 = \begin{vmatrix} e^{-2Ka} & 0 \\ 0 & e^{2Ka} \end{vmatrix}. \tag{3.9}$$

Using the boundary conditions at the interface of the 2 and 3 regions ($z = a$), we obtain

$$a_2' + b_2' = a_3 + b_3,$$

and

$$\frac{K}{m_2{}^*}(a_2' - b_2') = \frac{ik}{m_1{}^*}(a_3 - b_3). \tag{3.10}$$

Define the transfer matrix,

$$\begin{pmatrix} a_2' \\ b_2' \end{pmatrix} = M_3 \begin{pmatrix} a_3 \\ b_3 \end{pmatrix}. \tag{3.11}$$

The transfer matrix M_3 can be calculated from Eq. 3.10,

$$M_3 = \frac{1}{2}\begin{vmatrix} \left(1+\frac{i}{r}\right) & \left(1-\frac{i}{r}\right) \\ \left(1-\frac{i}{r}\right) & \left(1+\frac{i}{r}\right) \end{vmatrix}. \tag{3.12}$$

The total transfer matrix M connects the wave function at the input end and that at the output end. Hence

$$\begin{pmatrix} a_1 \\ b_1 \end{pmatrix} = M \begin{pmatrix} a_3 \\ b_3 \end{pmatrix}, \tag{3.13}$$

where

$$M = M_1 M_2 M_3.$$

Suppose the coefficient of the injected wave function e^{ikz} at the input end $a_1 = 1$; then b_1 represents the amplitude of the reflective wave e^{-ikz}. At the output end the coefficient of the transmitted wave e^{ikz} is a_3 and the coefficient of the returning wave e^{-ikz} $b_3 = 0$. Thus from Eq. 3.13,

$$\begin{pmatrix} 1 \\ b_1 \end{pmatrix} = \begin{pmatrix} M_{11} & M_{12} \\ M_{21} & M_{22} \end{pmatrix} \begin{pmatrix} a_3 \\ 0 \end{pmatrix}. \tag{3.14}$$

We obtain

$$a_3 = 1/M_{11} \quad \text{and} \quad b_1 = M_{21}a_3 = M_{21}/M_{11}. \tag{3.15}$$

The transmission probability and the reflection probability are, respectively,

$$T = |a_3|^2 \quad \text{and} \quad R = |b_1|^2. \tag{3.16}$$

The transfer matrix elements M_{11} and M_{21} in Eq. 3.15 can be calculated from Eq. 3.13 and Eqs. 3.7, 3.9, and 3.12,

$$\begin{aligned} M_{11} &= \frac{1}{4}\left[\left(2 - ir + \frac{i}{r}\right)e^{-2Ka} + \left(2 + ir - \frac{i}{r}\right)e^{2Ka}\right] \\ &= \cosh(2Ka) - \frac{i}{2}\left(r - \frac{1}{r}\right)\sinh(2Ka), \end{aligned}$$

and

$$\begin{aligned} M_{21} &= \frac{1}{4}\left[\left(ir + \frac{i}{r}\right)e^{-2Ka} + \left(-ir - \frac{i}{r}\right)e^{2Ka}\right] \\ &= -\frac{i}{2}\left(r + \frac{1}{r}\right)\sinh(2Ka). \end{aligned} \tag{3.17}$$

Then from Eqs. 3.15 and 3.16 we obtain

$$T = \frac{1}{1 + \left(r + \frac{1}{r}\right)^2 \sinh^2(2Ka)},$$

and

$$R = \frac{\left(r + \frac{1}{r}\right)^2 \sinh^2(2Ka)}{1 + \left(r + \frac{1}{r}\right)^2 \sinh^2(2Ka)}. \tag{3.18}$$

It is deduced from Eq. 3.18 that $T + R = 1$, which means the conservation of particle number.

The problem of the barrier tunneling is a nonstatic problem. We only know the amplitude of the injected wave and need to calculate simultaneously the amplitudes of the reflective wave and transmitted wave. The transfer matrix method is suitable for the two-terminal device with a complicated structure in the middle. For the multiple terminal devices, the scattering matrix method is useful.

Suppose there is an M terminal device, there are injected wave and transmitted wave at each terminal, and their coefficients are b_i and a_i ($i = 1, 2, \ldots, M$), respectively. The scattering matrix S connects the two sets of coefficients,

$$\begin{pmatrix} a_1 \\ a_2 \\ \vdots \\ a_M \end{pmatrix} = (S(E)) \begin{pmatrix} b_1 \\ b_2 \\ \vdots \\ b_M \end{pmatrix}. \tag{3.19}$$

If the coefficient of the injected wave at the j-th terminal $b_j = 1$, those at other terminals all equal zero. Then the coefficients of the transmitted waves at all other terminals and that of the reflective wave at the j-th terminal can be calculated from Eq. 3.19,

$$a_i = S_{ij} \quad (i = 1, \cdots M, \neq j)$$

and

$$a_j = S_{jj}. \tag{3.20}$$

We take the single-barrier tunneling as an example to calculate the scattering matrix. Define $b_2 e^{-Kz}$ as the wave that travels toward right and $a_2 e^{Kz}$ as the wave that travels toward left. Then the scattering matrix at the boundary $z = -a$ is written as

$$\begin{pmatrix} b_1 \\ b_2 \end{pmatrix} = (S_1) \begin{pmatrix} a_1 \\ a_2 \end{pmatrix}. \tag{3.21}$$

The scattering matrix S_1 can be calculated from Eq. 3.5,

$$S_1 = \frac{1}{1+ir} \begin{pmatrix} 1-ir & 2ir \\ 2 & -1+ir \end{pmatrix}. \tag{3.22}$$

In the barrier 2 region the scattering matrix is

$$\begin{pmatrix} a_2 \\ b_2' \end{pmatrix} = (S_2) \begin{pmatrix} b_2 \\ a_2' \end{pmatrix} \tag{3.23}$$

and

$$S_2 = \begin{pmatrix} 0 & e^{-2Ka} \\ e^{-2Ka} & 0 \end{pmatrix}. \tag{3.24}$$

The scattering matrix at the boundary $z = a$ is

$$\begin{pmatrix} a_2' \\ a_3 \end{pmatrix} = (S_3) \begin{pmatrix} b_2' \\ b_3 \end{pmatrix}. \tag{3.25}$$

S_3 can be calculated from Eq. 3.10,

$$S_3 = \frac{1}{1+ir} \begin{pmatrix} -1+ir & 2 \\ 2ir & 1-ir \end{pmatrix}. \tag{3.26}$$

The total scattering matrix in the single-barrier tunneling case is

$$\begin{pmatrix} b_1 \\ a_3 \end{pmatrix} = (S) \begin{pmatrix} a_1 \\ b_3 \end{pmatrix}. \tag{3.27}$$

But the total scattering matrix is not the multiplication of three matrices S_1, S_2, and S_3 but equals a special multiplication of three matrices introduced by Ando et al. [7],

$$S = S_1 \otimes S_2 \otimes S_3. \tag{3.28}$$

Suppose that there are two scattering matrices,

$$S_1 = \begin{pmatrix} r_1 & t_1' \\ t_1 & r_1' \end{pmatrix} \text{ and } S_2 = \begin{pmatrix} r_2 & t_2' \\ t_2 & r_2' \end{pmatrix}. \tag{3.29}$$

The matrix elements of the multiplication of S_1 and $S_2 S_{12} = S_1 \otimes S_2$ are

$$t_{12} = t_2(1 - r_1' r_2)^{-1} t_1,$$
$$t_{12}' = t_1'(1 - r_2 r_1')^{-1} t_2',$$
$$r_{12} = r_1 + t_1' r_2 (1 - r_1' r_2)^{-1} t_1,$$

and

$$r_{12}' = r_2' + t_2 r_1' (1 - r_2 r_1')^{-1} t_2'. \tag{3.30}$$

The results obtained from the transfer matrix method and the scattering matrix methods are the same. The transfer matrix method is convenient for the two-terminal devices, but for the multi-terminal devices we can only use the scattering matrix method. Besides, if the length of the barrier region a is too large the transfer matrix element (Eq. 3.9) e^{2Ka} from the evanescent wave will approach infinite, resulting in calculation divergence difficulty. While in the scattering matrix (Eq. 3.24) where the two matrix elements are e^{-2Ka}, the divergence difficulty does not appear.

In Eq. 3.16 the transmission probability T and reflection probability R equal the square of the coefficients of the transmitted wave a_3 and the reflective wave b_1, respectively. In the general cases, they should equal

$$T = |a_3|^2 v_2 \quad \text{and} \quad R = |b_1|^2 v_1 . \tag{3.31}$$

The injected electron current,

$$I = |a_1|^2 v_1, \tag{3.32}$$

where v_1 and v_2 are the velocities of the electron waves at the input end and output end, respectively. For the conduction band electron the velocity is proportional to the wave vector, $v = \hbar k/m^*$. In the case of a single barrier (Fig. 3.1) $k_1 = k_2$, then Eq. 3.16 is valid, but is a special case.

To illustrate the meaning of Eq. 3.31 we consider a non-symmetric single potential barrier as shown in Fig. 3.2, where the energy bottom of the output region is lower than those of the input and barrier regions $-V_1$. In this case, the transfer matrices M_1 and M_2 are the same as Eqs. 3.7 and 3.9, while

$$M_3 = \frac{1}{2}\begin{vmatrix} \left(1+\frac{i}{r'}\right) & \left(1-\frac{i}{r'}\right) \\ \left(1-\frac{i}{r'}\right) & \left(1+\frac{i}{r'}\right) \end{vmatrix}, \tag{3.33}$$

where

$$r' = \frac{m_1{}^* K}{m_2{}^* k'} \quad \text{and} \quad k' = \sqrt{\frac{2m_1{}^*(E+V_1)}{\hbar^2}}. \tag{3.34}$$

Suppose the injected electron current is 1. From Eqs. 3.31 and 3.32 we define

$$a_1 \sim \frac{1}{\sqrt{k}}, \quad a_3 \sim \frac{t}{\sqrt{k'}}, \quad \text{and} \quad b_1 \sim \frac{r}{\sqrt{k}}. \tag{3.35}$$

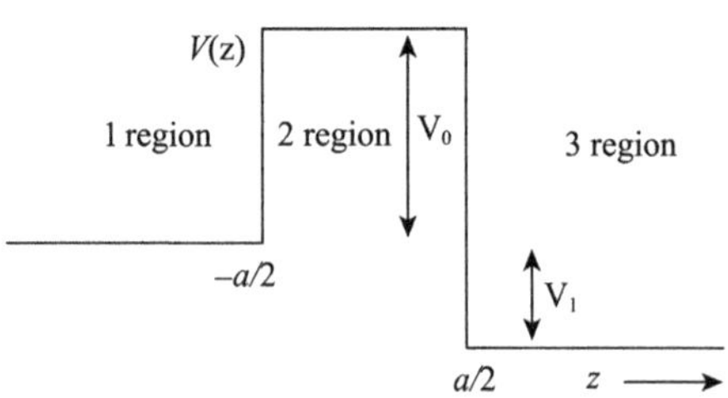

Figure 3.2 Non-symmetric single potential barrier schematic diagram.

The transmission probability and reflection probability are, respectively,

$$T = |t|^2 \quad \text{and} \quad R = |r|^2. \tag{3.36}$$

Equation 3.14 is changed to

$$\begin{pmatrix} 1/\sqrt{k} \\ r/\sqrt{k} \end{pmatrix} = \begin{pmatrix} M_{11} & M_{12} \\ M_{21} & M_{22} \end{pmatrix} \begin{pmatrix} t/\sqrt{k'} \\ 0 \end{pmatrix}, \tag{3.37}$$

$$\begin{aligned} \frac{1}{\sqrt{k}} &= \frac{M_{11}t}{\sqrt{k'}}, \quad t = \sqrt{\frac{k'}{k}}\frac{1}{M_{11}}, \\ \frac{r}{\sqrt{k}} &= \frac{M_{21}t}{\sqrt{k'}}, \quad r = \frac{M_{21}}{M_{11}}. \end{aligned} \tag{3.38}$$

Meanwhile, Eqs. 3.17 and 3.18 are changed as

$$M_{11} = \frac{1}{2}\left(1 + \frac{r}{r'}\right)\cosh 2Ka - \frac{i}{2}\left(r - \frac{1}{r'}\right)\sinh 2Ka,$$

and

$$M_{21} = \frac{1}{2}\left(1 - \frac{r}{r'}\right)\cosh 2Ka - \frac{i}{2}\left(r + \frac{1}{r'}\right)\sinh 2Ka. \tag{3.39}$$

Similarly, the scattering matrix should be correspondingly changed [8]. The wave function in the l-th channel is written as

$$\varphi_l(z) = \frac{1}{\sqrt{k_l}}\left(a_l e^{ik_l z} + b_l e^{-ik_l z}\right). \tag{3.40}$$

The scattering matrix is defined as

$$\begin{pmatrix} a_1 \\ a_2 \\ \vdots \\ a_M \end{pmatrix} = (S(E)) \begin{pmatrix} b_1 \\ b_2 \\ \vdots \\ b_M \end{pmatrix}, \tag{3.41}$$

where $a_l/\sqrt{k_l}$ and $b_l/\sqrt{k_l}$ are the coefficients of the transmitted and injected waves at the l-th channel, respectively.

For the non-symmetric single barrier (Fig. 3.2), the coefficient of the injected wave is $b_1/\sqrt{k_1} = 1/\sqrt{k_1}$ and the amplitudes of the reflective and transmitted waves are, respectively,

$$r = \sqrt{k_1} \cdot \left(\frac{a_1}{\sqrt{k_1}}\right) = a_1 = S_{11}$$

and

$$t = \sqrt{k_2} \cdot \left(\frac{a_2}{\sqrt{k_2}} \right) = a_2 = S_{21}. \tag{3.42}$$

Therefore, the scattering matrix defined in Eq. 3.41 satisfies the unitarity, that is,

$$S^+ S = 1. \tag{3.43}$$

In the two-terminal case, we have

$$|S_{11}|^2 + |S_{21}|^2 = |t|^2 + |r|^2 = 1. \tag{3.44}$$

In the n-terminal case,

$$\sum_l S_{nl} S_{ml}^* = \delta_{nm}. \tag{3.45}$$

The transmission and reflection probabilities are, respectively,

$$T_{nm} = |S_{nm}|^2, \quad m \neq n,$$

and

$$R_n = |S_{nn}|^2. \tag{3.46}$$

If there are no applied magnetic field and spin-orbital coupling, for the real energy E the wave functions ψ and ψ^* are all the solutions of Schrödinger equation and hence the S matrix is symmetric, that is,

$$S_{mn} = S_{nm}. \tag{3.47}$$

Equation 3.47 represents an important result: detailed balance principle $T_{mn} = T_{nm}$, that is, for any structure the transmission probability of the positive injection path equals that of the anti-injection path. It is also indicated from Eq. 3.47 that not only the amplitudes but also the phases are all equal.

In the actual case the chances of using the transfer matrix or scattering matrix to solve analytically the transport problem are less. Even in the single-barrier problem as shown in Fig. 3.1, the tunneling current is measured in the electric voltage bias V, that is, the barrier is under an applied electric field F. The electron motion equation includes a potential energy term,

$$V(z) = V_0(z) - eFz, \tag{3.48}$$

where $V_0(z)$ is the potential without the electric field, as shown in Fig. 3.1, the second term is the additional electric field potential term, which makes the potential energy inclining downward. This time the electron wave function is not a plane wave but a special function $A_i(z)$ and it is nearly impossible to use this function to calculate the transfer or scattering matrix.

Generally one uses the numerical method to solve the electron wave propagation problem in a structure with an arbitrary form of potential [9]. The electron motion Schrödinger equation (in atomic units, length = Born radius a_B and energy = Rydberg R) is written as

$$-\frac{1}{2m^*}\frac{\partial^2}{\partial z^2}\varphi(z) + V(z)\varphi(z) = E\varphi(z) \tag{3.49}$$

or

$$\frac{\partial^2\varphi(z)}{\partial z^2} = -2m^*[E - V(z)]\varphi(z). \tag{3.50}$$

Suppose that the wave function at the output end is $e^{ik'z}$. Then the boundary conditions at the interface between the barrier (2 region) and the output end (3 region) are

$$\varphi(z = a) = 1$$

and

$$\frac{d\varphi}{dz}(z = a) = ik'. \tag{3.51}$$

Starting from the initial condition (Eq. 3.51), integrating Eq. 3.50 from right to left, we obtain the values of the wave function and its differential U and U' at $z = -a$. The wave function at the input end is

$$\varphi(z) = a_1 e^{ikz} + b_1 e^{-ikz}. \tag{3.52}$$

The values of the wave function and its differential at $z = -a$ are

$$\varphi(z = -a) = a_1 + b_1 = U_1$$

and

$$\frac{d\varphi}{dz}(z = -a) = ik(a_1 - b_1) = U_1'. \tag{3.53}$$

The coefficients a_1 and b_1 can be calculated from Eq. 3.53. According to the definition of the transfer matrix (Eq. 3.13),

$$\begin{pmatrix} a_1 \\ b_1 \end{pmatrix} = (M) \begin{pmatrix} 1 \\ 0 \end{pmatrix}. \tag{3.54}$$

Hence,

$$a_1 = M_{11} \quad \text{and} \quad b_1 = M_{21}. \tag{3.55}$$

This numerical method is suitable for arbitrary potential barrier form or hole tunneling (heavy hole and light hole, and there is coupling between them) case [9].

3.2 Resonant Tunneling of Double Potential Barriers

Similar to the symmetry of the scattering matrix S (Eq. 3.47), we give the symmetry of the transfer matrix. In the case of no magnetic field and spin-orbital coupling the wave functions $\varphi(z)$ and $\varphi^*(z)$ are all the solutions of the Schrödinger equation. Thus

$$\varphi_1{}^*(z) = a_1{}^* e^{-ikz} + b_1{}^* e^{ikz}$$

and

$$\varphi_3{}^*(z) = a_3{}^* e^{-ikz} + b_3{}^* e^{ikz}. \tag{3.56}$$

From the definition of the transfer matrix Eq. 3.13,

$$\begin{pmatrix} b_1{}^* \\ a_1{}^* \end{pmatrix} = \begin{pmatrix} M_{11} & M_{12} \\ M_{21} & M_{22} \end{pmatrix} \begin{pmatrix} b_3{}^* \\ a_3{}^* \end{pmatrix}. \tag{3.57}$$

Take the complex number of Eq. 3.57

$$\begin{pmatrix} b_1 \\ a_1 \end{pmatrix} = \begin{pmatrix} M_{11}{}^* & M_{12}{}^* \\ M_{21}{}^* & M_{22}{}^* \end{pmatrix} = \begin{pmatrix} b_3 \\ a_3 \end{pmatrix} \tag{3.58}$$

and rearrange the order,

$$\begin{pmatrix} a_1 \\ b_1 \end{pmatrix} = \begin{pmatrix} M_{22}{}^* & M_{21}{}^* \\ M_{12}{}^* & M_{11}{}^* \end{pmatrix} = \begin{pmatrix} a_3 \\ b_3 \end{pmatrix}. \tag{3.59}$$

Then we obtain the symmetry relation,

$$M_{11}{}^* = M_{22} \quad \text{and} \quad M_{12}{}^* = M_{21}. \tag{3.60}$$

For single potential barrier structure we obtained the transfer matrix from Eq. 3.15,

$$M = \begin{vmatrix} 1/t_1 & r_1^*/t_1^* \\ r_1/t_1 & 1/t_1^* \end{vmatrix}, \tag{3.61}$$

where r_1 and t_1 are amplitudes of the reflective and transmitted waves, respectively. For the double-barrier structure, suppose the width of the middle potential well is w. Then the total transfer matrix is

$$M = \begin{vmatrix} 1/t_1 & r_1^*/t_1^* \\ r_1/t_1 & 1/t_1^* \end{vmatrix} \cdot \begin{vmatrix} e^{-ikw} & 0 \\ 0 & e^{ikw} \end{vmatrix} \cdot \begin{vmatrix} 1/t_1 & r_1^*/t_1^* \\ r_1/t_1 & 1/t_1^* \end{vmatrix}. \tag{3.62}$$

The matrix element

$$M_{11} = e^{-ikw}/t_1^2 + e^{ikw} R_1/T_1, \tag{3.63}$$

where $R_1 = |r_1|^2$ and $T_1 = |t_1|^2$ are the reflection and transmission probabilities, respectively, for the single-barrier structure. The total transmission probability can be calculated from Eq. 3.63,

$$T = 1/|M_{11}|^2 = \left[1 + \frac{4R_1}{T_1^2}\cos^2(kw + \theta)\right]^{-1}, \tag{3.64}$$

where θ is the phase angle of t_1 and $t_1 = |t_1|e^{i\theta}$.

From Eq. 3.64 we see that though the transmission probability T_1 of the single barrier is small, when $kw + \theta = (n + 1/2)\pi$ the transmission probability T of the double barrier equals 1. Physically, because the electron energy equals the energy of the confined state in the quantum well there occurs RT and the transmission probability can reach 1. If the electron energy deviates the resonant energy, the transmission probability descends rapidly, even several orders of magnitude.

Figure 3.3 shows the calculated transmission probabilities of an AlAs/GaAs/AlAs double potential barrier structure as functions of electron energy [10]. The barrier height $V_0 = 1.355$ eV, barrier width $L_B = 2.3$ nm, and the three curves correspond to GaAs potential well widths $L_W = 5$ nm, 7 nm, and 9 nm, respectively. When the electron energy equals the energy of a quasi-confined state there is a RT peak and the transmission probability reach 1. For a narrow quantum well $L_W = 5$ nm the confined states are less and their energies are

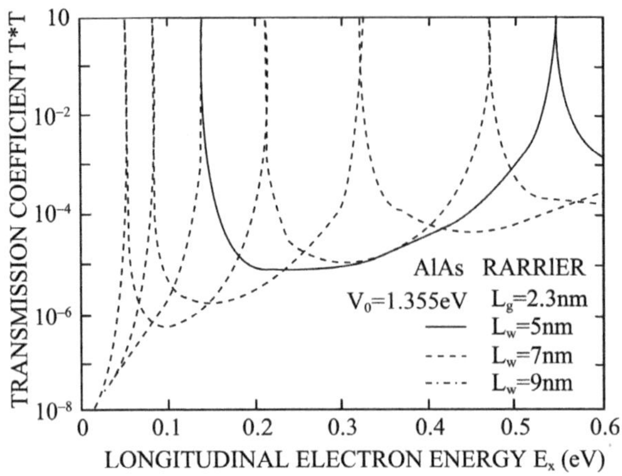

Figure 3.3 Calculated transmission probabilities of an AlAs/GaAs/AlAs double potential barrier structure as functions of electron energy.

higher. There are only two resonant peaks in the energy range of $E = 0 \approx 0.6$ eV. For a wide quantum well $L_W = 9$ nm there are three resonant peaks at lower energies.

Expanding the formula of the RT probability Eq. 3.64 near the resonant energy E_n, we obtain the Lorentz line-shape,

$$T(E) = \frac{\Gamma_n^2/4}{\Gamma_n^2/4 + (E - E_n)^2}, \tag{3.65}$$

where Γ_n is the half-height width of the resonant peak,

$$\Gamma_n = \left(\frac{\hbar^2 E_n T_1^2}{2m^* w^2 R_1}\right)^{1/2}. \tag{3.66}$$

The confined state in the quantum well of a double-barrier structure is a quasi-confined state. If an electron stays at the state, it will escape from the well and thus the energy of the quasi-confined state is a complex number,

$$E = E_0 - i\Gamma_n/2. \tag{3.67}$$

The wave function of electron state,

$$\begin{aligned}\varphi(t) = e^{-i\frac{E}{\hbar}t} &= e^{-i\frac{t}{\hbar}(E_0 - i\Gamma_n/2)} \\ &= e^{-i\frac{E_0}{\hbar}t - \frac{\Gamma_n}{2\hbar}t}.\end{aligned} \tag{3.68}$$

From Eq. 3.68 the electron density obtained is

$$|\varphi(t)|^2 = e^{-\frac{\Gamma_n}{\hbar}t}. \tag{3.69}$$

It means that in the well the electron density decays with time. Then we define the electron lifetime

$$\tau = \frac{\hbar}{\Gamma_n}. \tag{3.70}$$

The above calculation results are obtained by assuming that the single electron has only momentum k in the z direction. Actually the electrons at the input end have momentum $\mathbf{k}$ in the three-dimensional (3D) space and obey the Fermi distribution,

$$f(\mathbf{k}) = \frac{1}{1 + e^{(E-E_F)/kT}}. \tag{3.71}$$

The tunneling current equals the integration of all electron states,

$$J = +e\frac{2}{(2\pi)^3}\int T(E_z)f(\mathbf{k})v_z(\mathbf{k})d\mathbf{k}, \tag{3.72}$$

where $v_z(\mathbf{k})$ is the velocity in the z direction,

$$v_z = \frac{1}{\hbar}\frac{\partial E(\mathbf{k})}{\partial k_z} = \frac{\hbar k_z}{m^*}. \tag{3.73}$$

The total electron energy,

$$E = E_z + E_t = \frac{\hbar^2 k_z^2}{2m^*} + \frac{\hbar^2 k_t^2}{2m^*}, \tag{3.74}$$

where

$$k_t^2 = k_x^2 + k_y^2.$$

The integration of Eq. 3.72 can be divided into integration over k_z and k_t,

$$J = \frac{em^*}{2\pi^2\hbar^2}\int_0^\infty dE_z T(E_z)\int_0^\infty dE_t\left[f_l(E_z, E_t) - f_r(E_z, E_t)\right], \tag{3.75}$$

where f_l and f_r are the Fermi distribution function (Eq. 3.71) of electrons at the left side and the right side of the barrier, respectively. If there is no bias voltage on the structure, $f_l = f_r$ and $J = 0$, there is no tunneling current. If a bias voltage is applied to the structure, the potential energy curve inclines toward right (reverse voltage), so $f_l > f_r$ and tunneling current is produced.

Integrating Eq. 3.75 for E_t,

$$\int_0^\infty dE_t\,[f_l(E_z, E_t) - f_r(E_z, E_t)]$$
$$= \int_0^\infty dE_t \left[\frac{1}{1+e^{(E_z+E_t-E_F)/kT}} - \frac{1}{1+e^{(E_z+E_t-E_F+eV)/kT}}\right]$$
$$= kT \ln\left(\frac{1+e^{(E_F-E_z)/kT}}{1+e^{(E_F-eV-E_z)/kT}}\right), \tag{3.76}$$

where E_F is the Fermi energy of the left side and that of the right side is $E_F - eV$ due to the bias voltage. Inserting Eq. 3.76 into Eq. 3.75 we obtain

$$J = \frac{em^*kT}{2\pi^2\hbar^2}\int_0^\infty dE_z T(E_z) \ln\left(\frac{1+e^{(E_F-E_z)/kT}}{1+e^{(E_F-eV-E_z)/kT}}\right). \tag{3.77}$$

Equation 3.77 was derived first by Tsu et al. [1].

When $T = 0$, the electron energy distribution is step-like,

$$\ln\left[1+e^{(E_F-E_z)/kT}\right] = \begin{cases} \dfrac{E_F - E_z}{kT}, & E_z < E_F \\ 0. & E_z > E_F \end{cases} \tag{3.78}$$

Thus Eq. 3.77 is written as

$$J = \frac{em^*}{2\pi^2\hbar^2}\left[\int_0^{E_F} dE_z T(E_z)(E_F - E_z) - \int_0^{E_F-eV} dE_z T(E_z)(E_F - eV - E_z)\right]. \tag{3.79}$$

If $E_F - eV < 0$, the Fermi energy level descends to the bottom of the energy band at the left side ($E = 0$). The right side is completely empty for the tunneling electron from the left side, so the second term in Eq. 3.79 equals zero.

At the neighbor of the resonant energy E_n the tunneling probability can be expanded as in Eq. 3.65. In the limit that Γ_n approaches zero, it changes to be a δ function,

$$\delta(E_z - E_n) = \frac{1}{\pi}\lim_{\Gamma_n\to 0}\frac{\Gamma_n/2}{(\Gamma_n^2/4) + (E_z - E_n)^2}. \tag{3.80}$$

Thus

$$T(E_z) \approx \pi \cdot \frac{\Gamma_n}{2}\delta(E_z - E_n). \tag{3.81}$$

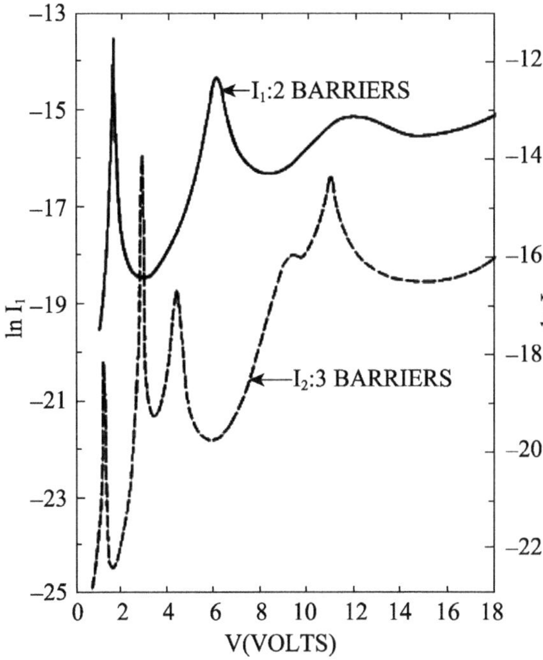

Figure 3.4 Calculated current density at 0 K for the double- and triple-barrier cases as a function of applied voltage.

Inserting Eq. 3.81 into Eq. 3.79, and assuming that $E_F - eV < 0$, we obtain

$$J = \frac{em^* T_{\text{res}} \Gamma_n}{4\pi \hbar^2}(E_F - E_n), \tag{3.82}$$

where T_{res} is a constant. From Eq. 3.82 we see that the tunneling current is proportional to $E_F - E_n$. When the E_n is far away from E_F, the tunneling current is larger, and when E_n approaches E_F, the tunneling current approaches zero.

Figure 3.4 shows the calculated current density at 0 K for the double- and triple-barrier cases, without the constant factor $em^*/2\pi^2\hbar^2$ as a function of applied voltage [1]. Note that the I–V characteristics indicate a fine structure having differential negative conductivities. The first peak for the double-barrier case is located approximately at 0.16 eV, which is about twice the transmission peak of 0.082 eV. This is because the bottom of the well shifts

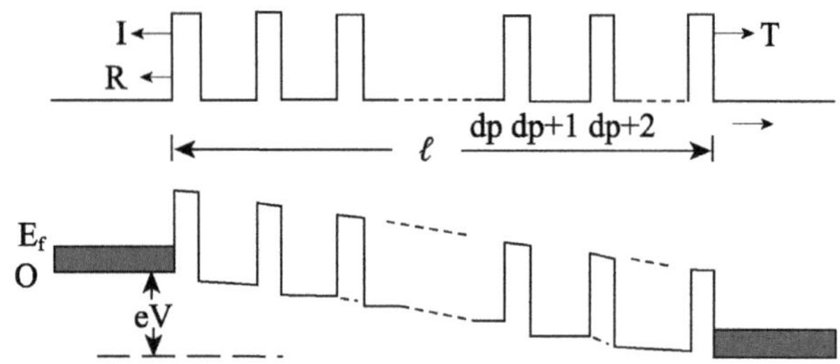

Figure 3.5 Schematic energy band of the finite superlattice: the upper part is without bias and the lower part is with bias.

only half the amount of the applied voltage for this case. When the voltage increases continuously, E_F approaches the energy of the second confined state of the well and there appears the second resonant current peak. For the triple-barrier case, the situation is more complicated, E_F can be resonant with the energy of the confined state in the first well or in the second well, and thus multiple resonant peaks appear.

Tsu et al. [1] calculated the tunneling probabilities of the superlattices composed of multi-barriers with the transfer matrix method. The schematic energy band of the finite superlattice is shown in Fig. 3.5: the upper part is without bias, and the lower part is with bias. Figure 3.6 shows in the case of no bias the transmission probabilities as functions of electron energy for the double, triple, and quintuple barriers. The barrier and well widths are 2 nm and 5 nm, respectively. The barrier height is 0.5 eV. Note that the resonant energies for the triple barrier case is split into doublets and those for the quintuple barrier case are split into quadruplets. The line widths are roughly determined by the tunneling probability of the barrier width. Generally, for n barriers, there will be an $(n-1)$-fold splitting. This splitting is caused by the coupling of the energy levels of the neighboring wells.

Using the negative resistance property produced by the RT effect one can design and fabricate the two-terminal RT oscillator. Figure 3.7 shows the simplest equivalent circuit of a two-terminal RT oscillator [11], where $-R_D$ and C_D represent the resistance and capacitance of the device, respectively. R_s and L_s are parasitic resistance and inductance of the lead, respectively. This equivalent

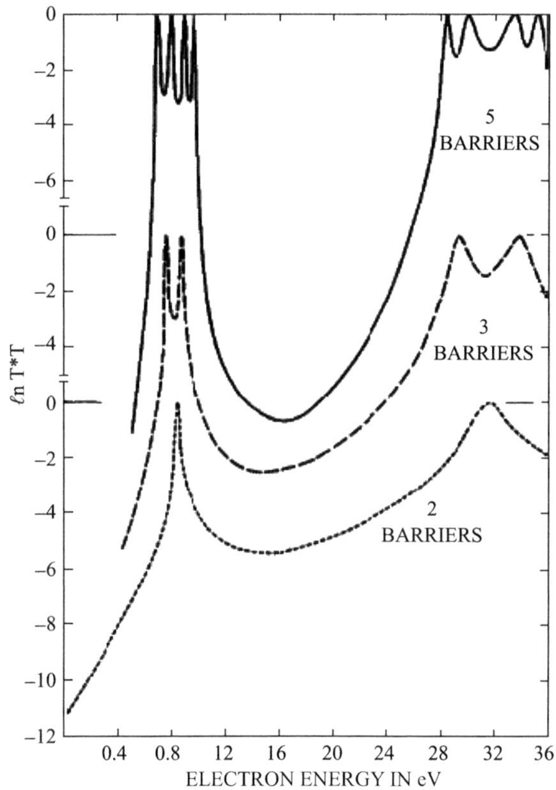

Figure 3.6 Transmission probabilities as functions of electron energy for the double, triple, and quintuple barriers.

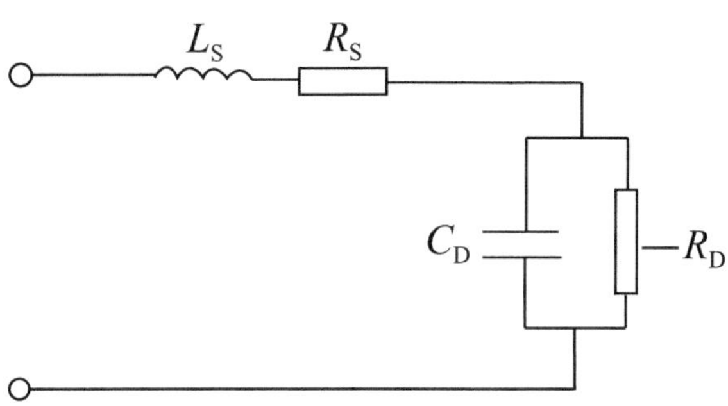

Figure 3.7 Equivalent circuit of a two-terminal RT oscillator.

circuit has been successfully applied to analyze the tunneling diodes, and the calculated I–V characteristics are in agreement with experimental results. The real part of the impedance in the equivalent circuit R_{eg} is

$$R_{eg} = R_s + \frac{-R_D}{1 + (\omega R_D C_D)^2}. \tag{3.83}$$

For steady oscillation R_{eg} should be negative; then the cutoff frequency can be calculated from Eq. 3.83,

$$f_{max} = \frac{1}{2\pi R_D C_D}\sqrt{\frac{R_D}{R_s} - 1}. \tag{3.84}$$

For raising the f_{max} the parasitic resistance R_s and the diode capacitance C_D should be minimum. Differentiating Eq. 3.84 to R_D, we obtain the condition that f_{max} is maximum and

$$R_D = 2R_s. \tag{3.85}$$

That means that the absolute value of the negative resistance R_D is also very small. Therefore, a steep drop of the current and high peak-valley ratio in the I–V characteristic curve will be helpful to raise the f_{max}. Another demand for the RT oscillator is large power output, generally,

$$P_{max} \approx (V_p - V_v)(I_p - I_v), \tag{3.86}$$

where V_p, I_p, V_v, and I_v are the voltage and current of the current peak and valley, respectively. Thus large peak-valley ratio and high current density are necessary for a high performance oscillator.

Brown et al. obtained oscillations at frequency 712 GHz in InAs/AlSb double-barrier resonant tunneling diodes (RTDs) at room temperature [12]. The InAs/AlSb materials system has several advantages over GaAs/AlAs for making high-speed RTDs. First, the InAs/AlSb band offset (staggered type II at the Γ pint) allows an electron to tunnel more easily through the AlSb barrier than the AlAs barrier (type I band offset). This leads to a larger difference of the peak and valley currents $\Delta I = I_p - I_v$ and a smaller R_D. A second advantage is that the electron effective mass in InAs (0.023 m_0) is smaller than that in GaAs (0.067 m_0), so the electrons will drift across a given depletion layer much more rapidly in InAs than

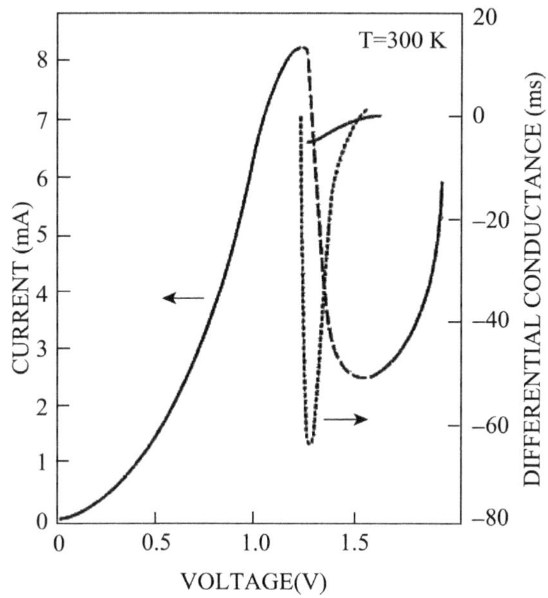

Figure 3.8 DC $I-V$ characteristic (solid line) and differential conductance (dotted line) of a 1.8 μm diameter diode.

in GaAs. A third advantage is that InAs RTDs have a lower total series resistance R_S.

Figure 3.8 shows the direct current (DC) I–V characteristic and differential conductance of a 1.8 μm diameter diode with a negative voltage applied to the top contact [12]. The I–V curve shows a peak-to-valley current ratio of about 3.4 at room temperature and a peak current density of 2.8×10^5 A cm^{-2}, corresponding to $\Delta I \cong 2.0 \times 10^5$ A cm^{-2}. The discontinuous nature of the experimental I–V curve in the NDC region is caused by self-rectification of the oscillations.

Figure 3.9 shows the highest power density as a function of the frequency obtained in the InAs/AlSb RTDs (dotted line) and GaAs/AlAs RTDs (solid line) [12]. At 360 GHz an absolute power of 3 μW was obtained, corresponding to a power density of 90 Wcm^{-2}. This is 50 times the power density obtained previously from GaAs/AlAs RTDs at 370 GHz. At 712 GHz a power of 0.3 μW was

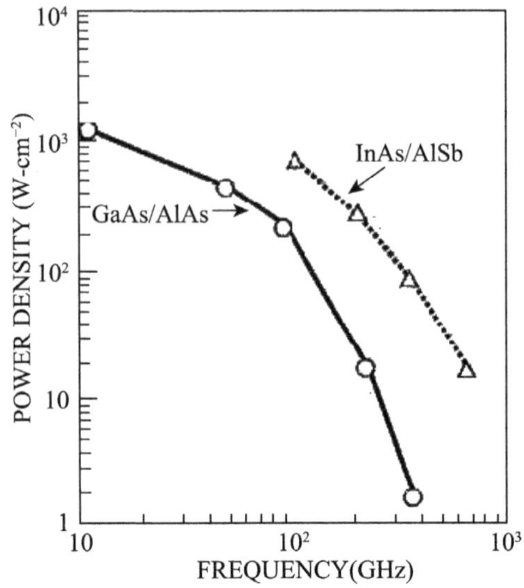

Figure 3.9 Highest power density as a function of the frequency obtained in the InAs/AlSb RTDs (dotted line) and GaAs/AlAs RTDs (solid line).

obtained, corresponding to a power density of 15 Wcm^2. The power density decreases with the oscillation frequency increasing.

The RTD oscillators have not applied on a large scale; the difficulties are operation at room temperature and large-scale integration.

3.3 Hole Resonant Tunneling

Mendez et al. first observed the hole RT in the GaAs/AlAs double-barrier structure [13]. The conductance (dI/dV) versus voltage bias of an undoped AlAs/GaAs/AlAs double-barrier structure for four temperatures is shown in Fig. 3.10 [13]. There are many conductance minima representing the positions of resonant peaks. On the basis of the temperature dependence behavior and the relative strength of the resonances, the authors assigned the high T set of structures to RT of light holes and the low T set to heavy hole tunneling. To compare with experiments they assumed that

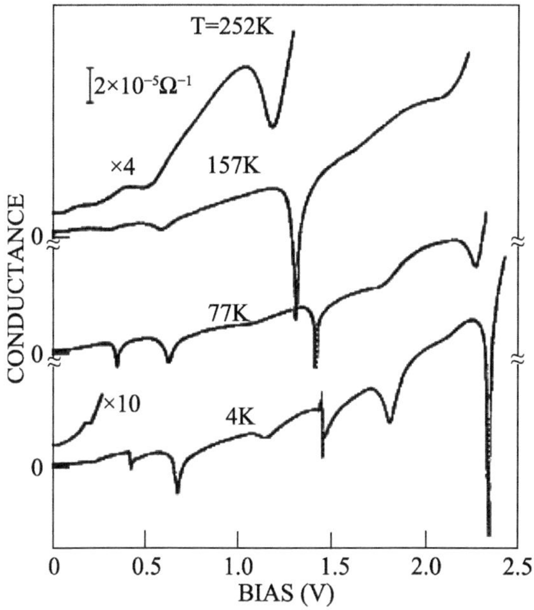

Figure 3.10 Conductance (dI/dV) versus voltage bias of an undoped AlAs/GaAs/AlAs double-barrier structure for four temperatures.

the effective masses of the light and heavy holes in GaAs are 0.1 m_0 and 0.6 m_0, respectively. The width of the GaAs and AlAs layers are 5 nm and the barrier height is 550 meV. Assuming that there is no coupling between the light hole and heavy hole, they calculated the tunneling probabilities as functions of energy separately for two kinds of holes; the results are shown in Fig. 3.11 [13]. It is considered approximately that the bias voltages to which the tunneling peaks correspond multiplied by the electron charge e are twice the energy to which the tunneling probability peaks correspond. From Fig. 3.11 the light hole resonant peaks should be at 0.168 and 0.634 V, which contrasts with the experimental values of 0.43, 0.67, and 1.45 V. The heavy hole resonant peaks should be at 0.038, 0.154, 0.344, 0.604, and 0.915 V, while experimentally only four peaks, at 0.20, 1.15, 1.81, and 2.33 V, were observed. The authors believed that non-parabolicity effects and band mixing (coupling between light hole and heavy hole) are probably the main reasons for the discrepancies found.

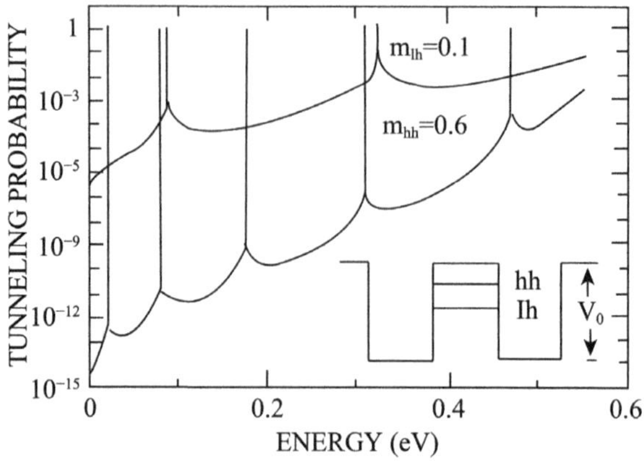

Figure 3.11 Calculated tunneling probabilities as functions of energy separately for two kinds of holes.

The authors also studied the effect of a strong magnetic field on the positions of resonant current peaks. The magnetic field is applied along the current direction. If the hole energy band is a simple parabolic band, the problem is simpler. The hole energy band in the plane perpendicular to the magnetic field direction is split into a series of Landau energy levels. The basis state energy equals $\hbar\omega_c/2 \approx B$. In the strong magnetic field the RT energy will increase linearly with the magnetic field. The surprising results are that with the magnetic field increasing some peak energy increases, but some peak energy decreases, which proves the complexity of the valence bands. We should consider the coupling between light and heavy holes and the non-parabolicity.

To solve the above problem, Xia proposed the hole RT theory [9]. In the double-barrier structure, the effective mass Hamiltonian is written as

$$H = H_{\mathrm{L}} + V(z), \tag{3.87}$$

where $V(z)$ is the effective potential of the structure,

$$H_{\mathrm{L}} = \frac{1}{2}\begin{vmatrix} P_1 & R & Q & 0 \\ R^* & P_2 & 0 & -Q \\ Q^* & 0 & P_2 & R \\ 0 & -Q^* & R^* & P_1 \end{vmatrix}, \tag{3.88}$$

$$\begin{aligned}P_1 &= (\gamma_1 + \gamma_2)P_{\|}^2 + (\gamma_1 - 2\gamma_2)P_z^2,\\ P_2 &= (\gamma_1 - \gamma_2)P_{\|}^2 + (\gamma_1 + 2\gamma_2)P_z^2,\\ Q &= -i2\sqrt{3}\gamma_3 P_z(P_x - iP_y),\\ R &= \sqrt{3}\left[\gamma_2(P_x^2 - P_y^2) - i2\gamma_3 P_x P_y\right],\end{aligned} \tag{3.89}$$

where $P_\perp$ and P_z are the momentum operators perpendicular and parallel to the z direction, respectively. γ_1, γ_2, and γ_3 are the Luttinger parameters.

For the superlattice or double-barrier structures only P_z is the operator; P_x and P_y can be replaced by their eigen-values k_x and k_y. To simplify the calculation of the transfer matrix, we transform the Hamiltonian (3.88) by a unitary transform proposed by Briodo et al. [14],

$$U = \begin{vmatrix} \frac{1}{\sqrt{2}}e^{-i\phi} & 0 & 0 & -\frac{1}{\sqrt{2}}e^{i\phi} \\ 0 & \frac{1}{\sqrt{2}}e^{-i\eta} & -\frac{1}{\sqrt{2}}e^{i\eta} & 0 \\ 0 & \frac{1}{\sqrt{2}}e^{-i\eta} & \frac{1}{\sqrt{2}}e^{i\eta} & 0 \\ \frac{1}{\sqrt{2}}e^{-i\phi} & 0 & 0 & \frac{1}{\sqrt{2}}e^{i\phi} \end{vmatrix}, \tag{3.90}$$

where ϕ and η are determined by k_x and k_y. The transformed Hamiltonian becomes two independent 2×2 matrices,

$$UH_{\mathrm{L}}U^{+} = \frac{1}{2}\begin{vmatrix} P_1 & i|Q|P_2 + |R| & 0 & 0 \\ -i|Q|P_2 + |R| & P_2 & 0 & 0 \\ 0 & 0 & P_2 & -i|Q|P_2 + |R| \\ 0 & 0 & i|Q|P_2 + |R| & P_2 \end{vmatrix}, \tag{3.91}$$

where

$$|R| = \sqrt{3}\left[\gamma_2^2(k_x^2 - k_y^2) + 4\gamma_3^2 k_x^2 k_y^2\right]^{1/2}$$

and

$$|Q| = 2\sqrt{3}\left[k_x^2 + k_y^2\right]^{1/2}. \tag{3.92}$$

Even with the 2×2 matrix the tunneling problem still cannot be solved analytically. We will use the numerical integration method [9]. We first consider the upper-left 2×2 matrix of Eq. 3.91; the result of the lower right 2×2 matrix is the same.

$$H_1 = \frac{1}{2}\begin{vmatrix} P_1 & i\,|Q|\,p_z - |R| \\ -i\,|Q|\,p_z - |R| & P_2 \end{vmatrix}. \tag{3.93}$$

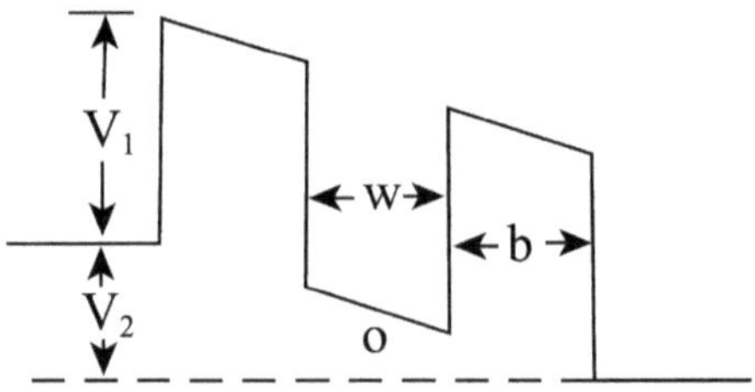

Figure 3.12 Potential barrier region for hole tunneling.

The potential barrier region is illustrated in Fig. 3.12. On the left side of the potential barrier region $V(z)$ is assumed to be zero. The hole wave function is of the form

$$\psi = \begin{pmatrix} a \\ b \end{pmatrix} e^{i\mathbf{k}_\parallel \cdot \mathbf{r}_\parallel + ik_z z}. \tag{3.94}$$

As the holes enter into the potential barrier region, where $V(z)$ is not a constant (see Fig. 3.12), the hole wave function becomes

$$\psi = \begin{pmatrix} U_1(z) \\ U_2(z) \end{pmatrix} e^{i\mathbf{k}_\parallel \cdot \mathbf{r}}, \tag{3.95}$$

where $\mathbf{k}_\parallel$ is still a good quantum number.

From the effective mass equation with the Hamiltonian (3.93) we obtain the differential equations satisfied by U_1 and U_2,

$$U_1'' = \frac{1}{\gamma_1 - 2\gamma_2}\{(\gamma_1 + \gamma_2)k_\parallel^2 U_1 - |R|U_2 + |Q|U_2' - 2[E - V(z)]U_1\},$$

and

$$U_2'' = \frac{1}{\gamma_1 + 2\gamma_2}\{(\gamma_1 - \gamma_2)k_\parallel^2 U_2 - |R|U_1 - |Q|U_1' - 2[E - V(z)]U_2\}. \tag{3.96}$$

From Eq. 3.96 we see that there is coupling between the heavy and light holes, so we cannot deal with the heavy hole and light hole independently.

First we calculate the hole wave function on the left side and right side of the barrier region. Because $V(z) = V_0$ is a constant on the left and right sides, inserting the hole wave function (Eq. 3.94) into the effective mass equation with the Hamiltonian (Eq. 3.93) we obtain the eigen-energy

$$E - V_0 = \frac{1}{2}\gamma_1 k^2 \pm \left[r_2^2 k^4 + 3(\gamma_3^2 - \gamma_2^2)(k_x^2 k_y^2 + k_y^2 k_z^2 + k_z^2 k_x^2)\right]^{1/2}, \tag{3.97}$$

where the sign $\pm$ corresponds to the light and heavy holes, respectively. For given k_x and k_y, the k_z can be calculated from Eq. 3.97. The coefficients a and b of the hole wave function (3.94) can be equally calculated.

When the energy and the parallel wave vectors k_x and k_y are given, there are generally four independent hole states on the left-hand side of the potential barrier region: the heavy hole states ψ_{h,k_h} and $\psi_{h,-k_h}$ with perpendicular wave vectors k_h and $-k_h$ and the light hole states ψ_{l,k_l} and $\psi_{l,-k_l}$ with perpendiculars k_l and $-k_l$. The k_h and k_l are calculated from Eq. 3.97 for given E, V_0, k_x, and k_y. At the left side and right side, the wave functions are, respectively,

$$\psi_l = \alpha\psi_{h,k_h} + \beta\psi_{h,-k_h} + \gamma\psi_{l,k_l} + \delta\psi_{l,-k_l}$$

and

$$\psi_r = \alpha'\psi_{h,k_h'} + \beta'\psi_{h,-k_h'} + \gamma'\psi_{l,k_l'} + \delta'\psi_{l,-k_l'}. \tag{3.98}$$

The coefficients $(\alpha, \beta, \gamma, \delta)$ and $(\alpha', \beta', \gamma', \delta')$ are connected by a transfer matrix,

$$\begin{pmatrix} \alpha \\ \beta \\ \gamma \\ \delta \end{pmatrix} = (M) \begin{pmatrix} \alpha' \\ \beta' \\ \gamma' \\ \delta' \end{pmatrix}. \tag{3.99}$$

Suppose at the right side a heavy hole state goes out; then the boundary conditions at the right barrier of the barrier U_1, U_1' and U_2, U_2' can be determined. Numerically integrating Eq. 3.96 from right to left (e.g., by the Adams method), we obtain the values of wave functions and their derivatives U_1, U_1' and U_2, U_2' at the left boundary of the barrier region.

The hole wave functions are given by Eqs. 3.98 and 3.94; thus their coefficients α, β, γ, and δ are determined by the following set of equations:

$$\begin{aligned}
&a_{h,k_h}\alpha + a_{h,-k_h}\beta + a_{l,k_l}\gamma + a_{l,-k_l}\delta = U_1, \\
&b_{h,k_h}\alpha + b_{h,-k_h}\beta + b_{l,k_l}\gamma + b_{l,-k_l}\delta = U_2, \\
&ik_h a_{h,k_h}\alpha - ik_h a_{h,-k_h}\beta + ik_l a_{l,k_l}\gamma - ik_l a_{l,k_l}\delta = U_1',
\end{aligned}$$

and

$$ik_h b_{h,k_h}\alpha - ik_h b_{h,-k_h}\beta + ik_l b_{l,k_l}\gamma - ik_l b_{l,k_l}\delta = U_2', \tag{3.100}$$

where (a_{hk_h}, b_{hk_h}) and (a_{lk_l}, b_{lk_l}) are the coefficients of the wave function (Eq. 3.94) for the heavy hole and light hole, respectively.

If there is a heavy hole at the right side ($k'_z > 0$), the transfer matrix equation (Eq. 3.99) will be

$$\begin{pmatrix} \alpha \\ \beta \\ \gamma \\ \delta \end{pmatrix} = (M) \begin{pmatrix} 1 \\ 0 \\ 0 \\ 0 \end{pmatrix}. \tag{3.101}$$

From Eq. 3.101 we obtain

$$M_{11} = \alpha, \quad M_{21} = \beta, \quad M_{31} = \gamma, \quad \text{and} \quad M_{41} = \delta. \tag{3.102}$$

Similarly if there is a light hole at the right side ($k'_z > 0$), we obtain

$$M_{13} = \alpha, \quad M_{23} = \beta, \quad M_{33} = \gamma, \quad \text{and} \quad M_{43} = \delta. \tag{3.103}$$

Knowing the transfer matrix (doesn't need all matrix elements), the transmission amplitudes T and the reflection amplitudes R can be calculated from Eq. 3.99,

$$\begin{aligned}
T_{\rm hh} &= \frac{M_{33}}{D}, \quad T_{\rm hl} = \frac{-M_{31}}{D}, \\
R_{\rm hh} &= \frac{M_{21}M_{33} - M_{23}M_{31}}{D}, \quad R_{\rm hl} = \frac{M_{41}M_{33} - M_{43}M_{31}}{D}, \\
T_{\rm lh} &= -\frac{M_{13}}{D}, \quad T_{\rm ll} = \frac{M_{11}}{D}, \\
R_{\rm lh} &= \frac{-M_{21}M_{13} + M_{23}M_{11}}{D}, \quad R_{\rm ll} = \frac{-M_{41}M_{13} + M_{43}M_{11}}{D},
\end{aligned} \tag{3.104}$$

and

$$D = M_{11}M_{33} - M_{13}M_{31}, \tag{3.105}$$

where $T_{\rm hh}$ represents the transmission amplitude from heavy hole state to heavy hole state, $T_{\rm hl}$ that from heavy hole state to light hole state, etc.

Figure 3.13 shows the transmission probabilities of the heavy and light hole $\log_{10}(T^*T)$ as functions of energy E at $F = 0$ and $k_\parallel = 0$ [9]. Since for $k_\parallel = 0$ there is no coupling between heavy and light holes and the resonant peaks correspond to the independent heavy and light hole states in the quantum well, similar to Fig. 3.11.

Figures 3.14 and 3.15 show the transmission probabilities $(T^*T)_{\rm hh}$ and $(T^*T)_{\rm hl}$ as well as $(T^*T)_{\rm ll}$ and $(T^*T)_{\rm lh}$ as functions of

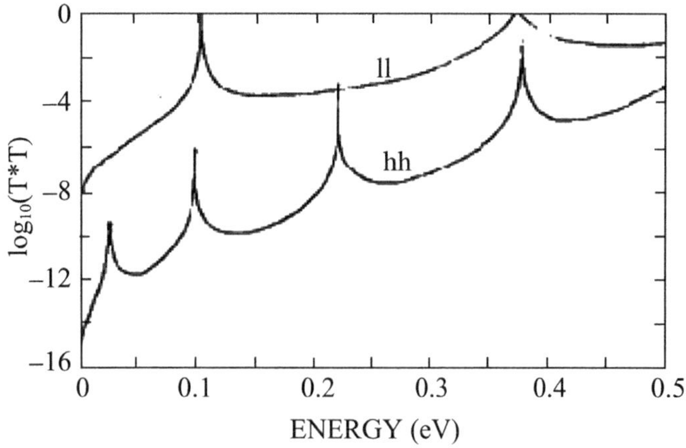

Figure 3.13 Transmission probabilities of the heavy and light hole $\log_{10}(T^*T)$ as functions of energy E at $F = 0$ and $k_{\|} = 0$.

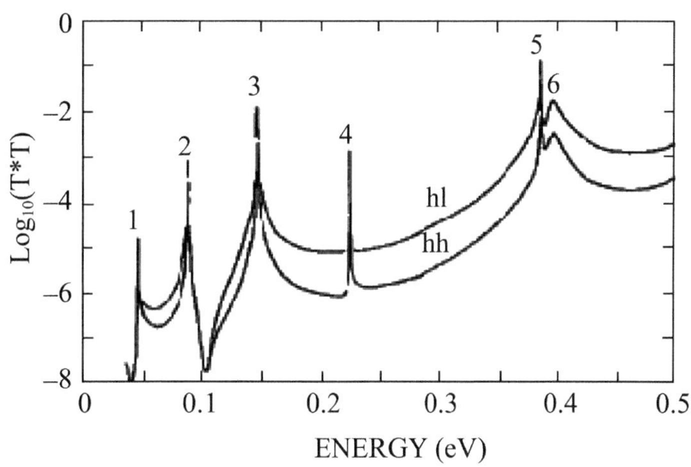

Figure 3.14 Transmission probabilities $(T^*T)_{\text{hh}}$ and $(T^*T)_{\text{hl}}$ as functions of energy E at $F = 0$ and $k_{\|} = 0.3$ ($2\pi/7$ nm).

energy E at $F = 0$ and $k_{\|} = 0.3$ ($2\pi/7$ nm), respectively [9]. From Fig. 3.14 we see that $(T^*T)_{\text{hh}}$ and $(T^*T)_{\text{hl}}$ contain almost all the resonant peaks of the heavy and light holes, which means that there is strong mixing between them. One peak is an exception: the fourth

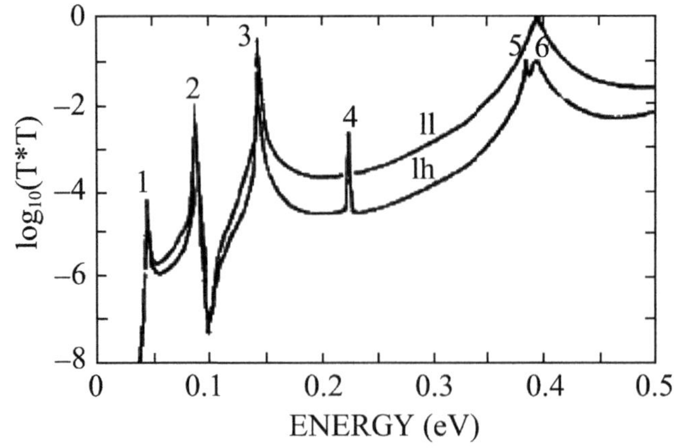

Figure 3.15 Transmission probabilities $(T^*T)_{\rm ll}$ and $(T^*T)_{\rm lh}$ as functions of energy E at $F = 0$ and $k_{\parallel} = 0.3$ $(2\pi/7$ nm).

peak appears in the hh curve but not in the hl curve. Similarly, in Fig. 3.15 the fourth peak appears only in the lh curve. It indicates that this peak is derived from a heavy hole resonance.

3.4 Resonant Tunneling in Dilute Magnetic Semiconductors

When magnetic ions, for example, Mn^{2+}, are doped in the semiconductor, then in the magnetic field the electronic energy levels with different spin orientations will split and the splitting energy is large, which is called giant Zeeman splitting energy. These kinds of semiconductors are called dilute magnetic semiconductors (DMSs). The giant Zeeman splitting energy

$$\Delta E = N_0 \alpha x_{\rm eff} \langle S_z \rangle \sigma_z, \tag{3.106}$$

where $N_0\alpha$ is the s-d exchange interaction energy. For $Zn_{1-x}Mn_xSe$ DMS, $N_0\alpha = 0.27$ eV. $x_{\rm eff}$ is the effective concentration of magnetic ions, $\langle S_z \rangle$ is the thermal average magnetic moment of magnetic ions:

$$\langle S_z \rangle = S B_J \left(\frac{S g u_{\rm B} B}{k_{\rm B}(T + T_0)} \right), \tag{3.107}$$

where B_J is the Brillouin function and J is the angular momentum quantum number of magnetic ion basis state. For Mn^{2+} ion, $S = J = 5/2$. σ_z is the spin of conduction electrons. For holes in valence band, Eqs. 3.106 and 3.107 are still valid, except the parameters are changed to those of the valence band.

If the magnetic ion concentration x is several percents, in the moderate magnetic field the giant Zeeman splitting energy can reach several even several tens of millielectron volt orders of magnitudes. This energy level splitting will have different effects on the electrons with positive and negative spin orientations. Chang et al. studied the RT of electrons through a DMS potential barrier structure [15].

When a small bias is applied across the structure, a non-equilibrium electron population will be generated. The current density $J = \Sigma_\sigma J^\sigma$ can be calculated,

$$J^\sigma = \frac{e^2 V}{2\pi^2 l_B^2} \sum_n \left(\frac{1}{2\pi}\right) \int_0^{k_n^F} dk_z \left(-\frac{\partial f_0}{\partial E}\right) T^\sigma v_z^\sigma, \tag{3.108}$$

where $T^\sigma(n, E_F)$ is the transmission probability at the Fermi energy for different spin orientations, $v_z^\sigma = \hbar k_z^\sigma / m$ is the group velocity, $(1/2)\pi l_B^2$ is the density of state of each Landau level, $l_B = \sqrt{\hbar/eB}$ is the magnetic length, and f_0 is the equilibrium distribution function. We use the approximation $-\partial f_0/\partial E \approx \delta(E - E_F)$ when $k_B T \ll E_F$. The low-temperature conductance is given by

$$\sigma^\sigma = \sigma_0 \sum_n T^\sigma(k_{nF}^\sigma), \tag{3.109}$$

where

$$k_{nE_F}^\sigma = \sqrt{\frac{2m}{\hbar^2}\left[E_F - \left(E_n \pm \frac{\Delta}{2}\right)\right]}, \tag{3.110}$$

$\sigma_0 = e^2/2\pi l_B^2 h$, $\Delta = J_{s-d}\langle S_z\rangle$ is the giant Zeeman splitting, and $E_n = (n + 1/2)\hbar\omega_c$ is the energy of the Landau level. The total conductivity is the sum of the conductivity of each Landau level at the Fermi energy and for each spin state.

The degree of spin polarization (SP) of the current density is defined by

$$P = \frac{J^\downarrow - J^\uparrow}{J^\downarrow + J^\uparrow}, \tag{3.111}$$

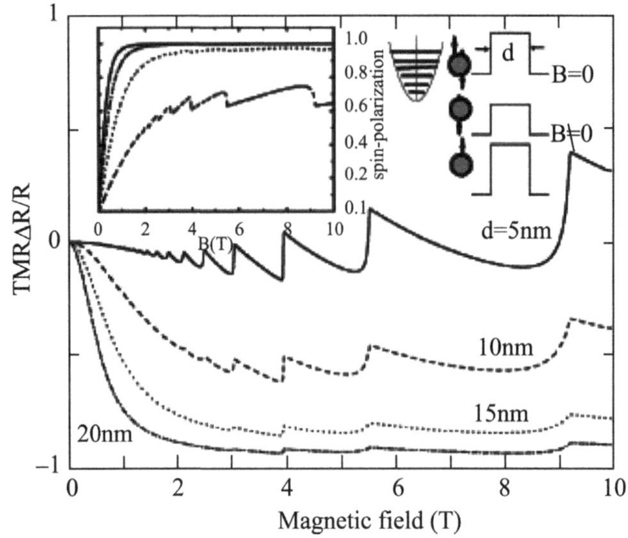

Figure 3.16 Electron tunneling through a single $ZnSe/Zn_{1-x}Mn_{0.07}Se$ ($x = 0.07$) barrier, TMR $\Delta R/R$, and spin polarization as functions of magnetic field for different DMS barrier thicknesses.

where $J^{\uparrow}$ ($J^{\downarrow}$) is the spin-up (spin-down) current density of the spin-polarized current. The tunneling magnetoresistance (TMR) as a result of tunneling through the NMR/DMS structures is defined by

$$\frac{\Delta R}{R} = \frac{R(B) - R(0)}{R(0)} = \frac{R(B)}{R(0)} - 1 = \frac{\sigma(0)}{\sigma(B)} - 1. \qquad (3.112)$$

Figure 3.16 shows the TMR $\Delta R/R$ as a function of the magnetic field for different single DMS barrier thicknesses [15]. The inset gives the SP versus the magnetic field. The potential profiles for $B = 0$ and $B \neq 0$ are also plotted. The solid, dashed, dotted, and dash-dotted curves correspond to different thicknesses of the DMS layer: 5, 10, 15, 20 nm, respectively. The other parameters for $ZnSe/Zn_{1-x}Mn_xSe$ are $m^* = 0.16\ m_0$, $T_0 = 1.4$ K, $N_0\alpha = 0.17$ eV, and potential barrier height $V_b = 10$ meV ($x = 0.07$). From Fig. 3.16 we see that the TMR decreases and oscillates with an increasing magnetic field. The oscillations of the TMR and the SP are weakened by increasing the DMS barrier thickness. These oscillations are mainly attributed to the oscillation of the spin-down conductivity component $\sigma^{\downarrow}/\sigma_0$,

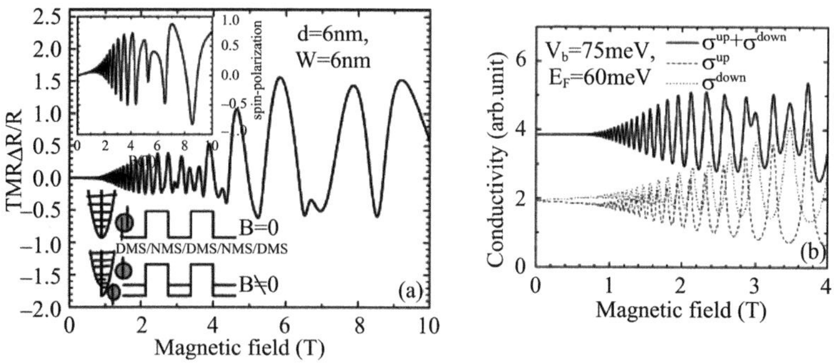

Figure 3.17 (a) Tunneling magnetoresistance (TMR) $\Delta R/R$ of a NMS double-barrier structure with DMS contacts as a function of magnetic field. The inset shows the spin polarization as a function of magnetic field. (b) Total conductivity (thick curve), spin-up (dotted), and spin-down (dashed) components as functions of magnetic field.

which is enhanced by an increasing magnetic field and weakened by the thickness of the DMS layer. The $\sigma^{\downarrow}/\sigma_0$ is larger than that of spin-up component $\sigma^{\uparrow}/\sigma_0$, since the barrier height seen by the spin-up electron is higher than that seen by the spin-down electron due to the magnetic field–induced s–p exchange interaction. Therefore the SP increases and saturates with an increasing magnetic field and barrier thickness.

Figure 3.17 shows the TMR $\Delta R/R$ of a non-magnetic semiconductor (NMS) double-barrier structure with a DMS well and contacts as a function of magnetic field [15]. The inset in Fig. 3.17a shows the SP as a function of magnetic field. The parameters are E_F $= 60$ meV and $V_b = 75$ meV for $Cd_{1-y}Mg_yTe/Cd_{1-x}Mn_xTe$ ($x = 0.04$, $y = 0.08$). From Fig. 3.17a we observe a peculiar beat pattern in the TMR and SP curves, which is directly related to the superposition of the s–p spin-split transmission channels. When the magnetic field increases, the landau levels are swept across the Fermi surface one by one, resulting in oscillations in the magnetoresistance, similar to those of Shubnikov de Haas (SdH) oscillations. And the s-d exchange interaction leads to a giant Zeeman splitting. The beating is a result of the fact that the total current is composed of spin-up and spin-down components. The interplay between the spin-up and spin-down channels results in the beat pattern in

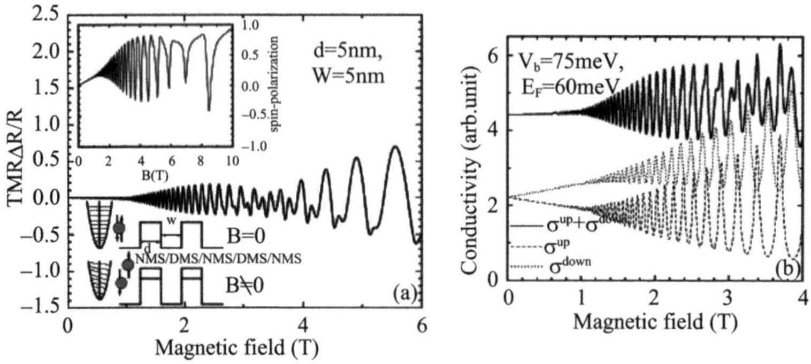

Figure 3.18 (a) Tunneling magnetoresistance (TMR) $\Delta R/R$ of a DMS double-barrier structure with NMS contacts as a function of magnetic field. The inset shows the spin polarization as a function of magnetic field. (b) Total conductivity (thick curve), spin-up (dotted), and spin-down (dashed) components as functions of magnetic field.

the magnetoresistance. This is clearly demonstrated in Fig. 3.17b, which shows the total conductivity (thick curve), spin-up (dotted), and spin-down (dashed) components. The phase difference of both currents results in the beat pattern of the total TMR and SP.

Figure 3.18a shows the TMR $\Delta R/R$ of a DMS double-barrier structure with a NMS well and contacts as a function of magnetic field [15]. The inset shows the SP as a function of magnetic field. The parameters are $E_F = 60$ meV and $V_b = 75$ meV for ZnSe/$Zn_{1-x}Mn_xSe$ ($x = 0.2$). Similar oscillating and beat behaviors as in Fig. 3.17a are found. Figure 3.18b shows the total conductivity and two components as functions of magnetic field. The left-down inset is the schematic diagram of the potential energy; in the magnetic field the potential heights for the spin-up and spin-down electrons are different, resulting in different tunneling probabilities $T^{\uparrow\downarrow}$. From Fig. 3.18a we see that the beat of the magnetoresistance is obvious. The SP oscillates with the magnetic field and is obviously larger than 1, that is, the spin-down current is dominant.

Grube et al. fabricated a BeTe/$Zn_{1-x}Mn_xSe$/BeTe double-barrier RTD and observed a SP of up to 80% in the tunneling current with a semimagnetic layer of only 3.5 nm thickness [16]. Figure 3.19 shows the schematic diagram of the potential energy of this device; the middle potential well is DMS $Zn_{1-x}Mn_xSe$, and the magnetic field

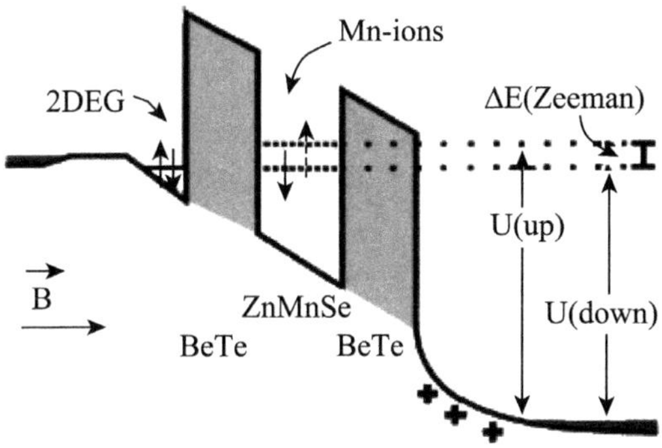

Figure 3.19 Schematic diagram of the potential energy of BeTe/$Zn_{1-x}Mn_xSe$/BeTe double-barrier resonant tunneling diode (RTD).

is applied in the z direction (perpendicular to the junction). Due to the giant Zeeman splitting effect the energy levels of the spin-up and spin-down electrons split. In the magnetic field $B = 2.5$ T the splitting energy is about 20 meV. When the bias is applied to the diode, if the Fermi energy level of the electron in the injecting region and the spin-down energy level in the well region coincide, there will be a tunneling current with spin-down polarization. At the same time the spin-up electron cannot tunnel through the device. Therefore in the collecting region we obtain electrons with only one spin orientation; the SP degree approaches 1 or -1.

To measure the SP degree a III-V $Al_{0.07}Ga_{0.93}As$/GaAs LED is grown directly on the bottom of the RTD. The tunneling current from the RTD is directly injected into the LED, and the spin-polarized electrons combine with holes in the quantum well. Measuring the circular polarization degree of the luminescent light, one can determine the SP degree according to the selected rule of the electron-hole transition [17].

The SP degree of injected current can be derived from the circular polarization degree of the LED luminescence [17],

$$P_{\text{opt}} = \frac{(3n^{\uparrow} + n^{\downarrow}) - (3n^{\downarrow} + n^{\uparrow})}{(3n^{\uparrow} + n^{\downarrow}) + (3n^{\downarrow} + n^{\uparrow})} = \frac{2n^{\uparrow} - 2n^{\downarrow}}{4n^{\uparrow} + 4n^{\downarrow}} = \frac{1}{2}P_{\text{J}}, \qquad (3.113)$$

where $n^{\uparrow}$ and $n^{\downarrow}$ are the occupied number of spin-up and spin-down electrons, respectively. P_{J} is the SP degree of the current; thus the SP

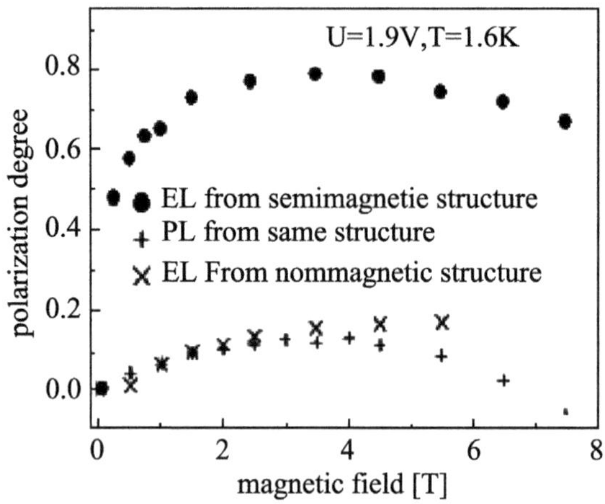

Figure 3.20 Magnetic dependence of the spin polarization degree (•) at a constant voltage of 1.9 V at the beginning of the first resonance in the AlGaAs/GaAs LED. For comparison the results for the nonmagnetic RTD are also shown (+, ×).

degree of the current is double of the circular polarization degree of luminescence.

Figure 3.20 shows the magnetic dependence of the SP degree (•) at a constant voltage of 1.9 V at the beginning of the first resonance in the AlGaAs/GaAs LED [16]. For comparison the results for the nonmagnetic RTD are also shown (+, ×). The results prove that the magnetic RT structure is the origin of the spin injection. From Fig. 3.20 we see that the SP degree increases with the magnetic field until it saturates at 80% for fields above 2–3 T, coinciding very well with the saturation of the giant Zeeman splitting in DMSs. Test measurements with optical excitation of nonpolarized carriers in the same structure with nonmagnetic BeTe-ZnSe tunneling structures reveal only a small polarization degree below 15%.

Figure 3.21 shows the voltage dependence of the SP degree and I–V curve at a constant magnetic field of 2.5 T around the first resonance of the 3.5 nm/3.0 nm BeTe/$Zn_{0.94}Mn_{0.06}Se$ RTD [16]. From Fig. 3.21 we see a clear reduction of the polarization degree over the resonance, which can be explained by the offset of the resonant spin-down level in the well (see Fig. 3.19). Although a

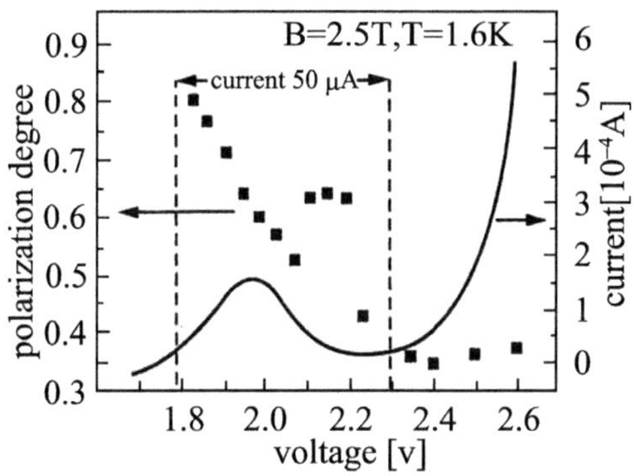

Figure 3.21 Voltage dependence of the spin polarization degree and I–V curve at a constant magnetic field of 2.5 T around the first resonance of the 3.5 nm/3.0 nm BeTe/$Zn_{0.94}Mn_{0.06}Se$ RTD.

reversal of the spin orientation has not been observed, the SP at a constant drive current of 50 μA can be from 80% down to 38% by merely changing the external voltage from 1.8 to 2.3 V. The reason that the spin-up polarization has not been observed is because the transit time is well above 10^{-7} s in the present RTD, whereas the spin-relaxation times in diluted magnetic semiconductors are in the range of 10^{-12} s. Thus, electrons that enter the ZnMnSe quantum well in resonance with the higher energy spin-split subband level will very likely relax into the lower energy spin-split level before they are injected into the III-V material.

Xia et al. studied theoretically the spin-polarized current through a RTD made of a semimagnetic semiconductor [18]. The structure is shown in Fig. 3.19; the parameters are the same as in Ref. [16]: $B = 2.5$ T, $T = 1.6$ K, $T_0 = 1.4$ K, and concentration of Mn^{2+} ions $x = 0.06$. Because the temperature is very low, we take $T = 0$ K in the calculation. Thus the tunneling current is given by Eq. 3.79. Because the RTD is in the magnetic field along the z direction (current direction), one should use the density of states of Landau energy levels instead of the two-dimensional density of states in Eq. 3.79,

$$J = \frac{e}{2\pi^2\hbar}\left(\frac{eB}{\pi\hbar c}\right)\int_0^{E_F} dE_z N(E_F - E_z)T(E_z), \qquad (3.114)$$

where $eB/(\pi\hbar c)$ is the density of states of each Landau energy level,

$$N(E_F - E_z) = \text{int}\left(\frac{E_F - E_z}{\hbar\omega_c} - \frac{1}{2}\right). \tag{3.115}$$

The transmission probability $T(E_z)$ is calculated by the numerical method.

The parameters of the RTD are well width 3.5 nm, barrier width 3 nm, and potential barrier height 1890 meV. The electron effective masses are assumed to be equal for the well and barrier, $m^* = 0.16\ m_0$. For the BeTe/ZnTe quantum well there are three confined states in the well, whose energies are 132, 521, and 1135 meV, respectively. The electron density n in the injection region is $10^{19}\ \text{cm}^{-3}$. Using the relation $E_F = \hbar^2(3\pi^2 n)^{2/3}/(2m^*)$, we obtain the Fermi energy $E_F = 105.8$ meV. In the calculation we take $E_F = 100$ meV.

Figure 3.22 shows the spin-polarized tunneling current (down ∇, up Δ), total current ($\square$), and SP degree ($\bullet$) as functions of bias voltage at $B = 2.5$ T when the Fermi level crosses over the first quasi-confined state [18]. From Fig. 3.22 we see that when the electric field is such that the Fermi level is near the first confined state there is only one kind of spin orientation, that is, spin-down, and the polarization degree reaches 1. As the electric field (voltage) increases, the current of the other kind of spin orientation, that is, spin-up, increases and the polarization degree decreases gradually. These results are basically consistent with

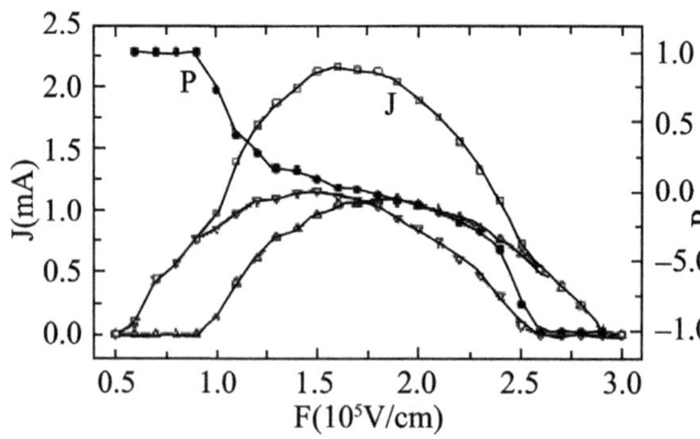

Figure 3.22 Spin-polarized tunneling current (down ∇, up Δ), total current ($\square$), and spin polarization degree ($\bullet$) as functions of bias voltage at $B = 2.5$ T when the Fermi level crosses over the first quasi-confined state.

the experimental results [16]. When the electric field increases continuously the opposite process occurs. The current of the spin-up becomes larger than that of the spin-down, and consequently, the polarization degree becomes negative. But this behavior has not been observed experimentally; the reason has been indicated above.

References

1. Tsu, R., and Esaki, L. (1973). Tunneling in a finite superlattice. *Appl. Phys. Lett.*, **22**, 562–564.
2. Chang, L. L., Esaki, L., and Tsu, R. (1969). Resonant tunneling in semiconductor double barriers. *Appl. Phys. Lett.*, **24**, 593–595.
3. Morkoc, H., Chen, J., and Reddy, U. K. (1986). Observation of a negative differential resistance due to tunneling through a single barrier into a quantum well. *Appl. Phys. Lett.*, **49**, 70–72.
4. Goodhue, W. D., Sollner, T. C. L. G., Le, H. Q., Brown, E. R., and Vojak, B. A. (1986). Large room-temperature effects from resonant tunneling through AlAs barriers. *Appl. Phys. Lett.*, **49**, 1086–1088.
5. Broekaert, T. P. E., Lee, W., and Fonstad, C. G. (1988). Pseudomorphic $In_{0.53}Ga_{0.47}As$/AlAs/InAs resonant tunneling diodes with peak-to-valley current ratios of 30 at room temperature. *Appl. Phys. Lett.*, **53**, 1545–1547.
6. Brown, E. R., Sollner, T. C. L. G., Parker, C. D., Goodhue, W. D., and Chen, C. L. (1989). Oscillations up to 420 GHz in GaAs/AlAs resonant tunneling diodes. *Appl. Phys. Lett.*, **55**, 1777–1779.
7. Tamura, H., and Ando, T. (1991). Conductance fluctuations in quantum wires. *Phys. Rev. B*, **44**, 1792–1800.
8. Price, P. J. (1993). Transmission and reflection peaks in multichannel ballistic transport. *Phys. Rev. B*, **48**, 17301–17307.
9. Xia, J. B. (1988). Theory of hole resonant tunneling in quantum well structures. *Phys. Rev. B*, **38**, 8365–8370.
10. Tsuchiya, M., and Sakaki, H. (1986). Dependence of resonant tunneling current on well widths in AlAs/GaAs/AlAs double barrier diode structures. *Appl. Phys. Lett.*, **49**, 88–90.
11. Luryi, S., and Zaslavsky, A. (1998). *Modern Semiconductor Device Physics*, ed. Sze, S. M., Chapter 5 "Quantum-effect and hot-electron devices" (John Wiley & Sons, Inc.).

12. Brown, E. R., Söderström, J. R., Parker, C. D., et al. (1991). Oscillations up to 712 GHz in InAs/AlSb resonant-tunneling diodes. *Appl. Phys. Lett.*, **58**, 2291–2293.
13. Mendez, E. E., Wang, W. I., Ricco, B., and Esaki, L. (2008). Resonant tunneling of holes in AlAs-GaAs-AlAs heterostructures. *Appl. Phys. Lett.*, **47**, 415–417.
14. Broido, D. A., and Sham, L. J. (1985). Effective masses of holes at GaAs-AlGaAs heterojunctions. *Phys. Rev. B*, **31**, 888–892.
15. Chang, K., Xia, J. B., and Peeters, F. M. (2002). Oscillating magnetoresistance in dilute magnetic semiconductor barrier structures. *Phys. Rev. B*, **65**, 115209 (1–5).
16. Gruber, Th., Keim, M., Fiederling, R., et al. (2001). Electron spin manipulation using semimagnetic resonant tunneling diodes. *Appl. Phys. Lett.*, **78**, 1101–1103.
17. Fiederling, R., Keim, M., Reuscher, G., et al. (1999). Injection and detection of a spin-polarized current in a light-emitting diode. *Nature*, **402**, 787–790.
18. Xia, J. B., Hai, G. Q., and Wang, J. N. (2003). Spin-polarized current produced by a double barrier resonant tunneling diode. *Solid State Commun.*, 489–492.

Chapter 4

Longitudinal Transport of Superlattices

Longitudinal transport in a superlattice is transport along the growth direction of the superlattice; the resonant tunneling discussed in the preceding chapter is one of the forms of longitudinal transports. The path of the longitudinal transport is very short, only several or several tenths of nanometers. The effect of scattering on electron motion is not obvious. Electron motion is mainly controlled by the quantum effect. At the same time, electron motion velocity is generally very higher than the thermal balance velocity of carriers; therefore these kinds of devices are called quantum effect devices or hot-electron devices [1]. The advantage of such a device is high velocity, and it can be used to fabricate high-frequency devices. But due to the delay of the circuit, for example, the RC time delay, the extremely high velocity in the active region cannot be represented in the whole device performance. Now people use the strong or modulated nonlinear current-voltage characteristics or special electrode symmetry to realize a more complex circuit performance and to replace the circuit unit constructed by a large number of transistors or passive circuits; for example, they use a few tunneling devices to realize a multiple value memory and logic circuit.

The largest obstacles of the practical application of quantum effect devices and hot-electron devices are the difficulties of room

Quantum Waveguide in Microcircuits
Jian-Bai Xia, Duan-Yang Liu, and Wei-Dong Sheng

ISBN 978-981-4669-85-6 (Hardcover), 978-1-315-36477-3 (eBook)
www.panstanford.com

temperature operation and large-scale integration, resulting in that they are now only used in some special cases.

4.1 Miniband Transport of a Superlattice

When the potential barrier width of a superlattice becomes gradually smaller, the confined states of neighboring wells will interact and the energy of a single confined state becomes a broad band, called a miniband. These neighboring confined states in quantum wells are similar to the atoms of a one-dimensional (1D) atomic chain. Assume that the energy of each atomic state is E_0, the interaction energy of neighboring atoms is V_0, and the distance between neighboring atoms is d; then the tight binding wave function of the atomic chain is

$$\psi_k = \frac{1}{\sqrt{N}}\sum_i e^{ikR_i}\phi_i(r), \tag{4.1}$$

where k is the wave vector, R_i is the coordinate of the i-th atom, $\phi_i(r)$ is the wave function of the i-th atom, and N is the total number of atoms. The energy of the atomic chain,

$$\begin{aligned} E = \psi^* H \psi &= \frac{1}{N}\sum_{ij} e^{-ikR_j}\phi_j^*(r) H e^{ikR_i}\phi_i(r) \\ &= E_0 + V_0 e^{ikd} + V_0 e^{-ikd} \\ &= E_0 + 2V_0\cos kd. \end{aligned} \tag{4.2}$$

Equation 4.2 can be also written as

$$E_z(k) = E_0 - \frac{\Delta}{2}\cos kd, \tag{4.3}$$

where $\Delta = 4|V_0|$ is the miniband width, which is proportional to the interaction energy V_0 of confined states in neighboring wells, that is, proportional inversely to the width of the barrier. Figure 4.1 shows Δ as functions of the barrier width for a fixed well width $w = 3.5$ nm in a GaAs/AlAs superlattice.

The miniband given by Eq. 4.3 is different from the ordinary energy band of the semiconductor in the following points: (i) The semiconductor energy band is three-dimensional isotropic, while the superlattice miniband is highly anisotropic; in the x and y

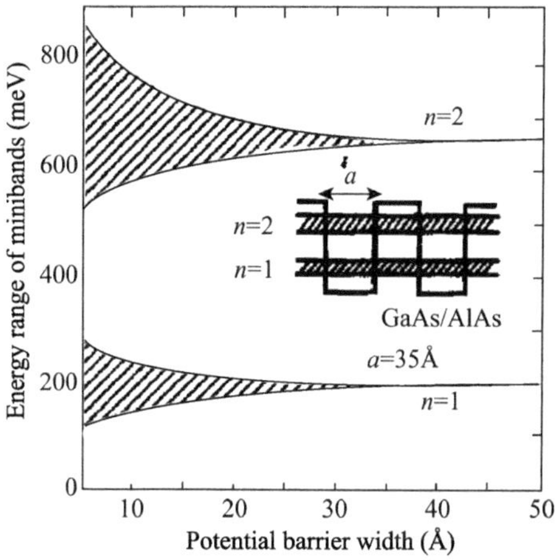

Figure 4.1 Δ as functions of the barrier width for a fixed well width $w = 3.5$ nm in a GaAs/AlAs superlattice.

directions it is same as the bulk energy band, but in the z direction it is a band with a small width Δ (generally several tenths of millielectron volts). (ii) A semiconductor energy band is defined in the Brillouin zone $-\pi/a < k < \pi/a$ for each direction, where a is the lattice constant. The miniband is defined in the Brillouin zone of z direction $-\pi/d < k < \pi/d$, where d is the period of the superlattice in the z direction. $d \gg a$, so the Brillouin zone of the miniband is very smaller than that of the bulk energy band. (iii) In the applied electric field the electrons in the bulk material move near the center of the Brillouin zone and are scattered by impurities or other scattering centers. The derivation of distribution function from the balance state is very small, so the transport can be treated by the perturbation method, for example, solving the Boltzmann equation. In the superlattice due to the small Brillouin zone in the z direction, in the electric field the electron can reach the edge of the Brillouin zone ($k = \pm\,\pi/d$) before it is scattered. At the edge of Brillouin zone the electron effective mass is negative, so negative conductance is possible.

The electron motion equation in a semiconductor is

$$\hbar\frac{d\mathbf{k}}{dt} = e\mathbf{F}, \tag{4.4}$$

where **k** is the wave vector and **F** is the applied electric field. In the electric field along the z direction the electron moves from the center of the Brillouin zone and after time τ reaches the edge of the Brillouin zone π/d. Then

$$\hbar k = \hbar\left(\frac{\pi}{d}\right) = eF\tau. \tag{4.5}$$

If the scattering relaxation time is longer than τ, then the electrons can reach the edge of the Brillouin zone and produce negative conductance. Esaki et al. predicted the Bloch oscillation is probably observed in superlattices on the basis of this idea [2]. Equation 4.5 becomes a necessary condition of occurrence of negative differential conductance (NDC). In the following we accept the relaxation approximation proposed by Huang et al. [3].

From Eq. 4.3 the electron velocity in the z direction

$$v = \frac{1}{\hbar}\frac{\partial E_z(k)}{\partial k} = \frac{\Delta d}{2\hbar}\sin kd. \tag{4.6}$$

From Eq. 4.4 the variation of the electron wave vector with time is

$$k = k_0 + \frac{eF}{\hbar}t, \tag{4.7}$$

where k_0 is the initial wave vector. Suppose the electron scattering time is τ; then the average drift velocity,

$$\begin{aligned} v_{\mathrm{d}}(k_0) &= \frac{1}{\tau}\int_0^\infty v(k_0, t)e^{-t/\tau}dt \\ &= \frac{\Delta eFd^2\tau}{2\hbar^2}\cdot\frac{\cos k_0 d + \frac{\hbar}{eFd\tau}\sin k_0 d}{1+\left(\frac{eFd\tau}{\hbar}\right)^2}. \end{aligned} \tag{4.8}$$

The electron total energy

$$E = E_z(k) + \frac{\hbar^2 k_{\|}^2}{2m^*}. \tag{4.9}$$

Assuming that the electrons satisfy the Boltzmann distribution, the electron density

$$\begin{aligned} n &= \frac{C}{4\pi^2}\int_{-\pi/d}^{\pi/d} dk \exp\left(-\frac{E_z(k)}{k_{\mathrm{B}}T}\right)\int_0^\infty dk_{\|}^2 \exp\left(-\frac{\hbar^2 k_{\|}^2}{2m^* k_{\mathrm{B}}T}\right) \\ &= C\cdot\frac{m^* k_{\mathrm{B}}T}{\pi\hbar^2 d} I_0\left(\frac{\Delta}{2k_{\mathrm{B}}T}\right), \end{aligned} \tag{4.10}$$

where I_0 is the zero-order Bessel function of an imaginary argument.

The calculation of the current density is similar to Eq. 4.10. Calculate the statistical average of the drift velocity $v_d(k)$,

$$j = C\frac{ev_{d0}}{4\pi^2}\cdot\frac{2m^*k_BT}{\hbar^2}\int_{-\pi/d}^{\pi/d} dk\cos kd\exp\left(-\frac{E_z(k)}{k_BT}\right)$$
$$= C\frac{ev_{d0}m^*k_BT}{\pi\hbar^2 d}I_1\left(\frac{\Delta}{2k_BT}\right)$$
$$= nev_{d0}\frac{I_1(\Delta/2k_BT)}{I_0(\Delta/2k_BT)}, \quad (4.11)$$

where

$$v_{d0} = \frac{\Delta eFd^2\tau}{2\hbar^2}\cdot\frac{1}{1+\left(\frac{eFd\tau}{\hbar}\right)^2}. \quad (4.12)$$

In calculating Eq. 4.11 the term sin kd in $v_d(k)$ (Eq. 4.8) is odd symmetric to k. Hence its contribution to the integration for k equals zero.

Therefore the current composes two parts: one is related to electric field strength F, which is included in v_{d0} (Eq. 4.12); the other is related to temperature, which is included in I_1/I_0. When the electric field is very small, $eFd\tau/h \ll 1$, then

$$v_{d0} = \frac{\Delta eFd^2\tau}{2\hbar^2} = \frac{eF\tau}{m_z{}^*}, \quad (4.13)$$

where $m_z{}^*$ is the effective mass in the z direction,

$$\frac{1}{m_z{}^*} = \frac{1}{\hbar^2}\left.\frac{\partial^2 E_z(k)}{\partial k^2}\right|_{k=0} = \frac{1}{\hbar^2}\frac{\Delta d^2}{2}. \quad (4.14)$$

Equation 4.13 is the result of the linear transport theory. If the electric field F and the relaxation time τ are large enough so $eFd\tau/h \approx 1$, then nonlinear conductance will appear and the current will not be proportional to the electric field.

Sibille et al. observed first the nonlinear conductance caused by the miniband transport [4]. They grew some GaAs/AlAs superlattice samples: the width of the GaAs layer is 10~20 monolayers (2.83 Å) and that of the AlAs layer is 3~7 monolayers. The I–V curves of three samples at 300 K are shown in Fig. 4.2 [4], where (12/4) represents that the monolayer number of GaAs and AlAs, 12 and 4, respectively. From Fig. 4.2 we see that when the bias voltage is very

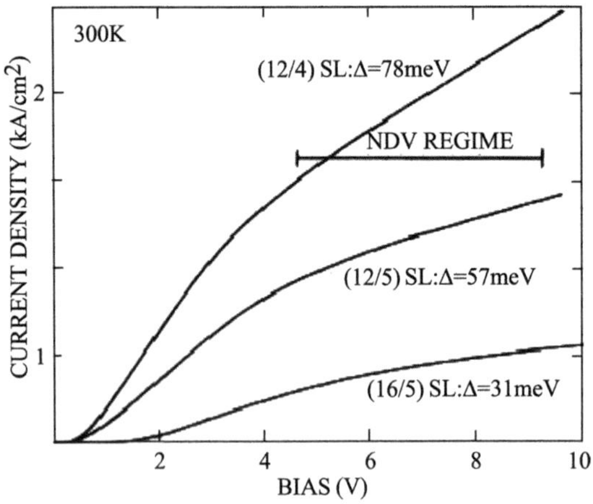

Figure 4.2 I–V curves of three samples at 300 K.

small (3 V) there appears nonlinear conductance. From Eq. 4.12 the drift velocity can be phenomenally written as

$$v_d(F) = \frac{\mu F}{1 + (F/F_0)^\beta}, \tag{4.15}$$

where β is a parameter. When $\beta = 2$, Eq. 4.15 is just Eq. 4.12. When $\beta > 1$, $v_d(F)$ reaches maximum if F equals a critical field F_c. When $F > F_c$, $v_d(F)$ decreases and exhibits a negative differential velocity (NDV). When $\beta = 1$, $v_d(F)$ approaches a saturated value; there is no maximum, as shown in Fig. 4.2. When $\beta = 2$, $v_d(F)$ reaches the maximum $v_p = \mu F_0/2$ at $F = F_0$.

Sibille et al. measured the I–V curves for another set of samples that have larger miniband widths Δ. The I–V curves for samples with $\Delta = 133$, 81, and 52 meV are shown in Fig. 4.3 [5]. Different from Fig. 4.2 the I–V curves in Fig. 4.3 show obvious NDC behavior.

A shown in Fig. 4.3 the samples are ohmic at a low bias and exhibit NDC beyond a critical voltage. The peak electron velocity v_p can be estimated from the peak current density J_p by applying $J_p = env_p$, where $n = 6 \times 10^{16}$ cm^{-3} is the electron density. For the (17/4) sample, $J_p = 40$ kA/cm^2 and $v_p = 4 \times 10^6$ cm/s; for the (13/3) sample, $J_p = 140$ kA/cm^2 and $v_p = 10^7$ cm/s. Because the electron velocity is very high, these samples can be used to fabricate high-frequency devices. For the highest value, a simple calculation leads

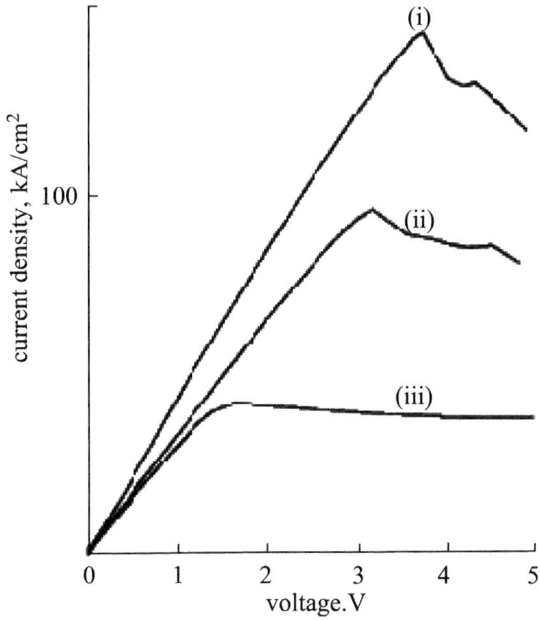

Figure 4.3 I–V curves for samples with $\Delta = 133$ (i), 81 (ii), and 52 (iii) meV.

to an expected maximum fundamental frequency $f_{\max} = v_{\mathrm{p}}/L$ of 200 GHz, where L is the device thickness $L = 0.5$ μm.

Another NDC mechanism was proposed, relying on a transition between Bloch miniband transport and hopping transport between Wannier–Stark quantized levels (WSL). To differentiate between the negative effective mass (NEM) and WSL mechanisms, the edF_{c} and v_{p}/d as a function of Δ for a series of samples are shown in Fig. 4.4 [4]. According to the NEM mechanism, Eqs. 4.12 and 4.15, ($\beta = 2$),

$$F_{\mathrm{c}} = \frac{\hbar}{ed\tau}, \quad edF_{\mathrm{c}} = \frac{\hbar}{\tau}, \tag{4.16}$$

and

$$v_{\mathrm{p}} = \frac{\mu F_{\mathrm{c}}}{2} = \frac{\Delta d}{4\hbar}, \quad \frac{v_{\mathrm{p}}}{d} = \frac{\Delta}{4\hbar}. \tag{4.17}$$

On the other hand, the WSL theory predicts $edF_{\mathrm{c}} \approx \Delta$ and a superlinear dependence of v_{p}/d on Δ. From Fig. 4.4 we see that the experimental values of edF_{c} rapidly and strongly deviate from the

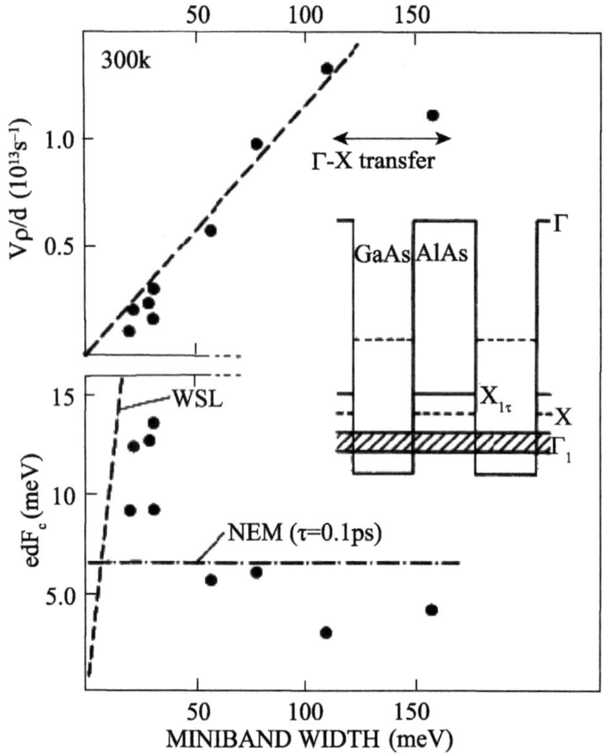

Figure 4.4 edF_c and v_p/d as a function of Δ for a series of samples. Inset: Conduction band diagram of the relevant levels.

line predicted by the WSL mechanism. Furthermore, v_p/d appears to vary linearly with Δ at least to $\Delta = 100$ meV. These two features strongly argue against the WSL mechanism and in favor of the NEM one.

Figure 4.5 shows the frequency dependence of the device conductance for several applied biases [6]. Both curves (two samples) exhibit sharp resonances, resulting in a large negative conductance at peak frequency f_m. The resonance frequencies are 2.7 GHz and 4.9 GHz for the samples of total thickness $L = 1.2$ μm and 0.6 μm, respectively. The f_m indeed scales almost linearly with the inverse of the square loop (SL) thickness, a logical consequence of a transit time effect.

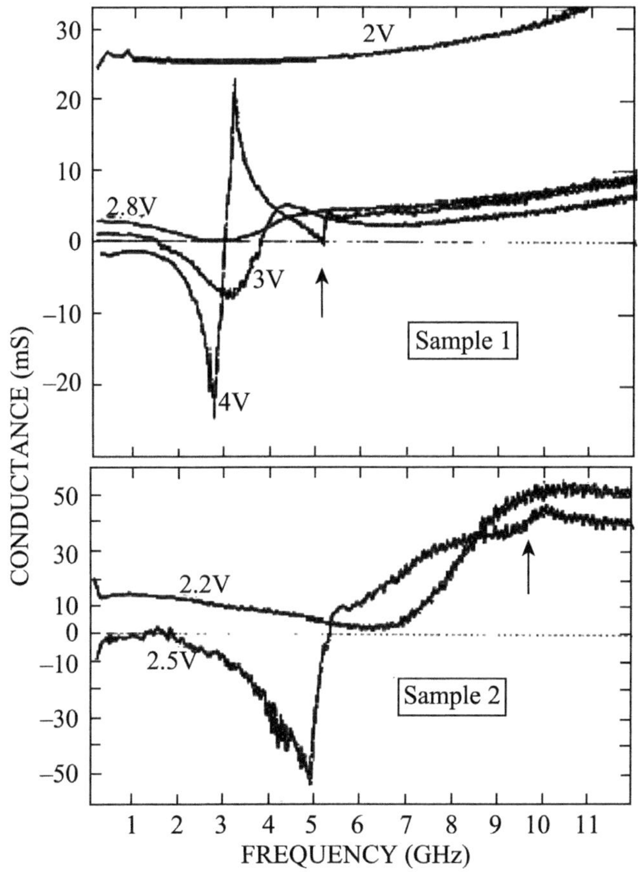

Figure 4.5 Microwave conductance as a function of frequency for several applied biases.

4.2 Bloch Oscillation in Superlattices

When Esaki et al. proposed the miniband transport of a superlattice, they predicted that it is possible to observe the Bloch oscillation in the superlattice [2]. If the collision relaxation time in the superlattice τ satisfies Eq. 3.5, then the Bloch oscillation can occur, whose period equals the time that the electron travels one circle along the Brillouin zone.

$$\hbar\frac{\Delta k}{T} = \hbar\left(\frac{2\pi}{d}\right)\frac{1}{T} = eF$$

$$T = \frac{\hbar}{eF}\left(\frac{2\pi}{d}\right), \quad \omega_B = \frac{2\pi}{T} = \frac{eFd}{\hbar}, \tag{4.18}$$

where ω_B is called Bloch oscillation frequency. To observe Bloch oscillation experimentally, people have made many years efforts, until 1996, when the strong terahertz photoelectric resonance at Bloch oscillation frequency was observed [7].

The experimental sample in the superlattice structure consists of 40 periods of 8 nm wide GaAs wells and 2 nm AlGaAs barriers (miniband width $\Delta = 22$ meV). The superlattice is homogeneously Si doped with a concentration of $n = 3 \times 10^{15}$ cm^{-3}. In the University of California, Santa Barbara (UCSB), free electron laser (FEL) were used as a terahertz radiation source, giving pulses of intense terahertz radiation with a pulse of several microseconds. Therefore the electric fields, including direct and alternating, are applied to the superlattice sample longitudinally.

$$F = F_0 + F_1 \cos\omega t. \tag{4.19}$$

Figure 4.6 shows the DC current-voltage curve for increasing FEL intensity. The FEL frequency was fixed to be 0.6 THz (Fig. 4.6a) and 1.5 THz (Fig. 4.6b) [7]. The curves are shifted downward for increasing laser intensity (F_1). From the figures we see that besides the NDC, there are a series of resonance peaks at the Bloch frequency and their harmonics. When the laser intensity is increased further the first peak starts to decrease and a second peak at about twice the voltage of the first peak is observed due to a two-photon resonance. At the highest intensities up to a four-photon resonance was observed. The authors attributed the first additional peak to a resonance of the external laser field where the Bloch frequency $\omega_B = \omega$. The other peaks are higher resonances, where $\omega_B = n\omega$.

To explain this behavior we still use the relaxation time approximation [3] used in the last section to calculate the current density in the presence of an alternating field. Similar to Eqs. 3.6 and 3.7, in the electric field (Eq. 4.19) we have

$$k = k_0 + \frac{eF_0}{\hbar}t + \frac{eF_1}{\hbar\omega}\sin\omega t. \tag{4.20}$$

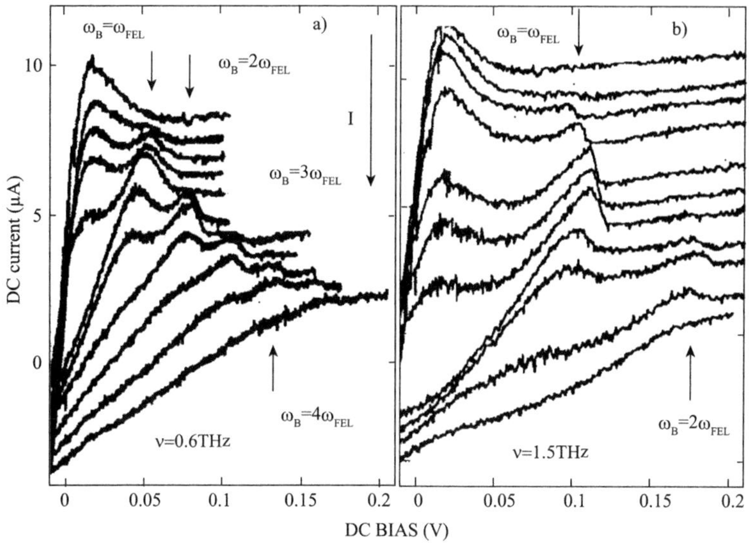

Figure 4.6 DC current-voltage curve for increasing FEL intensity. The FEL frequency was fixed to 0.6 THz (a) and 1.5 THz (b).

$$\begin{aligned} v(t) &= \frac{\Delta d}{2\hbar}\sin kd \\ &= \frac{\Delta d}{2\hbar}\sin\left(k_0 + \frac{eF_0 t}{\hbar} + \frac{eF_1}{\omega}\sin\omega t\right)d \\ &= \frac{v_0}{2i}\left[e^{i(\alpha+\beta\sin\omega t)} - e^{-i(\alpha+\beta\sin\omega t)}\right]. \end{aligned} \tag{4.21}$$

Expanding Eq. 4.21 to t, we obtain

$$\begin{aligned} v(t_0) = v_0 \Bigg\{ &\sin\alpha\left[J_0(\beta) + 2\sum_{k=1}^{\infty} J_{2k}(\beta)\cos 2k\omega t\right] \\ &+ \cos\alpha\left[2\sum_{k=0}^{\infty} J_{2k+1}(\beta)\sin(2k+1)\omega t\right]\Bigg\}. \end{aligned} \tag{4.22}$$

where

$$v_0 = \frac{\Delta d}{2\hbar}, \quad \alpha = \frac{eF_0 d}{\hbar}t + k_0 d, \quad \text{and} \quad \beta = \frac{eF_1 d}{\hbar\omega}. \tag{4.23}$$

When the collision relaxation is taken into account, the electron drift velocity equals

$$v_d(k_0) = \frac{1}{\tau}\int_0^{\infty} v(k_0, t)e^{-t/\tau}dt. \tag{4.24}$$

Inserting Eq. 4.23 into Eq. 4.24, at last we obtain

$$v_{d0} = \frac{\Delta eFd^2\tau}{2\hbar^2} \sum_{n=0}^{\infty} J_n\left(\frac{eF_1d}{\hbar\omega}\right) Q_n,$$

$$Q_n = \begin{cases} \dfrac{1}{1+\left(\dfrac{eF_0d\pi}{\hbar}\right)^2}, & n=0 \\ \dfrac{1+\dfrac{n\omega\hbar}{eF_0d}}{1+\left(\dfrac{eF_0d}{\hbar}+n\omega\right)^2\tau^2} \pm \dfrac{1-\dfrac{n\omega\hbar}{eF_0d}}{1+\left(\dfrac{eF_0d}{\hbar}-n\omega\right)^2\tau^2}. & \begin{matrix} n=2k \\ n=2k+1 \end{matrix} \end{cases} \tag{4.25}$$

Phenomenally we can write Eq. 4.25 as follows:

$$v_{d0} = \sum_{n=0}^{\infty} v_{dn}(F_0),$$

$$v_{dn}(F_0) = \frac{\mu_n F_0}{1+\left(\frac{F_0}{F_c} \pm n\omega\tau\right)^2}. \tag{4.26}$$

Equation 4.26 can be used to explain the peak positions in Fig. 4.6. Differentiating $v_{dn}(F_0)$ in Eq. 4.26 to F_0, we obtain

$$F_0 = n\omega\tau F_c = n\omega\tau \cdot \frac{\hbar}{ed\tau}, \quad \text{where} \quad n\omega = \frac{F_0ed}{\hbar} = \omega_B. \tag{4.27}$$

$v_{dn}(F_0)$ have maximum values. This explains the peaks corresponding to $n\omega_{FEL}$ in the I–V curve of Fig. 4.6, that is, the terahertz laser excites the Bloch oscillation in the superlattice. When the laser intensity F_1 increases, the amplitudes of peaks change according to the expanding coefficients in Eq. 4.25 $J_n(eF_1d/\hbar\omega)$, which oscillates as F_1 increases.

We calculated the direct current (DC)'s conductance with the above relaxation time approximation theory. In the following we will use the simplified balance equation theory [8] to study the dynamic behavior of the superlattice in the DC and alternating current (AC) electric fields,

$$\frac{dv_d}{dt} = \frac{eF(t)}{m_z{}^*(\varepsilon)} - \frac{v_d}{\tau_v},$$

$$\frac{d\varepsilon}{dt} = eF(t)v_d - \frac{(\varepsilon - \varepsilon_T)}{\tau_\varepsilon}, \tag{4.28}$$

where $v_{\rm d}$ is the drift velocity; ε is the electron energy; $m_z{}^*(\varepsilon)$ is the electron effective mass,

$$\frac{1}{m_z{}^*(\varepsilon)} = \frac{1}{\hbar^2}\frac{\partial^2 E_z(k)}{\partial k^2} = \frac{\Delta d^2}{2\hbar^2}\cos kd = \frac{1}{m_z{}^*(0)}\left(1-\frac{2\varepsilon}{\Delta}\right); \quad (4.29)$$

$\varepsilon_{\rm T}$ is the electron average thermal energy,

$$\varepsilon_{\rm T} = \frac{\Delta}{2}\left[1-\frac{I_1(\Delta/2kT)}{I_0(\Delta/2kT)}\right]; \quad (4.30)$$

and τ_v and τ_ε are the electron momentum and energy scattering relaxation times, respectively.

To check the simplified balance equation (Eq. 4.28), we calculate the steady solution of Eq. 4.28 in the DC bias voltage. Let $eF(t) = eF$ and $dv_{\rm d}/dt = d\varepsilon/dt = 0$. We obtain

$$\varepsilon = \frac{C+\varepsilon_{\rm T}}{1+2C/\Delta}, \quad C = \frac{(eF)^2\tau_{\rm v}\tau_\varepsilon}{m_z^*(0)}. \quad (4.31)$$

$$v_{\rm d} = \frac{1}{eF\tau_\varepsilon}[\varepsilon-\varepsilon_{\rm T}] = \frac{1}{eF\tau_\varepsilon}C\cdot\frac{I_1/I_0}{1+\frac{2}{\Delta}C} = v_{\rm d0}\cdot\frac{I_1}{I_0}, \quad (4.32)$$

$$v_{\rm d0} = \frac{\Delta eFd^2\tau_{\rm v}}{2\hbar^2}\cdot\frac{1}{1+\left(\frac{eFd\tau}{\hbar}\right)^2}, \quad \tau = \sqrt{\tau_{\rm v}\tau_\varepsilon}. \quad (4.33)$$

Equation 4.32 is just Eq. 4.11 and Eq. 4.12; only the relaxation time τ is replaced by τ_v and τ_ε.

If the peak value of the drift velocity $v_{\rm p}$ and the critical electric field $E_{\rm c}$ are known from the experiment, then the τ_v and τ_ε can be calculated from Eq. 4.32. For example, for the GaAs/AlAs superlattice, $T = 300$ K, $\Delta = 110$ meV, $v_{\rm p}/d = 1.4\times10^{12}$ s^{-1}, and $eE_{\rm c}d = 3.1$ meV and we obtain $\tau_\varepsilon = 2.2\times10^{12}$ s^{-1}, and $\tau_{\rm v} = 1.1\times10^{13}$ s^{-1} [8].

Introduce the efficiency of oscillator η,

$$\eta(f) = \frac{P_{\rm alt}}{P_{\rm bias}} = \frac{\int v(t)F_1\cos\omega t dt}{\int v(t)F_0 dt}, \quad (4.34)$$

where $P_{\rm bias}$ and $P_{\rm alt}$ are the powers absorbed from the bias source and the alternating field, respectively. The integration is taken over an oscillation period, and $f = \omega/2\pi$ is the frequency of the alternating field. If $v(t)$ and alternating field $F_1\cos\omega t$ have the same phases, then $P_{\rm alt} > 0$ $(\eta > 0)$ energy of the alternative field

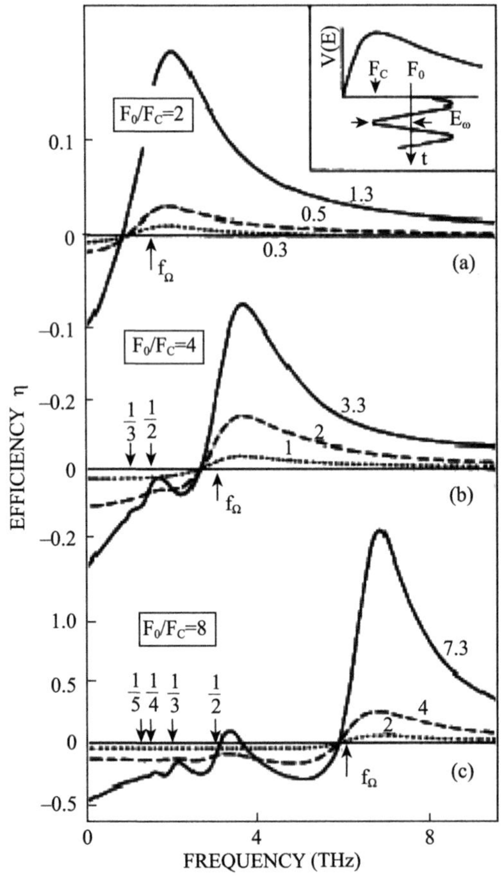

Figure 4.7 Calculated efficiencies as a function of frequency for the mentioned superlattice parameters [8]; (a), (b), and (c) correspond to different DC biases $F_0/F_c = 2, 4$, and 8.

is absorbed by the superlattice. If $v(t)$ and $F_1 \cos\omega t$ have opposite phases $P_{alt} < 0$ $(\eta < 0)$ energy is transferred to the alternating field, that is, the alternating field is amplified and, in principle, oscillation of the system is possible.

Figure 4.7 shows the calculated efficiencies as a function of frequency for the mentioned superlattice parameters [8]; (a), (b), and (c) correspond to different DC biases $F_0/F_c = 2, 4$, and 8. The number marked at each curve is the strength of the alternating field F_1/F_c. From the figure we see that the frequency range of amplification ($\eta < 0$) extends from almost DC to about the Bloch frequency $f_\Omega = eF_0 d/h$ that lies in the terahertz frequency range. With an increasing bias field the $\eta(f)$ curves show a fine structure near the subharmonics $f_n = f_\Omega/n$, where $n = 2, 3, \ldots$

Experimentally Wankle et al. have observed that when a microwave of 600 GHz irradiates on the GaAs/$Al_{0.3}Ga_{0.7}As$ superlattice, a strong third-order harmonic wave related to the injection power can be excited [9]. The transfer efficiency can reach 0.1%.

4.3 Hopping Conduction between Wannier–Stark States

Wannier [11] predicted early that when a quasi-continuous band is under an applied electric field, it can split into a serious of discrete energy states and the wave function changes from the expanded state to the local state. Later these states are called Wannier–Stark states. In the preceding section we discussed the longitudinal miniband transport in a superlattice. When the applied electric field along the z direction F is large enough, so that $eFd > \Delta$ (miniband width), that is, the potential difference between neighboring wells is larger than Δ, then the miniband doesn't exist, which splits into a series of discrete energy levels. The electron state is localized in a quantum well, and becomes the Wannier–Stark state. In this case the conduction is determined by the hopping conduction of electron states of neighboring quantum wells, as shown in Fig. 4.8 [12]. Figure 4.8 shows the energy bands of neighboring two quantum wells with s distance d in the applied electric field F. The potential difference is eFd. If eFd is such that level 1 coincides with level $2'$, electrons may tunnel resonantly from 1 to $2'$, marked by (a), followed by an inelastic scattering process marked by (b) to level $1'$, in order to repeat the process onto the next cell. Another process is the direct inelastic scattering process from 1 to $1'$, marked by (c). These two processes all need the participation of phonons; thus the hopping conductance is obviously lower than that within one band, resulting in NDC.

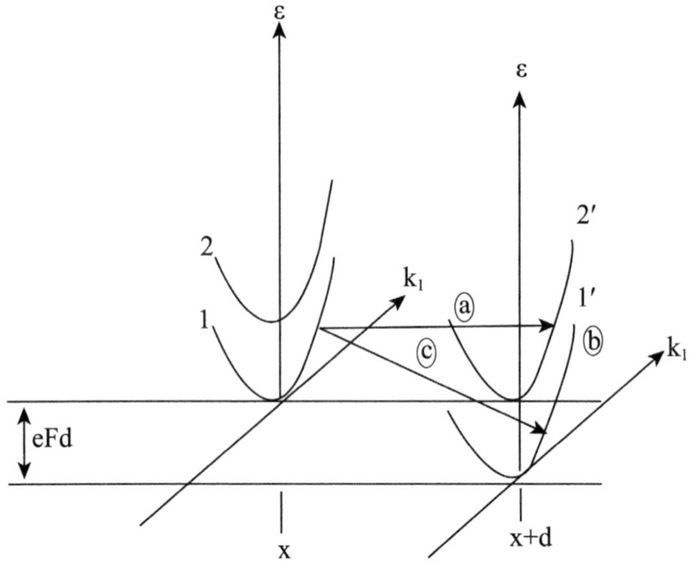

Figure 4.8 Energy bands of two neighboring quantum wells with a distance d in the applied electric field F.

To study the hopping conductance of Wannier–Stark states, we used the one-band model to calculate the Wannier–Stark state [13]. The effective mass Hamiltonian of electron in the electric field along the z direction is

$$H = E(k) + eFz, \tag{4.35}$$

where $E(k)$ is the 1D energy band dispersion relation as shown in Eq. 4.3. We write the Schrödinger equation in the momentum k space,

$$\left[E(k) + eFi\frac{d}{dk}\right]\psi(k) = E\psi(k), \tag{4.36}$$

where the coordinate z becomes an operator in the momentum space:

$$z = i\frac{d}{dk}. \tag{4.37}$$

The solution of Eq. 4.36 is easily obtained,

$$\psi(k) = C\exp\left\{-\frac{i}{eF}\int_0^k [E - E(k')]dk'\right\}, \tag{4.38}$$

where C is a normalization constant. Because $E(k)$ is a periodic function of k, $\psi(k)$ must be a periodic function in momentum space with period $2\pi/d$, which demands that

$$\frac{1}{eF}\int_{-\pi/d}^{\pi/d}[E - E(k)]dk = 2\pi n. \tag{4.39}$$

The eigenenergy is obtained from Eq. 4.39,

$$E = eFnd + \frac{d}{2\pi}\int_{-\pi/d}^{\pi/d} E(k)dk. \tag{4.40}$$

Equation 4.40 is just the Wannier–Stark ladder formula first derived by Wannier [12]. The second term in Eq. 4.40 is the average energy of the energy band.

The energy band $E(k)$ can be expanded by a series of cosine functions,

$$E(k) = \sum_{n=0}^{N}\lambda_n\cos(nkd). \tag{4.41}$$

Then the eigenenergy in Eq. 4.40 is

$$E = eFnd + \lambda_0. \tag{4.42}$$

Equation 4.42 represents the energy of the electron state in each quantum well, called the Wannier–Stark ladder.

The normalization constant $C = \sqrt{d}$ in a wave function (Eq. 4.38) is obtained from the normalization condition,

$$\frac{1}{2\pi}\int_{-\pi/d}^{\pi/d}|\psi(k)|^2dk = 1. \tag{4.43}$$

With the eigenenergy (Eq. 4.42) we transform the wave function $\psi(k)$ (Eq. 4.38) into the coordinate representation,

$$\begin{aligned}\psi(z) &= \frac{\sqrt{d}}{2\pi}\int dk\varphi_k(z)\exp\left\{-i\frac{1}{eF}\int_0^k[E - E(k')]dk'\right\}\\ &= \frac{\sqrt{d}}{2\pi}\int_{-\pi/d}^{\pi/d}dkU_k(z')\exp\left\{iz'k+\frac{1}{eFd}\sum_{n=1}^{N}\frac{\lambda_n}{n}\sin(ndk)\right\},\end{aligned} \tag{4.44}$$

where $z' = z\text{-}nd$ and $\varphi_k(z)$ is the Bloch function with wave vector k in the single band,

$$\varphi_k(z) = e^{ikz}U_k(z). \tag{4.45}$$

Equation 4.44 gives a general formula of the wave function for any form of band energy $E(k)$. If we take only two terms in the band energy expansion (Eq. 4.41),

$$E(k) = \lambda_0 + \lambda_1 \cos kd, \tag{4.46}$$

and let $z'/d = \nu - n$ (i.e., the coordinate at the center of the well) and let $U_k(z) = U_0$ be a constant, from Eq. 4.44 we obtain

$$\psi(z) = \frac{1}{\sqrt{d}} J_{n-\nu}\left(\frac{\lambda_1}{eFd}\right) U_0. \tag{4.47}$$

Equation 4.47 is just the result obtained by Bastard et al. [14] with the one-band tight-binding model.

At the same time Xia et al. used a finite Kronig–Penny model and series expansion method to calculate the eigenenergies and eigenstates of the Wannier–Stark state. Because the Wannier–Stark state is a local state, we take a large potential well with a finite number of quantum wells and an infinite high barrier at the two edges. We expand the wave function in a series of sine functions,

$$\psi(z) = \sqrt{\frac{2}{L}} \sum_n C_n \sin\left(\frac{n\pi z}{L}\right), \tag{4.48}$$

where L is the width of the large well, the sine function guarantees that the wave function equals zero at the edges, and the origin of the z coordinate is taken at the left edge. Inserting the wave function (Eq. 4.48) into the equation,

$$-\frac{1}{2m^*}\frac{d^2\psi}{dz^2} + [V(z) + eFz]\psi = E\psi, \tag{4.49}$$

where m^* is the effective mass and $V(z)$ is the Kronig–Penny potential (finite superlattice potential), we obtain the secular equation for the expansion coefficients C_n in an expanded form (Eq. 4.48).

In calculation we take the parameters for the GaAs/$Al_{0.35}Ga_{0.65}As$ superlattice: $m^* = 0.085\ m_0$, potential barrier height 0.26 eV, and widths of the well and the barrier 3 nm and 3.5 nm, respectively. Figure 4.9 shows the distribution of the wave functions along the z direction for the electric field 2×10^4 Vcm^{-1} (curve 1) and 5×10^4 Vcm^{-1} (curve 2) [13]. The unit of the abscissa is the superlattice d. From Fig. 4.9 we see that when the electric field is small (curve 1) the

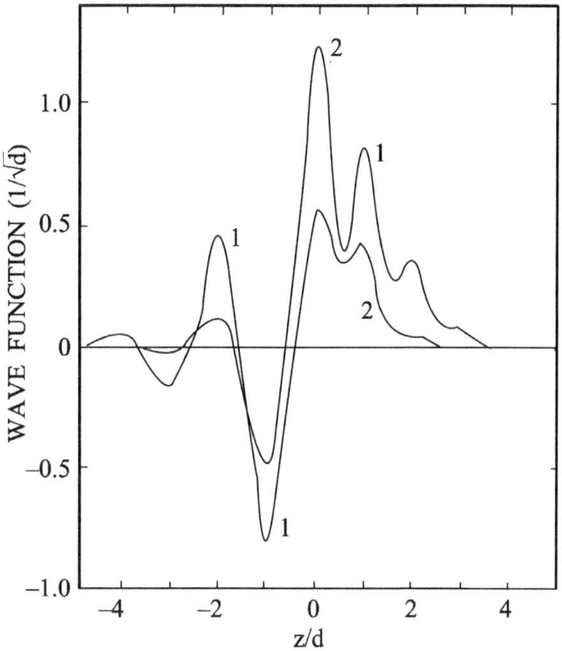

Figure 4.9 Distribution of the wave functions along the z direction for the electric field 2×10^4 Vcm^{-1} (curve 1) and 5×10^4 Vcm^{-1} (curve 2).

wave function extends over 10 periods and when the electric field is large (curve 2) the wave function extends over 7 periods, more local than the former. It is also to be noted that the wave function is not symmetrical with respect to the origin: on the left-hand side (lower potential) the wave function is oscillatory, taking positive and negative values at successive wells, while on the right-hand well (higher potential) the wave function is always positive, with the maxima at the successive wells. It is also found that the wave function values calculated from the numerical method and Eq. 3.47 are in good agreement.

Tsu et al. calculated inelastic scattering probabilities of process (c) in Fig. 4.8 for phonon emission at 300 K as a function of F, at fixed transverse energies $\varepsilon_\perp = \hbar^2 k_\perp^2/2m^* = 0.1$ eV [12]. Three curves in Fig. 4.10 correspond to the total energy of the first well $\varepsilon_1 = 0.01$, 0.02, and 0.1 eV (in the figure $\varepsilon_1 = 0.2$ eV is wrong; it should be

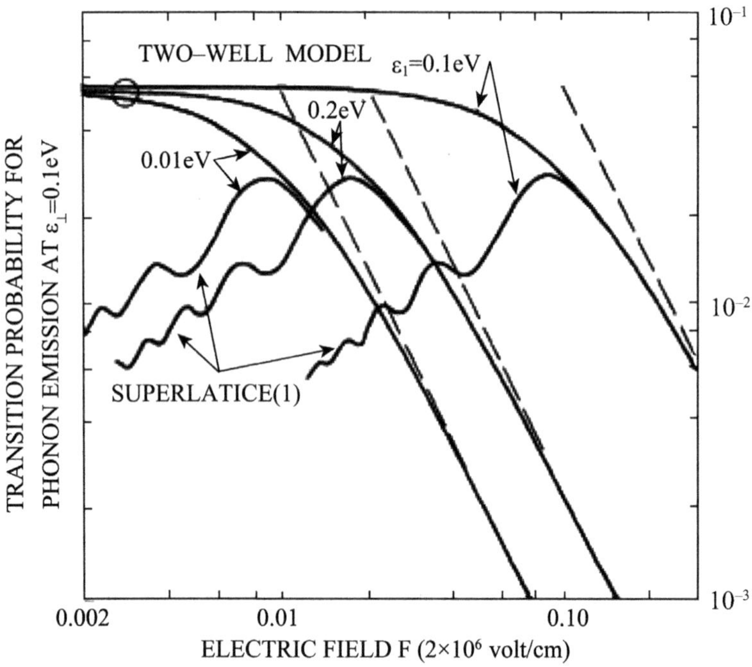

Figure 4.10 Transition probabilities of process (c) in Fig. 4.8 for phonon emission at 300 K as a function of F, at fixed transverse energies $\varepsilon_{\perp} = \hbar^2 k_{\perp}^2/2m^* = 0.1$ eV. Three curves correspond to the total energy of the first well $\varepsilon_1 = 0.01$, 0.02, and 0.1 eV.

0.02 eV).

$$\varepsilon_1 = E_0 + \left[V^2 + \alpha^2\right]^{1/2} + \frac{\hbar^2 k_{\perp}^2}{2m^*}, \tag{4.50}$$

where E_0 is the energy of the confined state in the quantum well, V is the interaction energy of neighboring wells, and 2α is the energy-level difference of the two wells. From Fig. 4.10 we see that the transition probability increases with increasing electric field F, reaches a maximum, and decreases as F increases continuously. The larger is the ε_1, the larger is the critical field F_c, at which the transition probability reaches the maximum. Thus F_c is proportional approximately to Δ, which corresponds to the formation of the Wannier–Stark state, $F_c \approx \Delta/ed$. When the electric field F is small, the transition probability oscillates with F. It is caused by the Bessel function factor in the Wannier–Stark wave function (4.47).

References

1. Luryi, S., and Zaslavsky, A. (1998). *Modern Semiconductor Device Physics*, ed. Sze, S. M., Chapter 5 "Quantum-effect and hot-electron devices" (John Wiley & Sons, Inc.).
2. Esaki, L., and Tsu, R. (1970). Superlattice and negative differential conductivity in semiconductors. *IBM J. Res. Dev.*, **14**, 61–65.
3. Huang, K., and Zhu, B. F. (1992). Temperature dependence of the low-field mobility of miniband conduction in superlattices. *Phys. Rev. B*, **45**, 14404–14406.
4. Sibille, A., Palmier, J. F., Wang, H., and Mollot, F. (1990). Observation of Esaki-Tsu negative differential velocity in GaAs/AlAs superlattices. *Phys. Rev. Lett.*, **64**, 52–55.
5. Hadjazi, M., Sibille, A., and Palmier, J. F. (1991). Negative differential conductance in GaAs/AlAs superlattices. *Electron. Lett.*, **27**, 1101–1103.
6. Sibille, A., Palmier, J. F., Wang, H., Esnault, J. C., and Mollot, F. (1990). dc and microwave negative differential conductance in GaAs/AlAs superlattices. *Appl. Phys. Lett.*, **56**, 256–258.
7. Unterrainer, K., Keay, B. J., Wanke, M. C., et al. (1996). *Hot Carriers in Semiconductors*, eds. Hess, K., Leburtor, J. P., and Rivaioli, U., "Strong terahertz-photocurrent resonances in miniband superlattices at the Bloch frequency" (Plenum, New York), pp. 135–138.
8. Ignatov, A. A., Renk, K. F., and Dodin, E. P. (1993). Esaki-Tsu superlattice oscillator: Josephson-like dynamics of carriers. *Phys. Rev. Lett.*, **70**, 1996–1999.
9. Wanke, M. C., Mankelz, A. G., Unterrainer, K., Allen, S. J., and Bhatt, R. (1996). *Hot Carriers in Semiconductors*, eds. Hess, K., Leburtor, J. P., and Rivaioli, U., "Third harmonic generation in a Gaas/Algaas superlattice in the Bloch oscillator regime" (Plenum, New York), pp. 161–163.
10. Xia, J. B. (1998). Theory of terahertz-photocurrent resonances in miniband superlattices. *Phys. Rev. B*, **58**, 3565–3567.
11. Wannier, G. H. (1962). Dynamics of band electrons in electric and magnetic fields. *Rev. Mod. Phys.*, **35**, 645–655.

12. Tsu, R., and Döhler, G. (1975). Hopping conduction in a "superlattice". *Phys. Rev. B*, **12**, 680–686.
13. Xia, J. B., and Huang, K. (1991). Wannier quantization of a superlattice subband under an electric field. *J. Phys. C*, **3**, 4639–4644.
14. Bleuse, J., Bastard, G., and Voisin, P. (1988). Electric-field induced localization and oscillatory electro-optical properties of semiconductor superlattices. *Phys. Rev. Lett.*, **60**, 220–223.

Chapter 5

Mesoscopic Transport

5.1 Contact Resistance

It is found experimentally that when we measure a sample of high mobility and small size, the current is always finite, though the transport is ballistic. There occurs a problem: where does the resistance come from?

Consider an experimental installation as shown in Fig. 5.1a [1]. A conductor of length L and width W is placed between contacts 1 and 2. According to the classical theory, the conductance of this conductor will equal $G = \sigma W/L$, where σ is the conductivity, independent of the sample dimensions. When the length L decreases, then we would expect the conductance to grow infinitely. Experimentally, however, it is found that the measured conductance approaches a limiting value G_c when the length of the conductor becomes much shorter than the mean free path $(L \ll L_m)$.

Theory analysis indicates that the resistance arises from the interface between the conductor and the contact; hence the resistance G_c^{-1} is called contact resistance. This contact resistance is not due to the difference of two materials. The current is carried in the contacts by infinitely transverse modes, but inside the conductor only a few modes. This requires a redistribution of the current

Quantum Waveguide in Microcircuits
Jian-Bai Xia, Duan-Yang Liu, and Wei-Dong Sheng

ISBN 978-981-4669-85-6 (Hardcover), 978-1-315-36477-3 (eBook)
www.panstanford.com

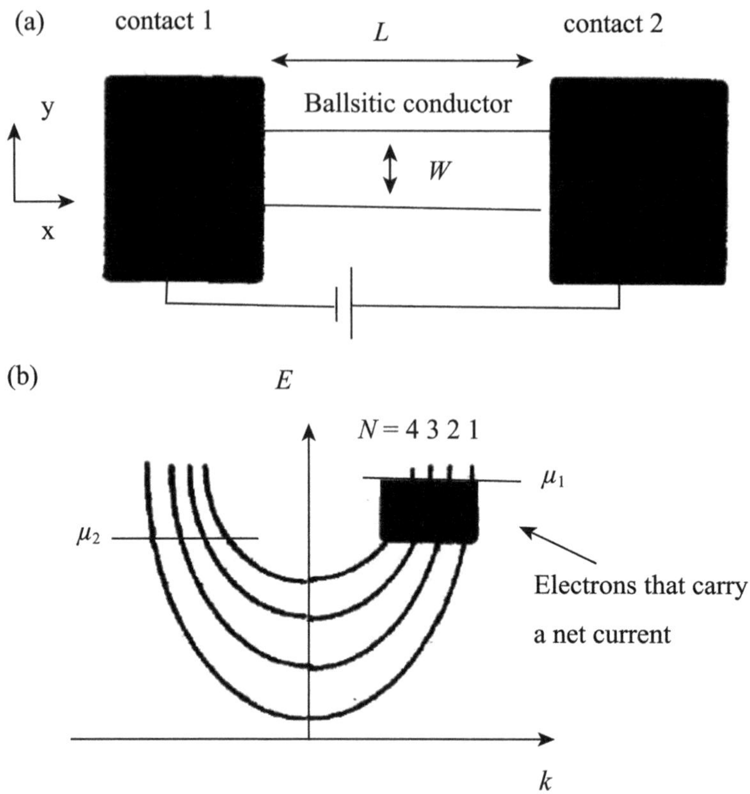

Figure 5.1 (a) A conductor connected with two contacts. (b) Conductor energy band and electron filling state.

among the current-carrying modes at the interface, leading to interface resistance.

To calculate the contact resistance G_c^{-1} we consider a ballistic conductor and calculate the current through it for a given applied bias $\mu_1 - \mu_2$. Numerical calculations indicate that an electron can exit from a narrow conductor into a wide contact with negligible probability of reflection [2]. Therefore, the reflection is negligible only when being transmitted from the narrow conductor to the wide contact. Going the other way, from the contact to the conductor, the reflections can be quite large.

The $+k$ state in the conductor is occupied by electrons coming from the left contact until μ_1, while the $-k$ state is empty because electrons are reflectionless through the right contact. The $-k$ state is occupied only by electrons coming from the right contact until μ_2, and the $+k$ state is empty because electrons are reflectionless through the left contact. The quasi-Fermi energy levels of $+k$ and $-k$ states are μ_1 and μ_2, respectively, when a bias $V = \mu_1 - \mu_2$ is applied (see Fig. 5.1b). At a low temperature the current equals that carried by the electrons in the states between μ_1 and μ_2 (shaded part of Fig. 5.1b).

The states in the narrow conductor belong to different transverse modes or subbands, as shown in Fig. 5.1b. Each mode has a dispersion relation $E(N, k)$ with a cut-off energy

$$\varepsilon_N = E(N, k = 0), \tag{5.1}$$

below which the current cannot propagate. The number of transverse modes at an energy E is obtained by counting the number of modes having cut-off energies smaller than E:

$$M(E) = \sum_N \theta(E - \varepsilon_N). \tag{5.2}$$

Consider a single transverse mode whose $+k$ state is occupied according to some distribution function $f^+(E)$. A uniform electron gas with n electrons per unit length moving with a velocity v carries a current equal to $en\mathbf{v}$. Since the electron density associated with a single k state in a conductor of length L is $(1/L)$ we can write the current I^+ carried by the $+k$ states as

$$I^+ = \frac{e}{L}\sum_k v f^+(E) = \frac{e}{L}\sum_k \frac{1}{\hbar}\frac{\partial E}{\partial k} f^+(E). \tag{5.3}$$

Changing the summation over k to the integration, we obtain

$$I^+ = \frac{e}{L}\cdot\frac{L}{\pi}\int dk\cdot\frac{1}{\hbar}\frac{\partial E}{\partial k} f^+(E) = \frac{2e}{h}\int_\varepsilon^\infty f^+(E)dE, \tag{5.4}$$

where ε is the cut-off energy of the transverse mode. If there are multi-modes then Eq. 5.4 can be written as

$$I^+ = \frac{2e}{h}\int_{-\infty}^\infty f^+(E)M(E)dE, \tag{5.5}$$

where $M(E)$ is given by Eq. 5.2. The general result given by Eq. 5.4 is that the current carried per mode per unit energy by an occupied state equals $2|e|/h$ (which is about 80 nA/meV).

At a low temperature the total current

$$I = I^+ - I^- = \frac{2e}{h}\left[\int_{-\infty}^{\mu_1} f^+(E)M(E)dE - \int_{-\infty}^{\mu_2} f^-(E)M(E)dE\right]. \tag{5.6}$$

The number of modes M is constant over the energy range $\mu_1 < E < \mu_2$, we can write

$$I = \frac{2e}{h}M\left[\int_{-\infty}^{\mu_1} f^+(E)dE - \int_{-\infty}^{\mu_2} f^+(E)dE\right]$$
$$= \frac{2e^2}{h}M\frac{(\mu_1 - \mu_2)}{e}, \tag{5.7}$$

$$G = \frac{2e^2}{h}M. \tag{5.8}$$

Equation 5.8 is a universal result, independent of the length and width of the conductor, the energy band dispersion, etc. The conductance is quantized, which is integral times of $2e^2/h$. The contact resistance is given by

$$G_c^{-1} = \frac{h}{2e^2 M} = \frac{12.9\,k\Omega}{M}. \tag{5.9}$$

The contact resistance goes down inversely with the number of modes. The contact resistance of a single-mode conductor is $\sim$12.9 kΩ, which is certainly not negligible. Only if the size of the sample reaches macro-size, the M approaches infinite, and the contact resistance can be neglected. Assuming that the width of the sample is W and the electron energy is E, we can estimate the number of modes M,

$$E = \frac{\hbar^2}{2m^*}\left(\frac{n\pi}{W}\right)^2$$

and

$$M = \mathrm{Int}\left[\frac{W}{\pi}\sqrt{\frac{2m^* E}{\hbar^2}}\right] = \mathrm{Int}\left[\frac{W}{\lambda_f/2}\right], \tag{5.10}$$

where λ_f is the Fermi wavelength and Int(x) represents the integer that is just smaller than x. If the typical electron density $n_s = 3.6 \times 10^{11}$ cm^{-2}, then $M = 1$ for $W = 22$ nm and $M = 47$ for $W = 1$ μm.

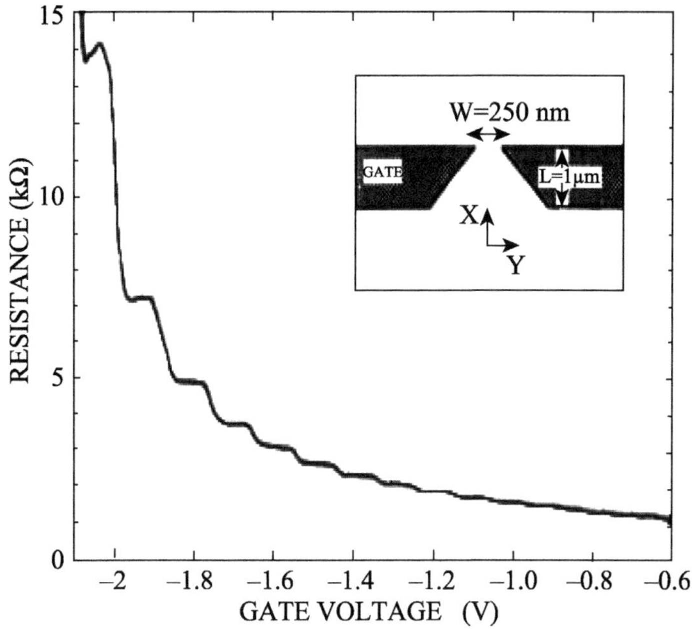

Figure 5.2 Point-contact resistance as a function of gate voltage at 0.6 K. Inset: Point-contact layout.

Wees et al. reported the first measurements of the conductance of single ballistic contacts in a two-dimensional electron gas (2DEG) [3]. A novel quantum effect is found: the conductance is quantized in units of $2e^2/h$, as shown in Eq. 5.8. A high-mobility 2DEG is formed on the interface of GaAs/AlGaAs heterostructure grown by molecular beam epitaxy. The electron density is 3.56×10^{11} cm^{-2}, and the mobility 85,000 cm^2/Vs (at 0.6 K). Using electron beam lithography, a metal gate is made on top of the heterostructure, with an opening 250 nm wide (inset in Fig. 5.2). The point contacts are defined by the application of a negative voltage to the gate. At $V_g = -0.6$ eV the electron gas underneath the gate is depleted, the conduction taking place through the point contact only. At this voltage the point contacts have their maximum width, about equal to the opening between the gates. By a further decrease of the gate voltage, the width of the point contacts can gradually be reduced, until they are fully pinched off at $V_g = -2.2$ eV.

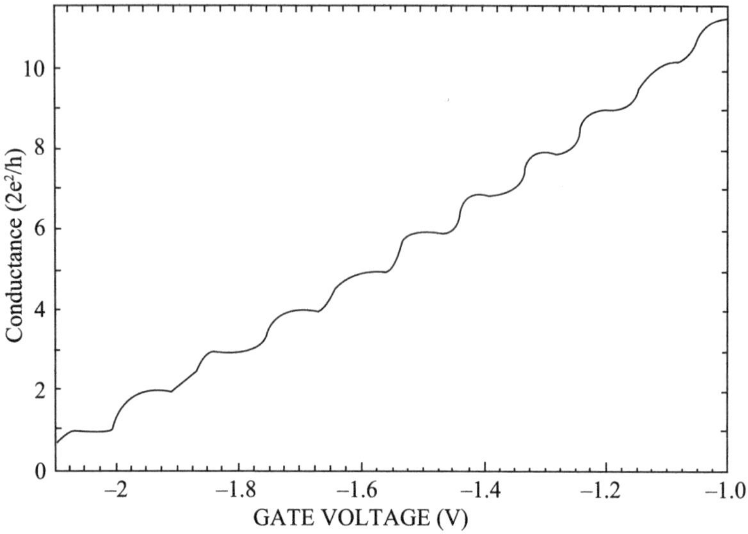

Figure 5.3 Point-contact conductance as a function of gate voltage, obtained from the data of Fig. 5.2 after subtraction of the lead resistance.

Figure 5.2 shows the measured resistance of a point contact as a function of gate voltage [3]. In total, 16 plateaus are observed when the gate voltage is varied from -0.6 to -2.2 V. The measured resistance consists of the resistance of the point contact, and a constant series resistance from the 2DEG leads to the point contact. The conductance calculated from the measured resistance after subtraction of a lead resistance of 400 Ω as a function of gate voltage is shown in Fig. 5.3 [3], which shows clear plateaus at integer multiples of $2e^2/h$, verifying the theoretical result of Eq. 5.8.

Equations 5.8 and 5.9 are general theoretical results. It is still not clear how is contact resistance is formed. Kirczenov calculated the conductance of a short, narrow ballistic channel in a 2DEG [4]. The model is of a heterostructure in the $x - y$ plane with a 2DEG occupying the left (L) and right (R) half-spaces, $x < -d$ and $x > d$, respectively, and a narrow channel (C) of length $2d$ centered on the x axis connecting the 2D regions; see Fig. 5.4 lower-right inset [4]. The shaded part is the infinite high potential barrier region produced by the metallic gate.

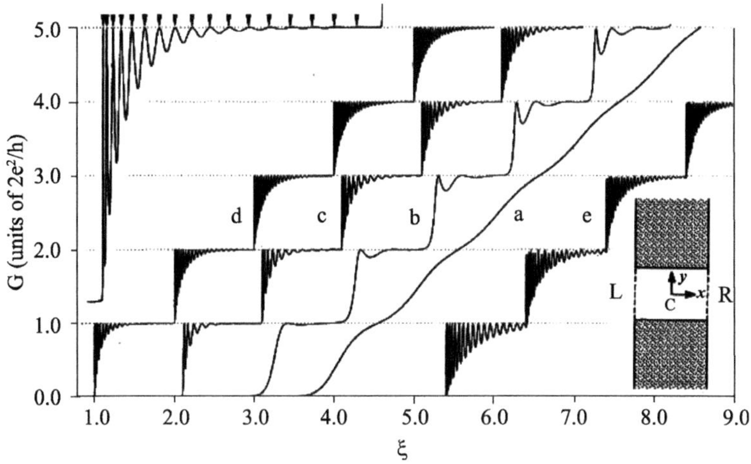

Figure 5.4 Conductance G as a function of the electron Fermi level ξ at $T = 0$ K. $U = 0$, $d = 0$, 1, 5, and 10 for curves a, b, c, and d. Curve e: $U = 2.5$ and $d = 10$.

Suppose that an electron moves from the left region into the channel region. Its energy is ε, wave vector is $\mathbf{k} = (k, K)$, and k and K are the components along the x and y directions, respectively. The wave function in the left region can be written as

$$\psi_k^L(\mathbf{r}) = e^{ikx}\phi_k(y) + \sum_{k'} a_{k'}^L e^{-ik'x}\phi_{k'}(y), \tag{5.11}$$

where $\phi_k(y) = e^{iky}$ and $k' = (2m^*\varepsilon_k/\hbar^2 - K'^2)^{1/2}$. The second term in Eq. 5.11 represents the reflection wave. The sum is over all transverse momentum K' so that imaginary values of k' (evanescent partial waves) are included. In the channel the wave function is

$$\psi_k^c(\mathbf{r}) = \sum_n \left(a_n^+ e^{iq_n x} + a_n^- e^{-iq_n x}\right)\phi_n(y), \tag{5.12}$$

where $\phi_n(y)$ is the eigenfunction of the n-th transverse eigenstate of the confining potential $U(y)$, $\phi_n = \sqrt{2/w}\sin(n\pi y/w)$, and $q_n = \left[2m^*\varepsilon_n/\hbar^2 - (n\pi/w)^2\right]^{1/2}$. In the right-hand region the transmitting wave (not including the reflection wave) is

$$\psi_k^R(\mathbf{r}) = \sum_{k'} a_{k'}^R e^{ik'x}\phi_{k'}(y). \tag{5.13}$$

Using the boundary conditions at $x = -d$ and $x = d$, the continuities of the wave function and its differential, we obtain four sets of equations of the coefficients $a^L_{k'}$, a^+_n, a^-_n, and $a^R_{k'}$. Eliminating $a^L_{k'}$ and $a^R_{k'}$ from the sets of equations yields the equations of a^+_n and a^-_n [4],

$$\sum_n \left[(T_{mn} + q_n\delta_{mn})e^{-iq_nd}a^+_n + (T_{mn} - q_n\delta_{mn})e^{ig_nd}a^-_n\right] = 2ke^{-ikd}M_{Km}$$

and

$$\sum_n \left[(T_{mn} - q_n\delta_{mn})e^{iq_nd}a^+_n + (T_{mn} + q_n\delta_{mn})e^{-ig_nd}a^-_n\right] = 0$$
$$(m = 1, 2, \cdots), \tag{5.14}$$

where

$$T_{mn} = \sum_{k'} k' M_{k'm} M_{-k'n}$$

and

$$M_{kn} = \int_{-w/2}^{w/2} \phi_k(y)\phi_n(y)dy. \tag{5.15}$$

In terms of a^+_n and a^-_n, the electric current carried through the channel by ψ_k is

$$i_x(k) = <\psi_k|j_x|\psi_k> = \frac{i\hbar e}{2m^*}\int_{-w/z}^{w/z}\left(\psi^*_k\frac{\partial\psi_k}{\partial x} - \psi_k\frac{\partial\psi^*_k}{\partial x}\right)dy$$
$$= -\frac{\hbar e}{m^*}\left[\mathrm{Re}\sum_n q_n(|a^-_n|^2 - |a^+_n|^2) + \mathrm{Im}\sum_n q_n(a^{+*}_n a^-_n - a^+_n a^{-*}_n)\right]. \tag{5.16}$$

Under the electric potential V, the electron Fermi circle shifts dk along the x direction. The total current J through the channel at $T = 0$ is given by the sum of the contributions of all states ψ_k in the k space, which is the difference of the Fermi circles before and after shift, and in the energy interval eV near the Fermi energy E_F, where V is the potential difference between the two 2DEG regions. The conductance is then

$$G = \left|\frac{J}{V}\right| = -2\int_{-a}^{a}\frac{m^*e}{h^2k}i_x(k)\,dK, \tag{5.17}$$

where $a = \left(2m^*E_F/\hbar^2\right)^{1/2}$ and $k = \left(2m^*E_F/\hbar^2 - K^2\right)^{1/2}$.

Figure 5.4 shows the calculated conductance as a function of electron Fermi energy [4], where the energy unit $\Delta = h^2/8m^*W^2$,

$\hat{E}_F = E_F/\Delta$, $\hat{U} = U_0/\Delta$, U_0 is the potential inside the channel, the aspect ratio $\hat{d} = 2d/W$, and the abscissa $\xi = \left(\hat{E}_F - \hat{U}\right)^{1/2}$. $\hat{U} = 0$ and $\hat{d} = 0, 1, 5$, and 10 for curves a, b, c, and d. Curve e: $\hat{U} = 2.5$ and $\hat{d} = 10$.

The horizontal scale is for curve d; the other curves are offset to the right by multiples of 1.1. Curve a is the limiting case of zero aspect ratio, $\hat{d} \to 0$. For this "ideal" point contact there is no quantization of conductance; a channel of nonzero length is necessary for quantization. In the cases of curves b, c, and d the conductance is close to $G = \nu 2e^2/h$ near the right-hand side of each plateau. But the rise to each plateau is oscillatory, the strength of the oscillations increasing with d and with ν. The $\nu = 1$ step of curve d is shown enlarged in the upper left. The resonance peaks correspond to the condition $n\lambda_f/2 = 2d$, where λ_f is the electron Fermi wavelength. This indicates that the open-ended channel supports longitudinal resonant states, i.e. the quasi-standing wave in the channel and at this time the conductance decreases. The curve e is for $\hat{U} = 2.5$ and $\hat{d} = 10$. The main effect is to increase the amplitude of the oscillations.

5.2 Landauer Formula

The last section discussed the case of an ideal conductor. Now if there is a scatterer in the conductor, as shown in Fig. 5.5, the carriers have a probability T for traveling of the scatterer and a probability R of being reflected. The left reservoir injects carriers into the perfect wire up to a quasi-Fermi energy μ_1, and the right reservoir emits carriers up to a quasi-Fermi energy μ_2 (see Fig. 5.4b). The net current, for two injection directions, is given by the sum of the contributions of all states in the energy range between μ_2 and μ_1,

$$I = ev\left(\frac{\partial n}{\partial E}\right)(\mu_1 - \mu_2), \tag{5.18}$$

where v is the Fermi velocity and $\partial n/\partial E$ is the density of states for two spin directions and for carriers with a positive velocity. In one dimension $\partial n/\partial E = 1/\pi$ and $\partial n/\partial E = 1/\pi\hbar v$. Thus, the total current emitted by the left reservoir due to the difference in the

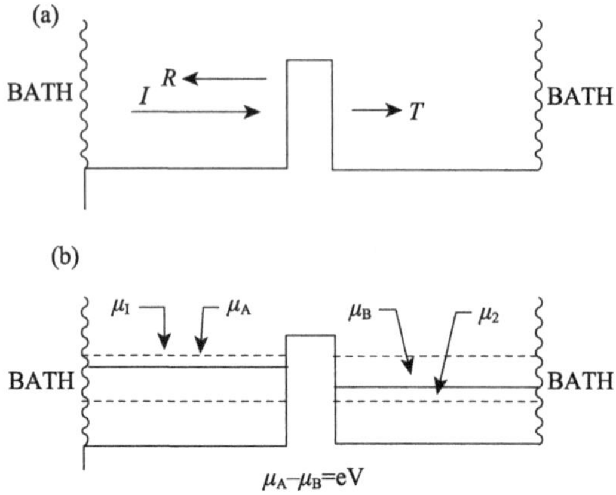

Figure 5.5 The scatterer is connected to two incoherent reservoirs by ideal 1D conductors.

quasi-Fermi levels is

$$I = \left(\frac{e}{\pi\hbar}\right)(\mu_1 - \mu_2). \tag{5.19}$$

When $T \neq 1$,

$$I = \left(\frac{e}{\pi\hbar}\right) T(\mu_1 - \mu_2). \tag{5.20}$$

Next, we have to determine the voltage across the scatterer. The carrier densities can be characterized by the chemical potentials μ_A and μ_B (see Fig. 5.5b). The respective levels μ_B, between μ_1 and μ_2, are determined such that the number of occupied states (electrons) above μ_B is equal to the number of empty states (holes) below μ_B. Since carriers have a transmission probability T, the number of occupied states is $T(\partial n/\partial E)(\mu_1 - \mu_B)$, and the number of unoccupied states is $(2 - T)(\partial n/\partial E)(\mu_B - \mu_2)$. Thus, the chemical potential μ_B is determined by

$$T\left(\frac{\partial n}{\partial E}\right)(\mu_1 - \mu_B) = (2 - T)\left(\frac{\partial n}{\partial E}\right)(\mu_B - \mu_2). \tag{5.21}$$

To the left of the barrier we have both incident carriers and reflected carriers. The number of occupied states is $(1 + R)(\partial n/\partial E)$ $(\mu_1 - \mu_A)$, and the number of unoccupied states is $[2 - (1 + R)]$ $(\partial n/\partial E)(\mu_A - \mu_2)$. Thus, the chemical potential μ_A is determined by

$$(1+R)\left(\frac{\partial n}{\partial E}\right)(\mu_1 - \mu_A) = [2 - (1 + R)]\left(\frac{\partial n}{\partial E}\right)(\mu_A - \mu_2). \tag{5.22}$$

From Eqs. 5.21 and 5.22 we obtain

$$\mu_{\mathrm{A}} - \mu_{\mathrm{B}} = R(\mu_1 - \mu_2). \tag{5.23}$$

The charge neutrality requires that the separation between the chemical potential μ_{A} or μ_{B}, respectively, and the band bottom be the same as in equilibrium. The conduction-band bottoms are displaced against each other by a potential difference,

$$eV = \mu_{\mathrm{A}} - \mu_{\mathrm{B}} = R(\mu_1 - \mu_2). \tag{5.24}$$

From Eqs. 5.20 and 5.24 we obtain the conductance,

$$G = \frac{I}{V} = \frac{2e^2}{h} \cdot \frac{T}{R}. \tag{5.25}$$

Equation 5.25 is called the Landauer formula.

In the case of measurement of mesoscopic systems we run into three separate problems [1]. Firstly, mesoscopic probes are often invasive, that is, they change what we are trying to measure. With macroscopic conductors, the probes represent a minor perturbation. But for a small conductor, the probe can very well be the dominant source of scattering (and hence resistance). But this is not the main problem. It is likely that there will be more of less-invasive microscopic measurements as nanotechnology progresses, for example, using weakly coupled scanning tunneling probes.

Secondly, mesoscopic probes are seldom identical so the two voltage probes could very well couple differently to the $+k$ and $-k$ states. Only if the two-voltage probes couple identically to the $+k$ and $-k$ states, the measurement result of resistance will be given by Eq. 5.25. Otherwise the measured resistance will lie somewhere between the extremes

$$\frac{h}{2e^2 M}\frac{1}{T} \quad \text{and} \quad \frac{h}{2e^2 M}\frac{1-2T}{T}. \tag{5.26}$$

Finally, mesoscopic measurements are strongly affected by quantum interference effects unless the distance of the probes from the scatterer is much greater than the phase-relaxation length. We would expect that a probe to the left of the scatterer to measure a potential of approximately 1 (equal to that of the left reservoir). However, due to quantum interference it could measure any potential between 0 and 1 depending on its distance from the scatterer. The reason is that the probe may not "see" the electrons from the left reservoir due to destructive interference between the incident wave and the reflected wave. Therefore, in phase-coherent conductors the $+k$ and $-k$ states can be strongly correlated so distribution functions only tell part of the story.

The above discussion of Eq. 5.25 is under the assumption that $T = 0$. When $T \neq 0$ we should consider the electron Fermi distribution $f(E)$. The net current flowing from the left reservoir to the right reservoir is now given by

$$I = \frac{2e}{h}\left[\int dE\left(-\frac{\partial f}{\partial E}\right)T(E)\right](\mu_1 - \mu_2), \qquad (5.27)$$

where

$$-\frac{\partial f}{\partial E} = [f(E-\mu_1) - f(E-\mu_2)]/(\mu_1 - \mu_2). \qquad (5.28)$$

Similarly, to determine the chemical potential we have to multiply Eqs. 5.21 and 5.22 by $-\partial f/\partial E$ and integrate over the energy. This yields a voltage

$$eV = \frac{\int dE(-\partial f/\partial E)R(E)(\partial n/\partial E)}{\int dE(-\partial f/\partial E)(\partial n/\partial E)}(\mu_1 - \mu_2). \qquad (5.29)$$

With Eqs. 5.27 and 5.29 we obtain the conductance

$$G = \frac{2e^2}{h}\left[\int dE\,(-\partial f/\partial E)\,T(E)\right] \times \frac{\int dE\,(-\partial f/\partial E)\,\upsilon^{-1}(E)}{\int dE\,(-\partial f/\partial E)\,R(E)\upsilon^{-1}(E)}, \qquad (5.30)$$

where we have used $\partial n/\partial E = 1/\pi\hbar v(E)$. At zero temperature we have $-\partial f/\partial E = \delta(E - E_F)$ and Eq. 5.30 reduces to Eq. 5.25.

5.3 Many-Channel Case

If the ideal conductors include N independent conducting channels, at zero temperature all the channels have the same energy. The electrons in these channels can be transmitted or reflected each other, having the probabilities T_{ji} and R_{ji}, respectively, as shown in Fig. 5.6 [5]. T_{ji} represents the transmission probability of electrons from the left i-th channel to right j-th channel, and R_{ji} represents the reflection probability of electrons from the left i-th channel to

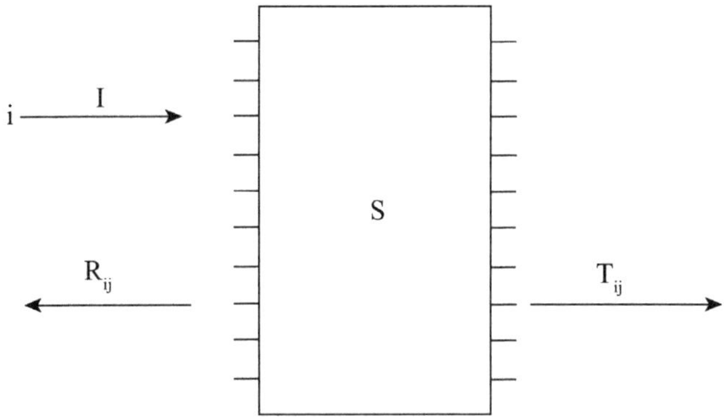

Figure 5.6 A multichannel system S. Indices i and j run from 1 to N.

left j-th channel. The scattering property can be described by a $2N \times 2N$ matrix S,

$$S = \begin{vmatrix} r & t' \\ t & r' \end{vmatrix}, \tag{5.31}$$

where r and t are the reflection and transmission coefficients of electrons from the left-hand side to right-hand side, respectively. The transmission probability $T_{ji} = |t_{ji}|^2$, and reflection probability $R_{ji} = |r_{ji}|^2$. r' and t' are those from the right-hand side to left-hand side.

The matrix S (Eq. 5.31) is unitary due to current conservation because T_{ij} and R_{ij} transform the lead currents. Furthermore, when time-reversal symmetry holds in the absence of a magnetic field,

$$SS^* = \mathbf{I} \quad \text{and} \quad S = \tilde{S}, \tag{5.32}$$

where the asterisk denotes complex conjugation, the tilde denotes the matrix transpose, and **I** is the unit matrix.

Assume that the interference effects between different input channels are neglected. The energy range is between μ_2 and μ_1, and carriers are injected into the perfect conductor only from the left-hand side reservoir. The current injected into the left channel j by the reservoir is $ev_j(\partial n_j/\partial E)(\mu_1 - \mu_2)$. The density of states (with a positive velocity) is given by $\partial n_j/\partial E = 1/\pi\hbar v_j$. Therefore, the current fed into the j-th channel is $(e/\pi\hbar)(\mu_1 - \mu_2)$, independent of the channel velocity. The current from the left j-th channel transmitted into the right i-th channel is $(e/\pi\hbar)T_{ij}(\mu_1 - \mu_2)$. The total current in the right i-th channel becomes

$$I_i = \frac{2e}{h}\left(\sum_{j=1}^{N} T_{ij}\right)(\mu_1 - \mu_2). \tag{5.33}$$

It is convenient to introduce a total transmission probability and reflection probability into the i-th channel,

$$T_i = \sum_j T_{ij}, \qquad R_i = \sum_j R_{ij}. \tag{5.34}$$

Thus the current in the right i-th channel is

$$I_i = \frac{2(\mu_1 - \mu_2)e}{h} T_i, \tag{5.35}$$

and the total current is given by

$$I_{\text{tot}} = \sum_i I_i = \frac{2(\mu_1 - \mu_2)e}{h} \sum_i T_i = \frac{2(\mu_1 - \mu_2)e}{h} \text{Tr}(tt^\dagger). \tag{5.36}$$

On the other hand, the current in the left i-th channel is

$$I_i = \frac{2(\mu_1 - \mu_2)e}{h}\left[1 - \sum_j R_{ij}\right] = \frac{2(\mu_1 - \mu_2)e}{h}(1 - R_i), \tag{5.37}$$

and the total current is

$$I_{\text{tot}} = \sum_i I_i = \frac{2(\mu_1 - \mu_2)e}{h} \sum_i (1 - R_i). \tag{5.38}$$

Comparing Eqs. 5.36 and 5.38, we find that current conservation implies

$$\sum_i T_i = \sum_i (1 - R_i). \tag{5.39}$$

Similar to the single-channel case (Eqs. 5.21 and 5.22), we determine the chemical potential μ_1 and μ_2. On the right side of the barrier the number of occupied states with energy higher than μ_{B} is

$$\sum_i T_i(\partial n_i/\partial E)(\mu_1 - \mu_{\text{B}}). \tag{5.40}$$

The number of unoccupied states with energy smaller than μ_{B} is

$$\sum_i (2 - T_i)(\partial n_i/\partial E)(\mu_{\text{B}} - \mu_2). \tag{5.41}$$

Again μ_B is determined such that the number of occupied states is equal to the number of unoccupied states,

$$\sum_i T_i \left(\frac{\partial n_i}{\partial E}\right)(\mu_1 - \mu_B) = \sum_i (2 - T_i)\left(\frac{\partial n_i}{\partial E}\right)(\mu_B - \mu_2). \quad (5.42)$$

Similarly, the chemical potential to the left is determined by

$$\sum_i (1 + R_i)\left(\frac{\partial n_i}{\partial E}\right)(\mu_1 - \mu_A) = \sum_i (1 - R_i)\left(\frac{\partial n_i}{\partial E}\right)(\mu_A - \mu_2). \quad (5.43)$$

Therefore, the voltage across the scatterer is given by

$$eV = \mu_A - \mu_B = \frac{\sum_i (1 + R_i + T_i)\upsilon_i^{-1}}{2\sum_i \upsilon_i^{-1}}(\mu_1 - \mu_2), \quad (5.44)$$

where we have used $\partial n_i/\partial E = 1/\pi\hbar v_i$. With the help of Eqs. 5.36 and 5.44 we obtain the conductance

$$G = \frac{2e^2}{h}\sum_i T_i \cdot \frac{2\sum_i \upsilon_i^{-1}}{\sum_i (1 + R_i - T_i)\upsilon_i^{-1}}. \quad (5.45)$$

5.4 Multi-Terminal Devices

Since 1985 many mesoscopic experiments have been conducted using miniature Hall bridges fabricated on both metallic and semiconducting samples. However, because of the reasons mentioned above (see Section 5.2), for a while there was serious confusion about how such four-terminal measurements should be interpreted. Büttiker [6, 7] found a simple and elegant solution to this problem. He noted that since there is really no quantitative difference between the current and the voltage probes, one could treat all the probes on an equal footing and simply extend the two-terminal linear response formula to a multi-terminal response formula.

Consider the conductor shown in Fig. 5.7 [6]. The leads in Fig. 5.7 are connected to reservoirs that are at chemicals μ_1, μ_2, μ_3, and μ_4, and the center conductor is an Aharonov–Bohm ring with a uniform magnetic flux through the hole. Assume that these perfect leads are strictly one-dimensional (1D) quantum channels, that is, there are

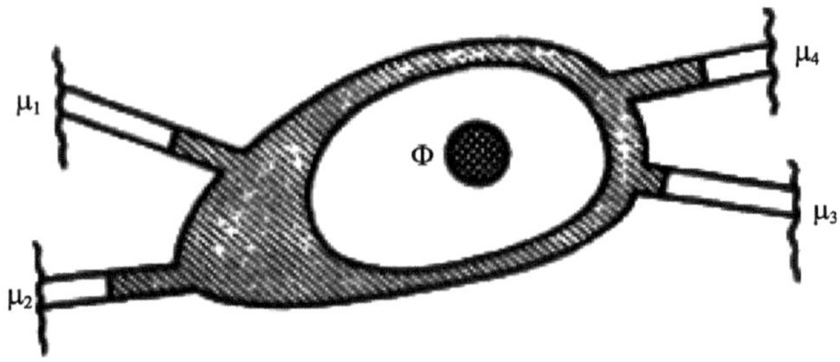

Figure 5.7 Conductor with four terminals connected via perfect leads to four reservoirs at chemical potentials μ_1, μ_2, μ_3, and μ_4. An Aharonov–Bohm flux Φ is applied through the hole of the sample.

only two states at the Fermi energy, one with positive velocity (taken to be the direction away from the reservoir) and one with negative velocity. Scattering in the sample is elastic. The elastic scattering properties of the sample are described by the probabilities $T_{ij}(\Phi)$ for carries incident in lead j to be transmitted into lead i and probabilities $R_{ii}(\Phi)$ for carriers to be reflected into lead i. Current conservation and time-reversal invariance in the presence of a flux imply

$$R_{ii}(\Phi) = R_{ii}(-\Phi), \quad T_{ij}(\Phi) = T_{ji}(-\Phi). \tag{5.46}$$

The potential μ_i are distributed in the range around the Fermi energy, which is so narrow that the energy dependence of the transmission and reflection probabilities in this range can be neglected. It is convenient to introduce a fifth chemical potential μ_0, which is smaller than the lowest of the four potentials μ_i. Below μ_0 the states with negative and positive velocities are filled and zero net current flows in each of the leads. The reservoir injects a current $e\mathbf{v}_i(dn_i/dE)\Delta\mu_i$ into lead i, $\Delta\mu_i = \mu_i - \mu_0$. Here v_i is the velocity at the Fermi energy in lead i and $dn_i/dE = 1/2\pi\hbar v_i$ is the density of states for carriers with a negative or a positive velocity at the Fermi energy. Thus the current injected by the reservoir i is $(e/h)\Delta\mu_i$. Consider the current in lead i. A current $(e/h)R_{ii}\Delta\mu_i$ is reflected back to the reservoir i. Carriers that are injected by the other reservoir j into lead i reduce the current in lead i by $-(e/h)T_{ij}\Delta\mu_j$. Collecting all results from lead j ($j \neq i$) we obtain the current in lead i,

$$I_i = \frac{e}{h}\left[(1 - R_{ii})\mu_i - \sum_{j\neq i} T_{ij}\mu_j\right]. \qquad (5.47)$$

Note that these currents are independent of the reference potential μ_0 since the coefficients multiplying the potentials add to zero. Equation 5.47 is called the Büttiker formula [6].

Consider a four-probe configuration as shown in Fig. 5.7 where a current I_1 is led into lead 1 and leaves through lead 3, and a current I_2 is fed into lead 2 and leaves the sample through lead 4. Thus we have to solve Eq. 5.47 under the condition that $I_1 = -I_3$ and $I_2 = -I_4$. We obtain the currents I_1 and I_2 as a function of differences of voltages, $V_i = \mu_i/e$,

$$I_1 = \alpha_{11}(V_1 - V_3) - \alpha_{12}(V_2 - V_4),$$

and

$$I_2 = -\alpha_{21}(V_1 - V_3) + \alpha_{22}(V_2 - V_4), \qquad (5.48)$$

where the conductance

$$\begin{aligned}
\alpha_{11} &= \left(\frac{e^2}{h}\right)[(-R_{11})S - (T_{14} + T_{12})(T_{41} + T_{21})]/S,\\
\alpha_{12} &= \left(\frac{e^2}{h}\right)(T_{12}T_{34} - T_{14}T_{32})/S,\\
\alpha_{21} &= \left(\frac{e^2}{h}\right)(T_{21}T_{43} - T_{23}T_{41})/S, \qquad (5.49)\\
\alpha_{22} &= \left(\frac{e^2}{h}\right)[(1 - R_{22})S - (T_{21} + T_{23})(T_{32} + T_{12})]/S,
\end{aligned}$$

and

$$S = T_{12} + T_{14} + T_{32} + T_{34} = T_{21} + T_{41} + T_{23} + T_{43}. \qquad (5.50)$$

Taking into account Eq. 5.46, we see that the diagonal elements are symmetric in the flux $\alpha_{11}(\Phi) = \alpha_{11}(-\Phi)$ and $\alpha_{22}(\Phi) = \alpha_{22}(-\Phi)$ and that the off-diagonal elements satisfy $\alpha_{12}(\Phi) = \alpha_{21}(-\Phi)$. Therefore, for the four-probe conductor the Onsager relations hold [6].

Suppose the current flows from lead 1 to lead 3. The potentials measured are $\mu_2 = eV_2$ and $\mu_4 = eV_4$ under the condition that the current in leads 2 and 4 is zero. Using Eq. 5.48 and taking

$I_2 = 0$, we obtain the current I_1 as a function of $V_2 - V_4$. Thus in this configuration the measured resistance is

$$R_{13,24} = \frac{V_2 - V_4}{I_1} = \frac{\alpha_{21}}{\alpha_{11}\alpha_{22} - \alpha_{12}\alpha_{21}}. \quad (5.51)$$

Since α_{21} is not symmetric the resistance $R_{13,24}$ is also not symmetric. Now we switch the current and the voltage leads but keep the flux fixed. This means that I_1 in Eq. 5.46 is zero. This yields a resistance

$$R_{24,13} = \frac{\alpha_{12}}{\alpha_{11}\alpha_{22} - \alpha_{12}\alpha_{21}}. \quad (5.52)$$

The sum of these two resistances is symmetric.

For a given flux there are generally six resistances,

$$R_{nm,kl} = \left(\frac{e^2}{h}\right)(T_{km}T_{ln} - T_{kn}T_{lm})\Big/ D, \quad (5.53)$$

where $D = (\alpha_{11}\alpha_{22} - \alpha_{12}\alpha_{21})S$. The resistances given by Eq. 5.53 obey $R_{mn,kl} = -R_{mn,lk} = -R_{nm,kl}$ and the reciprocity relation $R_{mn,kl}(\Phi) = R_{kl,mn}(\Phi)$. The reciprocity relation states that the resistance measured in the presence of a flux Φ is equal to the resistance measured in the presence of a flux $-\Phi$ if the reversal of the flux is accompanied by an exchange in the role of the current and voltage leads.

If the lead has a definite width, there are many states at the Fermi energy. Motion in the transverse direction is quantized and characterized by a set of discrete energies, E_n. To this energy we have to add the kinetic energy for motion along the direction of the lead, $\hbar^2k^2/2m$, such that $E_F = \hbar^2k^2/2m + E_n$. Each transverse state provides a channel. Suppose all the leads are identical and support N quantum channels. The probability of a carrier incident in channel n in lead i to be reflected into the same lead into channel m is denoted by $R_{ii,mn}$, and the probability of a carrier incident in lead j in channel n to be transmitted into lead i into channel m is $T_{ij,mn}$. Then the scattering matrix (Eq. 5.31) becomes a $4N \times 4N$ matrix.

Now we apply the Büttiker formula (Eq. 5.47) to the multichannel case. Assume that the reservoir feeds all channels equally up to the chemical potential μ_j. The current injected into each channel of lead j is $(e/h)\Delta\mu_j$ independent of the velocity and the density of states of this channel. The current in lead i due to the carriers injected in lead j is $I_{ij} = -(e/h)\Sigma_{mn} T_{ij,nm} \Delta\mu_j$. Therefore, if we introduce the trace $R_{ii} = \Sigma_{mn} R_{ii,mn}$, we can get $T_{ij} = \Sigma_{mn} T_{ij,mn}$, which has the symmetry properties given in Eq. 5.46. The conductance in the multichannel case is given by Eq. 5.47, except that $1 - R_{ii}$ in the single-channel case is replaced by $N - R_{ii}$ in the multichannel case. Thus the symmetry properties of the multichannel case are the same as those for the single-channel case.

5.5 Some Applications of the Büttiker Formula

5.5.1 Three-Probe Conductor

The three-probe conductor is shown in Fig. 5.8 [7], where probe 3 is used to measure the chemical potential μ_3. In general, the Büttiker formula can be written as a matrix form, in the case of a three-probe conductor,

$$\begin{pmatrix} I_1 \\ I_2 \\ I_3 \end{pmatrix} = \left(\frac{e^2}{h}\right) \begin{pmatrix} T_{12}+T_{13} & -T_{12} & -T_{13} \\ -T_{21} & T_{21}+T_{23} & -T_{23} \\ -T_{31} & -T_{32} & T_{31}+T_{32} \end{pmatrix} \begin{pmatrix} V_1 \\ V_2 \\ V_3 \end{pmatrix}. \tag{5.54}$$

Suppose the current always leaves the conductor through lead 2. V_2 is the lowest, and thus V_2 can be taken to be zero. Because of

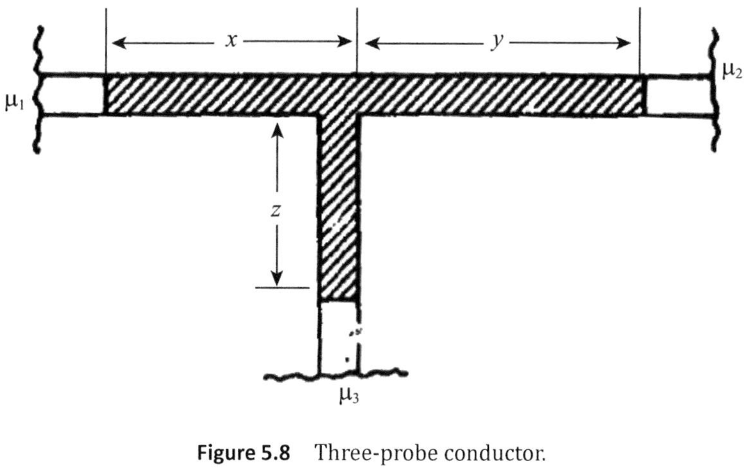

Figure 5.8 Three-probe conductor.

the current conservation, $I_1 + I_2 + I_3 = 0$, so the three equations in Eq. 5.54 are not independent. Equation 5.54 can be simplified to be 2×2 dimensional,

$$\begin{pmatrix} I_1 \\ I_3 \end{pmatrix} = \left(\frac{e^2}{h}\right) \begin{pmatrix} T_{12} + T_{13} & -T_{13} \\ -T_{31} & T_{31} + T_{32} \end{pmatrix} \begin{pmatrix} V_1 \\ V_3 \end{pmatrix}. \tag{5.55}$$

The inverse equation of Eq. 5.55 is

$$\begin{pmatrix} V_1 \\ V_3 \end{pmatrix} = \begin{pmatrix} R_{11} & R_{12} \\ R_{21} & R_{22} \end{pmatrix} \begin{pmatrix} I_1 \\ I_3 \end{pmatrix}, \tag{5.56}$$

where

$$(R) = \left(\frac{h}{e^2}\right) \begin{pmatrix} T_{12} + T_{13} & -T_{13} \\ -T_{31} & T_{31} + T_{32} \end{pmatrix}^{-1}. \tag{5.57}$$

Suppose that the currents from lead 1 to lead 2, the voltage is $V_1 - V_3$, thus $I_2 = -I_1$, $I_3 = 0$, and From Eq. (5.56) can calculate the resistance,

$$V_1 = R_{11} I_1, \quad V_3 = R_{21} I_1,$$

and

$$R_{12,13} = (V_1 - V_3)/I_1 = R_{11} - R_{21}. \tag{5.58}$$

Using Eq. 5.57 yields

$$R_{11} = \left(\frac{h}{e^2}\right) \frac{1}{D}(T_{31} + T_{32}), \quad R_{21} = \left(\frac{h}{e^2}\right) \frac{T_{31}}{D},$$

and

$$D = T_{12} T_{31} + T_{12} T_{32} + T_{13} T_{32}. \tag{5.59}$$

where D is the determinant of the matrix in Eq. 5.57. Inserting Eq. 5.59 into Eq. 5.58 yields

$$R_{12,13} = \left(\frac{h}{e^2}\right) \frac{T_{32}}{D}. \tag{5.60}$$

Similarly,

$$R_{12,32} = \frac{V_3}{I_1} = R_{21} = \left(\frac{h}{e^2}\right) \frac{T_{31}}{D}. \tag{5.61}$$

The determinant D is invariant under flux reversal, $D(\Phi) = D(-\Phi)$. The diagonal elements in the matrix of Eq. 5.57 are, respectively,

$$1 - R_{11} = T_{12} + T_{13} = T_{21} + T_{31}$$

and

$$1 - R_{33} = T_{31} + T_{32} = T_{13} + T_{23}. \tag{5.62}$$

Thus

$$D(-\Phi) = T_{21}T_{13} + T_{21}T_{23} + T_{31}T_{23}(\Phi). \tag{5.63}$$

The resistances $R_{12,13}$ and $R_{12,32}$ in Eqs. 5.60 and 5.61 are neither symmetric nor asymmetric under flux reversal due to T_{32} and T_{31}. However the combined resistance (the two-terminal resistance)

$$R_{12,12} = \frac{V_1 - V_2}{I} = \left(\frac{h}{e^2}\right)\frac{T_{31} + T_{32}}{D} \tag{5.64}$$

is symmetric. Thus, with regard to the two-terminal conductance, the fact that we have an additional lead does not change the symmetry.

Two-terminal conductance in the presence of an additional lead $G = (R_{12,12})^{-1}$ differs now from Eq. 5.25. It is given by

$$G = \left(\frac{e^2}{h}\right)(T_{\text{el}} + T_{\text{in}}), \tag{5.65}$$

where the elastic transmission probability describing the transmission of carriers that emanate from lead 1 and end up in lead 2 without entering reservoir 3 is given by

$$T_{\text{el}} = T_{21}. \tag{5.66}$$

The inelastic transmission probability T_{in} describes carriers that emanate from lead 1 and reach reservoir 3 and from reservoir 3 reach reservoir 2. Comparing Eq. 5.65 with Eq. 5.64 yields

$$T_{\text{in}} = \frac{T_{31}T_{23}}{T_{31} + T_{32}}. \tag{5.67}$$

Thus, the additional lead connected to an electron reservoir acts like an inelastic scatterer.

Equation 5.65 allows us to describe the continuous transition from completely coherent transmission through the conductor to completely incoherent or sequential transmission. In the coherent transmission case, carriers are not allowed to enter reservoir 3, Consequently, $T_{13} = T_{32} = 0$, and two-terminal conductance is given by Eq. 5.25, that is, $T_{\text{el}} = T$ and $T_{\text{in}} = 0$. In the completely incoherent case, $T_{21} = T_{\text{el}} = 0$. In this case Eq. 5.64 yields

$$R_{12,12} = \left(\frac{h}{e^2}\right)\left(\frac{1}{T_{31}} + \frac{1}{T_{23}}\right). \tag{5.68}$$

Equation 5.68 is just the classical addition of series resistors.

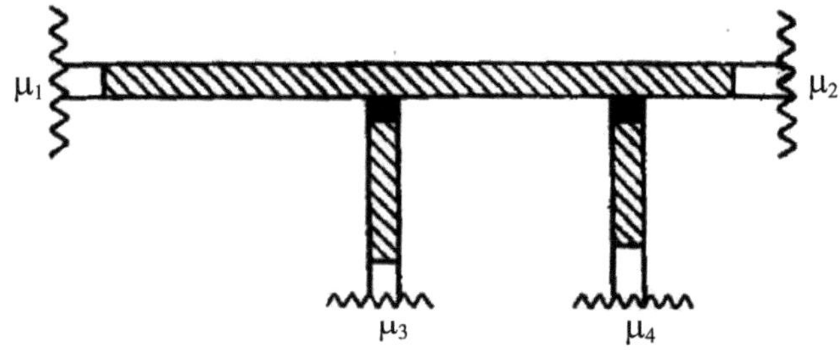

Figure 5.9 Four-probe conductor with tunneling barrier junctions (dark areas) for two of the probes.

5.5.2 Four-Probe Conductor

The four-probe conductor is shown in Fig. 5.9 [7].

Current is fed in at probe 1 and taken out at probe 2. Probes 3 and 4 serve to measure the voltage and are weakly coupled via tunneling barriers to the conductor, as shown in the dark parts in Fig. 5.9. The probabilities for transmission from probe 3 or 4 into the conductor and into reservoir 1 or 2 are small, denoted by ε. If the transmission probability T_{12} is zero order of ε; then T_{13}, T_{14}, T_{23}, and T_{24} are first order; and T_{34} is second order. Evaluation of Eq. 5.53 yields a resistance that reserves the lowest order of ε,

$$R_{12,34} = \frac{h}{e^2}\frac{1}{T_{12}}\frac{T_{31}T_{42} - T_{32}T_{41}}{(T_{31} + T_{32})(T_{41} + T_{42})}. \qquad (5.69)$$

$T = T_{21} = T_{12}$ has the symmetry of the transmission probability, and the sums $T_{31} + T_{32}$ and $T_{41} + T_{42}$ are also symmetric with regard to flux reversal. Because $1 - R_{33} = T_{31} + T_{32} + T_{34}$, since T_{34} is zero to order ε, so $T_{31} + T_{32}$ is symmetric. Therefore, Eq. 5.69 has precisely the symmetry required by the reciprocity theorem,

$$R_{12,34}(\Phi) = R_{34,12}(-\Phi). \qquad (5.70)$$

5.6 Experimental Results

5.6.1 Two-Terminal Conductor

Using molecular beam epitaxy, it is possible to grow AlGaAs-GaAs heterojunctions routinely with two-dimensional (2D) electron

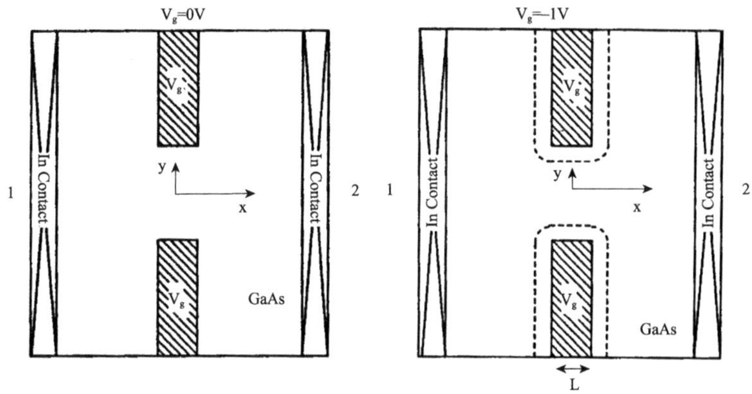

Figure 5.10 AlGaAs/GaAs-modulated doped heterojunctions with the electrodes over the 2DEG; (a) $V_g = 0$ V and (b) $V_g = -1$ V.

mobility $\mu \geq 10^6$ cm^2/Vs for a carrier density of $n \approx 3 \times 10^{11}$ cm^{-2}. The metallic electrodes are made over the 2DEG by using the electron beam lithography as shown in Fig. 5.10a. Timp [8] used the electrostatic potential provided by a split gate geometry to constrain laterally electron gas to the region within the gap between the gates to make a 1D constriction. Figures 5.10a and b schematically represent a typical device in which both gate electrodes are biased at $V_g = 0$ V and -1 V, respectively. In the case of a negative bias voltage the 2DEG at the AlGaAs/GaAs interface immediately beneath the gate electrodes is depleted and so the 2DEG is laterally constrained along the y axis and the electron gas becomes 1D.

Figure 5.11 shows the two-terminal resistance (conductance), $R_{12,12}$ ($G_{12,12}$), as a function of the applied gate voltage [8]; (a) and (b) correspond to the gate widths 200 nm and 600 nm. The series resistance, found at $V_g = 0$ V, was subtracted from the measured resistances. From Fig. 5.11 we see that the average conductance is approximately $2e^2N/h$, with N an integer ranging from 1 to about 10, and evidently is quantized in steps of $2e^2/h$ with about $1 - 5\%$ accuracy as an increasing negative gate voltage makes the constriction narrower. These results verify the theoretical results of Figs. 5.2 and 5.3. When the gate width increases from 200 nm to 600 nm (Fig. 5.11b) the quantized degree of the conductance becomes worse.

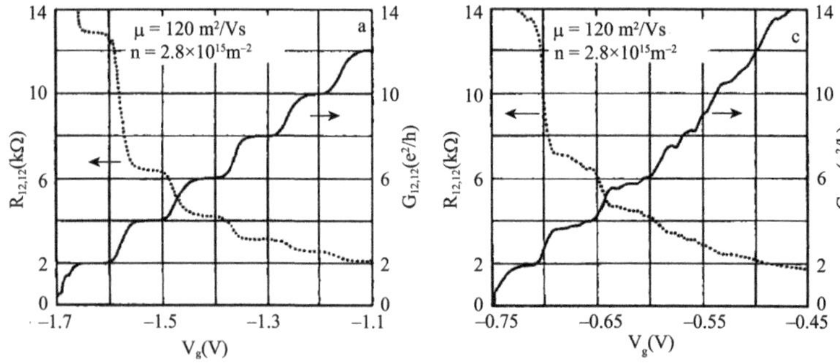

Figure 5.11 Two-terminal resistances (conductance), $R_{12,12}$ ($G_{12,12}$), as a function of the applied gate voltage; (a) and (b) correspond to the gate widths 200 nm and 600 nm.

5.6.2 Two-Terminal Device in the Magnetic Field

Consider an ideal 2D conductor without impurities or inhomogeneity of width w connecting two electron reservoirs as shown in Fig. 5.12 [9]. The chemical potentials of reservoirs are μ_1 and μ_2, respectively, the conductor is along the x direction, the transverse direction is the y direction, and the magnetic field is in the z direction. The electron Hamiltonian is

$$H = \frac{1}{2m^*}\left(\mathbf{p} - \frac{e\mathbf{A}}{\mathbf{c}}\right)^2 + V(y). \qquad (5.71)$$

Take the vector potential

$$\mathbf{A} = (-By, 0, 0), \qquad (5.72)$$

and let the electron wave function

$$\psi_{jk} = e^{ikx} f_{jk}(y). \qquad (5.73)$$

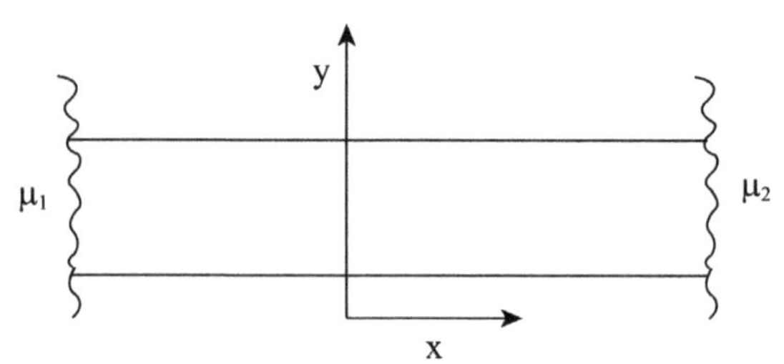

Figure 5.12 Perfect two-dimensional conductor connected to reservoirs.

We obtain the equation of the transverse wave function f,

$$\left[-\frac{\hbar^2}{2m^*}\frac{\partial^2}{\partial y^2}+\frac{1}{2}m^*\omega_c^2(y-y_0)^2+V(y)\right]f=Ef, \quad (5.74)$$

where $\omega_c = eB/m^*c$, $y_0 = kl_B^2$, and $l_B = (\hbar c/eB)^{1/2}$ is the magnetic length. Therefore, the effect of the magnetic field is to add a parabolic potential to the original transverse potential; the origin of the parabolic potential is at y_0.

Suppose the transverse potential is a square wall with infinite barriers at the edges y_1 and y_2 of the conductor. Solving Eq. 5.74 yields the electron energy levels as a function of y_0 as shown in Fig. 5.13 [9]. When y_0 is near the center of the well, far from y_1 and y_2, the electron is less effected by the $V(y)$, and thus the energy levels are Landau levels,

$$E_{jk}=\hbar\omega_0\left(j+\frac{1}{2}\right). \quad (5.75)$$

When y_0 is near the edges, the energy of a state depends on the y_0 through the distance $y_1 - y_0$ to the lower edge and $y_2 - y_0$ to the upper edge, as shown in Fig. 5.13. In general, the energy of a state is determined by

$$E_{jk}=E\left(j,\omega_c,y_0(k)\right). \quad (5.76)$$

The carriers in an edge state acquire a longitudinal velocity,

$$v_{jk}=\frac{1}{\hbar}\frac{dE_{jk}}{\partial k}=\frac{1}{\hbar}\frac{dE_{jk}}{dy_0}\cdot\frac{dy_0}{dk}, \quad (5.77)$$

which is proportional to the slope of the Landau level. dE/dy_0 is positive at the upper edge y_2 and negative at the lower edge (see Fig. 5.13). While $dy_0/dk = l_B^2$ is positive, therefore, the velocity is positive along the upper edge and negative along the lower edge. Note that it is only the edge states that contribute to carrier flow because the bulk Landau states have no velocity, as the region in Fig. 5.13, where E is independent of y_0.

Figure 5.14 depicts a single impurity near the edge of a sample. The quasi-classical skipping orbits are scattered by this impurity [9], but due to the magnetic field the scattered orbits are never further then a cyclotron radius away from the edge. After scattering by the impurity, the orbits return to the edge and continue to follow the

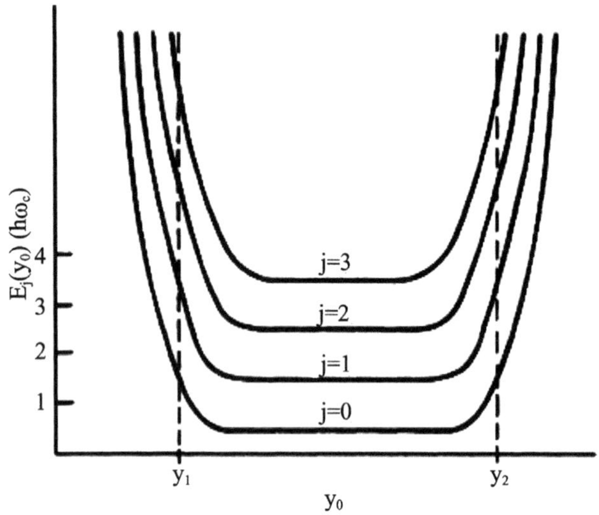

Figure 5.13 Energy spectrum of a perfect conductor in a high magnetic field for a rectangular confining potential (walls at y_1 and y_2).

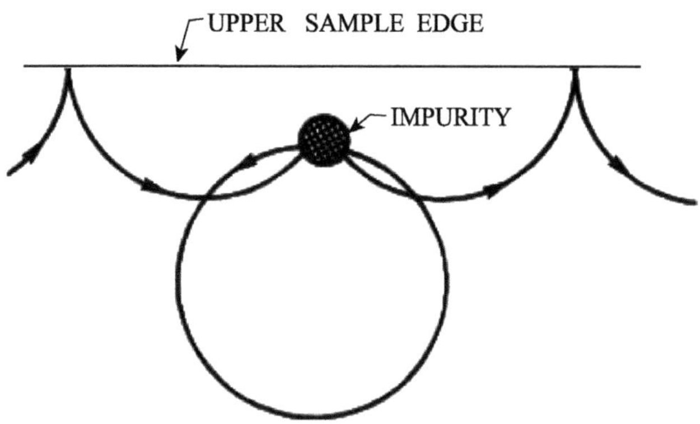

Figure 5.14 Quasi-classical skipping orbits along the upper edge of the sample in the presence of a localized impurity.

edge, and the velocity is positive. The key point is that an impurity cannot effectively reverse the direction of motion of a carrier. There is no scattering backward against the flow of carriers if the average distance between impurities is larger than the cyclotron radius.

To obtain the criterion for the strength of the field we can make use of the fact that the Landau states are a harmonic-oscillator wave function. The cyclotron radius of a state in the j-th Landau level is

$$\left\langle \Delta y^2 \right\rangle^{1/2} = l_{\mathrm{B}} \left(j + \frac{1}{2} \right)^{1/2} . \tag{5.78}$$

From Eq. 5.78 we obtain the critical magnetic field B_{crit} for the onset of backscattering,

$$2\pi l_e^2 B_{\mathrm{crit}} > \Phi_0 \left(N + \frac{1}{2} \right), \tag{5.79}$$

where $\Phi_0 = hc/e$ is magnetic flux quanta and N is the largest index of Landau state. l_e is the average distance between impurities. Therefore, Eq. (5.79) can be looked as the condition that the backscattering cannot be occurred.

In a strong magnetic field $B > B_{\mathrm{crit}}$ the current fed into an edge state by a reservoir is the same as the current fed into a quantum channel in a zero-field perfect conductor. The resulting two-terminal resistance for a perfect conductor in a high magnetic field is thus

$$R = \frac{h}{e^2} \cdot \frac{1}{N}, \tag{5.80}$$

where N is the number of edge states (with a positive velocity).

If the conductor has a disordered section connected at its left and right ends to ideal perfect conductors, the disordered part of the conductor mixes the channels of the perfect conductors. Carriers incident in channel j (edge state j) from the left have a probability amplitude t_{ij} for transmission into channel i and a probability amplitude r_{ij} for reflection into channel i. Therefore, the transmitted current is

$$I_i = \frac{e}{h} \sum_{j=1}^{N} T_{ij} \Delta\mu, \tag{5.81}$$

where $T_{ij} = |t_{ij}|^2$. Summing over all incident channels gives a total transmitted current,

$$I = \frac{e}{h} \sum_{i,j=1}^{N,N} T_{ij} \Delta\mu. \tag{5.82}$$

The voltage drop is $eV = \Delta\mu$, and the Landauer resistance in this case is

$$R = \frac{h}{e^2} \cdot \frac{1}{T}, \quad T = \sum_{i,j=1}^{N,N} T_{ij}. \tag{5.83}$$

5.6.3 Quantum Hall Effect

We discuss how the quantum Hall effect is established in an open conductor with current probes and Hall bars. Figure 5.15 shows a conductor where the Hall bars are of the same width as the probes connected to the current source and sink [9]. In the conductor of Fig. 5.15, N edge states connect the four contacts in a cyclical fashion. Assume that all the contacts are ideal and same and there is no scattering from one edge to the other edge. Under these circumstances, the edge states provide perfect transmission channels for carriers and lead to transmission probabilities, $T_{41} = T_{34} = T_{23} = T_{12} = N$. All the other transmission probabilities are zero. The Hall resistance $R_{13,42}$ is determined by $T_{41}T_{23} - T_{43}T_{21}$, which is equal to N^2. Evaluation of the subdeterminant D in Eq. 5.53 yields $D = N^3$. All Hall resistance values of the conductor of Fig. 5.15 are quantized and given by $\pm(h/e^2)(1/N)$.

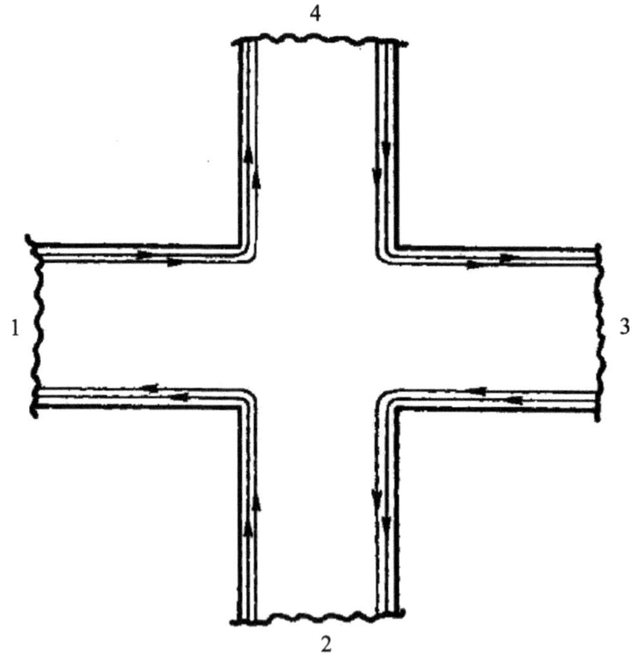

Figure 5.15 Ideal Hall conductor.

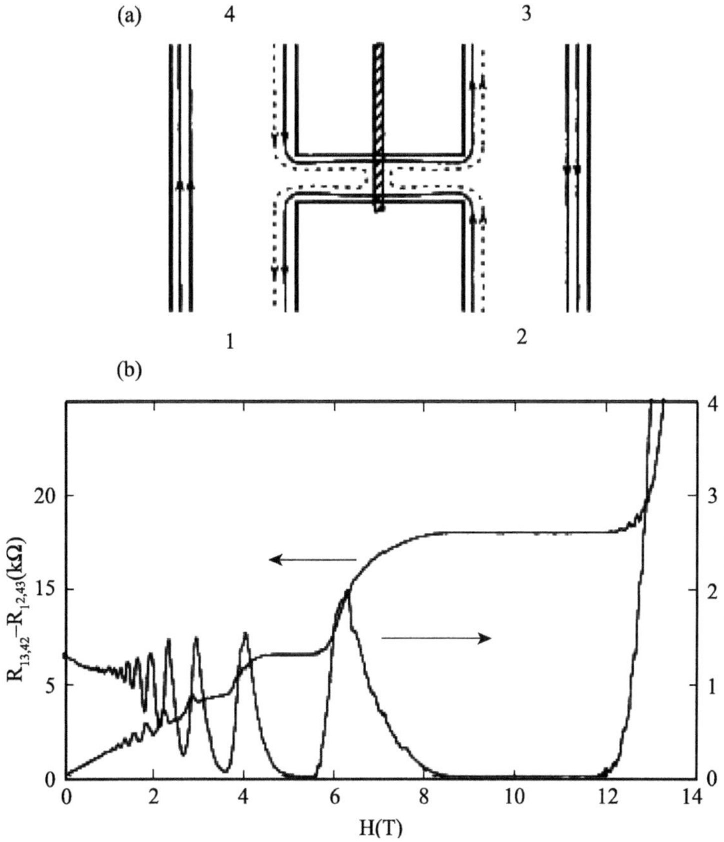

Figure 5.16 (a) A schematic view of the four-probe GaAs-Al$_x$Ga$_{1-x}$As wire with a narrow cross gate. (b) $R_{12,43}$ and $R_{13,42} - R_{12,43}$ at V_g as functions of magnetic field.

The longitudinal resistance, for example, $R_{12,43}$ are zero, since in the products forming the expression, $T_{41}T_{32} - T_{42}T_{31}$, at least one transmission probability always is zero.

The above conductor is an ideal conductor. Washburn et al. [10] added a potential barrier in this conductor, as shown in Fig. 5.16. They manufactured a narrow gate on the circuit center. Applying a negative bias voltage on the gate is equal to adding a potential barrier in the circuit; the barrier height is controlled by the bias voltage. Because the barrier is higher in the center region and lower in the edge region, the edge states near the edge (solid lines) can tunnel through the barrier. Those near the center region (dashed lines) are reflected into the opposite edge and move in the opposite direction, as shown in Fig. 5.16.

Assuming that there are K edge states that are reflected, we have $T_{41} = N$, $T_{34} = N - k$, $T_{14} = K$, $T_{23} = N$, $T_{12} = N - k$, and $T_{32} = K$ and all other T_{ij} equal zero. It can be proved from Eq. 5.53 that $D = N^2(N - k)$,

$$R_{13,42} = \left(\frac{h}{e^2}\right)(T_{41}T_{23} - T_{43}T_{21})/D$$
$$= \left(\frac{h}{e^2}\right)\frac{1}{N - K},$$
$$R_{42,13} = \left(\frac{h}{e^2}\right)(T_{14}T_{32} - T_{12}T_{34})/D$$
$$= -\left(\frac{h}{e^2}\right)\frac{N - 2K}{N(N - K)},$$

and

$$R_{12,43} = \left(\frac{h}{e^2}\right)(T_{41}T_{32} - T_{42}T_{31})/D$$
$$= \left(\frac{h}{e^2}\right)\frac{K}{N(N - K)}. \tag{5.84}$$

Figure 5.16b shows $R_{12,43}$ and $R_{13,42} - R_{12,43}$ as functions of magnetic field H at $V_g = 0$ [10]. These combinations are the nearest correspondence to the classical resistance ρ_{xx} and ρ_{xy}, which are the parameters usually studied in large samples. From the figure we see that $R_{12,43}$ approaches zero over wide regions of field ($4.9 < H < 5.5$ T and $8.5 < H < 10$ T), and in the same ranges $R_{13,42}$ is quantized to $h/4e^2$ and $h/2e^2$, respectively.

Figure 5.17 shows $R_{13,42}$ as a function of gate voltage for several values of the magnetic field [10]. From the figure we see that when $V_g = 0$, $R_{13,42}$ changes from $h/(5e^2)$ and $h/(4e^2)$ to $h/(2e^2)$ with magnetic field increasing, indicating that the number of occupied Landau levels decreases. When V_g decreases, K changes from 0 to 1 or 2, and from Eq. 5.84 $R_{13,42}$ increases and raises to the next plateau, for example, from $h/(4e^2)$ to $h/(2e^2)$. From the above discussion we conclude that backscattering by the gate potential

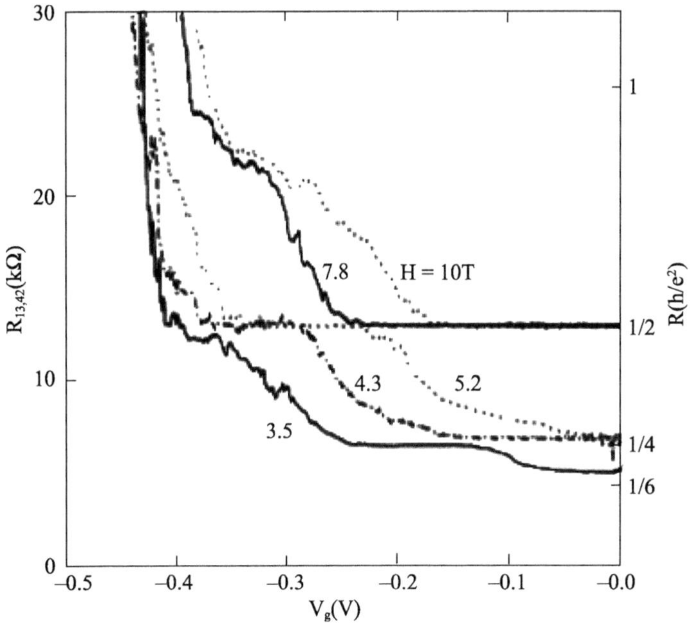

Figure 5.17 $R_{13,42}$ as a function of gate voltage for several values of the magnetic field.

does not destroy the quantized Hall effect. Instead, there is always a region in which the various four-probe resistances are quantized to h/e^2i.

References

1. Datta, S. (1995). *Transport in Mesoscopic Systems* (Cambridge, London).
2. Szafer, A., and Stone, A. D. (1989). Theory of quantum conduction through a constriction. *Phys. Rev. Lett.*, **62**, 300–303.
3. van Wees, B. J., van Houten, H., Beenakker, W. J., et al. (1988). Quantized conductance of point contacts in a two-dimensional electron gas. *Phys. Rev. Lett.*, **60**, 848–850.
4. Kirczenow, G. (1989). Resonant conduction in ballistic quantum channels. *Phys. Rev. B*, **39**, 10452–10455.

5. Büttiker, M., Imry, Y., Landauer, R., and Pinhas, S. (1985). Generalized many-channel conductance formula with application to small rings. *Phys. Rev. B*, **31**, 6207–6215.
6. Büttiker, M. (1986). Four-terminal phase-coherent conductance. *Phys. Rev. Lett.*, **57**, 1761–1764.
7. Büttiker, M. (1988). Symmetry of electrical conduction. *IBM J. Res. Dev.*, **32**, 317–334.
8. Timp, G. (1996). *Semiconductors and Semimetals*, Vol. 35, ed. Reed, M. (Academic Press, New York), p. 113.
9. Büttiker, M. (1988). Absence of backscattering in the quantum Hall effect in multiprobe conductors. *Phys. Rev. B*, **38**, 9375–9389.
10. Washburn, S., Fowler, A. B., Schmid, H., and Kern, D. (1988). Quantized Hall effect in the presence of backscattering. *Phys. Rev. Lett.*, **61**, 2801–2804.

Chapter 6

Transport in Quantum Dots

Since the single-electron effect in quantum dots and single-electron transistor were discovered, many new physical behaviors have been discovered, for example, core shell-like filling of electrons in quantum dots of regular shapes, electron levels of quantum dots in a perpendicular magnetic field, form of molecular state in two or three coupling quantum dots, coherent molecular states, covalent states, and ionic states. The high-order effects include resonant tunneling, Kondo effect caused by a strong coupling, mixed valence physics connected with the Anderson model, Fano resonance produced by the existence of resonance or non-resonance channels, etc. In the application aspects, many interesting proposals are suggested, for example, single-electron transistors (SETs) and quantum bite based on the electron spin used for quantum calculation. Some noticeable and useful devices have been invented, for example, scanning SET used to detect the local electric field and radio frequency (RF) SET used to detect electric charge at the level of $10^{-5}e/\sqrt{Hz}$.

Quantum Waveguide in Microcircuits
Jian-Bai Xia, Duan-Yang Liu, and Wei-Dong Sheng

ISBN 978-981-4669-85-6 (Hardcover), 978-1-315-36477-3 (eBook)
www.panstanford.com

6.1 Single-Electron Effect and Single-Electron Transistor

In the beginning of the twentieth century, physicist Millikan made the famous oil-drop experiment. He found that the electric charges brought by the tiny broken oil drops are always integral times of a basic electric quantity; then he deduced that the particle bringing the basic electric quantity is an electron and the basic electric quantity $e = 1.602 \times 10^{-19}$ C. But at that time Millikan could not obtain a single electron. Today the development of micro-lithography technology has made it possible to fabricate semiconductor micro-structures with a scale smaller than 100 nm. In this kind of structure one can operate electron motion one by one through a changing voltage. This is the single-electron effect.

In 1989 Scott-Thomas et al. created a dual-gate device with a 70 nm gap in the lower gate on narrow Si inversion layers. Figure 6.1 shows the schematic cross section (a) and the top view (b) of the slotted-gate device [1]. The inversion layer, formed by the positively biased upper gate, is confined by the lower gate. The width of the channel is controlled by the lower gate, and the electron density in

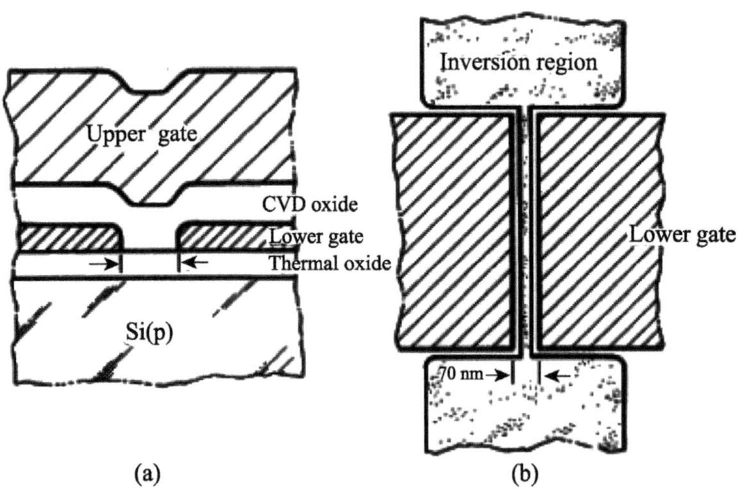

Figure 6.1 Schematic cross section (a) and top view (b) of the slotted-gate device.

the inversion layer is controlled by the upper gate voltage (positive). The width of the narrow channel is 20 nm.

Earlier, people also experimented with electrons through a narrow channel but did not obtained any regular results. Due to the limitation of the lithography technology the width of the channel is $3 \approx 5$ times of the present channel. Besides the electron mobility is lower. The experimental results of conductance from the device of Fig. 6.1 are shown in Fig. 6.2 [1]. The top panel shows G for a 10 μm long metal-oxide semiconductor field-effect transistor (MOSFET) as a function of the voltage on the upper gate V_G, which is proportional to the number of electrons per unit length. The periodic oscillations can be clearly identified, although they are accompanied by random, see [1]. That the oscillations are truly periodic is determined in the next three panels, which show the power spectral density, that is, the square of the modulus of the Fourier transform, for devices of 10, 2, and 1 μm lengths. Each device has a peak in its spectrum at a nonzero frequency. For a $L = 10$ μm device (second panel), the peak is at $1/\Delta V_G = 43\ \text{V}^{-1}$, that is, the oscillation period of the V_G is $\Delta V_G = 0.023$ V.

The electron charges in the channel equal the channel capacitance multiplied by V_G, C/L is the capacitance of unit length, and $e(N/L) = (C/L)V_G$. Therefore, in Fig. 6.2 G can be looked at as a function of number of electrons N. The oscillation of G with V_G is equivalent to that with N. The voltage difference ΔV_G for one period of oscillation is necessary for adding an electron. The experiments found that there is no correlation between ΔV_G and the channel length L, as shown in the next three panels of Fig. 6.2. The authors thought that the actual length of a channel is determined by the distance between two impurities in the channel, not the apparent length L as shown in Fig. 6.1b. The electrostatic potential produced by the impurities forms a barrier for electrons, forming a quantum dot. Thus, the period ΔV_G of G oscillation is decided by the distance between two impurities, not L. The bottom panel of Fig. 6.2 is the Fourier spectra for the 1 μm long channel in a magnetic field. Comparing the two lowest panels we found that the oscillation period of G is independent of the magnetic field.

The above impurity barrier model is only a surmise and has not been verified experimentally. To study the relation between

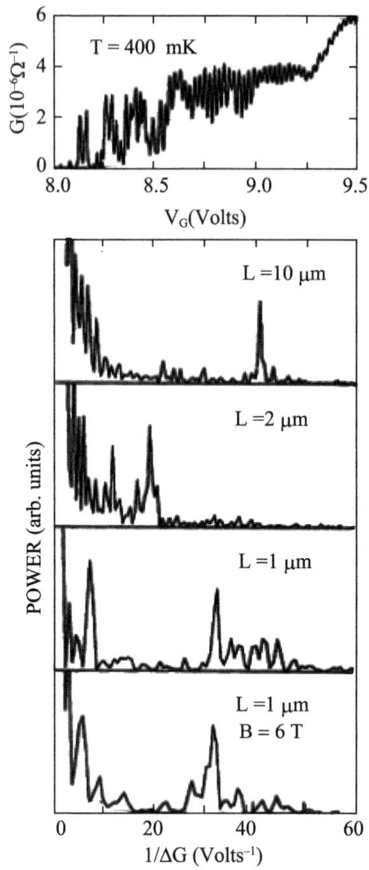

Figure 6.2 Top panel: G versus V_G for a 10 μm long inversion layer. Next three panels: Fourier power spectra of the data of the top panel and for 2 and 1 μm long channels. Bottom panel: Fourier spectra for the 1 μm long channel in a magnetic field.

the oscillation period of G, ΔV_G, and channel length Meirav et al. used a GaAs/AlGaAs-modulated doping heterojunction instead of a Si inversion layer and made the metal gate with two constrictions as shown in Fig. 6.3 [2]. Each constriction is about 100 nm long, defining a segment of length L_0 between them. When a negative V_b is applied, these constrictions induce saddle-shaped potential barriers for electrons moving along the channel.

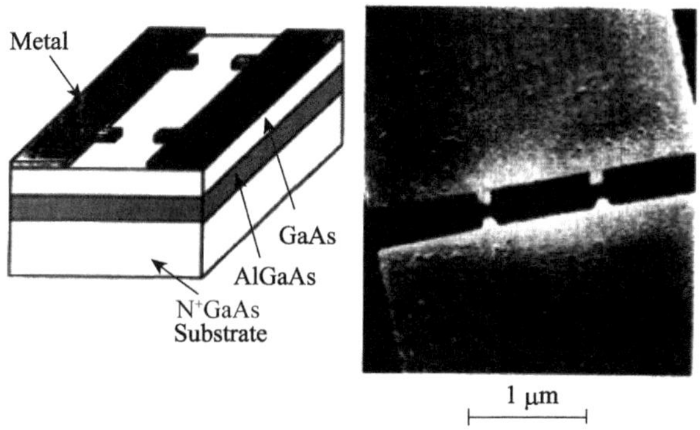

Figure 6.3 Schematic drawing of a device structure along with a scanning electron micrograph of one sample.

The measured G as a function of $V_g - V_t$ are shown in Fig. 6.4 [2], where V_t is a sample-dependent threshold and V_b was held fixed, typically at about -0.5 V. Figures 6.4a and 6.4b show data for two samples, which had the same geometry $L_0 = 1$ μm. The periodic oscillations are clearly seen, with the same period in both samples. The channels without constrictions had monotonic dependence or, occasionally, random fluctuation patterns, but no similar periodic behavior. Figures 6.4c and 6.4d show results for samples with progressively shorter lengths and correspondingly longer periods, consistent with the geometry.

The oscillations in Fig. 6.4 recurred with the exact same period even after samples were warmed to room temperature and cooled again, as shown in Fig. 6.5 [2]. In previous experiments, such thermal cycling invariably led to random changes or total disappearance of the periodicity, understood as the result of the redistribution of interface charges (impurities). Here no such randomness is seen. Thus, for the first time, we can control the period of the oscillation by the geometry of the devices. This is because the GaAs/AlGaAs heterostructure material is rather clean, making the incidence of charged impurities in the channel less common than in Si inversion layers.

There is still one problem: whether each oscillation corresponds to precisely one electron added to the system. We should estimate the increment in V_g required to add one electron to the segment

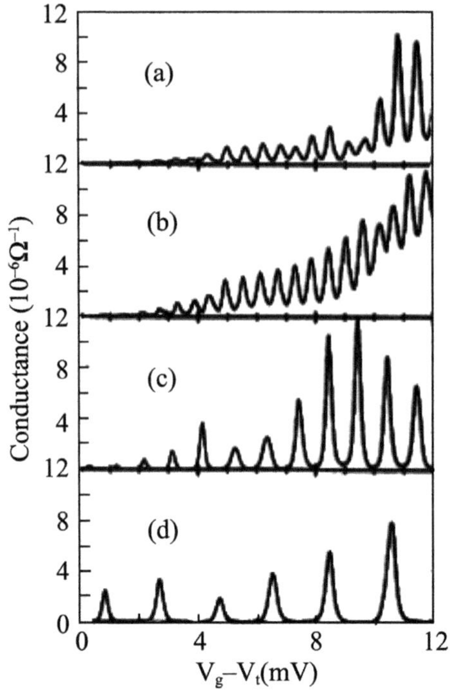

Figure 6.4 G as a function of $V_g - V_t$ for four samples of different L_0: (a) 1 μm, (b) 1 μm, (c) 0.8 μm, and (d) 0.6 μm.

of the channel between the two constrictions. Three-dimensional computer simulations of these structures gave estimates of the relation between V_g and the total charge in the channel. For all samples shown the estimated charge increase per ΔV_g is remarkably close to one electron, within 10% for most samples. The possibility of more than one electron per ΔV_g is outside the error margin.

Kouwenhoven et al. studied similar single charging effects in a lateral split-gate quantum dot defined by metal gates in the two-dimensional electron gas (2DEG) of a GaAs/AlGaAs heterostructure [3]. Figure 6.6 shows a scanning electron microscope (SEM) photograph of the gate geometry, which is fabricated on top of a GaAs/AlGaAs heterostructure containing 2DEG [3]. The gate F is denoted as the finger gate, gates 1 to 4 as quantum point contact (QPC) gates, and gate C as the center gate. A negative voltage −0.4 V

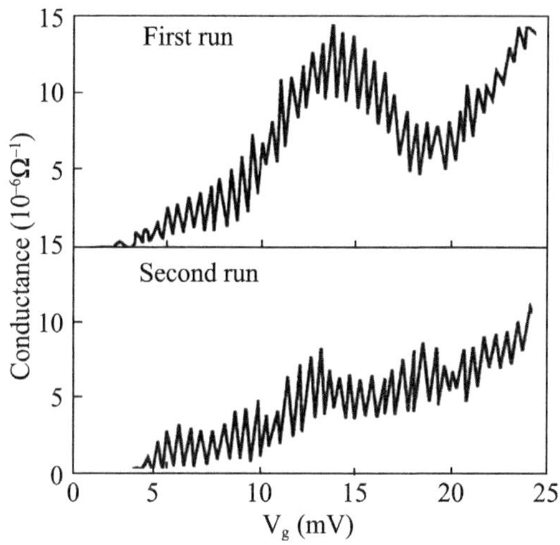

Figure 6.5 Conductance versus gate voltage for one sample taken in different runs, between which the sample was warmed to 300 K.

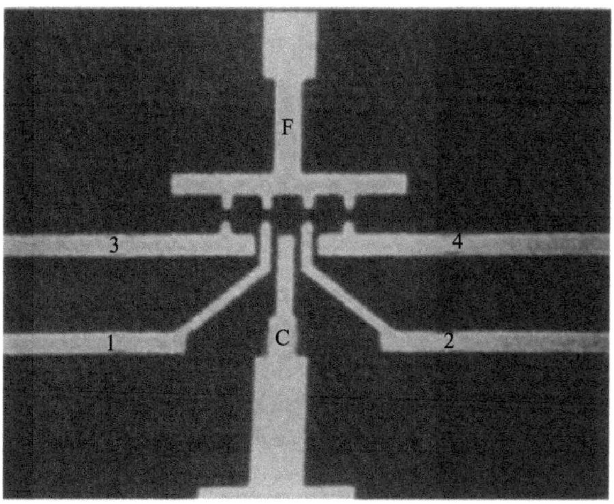

Figure 6.6 SEM photograph of the gate geometry, which is fabricated on top of a GaAs/AlGaAs heterostructure containing 2DEG.

depletes the 2DEG underneath the gates. The narrow channels between gates 3–1, 1–C, C–2, and 2–4 are completely pinched off at this gate voltage. Applying a negative voltage to the gates F, 1, 2, and C forms a dot in the 2DEG. The radius of the dot is estimated as 300 nm. QPC gates 1 and 2 are used to control the conductance of the tunneling barrier between the dot and the wide 2DEG regions, and the center gate is used to vary the number of electrons in the dot. This gate structure allows an independent control of the conductance of the two 2DEG leads and enables you to vary the number of electrons that are localized in the dot.

The gate voltages V_3 and V_4 are taken to be zero, so there is no quantum dot formed between gates 3, 4, and F. The gate voltages V_1 and V_2 are taken to be smaller than -1.4 V, so G_1 and $G_2 \ll 2e^2/h$. The measured conductance of the dot versus center gate voltage V_C is shown in Fig. 6.7 [3]. The oscillations appear as sharp peaks with an amplitude up to e^2/h. Experiments found that only when both QPC conductance values are below the quantized plateau value $2e^2/h$ does the amplitude of the Coulomb oscillations increase as the QPC conductance values decrease. From Fig. 6.7 the oscillation period $\Delta V_C = 8.3$ mV, a capacitance between the dot and the center

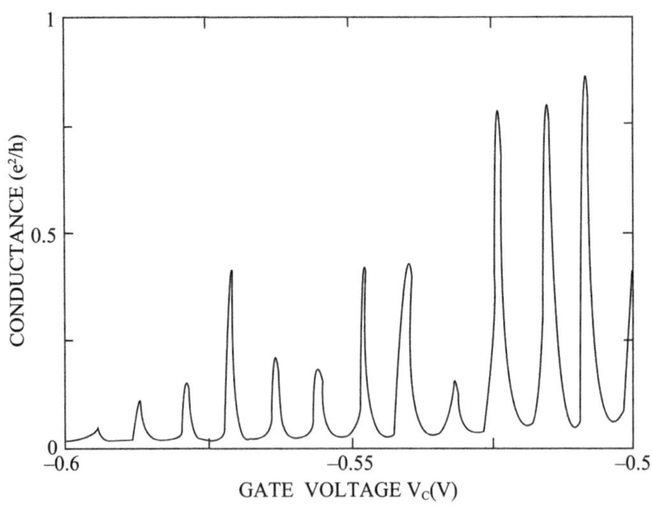

Figure 6.7 Conductance of the dot versus center gate voltage V_C for G_1 and $G_2 \ll 2e^2/h$.

gate is derived $C_C = e/\Delta V_C = 0.19 \times 10^{-16}$ F. To determine the total capacitance between the dot and the six gates of the sample, the authors measured the oscillations by varying the voltage on the different gates, while keeping the voltage on the remaining gates fixed. Then they obtained the capacitances between the dot and each gate, added these capacitances, and obtained the total capacitance $\Sigma C_g = 1.71 \times 10^{-16}$ F.

Using QPC gates 3 and 4, one can increase the dot size to two strongly coupled dots (i.e., one dot with a double size) and one dot with three times the size. Figure 6.8 shows the Coulomb oscillations versus the center gate voltage. The periods in the gate voltage are $\Delta V_{1\text{dot}} = 9.0$ mV, $\Delta V_{2\text{dot}} = 5.3$ mV, and $\Delta V_{3\text{dot}} = 3.6$ mV, yielding capacitances between the center gate and the dot $C_{C,1\text{dot}} = 1.8 \times 10^{-17}$ F, $C_{C,2\text{dot}} = 3.0 \times 10^{-17}$ F, and $C_{C,3\text{dot}} = 4.4 \times 10^{-17}$ F, which have the ratios 1.2:2:3. This result shows that the gate capacitance scales with the size of the dot.

The charging effect can be described in terms of the capacitance C between the dot and its environment. An estimate of C is obtained from the self-capacitance $C_0 = 8\varepsilon_r\varepsilon_0 R$ between a 2D dot with a disc shape and infinity, where R is the radius of the disc, ε_0 is the vacuum dielectric constant, and $\varepsilon_0 = 8.854 \times 10^{-12}$ F/m. A dot with $R =$ 300 nm and $\varepsilon_r = 13$ in GaAs gives $C_0 = 2.8 \times 10^{-16}$ F and a charging energy $e^2/C_0 = 0.6$ meV, which exceeds the thermal energy $k_B T$ for temperatures below 4 K. From the electron density of the ungated 2DEG and the dot area, the number N of electrons in the dot is estimated to be about 500. The average energy separation between the discrete states $2E_F/N$ is therefore $\sim$0.03 meV, where $E_F = 7$ meV is the 2DEG Fermi energy. This is less than one-tenth of the charging energy, so the charging effect is dominant in the electron transport process.

The transport of a quantum dot can be described schematically by Fig. 6.9 [3], where μ_l and μ_r denote the chemical potentials of left and right electron reservoirs, respectively, and $\mu_l > \mu_r$. The center part is the dot, separated from the reservoirs by the barriers, $e\varphi_n$ is the electrostatic energy of N electrons. At temperature $T = 0$ K, the ground state energy of N electrons is the sum of single electron

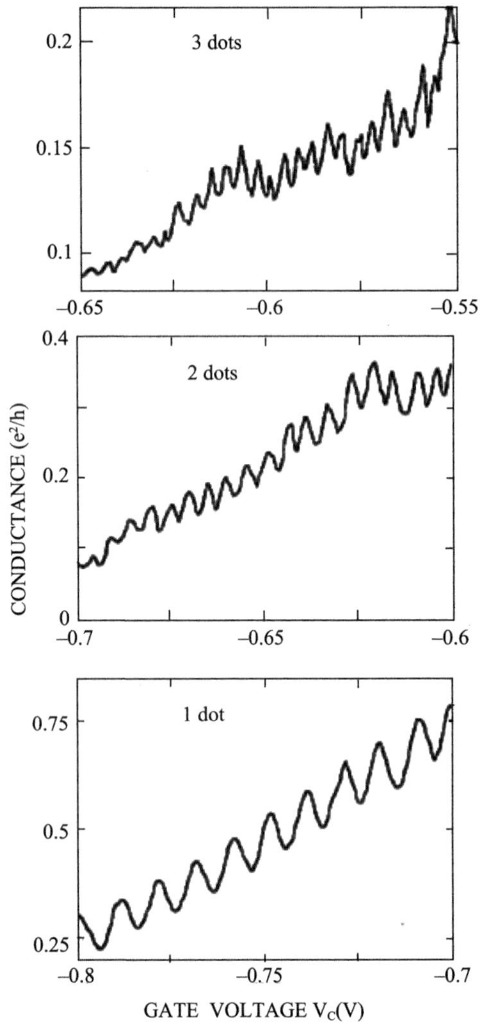

Figure 6.8 Conductance of the dot versus the center gate voltage V_C for different sizes of the dot.

energy E_p plus the electrostatic energy,

$$U(N) = \sum_{P=1}^{N} E_P + \frac{(-eN + C_g V_g)^2}{2C}, \tag{6.1}$$

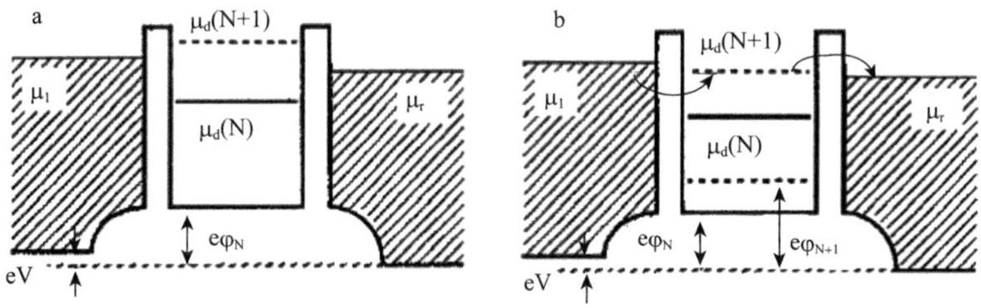

Figure 6.9 Two situations for different gate voltages. (a) Coulomb blockade of electron tunneling. (b) One-by-one electron tunneling at the $N \rightarrow N+1$ transition.

where C_{g} is the capacitance between the dot and one gate (e.g., the center gate) and C is the total capacitance between the dot and all gates.

The minimum energy necessary to add the N-th electron to the dot is

$$\mu_{\mathrm{d}}(N) = U(N) - U(N-1)$$
$$= E_N + \frac{(N-1/2)e^2}{C} - e\frac{C_{\mathrm{g}}}{C}V_{\mathrm{g}}. \qquad (6.2)$$

Thus, the difference of the chemical potentials of the $(N+1)$ and N electrons,

$$\mu_{\mathrm{d}}(N+1) - \mu_{\mathrm{d}}(N) = E_{N+1} - E_N + e^2/C. \qquad (6.3)$$

This energy gap leads to blockade for tunneling of an electron into and out of the dot, as shown schematically in Fig. 6.9a, where N electrons are localized in the dot. The $(N+1)$th electron cannot tunnel into the dot because the resulting electrochemical potential $\mu_{\mathrm{d}}(N+1)$ is higher than the electrochemical potentials of the reservoirs. So for $\mu_{\mathrm{d}}(N) < \mu_{\mathrm{l}}$ and $\mu_{\mathrm{l}} < \mu_{\mathrm{d}}(N+1)$ the electron transport is blocked, which is known as the Coulomb blockade (CB). The CB can be eliminated by increasing the center gate voltage, so $\mu_{\mathrm{d}}(N+1)$ is lined up between μ_{l} and μ_{r} $[\mu_{\mathrm{l}} < \mu_{\mathrm{d}}(N+1) < \mu_{\mathrm{r}}]$, as illustrated in Fig. 6.9b. In this case, the $(N+1)$th electron can tunnel into the dot and then tunnel out of the dot to the right 2DEG reservoir, causing the electrochemical potential to drop to $\mu_{\mathrm{d}}(N)$. Now a new electron can tunnel into the dot and repeat the cycle. This process, where current is carried by successive discrete charging and discharging of the dot, is known as single-charge tunneling.

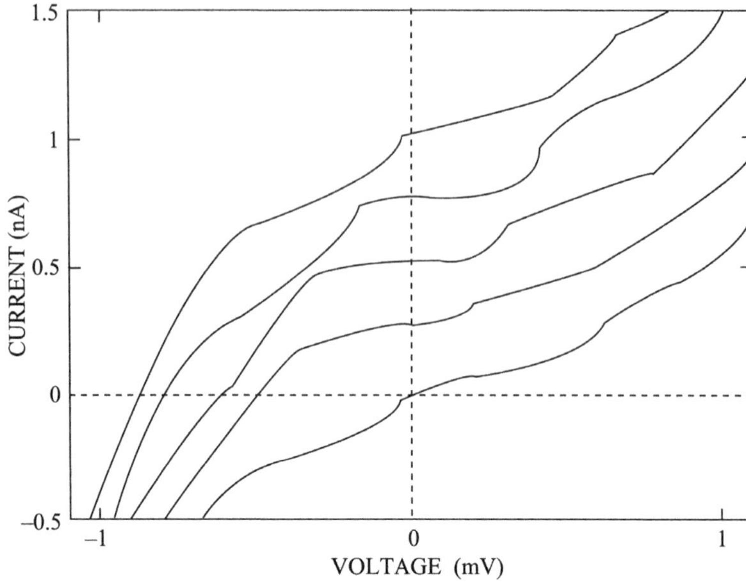

Figure 6.10 I–V characteristics for different center gate voltages, demonstrating the Coulomb staircase. The curves correspond to different values of V_C (in steps of 1 mV) and are offset for clarity ($I = 0$ occurs at $V = 0$).

In the case of Fig. 6.9b the potential difference of left and right reservoirs $eV = \mu_l - \mu_r$ is small, so only one electron is allowed to move through the dot, that is, the dot only opens a one-electron channel. If the bias voltage eV increases continuously, so the chemical potential difference $\mu_l - \mu_r$ can include two electron states, then the dot opens a second electron channel. Therefore, in the I–V characteristic curve, when V increases, the current will step-likely increase, as shown in Fig. 6.10 [3], where each step corresponds to one electron transport. This I–V curve is called the Coulomb staircase. The current steps $\Delta I \approx 0.2$ nA occur at voltage intervals $\Delta V \approx 0.67$ mV. This voltage difference is a direct measure of the charging energy in the sample $\Delta V = e/C$, which yields a total capacitance $C = 2.4 \times 10^{-16}$ F. Suppose that the total tunnel conductance is G. One extra elementary charge e is transported through the dot in a typical time C/G, yielding $\Delta I \approx eG/C$. This gives $G \approx (4\ \text{M}\Omega)^{-1}$ and the tunnel time $C/G \approx 10^{-9}$ s.

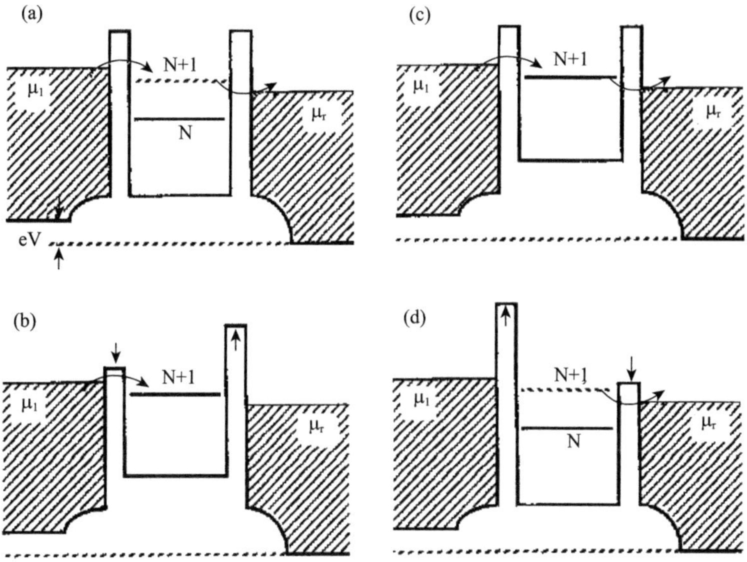

Figure 6.11 Schematic potential landscape through the quantum dot. (a) to (d) represent 4 stages of potential barrier height variation in a RF cycle.

When the two gates (gates 1 and 2 in Fig. 6.6) are applied alternating voltages with phase difference π (frequency $f = 10$ MHz), in one period the heights of two barriers beside the dot vary such as shown in Fig. 6.11a–d. The solid arrow denotes allowed electron motion, and the dashed arrow denotes forbidden electron motion. Thus, in one period of voltage variation just one electron tunnels through the dot. The AC frequency is f, and the current $I = ef$. If the bias voltage V is increased, so that the number of charge states in the interval between μ_l and μ_r increases to n, then n electrons can tunnel through the dot per radio-frequency (RF) cycle, yielding a quantized current $I = nef$.

The measured I–V curves for RF signals with a phase difference of π applied to gates 1 and 2 are shown in Fig. 6.12 [4]. The I–V curves have current plateaus at multiple values of ef, demonstrating that a discrete number of electrons are transferred through the quantum dot for each RF cycle. The curves correspond to different center gate voltages V_C (in steps of 1 mV) and are offset for clarity

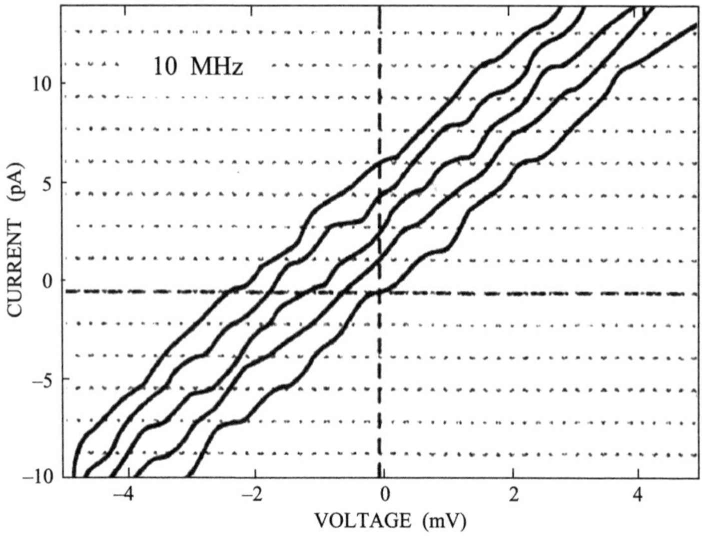

Figure 6.12 I–V characteristics when two phase shifted RF signals are applied with a frequency $f = 10$ MHz. The curves correspond to different center gate voltages V_C (in steps of 1 mV) and are offset for clarity by an integer times *ef*. Dotted lines show the current plateaus at integer values of *ef*.

by an integer times *ef* ($I = 0$ occurs at $V = 0$). The height of each plateau is $e \times 10$ MHz $= 1.6$ pA.

Figure 6.13 shows I–V characteristics for different frequencies $f = 5$, 10, and 20 MHz. The different curves in each group correspond to different V_C [4]. The current is proportional to f, varying in the interval between *nef* and $(n + 1)$*ef*. This behavior of transport in the RF field is called a turnstile effect, which is like the turnstile in the hotel allowing one or several people through it in each cycle. Comparing Figs. 6.12 and 6.10, we found that the current scales are pA and nA for the turnstile effect and the Coulomb staircase, respectively.

The most hopeful application of the single-electron effect is the single-electron transistor (SET), which can be used to fabricate memory of a large capacity. Now in the 4G DRAM, each bite accumulates about 500,000 electrons, dissipating a lot of energy. If we would fabricate 16 T memory, we should reduce largely

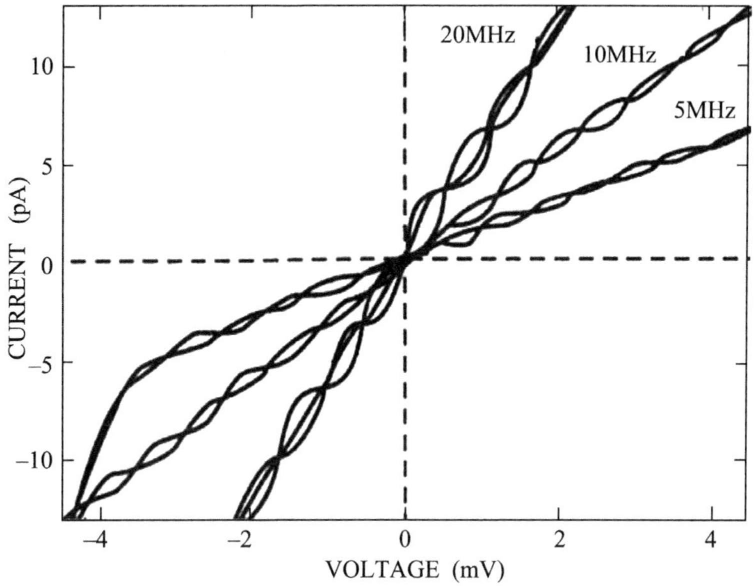

Figure 6.13 I–V characteristics for different frequencies $f = 5$, 10, and 20 MHz.

the number of electrons in each bite, for example, to less than 100. Therefore, the SET is the best choice of future large-capacity memory. But now it is far from the actual application of the SET, its volume is not small enough, the capacitance is too large and so the charging energy e^2/C is too small, and the device should operate at an ultra-low temperature so $k_B T \ll e^2/C$. The goal is to reduce the size of the quantum dot, reduce the capacitance and the number of electrons in the dot, and raise the operating temperature.

6.2 Transport of a Quantum Dot in a Magnetic Field

Experiments found that the conductance oscillation with the gate voltage exists for a quantum dot even in the perpendicular magnetic field. The geometry of the device is shown schematically in Fig. 6.14a [5]. It is a modulation doping GaAs/AlGaAs heterostructure, in which

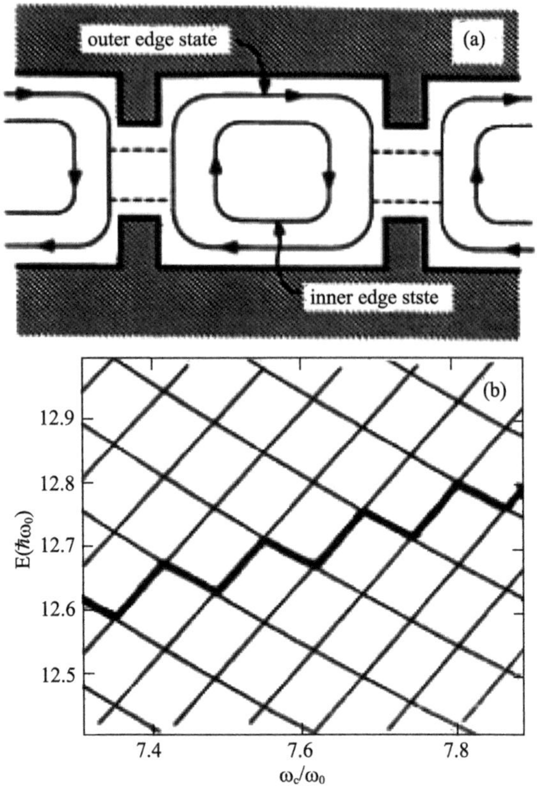

Figure 6.14 Schematic top view of the device, showing the path of the edge states associated with the lowest two Landau levels. The lithographic dimension is 500 nm by 700 nm. (b) Energy levels of a dot with a parabolic confining potential as a function of $\omega_c = eB/m^*$.

the upper gate (a negative bias) is used to define the dot and the lower gate (a positive bias) is to adjust the electron density. The magnetic field is perpendicular to the 2DEG, which forms the edge states in the dot. Figure 6.14b shows the calculated magnetic energy levels as functions of magnetic field ω_c/ω_0 in the parabolic confining potential $(1/2)m^*\omega_0^2 r^2$. The heavy line represents the energy of the single-particle state that is 78th lowest in energy.

The conductance G versus the gate voltage V_g applied to the lower gate is shown in the inset of Fig. 6.15 [5]. The conductance

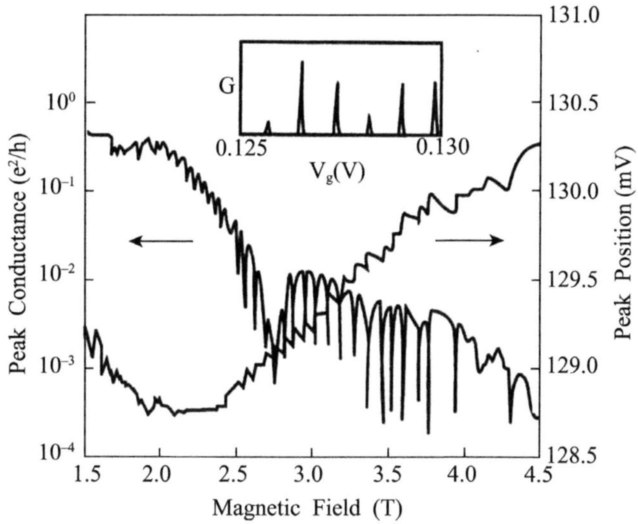

Figure 6.15 Amplitude and position of a conductance peak as a function of magnetic field at $T = 0.1$ K. Inset: Conductance versus V_g for the device at $\mathbf{B} = 3$ T.

consists of a periodic series of sharp peaks, but the amplitudes are much smaller than those in the absence of a magnetic field. The full scale of the ordinate is 0.03 e^2/h. The amplitude and position of a particular conductance peak as a function of magnetic field for $\mathbf{B} = 1.5 - 4.5$ T is shown in Fig. 6.15. The amplitude oscillates periodically with the magnetic field and drops by as much as orders of magnitude. Commensurate with these dips, oscillations are observed in the position of the peak. This structure washes out rapidly with an increasing temperature and is almost entirely destroyed by $T \approx 0.3$ K.

The conductance oscillation in the inset of Fig. 6.15 can be explained by the standard CB model (see Fig. 6.9). The gate voltage corresponding to a conductance peak is given from Eq. 6.2,

$$V_g(N) = \frac{\mu_d(N) - \mu}{ae} = \left(\frac{1}{ae}\right)\left[\left(N - \frac{1}{2}\right)U + (E_N - \mu)\right] + \text{const}, \tag{6.4}$$

where $U = e^2/C$ is the electron Coulomb energy, μ is the chemical potential in the leads, and a is a dimensionless constant, which can be determined from the temperature dependence of the width of a conductance peak and is found to be 0.4 for this device. Therefore, the position of a conductance peak is determined mainly by the Coulomb term $(N - 1/2)U$ and the single-particle term E_N-μ. The Coulomb energy does not vary with the magnetic field, so the variation of the position of the peak shown in Fig. 6.15 results from variation in E_N.

The single-particle energy levels as a function of magnetic field is shown in Fig. 6.14b, which consists of two Landau levels (LLs). Due to the confinement potential of the dot the LLs are composed of discrete nondegenerate states. States in the first LL fall in energy with increasing B, while those in the second LL rise. The electron alternately occupies a state in the first LL and a state in the second LL as the magnetic field is increased, as shown by the dark line in Fig. 6.14b. Consequently, the position of the N-th peak oscillates.

At a particular B, if the N-th single-particle state is in the first LL (the outer-edge state shown in Fig. 6.14a), it couples well to the leads and transport can occur by resonant tunneling through this state. If the N-th state is in the second LL (the inner-edge state), the coupling to the lead is weak and the peak amplitude is suppressed. A dip in amplitude is thus expected whenever the N-th state is in the second LL, that is, when the position of the peak is moving up in energy. The dip in conductance disappears when $k_B T$ becomes comparable to the single-particle level spacing in the first LL, since transport can then occur by thermal activation to the nearest energy state in the first LL.

The above discussion has not taken into account electron spin. Experiments found that the difference between an even- and odd-numbered finite fermion system, known as the even-odd parity effect, is a distinct feature reflecting the unique behavior of fermions in the presence of both orbital and spin degrees of freedom. The peak spacing fluctuation in CB peaks provides unique information about single-particle energy level, many-body interaction effect, and the parity of electron numbers. To study the parity effect of the CB peaks, Chang et al. fabricated a quantum dot of a small diameter (lithographic diameter 160 nm), as shown in Fig. 6.16a [6], which contains the number of electrons $N \approx 10$, made from a crystal of

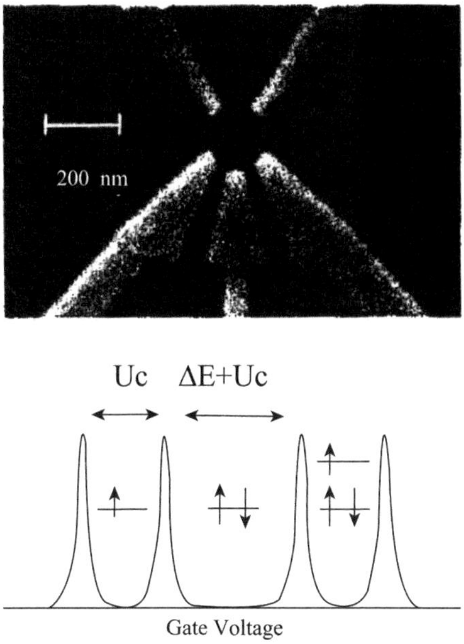

Figure 6.16 Scanning electron micrograph of a small-scale device (top). Schematic diagram of the peak positions as a function of gate voltage (bottom).

density $n = 3.5 \times 10^{11}$ cm^{-2}. According to the interaction model, the spacing between conductance peaks should be

$$\Delta V_g = \frac{C}{eC_g}\left(\Delta E + \frac{e^2}{C}\right), \tag{6.5}$$

where ΔE is the interaction energy of an even number of particles. The theoretical conductance versus the V_g curve will be shown as Fig. 6.16 (bottom).

Figure 6.17 shows the fluctuation of peak spacing in device 2 for a strong coupling case (a) and a weak coupling case (b) at $T = 75$ mK [6]. The lithographic diameter of device 2 is 230 nm, which contains about 50 electrons, with the electron density 3.5 $\times$ 10^{11} cm^{-2} ($r_s = 0.93$). For the strong coupling case (Fig. 6.17a) the peak pairing is observable obviously. The spacing of 2, 4, 6, 8, ... is larger than that of 1, 3, 5, 7, ... Moreover, peak height pairing is also visible over several peaks. On the other hand, for

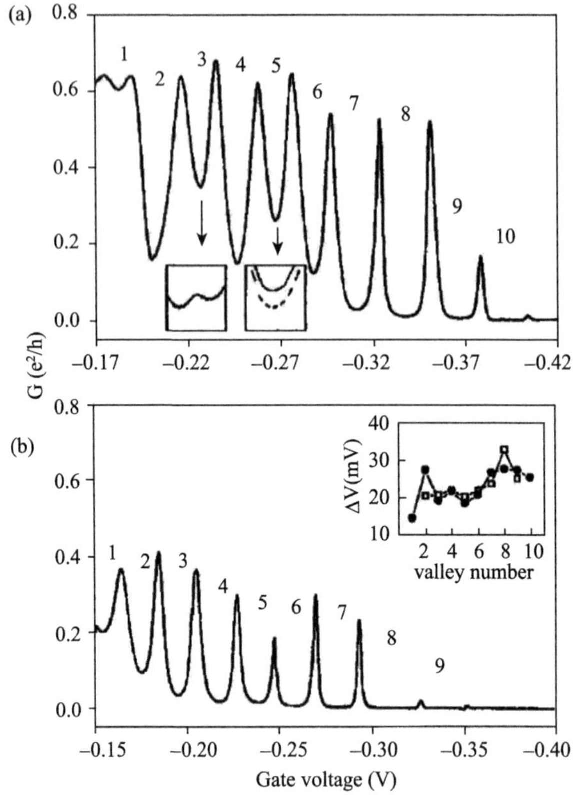

Figure 6.17 Fluctuation of peak spacing in device 2 in the case of strong coupling to the leads (a) and in the case of weak coupling (b) at $T = 75$ mK. Inset in (b): Spacing of conductance peaks as a function of order number of valleys; solid circles for the case of strong coupling and empty squares for weak coupling.

the weak case (Fig. 6.17b) the peak pairing behavior is not as obvious as that for device 2. The difference in behavior is believed to be a consequence of the modulation in the electron–electron interaction due to the difference of coupling strengths in two cases and suggests that strong Coulomb interaction plays an important role in deciding the peak spacing fluctuation. The inset in Fig. 6.17a shows several features of the Kondo effect. The Kondo valley shows the characteristic of unpaired electrons.

6.3 Kondo Effect in Quantum Dot Transport

In the preceding section it was found that the spacing of conductance peaks for even and odd numbers of electrons is non-equal (see Fig. 6.17). This behavior can be explained by Eq. 6.5. Experiments found further that when the temperature descends to very low the conductance valley of the odd number of electrons rises with a decreasing temperature, approaching the limiting value $2e^2/h$. This behavior cannot be explained by the single-electron energy and the Coulomb energy (Eq. 6.5).

In 1964 Kondo explained the anomalous temperature dependence of the resistance of metal. When the temperature is decreased, the resistance of a pure metal decreases, and at a certain temperature it is saturated. The temperature dependence changes considerably when a small concentration of magnetic atoms, such as cobalt, is added to the metal. Rather than getting saturated at a low temperature, the resistance increases as the temperature is lowered further, as shown in Fig. 6.18, where the solid line is for the pure metal and the dotted line is for the doped metal. Because in 1964 Kondo provided a theoretical explanation, since

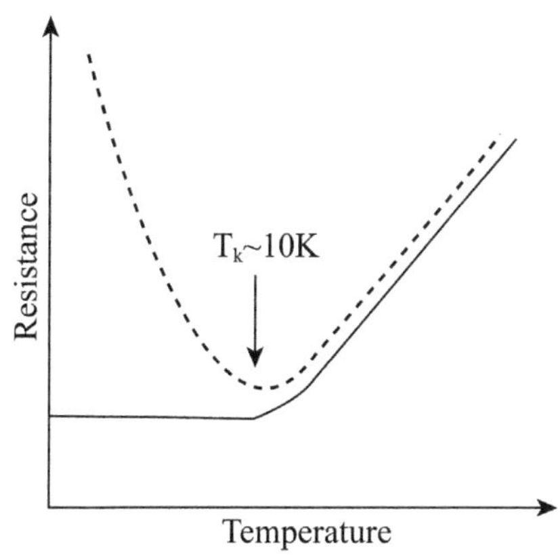

Figure 6.18 Schematic temperature dependence of the resistance of a pure metal (solid line) and metal with a small concentration of magnetic impurity atoms (dashed line). The latter curve shows a minimum around the Kondo temperature.

then the phenomenon has been referred to as the Kondo effect, and the turning temperature ($\sim$10 K) in Fig. 6.18 is called the Kondo temperature.

When the temperature is lower than T_K, the mobile electrons in the host metal tend to screen the non-zero total spin of the electrons in the magnetic impurity atom. In the simplest Anderson model of a magnetic impurity, there is only one electron level with energy ε_0 and the impurity spin is 1/2. The exchange processes can effectively flip the impurity spin while simultaneously creating a spin excitation in the Fermi sea. When many such processes are added coherently, a new state—the Kondo resonance—is generated with the same energy as the Fermi level. Such resonance is very effective at scattering electrons with energies close to the Fermi level. The strong scattering contributes greatly to the resistance. The whole system, that is, the magnetic impurity atom plus its surrounding electrons, forms a spin singlet. The energy scale for this singlet state is the Kondo temperature.

A quantum dot connected to source and drain leads can nicely mimic the above situation of a localized spin impurity in a Fermi sea. Therefore, the Kondo effect was expected to occur in quantum dot systems as well. However, there is an important difference between metal and quantum dot systems. In a metal, electrons are described by plane wave functions. Scattering from impurities mixed electron waves with different momentums. The momentum transfer increases the resistance. In a quantum dot, on the contrary, all the electrons have to travel through the device as there is no electrical path around it. In this case, the Kondo resonance makes it easier for states belonging to a bulk metal. Figure 6.19 shows the Anderson model of a magnetic impurity, applied to a single-level quantum dot connected to source and drain leads [7]. The level has an energy ε_0 below the Fermi energy of the leads and is initially occupied by one spin-up electron (leftmost diagram of Fig. 6.19). Adding another electron is prohibited by the charging energy E_C. By virtue of quantum uncertainty, the spin-up electron can momentarily tunnel out of the dot, leaving the dot-lead system in a classically forbidden virtual state (middle diagram of Fig. 6.19). If the spin-up electron is replaced by a spin-down electron from the leads (rightmost diagram of Fig. 6.19), the dot spin has effectively

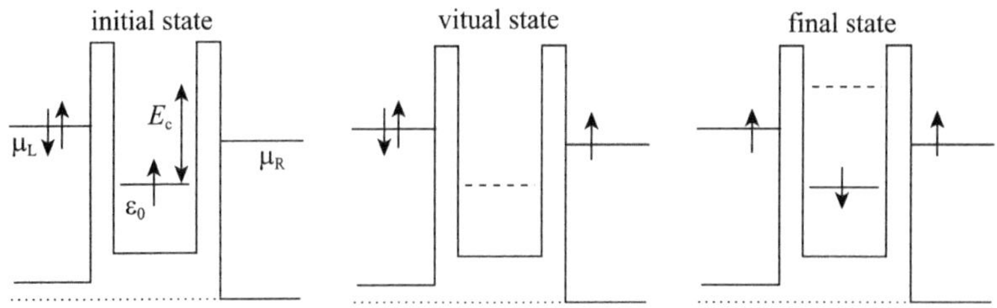

Figure 6.19 The Anderson model of a magnetic impurity, applied to a single-level quantum dot connected to source and drain leads.

been flipped. Many such events combine to produce the Kondo effect in quantum dots, which leads to the formation of an extra resonance at the Fermi level of the leads.

When the energy level ε_0 is occupied by two electrons, the total spin is zero, the virtual state does not exist, and thus there is no spin exchange interaction, that is, no resonant tunneling caused by the Kondo state. Only when the E_C is lowered to the Fermi level of the lead can conductance occur. The conductance as a function of the gate voltage V_g is shown in Fig. 6.20 [7], where the solid curve is for $T \ll T_K$, the dotted curve for $T \approx T_K$, and the dashed curve for $T < T_K$. Although the dot has two tunnel barriers and the charging energy tends to block electrons from tunneling into or out of it, the Kondo effect ensures that electrons are transmitted perfectly through the dot. The Kondo effect only occurs for odd electron numbers, resulting in the odd-even asymmetry between the different Coulomb valleys. Figure 6.20b shows that in the Kondo valleys conductance increases logarithmically with a lowering temperature, getting saturated at $2e^2/h$. Figure 6.20c shows that the Kondo resonance leads to a zero-bias resonance in the differential conductance, dI/dV, versus the bias voltage V.

Haldane [8] derived the Kondo temperature using the parameters of the Anderson model,

$$T_K = \frac{\sqrt{\Gamma E_C}}{2} e^{\pi \varepsilon_0 (\varepsilon_0 + E_C)/\Gamma E_C}, \tag{6.6}$$

where Γ is the width of the dot level, which is broadened by electrons tunneling to and from it. So the parameters that characterize the single-level dot system—E_C, ε_0, and Γ—can be replaced by a single energy scale, T_K. The advantage of quantum dots

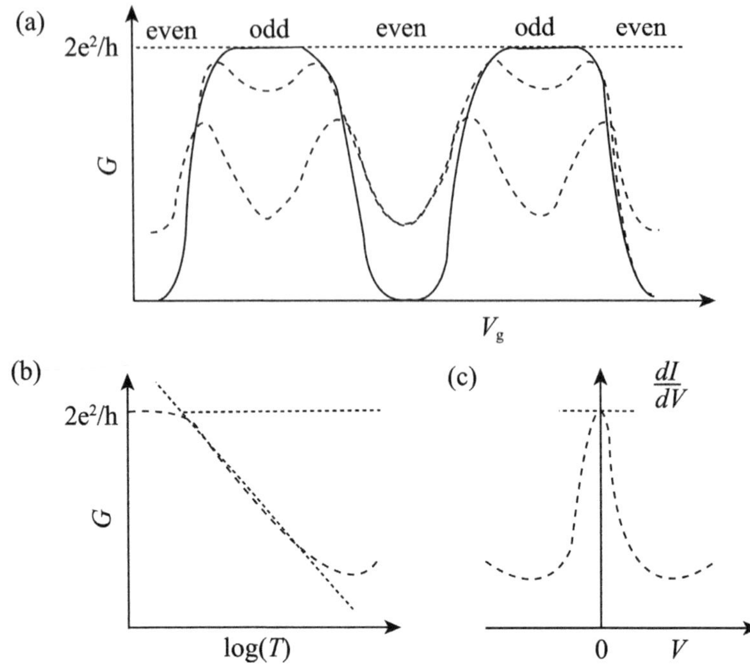

Figure 6.20 (a) Conductance as a function of the gate voltage V_g, where the solid curve is for $T \ll T_K$, the dotted curve for $T \approx T_K$, and the dashed curve for $T < T_K$. (b) In the Kondo valley G as a function of $\log(T)$. (c) Differential conductance dI/dV versus bias voltage V.

in studying the Kondo effect is that the parameters that determine the Kondo temperature can be easily changed by adjusting the voltages on the gates.

As shown in Fig. 6.20b in the Kondo valleys conductance increases logarithmically with a lowering temperature, getting saturated at $2e^2/h$, which is called "unitary limit" of conductance. Van der Wiel et al. [9] first observed experimentally the Kondo effect of the quantum dot in the unitary limit, that is, the CB for electron tunneling is overcome completely by the Kondo effect.

In Fig. 6.21a [9] an AB ring is defined in a 2DEG; in both arms of the ring a quantum dot can be defined by applying negative voltages to the gate electrodes. A quantum dot of size $\sim 200 \times 200$ nm, containing ~ 100 electrons, is formed in the lower arm using gate

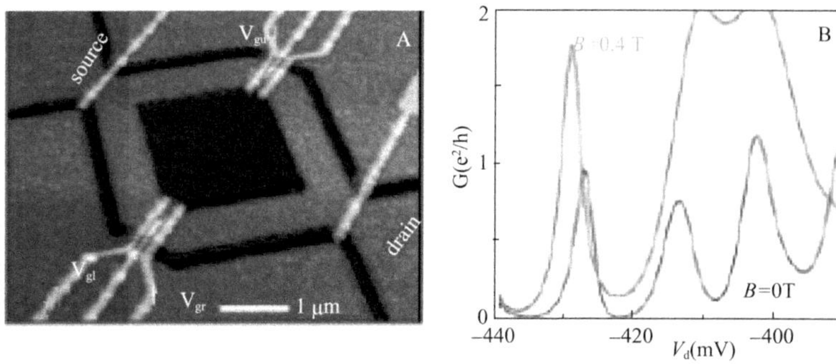

Figure 6.21 (a) Device structure diagram. (b) G as a function of V_{gl} for $B = 0$ T and 0.4 T at $T = 15$ mK.

voltages V_{gl} and V_{gr}. The gate voltage of the upper arm V_{gu} is kept at zero. The energy-level spacing of a single electron in the dot is about 100 μeV. Figure 6.21b shows G as a function of the left gate voltage. The right gate voltage is fixed at $V_{gr} = -488$ meV. At $B = 0$ regular Coulomb oscillations are observed with low valley conductance, while in the magnetic field the valley conductance increases considerably and can even reach $2e^2/h$. The pronounced peak reflects the Kondo resonance at the Fermi energy at the unitary limit.

More detailed results are shown in Fig. 6.22 [9]. Figure 6.22a shows Coulomb oscillations for different temperatures. At the base temperature, the valley $V_{gl} = -413$ and -372 mV reach the maximum possible conductance value of $2e^2/h$. When the temperature is increased, two separate Coulomb peaks develop with growing peak spacing. The conductance in the center of the valley has a logarithmic T dependence with a saturation at $2e^2/h$ for a low T. Figure 6.22b shows the differential conductance for different T values in the middle of the Kondo plateau at $2e^2/h$. The pronounced peak around $V_{SD} = 0$ reflects the Kondo resonance at the Fermi energy. The peak height has the same T dependence as shown in Fig. 6.22a, right inset. The width of the peak increases linearly with temperature (Fig. 6.22b, inset).

Last we return to the effect of a magnetic field. Experiments found near $\mathbf{B} = 0$, regular Coulomb oscillations are observed, but the Kondo effect typically changes the valley conductance by only

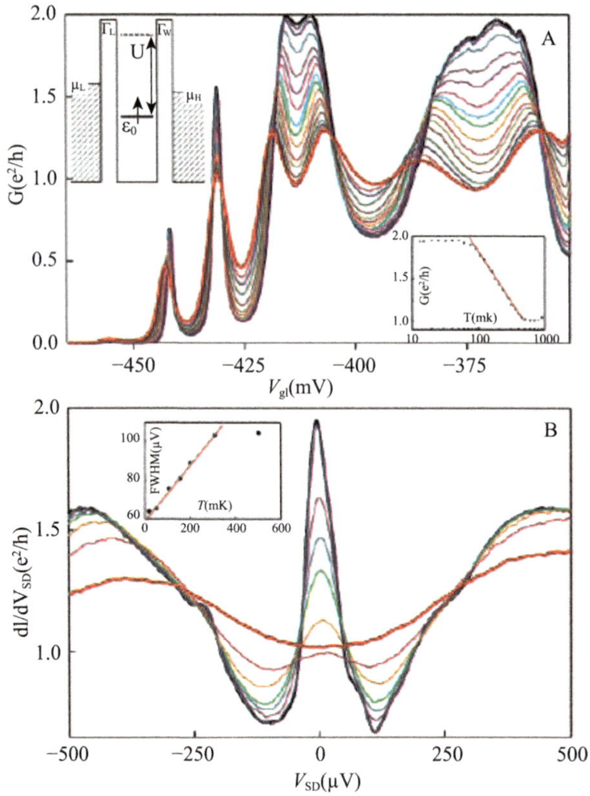

Figure 6.22 (a) Coulomb oscillations in G versus V_{gl} at $B = 0.4$ T for different temperatures. T ranges from 15 mK (thick black trace) to 800 mK (thick red trace). V_{gr} is fixed at -448 mV. The right inset shows the logarithmic T dependence between $\sim$90 and $\sim$500 mK for $V_{gl} = -413$ mV. (b) Differential conductance dI/dV_{SD} versus dc bias voltage between source and drain contacts V_{SD} for T ranging from 15 mK up to 900 mK. The inset shows that the width of the zero-bias peak measured from the FWHM increases linearly with T.

$\sim$20%. A big change occurs at $B \approx 0.1$ T, reflecting the onset of a different transport regime, an observation that seems common for half-open quantum dots. The magnetic scale corresponds to adding a flux quantum to the area of the dot, implying that time-reversal symmetry is broken.

6.4 Single-Electron Transport in Vertical Quantum Dots

Apart from the quantum dot defined on the 2DEG by the gate voltage, there is another kind of quantum dot—the three-dimensional (3D) quantum dot fabricated by the lithography technology, which has a well-defined confinement potential. Such a quantum dot can be regarded as an artificial atom. Associated with the rotational symmetry, as well as the parabolicity in the in-plane 2D harmonic confinement potential, atom-like properties such as shell-filling and abidance of Hund's first rule are all observed. Furthermore, this allows us to discuss the way of spin-filling for a given characteristic of the quantum state. When the single-particle states in the dot are separated by a large energy ΔE, an antiparallel spin-filling, forming a singlet state, is favored. For a small ΔE, parallel filling, forming a triplet state, is observed, which is in line with Hund's first rule. The magnetic field B can be used to tune $\Delta E(B)$; this allow us to alter the way of spin-filling.

6.4.1 Quantum Dot and Single-Electron Energy Levels

The schematic diagram of the device is shown in Fig. 6.23 [10]. The vertical quantum dot is fabricated by a double-barrier structure (DBS), which consists of an undoped 12 nm $In_{0.05}Ga_{0.95}As$ well and two undoped $Al_{0.22}Ga_{0.78}As$ barriers of thicknesses 9.0 and 7.5 nm, respectively. This is processed to form a circular mesa with a nominal top-contact diameter D of 0.54 μm. Figure 6.23b shows typical scanning electron micrographs of a circular mesa and a rectangular mesa. The dot is strongly confined in the vertical direction by the heterostructures, whereas it is softly confined in the lateral direction by the Schottky-gate-induced depletion region. This depletion region is well approximately by a harmonic potential, and the characteristic energy $\hbar\omega_0$ is evaluated from measurements of the magnetic field dependence of the Coulomb oscillations. The values of $\hbar\omega_0$ obtained for various numbers of electrons in the dot are shown in Fig. 6.23c. The effective lateral confinement becomes weak as the number of electrons in the dot increases, due to the effect of Coulomb screening.

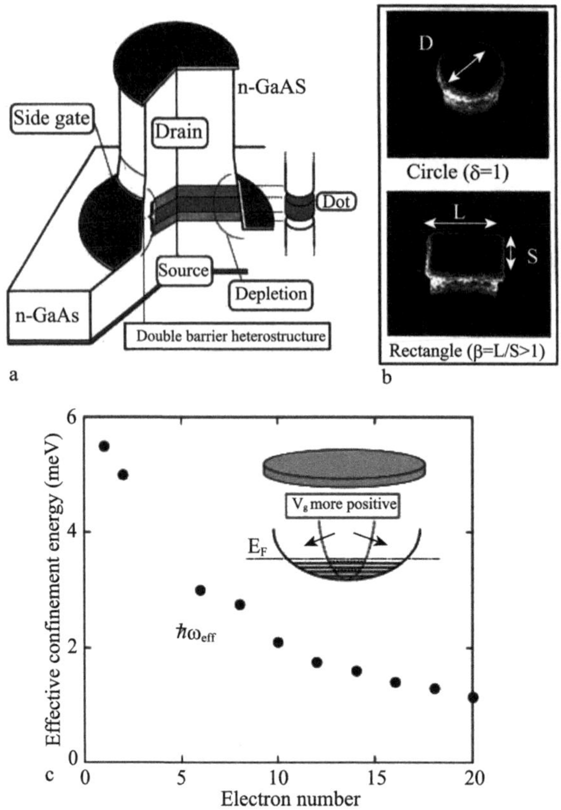

Figure 6.23 (a) Schematic diagram of the device. (b) Scanning electron micrographs of a circular mesa and a rectangular mesa. (c) Values of $\hbar\omega_0$ as a function of number of electrons in the dot.

The eigenstates for a 2D harmonic quantum dot in the perpendicular magnetic field are the Fock–Darwin states, and their energies are expressed by

$$E_{n,l} = -\frac{l}{2}\hbar\omega_0 + \left(n + \frac{1}{2} + \frac{1}{2}|l|\right)\hbar\sqrt{4\omega_0^2 + \omega_c^2}, \qquad (6.7)$$

where n and l are the radial quantum number and angular momentum quantum number, respectively, and $\hbar\omega_c = eB/m^*$ is the cyclotron energy.

6.4.2 Shell Filling and Hund's First Rule

The Coulomb oscillations in the current versus gate voltage at $B = 0$ T for a $D = 0.5$ μm dot is shown in Fig. 6.24a, and Fig. 6.24b shows the addition energy versus electron number for two different dots with $D = 0.5$ and 0.44 μm [11]. This series of current peaks is caused by electrons filling in the dot from $N = 1$, but the spacing between peaks is not equal, differing from that on the 2DEG.

From Eq. 6.7, when $\omega_c = 0$,

$$E_{n,l} = (2n + 1 + |l|)\,\hbar\omega_0. \tag{6.8}$$

Thus, according to the energy the electron energy level forms various shells: $(n, l) = (0, 0)$, $\hbar\omega_0$; $(0, \pm 1)$, $2\hbar\omega_0$; $(1, 0)$, $(0, \pm 2)$, $3\hbar\omega_0$.... Each orbital state fills two electrons, then the first three shells fill 2, 4, and 6 electrons. The current peak spacing in Fig. 6.24a is caused by Coulomb energy and also by the energy-level spacing $\hbar\omega_0$. Thus the spacing of current peaks after 2, 6, and 12 electrons is larger than others. This is also reflected in Fig. 6.24b, which shows the addition energy as a function of electron number for two dots.

The electronic states are expected to be significantly modified by a magnetic field B perpendicular to the dot. The B dependence on the position of the current oscillations is shown in Fig. 6.25 for B increasing from 0 to 3.5 T in steps of 0.05 T [11]. The positions of first three peaks depend monotonously on B, whereas the other peaks oscillate back and forth a number of times. The number of wiggles increases with N. A close inspection of the figure reveals that the current peaks generally shift in pairs with B. This even-odd effect persists up to $N = 40$.

For the simplest explanation of the magic number and the B dependence we ignore, for the moment, the Coulomb interaction. The magnetic energy spectrum is given in Eq. 6.7. At $B = 0$, E_{nl} has degenerate sets of states, which are separated by $\hbar\omega_0$ from each other and are completely filled by $N = 2$, 6, 12, 20, etc., as shown in Fig. 6.24. When B increases the original degenerate states split into a series of singlet states. The rearrangement of the pairing can be understood in terms of Hund's rule. Hund's rule favors the filling of electrons with spin-up and spin-down in a singlet state, decreasing the interaction energy. The detailed discussion can be seen in Refs. [10] and [11].

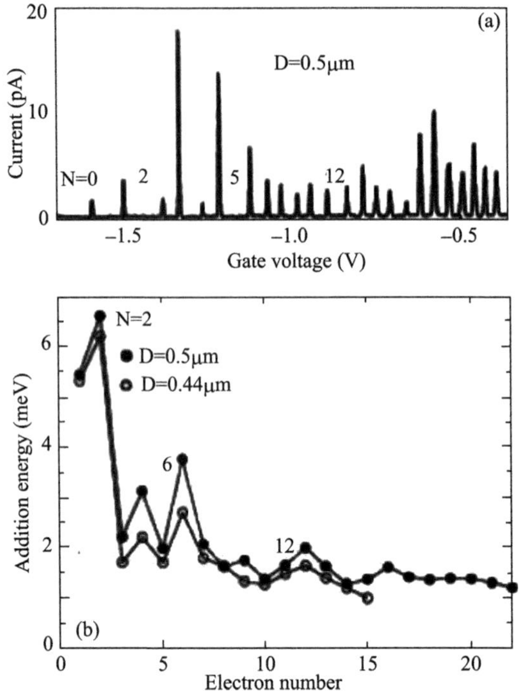

Figure 6.24 (a) Coulomb oscillations in the current versus gate voltage at $\mathbf{B} = 0$ T for a $D = 0.5$ μm dot. (b) Addition energy versus electron number for two different dots with $D = 0.5$ and 0.44 μm.

6.4.3 Single-Electron Tunneling Spectrum in the Magnetic Field

Below we introduce the elastic tunneling between two vertical coupled quantum dots [12]. The vertical double quantum dot device is like that shown in Fig. 6.23, but is made from a triple barrier heterostructure (TBS) and is located in a cylinder mesa whose diameter is 0.6 μm.

By appropriately tuning both V_G and the source-drain voltage V_S one can obtain configurations as shown in Fig. 6.26 [12]. The lowest $(n,l) = (0,0)$ orbital state of the left dot is aligned with the Fermi level of the left reservoir (source), and the lowest orbital state of the right dot is always located below the lowest orbital state of the left dot, and above the Fermi level of the right reservoir (drain). In

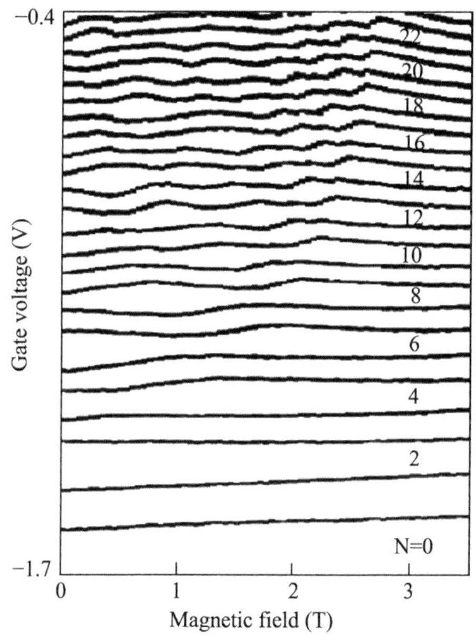

Figure 6.25 Gate voltage positions of the current oscillations versus magnetic field for a dot with $D = 0.5$ μm.

such a configuration, due to the CB in each dot, as well as inter-dot electrostatic interactions, the left dot acts as a "turnstile" so that the electron number in the right dot is always zero or one, no matter how large the source-drain voltages are. When the source-drain voltage is turned in such a way that a higher orbital (n,l) state in the right dot is aligned with the left (0,0) state in the left dot, elastic tunneling gives rise to a peak of current. This "inter-dot tunneling spectroscopy" enables us to demonstrate the single-particle nature of electronic states in the right dot.

The positions of the current peaks changing with magnetic field B are plotted in Fig. 6.27a [12]. The positions agree well with the dependence of the calculated Fock–Darwin states $E_{n,l}$ after subtracting $E_{0,0}$, that is, the B dependence of the orbital states of the right dot. Thus we can label (n,l) for each current peak by comparison with the Fock–Darwin diagram. The peak heights measured 30 mV above in V_G from the threshold line are plotted in Fig. 6.27c. It is clear that the current peak is significantly smaller

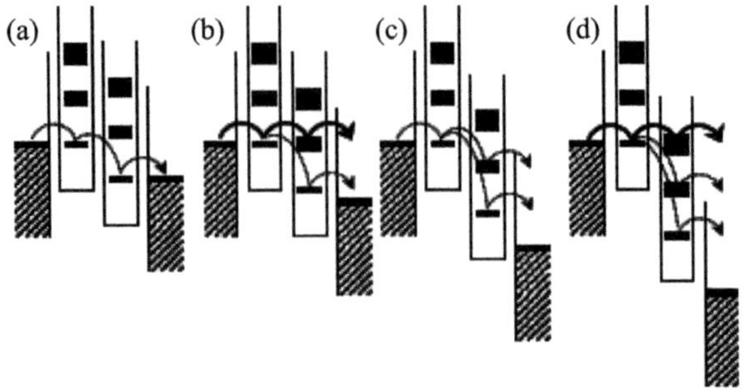

Figure 6.26 Potential landscape for the double quantum dot structure at various source-drain voltages. The horizontal lines in each dot represents single-particle energy levels at zero magnetic field. Solid (dotted) arrows indicate elastic (inelastic) three-step sequential tunneling processes via two 0D states.

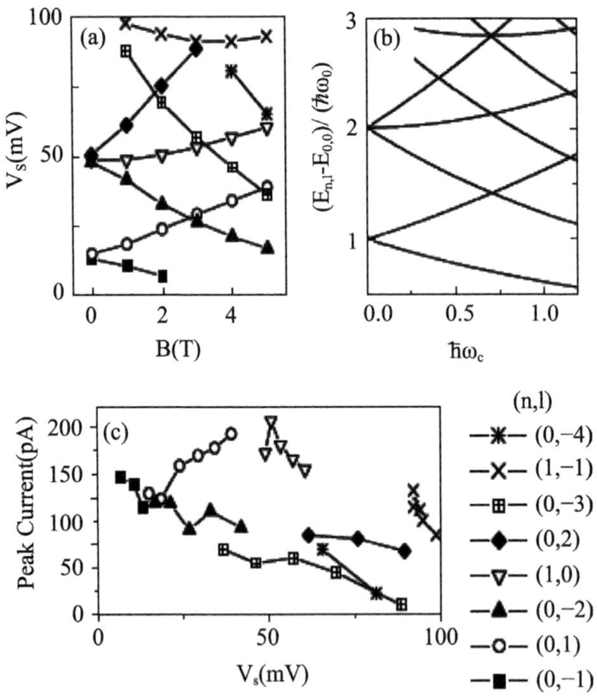

Figure 6.27 (a) Experimental data showing the positions in V_S on the varies current peaks. (b) Theoretically calculated Fock–Darwin states. (c) Heights of the current peaks shown in (a).

when the peak is associated with a higher angular momentum state. This demonstrates the existence of angular momentum selectivity for the electron inter-dot tunneling between the (0,0) state of the left dot and the higher orbital state of the right dot. The tunneling probability between the (0,0) state and the higher orbital states is small but not zero. For explanation of this, the authors proposed an incoherent sequential tunneling model; the tunneling probability is proportional to the product of the "local density of state,"

$$T \propto \int dxdy|\psi_{0,0}(x, y)|^2|\psi_{n,l}(x, y)|^2. \qquad (6.9)$$

The transmission becomes small (but are non-zero) when the angular momentum of $\psi_{n,l}$ is large.

6.4.4 Spin Blockade Effect

Except the CB effect, one also observed the spin blockade effect caused by the Pauli exclusion principle, which prevents two electrons of parallel spin from occupying a single spatial orbital. Ono et al. [13] found that the Pauli effect, in combination with the CB, can be used to block current altogether in one direction while permitting it to flow in the opposite direction, thereby realizing a fully controllable spin-Coulomb rectifier.

The schematic of the double-dot device is shown in Fig. 6.28b, and the electron transport in the forward bias (upper) and backward bias (down) is shown in Fig. 6.28a [13]. Suppose there are two sites, site 1 and site 2, weakly coupled together and one electron is permanently localized on site 2. Now consider the transport of a second electron through the system between two contact leads. The number of electrons on site 1 (or site 2), $N1$ ($N2$), varies between 0 and 1 (1 and 2). Crucially, the spin effect also markedly influences electron transport. Because the tunnel coupling between the two sites is sufficiently weak, the ($N1$,$N2$) $=$ (1,1) spin singlet and spin triplet are practically degenerate. For ($N1$,$N2$) $=$ (0,2), only a spin singlet is permitted because of Pauli exclusion. Therefore, electron transport is only allowed for a channel made from the (1,1) and (0,2) singlet states. For a forward bias, either the (1,1) singlet or triplet can be populated with the same probability by injection of an electron onto site 1 from the left lead. If the (1,1) singlet is populated,

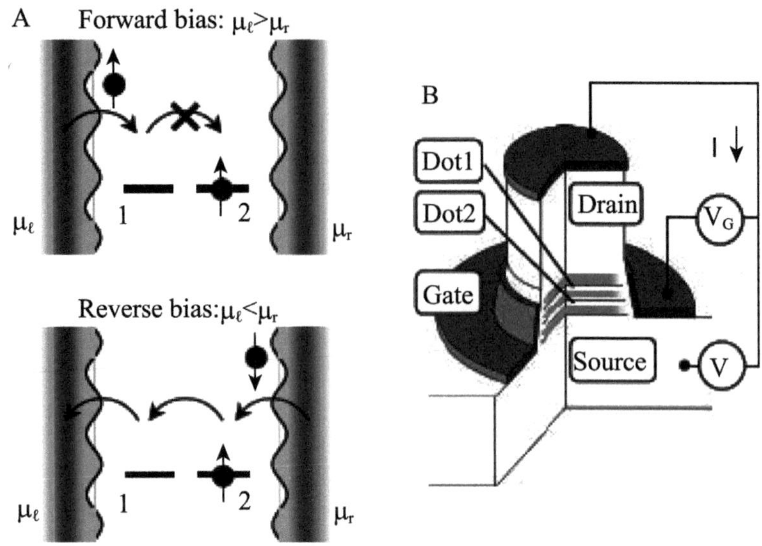

Figure 6.28 (b) Schematic of the double-dot device. (a) Electron transport in the forward bias (upper) and backward bias (down).

a single-electron tunneling current can flow through the singlet state. Once the triplet is populated, however, subsequent electron transfer from site 1 to 2 is blockaded by Pauli exclusion. Note that an electron arriving on site 1 usually cannot go back to the left lead because of the fast relaxation of the hole state left behind the lead. Thus the (1,1) triplet will sooner or later be occupied on a time scale sufficiently longer than the electron tunneling time between the leads and this should lead to clear current suppression. Because this blockade is due to spin and not charge, we hereafter refer to this process as a "spin blockade." On the other hand, for a reverse bias an antiparallel spin electron can always be injected onto site 2 from the right lead.

The differential conductance dI/dV and current I, flowing vertically through the two dots as a function of V_G and V, is shown in Fig. 6.29 [13]. V_G and V are used to change the electrostatic potential of the two dots together (number of electrons) and the potential offset between the two dots, respectively. In the lower-right inset

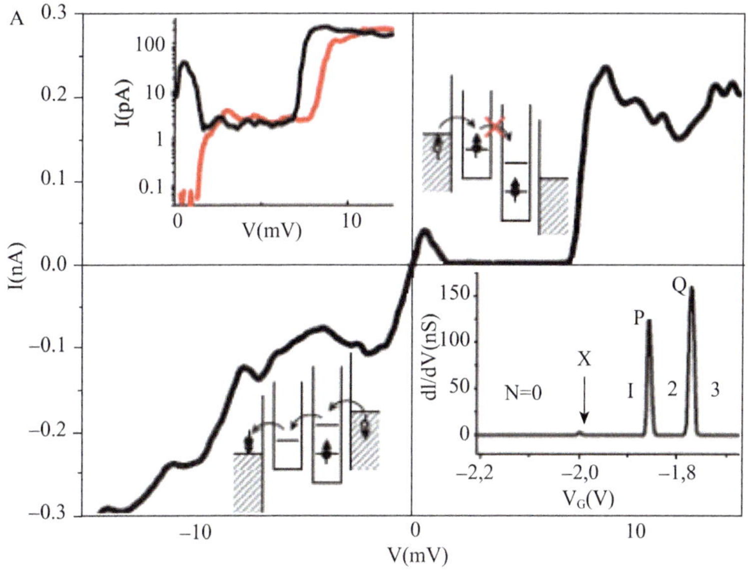

Figure 6.29 The differential conductance dI/dV and current I flowing vertically through the two dots as a function of V_G and V. Lower-right inset: $dI/dV \approx V_G$ measured for a small V ($\sim$0 V). Upper-left inset: magnified plots of I versus V for V_G fixed at peak P (black curve) and in the middle between the peaks P and Q (red curve) on a logarithmic scale.

$dI/dV \approx V_G$ measured for a small V ($\sim$0 V) shows clear Coulomb oscillation peaks. The second peak (P) and the third peak (Q) are much large. This implies that tunneling is elastic between the source and drain leads for $N = 1 \rightarrow 2$ and $2 \rightarrow 3$. For $|V| \geq 1$ mV, transport is nonlinear (see potential diagrams in the main diagram). The current is clearly suppressed in the forward bias because of a spin blockade, whereas a large current still flows in the reverse bias because of inelastic tunneling via the singlet states. The upper-left inset shows magnified plots of I versus V for V_G fixed at peak P (black curve) and in the middle between the peaks P and Q (red curve) on a logarithmic scale. Both curves show strong current suppression ($I \approx 2$ pA) due to the spin blockade. In the vicinity of $V = 0$ V, the red curve shows strong current suppression due to a CB.

6.4.5 Single-Electron Tunneling in Coupled Quantum Dots

Using the coupled quantum dots structure (e.g., Fig. 6.28b) the electron filling and the CB effects can also be studied by changing the gate voltage V_G. Figure 6.30a shows calculated addition energy spectra, $\Delta_2(N) = U(N + 1) - 2U(N) + U(N - 1)$ for different spacings between two dots b [14]. $U(N)$ is the total energy of the N-electron system, and $\Delta_2(N)$ can reveal a wealth of information about the energy required to place an extra electron into a quantum dot system. When b is small the coupled quantum dot is rather similar to a single quantum dot. At intermediate dot separation, the spectra pattern becomes more complex. However, at a larger inter-dot distance, a simple picture emerges that the coupled quantum dot is about to dissociate. For example, at $b = 7.2$ nm a strong peak at $N = 2$, 4, and 12 and a weaker peak at $N = 8$ appear that can be easily interpreted from the peaks appearing in the single quantum dot spectrum. The peaks at $N = 4$ and 12 are a consequence of symmetric dissociation into two closed shells $N = 2$ and 6 of quantum dots, respectively, whereas the peak at $N = 8$ corresponds to the dissociation into two identical stable quantum dots holding four electrons each, filled according to Hund's rule to give maximal spin. The peak at $N = 2$ is related to the localization of one electron on each constituent dot, the two-electron state being a spin-singlet configuration.

Due to the difficulty in fabricating two perfectly identical constituent quantum dots in the coupled quantum dot, the experimental spectra (Fig. 6.30b) are different from those of theoretical spectra. (i) The spectrum for the most strongly coupled quantum dot ($b =$ 2.5 nm) resembles that of the quantum dot up to the third shell ($N = 12$). (ii) For intermediate coupling ($b = 3.2$ to 4.7 nm), the spectra are quite different from the quantum dot spectrum, and a fairly noticeable peak appears at $N = 8$. (iii) For weaker coupling ($b = 6.0$ and 7.5 nm) the spectra are different again, with prominent peaks at $N = 1$ and 3.

In calculation the authors took the well width $w = 12$ nm, the well depths $V_0 \pm d$, $V_0 = 225$ meV, $d = 0$ or a realistic

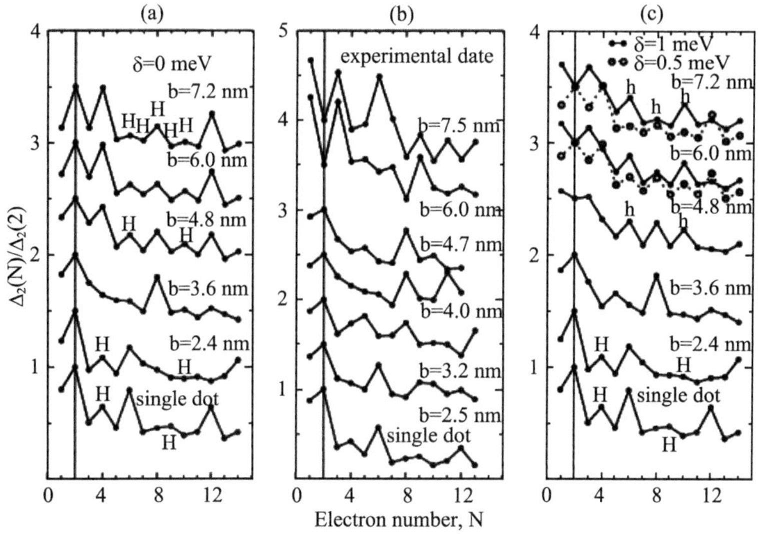

Figure 6.30 (a) Calculated $\Delta_2(N)/\Delta_2(2)$ for coupled QDs with different inter-dot distances b. Also shown is the calculated reference spectrum for a single QD. (b) Experimental $\Delta_2(N)/\Delta_2(2)$ for several inter-dot distances between 2.5 and 7.5 nm. (c) Same as panel (a), but for coupled QDs obtained using $\delta = 1$ or 0.5 meV.

value 0.5 or 1 meV. Taking into account this mismatch of well depth the authors confirmed the spectra character of the coupled quantum dot by performing the theoretical calculations with $\delta =$ 1 or 0.5 meV. The results are shown in Fig. 6.30c. The overall agreement between theory and experiment of the general spectral shape is quite good, indicating the crucial role played by a mismatch. In particular, the appearance of the spectra in the weak coupling limit for small N values is now correctly given, as well as the evolution with b of the peak appearing at $N = 8$ for intermediate coupling. A comparison between Figs. 6.30b and 6.30c reveals that for small values of b ($\leq$4.8 nm), for a reasonable choice of parameters (w, δ), a mismatch does not produce sizable effects.

References

1. Scott-Thomas, J. H. F., Field, S. B., Kastner, M. A., Smith, H. I., and Antoniadis, D. A. (1989). Conductance oscillations periodic in the density of a one-dimensional electron gas. *Phys. Rev. Lett.*, **62**, 583–586.
2. Meirav, U., Kastner, M. A., and Wind, S. J. (1990). Single-electron Charging and periodic conductance resonances in GaAs nanostructures. *Phys. Rev. Lett.*, **65**, 771–774.
3. Kouwenhoven, L. P., van der Varrt, N. C., Johnson, A. T., et al. (1991). Single electron charging effects in semiconductor quantum dots. *Z. Phys. B*, **85**, 367–373.
4. Kouwenhoven, L. P., Johnson, A. T., van der Vaart, N. C., et al. (1991). Quantized current in a quantum dot turnstile. *Z. Phys. B*, **85**, 381–388.
5. McEuen, P. L., Foxman, E. B., Meirav, U., Kastner, M. A., Meir, Y., and Wingreen, N. S. (1991). Transport spectroscopy of a Coulomb island in the quantum Hall regime. *Phys. Rev. Lett.*, **66**, 1926–1929.
6. Chang, A. M., Jeong, H., and Melloch, M. R. (2003). *Electron Transport in Quantum Dots*, ed. Bird, J. P., "Novel phenomena in small individual and coupled quantum dots" (Kluwer Academic Publishers, Boston/Dordrecht/London), pp. 123–157.
7. Tarucha, S., Ono, K., Fujisawa, T., van der Wiel, W. G., and Kouwenhoven, L. P. (2003). *Electron Transport in Quantum Dots*, ed. Bird, J. P., "Interactions, spins and the Kondo effect in quantum-dot systems" (Kluwer Academic Publishers, Boston/Dordrecht/London), pp. 1–42.
8. Haldane, F. D. M. (1978). Scaling theory of the asymmetric Anderson model. *Phys. Rev. Lett.*, **40**, 416–419.
9. van der Wiel, W. G., De Franceschi, S., Fujisawa, T., et al. (2000). The Kondo effect in the unitary limit. *Science*, **289**, 2105–2108.
10. Tarucha, S., Austing, D. G., Sasaki, S., Tokura, Y., van der Wiel, W., and Kouwenhoven, L. P. (2000). Effect of Coulomb interactions on spin states in vertical semiconductor quantum dots. *Appl. Phys. A*, **71**, 367–378.
11. Tarucha, S., Austing, D. G., Honda, T., van der Hage, R. J., and Kouwenhoven, L. P. (1996). Shell filling and spin effect in a few electron quantum dot. *Phys. Rev. Lett.*, **77**, 3613–3616.
12. Ono, K., Austing, D. G., Tokura, Y., and Tarucha, S. (2002). Angular momentum selectivity in tunneling between two quantum dots. *Physica B*, **314**, 450–454.

13. Ono, K., Austing, D. G., Tokura, Y., and Tarucha, S. (2002). Current rectification by Pauli exclusion in a weakly coupled double quantum dot system. *Science*, **297**, 1313–1317.

14. Pi, M., Emperador, A., Barranco, M., Garcias, F., et al. (2001). Dissociation of vertical semiconductor diatomic artificial molecules. *Phys. Rev. Lett.*, **87**, 066801(1–4).

Chapter 7

Silicon Single-Electron Transistor

The operation principle of the single-electron transistor (SET) is to control one electron through a very small quantum dot. The performance of the SET is enhanced with the decreasing scale of the quantum dot. Therefore, the quantum dot is generally smaller than 10 nm, very suitable to be high-density integrated. Meanwhile, the property of a single electron permits it to operate at ultra-low power because the power dissipated in the circuit is proportional to the number of participating electrons. SETs have a peculiar I–V characteristic, which is absent for a general MOSFET. All these properties make it possible for SETs to become high-performance circuits in a very small area.

At the early stage of single-electron transistor research the used materials are metals or compound semiconductors, mainly studying quantum dot physics. But considering the application of the SET, the most suitable material is silicon. Because Si SETs are compatible with general MOSFETs, it is easier to integrate a Si SET into the present very large scale integration (VLSI). Another convenience is that one can use the present mature microprocessing technology to fabricate a SET. Now the Si SET has been considered as one of the most suitable candidates of the unit device in future ultra-high density and ultra-low power VLSI.

Quantum Waveguide in Microcircuits
Jian-Bai Xia, Duan-Yang Liu, and Wei-Dong Sheng

ISBN 978-981-4669-85-6 (Hardcover), 978-1-315-36477-3 (eBook)
www.panstanford.com

7.1 Principle of a Single-Electron Transistor

Figure 7.1a is a schematic diagram of the equivalent circuit of a single-electron quantum dot [1]. The two leads of the dot are connected with the source and gate, and C_t and C_g are the tunneling capacitance and gate capacitance, respectively.

When an electron tunnels into the dot, the electrostatic energy (Coulomb energy) changes,

$$\Delta U = \frac{e^2}{2C_{dot}}, \tag{7.1}$$

where C_{dot} is the total capacity of the dot. If the dot is small enough, ΔU can be comparable with the thermal energy, even larger than it, thus only when the gate provides the extra energy can the electron tunnel into the dot. This is the Coulomb blockade (CB) effect, which is the foundation of the single-electron transistor (SET). A more detailed description of a SET is that the electrostatic energy of the system

$$U = \frac{Q_{dot}^2}{2C_{dot}} + \left(\frac{C_g}{C_{dot}}\right) Q_{dot} V_g + \text{const.}, \tag{7.2}$$

where $Q_{dot} = -N_{dot}e$ is the charge in the dot and C_g is the gate-dot capacitance. U can be rewritten as

$$U = \frac{\left(N_{dot}e - C_g V_g\right)^2}{2C_{dot}}. \tag{7.3}$$

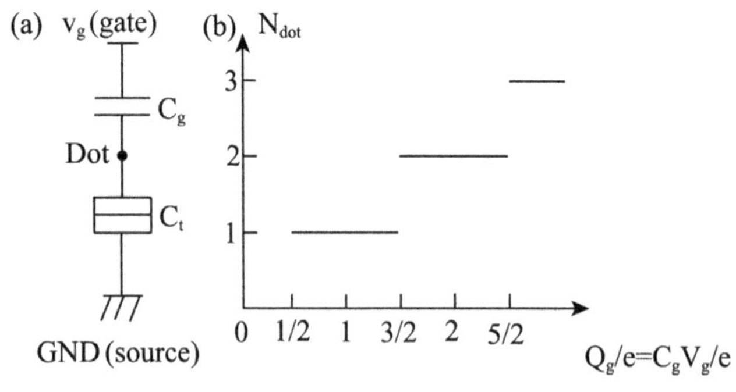

Figure 7.1 (a) Schematic diagram of the equivalent circuit of a single-electron quantum dot. (b) N_{dot} as a function of $Q_s = C_g V_g$ at $T = 0$ K.

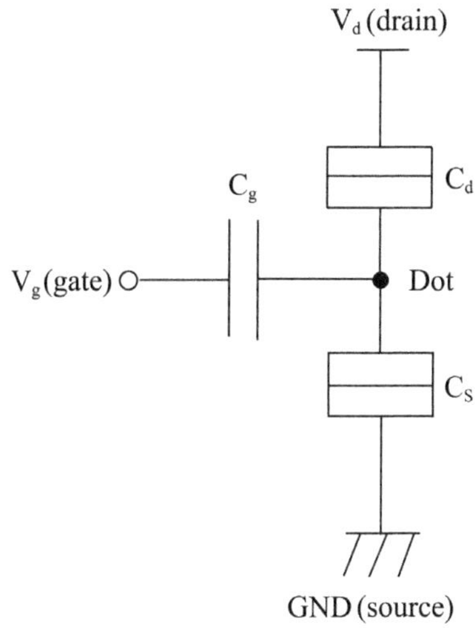

Figure 7.2 Equivalent circuit of the SET.

At $T = 0$ K, taking U as the minimum, one obtains N_{dot} as a function of V_g, as shown in Fig. 7.1b. When V_g increases by each e/C_g, N_{dot} increases one step. At a finite temperature, this step character becomes indistinct due to thermal fluctuation.

Figure 7.2 is the equivalent circuit diagram of a SET [1], where the dot is connected with the source and drain by the tunneling barriers C_s and C_d, respectively. Meantime, it is connected with the gate by the capacitively coupling, so it becomes a three-terminal device similar to the metal-oxide semiconductor field-effect transistor (MOSFET). Different from the single-electron quantum dot shown in Fig. 7.1a, in a SET there is current flowing from the source to the drain under the control of the gate.

The total energy of the N electrons in the dot is

$$E(N) = U(N) + \sum_{k=1}^{N} \varepsilon_k = \frac{\left(Ne - C_g V_g - C_d V_{ds}\right)^2}{2C_{\text{dot}}} + \sum_{k=1}^{N} \varepsilon_k, \quad (7.4)$$

where C_d is the source-dot capacitance, V_{ds} is the source-drain voltage, and ε_k is the k-th quantum level of the quantum dot. The

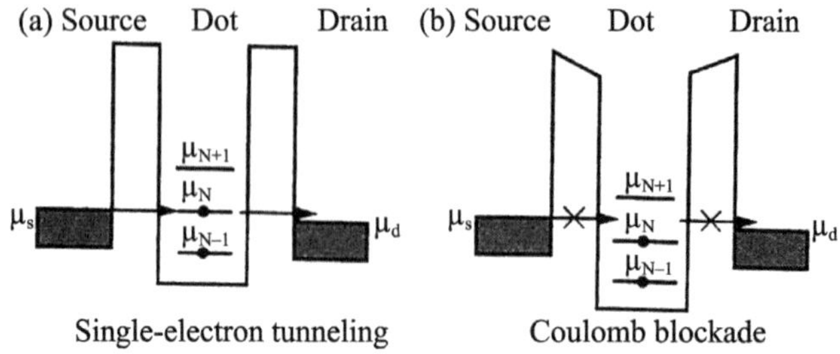

Figure 7.3 Conduction band potential energy diagram of the SET. (a) Condition for single-electron tunneling. (b) Condition for a Coulomb blockade.

chemical potential of the N-th electron in the quantum dot is

$$\mu_N = E(N) - E(N-1) = \frac{(2N-1)e^2 - 2eC_g V_g - 2eC_d V_{ds}}{2C_{dot}} + \varepsilon_N. \quad (7.5)$$

Figure 7.3 is the conduction band potential energy diagram of the SET [1]. When the chemical potential of the electron in the quantum dot satisfies

$$\mu_{N+1} > \mu_s \geq \mu_N \geq \mu_d > \mu_{N-1}, \quad (7.6)$$

the electron can enter the quantum dot from the source and then move out to the drain, as shown in Fig. 7.3a, where μ_s and μ_d are the chemical potential of the source and drain, respectively. Because only one electron can enter into and move out of the quantum dot, the transport is called single-electron tunneling. When V_g increases, so μ_N is lower than μ_d,

$$\mu_{N+1} > \mu_s \geq \mu_d > \mu_N, \quad (7.7)$$

the electron cannot tunnel into the dot and this case is called a CB. Thus the drain current oscillates with the gate voltage, as shown in Fig. 7.4 [4], where each peak represents the flowing of one electron.

Define the energy needed to increase an electron in the quantum dot as the single electron additional energy E_a,

$$E_a = \mu_N - \mu_{N-1} = \frac{e^2}{C_{dot}} + (\varepsilon_N - \varepsilon_{N-1}) = E_C + \Delta E, \quad (7.8)$$

where E_C is the Coulomb charge energy of a single electron and ΔE is the spacing of the quantum levels. When the potential energy

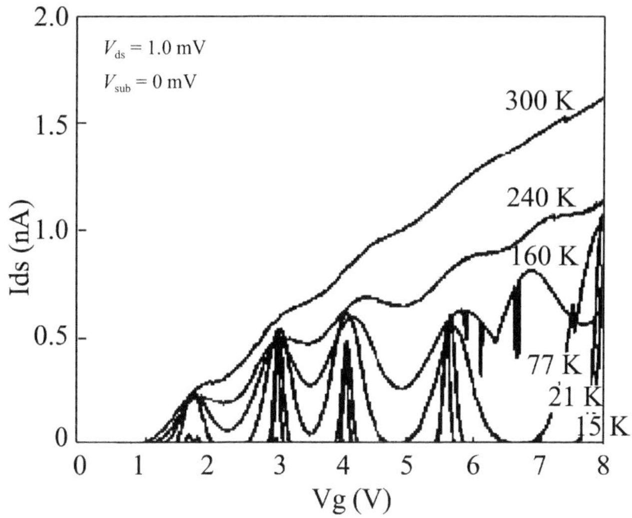

Figure 7.4 $I_d - V_g$ curves for $V_{ds} = 1.0$ mV; the temperature decreases from room temperature to 15 K.

of the quantum dot increases to E_a, it satisfies the single-electron-tunneling condition in Eq. (7.6). In the I–V curve (Fig. 7.4) the oscillation period is

$$\Delta V_g = \frac{E_a}{e\alpha} = \frac{C_{dot}}{eC_g}E_a = \frac{e}{C_g} + \frac{C_{dot}}{eC_g}\Delta E, \qquad (7.9)$$

where $\alpha = C_g/C_{dot}$ is a gain modulation factor, which changes the dot potential into V_g. When the dot is large enough, ΔE can be neglected compared with E_C and ΔV_g is approximately a constant; this case is called the Coulomb oscillation.

Figure 7.4 shows the $I_d - V_g$ curves for $V_{ds} = 1.0$ mV [4]. When V_g is fixed at the peak value of the Coulomb oscillation, I_d increases monotonously with an increasing V_{ds}, as shown in Fig. 7.5. When V_g is fixed at the CB regime, I_d keeps a low value as V_{ds} increases until V_{ds} is larger than a definite value so that μ_d is lower than μ_N; then I_d increases continuously with V_{ds}, as shown in Fig. 7.5.

Figure 7.6 shows the contour plot of I_d in a SET as a function of V_g and V_{ds} [1], which gives the whole picture of the CB characteristic. At a low V_{ds} along the V_g axis, there are a series of rhombus current blockade regimes (deep gray), called the CB regime or the Coulomb

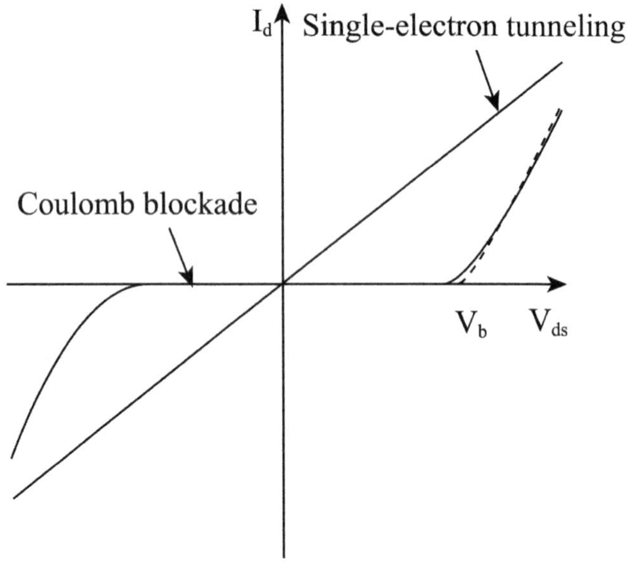

Figure 7.5 $I_d - V_{ds}$ characteristic curve of a SET under the single-electron-tunneling condition and the Coulomb blockade condition.

diamond. In each CB regime the number of electrons keeps an integer number. Between two neighboring CB regimes there exist light-gray regimes called single-electron-tunneling regimes. In each single-electron-tunneling regime the number of electrons jumps between $N - 1$ and N and the electron flows from the source to the drain, producing a tunneling current.

The slope of the boundary between the CB regime and the single-electron-tunneling regime reflects the difference of the influence of V_g and V_{ds} to the quantum dot potential; thus they are determined by the ratio of capacitances of the SET. The slope of the descending boundary of the diamond is C_g/C_d, and the slope of the raising boundary is $C_g/(C_g + C_s)$. The slope of the descending boundary corresponds to the voltage gain of the SET, which has an important influence on the performance of the SET circuit.

The operation of the SET has to meet two conditions; the first is that the Coulomb charging energy is much larger than the thermal energy,

$$E_a > 20 - 100\,k_B T. \tag{7.10}$$

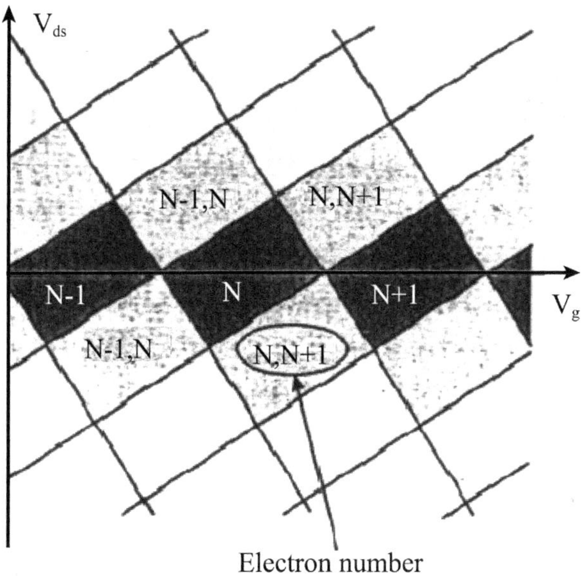

Figure 7.6 Contour plot of I_d in a SET as a function of V_g and V_{ds}.

If the temperature is not low enough, even in the case that the condition (7.6) does not satisfy, the thermally exited electron will tunnel through the quantum dot, resulting in closing of the neighboring CB peaks and increase of the valley current of the CB oscillation. Theoretically, the full width at half maximum (FWHM) of the CB peak is proportional to $k_B T/(\alpha e)$. While the spacing between gate voltages of peaks $\Delta V_g = E_a/(\alpha e)$, the ratio of ΔV_g and FWHM demonstrates the ratio of peak to valley of a CB oscillation $E_a/k_B T$. To increase the ratio of peak to valley the condition (Eq. 7.10) should be satisfied.

Figure 7.7 shows calculated E_a, E_C, and ΔE of a Si SET as a function of quantum dot size. The Si SET is a spherical Si quantum dot buried in the SiO^2 base [1]. From the figure we see that the room operation of the SET demands that the size of the SET be smaller than 2 or 3 nm. The capacitance of this ultra-small quantum dot is smaller than 1 aF. In this condition the proportion of the ΔE in the total energy will increase rapidly and there will appear the quantum effect in the SET characteristics.

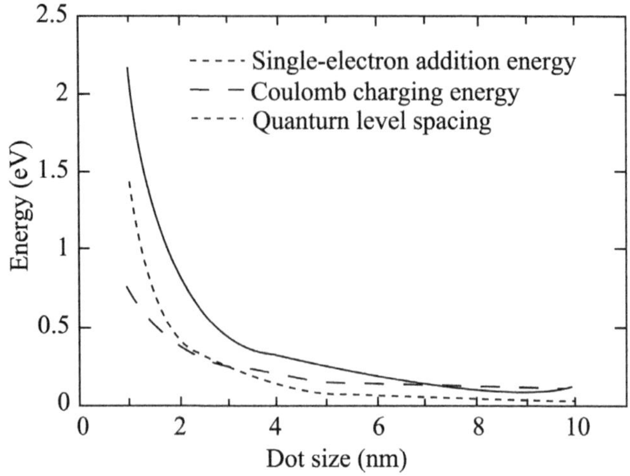

Figure 7.7 Calculated E_a, E_C, and ΔE of a Si SET as a function of QD scale.

The second condition comes from the uncertainty relation. To avoid the fluctuation or uncertainty of the number of electrons in a quantum dot, the electron should be localized well in the quantum dot, separated from the source and drain, which gives the condition

$$R_t \gg h/e^2 = 25.8\ \text{k}\Omega, \tag{7.11}$$

where R_t is the resistance of the tunneling barrier. $R_q = h/e^2$ is called the quantum resistance. A too-high tunneling resistance will result in very low drain current and low drivability, which is the main shortcoming of the SET.

7.2 Early Works of Set Operating at Room Temperature

Takahashi et al. [2] fabricated a Si SET by converting a one-dimensional (1D) Si wire substrate into a small Si island with a tunneling barrier at each end by means of pattern-dependent oxidation of a very thin Si layer on SiO_2. With this structure, the total capacitance was reduced to ~2 aF, which enabled conductance oscillation of the SET at room temperature.

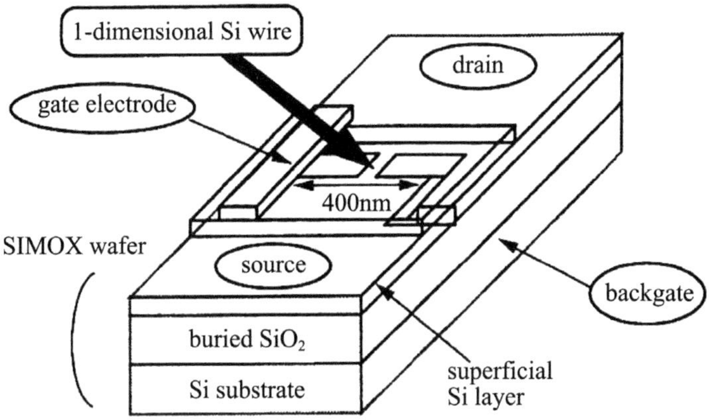

Figure 7.8 Schematic diagram of the Si SET.

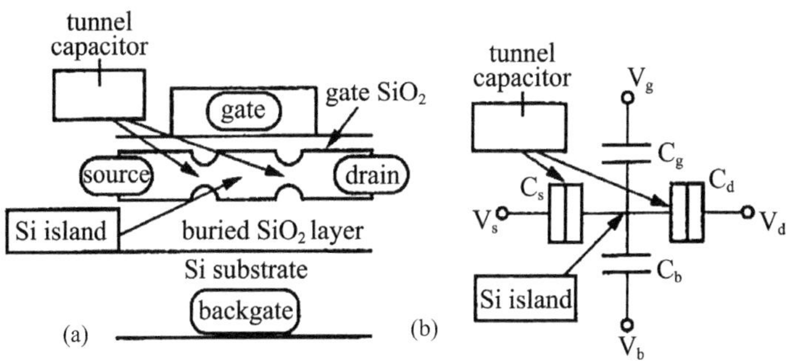

Figure 7.9 Cross-sectional view of a SET (a) and an equivalent circuit (b).

Figure 7.8 shows the schematic diagram of the Si SET [2]. Figure 7.9 shows the cross-sectional view of a SET (a) and an equivalent circuit (b) [2].

The conductance as a function of gate voltage in different temperatures is shown in Fig. 7.10 [2]. Here, the drain voltage was 1 mV and the source and back-gate voltages were fixed at 0 V. Conductance oscillations are observed even at room temperature. These oscillations are due to the CB by tunneling barriers with a very small capacitance. The capacitance can be estimated from the conductance characteristics. From the oscillation period ΔV_g in the gate voltage, ~500 mV, the gate capacitance C_g is calculated to be

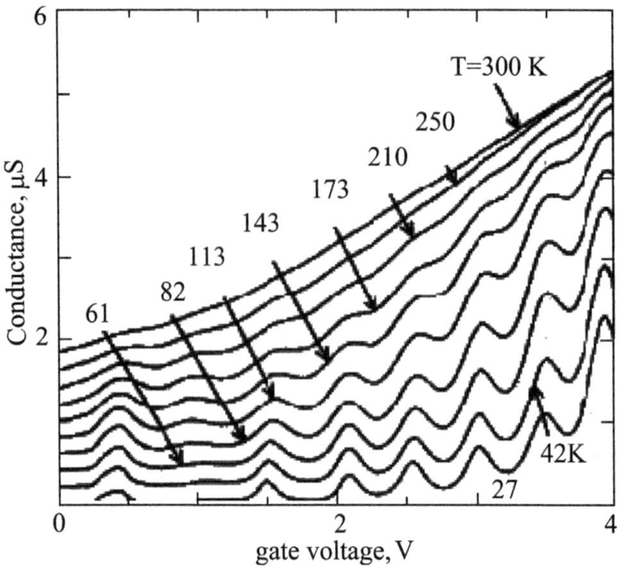

Figure 7.10 Conductance as a function of gate voltage in different temperatures.

~0.3 aF according to $C_g = e/\Delta V_g$. This value is consistent with the capacitance estimated from the dimensions of the structure. Hence, the back-gate capacitance C_b is determined to be ~0.01 aF because the cycle of the conductance oscillation as a function of the back-gate voltage is 30 times that for the front-gate voltage.

In Fig. 7.11 the source-drain current as a function of drain voltage V_d at the gate voltage corresponding to the conductance valley is shown [2]. The figure is similar to Fig. 7.5 in the CB condition. The gate voltage V_g and back-gate voltage are fixed at 0.7 and 0 V, respectively. The drain current is blocked over a V_d range of 160 mV. The drain capacitance C_d is found to be ~1 aF on the basis of the offset in the drain voltage of 160 mV. Taking into account that the source capacitance C_s does not exceed C_d in the present structure, one obtains the total capacitance $C_t = C_s + C_d + C_g + C_b < 2.3$ aF. This small value corresponds to a very large charging energy (e^2/C_t) of 70 meV, ensuring conductance oscillation at room temperature.

Ono et al. [3] developed a new oxidation method related to the original pattern-dependent oxidation (PADOX) method,

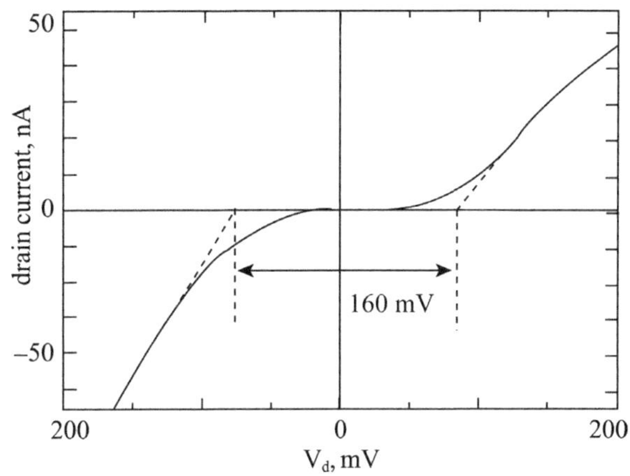

Figure 7.11 Source-drain current as a function of drain voltage V_d at the gate voltage corresponding to the conductance valley.

the vertical pattern-dependent oxidation (V-PADOX). The method applies thermal oxidation to a Si wire with a fine trench across it on a silicon-on-insulator substrate. During the oxidation, the Si wire with the fine trench is converted, in a self-organized manner, into a twin SET structure with two single-electron islands, one along each edge of the trench, due to position-dependent oxidation rate modulation caused by stress accumulation. Figure 7.12 shows the Si wire with a fine trench across it [3]. The key aspect of the method, thermal oxidation, is carried out just after the wire with a fine

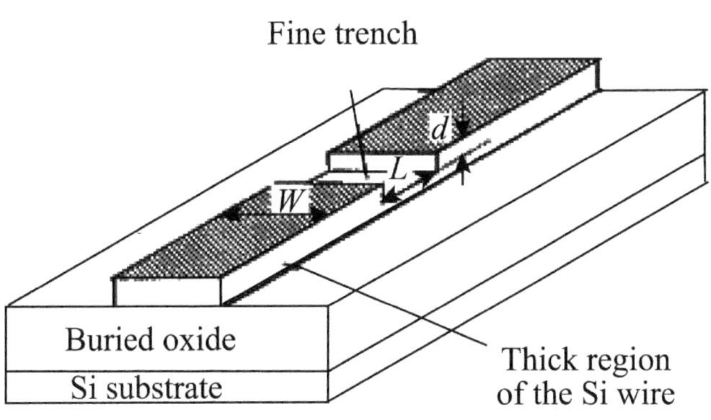

Figure 7.12 Si wire with a fine trench across it.

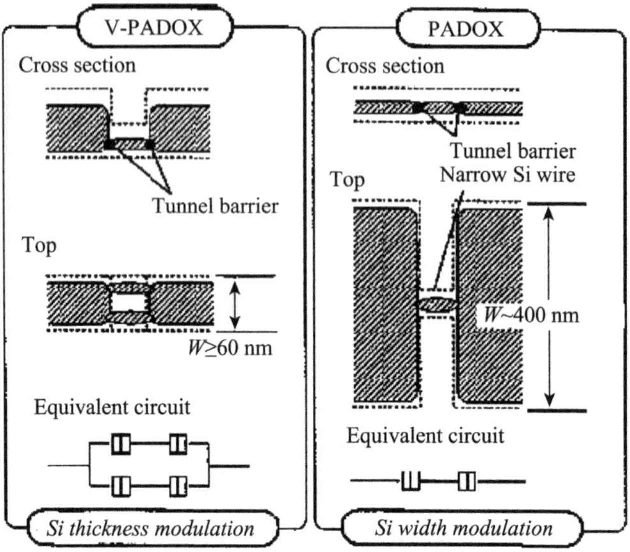

Figure 7.13 Resulting SET structure and the corresponding equivalent circuit. Those for the original PADOX are also shown for comparison.

trench is defined. During the oxidation the region below the trench is turned into twin Si islands, one along each edge of the trench. The resulting SET structure and the corresponding equivalent circuit are schematically shown in Fig. 7.13 [3]. Those for the original PADOX are also shown for comparison. In this figure, the broken lines represent preoxidation Si patterns and the hatched regions represent islands and leads after oxidation. The width of the island is 60 nm, and the length is 30 nm.

Figure 7.14 shows the conductance G, measured at 40 K with a drain voltage of 10 mV, as a function of the top-gate voltage V_g, the side-gate voltage $V_A = -4$ V, and $V_B = 0$ V [3]. Three peaks are observed, peaks A1, B1, and B2. Changing the side-gate voltages V_A and V_B, one can demonstrate that peak A1 originates from island A, which is closer to side gate A than island B is, and peaks B1 and B2 originate from island B. This confirms that a SET is formed along each edge of the fine trench and both SETs can be individually controlled. But in the present device the independent control effect of the side gate is not obvious.

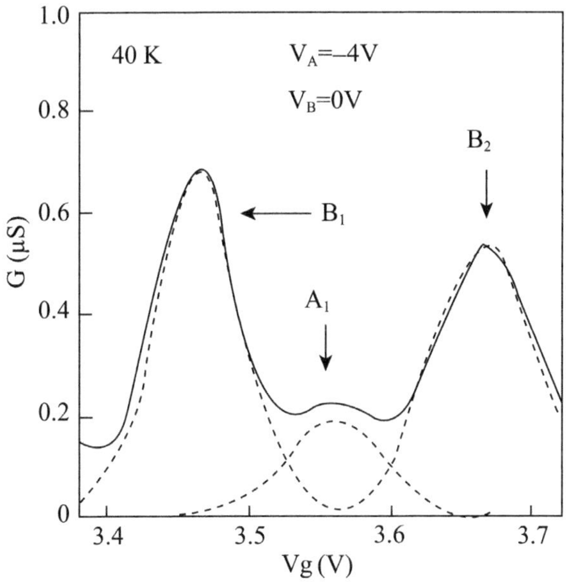

Figure 7.14 Conductance G, measured at 40 K with a drain voltage of 10 mV, as a function of the top-gate voltage V_g.

7.3 Si Set Operating at Room Temperature

In Section 7.1 we discussed the condition of operation of a SET at room temperature. As in Eq. 7.10 and Fig. 7.7, the size of the quantum dot should be smaller than 2 or 3 nm. In this case the spacing between single-electron energy levels ΔE will be much larger than the thermal energy and there will appear new quantum effects. Ishikuro et al. [4] fabricated the SET in the form of point-contact MOSFETs with various channel widths using electron beam lithography and the anisotropic etching technique on a silicon-on-insulator substrate. The device with an extremely narrow channel shows CB oscillations at room temperature. At a low temperature, negative differential conductance and fine structures are superposed on the device characteristics, which are attributed to the quantum mechanical effects in the quantum dot.

The schematic view of the point-contact MOSFET is shown in Fig. 7.15 [4]. It is found that the device with a 30 nm width shows

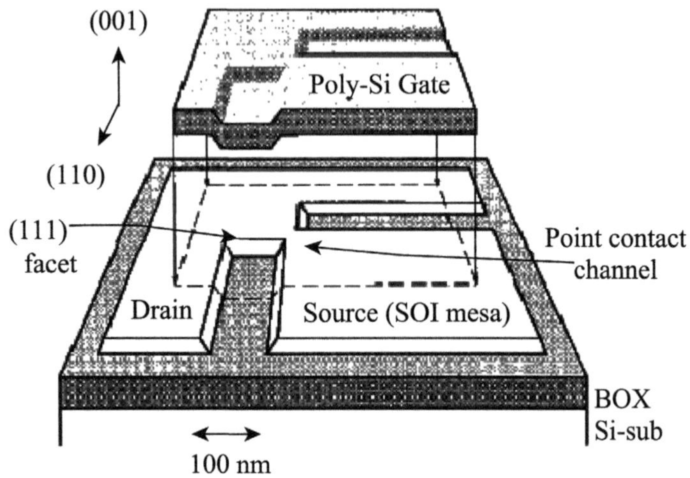

Figure 7.15 Schematic view of the point-contact MOSFET.

normal MOSFET operation even at 4.2 K. As the width decreases, the drain current decreases and, when the channel is extremely narrow, the device shows clear CB oscillations, which indicates that the channel is separated by tunnel barriers.

Figure 7.4 shows the drain current as a function of V_g. The temperature is changed from room temperature down to 21 K. The CB oscillation can be observed even at room temperature. Different from the CB characteristics of the semi-classical model, (i) the intervals between the peaks are not constant and (ii) negative differential conductance (NDC) and the fine structures are superposed on the $I_{ds} - V_{ds}$ characteristics. From the experimental results one can estimate that the single-electron charging energy $E_C = 58$ meV and the spacing between quantum levels $\Delta E =$ 30 meV, which are all much larger than the thermal energy at room temperature. Knowing E_C, one obtains $C_g = 0.085$, $C_d = 0.50$, $C_s =$ 0.80, and $C_{sub} = 0.009$ aF. Suppose the quantum dot is spherical and its diameter is estimated to be 6 nm.

Figure 7.16 shows the three-dimensional (3D) plot of the I_{ds} as a function of the V_g and V_{ds} at 4.2 K [4]. Clear rhombus shapes caused by CB oscillations are observed. NDCs and fine structures appear in parallel with the sides of the rhombus shapes.

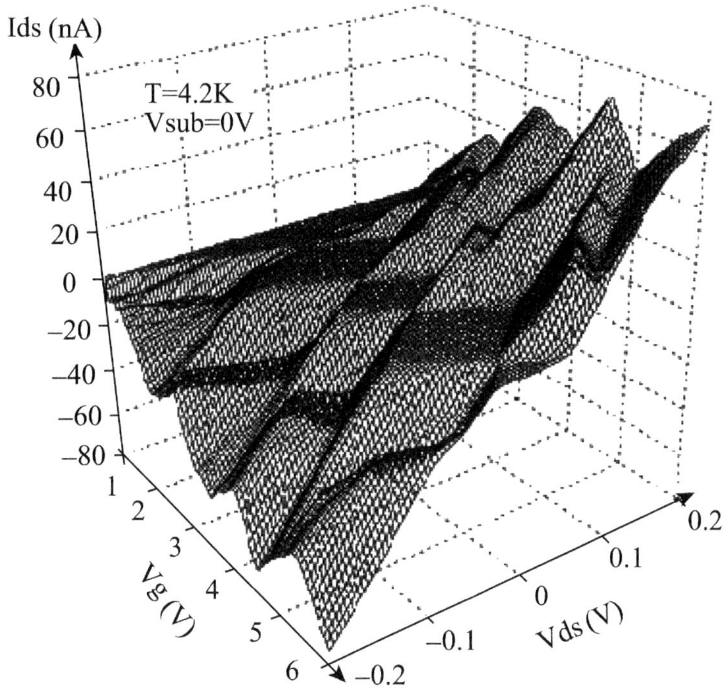

Figure 7.16 Three-dimensional plot of the I_{ds} as a function of the V_g and V_{ds} at 4.2 K.

Saitoh et al. [5] reported room temperature (RT) observation of NDC in a silicon single-dot single-hole transistor (SHT). They reduced the dot size to as small as 2 nm by improving the fabrication technique. In the single-dot SHT, both large CB oscillation and clear NDC due to large quantum-level spacing ΔE are observed at RT. The NDC appears as clearly as CB oscillations in the present SHT so the merged current blockade region (extended CB region) is observed.

The schematic of the point-contact MOSFET SHT is shown in Fig. 7.17a [5]. Two rectangles A and A' form the source and drain, and at the opposite angles a SHT (a single dot sandwiched by two tunneling barriers) is self-formed in the point-contact channel. To reduce the channel thickness as well as the channel width, they removed the buried oxide (BOX) just under the point-contact channel by hydrogen fluoride (HF). As a result, the etching of

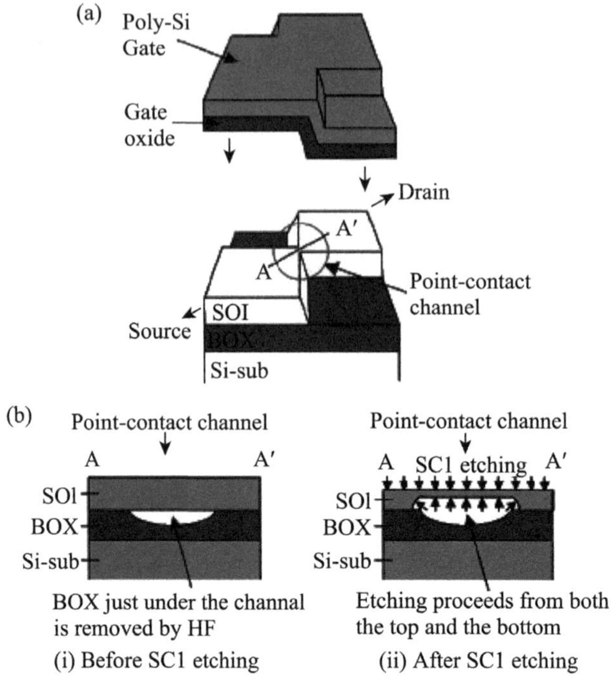

Figure 7.17 (a) Schematic of the point-contact MOSFET SHT. (b) The point-contact channel before and after SCI ($NH_4OH/H_2O_2/H_2O$) etching.

the channel proceeds from both the top and the bottom and the channel thickness is effectively reduced while the source/drain silicon on insulator (SOI) regions are kept relatively thick, as shown in Figs. 7.17b and 7.17c. The height and the width of the final channel are estimated to be less than 5 nm.

The drain current I_d as a function of the gate voltage V_g at RT is shown in Fig. 7.18a [5]. A large CB oscillation with one current peak is observed. The peak-valley current ratio (PVCR) is as high as 40.4. An enormously high PVCR of the observed CB oscillation indicates an ultra-small dot is successfully formed in the extremely constricted channel. Figure 7.18b shows I_d as a function of the drain voltage V_{ds} at RT. In the negative V_{ds} region, clear NDC with the PVCR of 11.8 is observed.

The most probable origin of clear NDC in the single-dot SETs/SHTs is the resonant tunneling at the source-side barrier due

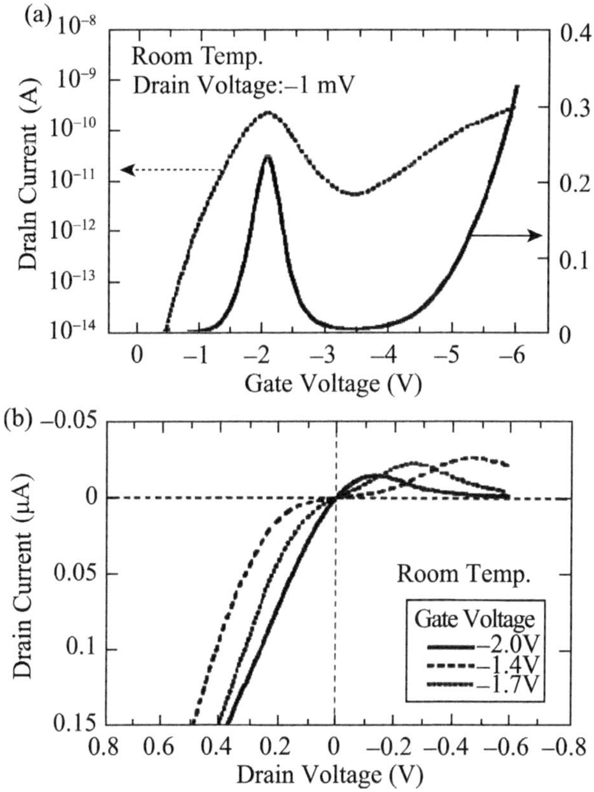

Figure 7.18 (a) Drain current I_d as a function of the gate voltage V_g at RT. (b) I_d as a function of the drain voltage V_{ds} at RT.

to large ΔE in the ultra-small dot. The schematics of the conduction band profile in a SET with an ultra-small dot are shown in Fig. 7.19a [5]. For simplicity, electron transport in SETs is considered instead of hole transport in SHTs. Since ΔE is much larger than the thermal energy at RT in the present device, electrons in the source cannot tunnel to the excited states in the dot and only ground state is accessible. At low V_{ds}, the tunneling rate of electrons from the source to the dot is relatively high because electrons tunnel through the thin tunneling barrier close to the Fermi level in the source. As V_{ds} increases, the energy levels in the dot fall down and electrons must tunnel through the thicker barrier close to the

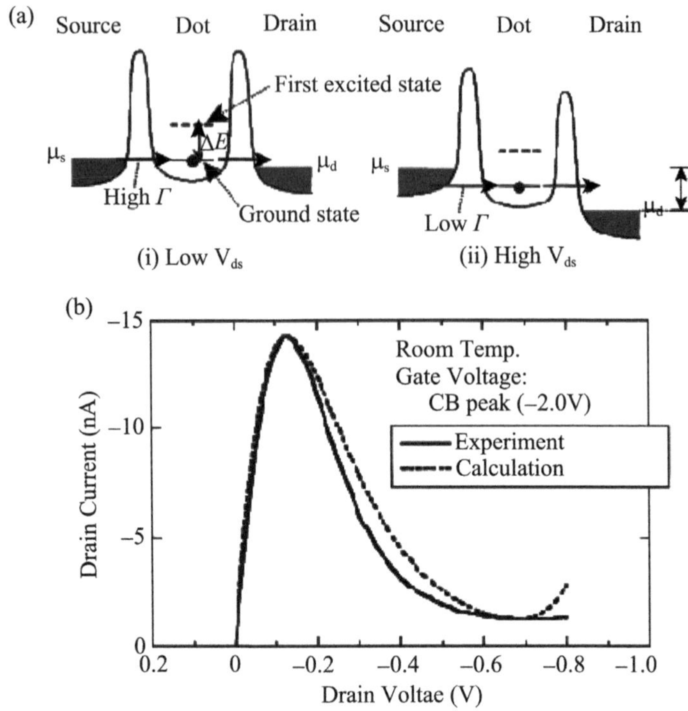

Figure 7.19 (a) Schematics of the conduction band profile in a SET with an ultra-small dot. (b) Comparison of the calculated $I_d - V_{ds}$ characteristics of the SHT with a 2 nm spherical silicon dot and the experimental data.

band edge in the source. Consequently, the tunneling rate decreases and NDC appears. Figure 7.18b compares the calculated $I_d - V_{ds}$ characteristics of the SHT with a 2 nm spherical silicon dot and the experimental data; the agreement is good.

The contour plots of the differential conductance $\partial I_d/\partial V_{ds}$ and I_d as a function of V_g and V_{ds} are shown in Figs. 7.20a and 7.20b, respectively [5]. In Fig. 7.20a two rhombus-shaped CB regions and a large NDC region are observed. In Fig. 7.20b the CB region is extended from low V_{ds} to negative and high V_{ds} as a result of the existence of the large NDC region. Such extended CB region and the NDC region have so far been observed only at a much low temperature. The NDC in a single-dot SHT is very simple and more suitable for circuit application.

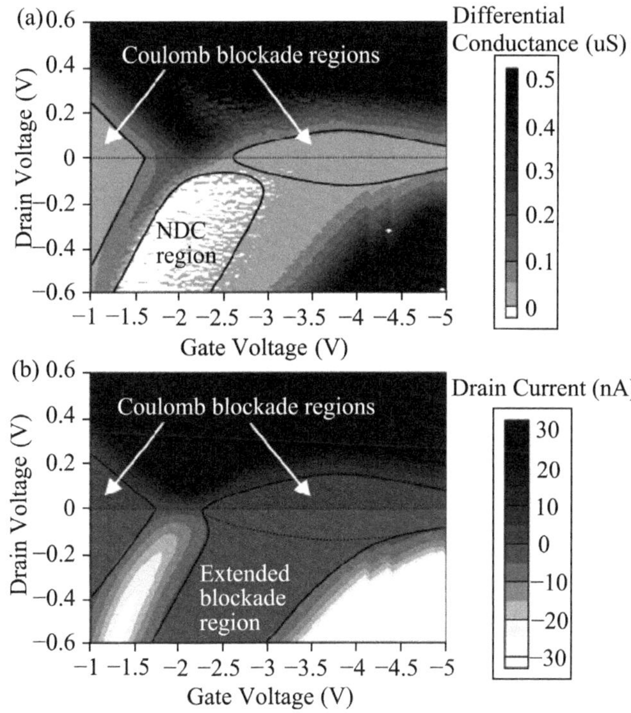

Figure 7.20 Contour plot of the differential conductance $\partial I_d/\partial V_{ds}$ (a) and I_d (b) as a function of V_g and V_{ds}, respectively.

7.4 Si Set Used as a Logic Circuit

The ultimate aim of the Si SET is to fabricate VLSI with ultra-high device density and ultra-low power loss. The single-electron logic circuit can be divided into two kinds: one is the CMOS-like SET logic circuit, in which the SET is used as an on/off switch device, similar to the general MOSFET in a CMOS logic circuit; and the other is the charging state logic circuit, where one bite is represented by one electron.

Ono et al. [6] fabricated a complementary single-electron inverter in which two identical SETs are packed on a silicon-on-insulator substrate (see Fig. 7.12). The resulting circuit occupies a very small area: 100 × 100 nm for each SET. For complementary

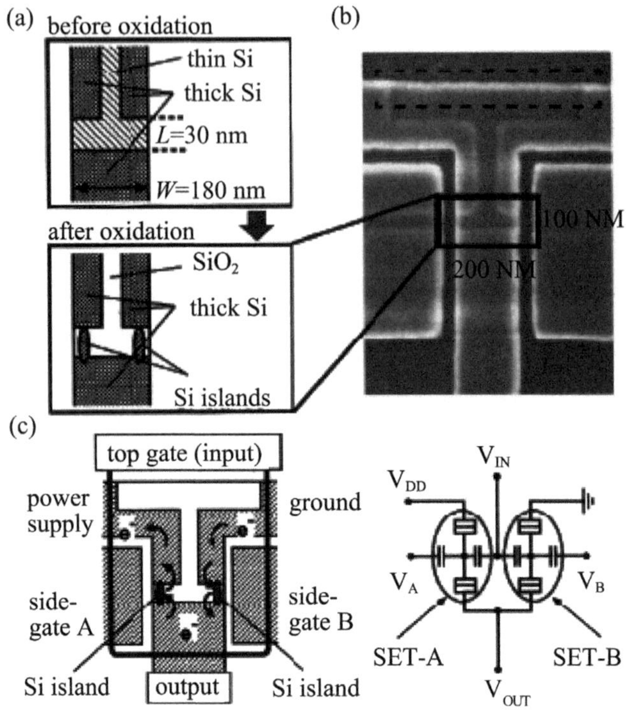

Figure 7.21 Structure of the complementary single-electron inverter. (a) Basic pattern before (top) and after (bottom) oxidation. (b) SEM image of the inverter. (c) Its equivalent circuit.

operation, the electric characteristics of one of the SETs are shifted using a side gate situated near the SET. The structure of the complementary single-electron inverter is shown in Fig. 7.21a [6], the equivalent circuit is shown in Fig. 7.21c, and the scanning electron microscope (SEM) image of the inverter is shown in Fig. 7.21b. The flow of electrons is indicated by the arrows. In the equivalent circuit, V_{IN} and V_{OUT} represent the input and output voltages. V_{DD}, V_A, and V_B are the voltages applied to the power-supply terminal and the two side gates, A and B, respectively.

Figure 7.22a shows input-output transfer characteristics of the inverter for a power-supply voltage V_{DD} of 20 mV [6]. For this measurement, a negative constant voltage ($V_B = -7$ V) was applied

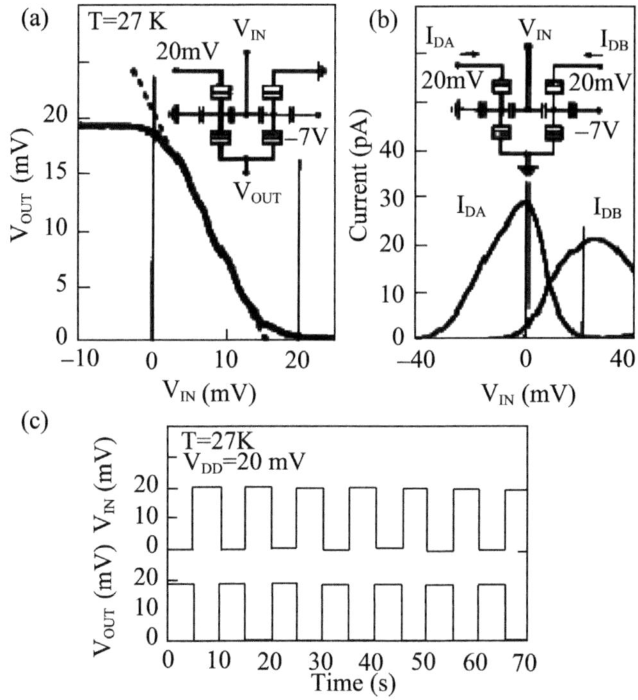

Figure 7.22 (a) Input-output transfer characteristics of the inverter for a power-supply voltage V_{DD} of 20 mV. (b) Drain-current characteristics of the two SETs for the drain voltage of 20 mV with the same side-gate voltage $V_A = 0$ V and $V_B = -7$ V. (c) Output voltage for a square-wave input with an amplitude of 20 mV.

to the side gate B to shift the current curve of SET B in the positive V_{IN} direction while gate A was grounded. Thus SET A and SET B operated as p- and n-type transistors, respectively. The drain-current characteristics of the two SETs for the drain voltage of 20 mV with the same side-gate voltage $V_A = 0$ V and $V_B = -7$ V are shown in Fig. 7.22b. The output voltage for a square-wave input with an amplitude of 20 mV is shown in Fig. 7.22c. The amplitude of the output is nearly the same as that of the input and the power supply voltage. But the switching speed is low, and it is caused by the slow response of the external circuit due to a large capacitance in the measurement system.

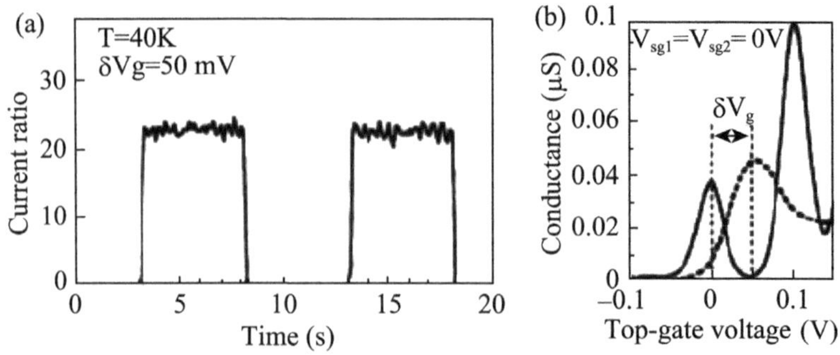

Figure 7.23 (a) Switching operation for a square-wave input with an amplitude of 50 mV. (b) Corresponding conductance characteristics of SET 1 (solid curve) and SET 2 (dotted curve).

Ono et al. [7] fabricated a Si SET current switching device on the basis of the Si SET inverter. The structure of the switching device is similar to that of the inverter. The switching operation for a square-wave input with an amplitude of 50 mV is shown in Fig. 7.23a [7], and the corresponding conductance characteristics of SET 1 (solid curve) and SET 2 (dotted curve) are shown in Fig. 7.23b. δV_g represents the amplitude of the square-wave input. Similarly, the switching speed is low.

The main shortcoming of the Si SET used as a device is that the speed is too slow. Apart from the tunneling resistance R_t, there is also the parasitic resistance of the external circuit. Due to the uncertainty relation R_t should be larger than the quantum resistance $h/e^2 \approx 25.8$ kΩ (see Eq. 7.11). The parasitic resistance comes from the undoped ultra-thin SOI region between the channel and the gate, which is serially connected with the intrinsic SET, resulting in large parasitic resistance. Although the upper limit of the peak conductance of SETs is determined by the quantum conductance ($= e^2/h \approx 38.8$ μS), further degradation of the peak conductance due to parasitic series resistance is a crucial issue.

Saitoh et al. [8] improved the silicon point-contact SET (see Fig. 7.17). By narrowing only the point-contact region and suppressing the parasitic series resistance, a peak conductance as large as 8.8 μS and single-electron addition energy as large as 128 meV are simultaneously obtained. Figure 7.24 shows the

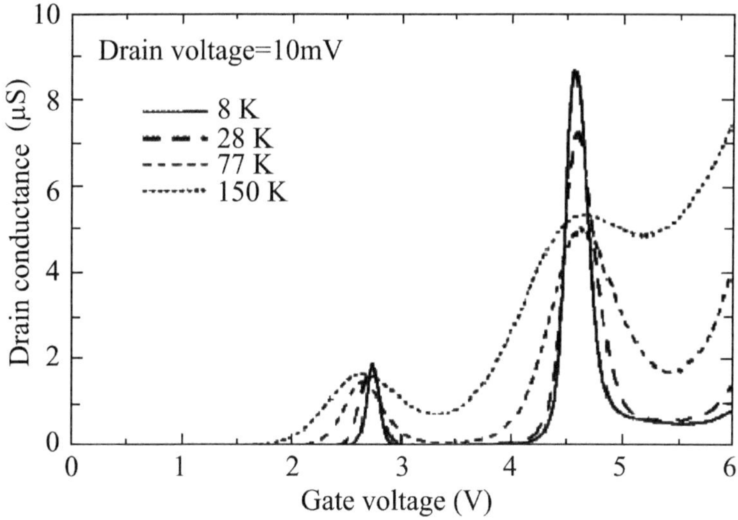

Figure 7.24 $I_d - V_g$ characteristics of the fabricated SET at a fixed $V_{ds} =$ 10 mV at several temperatures.

$I_d - V_g$ characteristics of the fabricated SET at a fixed $V_{ds} =$ 10 mV at several temperatures [8]. In Fig. 7.24 the conductance of the second peak at 8 K is 8.8 μS, which is much larger than the reported values (usually about 0.1 μS). This indicates that the relatively thick SOI layer successfully suppresses the parasitic series resistance. In the meantime, the height of the second peak decreases with an increasing temperature from 8 to 77 K. This temperature dependence is quite different from previously reported Si SETs, where the peak current increases with an increasing temperature. Since in this SET the quantum-level spacing ΔE is sufficiently large, only one quantum level, closest to the Fermi level, contributes significantly to one current peak when $k_B T \ll \Delta E$; the integrated area of one peak is independent of temperature. Therefore, the peak conductance decreases as the temperature increases and the peak width broadens. However, the first current peak keeps almost constant with an increasing temperature. This is because the conductance of the first peak is easily affected by the tunneling through the next level with higher coupling to reservoirs at a relatively high temperature.

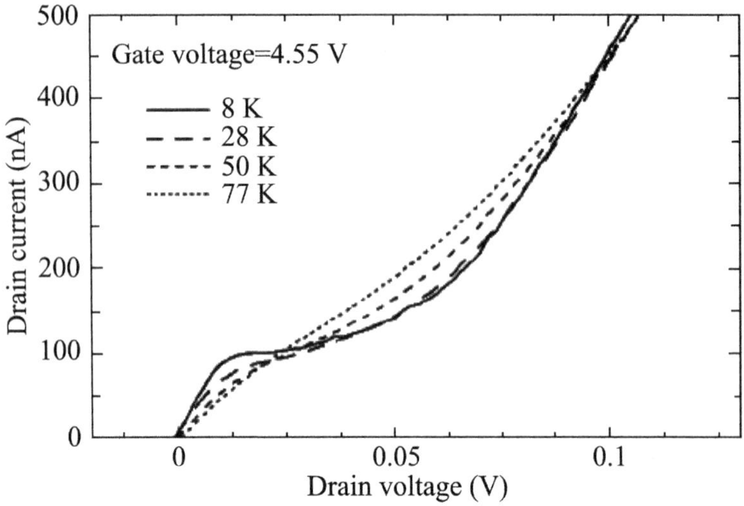

Figure 7.25 $I_d - V_{ds}$ characteristics at a fixed $V_g = 4.55$ V, where the $I_d - V_g$ curve has its peak, at several temperatures.

Figure 7.25 shows the $I_d - V_{ds}$ characteristics at a fixed $V_g = 4.55$ V, where the $I_d - V_g$ curve has its peak, at several temperatures [8]. A current staircase is observed at 8 K, and the fine structure (nonlinear behavior) persists up to 77 K. In this case, the staircase feature arises from the discreteness of quantum levels. When $k_B T \ll \Delta E$, only the ground state is accessible for an electron for a low drain voltage and the current is kept constant until a drain voltage at which the first excited state becomes aligned with the Fermi level in the reservoirs and begins to contribute to conduction. Thus, each plateau of the staircase corresponds to a different quantum state in the dot.

The energy spacing between the ground state and the first excited state ΔE can be derived from the drain voltage at which the drain current starts to increase from the first plateau, because the first excited state starts to contribute to electron transport at this drain voltage. Because the onset drain voltage is about 0.05 V in Fig. 7.25, the quantum-level spacing is estimated to be about 19 meV. The coulomb charging energy is roughly estimated to be 109 meV as the difference between the single-electron addition energy and the quantum-level spacing.

References

1. Saitoh, M., and Hiramoto, T. (2006). *Handbook of Semiconductor Nanostructures and Nanodevices*, Vol. 3, eds. Baladin, A. A., and Wang, K. L. (American Scientific Publishes, Los Angeles), p. 279.
2. Takahashi, Y., Nagase, M., Namatsu, H., et al. (1995). Fabrication technique for Si single-electron transistor operating at room temperature. *Electron. Lett.*, **31**, 136–137.
3. Ono, Y., Takahashi, Y. Yamazaki, K., et al. (2000). Fabrication method for IC-oriented Si single-electron transistors. *IEEE Trans. Electron Devices*, **47**, 147–153.
4. Ishikuro, H., and Hiramoto, T. (1997). Quantum mechanical effects in the silicon quantum dot in a single-electron transistor. *Appl. Phys. Lett.*, **71**, 3691–3693.
5. Saitoh, M., and Hiramoto, T. (2004). Extension of Coulomb blockade region by quantum confinement in the ultrasmall silicon dot in a single-hole transistor at room temperature. *Appl. Phys. Lett.*, **84**, 3172–3174.
6. Ono, Y., Takahashi, Y., Yamazaki, K., Nagase, M., and Namatsu, H. (2000). Si complementary single-electron inverter with voltage gain. *Appl. Phys. Lett.*, **76**, 3121–3123.
7. Ono, Y., Takahashi, Y., Yamazaki, K., et al. (2000). Single-electron transistor and current-switching device fabricated by vertical pattern-dependent oxidation. *Jpn. J. Appl. Phys.*, **39**, 2325–2328.
8. Saitoh, M., and Hiramoto, T. (2002). Observation of current staircase due to large quantum level spacing in a silicon single-electron transistor with low parasitic series resistance. *J. Appl. Phys.*, **91**, 6725–6728.

Chapter 8

Silicon Single-Electron Memory

Memory is the first and foremost application of silicon single-electron devices (SEDs) and has been extensively researched. One reason is that the SEDs can operate in smaller dimensions and this directly leads to the increased memory density. Another is that memory usually has a periodic and simple structure and this is expected to make the implementation of the emerging devices straightforward. The scaling limit in the current silicon memories, both flash memory and dynamic random access memory (DRAM), also adds to the demand for single-electron memories.

The memory unit with a discrete trap-like memory node has attracted much attention because it operates using fewer electrons and can possibly operate at a high density, a high speed, and low power dissipation. In these memories, the memory node includes floating-node type or natural nitride trap and semiconductor nanocrystals. The electrons are injected into the memory node, causing the shift of the critical voltage, whose principle is the same as that of general erasable programmable read-only memories (EPROMs) or electrically erasable and programmable read-only memories (FEPROMs), but the total number of electrons involved in the memory node is far less than the latter. This kind of memory is called a few-carriers memory.

Quantum Waveguide in Microcircuits
Jian-Bai Xia, Duan-Yang Liu, and Wei-Dong Sheng

ISBN 978-981-4669-85-6 (Hardcover), 978-1-315-36477-3 (eBook)
www.panstanford.com

8.1 Memory of Floating-Gate-Node Type

Most of the proposed single-electron memories are floating-node types, in which a limited number of electrons are stored in the floating memory node and the presence of the charge is detected by a charge-sensing device. SEDs can be used in either electron storage or charge sensing schemes. Both schemes are shown in Figs. 8.1 and 8.2 [1], respectively. Possible combinations of them are numerous.

A distinctive device in electron storage schemes is the electron trap, which consists of one, two, or more serial tunnel junctions and a capacitor (Fig. 8.1a–c). Another electron storage scheme is based on a serially connected transistor and a storage capacitor (Figs. 8.1d and 8.1e). Since transistors are three-terminal devices, this scheme provides flexibility in memory operations. Figure 8.2 shows various kinds of charge-sensing devices used in single-electron memories. Their drain current is modulated by the charge in the memory node. Thus the memory charge can be detected by the current of the sensing line. Apart from the single-electron transistor (SET)

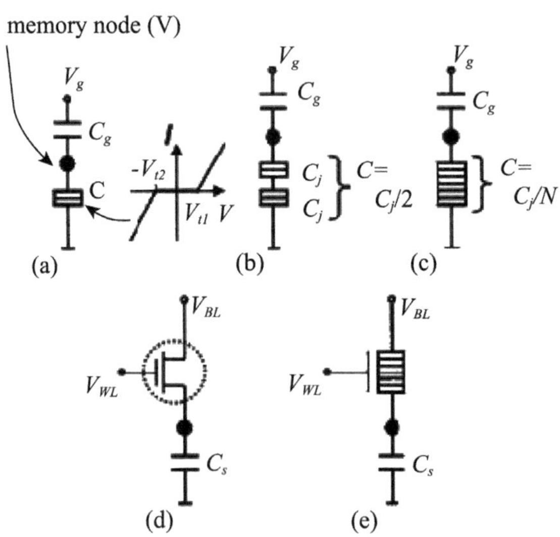

Figure 8.1 Various electron storage schemes used in single-electron memories.

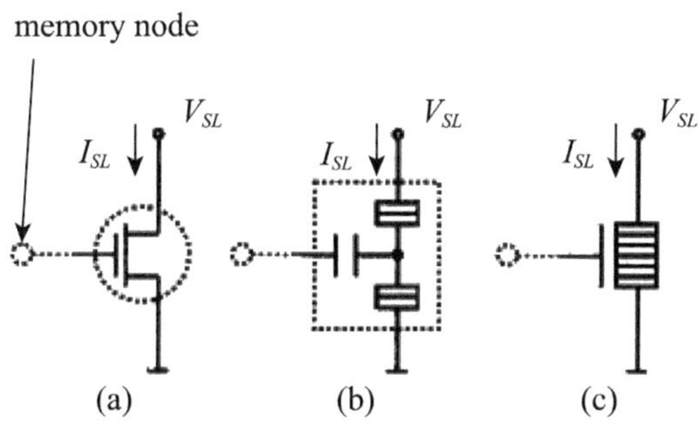

Figure 8.2 Various kinds of charge-sensing devices used in single-electron memories.

and multiple-tunnel-junction (MTJ) SET, the minimum metal-oxide semiconductor field-effect transistor (MOSFET) is also sensitive enough to detect a single electron.

In the relationship between the potential of the memory node V and the gate voltage V_g, Fig. 8.3 [1], tunneling of the electron into and out of the memory node is prohibited by the Coulomb blockade (CB) in the region $-Q_c/C < V < Q_c/C$. The critical charge Q_c is given by

$$Q_c = \frac{eC}{C_\Sigma}\left(\frac{1+\Delta}{2}\right), \tag{8.1}$$

where C_Σ is the total capacitance $C + C_g$, C is the capacitance of the MTJ, and C_g is the gate capacitance. Δ determines a multiple value

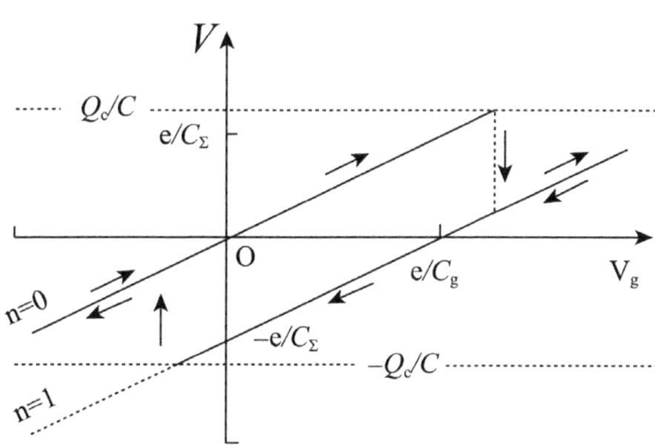

Figure 8.3 Potential of the memory node V as a function of gate voltage V_g for double- and multiple-tunnel-junction traps.

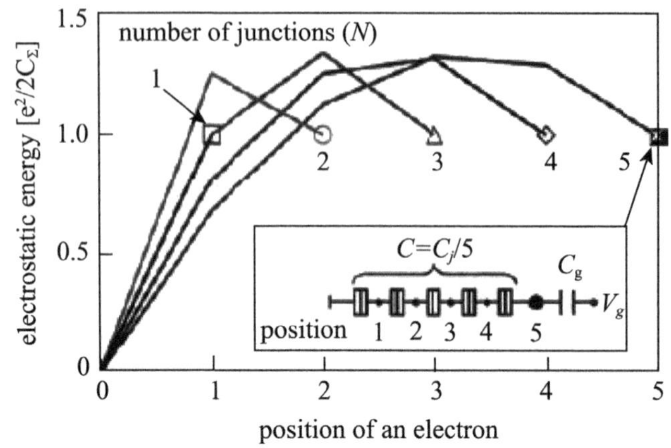

Figure 8.4 Electrostatic energy of the MTJ trap system with an extra electron as a function of its position when $V_g = 0$ and $C_g/C = 3$ [1].

condition, given by

$$\Delta = \left(1 - \frac{1}{N}\right)\frac{C_g}{C}, \qquad (8.2)$$

where N is the number of serially connected tunnel junctions.

The operation principle of the memory is shown in Fig. 8.3 [1]. V increases with a slope of C_g/C_Σ until the boundary of the CB regime ($V = Q_c/C$) is reached, where an electron tunnels into the memory node and the V drops abruptly by e/C_Σ. Even if the V_g sweep is reversed, the electron is trapped until the sweep reaches the other boundary ($V = -Q_c/C$), where the electron tunnels out of the memory node. Thus a hysteresis loop appears, and bistability is attained at $V_g = 0$ for $1 < \Delta < 3$.

The stability of a trapped electron can be assessed by calculating the electrostatic energy of the system as a function of the position of an extra electron, see Fig. 8.4 [1]. For the number of tunnel junctions more than one ($N > 1$), the curves become convex and an energy barrier appears between states with and without an extra electron in the memory node. This results in the stable storage of an electron in the node. If there is only one tunnel node ($N = 1$) the stable storage is impossible, only if the tunnel resistance is nonlinear, as shown in Fig. 8.1a.

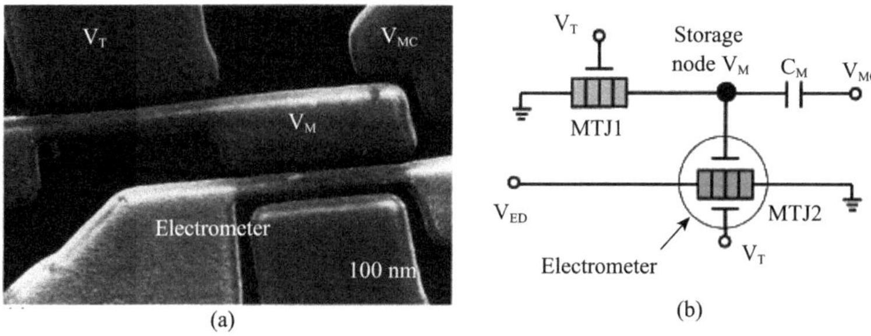

Figure 8.5 (a) Scanning electron micrograph of the compact silicon single-electron memory cell. (b) Equivalent circuit of the memory cell.

8.2 Si Set Used as Memory

Stone et al. [2] fabricated a compact single-electron memory in silicon, which is based on the CB effect observed in highly doped silicon nanowires. The circuit shows clear memory operation with a $>$ 100 mV gap between "0" and "1" levels when tested at a temperature of 4.2 K. The response of the circuit to write and erase pulse sequences is also presented. The silicon nanowires used as MTJs are 500 nm in length and have a width of 50 nm. The devices were fabricated in a silicon-on-insulator (SOI) material. Figure 8.5 shows a scanning electron micrograph of the compact cell after oxidation, and the equivalent circuit diagram is shown in Fig. 8.5b [2]. The memory cell consists of MTJ1 and a memory node that occupies an area of only 0.5 μm^2. The second device, MTJ2, forms an electrometer that has the function of detecting the state of the memory node. Each MTJ has a side gate to trim its operating point. The voltage V_{MC} controls the amount of charge on the memory node via capacitor C_M.

Memory operation is demonstrated by the two distinct levels in the memory node voltage as the voltage V_{MC} is scanned over a range as shown in Fig. 8.6a [2]. If V_{MC} is increased positively from zero the voltage on the memory node V_M increases until it reaches $+V_C$, the CB voltage. Further increase of V_{MC} results in a single electron flowing through MTJ1 onto the memory node, and the node voltage V_M then falls back below the Coulomb gap voltage $+V_C$ by

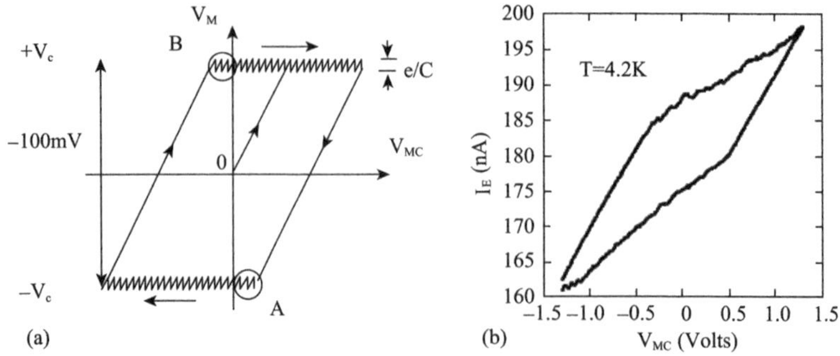

Figure 8.6 (a) Schematic representation of the hysteresis loop in a memory node voltage V_M as capacitor voltage V_{MC} is swept. (b) Hysteresis loop at 4.2 K. V_{MC} is swept in the range of ± 1.3 V.

an amount e/C (where C is the self-capacitance of the memory node). A subsequent increase of V_{MC} adds electrons to the memory node one by one. If V_{MC} is reduced toward zero the memory node voltage will fall finally to $-V_C$. The excess electrons at A in Fig. 8.6a leave the memory node via MTJ, and V_M is held at $-V_C$. The remaining electrons are trapped on the node. If a negative voltage V_{MC} is applied to the capacitor electrons are removed one by one from the node, which remains clamped at $-V_C$. The cyclic operation of V_{MC} results in the two levels as shown in Fig. 8.6a as parts of a hysteresis loop—the basis of memory operation. Figure 8.6b shows the measured current of the MTJ2 I_E as a function of V_{MC} at 4.2 K, showing the hysteresis loop.

The response of the memory to "write" and "erase" pulses is shown in Fig. 8.7 [2]. Positive and negative voltages were applied alternatively by V_{MC} separated by read periods of 0 V, while the memory current was monitored. During the read periods two distinct levels can be seen at B and D, signifying the "0" and "1" states. The change in current between B and D is determined by the CB gap, which is set by the trimming gate V_T of MTJ1. The self-capacitance of the island was estimated to be 100 aF. For a Coulomb gap of 0.05 V this would give an excess or shortfall of 30 electrons at two levels of V_M in Fig. 8.7b.

Takahashi et al. [3] fabricated a Si memory device composed of a small one-dimensional (1D) Si-wire MOSFET and a SET. The 1D

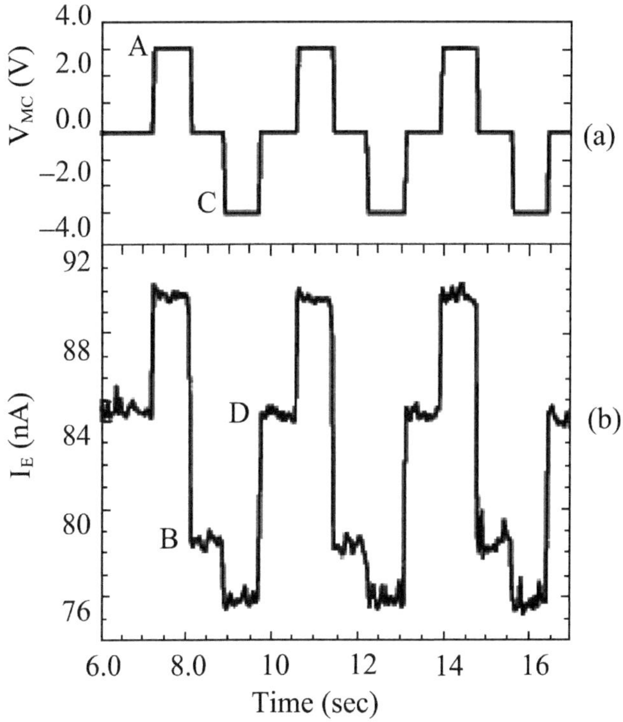

Figure 8.7 Memory read-write characteristics of single-electron memory. (a) Drive pulse wave form. (b) Electrometer output pulses monitoring the memory node.

MOSFET provides a very steep subthreshold slope that is very close to the physical limit at room temperature. This guarantees a low-voltage operation as well as a small size. The very small number of stored electrons is detected by a highly sensitive SET electrometer. The device can operate with an extremely small number of electrons, which ensures ultra-low-power and high-speed operation.

The SEM image of the Si memory device is shown in Fig. 8.8a, and its equivalent circuit is shown in Fig. 8.8b [3]. The memory node is connected via the 1D MOSFET to an electron reservoir (side electrode). By using the MOSFET to control electron transport between the memory node and the side electrode, high write/erase speed can be achieved without sacrificing retention time. This is

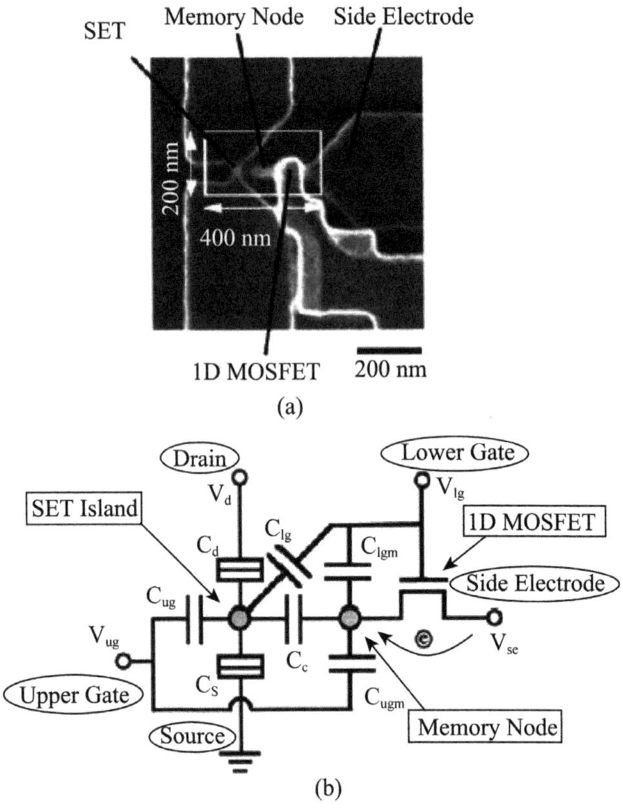

Figure 8.8 (a) SEM image of the Si memory device. (b) Its equivalent circuit.

in contrast to flash-memory-type single-electron memories, whose operating speed is limited by the low tunneling rate between the memory island and the channel to ensure sufficient storage time. The SET is used to sense a small number of electrons stored in the memory node. The $I_d - V_d$ characteristic of the device with the initially 30 nm wide 1D MOSFET with the 80 nm long gate shows that the conductance is remarkably high in spite of a channel width of only 20 nm. This guarantees a high driving capacity of the 1D MOSFET connected to the small memory node.

Figure 8.9 shows how the device state evolves as the lower-gate voltage (V_{lg}) is scanned in the positive direction and then in the reverse direction [3]. Initially, V_{lg} was set at a low voltage of −2.7 V,

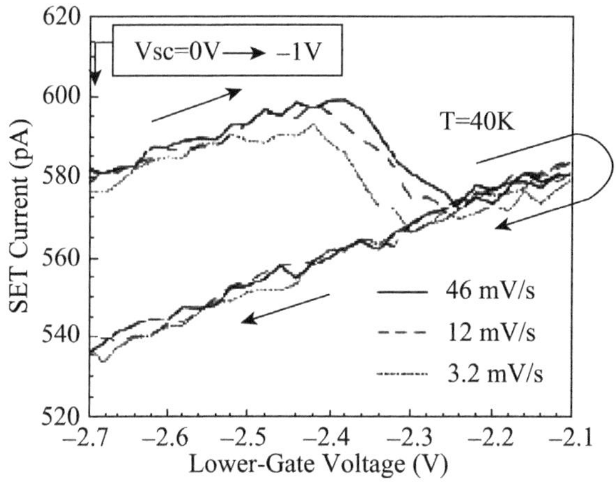

Figure 8.9 Hysteresis characteristics of the SET current representing the "write" and "erase" actions of the Si memory device.

at which the channel of the 1D MOSFET was closed. Then the side-electrode voltage V_{se} was changed from 0 V to -1 V before the start of the $V_{\rm lg}$ scan at various scan speeds. The rapid fall of the SET current at $V_{\rm lg}$ of about -2.3 V, where the 1D MOSFET is turned on, corresponds to the "write" action. The written information is held while $V_{\rm lg}$ is scanned back because the 1D MOSFET is turned off. The number of electrons in the memory node for a "write" voltage is estimated to be about 100. In Fig. 8.9 the threshold gate voltage at which the write operation occurs becomes lower as the scanning speed of $V_{\rm lg}$ decreases. This indicates that electron writing proceeds very slowly through the 1D MOSFET at gate voltages slightly lower than the threshold.

8.3 Floating Gate Memory Operating at Room Temperature

Guo et al. [4] fabricated a room-temperature silicon SET memory that consists of (i) a narrow channel MOSFET with a width ($\sim$10 nm) smaller than the Debye screening length of single electron and (ii) a nanoscale polysilicon dot (7 nm $\times$ 7 nm) as the floating gate

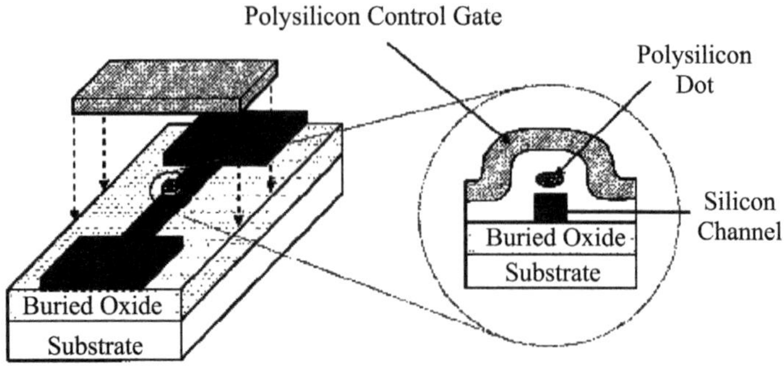

Figure 8.10 Schematic of a single-electron MOS memory that has a narrow silicon channel and a nanoscale polysilicon dot as the floating gate. The cross-section view illustrates the floating gate and the channel region.

embedded between the channel and the control gate. They observed that storing one electron on the floating gate can significantly screen the channel from the potential on the control gate, leading to a discrete shift in the threshold voltage, a staircase relationship between the charging voltage and the threshold shift.

Figure 8.10 shows the schematic of the single-electron MOS memory [4]. The polysilicon dot and the Si channel is formed by thermal oxidation, which would consume silicon, reducing the thickness of the polysilicon dot by about 9 nm and the lateral size of the dot and the silicon channel width by about 18 nm. It is noted that no tunnel oxide is intentionally added between the channel and the polysilicon floating gate. This will allow fast charging and minimize the potential difference between the channel and the floating dot during the charging process, so the CB effect can regulate the number of electrons stored on the floating dot gate for a given charging voltage. The potential barrier still exists between the channel and the floating gate because of the grain boundary and a thin native oxide.

First, a voltage pulse positive relative to the ground source was applied to the control gate and the drain voltage was maintained at 50 mV. This caused the electrons to tunnel from the channel to the floating dot. At various gate pulse voltages from 2 to 14 V the measured I–V characteristics are shown in Fig. 8.11 [4]. Despite a continuous charge voltage, the threshold voltage (defined as the

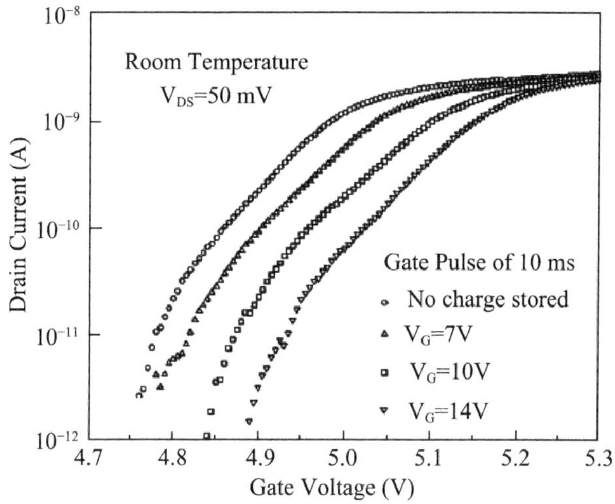

Figure 8.11 Room temperature I–V characteristics of the device before and after the charges are stored onto the floating dot.

gate voltage at which the drain current reaches 100 pA) always shifts a discrete increment of about 55 mV and each threshold shift corresponds to a charging voltage interval of ~4 V.

Therefore, there is a staircase relation between the threshold voltage shift and the charging voltage, as shown in Fig. 8.12a [4]. Moreover, for a given charging voltage, the threshold shift is self-

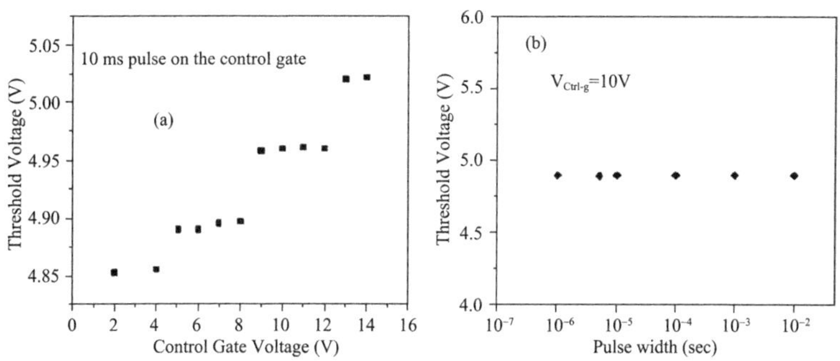

Figure 8.12 (a) Threshold voltage as a function of the charging voltage on the control gate, showing a staircase relation with ~4 V for each stair. (b) Threshold voltage as a function of the charging time, while the charging voltage is fixed at 10 V.

limited, the threshold voltage shift is independent of the charging time, as shown in Fig. 8.12b. Since there is no intentional tunnel oxide, the charge stored at the floating gate can be held for an average of 5 s after the control-gate potential is set back to the ground, and after 5 s the threshold voltage of the device returns to its origin value (the first I–V on the left in Fig. 8.11).

Nakajima et al. [5] fabricated seemingly at the same time a Si single-electron field-effect transistor (FET) memory device having a self-aligned floating dot gate. This device demonstrates single-electron memory operation at room temperature. Figure 8.13a shows the structure of this FET memory and 8.13b the cross-section view of the structure along the $a - a'$ line in Fig. 8.13a [5]. By use of the self-aligned manufacture a floating dot having a side length of about 30 nm is located on a narrow channel wire. The channel width is equal to or slightly larger than the floating dot. Finally, a second gate oxide 200 nm thick and a poly-Si control gate were deposited by low-pressure chemical vapor deposition (LPCVD).

Figure 8.14 shows the typical drain current I_{d} versus gate voltage V_{g} characteristics of the device [5]. For the device having a floating dot (Fig. 8.14a), an increasing V_{g} produced an I_{d} shift at a V_{g} of 3.9 V. However, with a decrease of V_{g}, the I_{d} shift did not occur, indicating a hysteresis of the $I_{\mathrm{d}} - V_{\mathrm{g}}$ curve. It means that the V_{g} reaches the CB boundary and an electron enters into the floating gate dot, resulting in the I_{d} shift. With a subsequent V_{g} increase (Fig. 8.14b), an additional I_{d} shift occurred at 5.1 V, the V_{g}, at which the I_{d} shift occurred, is called threshold voltage V_{th} (3.9, 5.1 V). For the device without a floating dot (Fig. 8.14c) such a quantized V_{th} shift and the $I_{\mathrm{d}} - V_{\mathrm{g}}$ curve hysteresis could not be observed.

From Figs. 8.14b and 8.14a the neighboring threshold voltages V_{th} separation ΔV_{w} is 1.2 V and the quantized threshold voltage ΔV_{th} is 0.1 V, which are related to the capacitances,

$$\Delta V_{\mathrm{w}} = \frac{e}{C_{\mathrm{gt}}},$$

and

$$\Delta V_{\mathrm{th}} = \frac{e}{C_{\mathrm{gc}} + C_{\mathrm{gt}}}, \tag{8.3}$$

where C_{gt} is the capacitance between the control gate and the floating dot gate, which is estimated to be 0.16 aF from the

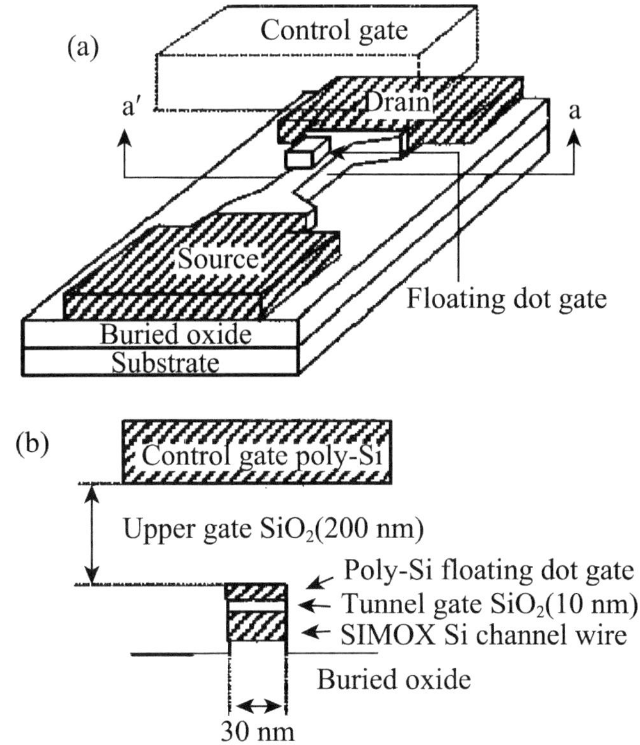

Figure 8.13 (a) Schematic diagram of Si single-electron FET memory with a self-aligned floating gate. (b) Cross-section view along the $a - a'$ line.

geometrical factors of the device. The ΔV_{w} is calculated to be 1.0 V, which is close to that obtained from measurement 1.2 V. C_{gc} is the capacitance between the control gate and the narrow channel wire, which is estimated to be 1.4 aF, giving ΔV_{th} a value of 0.1 V, in agreement with the measurement result.

8.4 Silicon Nanocrystal-Based Memory

The floating gates introduced in above sections are fabricated by lithography technology. The size of dots is limited by the manufacture condition. This section introduces a new kind of quantum dot (nanocrystals) formed by the chemical method. Tiwan

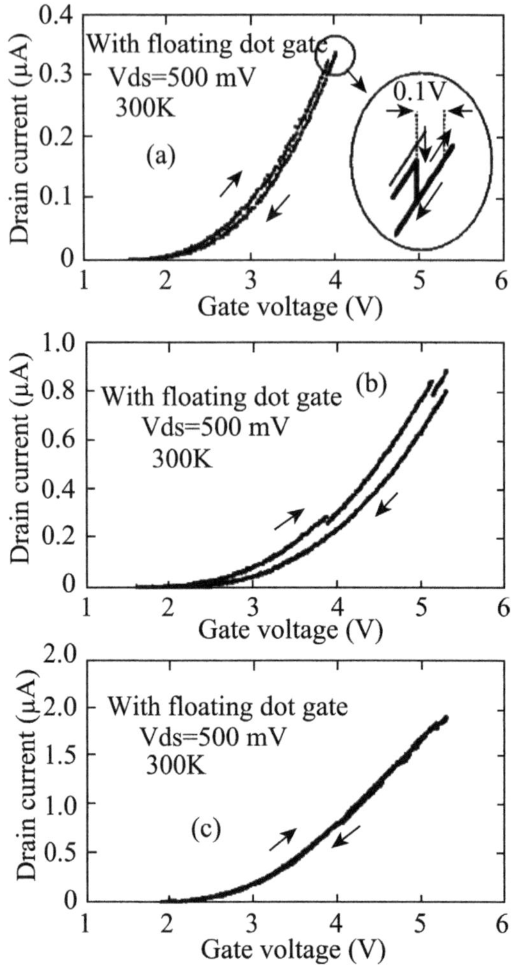

Figure 8.14 Drain current versus control gate voltage at room temperature for (a) and (b) FET with a floating dot gate and (c) FET with no floating dot gate.

et al. [6] fabricated a new memory structure using threshold shifting from charge stored in nanocrystals of silicon (~5 nm in size). A threshold voltage shift of 0.2–0.4 V with read and write times less than hundreds of a nanosecond at an operating voltage below 2.5 V has been obtained experimentally. The retention times are measured

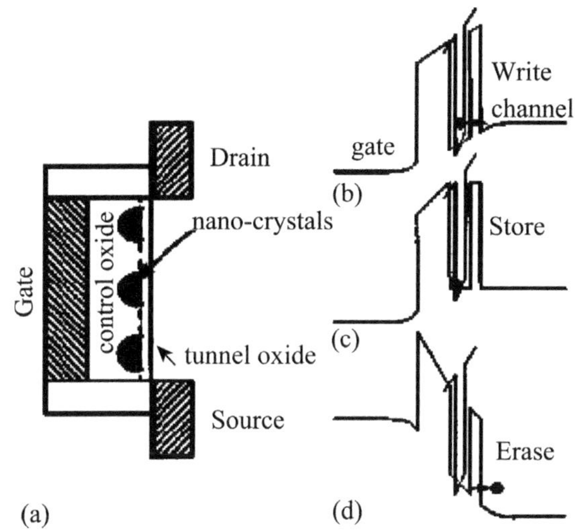

Figure 8.15 (a) Schematic cross section of the device. (b–d) Band diagram for (b) injection, (c) storage, and (d) removal of an electron from a nanocrystal.

in days and weeks, and the structure has been operated in excess of 10^9 cycles without degradation in performance.

Figure 8.15 shows a schematic cross section and band diagram during injection (write cycle), storage (store), and removal (erasure) of an electron in the device [6]. A thin tunneling oxide (1.1–1.8 nm thick) separates the inversion surface of an n-channel silicon FET from a distributed film of nanocrystals of silicon that covers the entire surface channel region. A thicker tunneling oxide (4.5 nm or thicker) separates the nanocrystals from the control gate of the FET. An injection of an electron occurs from the inversion layer via direct tunneling when the control gate is forward biased with respect to the source and drain. The resulting stored charge screens the gate charge and reduces the conduction in the inversion layer, that is, it effectively shifts the threshold voltage of the device to be more positive, whose magnitude for a single electron per nanocrystal is approximately given by

$$\Delta V_{\text{th}} = \frac{en_{\text{w}}}{\varepsilon_{\text{ox}}}\left(t_{\text{c}} + \frac{1}{2}\frac{\varepsilon_{\text{ox}}}{\varepsilon_{\text{Si}}}t_{\text{w}}\right), \tag{8.4}$$

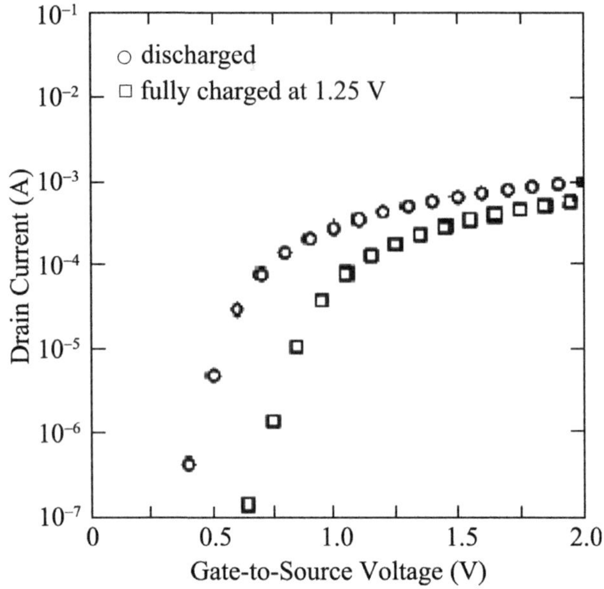

Figure 8.16 A demonstration of the bistability as a result of injection of electrons into nanocrystals. The characteristics are measured with a 20 ns gate voltage pulse.

where ΔV_{th} is the threshold voltage shift, t_c is the thickness of the control oxide under the gate, t_w is the linear dimension of the nanocrystal well, the ε's are the permittivities, q is the magnitude of the electronic charge, and n_w is the density of nanocrystals. For $t_w =$ 5 nm, 5 nm apart, $n_w = 1 \times 10^{12}$ cm^{-2}, $t_c = 7$ nm, and the threshold shift is nearly 0.36 V for one electron per nanocrystal. This is easily current-sensed.

Figure 8.16 shows the drain current-gate voltage characteristics in the presence and absence of electrons in nanocrystals [6]. The characteristics are obtained using 20 ns pulses, applied between gate and grounded source, with the drain maintained at 100 mV. The threshold shift of $\sim$0.25 V under a 1.25 V static gate bias shows the effect of the storage of electrons, estimated to be one electron per nanocrystal. At a 3 V static gate bias the threshold shift is nearly 1.2 V, corresponding to a larger number of electrons per nanocrystal.

The refresh times for the structures are very large, that is, the stored charge does not leak out in accurately measurable times at room temperature. Leakage of the charge occurs either laterally by conduction between the nanocrystals or from the silicon surface with an eventual path to the n^+-doped source and drain regions. The band alignment is unfavorable for tunneling, and the charge movement within the bulk silicon requires diffusion of carriers. Thus, the nanomemory has a long retention time. The write time constants are about 100 ns, which are in the range of theoretical expectations, and should scale exponentially with a reduction in the tunneling oxide thickness. The corollary to the long refresh time is an increase in erase times for the charge. Complete removal of the charge requires milliseconds at voltages of 3 V and above.

Applying a pulse voltage of $\pm$2.5 V can complete a circle of writing (1 μs) and erasing (1 ms). The test shows that after 10^9 circles the threshold voltages persist basically unchanged. It is due to direct tunneling in the charging and discharging of the structure to prevent hot-carrier degradation. Besides, the test used a smaller nanocrystal density to limit power dissipation.

8.5 Retention Property of Nanocrystal Floating Memory

The key of the non-volatility memory of the nanocrystal floating memory is the long period retention property of the electrons in the memory. When some electrons are stored in the nanocrystals, under a selected voltage the stored electrons have a probability to tunnel out of the nanocrystal, leading to a gradual change of the channel current. This gradual change reflects directly the information of the potential height/width, internal electric field, defects, interface states, etc. Thus, research of the time variation of the memory window and the charging and discharging behavior of the Si nanocrystal will clearly explain the retention property of the Si nanocrystal memory devices.

Hinds et al. [7] studied the lifetime of the emission of a single electron stored in a nanocrystalline Si (nc-Si) dot in order to

a)

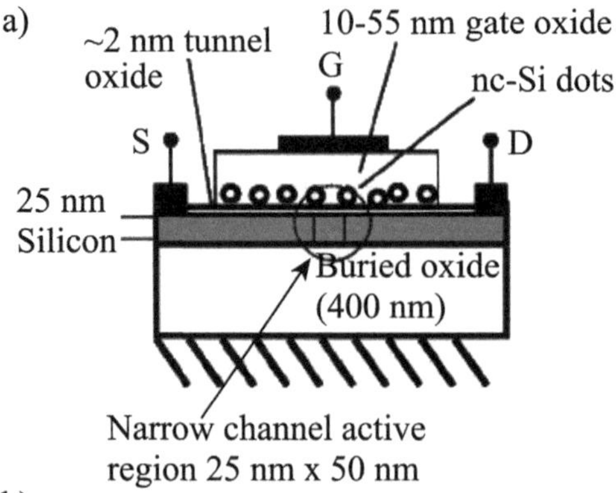

b)

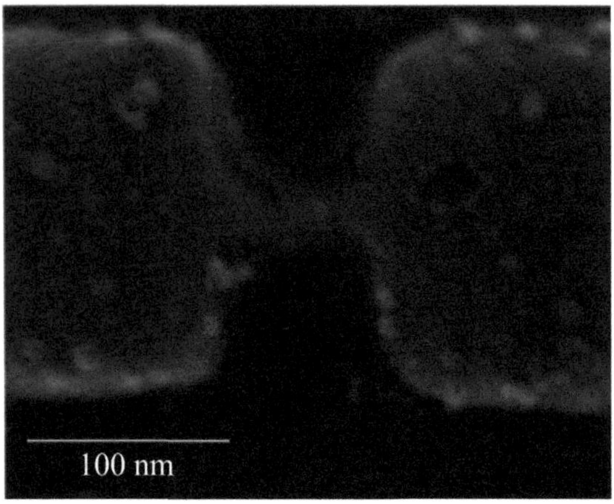

Figure 8.17 (a) Schematic of a single-electron memory device isolating a single nc-Si and a floating gate memory node. (b) Planar scanning electron microscopy view of a representative memory device showing a single nc-Si dot near the center of the narrow channel active region.

understand the physical processes for memory application. The schematic of the FET with nc-Si floating gate nodes is shown in Fig. 8.17a [7]. A small active area FET channel (50 × 25 nm) is defined by electron beam lithography on a thin (20 nm) SOI channel and allows for the electric isolation of a single nc-Si dot. Remote plasma-enhanced chemical vapor deposition is used to form 8 ±

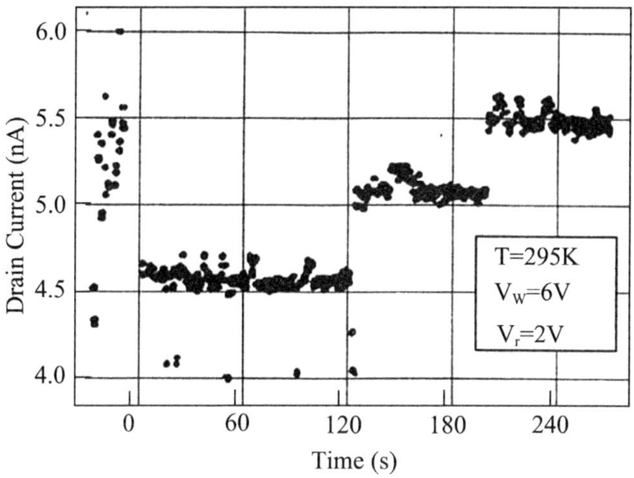

Figure 8.18 Time dependence of the channel current after the writing process.

1 nm diameter nc-Si dots. Electrons stored in a dot result in an observed discrete threshold shift of 90 mV.

For a 25 nm wide channel and a gate oxide thickness of 50 nm the observed shift in V_{th} is 90 mV. Notable is the discrete step in drain current at a constant gate bias after a writing pulse as shown in Fig. 8.18 [7]. A stepwise increase in drain current clearly shows the discrete emission of an electron from the nc-Si dot. The data shown in Fig. 8.18 is a representative example of memory lifetime, and there was a significant distribution of lifetimes for other pulses under the same conditions. For the erase voltage $V_e = -2.25$ to -0.25 V and $T = 295$ K the distribution of the measured memory lifetime is quite broad, with the mean value being nearly equal to the standard deviation. The median lifetime as a function of gate bias is shown in Fig. 8.19 [7]. The shown curves are calculated from a polarizable Schrodinger equation for a 1D confined potential well at the given nc-Si dot diameter. Most notable is the rather small dependence of lifetime on bias over a large voltage range and different slopes for positive and negative biases. The temperature dependence of lifetime is seen to be proportional to $1/T^2$, which is consistent with a direct tunneling process.

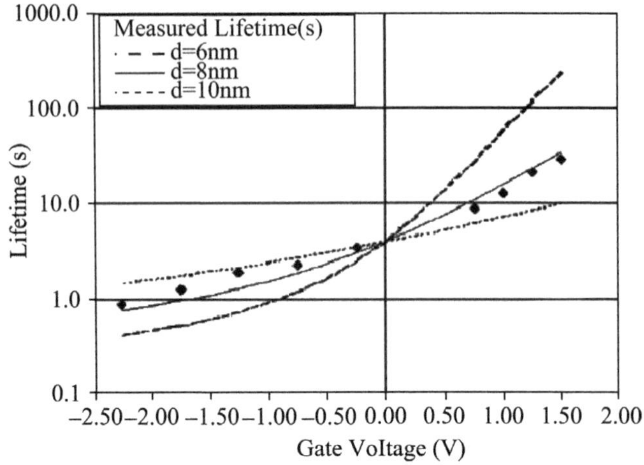

Figure 8.19 Observed median lifetime (solid points) of a nc-Si memory device as a function of applied gate bias.

Because the lifetime has a weak dependence on the gate bias, it is able to infer that the observed electron emission in the nc-Si memory is not from a defect site on the SOI channel/SiO_2 interface or from the nc-Si/SiO_2 interface. Thus, the stored electron behaves as if it were delocalized over the whole dot. To explain the lifetime as a function of applied gate bias, an important concept is that the electron will be attracted to the top of the dot with a positive bias, thus reducing the tunnel current from the bottom of the dot into the channel. And in the negative bias the electron will be attracted to the bottom of the dot, increasing the tunnel current. Figure 8.19 shows the calculated lifetimes as a function of gate bias for three different nc-Si dot diameters. The lifetime can be improved by increasing the tunnel oxide thickness, but this would also increase the write and erase times in a similar fashion. To improve the retention time while not increasing write and erase times it is possible to take advantage of the shallow interfacial traps on the nc-Si interface, for example, the Si_3N_4 trap.

Saitoh et al. [8] proposed an ultra-narrow silicon floating gate memory, in which the channel width is scaled to sub-10 nm. In this ultra-narrow-channel memory a larger threshold voltage shift has been observed than in the wide-channel memory. From the

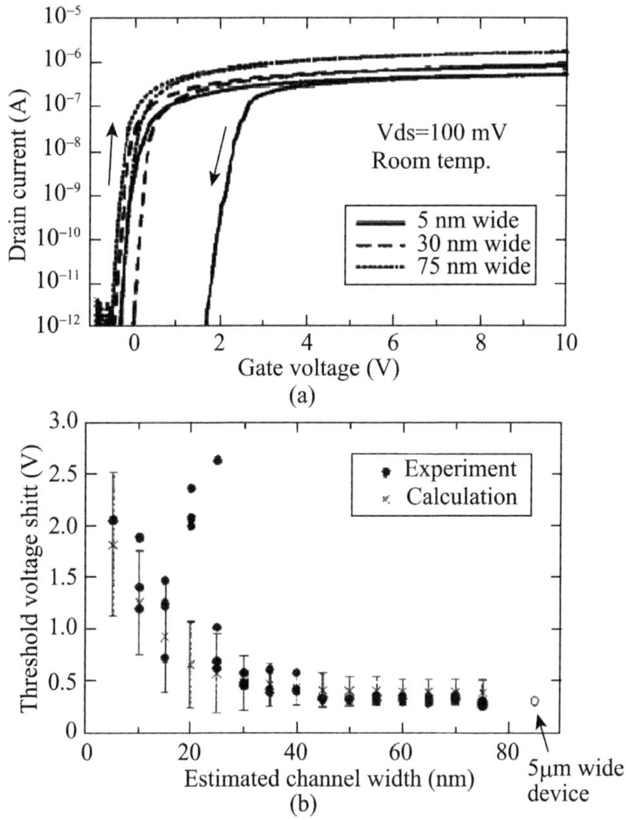

Figure 8.20 (a) Room-temperature hysteresis characteristics of the devices with various channel widths. (b) Measured and calculated results of the channel width dependence of ΔV_{th}.

numerical calculation, it turns out that this is caused by bottleneck regions that dominate the conductance of the whole channel in the ultra-narrow channel. Moreover, a longer charge-retention time has been also obtained in this device.

Figure 8.20a shows the drain current I_{d} as a function of the gate voltage V_{g} with a drain voltage $V_{\text{ds}} = 100$ mV for different channel widths at room temperature [8]. V_{g} scan proceeds from -1 to 10 V and back to -1 V. Hysteresis loops are observed in all the devices, and ΔV_{th} increases as the channel width decreases. Figure 8.20b shows measured ΔV_{th} as a function of estimated channel width.

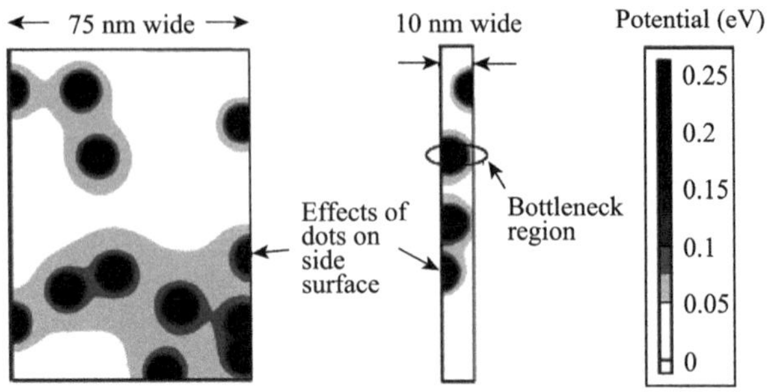

Figure 8.21 Calculated results of the potential distribution in a 75 nm wide channel and a 10 nm wide channel.

When the channel is narrower than 25 nm, ΔV_{th} rapidly increases. The characteristics of 5 μm wide devices (also shown in Fig. 8.20b) are almost the same as 75 nm wide channel devices. From ΔV_{th} in the wide-channel devices, the average number of electrons per dot is estimated to be approximately 0.25.

To understand the mechanism of the large ΔV_{th} in the ultra-narrow channel, the potential distributions are calculated in a 75 nm wide channel and a 10 nm wide channel when one-fourth of the dots are occupied by one electron, and the results are shown in Fig. 8.21 [8]. In the wide channel, the current can flow through the wide and low-potential region. In the ultra-narrow channel, the current path is completely blocked at the bottleneck region where one dot covers almost the entire channel (bottleneck effect). Moreover, the average potential in the ultra-narrow channel is higher than in the wide channel because of the effects of dots on the side surfaces. These effects are the origins of large ΔV_{th} in the ultra-narrow devices.

Figure 8.22a shows the measured retention characteristics [8]. First change the gate voltage from 0 to 10 V (write) or -10 V (erase), and then suddenly change the gate voltage to 0 at a time $t = 0$. V_{th} was measured several times afterward. It is apparent that the ultra-narrow channel (5 nm) device has a wider memory window than the wide channel (5 μm) device at 10^4 s after programming. Even in comparison to normalized ΔV_{th}, the ultra-narrow channel device has longer retention time, as shown in Fig. 8.22b. In the time scale, the retention time in the 5 nm wide channel device is five times longer.

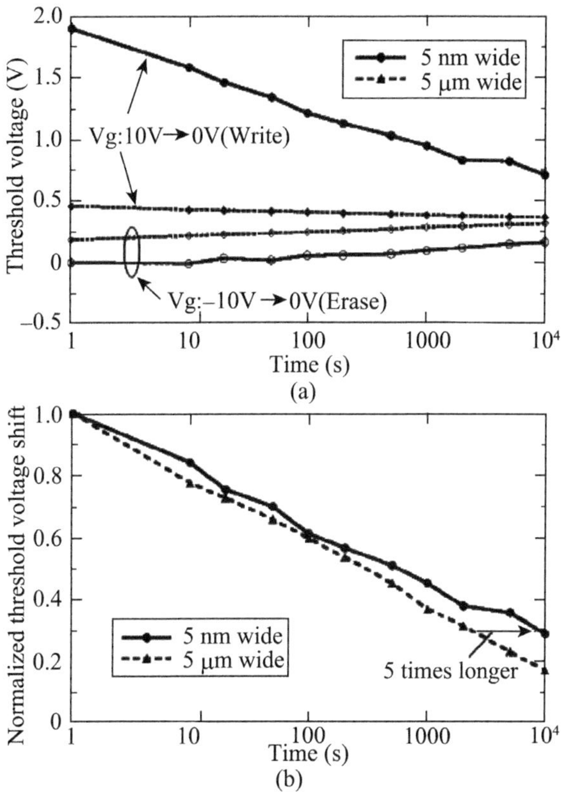

Figure 8.22 (a) Measured retention characteristics in a 5 nm wide device and a 5 μm wide device. (b) Retention characteristics when ΔV_{th} is normalized to the value at 1 s.

Longer retention time in the ultra-narrow-channel devices can be explained by the following two mechanisms. One is a classical bottleneck effect. The linear relationship between ΔV_{th} and the total number of electrons in dots is valid for the wide channel device, while a strong nonlinear relationship exists for the ultra-narrow-channel device. This is because a small number of electrons in several bottleneck regions dominate the conductance of the whole channel and the influence of one electron is much larger in the ultra-narrow-channel devices. It is found that when electrons are emitted from dots and the total number of electrons is decreased by 90%,

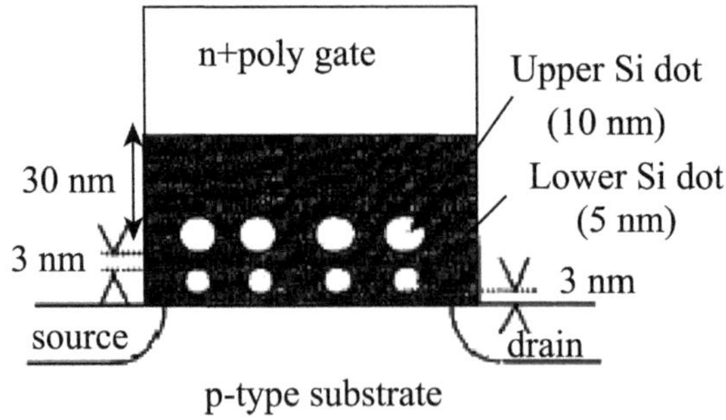

Figure 8.23 Schematic diagram of Si self-aligned doubly stacked dot memory.

ΔV_{th} decreases by 90% in the 75 nm wide channel device and by 61% in the 5 nm wide channel device. The other mechanism is the quantum confinement effect. The tunneling rate from a dot to the ultra-narrow channel is lower than that to the wide channel because the ground energy level in the ultra-narrow channel is lifted up due to the increased quantum confinement.

The manufacture of an ultra-narrow channel is difficult. Ohba et al. [9] proposed a Si dot memory whose floating gate consists of self-aligned doubly stacked Si dots, as shown in Fig. 8.23. A smaller Si dot exists immediately below an upper dot and lies over the thin tunnel oxide. It is experimentally shown that charge retention is improved compared to the usual single layer Si dot memory. Due to the quantum confinement effect and the CB effect of the lower layer dots, the energy of electronic states increases and the tunneling rate of electrons in the upper layer dots through the lower layer dots decreases, leading to increase of the retention time.

The upper diagram in Fig. 8.24 shows the energy band diagrams in a low-gate-voltage (V_g) region [9], and V_{eff} represents the voltage difference between the channel and the charged Si dot. In the usual single-dot memory the electrons only pass through a thin tunnel oxide. However, in the doubly stacked dot memory, the tunnel probability P_t will decrease by the energy barrier height ΔE, which is due to CB and quantum confinement in the lower Si dot. Since the lower dot is smaller than the upper dot, ΔE will be determined by the lower dot size effects. The ratio of tunnel probability $\alpha_{ret} = P_{tsingle}/P_{tdouble}$ in a low-voltage region is a measure of

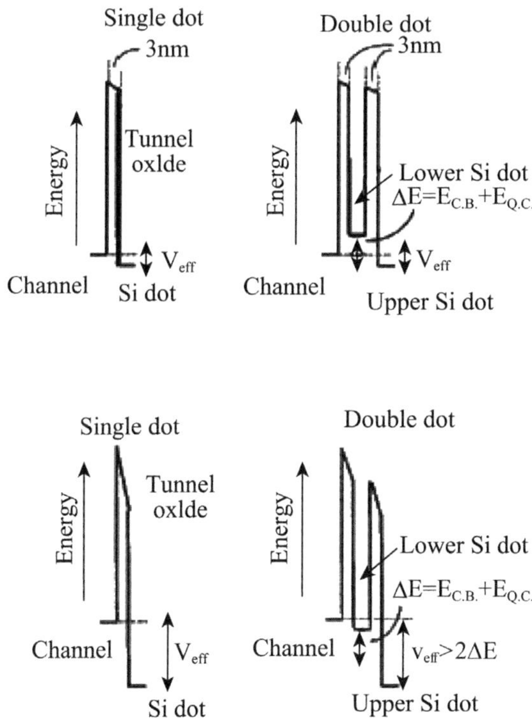

Figure 8.24 Upper diagram: In a low V_g region. Lower diagram: In write operation the energy band diagrams for single and double-dot memory.

retention improvement of the double-dot memory compared to the single-dot one. The retention improvement factor is obtained as follows:

$$\alpha_{\text{ret}} = \alpha\left(V_{\text{eff}} \approx 0\right) = \left(\frac{2k_{\text{B}}T}{\Delta E}\right) \sinh\left(\frac{\Delta E}{k_{\text{B}}T}\right). \quad (8.5)$$

The exponential dependence on ΔE is very important.

Figure 8.25 shows the retention factor α_{ret} as a function of ΔE at 300 K. With a decrease of the lower dot diameter the α_{ret} increases in orders of magnitude. Though the w/e speed reduction factor $\alpha_{\text{w/e}}$ is small and less than 10, the retention is improved exponentially.

The lower diagram of Fig. 8.24 shows the band diagram in write operations. When the write/erase process is in the $|V_{\text{eff}}| > 2\Delta E$, a high speed will be possible in the double-dot memory because there is no energy barrier in the tunneling process. As in the retention

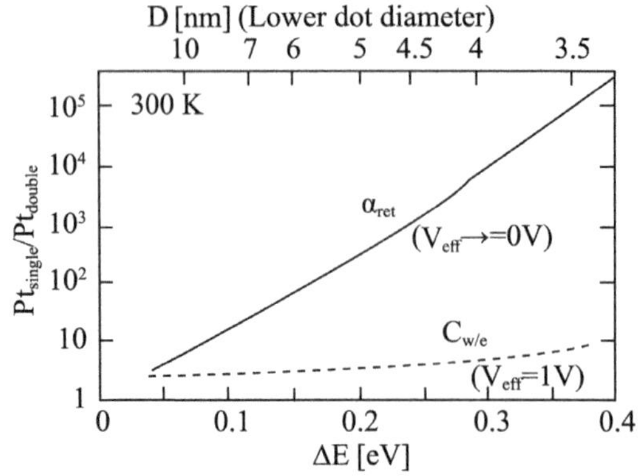

Figure 8.25 Retention improvement factor α_{ret} as a function of ΔE. The corresponding lower Si dot diameter D is plotted in the upper abscissa. $\alpha_{\text{w/e}}$ is the velocity reduction factor.

case, the current ratio $\alpha_{\text{w/e}}$ is a measure of the speed reduction. The speed reduction factor is approximately expressed as

$$\alpha_{\text{w/e}} = \alpha\left(V_{\text{eff}} > \frac{2\Delta E}{e}\right) = \frac{2}{\left[1 - \left(\frac{2\Delta E}{V_{\text{eff}}}\right)\right]}. \tag{8.6}$$

It is important that $\alpha_{\text{w/e}}$ have no exponential dependence on ΔE.

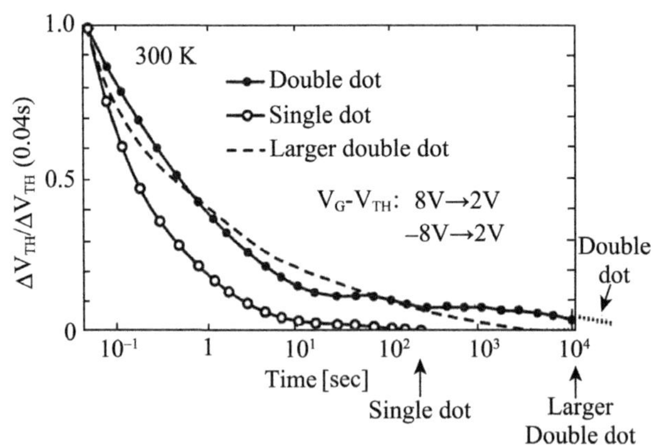

Figure 8.26 Time dependence of the memory window at the same bias condition for the double-dot memory, the double-dot memory with larger dots, and the single-dot memory.

Figure 8.26 shows the time dependence of the memory window at the same bias condition for the double-dot memory, the double-dot memory with larger dots, and the single-dot memory [9]. The value for a 5 nm lower dot memory (solid dots) is larger than that for the single-dot memory (empty circle) by more than 10^2 times, consistent with the retention factor $\alpha_{\mathrm{ret}} \approx 300$ in Fig. 8.25. For the larger double-dot memory (dashed line) ΔV_{th} disappears at 10^4 s, corresponding to $\alpha_{\mathrm{ret}} \approx 30$ in Fig. 8.25.

References

1. Takahashi, Y., Ono, Y., Fujiwara, A., and Inokawa, H. (2002). Silicon single-electron devices. *J. Phys. C*, **14**, R995–R1033.
2. Store, N. J., and Ahmed, H. (1998). Silicon single electron memory cell. *Appl. Phys. Lett.*, **73**, 2134–2136.
3. Takahashi, Y., Fujiwara, A., Yamazaki, K., et al. (1999). A Si memory device composed of a one-dimensional metal-oxide-semiconductor field effect-transistor switch and a single-electron-transistor detector. *Jpn. J. Appl. Phys.*, **38**, 2457–2461.
4. Guo, L., Leobandung, E., and Chou, S. Y. (1997). A room-temperature silicon single-electron metal-oxide-semiconductor memory with nanoscale floating-gate and ultranarrow channel. *Appl. Phys. Lett.*, **70**, 850–852.
5. Nakajima, A., Futasugi, T., Kosemura, K., Fukano, T., and Yokoyama, N. (1997). Room temperature operation of Si single-electron memory with self-aligned floating dot gate. *Appl. Phys. Lett.*, **70**, 1742–1744.
6. Tiwari, S., Rana, F., Hanafi, H., Harstein, A., Crabbe, E. F., and Chan, K. (1996). A silicon nanocrystals based memory. *Appl. Phys. Lett.*, **68**, 1377–1379.
7. Hinds, B. J., Yamanaka, T., and Oda, S. (2001). Emission lifetime of polarizable charge stored in nano-crystalline Si based single-electron memory. *J. Appl. Phys.*, **90**, 6402–6408.
8. Saitoh, M., nagata, E., and Hiramoto, T. (2003). Large memory window and long charge-retention time in ultranarrow-channel silicon floating-dot memory. *Appl. Phys. Lett.*, **82**, 1787–1789.
9. Ohba, R., Sugiyama, N., and Uchida, K. (2002). Nonvolatile Si quantum memory with self-aligned doubly-stacked dots. *IEEE Trans. Electron Devices*, **49**, 1392–1398.

Part II

Quantum Waveguide Theory in Mesoscopic Systems

Chapter 9

Properties of Quantum Transport

9.1 Characteristic Length [1]

In traditional transistors, the electron's movement is classical. But when the scale of the device is so small that its scale is about equal to or smaller than some characteristic lengths, there will be distinct quantum effects of current.

Electrons in two-dimensional electron gas (2DEG) degenerate at a low temperature, so their Fermi wave vector can be written as

$$k_F = \sqrt{2\pi n_s}, \tag{9.1}$$

where n_s is the area density of 2DEG. The electrons' Fermi wavelength is

$$\lambda_F = \frac{2\pi}{k_F} = \sqrt{\frac{2\pi}{n_s}}. \tag{9.2}$$

For electrons with an area density $n_s = 5 \times 10^{11}$ cm^{-2}, the Fermi wavelength is about 35 nm, so it is obviously comparable to the scale of mesoscopic devices. At a low temperature, the electric current is contributed mostly by electrons near the Fermi energy; other electrons with energy less than the Fermi energy do not contribute to the conductance. Therefore the Fermi wavelength is associated with the quantum effect of current.

Quantum Waveguide in Microcircuits
Jian-Bai Xia, Duan-Yang Liu, and Wei-Dong Sheng

ISBN 978-981-4669-85-6 (Hardcover), 978-1-315-36477-3 (eBook)
www.panstanford.com

Electrons that move in a semiconductor will be scattered by impurities, defects, or phonons. Their momentum relaxation time τ_m and scattering time τ_s have the relationship

$$\frac{1}{\tau_m} = \frac{1}{\tau_s}\alpha_m, \tag{9.3}$$

where α_m is a constant between 0 and 1, and it denotes effectiveness for momentum relaxation of different scatterings.

The mean free path L_m is defined as the average distance traveled by an electron before it loses its momentum. So it can be written as

$$L_m = k_F \tau_m, \tag{9.4}$$

where k_F is the Fermi velocity, and for electrons with an area density $n_s = 5 \times 10^{11}$ cm^{-2}, on the basis of Eq. 9.1, we obtain:

$$k_F = \frac{\hbar k_F}{m^*} = \frac{\hbar}{m^*}\sqrt{2\pi n_s} = 3 \times 10^7 \text{ cm/s}, \tag{9.5}$$

where m^* is the electron's effective mass and m_0 is the rest mass of an electron. If $m^* = 0.067\ m_0$ and $\tau_m \cong 100$ ps, then from Eq. 9.4 $L_m = 30$ μm can be obtained.

The phase relaxation length is defined as the average distance traveled by an electron before the electron wave loses its phase. Similar to the momentum relaxation time τ_m, the phase relaxation time τ_φ has the following relationship with the scattering time τ_s:

$$\frac{1}{\tau_\varphi} = \frac{1}{\tau_c}\alpha_\varphi, \tag{9.6}$$

where α_φ is a constant between 0 and 1, and it denotes the effectiveness for phase destruction of different scattering.

To understand the concept of phase destruction, we imagine an experiment of an Aharonov–Bohm (AB) ring. The incident electron beam splits into two at one end of the ring, moves up and down the two arms, then meets at the other end of the ring. If the lengths of both arms are the same and the phases of the two waves at the meeting point are equal, then the amplitude rises. Assume that there are impurities or defects (named scatterers) randomly distributed in each arm. They will scatter the passing electron wave. Because these scatterers are static and elastic, they do not change the electron's energy, just change its phase. When the two electron waves meet, their phases are unequal and so interference reduces the amplitude.

Because the scatterers are static, the phase relationship between the two paths is definite.

If we add a magnetic field perpendicular to the ring, the electron wave moving up or down an arm get a extra positive or negative phase shift, which is in proportion to the magnetic flux Φ through the ring. Therefore the amplitude of the output electron wave oscillates with Φ, and it is the AB effect. In the case that there are scatterings in the arms, although the amplitude reduces when $\Phi = 0$ (the magnetic field is zero), when the strength of the field increases, the amplitude's oscillation with Φ doesn't change. When Φ reaches a certain value, the amplitude reaches its maximum. We can say that the loss of the phase at the scatterings was compensated by the magnetic field. In this condition, we can consider

$$\alpha_\varphi = 0,\ \tau_\varphi \to \infty, \tag{9.7}$$

that is, the elastic scattering of static scatterings doesn't affect the phase relaxation time. This fact has been proved by the experiment. Experiments found that the length of two arms of an AB ring is much larger than the mean free path L_{m} in general, that is, an electron has experienced repeatedly the momentum elastic scattering but experiments still observe the AB oscillation.

A major factor that affects phase relaxation is the inelastic scattering of electron-phonon. A phonon is one quantum mode of the lattice vibrations, which is not a static point as an impurity or a defect, so its scattering on electrons has the property of being random. As it is inelastic scattering, in every scattering the electron's energy will increase or decrease the energy of a phonon. When two electron waves scattered by phonons meet, the relationship of their phases is irregular, so the average amplitude of the electron wave reduces. In summary, rigid scatterers do not contribute to phase relaxation, only fluctuating scatterers do.

Assume that after time τ_φ, the mean square energy that the electron gains in phonon scattering is equal to the square of energy that the electron gains each time multiplied by the number of scattering:

$$(\Delta\varepsilon)^2 = (\hbar\omega)^2 \left(\tau_\varphi / \tau_{\text{s}}\right), \tag{9.8}$$

where $\hbar\omega$ is the energy of a phonon. The phase relaxation time is defined as that after time τ_φ the mean square value of an electron's phase change is roughly equal to 1:

$$\Delta\varphi \sim (\Delta\varepsilon)\,\tau_\varphi/\hbar \sim 1. \tag{9.9}$$

It can be obtained from Eq. 9.8 and Eq. 9.9:

$$\tau_\varphi = \left(\frac{\tau_S}{\omega^2}\right)^{1/3}. \tag{9.10}$$

Therefore for the low-frequency phonon (acoustic phonon), its influence on the phase relaxation is small. A major factor of phase relaxation is the optical phonon.

At a low temperature, a major factor of the phase relaxation is electron–electron scattering. The frequency of electron–electron scattering is determined by the difference of electron energy E and Fermi energy E_F: $\Delta = E - E_F$. Because Δ is smaller, the states that can be scattered are very few because of the Pauli exclusion principle. So the probability of scattering goes to zero. In 2DEG, it has been proved that

$$\frac{\hbar}{\tau_\varphi} \sim \frac{\Delta^2}{E_F}\left[\ln\left(\frac{E_F}{\Delta}\right) + \text{const.}\right]. \tag{9.11}$$

Because the hot electron's average energy $\Delta \approx k_B T$, the relationship between τ_φ and T is the formula when Δ is replaced by $k_B T$ in Eq. 9.11.

9.2 Phase-Coherent Effect [2]

When electrons pass through a device, if the size of the device is smaller than electrons' coherent length (inelastic mean free path), different waves will interfere. The coherent effect will result in additional scattering, then reduce the conductivity. In addition, the coherent effect will result in the AB effect, universal conductance fluctuation, etc.; all these are named mesoscopic effects.

One of important problems is the conductance fluctuation caused by the quantum effects. Assume the action area of the gate is 0.1 $\times$ 0.05 μm^2 and the carrier concentration in the inversion layer is 2×10^{12} cm^{-2}. Then there are only 100 electrons under the gate. The conductance's change caused by the phase coherence is on the order of e^2/h, about 40 μS. If the normal conductivity is 1000 mS/mm, then for a device with a gate width 0.1 μm, the total conductance is 100 μS. Therefore the conductance fluctuation caused by the phase coherence is 40% of total conductance, so it will limit the performance of the device greatly.

In addition, if the orbit of a ballistic electron surrounds an obstacle, such as an impurity atom, then interference between two orbits will also result in the phase coherent effect. Especially when there is a perpendicular magnetic field in the area surrounded by two orbits, the AB effect will occur. Here the wave function in the closed loop can be expressed by the integral along the loop:

$$\Psi \sim \exp\left[\frac{e}{\hbar}\left(\int_1 \mathbf{A}\cdot d\mathbf{l} - \int_2 \mathbf{A}\cdot d\mathbf{l}\right)\right] = \exp\left[\frac{e}{\hbar}\oint \mathbf{B}\cdot d\mathbf{S}\right] = \exp\left(\frac{\Phi}{\Phi_0}\right), \quad (9.12)$$

where $\Phi_0 = h/e$ is the magnetic flux quantum. The electric current passing through the closed loop will oscillate periodically with the magnetic flux. When a current of 10 mA pass through the loop, if there is a magnetic field of 0.02 T, then the AB effect can result in distinct fluctuation.

9.3 Coulomb Blockade Effects

Experiments found that for a small quantum dot, only when the electric voltage is larger than a certain value, the electron can pass through the dot. The reason is that the Coulomb interaction between the electron in a quantum dot and the electron in a circuit will reject the entry of the second electron to the quantum dot. Only when the energy of the electron exceeds the Coulomb interaction energy, the second electron can enter the quantum dot and the current can occur. This appearance is named Coulomb blockade (CB) effects, and the relationship curve between voltage and current has the shape of a step, which is named the Coulomb staircase. The CB effects have been observed in 2DEG systems in Si metal-oxide semiconductor field-effect transistor (Si-MOSFET) and GaAs heterojunction.

From the point of view of a large-scale integrated circuit, all effects above are unfavorable, and we should avoid these in design.

On the other hand, these mesoscopic effects may be utilized in the new generation of electronic devices. For example, in a device that has a size smaller than the inelastic scattering mean free path, electrons follow the motion law of quantum mechanics, so we can utilize properties of quantum interference and quantum waveguide to design the device and to control the movement of electrons. And we can design a single-electron transistor by using CB effects, which can greatly reduce the number of electrons stored in one bit and can reduce power dissipation of memory devices. Because spin of an electron has a much longer scattering time and distance than that of electric charge, we can utilize spin as the information carrier to design spintronics devices and so on.

9.4 Landauer–Büttiker Formula

Datta first proposed the concept of a quantum device in 1989 [3], which can only be understood by considering an electron's wave property in simple terms. Concepts that can describe an electron's movement are no longer scattering probability, relaxation time, mobility. and so on. For a two-terminal device, assume that a^+ and a^- are amplitudes of the electron wave in the income circuit and b^+ and b^- are amplitudes of the electron wave in the outcome circuit. Then for a definite energy E, they can be related by a scattering matrix

$$\begin{pmatrix} a^- \\ b^- \end{pmatrix} = \begin{pmatrix} r(E) & t'(E) \\ t(E) & r'(E) \end{pmatrix} \begin{pmatrix} a^+ \\ b^+ \end{pmatrix}, \tag{9.13}$$

where $r(E)$ and $r'(E)$ denote reflection coefficients and $t(E)$ and $t'(E)$ denote transmission coefficients, which are determined by the internal potential and structure.

The circuit has a certain width. Then there are transverse modes with different energies. In common, the transport in the longitudinal direction is multimode, so the amplitudes a^+ and a^- are column matrices of size $(M_\mathrm{a} \times 1)$ and b^+ and b^- are column matrices of size $(M_\mathrm{b} \times 1)$. Similarly, r is a matrix with size $(M_\mathrm{a} \times M_\mathrm{b})$, t is a matrix with size $(M_\mathrm{b} \times M_\mathrm{a})$, and so on. M_a and M_b are the number of transverse modes in the income circuit and outcome circuit, respectively.

In Landauer–Büttiker formula, conductance is expressed by the scattering performance, so this theory is suitable for solving conductance of a system that is made of different materials or conductors of different shapes in contact with each other. This theory is the basic theory in the research on mesoscopic transport.

Suppose an electron moves in an infinite ideal conductor along the z axis and ignore the positive ions in lattice points and the scattering of positive electric charge on the electron. In the absence of a magnetic field (so take no account of the spin), the Hamiltonian of the electron is

$$H = \frac{p^2}{2m} + V(x, y), \tag{9.14}$$

where $V(x, y)$ is the lateral confinement potential in the wire. On the basis of the Hamiltonian (Eq. 9.14), we can obtain the system's eigenstate

$$\Psi_{\alpha k}(x, y, z) = \frac{1}{\sqrt{2\pi}} e^{ikz} \phi_\alpha(x, y), \tag{9.15}$$

where k is the wave vector along the z direction of the wire, α denotes the α-th transverse eigenstate, and the eigenenergy corresponding to the α-th eigenstate is $E_{\alpha k} = E_\alpha + \hbar^2 \mathrm{k}^2/2\ \mathrm{m}$. The first term and the second term are lateral and longitudinal energy, respectively, and the lateral energy E_α is determined by the lateral confinement potential $V(x, y)$. We can use the square potential well to express the lateral confinement potential of an ideal wire. Suppose the well in one direction is very narrow and the width in another direction is W. Then the lateral energy $E_\alpha = (\mathrm{n}\hbar\pi)^2/2\,mW^2$ has discrete energy levels. According to this, the energy spectrum of the system is made up of a series of parabolic and discrete energy bands and the minimum value of the corresponding curve is E_α. As shown in Fig. 9.1, every parabola denotes a lateral energy band, which is named the allow mode.

When $T = 0$ K, the current in the α-th channel of the wire can be expressed as

$$I_\alpha = \frac{2}{2\pi}\int_0^{k_{\max}} ev_{\alpha k} dk = \frac{2}{2\pi}\int_0^{k_{\max}} ev_{\alpha k}\frac{dk}{dE_{\alpha k}} dE_{\alpha k} = \frac{2e}{h}(\mu - E_\alpha), \tag{9.16}$$

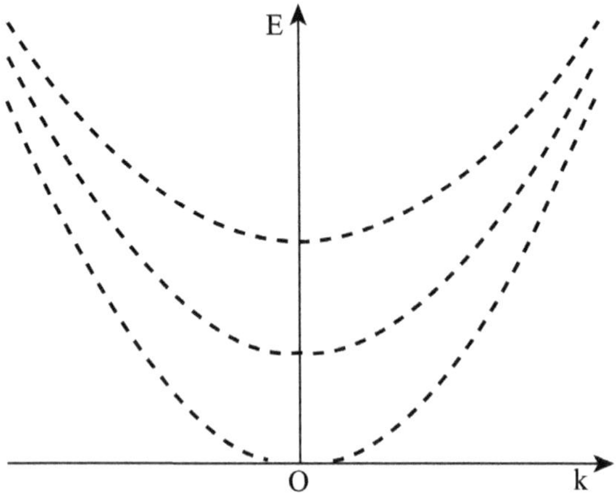

Figure 9.1 Dispersion relation $E(k)$ as the function of k.

where $v_{\alpha k} = 1/\hbar \times dE_{\alpha k}/dk$ is electron's group velocity and μ is the chemical potential (Fermi energy level).

If the width of the ideal conductor is small enough, then the energy gap between two energy bands will be large enough for the electron to just occupy the lowest energy band, and then this energy band will become the one and only allow channel. At present we can calculate the net current in the wires with the chemical potentials μ_1 and μ_2 connected to each other:

$$I = I_1 - I_2 = \left(\frac{2e}{h}\right)\mu_1 - \left(\frac{2e}{h}\right)\mu_2 = \left(\frac{2e^2}{h}\right)(V_1 - V_2). \quad (9.17)$$

Therefore the conductance of a two-terminal, single-channel device is

$$G = \frac{I}{V_1 - V_2} = \frac{2e^2}{h}. \quad (9.18)$$

This is the Landauer formula of a two-terminal, single-channel system; $2e^2/h$ is called the quantum conductance.

If the wire has a finite width, the electron may occupy several energy bands. Assume that N channels have been filled in and $f(E)$ denotes the probability that the channel has been occupied by the electron. At present the current can be written as

$$I = \frac{2e}{h}\int_0^\infty dE\left[f_1(E)\sum_i T_i(E) - f_2(E)\sum_i T_i(E)\right], \quad (9.19)$$

where $T_i = \sum_j T_{ij} = \sum_j |t_{ij}|^2$ denotes the total transmission probability of an electron transport from all channels of wire 1 to the i-th channel of wire 2. $f_1(E)$ and $f_2(E)$ are the Fermi–Dirac distribution function in wire 1 and wire 2, respectively. Therefore the current of the system is

$$I = \frac{2e}{h}\int dE\,[f(E) - f(E + V_D)]T(E), \tag{9.20}$$

where $f(E)$ is the Fermi–Dirac distribution function, $V_D = V_1 - V_2$ is the bias voltage of the system, and $T(E) = \Sigma_i T_i(E)$ is the total transmission probability. For a small bias, Eq. 9.20 can be simplified as

$$G = \frac{I}{V_D} = \frac{2e^2}{h}\int dE\left(-\frac{\partial f}{\partial E}\right)T(E). \tag{9.21}$$

At a low temperature, $-\partial f/\partial E = \delta(E - E_F)$. So in the end, we obtain

$$G = \frac{2e^2}{h}T(E_F) = \frac{2e^2}{h}\sum_{i=1}^{M_a}\sum_{j=1}^{M_b}\left|t_{ij}(E_F)\right|^2, \tag{9.22}$$

where $t_{ij}(E_F)$ is the transmission coefficient shown in Eq. 9.13, and Eq. 9.22 is the Landauer–Büttiker formula for the two-terminal, multichannel device. It follows that the key point of utilizing the Landauer–Büttiker formula is solving the transmission coefficient matrix t. Most research on mesoscopic transport focuses on this problem, so next we will introduce three methods that are widely used to calculate the transmission coefficient matrix.

The two-terminal Landauer formula can be extended to the multi-terminal device. Considering a three-terminal device, we can write its scattering matrix functions similar to Eq. 9.13:

$$\begin{pmatrix} a^- \\ b^- \\ c^- \end{pmatrix} = \begin{pmatrix} r_{aa} & t_{ab} & t_{ac} \\ t_{ba} & r_{bb} & t_{bc} \\ t_{ca} & t_{cb} & r_{cc} \end{pmatrix}\begin{pmatrix} a^+ \\ b^+ \\ c^+ \end{pmatrix}. \tag{9.23}$$

Büttiker has proved that the current I_i ($i = a, b, c$) has the following relationship with the chemical potential of every circuit μ_i:

$$I_i = \frac{2e^2}{h}\sum_{j=a,b,c}\left(T_{ij}\mu_j - T_{ji}\mu_i\right), \tag{9.24}$$

where

$$T_{ij} = \sum_{m,n=1}^{M} \left|(t_{ij})_{mn}\right|^2. \tag{9.25}$$

When there is no external field, $T_{ij} = T_{ji}$ and Eq. 9.24 can be written as

$$I_i = \frac{2e^2}{h} \sum_{j=a,b,c} T_{ij}\left(\mu_j - \mu_i\right), \tag{9.26}$$

where $\mu_j - \mu_i$ corresponds to the bias voltage between two circuits. The conductance between each pair of circuits can be defined as

$$G_{ij} = \frac{2e^2}{h} T_{ij}, \quad i, j = a, b, c\,(i \neq j). \tag{9.27}$$

Equations 9.22 and 9.27 are the fundamental formulas of quantum conductance. They form the theoretical basis of future quantum devices. For a certain device, we should obtain scattering matrices $r_{aa}(E)$, $t_{ab}(E)$, ... It is shown in Eq. 9.24 that the quantum device is non-local, and change of any terminal's chemical potential will influence currents in all circuits.

9.5 Spintronics

Electron spin, or intrinsic electronic angular momentum, is another intrinsic property of an electron besides electric charge. The electron spin has two discrete values $\pm\hbar/2$, which are commonly named the spin-up state and the spin-down state. This is very similar to the high and low levels or switch off and switch on used to realize logic '1' and '0' states. Moreover, a 1/2-spin system is an ideal two-level system, and spin-up and spin-down states are an ideal choice to realize the quantum bit (qubit) in quantum calculation. Recently in the traditional electronic industry, devices are getting more and more integrated and the size of devices is getting smaller and smaller, which results in distinct quantum effects and too much energy consumption. Therefore, naturally, people think of utilizing spin-free degree, which always was neglected formerly, to replace or to combine the charge-free degree. Therefore, the research on how to control spin-free degree effectively has attracted wide attention of scientists and was named "spintronics" by Wolf et al. formally in 2001 [4]. Spintronics researches a particle's spin in a solid and applies it in devices, and it contains spin polarization's production, control, transport, and exploration. It is an interdiscipline field that involves electronics, magnetism, optics, and micro- and nanoprocessing technology. According to the materials researched, it can be grouped into two areas: metal spintronics and semiconductor spintronics.

Ideal spintronics devices realize functions by coupling of spin orientation and spin, so they may not be restricted by the number of electric charges and energy dissipation, and they have a lower power dissipation and a faster running speed. Moreover, electronic storage devices based on spin have the advantage of nonvolatility. This shows clearly that spintronics will have wide prospects of development and application in areas of quantum calculation, communication, molecules, chemistry, and so on. Therefore people expect that spintronics can construct the physical foundation of a new generation of nanoelectronics and the spintronics device will replace the current microelectronics devices.

The symbol of spintronics' birth is the discovery of the giant magnetoresistance (GMR) of the metallic multilayer structure in 1988 [5, 6]. The proposition of spin-vales and room-temperature magnetic sensor utilizing anisotropic magnetoresistance makes for great success of GMR in commerce. Nowadays a new generation of the magnetic heads of high-density disks is using the GMR principle. Now thanks to the high sensitivity to the magnetic field of GMR, each GMR magnetic head has to be reduced to 30–50 nm and more than 4 T volume in desktops and more than 1 T volume in laptops have been realized.

Now spintronics devices are mostly made of metal magnetic materials, which belong to the first category of spintronics, that is, magnetoelectronics. In 1995 scientists found a new phenomenon, tunneling magnetoresistance (TMR) [7], which has larger magnetoresistance and smaller coercive force. The magnetic tunnel junction (MTJ) utilizing the TMR technology has been created, and new magnetoresistive random access memory (MRAM) is expected to replace nonvolatile memory based on the complementary metal-oxide semiconductor (CMOS). This new generation of memory has advantages such as no data loss on power failure, a rapid reading speed comparable to static random access memory (SRAM), and large memory space comparable to dynamic random access memory (DRAM), so it has wide application prospects.

The second category of spintronics mainly studies semiconductors, and it hopes to create an imbalance of the spin number to realize spin transistors and spin valves and then replace traditional electronic devices. These new spintronics devices have characteristics such as low energy consumption and rapid switching speed. Because ready-made mature semiconductor technology and equipment can be used to reduce the developing cost, these devices have attracted wide attention. To utilize spin-free degree in semiconductors, we must produce, keep, control, and detect the spin polarization of carriers.

There are several methods that can produce spin current: ohmic injection, tunnel injection, ballistic electron injection, utilizing the giant Zeeman splitting of a dilute magnetic semiconductor (DMS) in a magnetic field, utilizing a ferromagnetic semiconductor (FMS) as a spin calibrator, the optical method, and so on. Ohmic injection means using a ferromagnetic metal (FM) as an electrode to inject spin-polarized electrons. If the ohmic contact is created in the junction between the FM and the semiconductor, then it can be expected that the spin-polarized current in the FM can be injected into the semiconductor. However, the ohmic contact by heavy doping produces scattering of the spin flip, which reduces spin polarization. At $T < 10$ K, from FM-InAs ohmic contact, spin-polarized electrons of 4.5% have been obtained [8]. At room temperature, from the Fe-GaAs contact, spin-polarized electrons of 2% have been obtained [9].

The scanning tunneling microscopy (STM) experiment has proved that a process of vacuum tunnel can inject spin-polarized electrons into a semiconductor effectively [10]. The FM-insulator-FM tunnel junction with a high magnetoresistance experiment has determined that the tunneling barrier can remain spin polarization of electrons in the tunneling process. This means tunneling is a more effective method of spin injection than diffusive transport. The two methods above both rely on the ferromagnetic film's epitaxial growth on a semiconductor and demand a sharp interface and a high-quality Schottky potential barrier between the metal and the semiconductor.

The third method is using ballistic transport. From the energy difference of the conduction bands of two kinds of spin in a ferromagnetic material and the conduction band of a semiconductor, we can determine the ballistic electron's spin transmissivity and reflectivity at the junction. If we create a point contact between a FM and a nonferromagnetic metal, experiments have proved that current with spin polarization up to 40% is realized in a nonferromagnetic metal by using a ballistic injection [11]. Using the DMS $Be_{0.07}Mn_{0.03}Zn_{0.9}Se$ as the spin aligner, at a low temperature ($\sim$10 K) and an external magnetic field (>1 T), spin polarization injection efficiency up to 90% is realized when electrons pass through the $Be_{0.07}Mn_{0.03}Zn_{0.9}Se$ with a width of 300 nm [12]. This is because in a magnetic field, a low concentration of Mn ions creates giant Zeeman splitting in the conduction and valence bands by the sp-d interaction and the electron's effective Lande g-factor may be up to 100. At a low temperature, electrons only occupy the lowest $S = -1/2$ band, so a spin polarization current is produced. Similarly, a FMS can be used as a spin aligner.

The optical method is an important method to produce a spin current, and it is also an important method to detect spin polarization of carriers. Assume that there is a sample of a GaAs quantum well, and its direction of growth is along the z axis. In the GaAs quantum well, the energies of the heavy hole and the light hole are split and the heavy hole state is the ground state, while the light hole state is the excited state. Using a beam of circularly polarized light (σ^+) with energy equal to a light exciton to radiate on the quantum well sample along its growth direction, due to the transition selection rule of heavy holes, light holes, and electrons, this beam of light can just excite electrons in light hole states of $L_z = -1/2$ to electron states of $S_z = 1/2$ ($\Delta L_z = +1$), so in the conduction band electrons with $S_z = 1/2$ are much more than electrons with $S_z = -1/2$. After the laser stops, electrons in the conduction band will recombine with the heavy hole and produce light with σ^+ polarization and σ^- polarization, which correspond to electron–heavy hole transition ($S_z = -1/2 \rightarrow L_z = -3/2$) and ($S_z =$

$+1/2 \to L_z = 3/2$), respectively. Therefore the intensity of light with σ^- polarization I_- is much larger than that of light with σ^+ polarization I_+, and I_+/I_- is equal to the ratio of numbers of electrons with $S_z = 1/2$ and electrons with $S_z = -1/2$.

About how to control spin polarization of carriers in a semiconductor, various semiconductor spintronics devices have been proposed. The original one is a spin field-effect transistor (SFET) proposed by Datta and Das in 1989 [13], which is also the most famous one. We will introduce it in detail in the next part. Other important ones are the graphene spin field-effect transistor, the metal-oxide-silicon spin field-effect transistor, the Johnson spin switch, the unipolar spin transistor, and so on. Although making great efforts, people have not succeeded even in the original Datta–Das transistor yet, which shows that we have a long way to go and there is much work to do.

The third category of spintronics is very different from the first two. It attempts to control spin the quantum state of a single electron or several electrons and then realize quantum calculation and quantum communication. In other words, it attempts to produce a qubit by using the two-quantum-state system of spin. The study of this kind of spintronics devices is in the very early stages. Due to the advantage that a qubit can be laid in solid materials, it has a better prospect than some other schemes of quantum calculation, such as iron trap and cavity quantum electrodynamics.

9.6 Rashba Spin-Orbit Interaction

Datta and Das first proposed the concept of the spin transistor, which is based on controlling the spin of an electron [13]. The paper's title is "Electronic Analog of the Electro-optic Modulator," and its principle is as shown in Fig. 9.2. Figure 9.2a is an electro-optic modulator, and Fig. 9.2b is a spin transistor similar to an electro-optic modulator.

The principle of the electro-optic modulator should be introduced first. A linearly polarized light at 45° to the y axis is radiated from the left of the electro-optic modulator along the x direction, and it can be represented as a combination of the z- and y-polarized

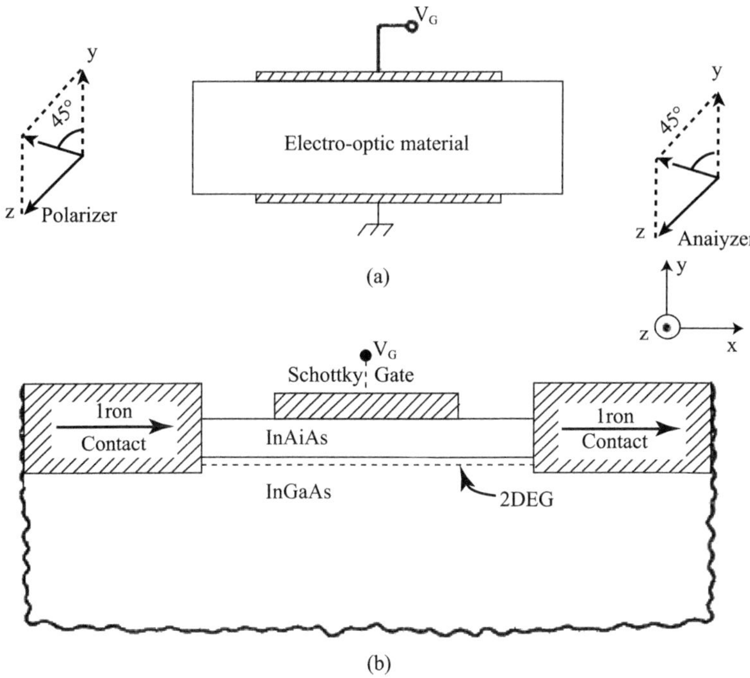

Figure 9.2 (a) Electro-optic modulator; (b) a spin transistor similar to an electro-optic modulator.

light

$$\begin{pmatrix} 1 \\ 1 \end{pmatrix}_{(45^\circ \text{ pol})} = \begin{pmatrix} 1 \\ 0 \end{pmatrix}_{(z \text{ pol})} + \begin{pmatrix} 0 \\ 1 \end{pmatrix}_{(y \text{ pol})} . \tag{9.28}$$

Because the electro-optic effect makes the dielectric constant ε_{zz} slightly different from ε_{yy}, as this light passes through the electro-optic material, the two polarizations suffer different phase shifts $k_1 L$ and $k_2 L$, where L denotes the length of the crystal. The light emerging from the electro-optic material is represented as $((e^{ik_1^L})/(e^{ik_2^L}))$. The analyzer at the output lets the light with polarization (1/1) pass through, so the output power P_o is given by

$$P_o \propto \left| \begin{pmatrix} 1 & 1 \end{pmatrix} \begin{pmatrix} e^{ik_1 L} \\ e^{ik_2 L} \end{pmatrix} \right|^2 = 4 \cos^2 \frac{(k_1 - k_2)\, L}{2} . \tag{9.29}$$

The light output is modulated by a gate voltage that controls the difference of the phase shifts $\Delta\theta = (k_1 - k_2)L$.

The theorem of the spin transistor is based on the interaction of the electron orbit and spin, that is, the Rashba interaction [14],

$$H_R = \frac{\alpha}{\hbar}(\sigma \times p)_y = i\alpha\left(\sigma_x \frac{\partial}{\partial z} - \sigma_z \frac{\partial}{\partial x}\right), \qquad (9.30)$$

where α is named as the Rashba coefficient and generally is $(1-10) \times 10^{-10}$ eVcm and σ_x and σ_z are the Pauli matrices.

In the spin transistor as shown in Fig. 9.2b, both ends are FM iron contacts, which are magnetized in the x direction and correspond to the polarizer and analyzer in the electro-optic modulator of Fig. 9.2a. Electrons injected through the source electrode are spin-polarized along the x direction, which can be represented as a linear combination of positive z-polarized and negative z-polarized electrons

$$\begin{pmatrix}1\\1\end{pmatrix}_{(+z\ \text{pol})} = \begin{pmatrix}1\\0\end{pmatrix}_{(+z\ \text{pol})} + \begin{pmatrix}0\\1\end{pmatrix}_{(-z\ \text{pol})}. \qquad (9.31)$$

Due to the Rashba term in the effective mass Hamiltonian (Eq. 9.30) $H_R = \alpha(\sigma_z k_x - \sigma_x k_z)$, in the absence of a magnetic field, the Rashba term causes the spin-up and spin-down states to split. If an electron is traveling in the x direction with $k_x \neq 0$ and $k_z = 0$, then considering the Rashba term, the energies of the electron can be written as

$$E\ (+z\ \text{pol}) = \frac{\hbar^2 k_{x1}^2}{2m^*} + \alpha k_{x1},$$

and

$$E\ (-z\ \text{pol}) = \frac{\hbar^2 k_{x2}^2}{2m^*} - \alpha k_{x2}. \qquad (9.32)$$

Electrons with two kinds of spin polarizations have the same energy, so

$$k_{x2} - k_{x1} = \frac{2m^*\alpha}{\hbar^2}. \qquad (9.33)$$

Therefore there is a differential phase shift for spin-up and spin-down electrons after they pass through the junction area, which is shown as

$$\Delta\theta = (k_{x2} - k_{x1})\,L = \frac{2m^*\alpha L}{\hbar^2}. \qquad (9.34)$$

For InGaAs/InAlAs heterostructures, from the experimentally observed zero-field spin splitting, α was estimated to be $\sim 3.9^{10}$ eV·cm.

To make a phase difference of π, L is about 0.67 μm, which is less than the mean free path (≥1 μm) in high-mobility semiconductors at low temperatures.

All the above discussion is in the condition $k_x \neq 0$ and $k_z = 0$. For a general case, both k_x and k_z should be taken into account, so the Hamiltonian is more complex. And If $k_z \neq 0$ and $k_x = 0$, the eigenstates are (1/1) and (1/(−1)) so the incoming beam is not split at all. It goes entirely into one of the eigenstates, and consequently no current modulation is expected. As the angle θ of propagation of the electrons with the x axis is increased, it can be shown that the effect is reduced gradually to zero at $\theta = 90°$. To prevent this effect, Datta and Das suggested a confining potential $V(z)$, which makes electrons form a series of discrete subbands in the z direction. If the confining potential is narrow enough so the different subbands are sufficiently far apart in energy, then subband mixing can be neglect. Then we return to the case $k_z = 0$, when the current modulation is the strongest.

Since Datta's paper was reported, many kinds of semiconductor spintronics devices have been proposed, almost all of which are based on the spin-orbit interaction (SOI), especially the Rashba spin-orbit interaction (RSOI) [14]. The SOI researched by spintronics can be classified into two classes: the RSOI and the Dresselhaus spin-orbit interaction (DSOI) [15]. The RSOI causes a spin split of electron states in the absence of an external field, that is, 1 order term of momentum arises in the Hamiltonian of the system, which makes the dispersion relation of the electron energy split from the single parabolic curve to two ones.

Both SOIs can be obtained from the Dirac relativistic wave equation and are related to the spin-orbit coupling term in the nonrelativistic limit, that is, the Thomas term. For a semiconductor heterojunction, if $V(z)$ is not inversion symmetric at the junction of 2DEGs, the Thomas term can be written as

$$H_{\mathrm{R}} = i\alpha \left(\sigma_y \frac{\partial}{\partial x} - \sigma_x \frac{\partial}{\partial y} \right),$$

which is just Eq. 9.30, and the Rashba coefficient α is related to the symmetry breaking of $V(z)$. On the other hand, if the system studied has the bulk crystal inversion asymmetry, such as diamond or zincblende semiconductor structures, the spin-orbit coupling term can be written as

$$H_{\mathrm{D}} = \beta\left[\sigma_x k_x\left(k_y^2 - k_z^2\right) + \sigma_y k_y\left(k_z^2 - k_x^2\right) + \sigma_z k_z\left(k_x^2 - k_y^2\right)\right], \tag{9.35}$$

where β is the strength coefficient of spin-orbit coupling, which is related to a specific material. This expression of spin-orbit coupling was first proposed by Dresselhaus in 1955 [15], so it is known as Dresselhaus spin-orbit interaction.

9.7 Quantum Waveguide Theory

It follows that the key point of utilizing the Landauer–Büttiker formula is solving the transmission coefficient matrix t. Actually most research on mesoscopic transport focuses on this problem. To calculate the scattering matrix, authors proposed and developed quantum waveguide theory, including one-dimensional quantum waveguide theory [16], two-dimensional quantum waveguide theory [17], and theory of one-dimensional quantum waveguide taking account of the Rashba interaction [18, 19]. In other chapters we will introduce these theories, related calculation methods, and some results.

References

1. Datta, S. (1995). *Electron Transport in Mesoscopic Systems* (Cambridge, London), p. 16.
2. Ferry, D. K., Takagaki, Y., and Zhou, J. R. (1994). *Jpn. J. Appl. Phys.*, **33**, 873.
3. Datta, S. (1989). *Superlatt. Microstruct.*, **6**, 83.
4. Wolf, S. A., Awschalom, D. D., Buhrman, R. A., et al. (2001). *Science*, **294**, 1488.
5. Baibich, M. N., Broto, J. M., Fert, A., et al. (1988). *Phys. Rev. Lett.*, **61**, 2472.
6. Binasch, G., Grunberg, P., Saurenbach, F., et al. (1989). *Phys. Rev. B*, **39**, 4828.

7. Moodera, J. S., Kinder, L. R., Wong, T. M., et al. (1995). *Phys. Rev. Lett.*, **74**, 3273.
8. Hu, C. M., et al. (2001). *Phys. Rev. Lett.*, **63**, 125333.
9. Zhu, H. J., et al. (2001). *Phys. Rev. Lett.*, **87**, 016601.
10. Alvorado, S. F., and Renand, Ph. (1992). *Phys. Rev. Lett.*, **68**, 1387.
11. Upadhyay, S. K., et al. (1998). *Phys. Rev. Lett.*, **81**, 3247.
12. Fiederling, R., Keim, M., Reuscher, G., et al. (1999). *Nature*, **402**, 787.
13. Datta, S., and Das, B. (1990). *Appl. Phys. Lett.*, **58**, 665.
14. Rashba, E. I. (1960). *Sov. Phys. Solid State*, **2**, 1109.
15. Dresselhaus, G. (1955). *Phys. Rev.*, **100**, 580.
16. Xia, J. B. (1992). *Phys. Rev. B*, **45**, 3593.
17. Sheng, W. D., and Xia, J. B. (1996). *J. Phys. C*, **8**, 3635.
18. Liu, D. Y., Xia, J. B., and Chang, Y. C. (2009). *J. Appl. Phys.*, **106**, 093705.
19. Liu, D. Y., and Xia, J. B. (2010). *J. Appl. Phys.*, **108**, 053717.

Chapter 10

One-Dimensional Quantum Waveguide Theory

In the 1980s, most of the initial work on electron transport in a small system dealt with metal samples, in which many transverse subbands were involved and the transport was diffusive. At the same time, advances in semiconductor microtechnology made it possible to fabricate extremely high mobility quantum wires with narrow widths, in which only a few of the lowest subbands are occupied and the transport is ballistic. The allowed modes in the channel are then the "waveguide" modes.

It follows from Chapter 9 that the key point of utilizing the Landauer–Büttiker formula is solving the transmission coefficient matrix t. Here we introduce the one-dimensional quantum waveguide theory [1, 2], which can be applied to one-dimensional quantum waveguide circuits of any shape and any structure. The so-called one-dimensional circuit means that the width of the circuit is narrow enough for the energy spacing between subbands produced by the transverse confinement to be much larger than the electron's longitudinal kinetic energy and there is only one mode of electron moving in the circuit. The single-mode movement of an electron is

Quantum Waveguide in Microcircuits
Jian-Bai Xia, Duan-Yang Liu, and Wei-Dong Sheng

ISBN 978-981-4669-85-6 (Hardcover), 978-1-315-36477-3 (eBook)
www.panstanford.com

described by the plane wave function with the wave vector k along the circuit's direction, which follows the quantum mechanics law.

10.1 Two Basic Equations

Let ψ_i be the wave function in the i-th circuit,

$$\psi_i = c_{1i}e^{ikx} + c_{2i}e^{-ikx}, \qquad (10.1)$$

where the coordinate x axis is along the longitudinal direction of the circuit.

The core of this theory is giving boundary conditions at each intersection crossed by more than two circuits, which is described by two basic equations. The first one is the continuity of the wave functions at the intersection, which can be written as

$$\psi_1 = \psi_2 = \psi_3 = \cdots = \psi_n, \qquad (10.2)$$

where ψ_i denotes the value of wave function in the i-th circuit at the intersection. The second equation is the conservation of the current density,

$$\sum_i \frac{\partial \psi_i}{\partial x_i} = 0, \qquad (10.3)$$

where all the coordinates x point to or back to the intersection.

In the general case, especially when there is spin-orbit interaction, we introduce a current density operator L_i, which has a more complex form than $\partial/\partial x_i$, as in Eq. 10.3. Generally we can obtain it from the Hamiltonian

$$L_i = -\frac{i}{\hbar}[l, H]. \qquad (10.4)$$

The second equation can be written as

$$\sum_i L_i \psi_i = 0. \qquad (10.5)$$

The completeness of Eqs. 10.2 and 10.3: From Eq. 10.1 there are $2n$ unknown coefficients for the n circuits crossing the intersection, among which the n coefficients can be determined by the n equations Eqs. 10.2 and 10.3. The other half of the coefficients will be determined by the boundary conditions at the other intersections or the conditions at the input or output terminals. Hence the set of equations Eqs. 10.2 and 10.3 at all intersections is complete for determining the wave function of the whole system.

10.2 Ring with Two Arms

To illustrate the application of the above theory, we consider the structure of a ring with two arms as shown in Fig. 10.1a in the absence of a magnetic field. The two arms of the ring have different lengths L_1 and L_2. We introduce the local coordinate system for each circuit such that the direction is along the electron-current direction and the origin is taken at the intersection. The choice of the coordinate origin is noncritical; it only affects a phase factor on the wave function.

We assume that an electron with a wave vector k enters through circuit 1 and departs from circuit 4. In the local coordinate system, the wave functions in circuits 1–4 shown in Fig. 10.1a can be written as

$$\begin{aligned}\psi_1 &= e^{ikx} + ae^{-ikx},\\ \psi_2 &= c_1 e^{ikx} + c_2 e^{-ikx},\\ \psi_3 &= d_1 e^{ikx} + d_2 e^{-ikx},\end{aligned} \tag{10.6}$$

and

$$\psi_4 = ge^{ikx},$$

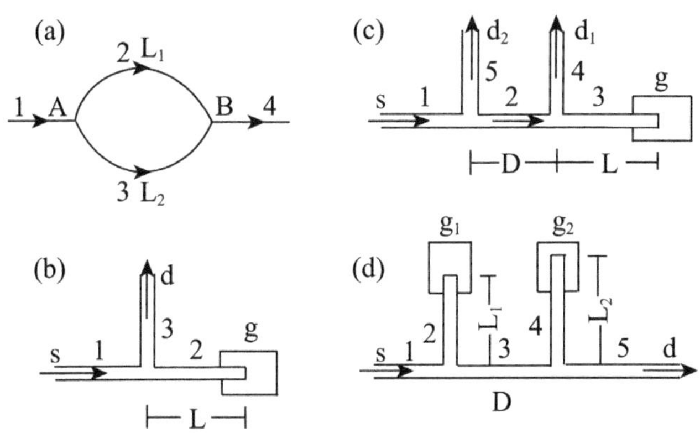

Figure 10.1 Various configurations of mesoscopic structures: (a) a ring with two arms, (b) a quantum interference transistor, (c) a quantum interference device with two drains, and (d) a quantum interference device with two gates. s, g, and d represent the source, gate, and drain, respectively.

where in ψ_1 the coefficient of the injected wave is 1, denoting that one electron enters, and in circuit 4, ψ_4 has only one term, denoting the output wave without the input wave. Thus the coefficients a and g are the reflection and transmission amplitudes, respectively.

The boundary condition equations Eq. 10.2 and Eq. 10.3 for the wave function (Eq. 10.6) can be written at the A and B points,

$$\begin{aligned}
1 + a &= c_1 + c_2, \\
1 + a &= d_1 + d_2, \\
1 - a &= c_1 - c_2 + d_1 - d_2, \\
c_1 e^{ikL_1} + c_2 e^{-ikL_1} &= g, \\
d_1 e^{ikL_2} + d_2 e^{-ikL_2} &= g,
\end{aligned} \tag{10.7}$$

and

$$c_1 e^{ikL_1} - c_2 e^{-ikL_1} + d_1 e^{ikL_2} - d_2 e^{-ikL_2} = g.$$

Solving the set of linear algebraic equations (10.7), we obtain the transmission function [1]

$$\begin{aligned}
T &= |g|^2 = \frac{64}{\Delta_L^2} \left[1 - \cos(kL)\right] \left[1 + \cos(k\Delta L)\right], \\
\Delta_L^2 &= 4 \left\{ \left[4 - 5\cos(kL) + \cos(k\Delta L)\right]^2 + \left[4 \sin(kL)\right]^2 \right\},
\end{aligned} \tag{10.8}$$

and

$$L = L_1 + L_2, \qquad \Delta L = L_2 - L_1.$$

From Eq. 10.8 we see that the amplitude of the output wave changes periodically not only with L but also with ΔL. It is caused by the phase-coherent effect. The T as a function of kL for different $k\Delta L$ and T as a function of $k\Delta L$ for different kL are shown in Figs. 10.2a and 10.2b, respectively.

10.3 Aharonov–Bohm Ring

The structure of the Aharonov–Bohm (AB) ring is the same as that in Fig. 10.1a. When a magnetic field is applied perpendicularly to the ring, in the magnetic field the Schrödinger equation is

$$\left[\frac{1}{2m^*}\left(\mathbf{p} + \frac{e}{c}\mathbf{A}\right)^2 + V(\mathbf{r})\right] \psi(\mathbf{r}) = E\psi(\mathbf{r}), \tag{10.9}$$

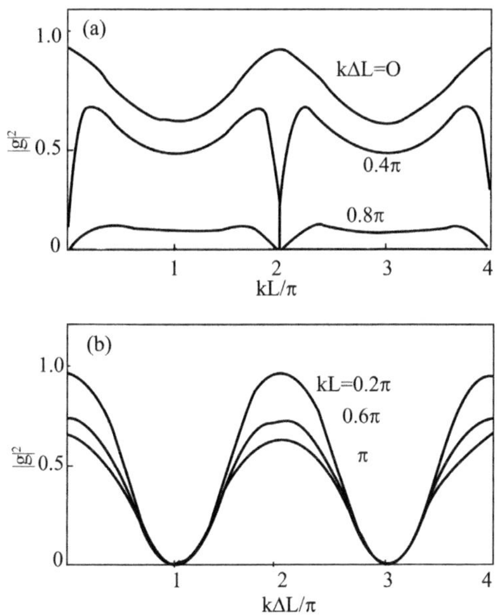

Figure 10.2 (a) T as a function of kL for different $k\Delta L$; (b) T as a function of $k\Delta L$ for different kL.

where **A** is the vector potential of the magnetic field **B**,

$$\mathbf{A} = \nabla \times \mathbf{B}. \tag{10.10}$$

As the magnetic field **B** is perpendicular to the ring plane, according to the Gauss theorem the vector potential **A** is along the ring direction and its magnitude

$$\mathbf{A} = \frac{\Phi}{L}, \tag{10.11}$$

where $\Phi = B \cdot S$ is the magnetic flux through the ring section area S and L is the ring round length.

Inserting Eq. 10.11 into Eq. (10.9), we obtain the one-dimensional (1D) Schrödinger equation,

$$\left[\frac{1}{2m^*}\left(\frac{\hbar}{i}\frac{d}{dx} - \frac{e}{c}\frac{\Phi}{L}\right)^2 + V(x)\right]\psi(x) = E\psi(x). \tag{10.12}$$

The wave function $\psi(x)$ is still a plane wave with wave vector k_1, its eigenenergy

$$E = \frac{\hbar^2}{2m^*}\left(k_1 - \frac{e\Phi}{\hbar c L}\right)^2, \tag{10.13}$$

which should be equal to the energy of the injected electron, $\hbar^2 k^2/2m^*$. Thus we have

$$k_1 = k + \frac{e\Phi}{\hbar c L}. \tag{10.14}$$

For the electron moving in the opposite direction in the ring, we obtain the wave vector of the electron,

$$k_2 = k - \frac{e\Phi}{\hbar c L}. \tag{10.15}$$

The wave functions in circuits 1-4 shown in Fig. 10.1a are written as

$$\begin{aligned} \psi_1 &= e^{ikx} + ae^{-ikx}, \\ \psi_2 &= c_1 e^{ik_1 x} + c_2 e^{-ik_2 x}, \\ \psi_3 &= d_1 e^{ik_2 x} + d_2 e^{-ik_1 x}, \end{aligned} \tag{10.16}$$

and

$$\psi_4 = ge^{ikx},$$

where k_1 and k_2 are given in Eqs. 10.14 and 10.15, respectively. Similarly, we can write down the boundary condition equations at the A and B points and obtain a set of linear algebraic equations for the coefficients a, c_1, c_2, d_1, d_2, and g. For the case $L_1 = L_2 = L_0$, we obtain [1]

$$g = \frac{8i}{\Delta_k} \left(\sin k_1 L_0 + \sin k_2 L_0\right)$$

and

$$\Delta_k = 2 + 8\cos\phi + 9e^{-ikL} - e^{ikL}, \tag{10.17}$$

where

$$\phi = (k_2 - k_1)\frac{L}{2} = \frac{e\Phi}{\hbar c}. \tag{10.18}$$

From Eq. 10.17 we obtain the transmission function

$$T = |g|^2 = \frac{64}{\Delta_k^2}\left(1 - \cos kL\right)\left(1 + \cos\phi\right),$$

where

$$\Delta_k^2 = 4\left[(1 + 4\cos\phi - 5\cos kL)^2 + (4\sin kL)^2\right]. \tag{10.19}$$

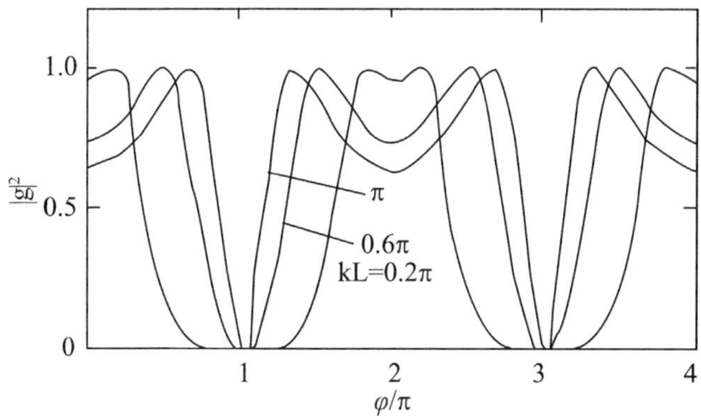

Figure 10.3 T as a function of ϕ/π for different kL values in the AB ring.

From Eq. 10.19 we see that the T varies periodically as the magnetic flux Φ changes with the period

$$\Phi = \frac{hc}{e}. \tag{10.20}$$

This is the basic result of the AB effect, which is in agreement with the results of Datta and Bandyopadhyay [3]. The T as a function of ϕ/π for several kL values is shown in Fig. 10.3. From the figure we see that when kL is close to 0 (or integer times of 2π) the wave's shape is close to the harmonic wave and when kL is close to π the wave's shape deviates from the harmonic wave, indicating there are components of higher harmonics.

10.4 Quantum Interference Devices

The quantum interference transistor [4, 5] as shown in Fig. 10.1b differs from the ordinary field-effect transistor (FET) in that the gate lies outside the classical path of electrons. Conductance oscillations as a function of the gate potential have been observed in such a structure. The wave functions in circuits 1–3 (Fig. 10.1b) can be written as

$$\begin{aligned}\psi_1 &= e^{ikx} + ae^{-ikx},\\ \psi_2 &= c\sin[k(x-L)],\end{aligned} \tag{10.21}$$

and

$$\psi_3 = g e^{ikx},$$

where it is assumed that the wave function at the gate is zero, that is, it is a standing wave in circuit 2, and L is the distance between the intersection and the gate.

Applying the boundary conditions (Eqs. 10.2 and 10.3), we obtain

$$1 + a = -c \sin kL,$$

$$1 + a = g,$$

and

$$1 - a + ic \cos kL = g. \tag{10.22}$$

From Eq. 10.22 it is easy to obtain

$$a = -\frac{i \cos kL}{2 \sin kL + i \cos kL}$$

and

$$g = \frac{2 \sin kL}{2 \sin kL + i \cos kL}. \tag{10.23}$$

The $T = |g|^2$ as a function of kL is shown in Fig. 10.4 (dashed line). It can be seen that the conductance curve is in good agreement with the experimental single-mode results [4]. This conductance oscillation is also caused by the phase-coherent effect. When the injected electron wave arrives at the intersection, one part goes to the gate and is reflected from the gate. On this path the phase change is $2kL$. This part of the wave meets the wave at the intersection, and there is an interference effect. Consequently, the amplitude of the output wave varies periodically with $2kL$, as shown in Fig. 10.4 (dashed line).

As a development of the interference device, we consider the structure with two drains controlled by one gate as shown in Fig. 10.1c, and the two drains are separated by a distance D. The wave functions in circuits 1–5 can be written as

$$\psi_1 = e^{ikx} + a e^{-ikx},$$

$$\psi_2 = c_1 e^{ikx} + c_2 e^{-ikx},$$

$$\psi_3 = d \sin\left[k\left(x - L\right)\right],$$

$$\psi_4 = g_1 e^{ikx}, \tag{10.24}$$

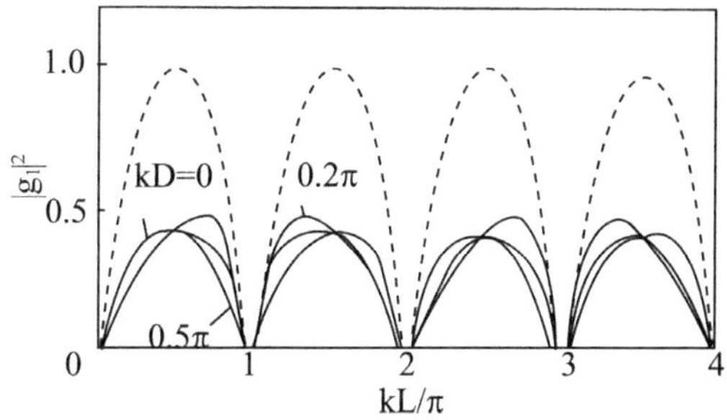

Figure 10.4 T as function of kL; dashed line for the single-drain structure in Fig. 10.1b; solid lines for different kD in the first drain of the structure in Fig. 10.1c.

and

$$\psi_5 = g_2 e^{ikx}.$$

Similarly applying the boundary conditions Eq. 10.2 and Eq. 10.3 we obtain the T_1 and T_2 as functions of kL for three kD values shown in Figs. 10.4 and 10.5, respectively. From Fig. 10.4 we see that in the drain near the gate, the conductance oscillations are nearly the same, independent of kD, and their magnitudes are about half of that in the single-drain structure (dashed line). In the drain far away from the gate, the conductance oscillations critically depend on the kD. When $kD = 0.5\,\pi$, the $T_2 = 1$ at $kL = \pi$. The results of the two-gate structure Fig. 10.1d are not given here; the reader can consult Ref. [1].

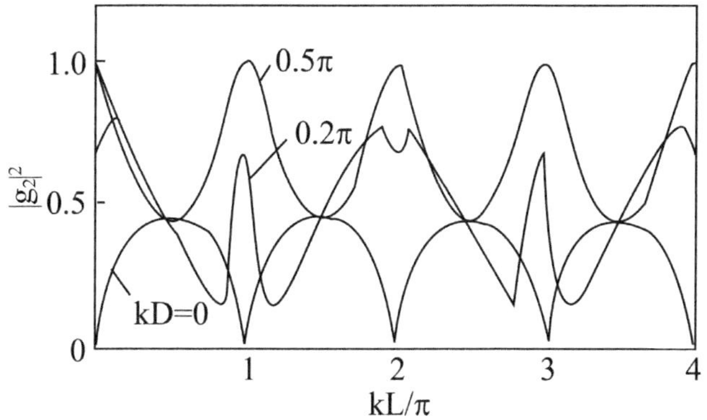

Figure 10.5 T_2 as a function of kL for different kD values in the second drain of the structure in Fig. 10.1c.

10.5 Stub Model

For comparison with the theoretical results of the ideal two-dimensional (2D) electron waveguide model [6], we calculate the transmission function T for the single- and double-gate (stub) structures (as shown in Fig. 10.1d) with the same parameters as in Ref. [6]. Of course, the width effect is neglected in our model. We take the electron effective mass $m^* = 0.05\ m_0$, the electron energy $E = 0.08$ eV, and the separation between two stubs $D = 95$ Å. In Fig. 10.6 the T for the structures of a single stub, two identical stubs, and two stubs with length difference are given, respectively. From the figure we see that there is qualitative agreement with the 2D theoretical results for the structure with equal length [6]. In the case of a single stub, the transmission valley is narrow, while in the case of two identical stubs the valley becomes broader. In the case of two stubs of different lengths, there appears an additional peak at the transmission valley. It is found that the height of the additional peak is sensitive to the kD, and the T as a function of kL^* (length of the shorter one of the two stubs) is shown in Fig. 10.6d. From the figure

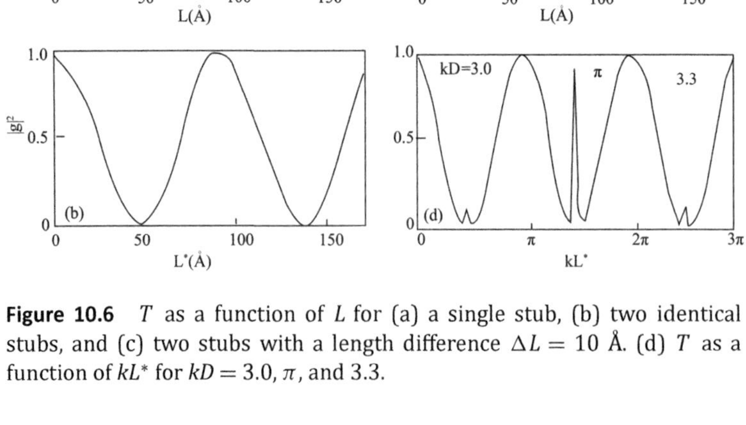

Figure 10.6 T as a function of L for (a) a single stub, (b) two identical stubs, and (c) two stubs with a length difference $\Delta L = 10$ Å. (d) T as a function of kL^* for $kD = 3.0, \pi$, and 3.3.

we see that if $kD = \pi$, there is a strong peak at the transmission valley; if kD deviates from π, the resonant peak decreases greatly.

10.6 One-Dimensional Waveguide Theory of Holes

On the basis of the 1D waveguide theory of electrons we developed the 1D waveguide theory of holes [2]. The hole has an orbital angle momentum $l = 1$ (p state), which is coupled with spin $s = 1/2$ to get the total angle momentum $J = 3/2$ and $1/2$. Generally, the $J = 3/2$ state is the basic state, that is, at the top of the valence band. Thus the hole wave function has four components, corresponding to $J = 3/2, 1/2, -1/2$, and $-3/2$ states. The motion of the hole can be described by the following 4×4 Luttinger Hamiltonian [7]

$$H = \frac{1}{2m_0}\begin{pmatrix} P_1 & Q & R & 0 \\ Q^* & P_2 & 0 & R \\ R^* & 0 & P_2 & -Q \\ 0 & R^* & -Q^* & P_1 \end{pmatrix}, \tag{10.25}$$

where

$$\begin{aligned} P_1 &= (\gamma_1 + \gamma_2)\left(p_x^2 + p_y^2\right) = (\gamma_1 - \gamma_2)\, p_z^2, \\ P_2 &= (\gamma_1 - \gamma_2)\left(p_x^2 + p_y^2\right) = (\gamma_1 + 2\gamma_2)\, p_z^2, \\ Q &= -i2\sqrt{3}\gamma_3\left(p_x - ip_y\right) p_z, \end{aligned} \tag{10.26}$$

and

$$R = \sqrt{3}\gamma_2\left(p_x^2 - p_y^2\right) - 2i\gamma_3 p_x p_y,$$

where γ_1, γ_2, and γ_3 are Luttinger effective mass parameters.

We assume that the hole is confined in the x–y plane; then the momentum p_z can be set to 0. Therefore, the Q term in Eq. 10.26 vanishes, and the Hamiltonian (Eq. 10.24) splits into two 2×2 equivalent blocks,

$$H = \frac{1}{2m_0}\begin{pmatrix} P_1 & R \\ R^* & P_2 \end{pmatrix}. \tag{10.27}$$

In the axial approximation $\gamma_2 = \gamma_3$ and $R = \sqrt{3}\gamma_2\left(\mathbf{p}_x - i\mathbf{p}_y\right)^2$.

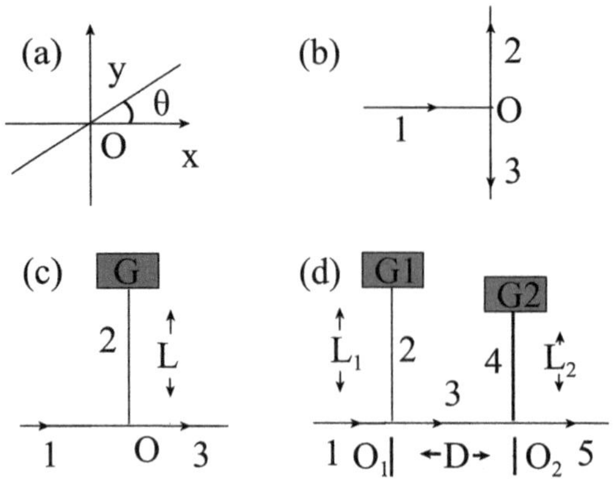

Figure 10.7 (a) Circuit 1 with a polar angle θ; (b) branch structure; (c) quantum-interference device with one gate; (d) quantum interference device with two gates.

The wave function of a hole in the 1D circuit is different from that of the electron. The electron wave function is a plane wave independent of the direction of the circuit, while the hole wave function is two components and dependent on the direction of the circuit. We study the hole wave function in the circuit shown in Fig. 10.7a with a polar angle of θ. The Hamiltonian can be written as

$$H = -\frac{\hbar^2}{2m_0}\begin{pmatrix} (\gamma_1+\gamma_2) & \sqrt{3}\gamma_2 e^{-2i\theta} \\ \sqrt{3}\gamma_2 e^{2i\theta} & (\gamma_1-\gamma_2) \end{pmatrix}\frac{d^2}{dl^2}, \tag{10.28}$$

where l is the coordinate along the circuit. We take the wave function as a plane wave form,

$$\phi = \begin{pmatrix} c_1 \\ c_2 \end{pmatrix} e^{ikl}, \tag{10.29}$$

where k is the wave vector and c_1 and c_2 are the coefficients to be determined. Substituting Eq. 10.29 into the effective mass equation $H\phi = E\phi$ will give rise to the following secular equation:

$$\begin{vmatrix} (\gamma_1+\gamma_2)-\varepsilon & \sqrt{3}\gamma_2 e^{-2i\theta} \\ \sqrt{3}\gamma_2 e^{2i\theta} & (\gamma_1-\gamma_2)-\varepsilon \end{vmatrix} = 0, \qquad \varepsilon = E\Big/\left(\frac{\hbar^2k^2}{2m_0}\right). \tag{10.30}$$

From Eq. 10.30 we obtain

$$\varepsilon = \gamma_1 \pm 2\gamma_2. \tag{10.31}$$

From the definition of ε in Eq. 10.30, m_0/ε corresponds to the effective mass of a hole. Then the values of ε in Eq. 10.31 correspond to the light hole state and the heavy hole state, respectively. The wave functions of the heavy hole state and light hole state are

$$\phi_{\mathrm{h}}(\theta, k) = \phi_{\mathrm{h}}(\theta)\, e^{ikl} = \begin{pmatrix} 1/2 \\ -\sqrt{3}e^{2i\theta}/2 \end{pmatrix} e^{ikl}$$

and

$$\phi_{\mathrm{l}}(\theta, k) = \phi_{\mathrm{l}}(\theta)\, e^{ikl} = \begin{pmatrix} \sqrt{3}e^{-2i\theta}/2 \\ 1/2 \end{pmatrix} e^{ikl}. \tag{10.32}$$

For the hole state with a given energy E, the general wave function in the circuit Fig. 10.7a can be written as

$$\Phi = c_1\phi_{\mathrm{h}}(\theta)\, e^{ik_{\mathrm{h}}l} + c_2\phi_{\mathrm{l}}(\theta)\, e^{ik_{\mathrm{l}}l} + c_3\phi_{\mathrm{h}}(\theta)\, e^{-ik_{\mathrm{h}}l} + c_4\phi_{\mathrm{l}}(\theta)\, e^{-ik_{\mathrm{l}}l}, \tag{10.33}$$

where

$$k_{\mathrm{h}} = \sqrt{2m_{\mathrm{h}}E}, \qquad k_{\mathrm{l}} = \sqrt{2m_{\mathrm{l}}E}$$

$$m_{\mathrm{h}} = \frac{m_0}{\gamma_1 - 2\gamma_2}, \quad \text{and} \quad m_{\mathrm{l}} = \frac{m_0}{\gamma_1 + 2\gamma_2} \tag{10.34}$$

are the wave vectors of the heavy hole and light hole, respectively; and c_1, c_2, c_3, and c_4 are the coefficients to be determined by the boundary conditions.

The first boundary condition for the hole wave functions are the same as that for the electron wave function (Eq. 10.2). The second boundary condition is given by Eqs. 10.4 and 10.5, namely the current density operator

$$L_{\mathrm{l}} = \frac{1}{m_0}\begin{pmatrix} (\gamma_1 + \gamma_2) & \sqrt{3}\gamma_2 e^{-2i\theta} \\ \sqrt{3}\gamma_2 e^{2i\theta} & (\gamma_1 - \gamma_2) \end{pmatrix} p_{\mathrm{l}}. \tag{10.35}$$

The corresponding boundary conditions at the intersection are

$$\Phi_1 = \Phi_2 = \cdots = \Phi_n$$

and

$$\sum_{i=1}^{n} L_i \Phi_i = 0. \tag{10.36}$$

10.7 Quantum Interference Device of a Hole

Obviously, the hole case is more complicated than the electron case, there are four unknown coefficients in each circuit, and generally we cannot obtain the analytical results from the set of linear equations of coefficients. In the following we consider the hole transport in the quantum interference transistors [4, 5] with one gate, as shown in Fig. 10.7c. We assume that an incident heavy hole wave with a wave vector k enters into source circuit 1 and departs from the drain circuits 3. Stub 2 is the gate, whose length L is controlled by the gate voltage. The wave function in stub 2 is a standing wave with its zero pint at the gate. If we choose the node 0 as the origin of all three circuits, then the wave functions can be written as

$$\Phi_1 = \phi_{\mathrm{h}}(0)\, e^{ikl_1} + a_1\phi_{\mathrm{l}}(0)\, e^{ik'l_1} + a_2\phi_{\mathrm{l}}(0)\, e^{-ik'l_1},$$

$$\Phi_2 = c_1\phi_{\mathrm{h}}(\pi/2)\sin\left[k\left(l_2 - L\right)\right] + c_2\phi_{\mathrm{l}}(\pi/2)\sin\left[k'\left(l_2 - L\right)\right],$$

and

$$\Phi_3 = d_1\phi_{\mathrm{h}}(0)\, e^{ikl_3} + d_2\phi_{\mathrm{l}}(0)\, e^{ik'l_3}, \qquad (10.37)$$

where k and k' are the wave vectors of a heavy hole and a light hole, respectively (see Eq. 10.34).

Applying the boundary conditions (Eq. 10.36) we obtain a set of linear algebraic equations of six coefficients in Eq. 10.37. The final results are given in Ref. [2]. It is noticed that the current densities of the heavy hole and light hole equal $\hbar k/m_{\mathrm{h}}$ and $\hbar k'/m_{\mathrm{l}}$ multiplied by their corresponding coefficients, respectively. The transmission and reflection functions can be written as

$$T_{\mathrm{hh}} = |d_1|^2, \quad T_{\mathrm{hl}} = |d_2|^2\frac{k}{k'},$$

$$R_{\mathrm{hh}} = |a_1|^2, \quad \text{and} \quad R_{\mathrm{hl}} = |a_2|^2\frac{k}{k'}, \qquad (10.38)$$

where T_{hh} represents the transmission probability of one heavy hole to one heavy hole, T_{hl} the transmission probability of one heavy hole to one light hole, R_{hh} the reflection probability of one heavy hole to one heavy hole, and R_{hl} the reflection probability of one heavy hole to one light hole.

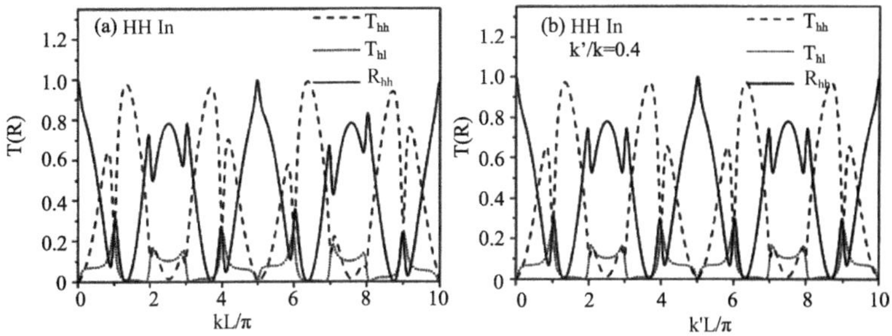

Figure 10.8 Transmission and reflection functions as functions of kL for the one gate structure shown in Fig. 10.7c. (a) $k'/k = 0.395$; (b) $k'/k = 0.4$.

The numerical calculation results for T_{hh}, T_{hl}, and R_{hh} as functions of kL are shown in Fig. 10.8a. In calculation we take the GaAs effective mass parameters $\gamma_1 = 6.85$ and $\gamma_2 = 10.5$. From the figure we see that the T_{hh}, T_{hl}, and R_{hh} all oscillate with kL in a period of about 5 π. With these parameters the ratio between the light hole and heavy hole wave vector k'/k is approximately 0.395. If we substitute it with a close value 0.4, then all the trigonometric functions in the results have a common period 5 π and we obtain a more regular oscillation shape, as shown in Fig. 10.8b.

The oscillation period for the electrons is π in the same single-stub structure [1]. The T_{hh} curve in Fig. 10.8b shows two main peaks and two main valleys in each period. Besides, at the positions of T_{hl} peaks, the T_{hh} curve shows a sharp dip around π and 3π. It means that one part of the heavy hole is converted to a light hole. This arises from the interference between the heavy hole and light hole waves. We also find that the peak value of T_{hl} is about 0.2, which means a relatively small fraction of the heavy hole wave can be converted into a light hole wave.

If an incident light hole wave with wave vector k' enters into source 1, the transmission and reflection functions can be calculated in a similar way and its numerical results are shown in Fig. 10.9. The ratio k'/k is chosen as 0.4 so that these functions have a period of 2π with respect to $k'L$. The peaks of R_{ll} are much sharper than that

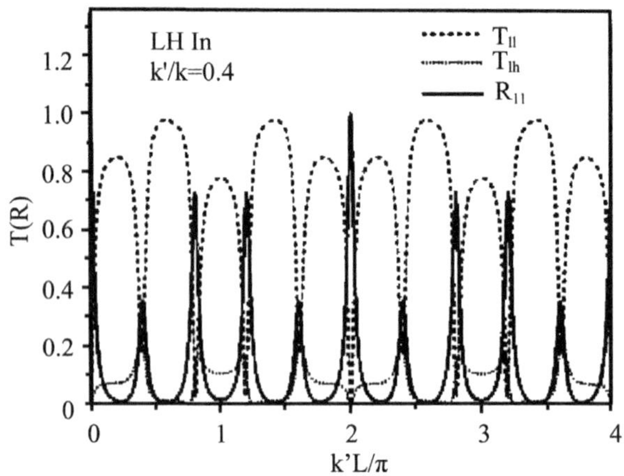

Figure 10.9 Transmission and reflection functions as functions of $k'L$ for the one-gate structure shown in Fig. 10.7c. k'/k is set to be 0.4.

of R_{hh} shown in Fig. 10.8b, and T_{ll} shows resonant plateaus rather than peaks.

References

1. Xia, J. B. (1992), *Phys. Rev. B*, **45**, 3593.
2. Wu, H. B., Xia, J. B., and Chang, K. (2003). *Solid State Commun.*, **128**, 125.
3. Datta, S., and Bandyopadhyay, S. (1987). *Phys. Rev. Lett.*, **58**, 717.
4. Datta, S. (1989). *Superlatt. Microstruct.*, **6**, 83.
5. Capasso, F., and Datta, S. (1990). *Phys. Today*, LB **(2)**, 74.
6. Sols, F., Macucci, M., Ravaioli, U., and Hess, K. (1989). *J. Appl. Phys.*, **66**, 3892.
7. Luttinger, J. M. (1956). *Phys. Rev.*, **102**, 1030.

Chapter 11

Two-Dimensional Quantum Waveguide Theory

Though many fundamental transport properties of quantum waveguides have been found in the study of idealized structures, in real waveguides the boundaries are usually defined via electrostatic confinement from metal gates and thus the geometries can be complicated. In this case, realistic lateral guiding potentials shall be taken into account, especially when the electrons are of high energies and would transport beyond the single-mode regime [1, 2]. When the width of the circuit is so large that the energy-level spacing between the transverse modes in the circuit is comparable to the electron kinetic energy, we should consider the transport of multiple transverse modes, that is, the two-dimensional waveguide theory. In this chapter, we will describe various theoretical approaches, such as the basic mode-matching technique, the transfer matrix, and the scattering matrix methods, to study electron transport through two-dimensional quantum waveguides. In the end, we will apply the theory to two-electron waveguide devices.

Figure 11.1 illustrates a typical two-dimensional quantum waveguide. The device can have several terminals, some of which may be used for input and the others for output. In general, one

Quantum Waveguide in Microcircuits
Jian-Bai Xia, Duan-Yang Liu, and Wei-Dong Sheng

ISBN 978-981-4669-85-6 (Hardcover), 978-1-315-36477-3 (eBook)
www.panstanford.com

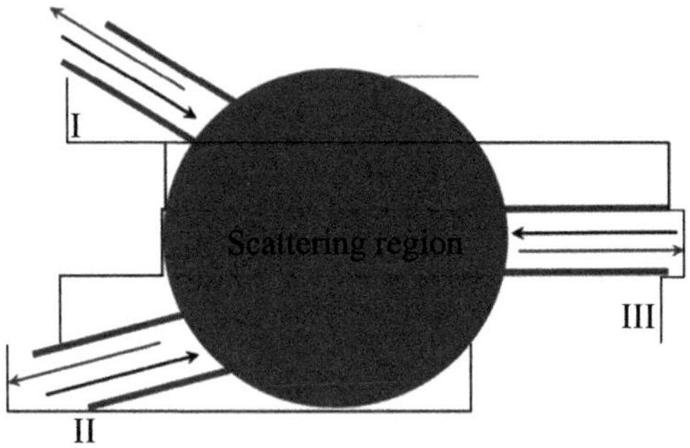

Figure 11.1 Schematic view of a two-dimensional multi-terminal quantum waveguide.

would like to know the output of the waveguide device if all the input information is given. Let $A_{\mathrm{I}}^{\mathrm{in}}$ and $A_{\mathrm{I}}^{\mathrm{out}}$ denote the incoming and outgoing electron waves to and from terminal I, respectively. All the outgoing waves can be related to the incoming waves by a matrix **S** in the linear response regime as follows:

$$\begin{bmatrix} A_{\mathrm{I}}^{\mathrm{out}} \\ A_{\mathrm{II}}^{\mathrm{out}} \\ A_{\mathrm{III}}^{\mathrm{out}} \end{bmatrix} = \begin{bmatrix} S_{11} & S_{12} & S_{13} \\ S_{21} & S_{22} & S_{23} \\ S_{31} & S_{32} & S_{33} \end{bmatrix} \begin{bmatrix} A_{\mathrm{I}}^{\mathrm{in}} \\ A_{\mathrm{II}}^{\mathrm{in}} \\ A_{\mathrm{III}}^{\mathrm{in}} \end{bmatrix}. \tag{11.1}$$

Here **S** is called the scattering matrix. For a scatterer, all the transport properties, including the transmission matrix, can be readily determined if the scattering matrix is obtained. In some simple cases, like for a two-terminal waveguide, it is common to use a transfer matrix method to obtain the transmission coefficient.

11.1 Transfer Matrix Method [3]

Let us start with a simple case, a two-terminal waveguide as illustrated in Fig. 11.2, as an example. The structure has two terminals L and R and a step-like interface between them. In terminals L and R, the electron wave functions can be written as

$$\varphi_{\mathrm{L}}(x,y) = \sum_{n=1}^{N_{\mathrm{L}}} \left(a_n^{\mathrm{L}} e^{ik_n^{\mathrm{L}}x} + b_n^{\mathrm{L}} e^{-ik_n^{\mathrm{L}}x} \right) \sqrt{\frac{2}{W_{\mathrm{L}}}} \sin\left(\frac{n\pi}{W_{\mathrm{L}}} y \right),$$

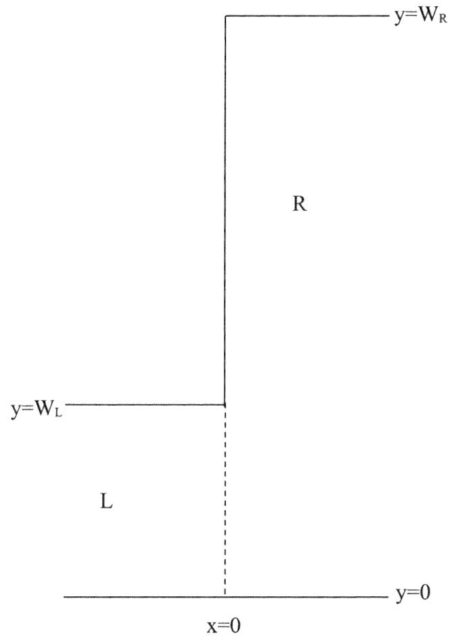

Figure 11.2 Schematic view of a two-terminal quantum waveguide.

and

$$\varphi_{\mathrm{R}}(x, y) = \sum_{n=1}^{N_{\mathrm{R}}} \left(a_n^{\mathrm{R}} e^{ik_n^{\mathrm{R}}x} + b_n^{\mathrm{R}} e^{-ik_n^{\mathrm{R}}x} \right) \sqrt{\frac{2}{W_{\mathrm{R}}}} \sin\left(\frac{n\pi}{W_{\mathrm{R}}} y \right), \quad (11.2)$$

where the longitudinal wave numbers k_n^{L} and k_n^{R} satisfy

$$\frac{\left(\hbar k_n^{\mathrm{L}}\right)^2}{2m^*} + \frac{\hbar^2}{2m^*} \left(\frac{n\pi}{W_{\mathrm{L}}} \right)^2 = E_{\mathrm{F}} \text{ and } \frac{\left(\hbar k_n^{\mathrm{R}}\right)^2}{2m^*} + \frac{\hbar^2}{2m^*} \left(\frac{n\pi}{W_{\mathrm{R}}} \right)^2 = E_{\mathrm{F}}. \quad (11.3)$$

Here E_{F} is the electron Fermi energy and N_{L} (N_{R}) is the number of transverse modes in terminal L(R). If one sets $x = 0$ at the interface, the continuity of the wave function requires

$$\sum_{n=1}^{N_{\mathrm{L}}} \left(a_n^{\mathrm{L}} + b_n^{\mathrm{L}} \right) \sqrt{\frac{2}{W_{\mathrm{L}}}} \sin\left(\frac{n\pi}{W_{\mathrm{L}}} y \right) = \sum_{n=1}^{N_{\mathrm{R}}} \left(a_n^{\mathrm{R}} + b_n^{\mathrm{R}} \right) \sqrt{\frac{2}{W_{\mathrm{R}}}} \sin\left(\frac{n\pi}{W_{\mathrm{R}}} y \right). \quad (11.4)$$

Similarly, matching the first derivatives of the wave functions at the interface gives

$$\sum_{n=1}^{N_\mathrm{L}} k_n^\mathrm{L}\left(a_n^\mathrm{L}-b_n^\mathrm{L}\right)\sqrt{\frac{2}{W_\mathrm{L}}}\sin\left(\frac{n\pi}{W_\mathrm{L}}y\right)=\sum_{n=1}^{N_\mathrm{R}} k_n^\mathrm{R}\left(a_n^\mathrm{R}-b_n^\mathrm{R}\right) \times\sqrt{\frac{2}{W_\mathrm{R}}}\sin\left(\frac{n\pi}{W_\mathrm{R}}y\right). \quad (11.5)$$

Supposing $W_\mathrm{L} < W_\mathrm{R}$. We multiply both sides of Eqs. 11.4 and 11.5 by $\sqrt{2/W_\mathrm{R}}\sin(m\pi y/W_\mathrm{R})$ and $\sqrt{2/W_\mathrm{L}}\sin(m\pi y/W_\mathrm{L})$, respectively, integrate from 0 to W_L, and obtain

$$\sum_{n=1}^{N_\mathrm{L}} C_{nm}\left(a_n^\mathrm{L}+b_n^\mathrm{L}\right)=a_m^\mathrm{R}+b_m^\mathrm{R} \quad (11.6)$$

and

$$k_m^\mathrm{L}\left(a_m^\mathrm{L}-b_m^\mathrm{L}\right)=\sum_{n=1}^{N_\mathrm{R}} C_{mn}k_n^\mathrm{R}\left(a_n^\mathrm{R}-b_n^\mathrm{R}\right), \quad (11.7)$$

where

$$C_{nm}=\frac{2}{\sqrt{W_\mathrm{L}W_\mathrm{R}}}\int_0^{W_\mathrm{L}}\sin\left(\frac{n\pi}{W_\mathrm{L}}y\right)\sin\left(\frac{m\pi}{W_\mathrm{R}}y\right)dy. \quad (11.8)$$

If the widths of the two terminals are not much different, that is, $W_\mathrm{L} \approx W_\mathrm{R}$, one may set $N_\mathrm{L} = N_\mathrm{R}$ and the above equations can be rewritten as

$$\begin{bmatrix}\mathbf{L}_a\\ \mathbf{L}_b\end{bmatrix}=\mathbf{T}\begin{bmatrix}\mathbf{R}_a\\ \mathbf{R}_b\end{bmatrix}=\frac{1}{2}\begin{bmatrix}\mathbf{M}_1+\mathbf{M}_2 & \mathbf{M}_1-\mathbf{M}_2\\ \mathbf{M}_1-\mathbf{M}_2 & \mathbf{M}_1+\mathbf{M}_2\end{bmatrix}\begin{bmatrix}\mathbf{R}_a\\ \mathbf{R}_b\end{bmatrix}. \quad (11.9)$$

Here $\mathbf{L(R)}_a=\left[a_1^{\mathrm{L(R)}}, a_2^{\mathrm{L(R)}}, \ldots, a_{N_{\mathrm{L(R)}}}^{\mathrm{L(R)}}\right]^T$ and $\mathbf{L(R)}_b=\left[b_1^{\mathrm{L(R)}}, b_2^{\mathrm{L(R)}}, \ldots, b_{N_{\mathrm{L(R)}}}^{\mathrm{L(R)}}\right]^T$ are the vectors for terminal L and R, respectively; $\mathbf{M}_1 = \left(\mathbf{C}^T\right)^{-1}$; and $\mathbf{M}_2 = \left(\mathbf{K}^\mathrm{L}\right)^{-1}\mathbf{C}\mathbf{K}^\mathrm{R}$. $\mathbf{C}$ is the matrix with elements C_{nm} as defined in Eq. 11.8, while $\mathbf{K}^\mathrm{L}$ and $\mathbf{K}^\mathrm{R}$are diagonal matrices with elements $(\mathbf{K}^\mathrm{L})_{nn} = k_n^\mathrm{L}$ and $(\mathbf{K}^\mathrm{R})_{nn} = k_n^\mathrm{R}$

T is commonly known as the transfer matrix that relates all the wave components in the output port to those in the input terminal. Once it is obtained, the transmission and reflection amplitudes can be calculated in a straightforward manner. For an example, supposing electrons propagate in the ground transverse mode from the left terminal, we have the incident wave $\mathbf{L}_a = \left[1/k_1^{\mathrm{L}},\ 0,\ \ldots,\ 0\right]^T$ and $\mathbf{R}_b = 0$. The transmitting wave can then be obtained by $\mathbf{R}_a = \left[t_{11}/k_1^{\mathrm{R}},\ t_{21}/k_2^{\mathrm{R}},\ \ldots,\ t_{n1}/k_n^{\mathrm{R}}\right]^T = 2\left(\mathbf{M}_1 + \mathbf{M}_2\right)^{-1}\mathbf{L}_a$, followed by the reflecting wave $\mathbf{L}_b = \left[r_{11}/k_1^{\mathrm{L}}, r_{21}/k_2^{\mathrm{L}},\ \ldots,\ r_{n1}/k_n^{\mathrm{L}}\right]^T = \frac{1}{2}\left(\mathbf{M}_1 - \mathbf{M}_2\right)\mathbf{R}_a$.

Beyond the single-mode regime, the total transmission and reflection amplitudes T and R are given by

$$T = \sum_{\mathrm{real}\, k_i^{\mathrm{R}}, k_j^{\mathrm{L}}} \left|t_{ij}\right|^2 \quad \text{and} \quad R = \sum_{\mathrm{real}\, k_i^{\mathrm{L}}, k_j^{\mathrm{L}}} \left|r_{ij}\right|^2. \tag{11.10}$$

It is noted that one needs to include only the propagating modes with real wave numbers as all the evanescent states would eventually decay in the terminals [4]. The unitary condition is now given by $T + R = N_{\mathrm{i}}$, where N_{i} is the number of propagating modes in the incident port.

For a general waveguide with two aligning terminals, it is possible to divide the structure into a number of uniform sections (see Fig. 11.3). In this way, the total transfer matrix can be constructed as a product of $\mathbf{T}_m$, which describes the scattering by the interface between the $(m-1)$-th and m-th section and $\mathbf{T}_m^{\mathrm{f}}$, which

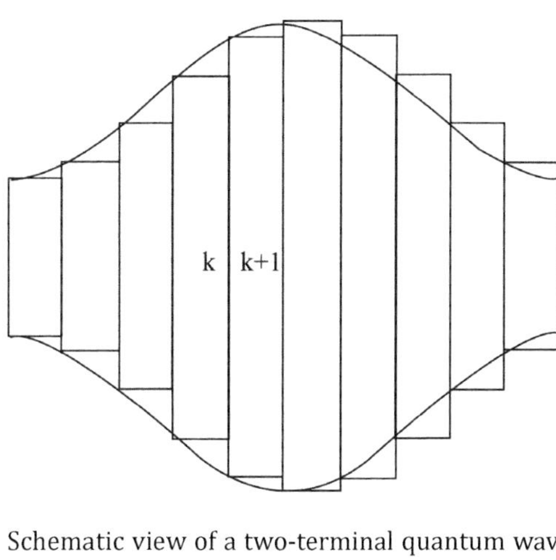

Figure 11.3 Schematic view of a two-terminal quantum waveguide that is divided into a number of transverse slices along its longitudinal direction.

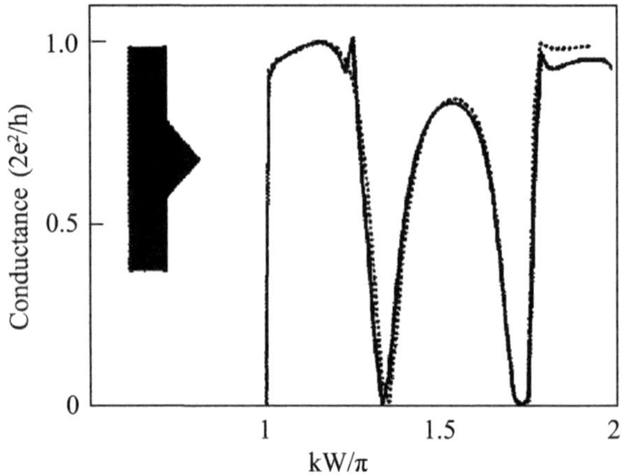

Figure 11.4 The conductance G in units of $2e^2/h$ versus kW/π for a triangular cavity structure as shown in the inset, where the solid line was calculated by the transfer method and the dotted line wa obtained by the recursive Green's function method.

describes free propagation from across the m-th section, that is,

$$\mathbf{T} = \prod_m \mathbf{T}_m \mathbf{T}_m^{\mathrm{f}} = \prod_m \mathbf{T}_m \begin{bmatrix} \mathbf{P}_m^- & 0 \\ 0 & \mathbf{P}_m^+ \end{bmatrix}, \tag{11.11}$$

where $\mathbf{P}_m^{\pm}$ are diagonal matrices with elements $\left(\mathbf{P}_m^{\pm}\right)_{nn} = e^{\pm i k_n^m L_m}$. L_m is the dimension of the m-th section along the propagating direction.

Figure 11.4 is the conductance G in units of $2e^2/h$ versus kW/π for a triangular cavity structure as shown in the inset, where the solid line was calculated by the above transfer matrix method and the dotted line was obtained by the recursive Green's function method [3]. From the figure we see that the agreement between the two results is good. In the numerical calculation of the transfer method, we divide the cavity into 20 segments along the longitudinal direction, and the transverse modes N is chosen to be 5. From Fig. 11.3 we see that when $kW/\pi = 1.3$ or 1.73, the conductance $G \approx 0$, that is, the two-dimensional (2D) circuit is blocked for electrons.

Figures 11.5a and 11.5b are the three-dimensional (3D) plots of the electron probability density ($|\Psi|^2$) in the triangular cavity

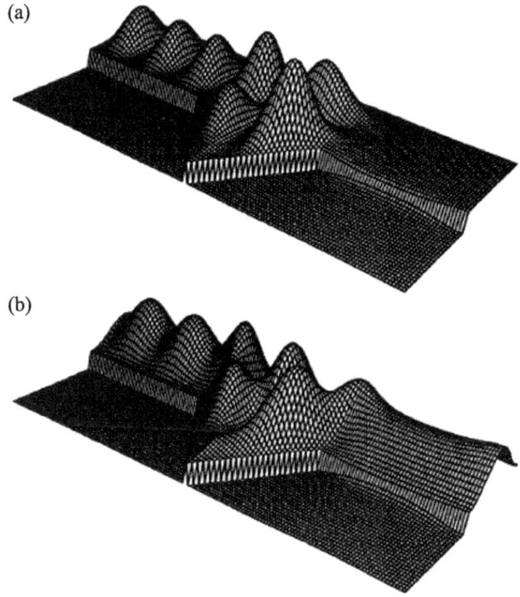

Figure 11.5 A three-dimensional plots of the electron probability density ($|\Psi|^2$) in the triangular cavity structure (a) for $kW/\pi = 1.73$ and $G = 0.04$ and (b) for $kW/\pi = 1.57$ and $G = 0.972$.

structure for which the transmission profile has been shown in Fig. 11.4 [3]. In the two figures, the electron is incident from the upper left. Figure 11.5a is for $kW/\pi = 1.73$ and $G = 0.04$, that is, the blocked case, and the electron density is concentrated mainly in the cavity, forming the standing wave (confined state), while on the right side of the cavity, there is nearly zero electron density. Figure 11.5b is for $kW/\pi = 1.57$ and $G = 0.972$, that is, the transmitted case, and the electron density at the input end (left) and the output end (right) are nearly same; the electron does not form the confined state in the cavity. This gives a physical picture of conductance in the 2D waveguide: if the electron forms a confined state in the cavity, the circuit is blocked and vice versa.

The transfer matrix method can be applied to many waveguides with different geometries, which most of the time gives reasonable results. However, the free propagation part $\mathbf{T}_m^{\mathrm{f}}$ contains both wave components $e^{ik_n^m L_m}$ and $e^{-ik_n^m L_m}$. For evanescent mode m, the wave number k_n^m becomes imaginary and thus $e^{ik_n^m L_m} = e^{-|k_n^m|L_m}$ can be very small while $e^{-ik_n^m L_m} = e^{|k_n^m|L_m}$ can be very big. Numerical errors would therefore inevitably accumulate during the calculation, which eventually destroys the unitary condition and renders the result useless [4]. In the next section, we will introduce a more stable method to calculate the scattering matrix directly.

11.2 Scattering Matrix Method [5]

For general waveguide devices, especially those with multiple terminals, each and every port can be used for input or output purpose. In this sense, it is the scattering matrix instead of the transfer matrix that represents its most fundamental property. Let us take an example of the two-terminal device as illustrated in Fig. 11.2. $\mathbf{L}_a(\mathbf{L}_b)$ and $\mathbf{R}_b(\mathbf{R}_a)$ denote the incoming (outgoing) wave components to ports L and R, respectively. Hence we may define $\mathbf{L}_{\text{in}} = \mathbf{L}_a$, $\mathbf{L}_{\text{out}} = \mathbf{L}_b$, $\mathbf{R}_{\text{in}} = \mathbf{R}_b$, and $\mathbf{R}_{\text{out}} = \mathbf{R}_a$ and look for the scattering matrix to relate every outgoing wave to all the incoming waves, that is,

$$\begin{bmatrix} \mathbf{L}_{\text{out}} \\ \mathbf{R}_{\text{out}} \end{bmatrix} = \mathbf{S} \begin{bmatrix} \mathbf{L}_{\text{in}} \\ \mathbf{R}_{\text{in}} \end{bmatrix} = \begin{bmatrix} \mathbf{S}_{11} & \mathbf{S}_{12} \\ \mathbf{S}_{21} & \mathbf{S}_{22} \end{bmatrix} \begin{bmatrix} \mathbf{L}_{\text{in}} \\ \mathbf{R}_{\text{in}} \end{bmatrix}. \tag{11.12}$$

For the interface between the two channels as illustrated in Fig. 11.2, the scattering matrices be derived from Eq. 11.9 in a straightforward manner as follows:

$$\mathbf{S}_{11} = -\left(\mathbf{M}_1^{-1} + \mathbf{M}_2^{-1}\right)^{-1}\left(\mathbf{M}_1^{-1} - \mathbf{M}_2^{-1}\right), \quad \mathbf{S}_{12} = 2\left(\mathbf{M}_1^{-1} + \mathbf{M}_2^{-1}\right)^{-1},$$
$$\mathbf{S}_{21} = 2\left(\mathbf{M}_1 + \mathbf{M}_2\right)^{-1}, \quad \text{and} \quad \mathbf{S}_{22} = -\left(\mathbf{M}_1 + \mathbf{M}_2\right)^{-1}\left(\mathbf{M}_1 - \mathbf{M}_2\right). \tag{11.13}$$

Free propagation across a uniform channel of length L is described by the scattering matrix

$$\mathbf{S}_{\text{f}} = \begin{bmatrix} 0 & \mathbf{P} \\ \mathbf{P} & 0 \end{bmatrix}, \tag{11.14}$$

where $\mathbf{P}$ is a diagonal matrix with elements $P_{nn} = e^{ik_n L}$.

The total scattering matrix for a general waveguide structure can be calculated in a way similar to what is depicted in Fig. 11.3. When combining two consecutive sections A and B into a single section A+B, the overall transfer matrix is just a simple matrix product of the two individual matrices, that is, $\mathbf{T}_{\mathrm{A+B}} = \mathbf{T}_{\mathrm{A}}\mathbf{T}_{\mathrm{B}}$. However, the overall scattering matrix $\mathbf{S}_{\mathrm{A+B}}$ can't be written as a simple function of $\mathbf{S}_{\mathrm{A}}$ and $\mathbf{S}_{\mathrm{B}}$. Let us start with the definition of $\mathbf{S}_{\mathrm{A}}$ and $\mathbf{S}_{\mathrm{B}}$,

$$\begin{bmatrix} \mathbf{L}_{\mathrm{A}}^{o} \\ \mathbf{R}_{\mathrm{A}}^{o} \end{bmatrix} = \mathbf{S}_{\mathrm{A}} \begin{bmatrix} \mathbf{L}_{\mathrm{A}}^{i} \\ \mathbf{R}_{\mathrm{A}}^{i} \end{bmatrix} = \begin{bmatrix} \mathbf{S}_{\mathrm{A}}^{11} & \mathbf{S}_{\mathrm{A}}^{12} \\ \mathbf{S}_{\mathrm{A}}^{21} & \mathbf{S}_{\mathrm{A}}^{22} \end{bmatrix} \begin{bmatrix} \mathbf{L}_{\mathrm{A}}^{i} \\ \mathbf{R}_{\mathrm{A}}^{i} \end{bmatrix} \tag{11.15}$$

and

$$\begin{bmatrix} \mathbf{L}_{\mathrm{B}}^{o} \\ \mathbf{R}_{\mathrm{B}}^{o} \end{bmatrix} = \mathbf{S}_{\mathrm{B}} \begin{bmatrix} \mathbf{L}_{\mathrm{B}}^{i} \\ \mathbf{R}_{\mathrm{B}}^{i} \end{bmatrix} = \begin{bmatrix} \mathbf{S}_{\mathrm{B}}^{11} & \mathbf{S}_{\mathrm{B}}^{12} \\ \mathbf{S}_{\mathrm{B}}^{21} & \mathbf{S}_{\mathrm{B}}^{22} \end{bmatrix} \begin{bmatrix} \mathbf{L}_{\mathrm{B}}^{i} \\ \mathbf{R}_{\mathrm{B}}^{i} \end{bmatrix}$$

and remind that the right port of section A aligns with the left port of section B, that is, $\mathbf{R}_{\mathrm{A}}^{i} = \mathbf{L}_{\mathrm{B}}^{o}$ and $\mathbf{R}_{\mathrm{A}}^{o} = \mathbf{L}_{\mathrm{B}}^{i}$. We may eliminate the connecting port and obtain the overall scattering matrix as follows:

$$\begin{bmatrix} \mathbf{L}_{\mathrm{A}}^{o} \\ \mathbf{R}_{\mathrm{B}}^{o} \end{bmatrix} = \mathbf{S}_{\mathrm{A+B}} \begin{bmatrix} \mathbf{L}_{\mathrm{A}}^{i} \\ \mathbf{R}_{\mathrm{B}}^{i} \end{bmatrix} = \begin{bmatrix} \mathbf{S}_{\mathrm{A+B}}^{11} & \mathbf{S}_{\mathrm{A+B}}^{12} \\ \mathbf{S}_{\mathrm{A+B}}^{21} & \mathbf{S}_{\mathrm{A+B}}^{22} \end{bmatrix} \begin{bmatrix} \mathbf{L}_{\mathrm{A}}^{i} \\ \mathbf{R}_{\mathrm{B}}^{i} \end{bmatrix}, \tag{11.16}$$

where

$$\begin{aligned} \mathbf{S}_{\mathrm{A+B}}^{11} &= \mathbf{S}_{\mathrm{A}}^{11} + \mathbf{S}_{\mathrm{A}}^{12}\mathbf{S}_{\mathrm{B}}^{11}\left(1 - \mathbf{S}_{\mathrm{A}}^{22}\mathbf{S}_{\mathrm{B}}^{11}\right)^{-1}\mathbf{S}_{\mathrm{A}}^{21}, \\ \mathbf{S}_{\mathrm{A+B}}^{12} &= \mathbf{S}_{\mathrm{A}}^{12}\left(1 - \mathbf{S}_{\mathrm{B}}^{11}\mathbf{S}_{\mathrm{A}}^{22}\right)^{-1}\mathbf{S}_{\mathrm{B}}^{12}, \\ \mathbf{S}_{\mathrm{A+B}}^{21} &= \mathbf{S}_{\mathrm{B}}^{21}\left(1 - \mathbf{S}_{\mathrm{A}}^{22}\mathbf{S}_{\mathrm{B}}^{11}\right)^{-1}\mathbf{S}_{\mathrm{A}}^{21}, \end{aligned} \tag{11.17}$$

and

$$\mathbf{S}_{\mathrm{A+B}}^{22} = \mathbf{S}_{\mathrm{B}}^{22} + \mathbf{S}_{\mathrm{B}}^{21}\mathbf{S}_{\mathrm{A}}^{22}\left(1 - \mathbf{S}_{\mathrm{B}}^{11}\mathbf{S}_{\mathrm{A}}^{22}\right)^{-1}\mathbf{S}_{\mathrm{B}}^{12}.$$

By defining a composition operator $\mathbf{S}_{\mathrm{A+B}} = \mathbf{S}_{\mathrm{A}} \otimes \mathbf{S}_{\mathrm{B}}$, we can express the overall scattering matrix for a waveguide as depicted in Fig. 11.3 as [5, 6]

$$\mathbf{S} = \mathbf{S}_{\mathrm{f}}^{1} \otimes \mathbf{S}_{12} \otimes \mathbf{S}_{\mathrm{f}}^{2} \ldots \otimes \mathbf{S}_{m,m+1} \otimes \mathbf{S}_{\mathrm{f}}^{m+1} \otimes \ldots \otimes \mathbf{S}_{\mathrm{f}}^{N}, \tag{11.18}$$

where $\mathbf{S}_{m,m+1}$ describes the scattering across the interface between the m-th and $(m+1)$-th sections, $\mathbf{S}_{\mathrm{f}}^{m}$ is for free propagation across section m, and N is the total number of sections. It is noted that the composition operator, like the matrix multiplication, satisfies the associative law but not the commutative law, that is,

$$(\mathbf{S}_A \otimes \mathbf{S}_B) \otimes \mathbf{S}_C = \mathbf{S}_A \otimes (\mathbf{S}_B \otimes \mathbf{S}_C), \mathbf{S}_A \otimes \mathbf{S}_B \neq \mathbf{S}_B \otimes \mathbf{S}_A.$$

The overall scattering matrix for a two-terminal waveguide device is commonly written in an intuitive way as $\mathbf{S} = \begin{bmatrix} \mathbf{r} & \mathbf{t}' \\ \mathbf{t} & \mathbf{r}' \end{bmatrix}$, where $\mathbf{t}$ and $\mathbf{r}$ are the transmission and reflection matrices, respectively.

Although the transfer matrix method is very efficient for structures whose dimensions are not very large, it is numerically singular for structures with dimensions much larger than the electron de Broglie wavelength, while the same problem does not exist in the scattering matrix method, and we found that numerical errors would not accumulated in the composition of scattering matrices. Figure 11.6 shows the conductance G versus kW/π for a multiple-stub structure shown in the inset [5]. The length of the channel linking the two adjacent stubs on one side of the main wire is set to be $2W$, where W is the width of the terminal as well as the width and height of the stub. Similar structures are found to exhibit perfect quantum-modulated transistor action.

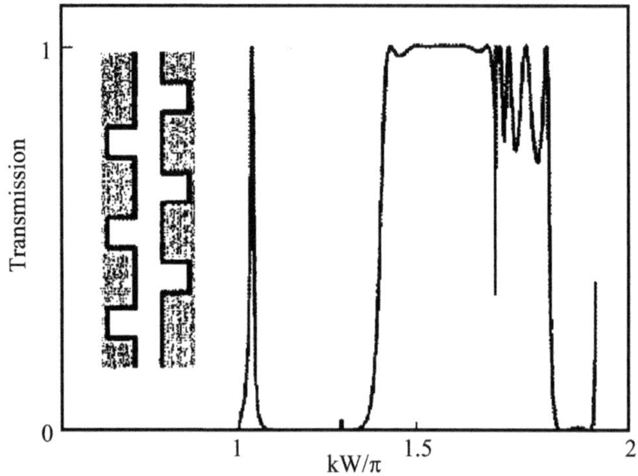

Figure 11.6 Conductance G versus kW/π for a multiple-stub structure shown in the inset.

11.3 Waveguide with Multiple Terminals

In many applications, such as quantum directional coupler [7], the waveguide device comes with multiple terminals. In this section, we will illustrate how to construct scattering matrices for two typical four-terminal structures.

The first device is depicted in Fig. 11.7, which can be regarded as two coupled parallel waveguides. The structure as shown is divided into three sections, the left two terminals L_1 and L_2, the connecting section W, and the right two terminals R_1 and R_2. Correspondingly, the overall scattering matrix can be expressed as

$$\mathbf{S} = \mathbf{S}_{L_1,L_2;W} \otimes \mathbf{S}_{\mathrm{W}}^{f} \otimes \mathbf{S}_{W;R_1,R_2}. \tag{11.19}$$

The scattering by the interface between L_1, L_2 and W is described by $\mathbf{S}_{\mathrm{L_1,L_2;W}}$, which is defined by $\left[\mathbf{A}_{\mathrm{L_1}}^{o};\mathbf{A}_{\mathrm{L_2}}^{o};\mathbf{A}_{\mathrm{W}}^{o}\right] = \mathbf{S}_{\mathrm{L_1,L_2;W}}$ $\left[\mathbf{A}_{\mathrm{L_1}}^{i};\mathbf{A}_{\mathrm{L_2}}^{i};\mathbf{A}_{\mathrm{W}}^{i}\right]$. By using the mode-matching technique, we have $\mathbf{M}_1\left[\mathbf{A}_{\mathrm{L_1}}^{i};\mathbf{A}_{\mathrm{L_1}}^{o};\mathbf{A}_{\mathrm{L_2}}^{i};\mathbf{A}_{\mathrm{L_2}}^{o}\right] = \mathbf{M}_2\left[\mathbf{A}_{\mathrm{W}}^{i};\ \mathbf{A}_{\mathrm{W}}^{o}\right]$, where

$$\mathbf{M}_1 = \begin{bmatrix} \mathbf{C}_1^T & \mathbf{C}_1^T & \mathbf{C}_2^T & \mathbf{C}_2^T \\ \mathbf{K}_{\mathrm{L}} & -\mathbf{K}_{\mathrm{L}} & 0 & 0 \\ 0 & 0 & \mathbf{K}_{\mathrm{L}} & -\mathbf{K}_{\mathrm{L}} \end{bmatrix}, \ \mathbf{M}_2 = \begin{bmatrix} 1 & 1 \\ \mathbf{C}_1\mathbf{K}_{\mathrm{W}} & -\mathbf{C}_1\mathbf{K}_{\mathrm{W}} \\ \mathbf{C}_2\mathbf{K}_{\mathrm{W}} & -\mathbf{C}_2\mathbf{K}_{\mathrm{W}} \end{bmatrix}. \tag{11.20}$$

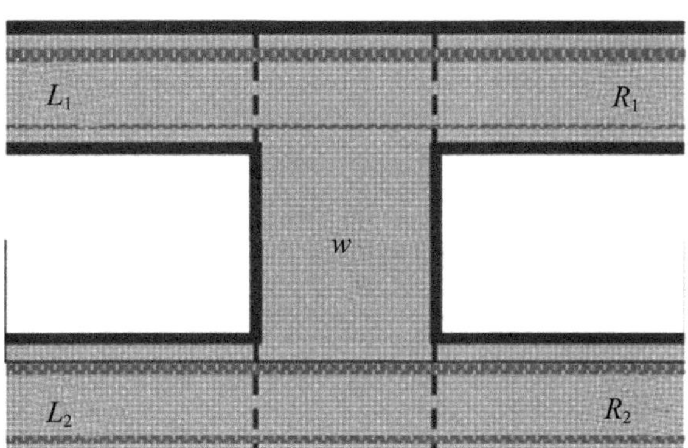

Figure 11.7 Schematic view of a four-terminal quantum waveguide.

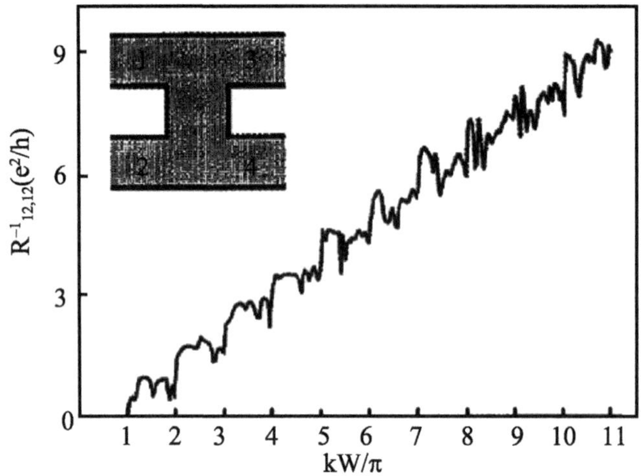

Figure 11.8 The inverse resistance $R^{-1}_{12,12}$ versus kW/π for the four-terminal structure shown in the inset.

Rearranging the above matrix equation, we can obtain $\mathbf{S}_{\mathrm{L_1,L_2;W}}$ as follows:

$$\mathbf{S}_{\mathrm{L_1,L_2;W}} = \begin{bmatrix} C_1^{\mathrm{T}} & C_2^{\mathrm{T}} & -1 \\ -K_{\mathrm{L}} & 0 & -C_1 K_{\mathrm{W}} \\ 0 & -K_{\mathrm{L}} & -C_2 K_{\mathrm{W}} \end{bmatrix}^{-1} \begin{bmatrix} -C_1^{\mathrm{T}} & -C_2^{\mathrm{T}} & 1 \\ -K_{\mathrm{L}} & 0 & -C_1 K_{\mathrm{W}} \\ 0 & K_{\mathrm{L}} & -C_2 K_{\mathrm{W}} \end{bmatrix}. \quad (11.21)$$

$\mathbf{S}_{\mathrm{W;R_1,R_2}}$ can be obtained in a similar way.

Figure 11.8 shows the calculated Büttiker resistance $R_{12,12}$ for the four-terminal structure as shown in the inset [5]. The parameters are taken to be the same as those adopted in Fig. 11.8 of Ref. [6]. A comparison of our results with those in Ref. [6] shows that the two results are consistent each other as $kW/\pi < 7$. When $kW/\pi > 7$, the profile of our results becomes more complicated while that in Ref. [6] becomes simpler. This is because when $kW/\pi > 7$, the mode-mixing effect is enhanced and the interference between various modes becomes more complicated for higher electron energies, which have not been considered in Ref. [6].

The second device, as illustrated in Fig. 11.9, is a cross structure with four ports. As the terminals don't align with each other like that shown in Fig. 11.7, it is not possible to construct the overall

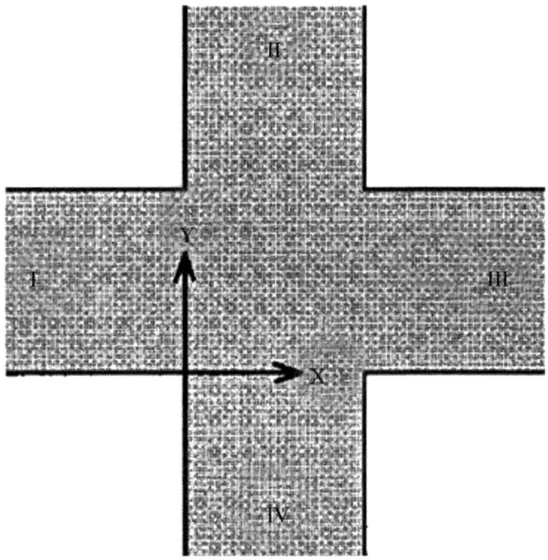

Figure 11.9 Schematic view of a quantum waveguide with a cross junction.

scattering matrix from those for the individual sections. Let us first expand the wave functions in I and III as well as II and IV onto the transverse modes $\phi_n(y) = \sqrt{\frac{2}{W}}\sin\left(\frac{n\pi}{W}y\right)$ and $\phi_n(x) = \sqrt{\frac{2}{W}}\sin\left(\frac{n\pi}{W}x\right)$, respectively, as in Eq. 11.2. Here W is the width of each of the four terminals. Next we introduce four auxiliary functions $\zeta_n^{\alpha}(xy)$ ($\alpha =$ I, II, III and IV) in the internal cross junction so that each of them matches the transverse mode in the corresponding terminal, that is, $\zeta_n^{\alpha}|_{\sigma_\alpha} = \phi_n^{\alpha}$. Thanks to the simple device geometry, ζ_n^{α}'s are found to be [8]

$$
\begin{aligned}
\zeta_n^1(x,y) &= \left(\cos k_n x - \frac{\sin k_n x}{\tan k_n W}\right)\varphi_n(y), \\
\zeta_n^2(x,y) &= \frac{\sin k_n y}{\sin k_n W}\phi_n(x), \\
\zeta_n^3(x,y) &= \frac{\sin k_n x}{\sin k_n W}\phi_n(y), \text{ and} \\
\zeta_n^4(x,y) &= \left(\cos k_n y - \frac{\sin k_n y}{\tan k_n W}\right)\varphi_n(x).
\end{aligned}
\qquad (11.22)
$$

Hence the wave function in the cross junction is given by

$$\psi(x,y)=\sum_{\alpha,n}\left(a_n^\alpha+b_n^\alpha\right)\zeta_n^\alpha(x,y) \tag{11.23}$$

and continuity of the first-order derivatives gives

$$\sum_n ik_n\left(a_n^\alpha-b_n^\alpha\right)\nabla\phi_n^\alpha\big|_{\sigma_\alpha}=\sum_{\alpha',n}\left(a_n^{\alpha'}+b_n^{\alpha'}\right)\nabla\zeta_n^\alpha\big|_{\sigma_{\alpha'}}. \tag{11.24}$$

By proper integration of the above equations, we may eliminate ζ_n^α and ϕ_n^α and obtain the overall scattering matrix for the cross junction, $\mathbf{S}_+=(i\mathbf{K}_4+\mathbf{D})^{-1}(i\mathbf{K}_4-\mathbf{D})$ where

$$\mathbf{K}_4=\begin{bmatrix}\mathbf{K}' & 0 & 0 & 0\\ 0 & \mathbf{K}' & 0 & 0\\ 0 & 0 & \mathbf{K}' & 0\\ 0 & 0 & 0 & \mathbf{K}'\end{bmatrix},\ D=\begin{bmatrix}-\mathbf{C}_1 & \mathbf{FA} & \mathbf{C}_2 & \mathbf{A}\\ \mathbf{AF} & -\mathbf{C}_1 & \mathbf{FAF} & \mathbf{C}_2\\ \mathbf{C}_2 & \mathbf{FAF} & -\mathbf{C}_1 & \mathbf{AF}\\ \mathbf{A} & \mathbf{C}_2 & \mathbf{FA} & -\mathbf{C}_1\end{bmatrix}. \tag{11.25}$$

with the matrix elements given by $\mathbf{K}'_{mn}=k'_n\delta_{mn}\,(k'_n=k_nW/\pi)$, $\mathbf{F}_{mn}=(-1)^{n+1}\delta_{mn}$, $\mathbf{A}_{mn}=2mn/\left[\pi m^2-\pi\left(k'_n\right)^2\right]$, $(\mathbf{C}_1)_{mn}=k'_n tgk'_n\pi\,\delta_{mn}$, and $(\mathbf{C}_2)_{mn}=\frac{k'_n}{sink'_n\pi}\delta_{mn}$. Similarly, we may obtain the scattering matrix for the L-shaped junction, which consists of ports I and II, as follows:

$$\mathbf{S}_L=\begin{bmatrix}i\mathbf{K}'-\mathbf{C}_1 & \mathbf{FA}\\ \mathbf{AF} & i\mathbf{K}'-\mathbf{C}_1\end{bmatrix}^{-1}\begin{bmatrix}i\mathbf{K}'+\mathbf{C}_1 & -\mathbf{FA}\\ -\mathbf{AF} & i\mathbf{K}'+\mathbf{C}_1\end{bmatrix}. \tag{11.26}$$

Further, the scattering matrix for the T-shaped junction, which consists of ports I, II, and III, can be given by

$$\mathbf{S}_T=\begin{bmatrix}i\mathbf{K}'-\mathbf{C}_1 & \mathbf{FA} & \mathbf{C}_2\\ \mathbf{AF} & i\mathbf{K}'-\mathbf{C}_1 & \mathbf{FAF}\\ \mathbf{C}_2 & \mathbf{FAF} & i\mathbf{K}'-\mathbf{C}_1\end{bmatrix}^{-1}\begin{bmatrix}i\mathbf{K}'+\mathbf{C}_1 & -\mathbf{FA} & -\mathbf{C}_2\\ -\mathbf{AF} & i\mathbf{K}'+\mathbf{C}_1 & -\mathbf{FAF}\\ -\mathbf{C}_2 & -\mathbf{FAF} & i\mathbf{K}'+\mathbf{C}_1\end{bmatrix}. \tag{11.27}$$

Figure 11.10 shows the transmission coefficients versus kW/π for the structure with rounded corners shown in the inset [8]. The solid line is for forward transmission, and the dotted line is for side transmission. From the figure we see that the forward transmission profile has a sharp dip (anti-resonance). It is attributed to the quantum bound state. The bound energy of the quantum bound state becomes larger with enlargement of the internal junction area.

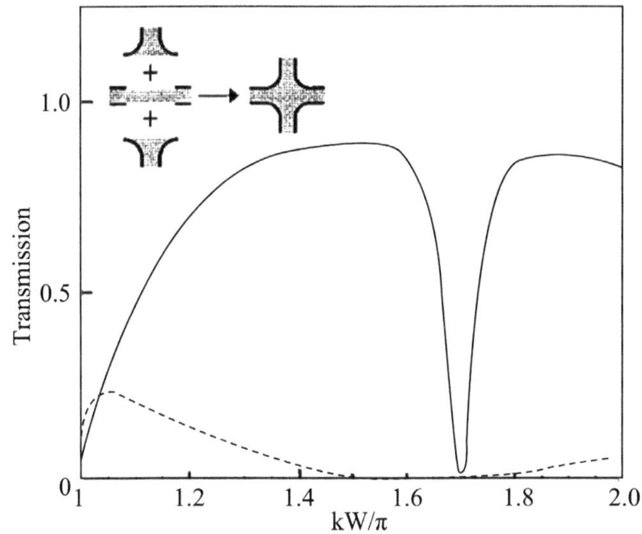

Figure 11.10 Transmission coefficients versus kW/π for the structure with rounded corners shown in the inset. The solid line is for forward transmission, and dotted line for side transmission.

Therefore the scattering of the propagating states with the bound state is enhanced. We also find the side transmission is much smaller due to the enhanced reflection.

References

1. Sheng, W.-D., and Xia, J. B. (1996). *Phys. Letts. A*, **220**, 268.
2. Xia, J. B., and Sheng, W.-D. (1996). *J. Appl. Phys.*, **79**, 7780.
3. Sheng, W.-D., and Xia, J. B. (1996). *J. Phys.: Condens. Matter*, **8**, 3635.
4. Sheng, W.-D., and Xia, J. B. (1997). *J. Appl. Phys.*, **81**, 734.
5. Sheng, W.-D. (1997). *J. Phys.: Condens. Matter*, **9**, 8369.
6. Wang, J., Wang, Y. J., and Guo, H. (1992). *Phys. Rev. B*, **46**, 2420.
7. Sheng, W.-D., and Xia, J. B. (1997). *Appl. Phys. A*, **64**, 167.
8. Sheng, W.-D. (1997). *J. Appl. Phys.*, **81**, 6210.

Chapter 12

One-Dimensional Quantum Waveguide Theory of a Rashba Electron [1]

Some of the first observations of quantum interference were made using thin metal films and silicon inversion layers [2, 3]. Since then most of the quantum interferences and ballistic transports are observed in two-dimensional systems. The physics of quantum interference includes the Aharonov–Bohm effect, quantum interference transistors, universal conductance fluctuations, ballistic electron transport and Landauer–Büttiker formula, quantized conductance in point contacts, multi-terminal devices, quantum dot resonant tunneling devices, etc. In these structures the electron movement is dominated by quantum mechanics, not classical mechanics. In the past 20 years, mesoscopic physics and spintronics have become two most active areas in condensed matter physics.

The nature of the spin of carriers in semiconductors has received considerable attention. With the rapid progress in semiconductor fabrication techniques, it is now possible to dope magnetic impurities inside semiconductors to produce diluted magnetic semiconductors (DMSs). The doped Mn ions interact with the carriers through sp-d exchange interaction, which results in a giant Zeeman splitting of the spin sublevels of the electron and hole.

Quantum Waveguide in Microcircuits
Jian-Bai Xia, Duan-Yang Liu, and Wei-Dong Sheng

ISBN 978-981-4669-85-6 (Hardcover), 978-1-315-36477-3 (eBook)
www.panstanford.com

A spin-polarized current can be produced by DMS-semiconductor heterostructures [4] or resonant tunneling with a DMS as a potential well [5] due to the giant Zeeman splitting. Now the spin coherence relaxation time has reached the nanosecond level at room temperature and the coherence distance exceeds 100 μm. The ability to preserve coherence spin states in semiconductors may enable quantum computing in the solid state. On the other hand, it was found that the Curie temperature T_C in a DMS in excess of 100 K has been realized in (GaMn)As systems [6]. The high T_C DMSs can be used as an efficient spin injector from a ferromagnetic DMS into a semiconductor without applying a magnetic field. Datta [7] has proposed a spin transistor device.

For a conduction-band electron in zinc-blende semiconductors the dominant spin-orbit interaction (SOI) in low-dimensional semiconductor structures comes from two physical factors: one is the Rashba SOI [8], which arises from the structure inversion asymmetry of the confined potential, for example, in a triangle well formed in modulated-doped heterojunctions or the external electric field. The other is the Dresselhaus SOI [9] induced by the lack of bulk inversion symmetry, for example, in III-V compounds. Sheng et al. [10] studied theoretically electron spin states in one-dimensional ring in the presence of both the Rashba SOI and the Dresselhaus SOI in a perpendicular magnetic field. They found that persistent charge current, persistent spin current, etc., are very sensitive to the strength of the Rashba and Dresselhaus SOI.

In this chapter, we apply the one-dimensional quantum theory [11] to the case of an electron with a spin in the presence of a Rashba SOI [8].

12.1 Rashba State Wave Function

In 1960 Rashba proposed Hamiltonian about an electron's spin in a semiconductor [8]

$$H_R = \alpha \left[\sigma \times \mathbf{k}\right] \cdot \mathbf{n}, \tag{12.1}$$

where σ is the Pauli matrix of an electron's spin, $\mathbf{k}$ is the wave vector of the electron, $\mathbf{n}$ is the unit vector perpendicular to the interface, and α is the Rashba coefficient. Andrada et al. [12] proved that when the potential $V(z)$ is asymmetric along the **n** direction, that is, $dV(z)/dz \neq 0$, α is not equal to zero, that is, there is a Rashba effect. In most two-dimensional electron gases (2DEGs) formed in the modulation doping heterojunction structure $V(z)$ is asymmetric, so in many modulation doping field-effect transistors (MODFET) there is a Rashba effect. Moreover, in the ordinary quantum well, if there is a, external electric field perpendicular to the interface, the Rashba effect will arise and the strength of the Rashba effect is proportional to $dV(z)/dz$. To fabricate spin-controllable devices by utilizing the Rashba effect, we have studied quantum waveguide theory of Rashba electrons [1].

According to Eq. 12.1, the Hamiltonian of an electron in the two-dimensional (2D) system with the Rashba spin-orbit interaction (RSOI) is

$$H = \begin{pmatrix} -\dfrac{\hbar^2}{2m^*}\nabla^2 + V(x, y) & \dfrac{\alpha}{\hbar}(ip_x + p_y) \\ \dfrac{\alpha}{\hbar}(-ip_x + p_y) & -\dfrac{\hbar^2}{2m^*}\nabla^2 + V(x, y) \end{pmatrix}, \tag{12.2}$$

where m^* is the electron effective mass and α is the Rashba coefficient. If the electron moves in a one-dimensional (1D) straight circuit with a polar angle θ(see Fig. 12.1a) and the potential is zero in the circuit, then the Hamiltonian can be written as

$$H = \begin{pmatrix} -\dfrac{\hbar^2}{2m^*}\dfrac{\partial^2}{\partial l^2} & \alpha e^{-i\theta}\dfrac{\partial}{\partial l} \\ -\alpha e^{i\theta}\dfrac{\partial}{\partial l} & -\dfrac{\hbar^2}{2m^*}\dfrac{\partial^2}{\partial l^2} \end{pmatrix}, \tag{12.3}$$

where l is the coordinate along the circuit. The electron wave function has the plane wave form,

$$\Phi = \begin{pmatrix} c_1 \\ c_2 \end{pmatrix} e^{ikl}. \tag{12.4}$$

Then the eigenenergies are determined as

$$E = \frac{\hbar^2}{2m^*}k^2 \pm \alpha k, \tag{12.5}$$

and the wave functions are calculated to be

$$\phi_1(\theta) = \frac{1}{\sqrt{2}}\begin{pmatrix} 1 \\ ie^{i\theta} \end{pmatrix} \text{ and } \phi_2(\theta) = \frac{1}{\sqrt{2}}\begin{pmatrix} 1 \\ -ie^{i\theta} \end{pmatrix}, \tag{12.6}$$

corresponding to the $-\alpha k$ and $+\alpha k$ terms in Eq. 12.5, respectively.

The spin orientations of the states ϕ_1 and ϕ_2 can be determined by $\phi_i^+ s_x \phi_i$ and $\phi_i^+ s_y \phi_i$, respectively, where s_x and s_y are the spin component operators along the x and y directions, respectively.

$$\begin{aligned} \bar{S}_{x1} &= -\sin\theta, \quad \bar{S}_{x2} = \sin\theta, \\ \bar{S}_{y1} &= \cos\theta, \quad \bar{S}_{y2} = -\cos\theta, \\ \bar{S}_{z1} &= 0 \quad \text{and} \quad \bar{S}_{z2} = 0. \end{aligned} \tag{12.7}$$

From Eq. 12.7 we found that the spin orientation of the ϕ_1 and ϕ_2 states are perpendicular to the circuit and the angles between the spin and the circuit are $+\pi/2$ and $-\pi/2$, respectively. Afterward, we call the spin with the angle $+\pi/2$ to the circuit as spin-up and that with the angle $-\pi/2$ as spin-down.

If the electron states ϕ_1 and ϕ_2 have the same energy E, from Eq. 12.5 we obtain their wave vectors,

$$\begin{aligned} k_1 &= k_0 + k_\delta, \quad k_2 = k_0 - k_\delta, \\ k_0 &= \frac{m^*}{\hbar^2}\sqrt{\alpha^2 + \frac{2\hbar^2}{m^*}E}, \quad \text{and} \quad k_\delta = \frac{m^*}{\hbar^2}\alpha. \end{aligned} \tag{12.8}$$

Therefore, due to the RSOI the electrons with the same energy will have different wave vectors and spin orientations. Note that there is another pair of solutions associated with $-k_0$.

Up to now, we have only considered that the electron can pass through the circuit freely. Now we consider the case with a ferromagnetic contact [7] (see Fig. 12.1b) or a gate [11] (see Fig. 12.1c) at the end of the circuit, and either the spin-up (or spin-down) electrons or all electrons cannot pass through the circuit. If the spin-up electrons are reflected, then the wave function in the circuit will not have the plane wave form as in Eq. 12.4. It has the form of a standing wave, as

$$\begin{aligned} \Phi &= \phi_1(\theta)\, e^{ik_1 l} - \phi_2(\theta + \pi)\, e^{-ik_2 l} \\ &= \phi_1(\theta)\, e^{ik_\delta l} \sin(k_0 l), \end{aligned} \tag{12.9}$$

where the origin of the coordinate l is at the contact or gate and we have used the relation $\phi_2(\theta + \pi) = \phi_1(\theta)$ and Eq. 12.8. If the spin-down electrons are reflected, the wave function will have the form

$$\Phi = \phi_2(\theta)\, e^{-ik_\delta l} \sin(k_0 l). \tag{12.10}$$

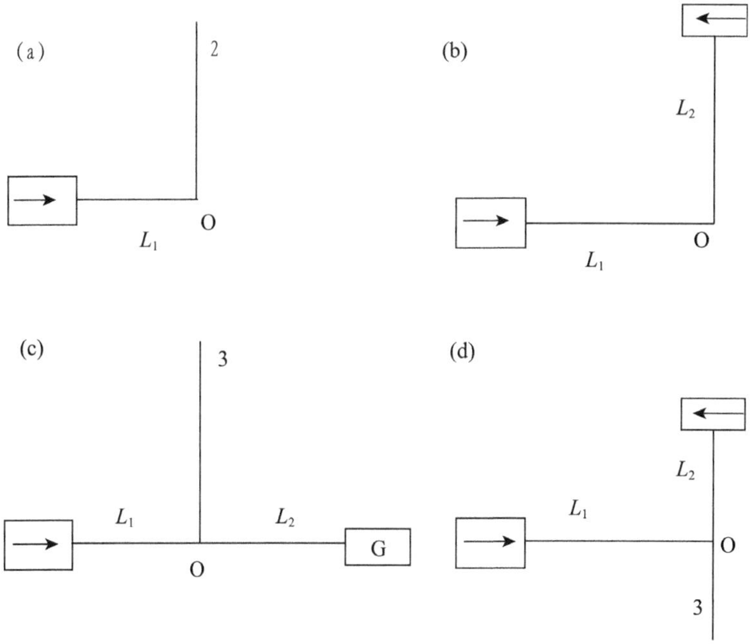

Figure 12.1 Several structures: (a) a turning structure, (b) a spin-polarized device, (c) a spin-polarized interference device, and (d) another spin-polarized interference device.

The main result of this section is that the phase of the Rashba wave function depends on the direction of the circuit θ, as shown in Eq. 12.6. The electron without considering the spin does not have this property [11], while the hole has a similar property, see Section 10.6.

12.2 Boundary Conditions of the Rashba Current

Now we know all wave functions in every circuits. Another main problem is the boundary conditions at the intersection. If the intersection is crossed by n circuits, let Φ_i be the wave function of the i-th circuit. At the intersection there are two boundary conditions: one is the continuity of the wave functions, and the other is the conservation of the current density. The first one is simple; it demands that

$$\Phi_1 = \Phi_2 = \cdots = \Phi_n. \tag{12.11}$$

The second one can be determined by the current density operator L_i, which is the operator of the derivative of the coordinate along the i-th circuit for the case of a simple electron. Now we calculate the form of the operator L_i from Eq. 12.3. Because the RSOI is related to the momentum, L_i is determined by the commutation relation as

$$L_i = -\frac{i}{\hbar}[l, H] = \frac{i}{\hbar}\begin{pmatrix} -\frac{\hbar^2}{m^*}\frac{\partial}{\partial l} & \alpha e^{-i\theta} \\ -\alpha e^{i\theta} & -\frac{\hbar^2}{m^*}\frac{\partial}{\partial l} \end{pmatrix}. \tag{12.12}$$

If we assign all positive directions of l_i to be pointing to the intersection, the second boundary condition has the form

$$\sum_{i=1}^{n} L_i \Phi_i = 0. \tag{12.13}$$

For the plane wave in Eq. 12.6, in spite of the spin-up or spin-down state, we get

$$L\Phi = \frac{\hbar k_0}{m^*}\Phi. \tag{12.14}$$

For the standing waves in Eqs. 12.9 and 12.10, with the coordinate origin at the intersection and L as the distance from the gate to the intersection, we get

$$L\Phi = -\frac{\hbar k_0}{m^*} i \cot\left[k_0 \left(l - L\right)\right]\Phi. \tag{12.15}$$

It can be expected that all $\hbar k_0/m^*$ terms in the equations of the second boundary condition (Eq. 12.13) can be counteracted. From Eq. 12.14 we see that though the Rashba states have different wave vectors of k_1 and k_2, their travel velocities are the same $\hbar k_0/m^*$. This will make the calculation more convenient.

12.3 Kinetic Property of a Rashba Wave in Branch Circuits

12.3.1 Turning Structure

First we consider the turning structure, the simplest situation in Fig. 12.1a. Suppose an incident electron with energy E enters circuit 1 (Fig. 12.1a). Then there will be transmitted waves in circuit 2 and reflected waves in circuit 1. The wave functions in circuits 1 and 2 can be written as

$$\Phi_1 = a_{10}\phi_1(0)\,e^{ik_1l_1} + a_{20}\phi_2(0)\,e^{ik_2l_1} + a_1\phi_1(\pi)\,e^{-ik_1l_1} + a_2\phi_2(\pi)\,e^{-ik_2l_1},$$

and

$$\Phi_2 = c_1\phi_1(\pi/2)\,e^{ik_1l_2} + c_2\phi_2(\pi/2)\,e^{ik_2l_2}, \qquad (12.16)$$

where a_{10} and a_{20} are the coefficients of the known incident wave functions, a_1 and a_2 are the coefficients of reflected wave functions, and c_1 and c_2 are the coefficients of transmitted wave functions. From the boundary condition Eq. 12.11, we obtain

$$A_{10}\begin{pmatrix}1\\ i\end{pmatrix}+A_{20}\begin{pmatrix}1\\ -i\end{pmatrix}+A_1\begin{pmatrix}1\\ -i\end{pmatrix}+A_2\begin{pmatrix}1\\ i\end{pmatrix}=c_1\begin{pmatrix}1\\ -1\end{pmatrix}+c_2\begin{pmatrix}1\\ 1\end{pmatrix}. \qquad (12.17)$$

From the boundary condition Eqs. 12.13 and 12.14, we obtain

$$A_{10}\begin{pmatrix}1\\ i\end{pmatrix}+A_{20}\begin{pmatrix}1\\ -i\end{pmatrix}-A_1\begin{pmatrix}1\\ -i\end{pmatrix}-A_2\begin{pmatrix}1\\ i\end{pmatrix}=c_1\begin{pmatrix}1\\ -1\end{pmatrix}+c_2\begin{pmatrix}1\\ 1\end{pmatrix}, \qquad (12.18)$$

where

$$A_{10} = a_{10}e^{ik_1L_1}, \qquad A_{20} = a_{20}e^{ik_2L_1},$$
$$A_1 = a_1e^{-ik_1L_1}, \qquad \text{and} \quad A_2 = a_2e^{-ik_2L_1}. \qquad (12.19)$$

We assumed that the coordinate origin of circuit 1 is at the magnetic contact, which is at a distance L_1 from the intersection point O, and the coordinate origin of circuit 2 is at the intersection point O.

The solutions of Eqs. 12.17 and 12.18 are

$$A_1 = A_2 = 0,$$
$$c_1 = \frac{1-i}{2}A_{10} + \frac{1+i}{2}A_{20},$$

and

$$c_2 = \frac{1+i}{2}A_{10} + \frac{1-i}{2}A_{20}. \qquad (12.20)$$

From Eq. 12.20, we see that in this structure there is no reflected wave. We can prove that for any simple turning structure, the reflected waves are zero, no matter what the turning angle is. If the incident wave has only one spin orientation, for example, spin-up, with the wave vector k_1, that is, $a_{20} = 0$ and $a_{10} = 1$, then from Eqs. 12.20 and 12.16 we see that it divides into two waves with the wave vectors k_1 and k_2 and the same probability 1/2. If the incident wave has the spin orientation in the positive x direction, then $a_{10} = 1/\sqrt{2}$ and $a_{20} = i/\sqrt{2}$. From Eq. 12.20 we obtain $c_1 = e^{ik_0 L_1} \sin(k_\delta L_1)$ and $c_2 = e^{ik_0 L_1} \cos(k_\delta L_1)$, that is, two incident waves with the wave vectors k_1 and k_2 have an interference effect as they arrive at point O. We find that the spin of the electron moving from circuit 1 to circuit 2 through the intersection has not changed. Generally, this conclusion is not related to the direction of circuit 2. So if there is no branch at the intersection like this one, the electron passes through the intersection just like in one circuit. The only difference is that the spin-up and spin-down components will be redistributed depending on the direction of circuit 2 and $k_\delta L_1$.

Figure 12.2 shows the transmission probabilities $T_{21} = |c_1|^2$ and $T_{22} = |c_2|^2$ as functions of α, when the incident electron has a spin in the positive x direction and $m^* = 0.1\ m_0$, $E = 10$ meV, and

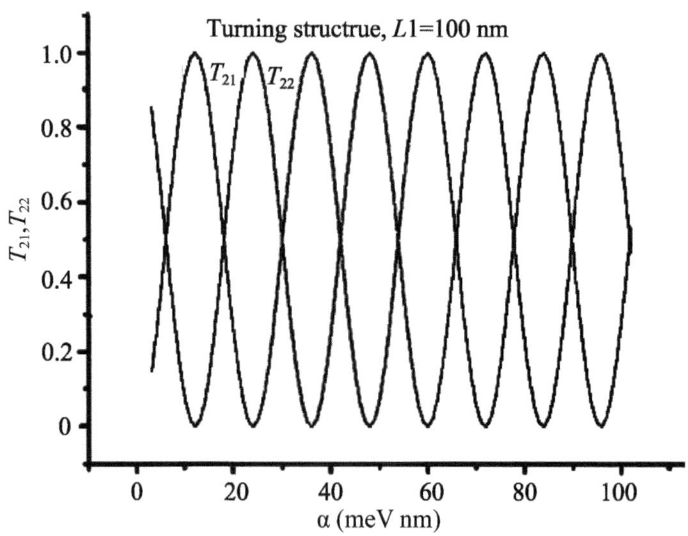

Figure 12.2 T_{21} and T_{22} of the turning structure in Fig. 12.1a as functions of the Rashba coefficient α for $m^* = 0.1\ m_0$, $E = 10$ meV, and $L_1 = 100$ nm.

$L_1 = 100$ nm. The parameters m^*, E, and L_1 are fixed in the following figures. We see that T_{21} and T_{22} change periodically with α. Due to the interference effect, when the spin at the intersection is polarized along the spin-up direction in circuit 2, $T_{21} = 1$ and $T_{22} = 0$. In the opposite case, $T_{21} = 0$, $T_{22} = 1$. It is noticed that the interference effect is only related to the phase $k_\delta L_1 \approx \alpha L_1$, independent of the electron energy E.

12.3.2 Spin-Polarized Device

Now we add a ferromagnetic contact that is magnetized in the spin-up direction in circuit 2 at the distance L_2 from the intersection O, as shown in Fig. 12.1b. According to the property of the ferromagnetic material, we expect to get a spin-polarized device. It will allow the spin-up electron to pass through completely in circuit 2 and forbid the spin-down electron from going through.

Again we assume that an incident electron with energy E and along the positive x direction enters circuit 1. The wave functions can be written as

$$\Phi_1 = a_{10}\phi_1(0)\,e^{ik_1l_1} + a_{20}\phi_2(0)\,e^{ik_2l_1} + a_1\phi_1(\pi)\,e^{-ik_1l_1} + a_2\phi_2(\pi)\,e^{-ik_2l_1},$$

and

$$\Phi_2 = c_1\phi_1(\pi/2)\,e^{ik_1l_2} + c_2\phi_2(\pi/2)\,e^{-ik_0l_2}\sin\left[k_0(l_2 - L_2)\right]. \quad (12.21)$$

Using the boundary conditions Eqs. 12.11 and 12.13 at the intersection O, the calculated results are

$$A_2 = -iA_1 = -\frac{A_{10} - iA_{20}}{2}e^{2ik_0L_2}$$

and

$$c_1 = \frac{1-i}{2}A_{10} + \frac{1+i}{2}A_{20}. \quad (12.22)$$

From Eq. 12.22 we see that the absolute values of c_1, A_1, and A_2 are not related to L_2, so we will neglect L_2 in the following discussion. The transmission probability $T_{21} = |c_1|^2 = \sin^2(k_\delta L_1)$ equals that in the above case, and there is no spin-down electron passing through the end of circuit 2. The reflection probability $R_{11} = R_{12} = \cos^2(k_\delta L_1)/2$, depending on the Rashba coefficient α. When

$k_\delta L_1 = m^*\alpha L_1/\hbar^2 = n\pi$, $T_{21} = 0$, and all electrons are reflected. When $k_\delta L_1 = m^*\alpha L_1/\hbar^2 = n\pi/2$, $T_{21} = 1$, and all electrons leave with spin up from circuit 2. So this structure is a polarization-modulation spin diode. If the ferromagnetic contact is magnetized in the spin-down direction in circuit 2, the reflection and transmission will be reversed.

12.3.3 Spin-Polarized Interference Device

Here we investigate the structure with a gate as shown in Fig. 12.1c. In this case, circuit 1 acts as the source, circuit 3 acts as the drain, and stub 2 acts as the gate, whose length L_2 can be controlled by a gate voltage. Again we assume that an incident electron with energy E and spin-polarized along the positive x direction enters circuit 1. The wave functions can be written as

$$\begin{aligned}\Phi_1 &= a_{10}\phi_1(0)\,e^{ik_1l_1} + a_{20}\phi_2(0)\,e^{ik_2l_1} + a_1\phi_1(\pi)\,e^{-ik_1l_1}\\ &\quad + a_2\phi_2(\pi)\,e^{-ik_2l_1},\\ \Phi_2 &= b_1\phi_1(0)\,e^{ik_\delta l_2}\sin\left[k_0\left(l_2 - L_2\right)\right]\\ &\quad + b_2\phi_2(0)\,e^{-ik_\delta l_2}\sin\left[k_0\left(l_2 - L_2\right)\right],\end{aligned}$$

and

$$\Phi_3 = c_1\phi_1(\pi/2)\,e^{ik_1l_2} + c_2\phi_2(\pi/2)\,e^{ik_2l_2}. \tag{12.23}$$

Using the boundary conditions Eqs. 12.11 and 12.13 at intersection 0, we obtain

$$\begin{aligned}A_2 &= -\frac{i}{D}\cos\left(k_0L_2\right)A_{10},\\ A_1 &= -\frac{i}{D}\cos\left(k_0L_2\right)A_{20},\\ c_1 &= \frac{i}{D}\sin\left(k_0L_2\right)\left[\frac{1-i}{2}A_{10} + \frac{1+i}{2}A_{20}\right],\end{aligned}$$

and

$$c_2 = \frac{i}{D}\sin\left(k_0L_2\right)\left[\frac{1+i}{2}A_{10} + \frac{1-i}{2}A_{20}\right], \tag{12.24}$$

where

$$D = 2\sin\left(k_0L_2\right) + i\cos\left(k_0L_2\right). \tag{12.25}$$

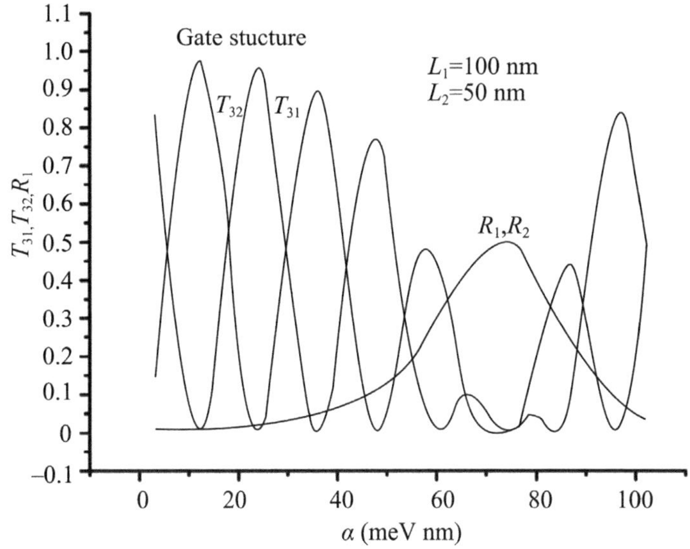

Figure 12.3 T_{31}, T_{32}, R_1, and R_2 of the spin-polarized interference device in Fig. 12.1c as functions of α for $L_2 = 50$ nm and other parameters the same as Fig. 12.2.

Comparing Eq. 12.24 to Eq. 12.20, we find that they are similar, c_1 and c_2 are multiplied by a coefficient that is only related to $|\sin(k_0L_2)/D|^2$, and the reflection is not zero now. These two effects are caused obviously by the gate. If there is no gate, the structure is the turning structure, as shown in Fig. 12.1a. The transmission probabilities T_{21} and T_{22} oscillate periodically with the Rashba coefficient α, as shown in Fig. 12.2. Now we can expect that they can be further controlled by the gate voltage.

Figure 12.3 shows the transmission and reflection probabilities as functions of α for $L_2 = 50$ nm. From Fig. 12.3 we see that T_{31} and T_{32} oscillate periodically with α, as in Fig. 12.2, but their amplitudes decrease with α, reach a minimum at $\alpha = 73$ meV nm, and then increase afterward. This modulation is caused by the interference effect related to $\cot(k_0L_2)$. Figure 12.4 shows the transmission and reflection probabilities as functions of α for $L_2 = 80$ nm. From Fig. 12.4 we see that when L_2 is changed by the gate voltage, the amplitudes of T_{31} and T_{32} increase with α, reach a maximum at

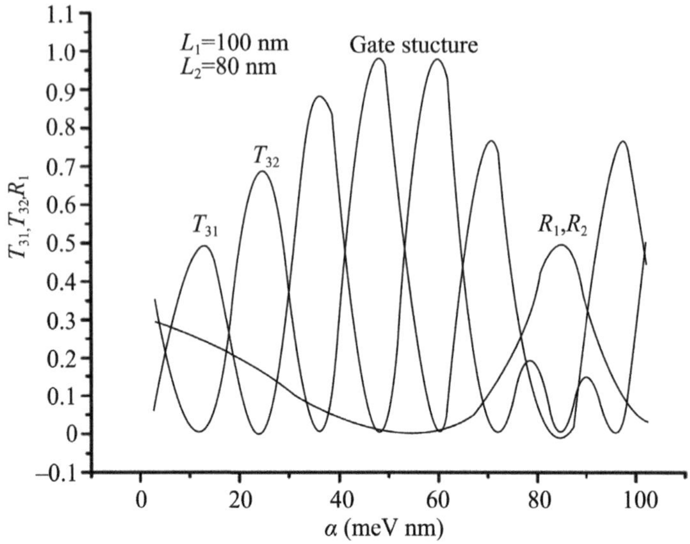

Figure 12.4 The same as Fig. 12.3 but for $L_2 = 80$ nm.

$\alpha = 50$ and 60 meV nm, then decrease to zero at $\alpha = 85$ meV nm. The interference effect of the gate is obvious, but it only changes the magnitude of T_{31} and T_{32} simultaneously, while the interference effect between electrons with spin-up and spin-down changes T_{31} and T_{32} alternatively, as shown in Fig. 12.2.

For showing the prominence of the gate, we keep the RSOI coefficient α as a constant and show the transmission probabilities T_{31}, T_{32}, R_1, and R_2 as functions of L_2 for $\alpha = 50$ meV nm in Fig. 12.5. From Fig. 12.5 we see that the amplitudes of T_{31} and T_{32} oscillate simultaneously with L_2 and their relative magnitudes are determined by the α. So making use of controlling the gate voltage, this structure is a spin-polarized interference device.

12.4 General Theory for a Structure with Multiple Branches

We assume that except the input circuit there are n_1 free output circuits ($j = 1, 2, \ldots, n_1$), n_2 circuits with gates ($k = n_1 + 1, \ldots,$

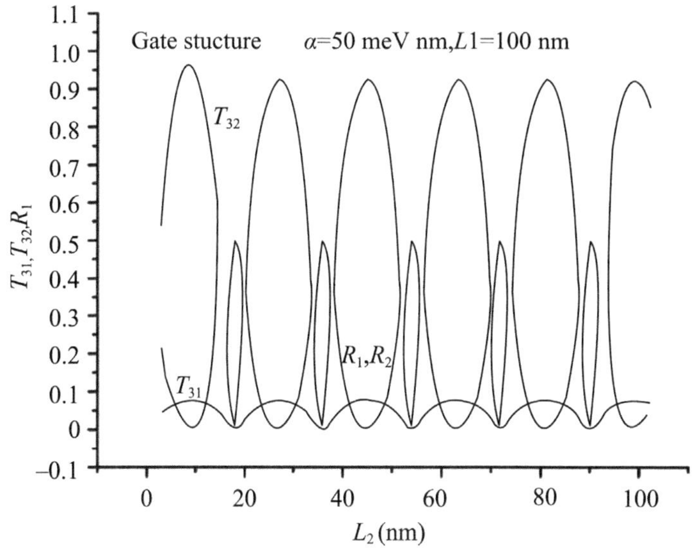

Figure 12.5 T_{31}, T_{32}, R_1, and R_2 of the spin-polarized interference device in Fig. 12.1c as functions of L_2 for $\alpha = 50$ meV nm and other parameters the same as Fig. 12.2.

$n_1 + n_2$), and n_3 circuits with ferromagnetic contacts, which allow spin-up or spin-down electrons to pass through ($m = n_1 + n_2 + 1, \ldots, n_1 + n_2 + n_3$). The orientation angle θ and the phase functions ϕ_1 and ϕ_2 (Eq. 12.6) of each circuit are denoted by the subscripts j, k, and m.

The wave functions in the input circuit are incident wave Φ_{i} and reflection wave Φ_{r},

$$\Phi_{\mathrm{i}} = a_{10} e^{ik_1 l_i} \phi_{i1} + a_{20} e^{ik_2 l_i} \phi_{i2},$$

and

$$\Phi_{\mathrm{r}} = a_1 e^{-ik_1 l_i} \phi_{i2} + a_2 e^{-ik_2 l_1} \phi_{i1}. \tag{12.26}$$

The output waves in the j-th circuit,

$$\Phi_j = a_{j1} e^{ik_1 l_j} \phi_{j1} + a_{j2} e^{ik_2 l_j} \phi_{j2}. \tag{12.27}$$

In the k-th circuit,

$$\Phi_k = a_{k1} e^{ik_\delta l_k} \sin\left[k_0 \left(l_k - L_k\right)\right] \phi_{k1} + a_{k2} e^{-ik_\delta l_k} \sin\left[k_0 \left(l_k - L_k\right)\right] \phi_{k2}. \tag{12.28}$$

In the m-th circuit,

$$\Phi_m = a_{m1}e^{ik_1 l_m}\phi_{m1} + a_{m2}e^{-ik_\delta l_m}\sin\left[k_0\left(l_m - L_m\right)\right]\phi_{m2} \qquad (12.29)$$

or

$$\Phi_m = a_{m1}e^{ik_\delta l_m}\sin\left[k_0\left(l_m - L_m\right)\right]\phi_{m1} + a_{m2}e^{ik_2 l_m}\phi_{m2} \qquad (12.30)$$

for spin-up and spin-down allowing circuits, respectively. The L_k and L_m are the distances from intersection O to the gate or contact.

The boundary conditions of the wave functions at intersection O are

$$\Phi_\mathrm{i} + \Phi_\mathrm{r} = \Phi_t, \quad t = 1, 2, \ldots n_1 + n_2 + n_3, \qquad (12.31)$$

and

$$\Phi_\mathrm{i} - \Phi_\mathrm{r} = \sum_{j=1}^{n_1}\Phi_j + i\sum_{k=n_1+1}^{n_1+n_2}\cot\left(k_0 L_k\right)\Phi_k + \sum_{m=n_1+n_2+1}^{n_1+n_2+n_3} J_m\Phi_m, \qquad (12.32)$$

where

$$J_m\Phi_m = a_{m1}\phi_{m1} + a_{m2}\left[-i\cos\left(k_0 L_m\right)\right]\phi_{m2}$$

and

$$J_m\Phi_m = a_{m1}\left[-i\cos\left(k_0 L_m\right)\right]\phi_{m1} + a_{m2}\phi_{m2} \qquad (12.33)$$

for the wave functions (Eq. 12.29 or Eq. 12.30), respectively.

Solving Eqs. 12.31 and 12.32 we can obtain the reflection coefficients a_1 and a_2 and the transmission coefficients of every circuits a_{t1} and a_{t2} for $t = 1, 2, \ldots, n_1, n_1 + n_2 + 1, \ldots, n_1 + n_2 + n_3$. For the circuits with gates $j = n_1 + 1, \ldots, n_1 + n_2$, there is no transmission wave in them, so we do not need to calculate the coefficients a_{j1} and a_{j2}. For the circuits with a ferromagnetic contact $m = n_1 + n_2 + 1, \ldots, n_1 + n_2 + n_3$, one spin wave is allowed to pass, another is forbidden, so we only need to calculate the coefficient of plane wave.

In terms of the transmission probability, in the circuits $1 \leq j \leq n_1$, $T_j = |a_{j1}|^2 + |a_{j2}|^2$, in the circuits $n_1 + 1 \leq k \leq n_1 + n_2$, $T_k = 0$, and in the circuits $n_1 + n_2 + 1 \leq m \leq n_1 + n_2 + n_3$, $T_m = |a_{m1}|^2$ or $|a_{m2}|^2$. The reflection probability $R = |a_1|^2 + |a_2|^2$. Because the travel velocities of the electrons with spin-up and spin-down are the same $\hbar k_0/m^*$, T and R are proportional to the square of the coefficients of the wave functions. For all the above cases we proved that $\sum T_t + R = 1$, that is, the conversation of the particle current.

For simplicity we first consider the case of $n_3 = 0$, that is, there is no circuit with a ferromagnetic contact. From the boundary condition Eqs. 12.31 and 12.32 we obtain

$$\Phi_{\rm i} - \Phi_{\rm r} = (n + i\,D)\,\Phi_{\rm j}, \quad D = \sum_{k=n_1+1}^{n_1+n_2} \cot\left(k_0\,L_k\right). \tag{12.34}$$

From Eqs. 12.31 and 12.32 we obtain

$$\Phi_{\rm i} = \frac{1}{2}\,(1 + n_1 + i\,D)\,\Phi_{\rm j},$$

$$\Phi_{\rm r} = \frac{1}{2}\,(1 - n_1 - i\,D)\,\Phi_{\rm j},$$

$$\Phi_{\rm j} = \frac{2}{1 + n_1 + i\,D}\left(A_{10}\phi_{\rm i1} + A_{20}\phi_{\rm i2}\right),$$

and

$$\Phi_{\rm r} = \frac{1 - n_1 - i\,D}{1 + n_1 + i\,D}\left(A_{10}\phi_{\rm i1} + A_{20}\phi_{\rm i2}\right). \tag{12.35}$$

From Eq. 12.35 we obtain

$$a_{\rm j1} = \frac{2}{1 + n_1 + i\,D}\left(A_{10}\phi_{\rm j1}^{+}\phi_{\rm i1} + A_{20}\phi_{\rm j1}^{+}\phi_{\rm i2}\right),$$

$$a_{\rm j2} = \frac{2}{1 + n_1 + i\,D}\left(A_{10}\phi_{\rm j2}^{+}\phi_{\rm i1} + A_{20}\phi_{\rm j2}^{+}\phi_{\rm i2}\right),$$

$$A_1 = \frac{1 - n_1 - i\,D}{1 + n_1 + i\,D}A_{20},$$

and

$$A_2 = \frac{1 - n_1 - i\,D}{1 + n_1 + i\,D}A_{10}. \tag{12.36}$$

The wave function in a circuit with a gate is similarly given by Eq. 12.35. Their coefficients can also be calculated. But the current in these circuits equals zero, so the calculated coefficients are meaningless.

We apply the above result to a few special examples:

- Consider a turning structure as in Fig. 12.1a, where $n_1 = 1$, $n_2 = 0$, $\theta_{\rm i} = 0$, and $\theta_{\rm j} = \pi/2$. From Eq. 12.36 we obtain

$$a_{\rm j1} = \frac{1 - i}{2}A_{10} + \frac{1 + i}{2}A_{20},$$

$$a_{\rm j2} = \frac{1 + i}{2}A_{10} + \frac{1 - i}{2}A_{20}, \tag{12.37}$$

and

$$A_1 = A_2 = 0.$$

just as Eq. 12.20.

- Consider a spin-polarized interference device as in Fig. 12.1c, where $n_1 = 1$, $n_2 = 1$, $\theta_{\mathrm{i}} = 0$, $\theta_{\mathrm{j}} = \pi/2$, and $\theta_k = 0$. From Eq. 12.36 we obtain

$$\begin{aligned} a_{j1} &= \frac{1-i}{2+i\cot(k_0 L_k)} A_{10} + \frac{1+i}{2+i\cot(k_0 L_k)} A_{20}, \\ a_{j2} &= \frac{1+i}{2+i\cot(k_0 L_k)} A_{10} + \frac{1-i}{2+i\cot(k_0 L_k)} A_{20}, \\ A_1 &= \frac{-i\cot(k_0 L_k)}{2+i\cot(k_0 L_k)} A_{20}, \end{aligned}$$

and

$$A_2 = \frac{-i\cot(k_0 L_k)}{2+i\cot(k_0 L_k)} A_{10}, \tag{12.38}$$

just as Eqs. 12.24 and 12.25.

- Another spin-polarized interference device with the free circuit and the circuit with gate exchanged, where $n_1 = 1$, $n_2 = 1$, $\theta_{\mathrm{i}} = 0$, $\theta_{\mathrm{j}} = 0$, and $\theta_k = \pi/2$. From Eq. 12.36 we obtain

$$\begin{aligned} a_{j1} &= \frac{2}{2+i\cot(k_0 L_k)} A_{10}, \\ a_{j2} &= \frac{2}{2+i\cot(k_0 L_k)} A_{20}, \\ A_1 &= \frac{-i\cot(k_0 L_k)}{2+i\cot(k_0 L_k)} A_{20}, \\ A_2 &= \frac{-i\cot(k_0 L_k)}{2+i\cot(k_0 L_k)} A_{10}. \end{aligned} \tag{12.39}$$

It means that there is no interference effect between the electrons with spin-up and spin-down and the two kinds of electrons move independently. The device behaves like an ordinary quantum interference device.

For the case that there is one circuit with a ferromagnetic contact, $n_3 = 1$, the boundary conditions Eqs. 12.31 and 12.32 become

$$\Phi_{\mathrm{i}} + \Phi_{\mathrm{r}} = \Phi_m = a_{m1}\left[-\sin(k_0 L_m)\right]\phi_{m2} \tag{12.40}$$

and

$$\Phi_{\mathrm{i}} - \Phi_{\mathrm{r}} = (1 + n_1 + i D)\, a_{m1}\phi_{m1} + \{(n_1 + i D)\,[-\sin(k_0 L_m)] + [-i \cot(k_0 L_m)]\}\, a_{m2}\phi_{m2}. \tag{12.41}$$

From Eqs. 12.40 and 12.41 we can calculate analytically the coefficients a_{m1} and a_{m2} and other coefficients a_{j1}, a_{j2}, a_{k1}, and a_{k2}.

$$\begin{aligned}
a_{m1} &= \frac{2}{2 + n_1 + i D}\left(A_{10}\phi_{m1}^{+}\phi_{i1} + A_{20}\phi_{m1}^{+}\phi_{i2}\right),\\
a_{m2} &= \frac{-2\left(A_{10}\phi_{m2}^{+}\phi_{i1} + A_{20}\phi_{m2}^{+}\phi_{i2}\right)}{(1 + n_1)\sin(k_0 L_m) + i\,[D \sin(k_0 L_m) + \cos(k_0 L_m)]},\\
a_{j1} &= a_{m1}\phi_{j1}^{+}\phi_{m1} + a_{m2}\,[-\sin(k_0 L_m)]\,\phi_{j1}^{+}\phi_{m2},\\
a_{j2} &= a_{m1}\phi_{j2}^{+}\phi_{m1} + a_{m2}\,[-\sin(k_0 L_m)]\,\phi_{j2}^{+}\phi_{m2},\\
a_{k1} &= -\frac{1}{\sin(k_0 L_k)}\{a_{m1}\phi_{k1}^{+}\phi_{m1} + a_{m2}\,[-\sin(k_0 L_m)]\,\phi_{k1}^{+}\phi_{m2}\},\\
a_{k2} &= -\frac{1}{\sin(k_0 L_k)}\{a_{m1}\phi_{k2}^{+}\phi_{m1} + a_{m2}[-\sin(k_0 L_m)]\,\phi_{k2}^{+}\phi_{m2}\},\\
A_2 &= a_{m1}\phi_{i1}^{+}\phi_{m1} + a_{m2}\,[-\sin(k_0 L_m)]\,\phi_{i1}^{+}\phi_{m2} - A_{10},
\end{aligned}$$

and

$$A_1 = a_{m1}\phi_{i2}^{+}\phi_{m1} + a_{m2}\,[-\sin(k_0 L_m)]\,\phi_{i2}^{+}\phi_{m2} - A_{20}. \tag{12.42}$$

We apply this to some special examples.

- Consider a turning structure with an output circuit with a ferromagnetic contact, as shown in Fig. 12.1b, where $n_1 = n_2 = 0$, $n_3 = 1$, $\theta_{\mathrm{i}} = 0$, and $\theta_m = \pi/2$. From Eq. 12.42 we obtain

$$\begin{aligned}
a_{m1} &= \frac{1 - i}{2}A_{10} + \frac{1 + i}{2}A_{20},\\
a_{m2} &= 2i e^{i k_0 L_m}\left(\frac{1 + i}{2}A_{10} + \frac{1 - i}{2}A_{20}\right),\\
A_2 &= -\frac{e^{2i k_0 L_m}}{2}\,(A_{10} - i A_{20}),
\end{aligned}$$

and

$$A_1 = -\frac{e^{2i k_0 L_m}}{2}\,(i A_{10} + A_{20}), \tag{12.43}$$

just as Eq. 12.22.

- Consider a branch structure with two output circuits, one with a ferromagnetic contact and one free, where $n_1 = 1$, $n_2 = 0, n_3 = 1, \theta_i = 0, \theta_j = -\pi/2$, and $\theta_m = \pi/2$, as shown in Fig. 12.1d. From Eq. 12.42 we obtain

$$
\begin{aligned}
a_{m1} &= \frac{1-i}{3}A_{10} + \frac{1+i}{3}A_{20},\\
a_{m2} &= -\frac{2}{2\sin k_0 L_m + i\cos k_0 L_m}\left(\frac{1+i}{2}A_{10} + \frac{1-i}{2}A_{20}\right),\\
a_{j1} &= \frac{2}{2 + i\cot k_0 L_m}\left(\frac{1+i}{2}A_{10} + \frac{1-i}{2}A_{20}\right),\\
a_{j2} &= a_{m1},\\
A_2 &= \frac{1}{3}\left(-2A_{10} + iA_{20}\right) + \frac{1}{2 + i\cot k_0 L_m}\left(A_{10} - iA_{20}\right),
\end{aligned}
$$

and

$$
\begin{aligned}
A_1 = &-\frac{1}{3}\left(iA_{10} + 2A_{20}\right)\\
&+\frac{1}{2 + i\cot k_0 L_m}\left(iA_{10} + A_{20}\right). \qquad (12.44)
\end{aligned}
$$

Figure 12.6 shows the transmission probabilities T_{21}, T_{31}, T_{32}, R_1, and R_2 as functions of α for $L_2 = 50$ nm. From Fig. 12.6 we see that $T_{21} = T_{32}$ and both are not influenced by the contact in circuit 2. T_{32} oscillates with α due to the inference effect related to $\cos^2(k_\delta L_1)$, is modulated simultaneously by the interference effect related to $1/(4 + \cot^2 k_0 L_2)$, and reaches a minimum at $\alpha = 73$ meV nm. So we can modulate the electron current of one kind of spin by using a ferromagnetic contact.

12.5 Summary

We have discussed the properties of the Rashba wave function in the planar 1D waveguide and obtain the following results. Due to the Rashba effect, the plane waves of an electron with energy E divide into two kinds of waves with the wave vectors $k_1 = k_0 + k_\delta$ and $k_2 = k_0 - k_\delta$, where k_δ is proportional to the Rashba coefficient, and their spin orientations are $+\pi/2$ (spin-up) and $-\pi/2$ (spin-down) with respect to the circuit, respectively. Unlike the electron

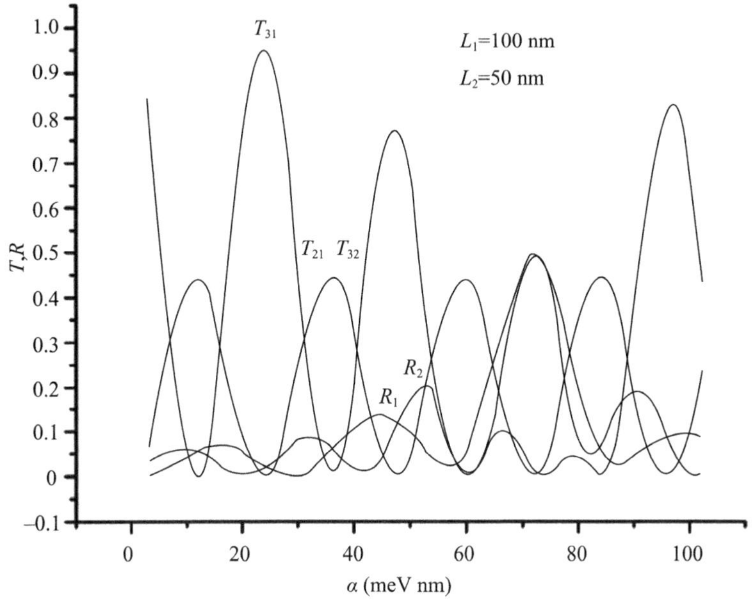

Figure 12.6 T_{21}, T_{31}, T_{32}, R_1, and R_2 of the spin-polarized interference device in Fig. 12.1d as functions of α for $L_2 = 50$ nm and other parameters the same as Fig. 12.2.

without considering the spin, the phase of the Rashba wave function depends on the direction angle θ of the circuit. The travel velocity of the Rashba waves with the wave vector k_1 or k_2 is the same, $\hbar k_0/m^*$. The boundary conditions of the Rashba wave functions at the intersection of circuits are given from the continuity of wave functions and the conservation of current density. We considered three cases: a free circuit, a circuit with a gate, and a circuit with a ferromagnetic contact. In the case of gate or ferromagnetic contact in the circuit, the Rashba wave function becomes a standing wave form $e^{\pm ik_\delta l} \sin[k_0 (l - L)]$, where L is the position coordinate of the gate or contact. Using the boundary conditions of Rashba wave functions we studied the transmission and reflection probabilities of a Rashba electron moving in several structures and found the interference effects of the two Rashba waves with different wave vectors and the Rashba waves with the gate and the ferromagnetic contact. Finally, we derived a general theory for a structure with multiple branches.

The theory of Rashba 1D waveguide, including the wave functions and the boundary conditions at the intersection, can be used to design various spin-polarized devices.

References

1. Liu, D. Y., Xia, J. B., and Chang, Y. C. (2010). *Sci. China: Phys. Mech. Astron.*, **53**, 1.
2. van Wees, B. J., van Houten, H., Beenakker, C. W. J., et al. (1998). *Phys. Rev. Lett.*, **60**, 848.
3. Wharam, D. A., Thornton, T. J., Newbury, R., et al. (1998). *J. Phys. C*, **21**, L209.
4. Fiederling, R., Keim, M., Reuscher, G., et al. (1999). *Nature*, **402**, 787.
5. Gruber, T., Keim, M., Fiederling, R., et al. (2001). *Appl. Phys. Lett.*, **78**, 1101.
6. Matsukura, F., Ohno, H., Shen, A., et al. (1998). *Phys. Rev. B*, **57**, R2037.
7. Datta, S., and Das, B. (1990). *Appl. Phys. Lett.*, **56**, 665.
8. Rashba, E. I. (1960). *Sov. Phys. Solid State*, **2**, 1109.
9. Dresselhaus, G. (1955). *Phys. Rev.*, **100**, 580.
10. Sheng, J. S., and Chang, K. (2006). *Phys. Rev. B*, **74**, 235315.
11. Xia, J. B. (1992). *Phys. Rev. B*, **45**, 3593.
12. Andrada, E. A., La Rocca, G. C., and Bassani, F. (1994). *Phys. Rev. B*, **50**, 8523.

Chapter 13

1D Quantum Waveguide Theory of Rashba Electrons in Curved Circuits

Since the Datta–Das spin field-effect transistor [1] was proposed, the Rashba spin-orbit interaction (RSOI) [2] has attracted considerable attention on account of its conceivable applications in spintronics. A great deal of spintronic devices based on RSOI have been proposed [3–6], most of which focus on ballistic straight waveguides [7–9] and rings or analogous structures [10–12]. They are expected to control spin-polarized transport on the basis of the interferences of different paths [13]. Conductance properties of rings or analogous structures with several diametrically connected leads have been discussed [5, 14]; some researchers consider similar structures as a spin filter [6, 12]. Földi et al. [10] accounted for the spin transformation properties of a quantum ring with RSOI and indicated that it can serve as a one-qubit quantum gate for electron spin, and Shelykh et al. [6] invested a gated ballistic AB ring with three asymmetrically situated electrodes and showed that it was able to demonstrate the properties of both the quantum splitter and spin filter. In recent years, there have also been experiments about the spin transport in these structures [15–17], where the AB effect plays an important role.

Quantum Waveguide in Microcircuits
Jian-Bai Xia, Duan-Yang Liu, and Wei-Dong Sheng

ISBN 978-981-4669-85-6 (Hardcover), 978-1-315-36477-3 (eBook)
www.panstanford.com

But the AB rings are not made of straight circuits such as structures discussed in Chapter 12, so transports in these rings cannot be studied using the theory in the previous chapter. Therefore we divide the curved part into N segments, where N is a big number so that every segment can be regarded as a small straight line. Then we investigate the electron's movement in every straight segment and every vertex. When every straight segment tends to be infinitely small, the wave function of the Rashba electron passing through a curve can be obtained.

13.1 Transfer Matrix of a Rashba Electron in a 1D Two-Terminal Structure [18]

Firstly, we apply boundary conditions in Chapter 12 to a turning structure. An incident electron with energy E enters circuit 1 at angle θ, passes through a corner, and then enters circuit 2 at angle ϕ. The wave functions in the circuits can be written as

$$\Phi_1 = a_{10}\phi_1(\theta)\, e^{ik_1 l_1} + a_{20}\phi_2(\theta)\, e^{ik_2 l_1} + a_1\phi_1(\theta+\pi)\, e^{-ik_1 l_1} + a_2\phi_2(\theta+\pi)\, e^{-ik_2 l_1}$$

and

$$\Phi_2 = c_1\phi_1(\varphi)\, e^{ik_1 l_2} + c_2\phi_2(\varphi)\, e^{ik_2 l_2}, \tag{13.1}$$

where a_{10} and a_{20} are amplitudes of the inject waves, a_1 and a_2 are those of the reflecting waves, and c_1 and c_2 are those of the output waves. l_1 and l_2 are the coordinates of circuits 1 and 2, respectively. ϕ_1 and ϕ_2 are the phase factors of spin-up and spin-down electrons, given in Eq. 12.6, k_1 and k_2 are the wave vectors, given in Eq. 12.8, respectively. Applying Eq. 13.11 and Eq. 13.13, we can find that there is no reflected wave function in circuit 1, at the intersection $a_1 = 0$, $a_2 = 0$.

In a circuit with angle θ, we can write the wave function as

$$\Phi = \{[\phi_1(\theta), \phi_2(\theta)]\}\, \Psi = [\phi_1(\theta), \phi_2(\theta)] \begin{pmatrix} a_1 \\ a_2 \end{pmatrix}. \tag{13.2}$$

In the following part of the chapter, we will adopt Ψ to describe the wave function in most time. If we take the origins of the coordinates

l_1 and l_2 all at the intersection, then Eq. 13.1 can be written as

$$[\phi_1(\varphi)\ \phi_2(\varphi)]\begin{pmatrix} c_1 \\ c_2 \end{pmatrix} = [\phi_1(\theta)\ \phi_2(\theta)]\begin{pmatrix} a_{10} \\ a_{20} \end{pmatrix}. \quad (13.3)$$

We can use a simple transfer matrix

$$\mathbf{M}_{\theta\to\varphi} = \begin{pmatrix} \phi_1^+(\varphi) \\ \phi_2^+(\varphi) \end{pmatrix}[\phi_1(\theta)\ \phi_2(\theta)] = \frac{1}{2}\begin{pmatrix} 1+e^{-i(\varphi-\theta)} & 1-e^{-i(\varphi-\theta)} \\ 1-e^{-i(\varphi-\theta)} & 1+e^{-i(\varphi-\theta)} \end{pmatrix} \quad (13.4)$$

to describe the transform of the wave function Ψ at the intersection of the turning structure. Accordingly the transfer matrix of one circuit with length L can be written as

$$\mathbf{M}_{\mathrm{L}} = \begin{pmatrix} e^{ik_1L} & 0 \\ 0 & e^{ik_2L} \end{pmatrix}. \quad (13.5)$$

In the following, we will calculate the spin transport on the basis of Eq. 13.4 and Eq. 13.5 when there is no branch. If at the intersection there are branches, we can calculate that by utilizing the boundary conditions Eq. 12.11 and Eq. 12.13.

All the results above are in the condition of no magnetic field. Now we consider the two-dimensional (2D) system in the external magnetic field perpendicular to the circuit plane. In this case, for a close ring the wave vector k in Hamiltonian will be replaced by

$$k_{\mathrm{eff}} = k \pm eA/\hbar, \quad (13.6)$$

where the $\pm$ sign depends on the relative orientations of the magnetic field and the k, $|A| = \Phi_m/L$ is the vector potential, and Φ_m and L are the magnetic flux through the closed loop and its perimeter, respectively. So if we substitute k_{eff} for k, the k_1 and k_2 in Eq. 13.1 and Eq. 13.5 will be changed to

$$k_1 = k_0 + k_\delta - k_A, \quad k_1 = k_0 - k_\delta - k_A,$$
$$k_0 = \frac{m^*}{\hbar^2}\sqrt{\alpha^2 + \frac{2\hbar^2}{m^*}E},\ k_\delta = \frac{m^*}{\hbar^2}\alpha, \quad \text{and} \quad k_A = \pm\frac{eA}{\hbar}. \quad (13.7)$$

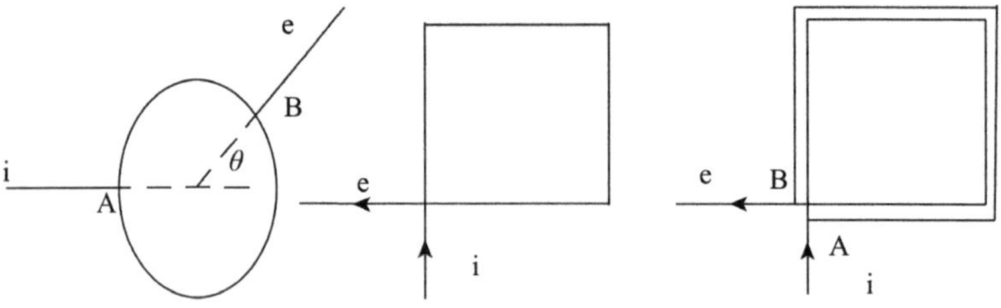

Figure 13.1 Several structures: (a) an AB ring, (b) an AB SL, and (c) a AB double SL.

13.2 Electron Structure of a Closed Circle [1]

The structures studied in this section are shown in Fig. 13.1. Figure 13.1a is an Aharonov–Bohm (AB) ring, and the angle between the inject circuit i and the output circuit e is θ. Figure 13.1b is an AB square loop structure, and Fig. 13.1c is an AB double square loop. First we calculate the electron structure of a closed circular ring (as Fig. 13.1a without inject and output circuits) by the transfer matrix method. According to Eq. 13.4 and Eq. 13.5, we can get the transfer matrix of arbitrary structure with no branches. For a closed circle, we divide the circle into N segments, each segment can be seen as a straight line segment, and we calculate the transfer matrices in every segments and every intersections. When the N is large enough, the product of all matrices according to the order of transport is the total transfer matrix M.

It can be inferred from Eq. 13.4 and Eq. 13.5 that the total transfer matrix $\mathbf{M}$ is just concerned with the electron energy E, the Rashba coefficient α, the external magnetic B, and the radius of the circle R. Now we fix up the last three coefficients, so the $\mathbf{M}$ can be written as $\mathbf{M}(E)$. It is noticed that the eigenstates of the circle exist just when $\mathbf{M}(E)$ has an eigen value of 1, that is, when

$$\det\left[\mathbf{M}\left(E\right) - I\right] = 0 \tag{13.8}$$

and the corresponding eigen vector describes the eigenstate in the form of Ψ.

Next we will give the analytical solution of this problem. We consider one segment and the intersection at its heel. If the N is large enough, the length of the segment can be written as $R\delta\theta$, and

$\delta\theta = (\phi - \theta)$ is the turning angle at the intersection in Eq. 13.4. If the wave vector is in the counter-clockwise (CCW) direction, $\delta\theta > 0$, and for the wave vector in the clockwise (CW) direction, $\delta\theta < 0$. $\delta\theta$ is an infinitesimal quantity, and $N\delta\theta = 2\pi$. For one segment, the transfer matrix is

$$\mathbf{M}_{\delta\theta} = \frac{1}{2}\begin{pmatrix} 1 + e^{-i\delta\theta} & 1 - e^{-i\delta\theta} \\ 1 - e^{-i\delta\theta} & 1 + e^{-i\delta\theta} \end{pmatrix}\begin{pmatrix} e^{ik_1 R\delta\theta} & 0 \\ 0 & e^{ik_1 R\delta\theta} \end{pmatrix}. \tag{13.9}$$

Because $\mathbf{M}_{\delta\theta}$ is very close to I, so we assume that its eigen value is $e^{im\delta\theta}$, where m is an integral. Ignoring twice and more power terms of $\delta\theta$ and solving the secular equation

$$\det\left(\mathbf{M}_{\delta\theta} - e^{im\delta\theta}\right) = 0, \tag{13.10}$$

we obtain the eigenenergy for $B = 0$,

$$\varepsilon = \left(m + \frac{1}{2}\right)^2 + \frac{1}{4} \pm \left(m + \frac{1}{2}\right)\sqrt{1 + \bar{\alpha}^2}, \tag{13.11}$$

where m is the quantum number of the quantum energy level. In this paper, we use the dimensionless physical quantities. If the energy unit $E_0 = \hbar^2/(2m^* R^2)$, then the energy $\varepsilon = E/E_0$, the magnetic field $b = (\hbar e B/m^* c)/E_0$, and the Rashba coefficient $\bar{\alpha} = (\alpha/R)/E_0 = \alpha(2m^* R/\hbar^2)$.

We can also get the eigen vectors of the transfer matrix $\mathbf{M}_{\delta\theta}$,

$$\mathbf{M}_{\delta\theta}\begin{pmatrix} \cos\varphi' \\ \sin\varphi' \end{pmatrix} = e^{im\delta\theta}\begin{pmatrix} \cos\varphi' \\ \sin\varphi' \end{pmatrix}, \tag{13.12}$$

where

$$\tan\varphi' = \bar{\alpha} \pm \sqrt{1 + \bar{\alpha}^2}.$$

Because the total transfer matrix $\mathbf{M} = (\mathbf{M}_{\delta\theta})^N$, these vectors are also the eigen vectors of $\mathbf{M}$, and the eigen value becomes $e^{im2\pi}$. It is obvious that when m is an integer, these states describe eigen Rashba states of the circle. In the presence of a magnetic field, the corresponding eigenenergy is

$$\varepsilon = \left(m + \frac{b}{4} + \frac{1}{2}\right)^2 + \frac{1}{4} \pm \left(m + \frac{b}{4} + \frac{1}{2}\right)\sqrt{1 + \bar{\alpha}^2}. \tag{13.13}$$

According to Eq. 13.2 and Eq. 13.12, the eigen Rashba states in the circle with a suffix m are

$$\Psi_{\mathrm{m}}(\theta) = [\phi_1(\theta)\ \phi_2(\theta)]\begin{pmatrix} \cos\varphi' \\ \sin\varphi' \end{pmatrix} = \frac{1}{\sqrt{2\pi}} e^{im\theta}\begin{pmatrix} \cos\varphi \\ \sin\varphi e^{i\theta} \end{pmatrix}, \tag{13.14}$$

where $\tan\varphi = (1+\sqrt{1+\bar{\alpha}^2})/\bar{\alpha}$ is for the + sign in Eq. 13.13 and $\tan\varphi = (1-\sqrt{1+\bar{\alpha}^2})/\bar{\alpha}$ is for the – sign, which are defined as spin-up and spin-down states, respectively. The spin orientation of each state can be described as a function of θ,

$$S(\theta) = \sin(2\varphi)\cos\theta\hat{e}_x + \sin(2\varphi)\sin\theta\hat{e}_y + \cos(2\varphi)\hat{e}_z. \quad (13.15)$$

We find that the spin-up and spin-down states have the opposite local spin orientation, and everywhere their components in the x–y plane point to the center along the radius, or in the opposite direction, respectively. These results are identical to those obtained from solving the Schrödinger equation with the Hamiltonian in the polar coordinates [19, 20]

$$H_{\mathrm{po}} = \begin{pmatrix} \left(-i\frac{\partial}{\partial\theta}+\frac{b}{4}\right)^2 & \frac{1}{2}\left[\alpha e^{-i\theta}\left(-i\frac{\partial}{\partial\theta}+\frac{b}{4}\right)+\alpha\left(-i\frac{\partial}{\partial\theta}+\frac{b}{4}\right)e^{-i\theta}\right] \\ \frac{1}{2}\left[\alpha e^{i\theta}\left(-i\frac{\partial}{\partial\theta}+\frac{b}{4}\right)+\alpha\left(-i\frac{\partial}{\partial\theta}+\frac{b}{4}\right)e^{i\theta}\right] & \left(-i\frac{\partial}{\partial\theta}+\frac{b}{4}\right)^2 \end{pmatrix} \quad (13.16)$$

Notice that the nondiagonal elements are written to ensure the Hermitian of the Hamiltonian. On the basis of Eq. 13.16, we can also obtain Eq. 13.13 to Eq. 13.15.

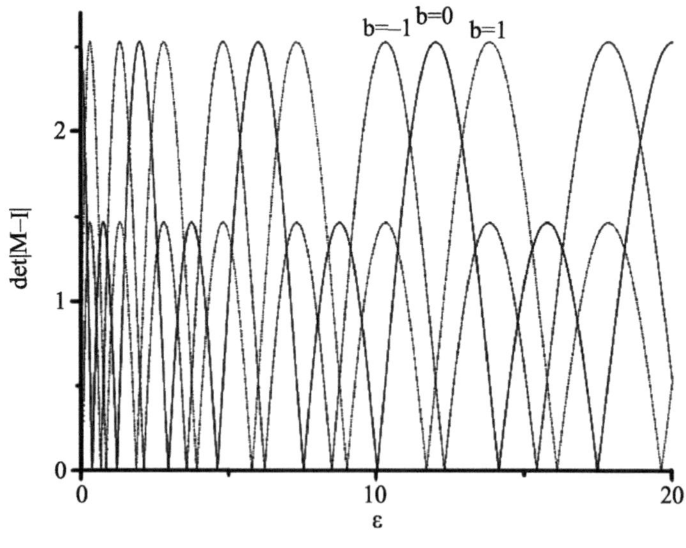

Figure 13.2 $|\det[\mathbf{M}(E)-I]|$ of the closed circular ring as functions of the electron energy ε for $\bar{\alpha}=1$ and $b = 0$, 1, and −1.

We calculate the eigenenergies numerically. Figure 13.2 shows the numerical results of the transfer matrix method, the $|\det(\mathbf{M}(E)-I)|$ as functions of ε for $\alpha = 1$ and $b = 0, 1$, and -1. From the figure we see that the zero points correspond to the energies of eigenstates, for example, in the case of $b = 0$, $\varepsilon = 0.38, 1.2, 3.0, 4.6, 7.6, 10.0, 14.1, 17.4$, etc., which are in agreement with the results of Eq. 13.13. In the calculation, we take $N = 1000$.

13.3 Electron Structure of a Closed Square Loop [18]

Although the spin states and electron structure in a close circle have been investigated in some literature [19, 20] by other methods, our method can be utilized to calculate more anomalistic geometry, such as a closed square loop (as in Fig. 13.1b without inject and output circuits). Assume that the side length of the square loop is L. We can get the transfer matrix for a CCW circuit as

$$\mathbf{M}_{\mathrm{SL}} = -\frac{1}{4}\begin{pmatrix} A^4 - 3A^3B - A^2B^2 - AB^3 & i\left(B^4 - B^3A - B^2A^2 + BA^3\right) \\ i\left(A^4 - 3A^3B - A^2B^2 + AB^3\right) & B^4 - B^3A - B^2A^2 - BA^3 \end{pmatrix}, \tag{13.17}$$

where $A = e^{ik_1^L}$, $B = e^{ik_2L}$, k_1, and k_2 are defined in Eq. 13.8. The matrix in CW is also easy to obtain. Similarly, we use the dimensionless physical quantities, taking the energy unit $E_0 = \hbar^2(2m^*L^2)$. Then the energy $\varepsilon = E/E_0$, the magnetic field $b = (\hbar eB/m^*c)/E_0 = 2eBL^2/\hbar c$, and the Rashba coefficient $\alpha = (\alpha/L)/E_0 = \alpha(2m^*L/\hbar^2)$. We can also get the eigenenergies and vectors on the basis of Eq. 13.8. From Eq. 13.8 and Eq. 13.17 we obtain the secular equation,

$$\begin{pmatrix} C - y & iD \\ iD^* & C^* - y \end{pmatrix} = 0, \tag{13.18}$$

where

$$C = -e^{2i\tilde{\alpha}} + 3e^{i\tilde{\alpha}} + 1 + e^{-i\tilde{\alpha}},$$
$$D = -e^{i\tilde{\alpha}} + 1 + e^{-i\tilde{\alpha}} - e^{-2i\tilde{\alpha}},$$
$$y = 4e^{-4ix},$$

and

$$x = k_0 L - k_A L = \sqrt{\left(\frac{\bar{\alpha}}{2}\right)^2 + \varepsilon} - \frac{b}{8}. \tag{13.19}$$

From Eq. 13.18 we obtain the eigenenergies of a closed square loop,

$$\varepsilon = \left(\pm\frac{\varphi}{4} + \frac{\pi}{2}m + \frac{b}{8}\right)^2 - \left(\frac{\bar{\alpha}}{2}\right)^2$$

and

$$\varphi = \arccos\left(\frac{1 + 4\cos\bar{\alpha} - \cos 2\bar{\alpha}}{4}\right), \tag{13.20}$$

where m is an integer and $\pm(\phi/4) + (\pi/2)m + (b/8) > 0$. As we know, this is the first result of eigenenergies of Rashba states in a square loop obtained by the transfer matrix method, which cannot be obtained by solving the Schrödinger equation. With the transfer matrix method we can calculate the eigenstates of a closed loop of any shape, for example, triangle, pentagon, hexagon, rectangle, and ellipse.

About the eigenstates, in the straight-line section, the states are just denoted by Eq. 13.4 and Eq. 13.6; the spin orientation of the Rashba states with the wave vectors k_1 and k_2 are all perpendicular to the circuit; the angles between the spin and the circuit are $+\pi/2$ and $-\pi/2$; respectively; and the coefficients of the spin-up and spin-down states, which describe eigenstates in the form of Ψ in Eq. 13.2, can be determined by $M_{\mathrm{SL}}\Psi = \Psi$.

13.4 Spin Interference in an AB Ring [18]

Now we consider an interference structure, the AB ring as in Fig. 13.1a. We use the transfer matrices Eq. 13.4 and Eq. 13.5 to describe the spin transport in a circular circuit, and the boundary conditions Eq. 13.11 and Eq. 13.13 to describe the transport through the intersection. We obtained the reflection and transmission coefficients in AB rings as functions of the electron energy ε, the Rashba coefficient α, and the external magnetic field B.

We assume that an electron with energy ε enters circuit i of the AB ring from left to intersection A, then two transmitted waves depart from intersection A, meet at intersection B, and depart from circuit e. At the same time, two reflected waves depart from circuit i. Write the wave functions in the four circuits of the AB ring and the boundary conditions at the intersections A and B. In the two arms of the AB ring, the wave functions at point B are related with those at point A by the transfer matrices. There will be 20 coefficients for all wave functions in all circuits. We have 12 equations from the boundary conditions at two intersections and 8 equations from the transfer matrices in two arms of the geometries. So we can solve this problem and get coefficients of reflection and transmission waves uniquely.

The transmission and reflection coefficients are $T_1 = |t_{\text{up}}|^2$, $T_2 = |t_{\text{down}}|^2$, and $R_1 = |r_{\text{up}}|^2$, $R_2 = |r_{\text{down}}|^2$. Figure 13.3 shows T_1, T_2, R_1, and R_2 as functions of the electron energy ε for the magnetic field $b = 0$, $\theta = 0$, $\bar{\alpha} = 1$, and coefficients of injected waves are $a_{10} = 1$ and $a_{20} = 0$. In this case, $R_1 = 0$ and $T_2 = 0$. From Fig. 13.3 we see that the zero points of the R_2 curve are $\varepsilon = 0.3$, 1.3, 2.8, 4.8, 7.3, 10.3, 13.8, 17.8, etc., which just correspond to the eigenenergies of eigenstates in the closed AB ring, calculated from Eq. 13.13. It

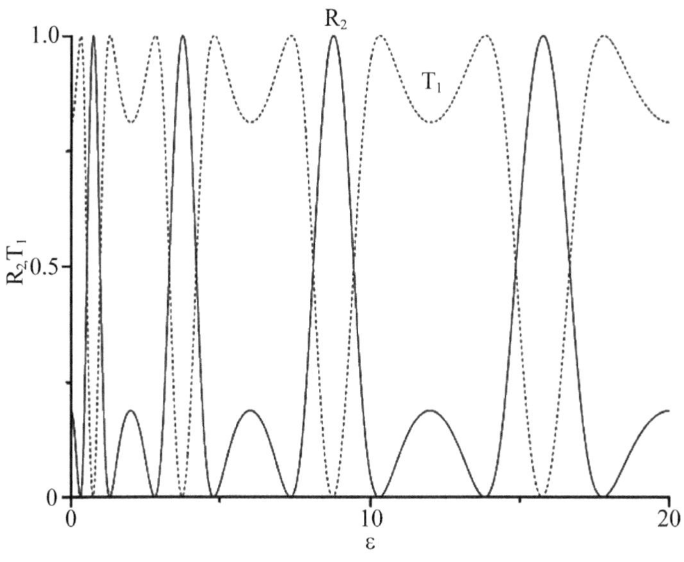

Figure 13.3 T_1 and R_2 of the AB ring in Fig. 13.1a as functions of ε for $\theta = 0$, $\bar{\alpha} = 1$, $b = 0$, $a_{10} = 1$, and $a_{20} = 0$.

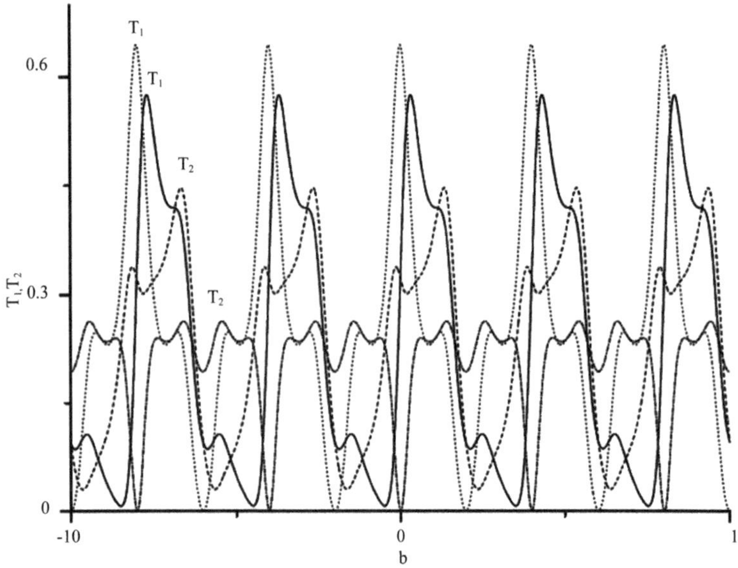

Figure 13.4 T_1 and T_2 of the AB ring in Fig. 13.1a as functions of **b** for $\theta = 0$, $\bar{\alpha} = 1$, $\varepsilon = 0.5$, and $a_{10} = 1$, $a_{20} = 0$ (T1,T2) and $a_{10} = 0.707$, $a_{20} = 0.707i$(T1',T2').

means that when the energy of the injected electron equals the energy of the eigenstate in the closed ring, there will be no reflection completely and there will be resonance.

Figure 13.4 shows the T_1 and T_2 as functions of the magnetic field b for the fixed electron energy $\varepsilon = 0.5$, $\theta = 0$, $\bar{\alpha} = 1$, and the coefficients of injected waves $a_{10} = 1$, $a_{20} = 0$, and $a_{10} = 0.7071$, $a_{20} = 0.7071i$. From Fig. 13.4 we see that for both cases, T_1 and T_2 curves all oscillate with the magnetic field b and the oscillating period is $b = 4$, though their zero points are different. From the definition of $b = 2eBR^2/c\hbar$, we obtain the period of the magnetic flux is $\Phi_m = hc/e$, independent of the magnitude of the ring. This is the first proof of the AB effect of the Rashba spin current.

13.5 Spin Interference in an AB Square Loop [18]

For comparing our results with the experiment in Ref. [15] and analytical account in Ref. [21] of Koga, we consider the spin interference in a square loop as shown in Fig. 13.1b, similar to the geometry of sample 2 in Koga's paper. We illustrate our method in detail. Using Eqs. 13.4 and 13.6, the wave functions in the input circuit i and the output circuit e can be written as

$$\Psi_{\mathrm{i}} = a_{10}\begin{pmatrix} 1 \\ -1 \end{pmatrix} e^{ik_1 l_1} + a_{20}\begin{pmatrix} 1 \\ 1 \end{pmatrix} e^{ik_2 l_1} + a_1\begin{pmatrix} 1 \\ 1 \end{pmatrix} e^{-ik_1 l_1} + a_2\begin{pmatrix} 1 \\ -1 \end{pmatrix} e^{-ik_2 l_1}$$

and

$$\Psi_{\mathrm{e}} = d_1\begin{pmatrix} 1 \\ -i \end{pmatrix} e^{ik_1 l_2} + d_2\begin{pmatrix} 1 \\ i \end{pmatrix} e^{ik_2 l_2}. \tag{13.21}$$

The wave functions in the closed square loop at points A and B can be written as

$$\Psi_{\mathrm{c}}(A) = b_1\begin{pmatrix} 1 \\ i \end{pmatrix} e^{ik_1 l_2} + b_2\begin{pmatrix} 1 \\ -i \end{pmatrix} e^{ik_2 l_2} + b_3\begin{pmatrix} 1 \\ -i \end{pmatrix} e^{-ik_1 l_2} + b_4\begin{pmatrix} 1 \\ i \end{pmatrix} e^{-ik_2 l_2}$$

and

$$\Psi_{\mathrm{c}}(B) = c_1\begin{pmatrix} 1 \\ 1 \end{pmatrix} e^{ik_1 l_2'} + c_2\begin{pmatrix} 1 \\ -1 \end{pmatrix} e^{ik_2 l_2'} + c_3\begin{pmatrix} 1 \\ -1 \end{pmatrix} e^{-ik_1 l_2'} + c_4\begin{pmatrix} 1 \\ 1 \end{pmatrix} e^{-ik_2 l_2'}, \tag{13.22}$$

where the origins of the coordinates l_2 and l_2' are at points A and B, respectively.

Using the boundary conditions Eqs. 13.11 and 13.13 we obtain the following group of equations:

$$a_{10} + a_{20} + a_1 + a_2 = b_1 + b_2 + b_3 + b_4,$$
$$-a_{10} + a_{20} + a_1 - a_2 = i\left(b_1 - b_2 - b_3 + b_4\right),$$
$$b_1 + b_2 + b_3 + b_4 = d_1 + d_2,$$
$$b_1 - b_2 - b_3 + b_4 = -d_1 + d_2,$$
$$c_1 + c_2 + c_3 + c_4 = d_1 + d_2,$$
$$c_1 - c_2 - c_3 + c_4 = i\left(-d_1 + d_2\right),$$
$$a_{10} + a_{20} - a_1 - a_2 + c_1 + c_2 - c_3 - c_4 = b_1 + b_2 - b_3 - b_4 + d_1 + d_2,$$

and

$$-a_{10} + a_{20} - a_1 + a_2 + c_1 - c_2 + c_3 - c_4 = i\left(b_1 - b_2 + b_3 - b_4 - d_1 + d_2\right). \quad (13.23)$$

The coefficients c_1, c_2, c_3, and c_4 are related to the coefficients b_1, b_2, b_3, and b_4 by the transfer matrices,

$$\begin{pmatrix} c_1 \\ c_2 \end{pmatrix} = \mathbf{M}_1 \begin{pmatrix} b_1 \\ b_2 \end{pmatrix}, \quad \begin{pmatrix} c_3 \\ c_4 \end{pmatrix} = \mathbf{M}_2 \begin{pmatrix} b_3 \\ b_4 \end{pmatrix}. \quad (13.24)$$

The transfer matrices $\mathbf{M}_1$ and $\mathbf{M}_2$ are calculated in a way similar to Eq. 13.17.

$$\mathbf{M}_1 = \frac{1}{4}\begin{pmatrix} (1+i)\left(-A^4 + 2A^3B + A^2B^2\right) & (1-i)\left(A^3B + AB^3\right) \\ (1-i)\left(A^3B + AB^3\right) & (1+i)\left(A^2B^2 + 2AB^3 - B^4\right) \end{pmatrix}$$

and

$$\mathbf{M}_2 = \frac{1}{4}\begin{pmatrix} (1+i)\left(-A^{*4} + 2A^{*3}B^* + A^{*2}B^{*2}\right) & (1-i)\left(A^{*3}B^* + A^*B^{*3}\right) \\ (1-i)\left(A^{*3}B^* + A^*B^{*3}\right) & (1+i)\left(A^{*2}B^{*2} + 2A^*B^{*3} - B^{*4}\right) \end{pmatrix}, \quad (13.25)$$

where $A = e^{ik_1^L}$ and $B = e^{ik_2L}$.

Equations 13.23 to 13.25 are for the case of no magnetic field. In the case of a magnetic field perpendicular to the loop plane, the k_1 and k_2 in Ψ_i and Ψ_e in Eq. 13.21 are $k_0 \pm k_\delta$, while those in Ψ_c in Eq. 13.22 are $k_0 \pm k_\delta + k_A$ and $k_A = \pm\, eA/\hbar = \pm\, e\Phi_m/\hbar L$, where the $\pm$ sign of k_A depends on the direction of the wave, CW or CCW (see Eq. 13.6).

Solving Eqs. 13.23 and 13.24 we obtain the T_1, T_2, R_1, and R_2 of the square loop as functions of electron energy ε for $b = 0$, $\bar{\alpha} = 1$, $a_{10} = 1$, and $a_{20} = 0$, as shown in Fig. 13.5. From Fig. 13.5 we see that $R_1 = 0$, $T_1 = T_2$, and the zero points of R_2 are $\varepsilon = 1.9$, 2.6, 8.9, and 10.4, which are just the energies of eigenstates in the closed square loop given by Eq. 13.20. Figure 13.6 shows the T_1, T_2, R_1, and R_2 of the square loop as functions of the magnetic field b for $\varepsilon = 0.5$, $\bar{\alpha} = 1$, $a_{10} = 1$, and $a_{20} = 0$. From Fig. 13.6 we see that the T_1, T_2, and R_2 all oscillate with the magnetic field and the oscillating period is $b = 12.5$. According to the definition of the b in the square loop $b = 2eBL^2/\hbar c$, the oscillating period corresponds to $\Phi_m = hc/e$, the same as the AB ring.

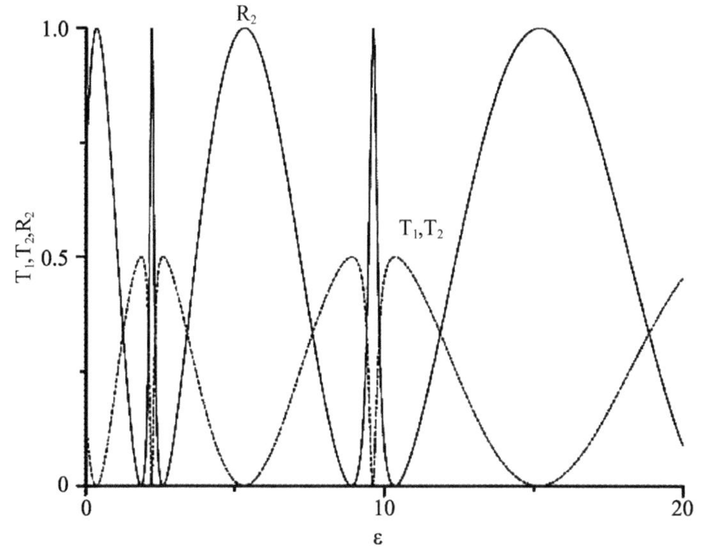

Figure 13.5 T_1, T_2, and R_2 of the AB SL in Fig. 13.1b as functions of ε for $b = 0, \bar{\alpha} = 1, a_{10} = 1$, and $a_{20} = 0$.

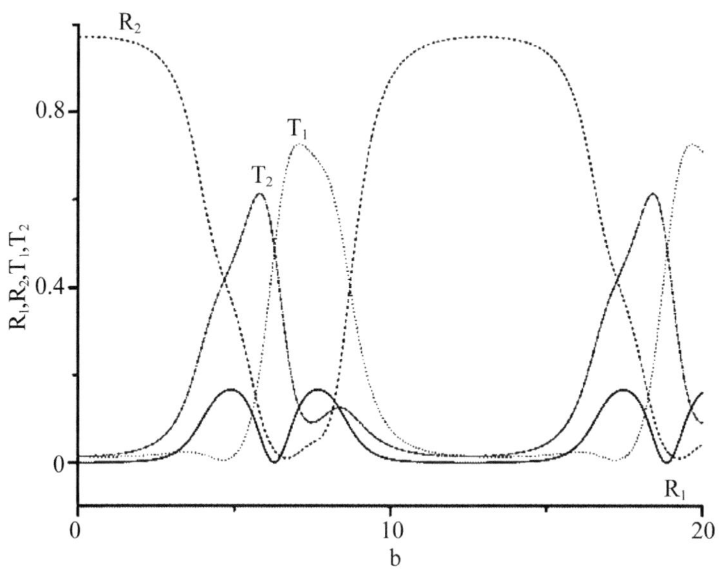

Figure 13.6 T_1, T_2, R_1, and R_2 of the AB SL in Fig. 13.1b as functions of b for $\varepsilon = 0.5, \bar{\alpha} = 1, a_{10} = 1$, and $a_{20} = 0$.

13.6 Spin Interference in an AB Double Square Loop [18]

In the experiment in Ref. [15] Koga et al. found that the period of the AB oscillation is $\Phi_m = hc/2e$, half of the theoretical prediction. We think that their circuit is actually an AB double square loop, as shown in Fig. 13.1c, and the Rashba electron travels twice in the loop. Similarly we write the wave functions in each circuit, and use the boundary conditions and the transfer matrices, and obtain the set of equations of wave function coefficients.

Solving the set of equations we obtain the T_1, T_2, R_1, and R_2 of the double square loop as functions of the electron energy ε for $b = 0$, $\bar{\alpha} = 1$, $a_{10} = 1$, and $a_{20} = 0$, as shown in Fig. 13.7. From Fig. 13.7 we see that $R_1 = 0$, $T_1 = T_2$, and the zero points of R_2 are $\varepsilon = 0.6$, 1.9, 2.6, 4.7, 6.0, 8.9, 10.4, 14.1, and 16.3, which are the energies of eigenstates in the closed double square loop. In there $\varepsilon = 1.9$, 2.6, 8.9, and 10.4 are the energies of eigenstates in the closed single square loop. So if the closed loop has n circles, there are n times of

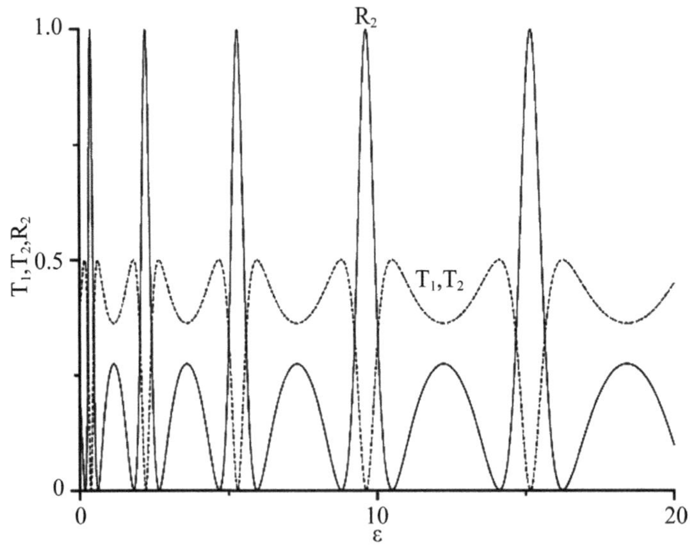

Figure 13.7 T_1, T_2, and R_2 of the AB double SL in Fig. 13.1c as functions of ε for $b = 0$, $\bar{\alpha} = 1$, $a_{10} = 1$, and $a_{20} = 0$.

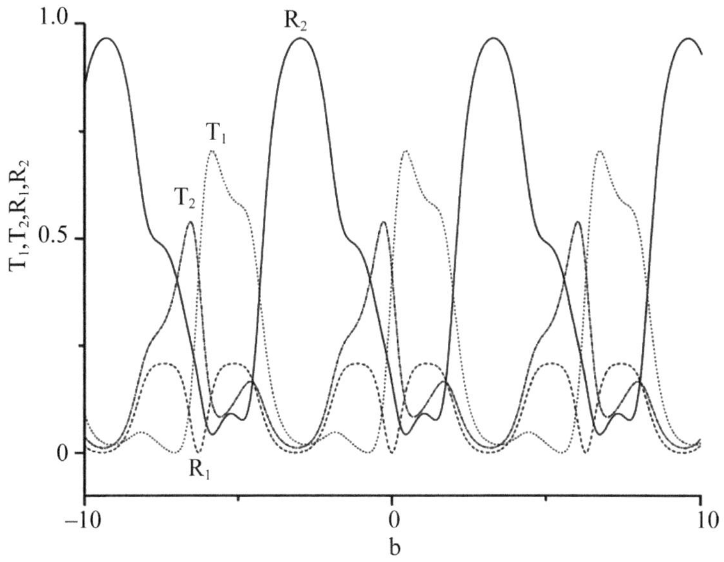

Figure 13.8 T_1, T_2, R_1, and R_2 of the AB double SL in Fig. 13.1c as functions of b for $\varepsilon = 0.5$, $\bar{\alpha} = 1$, $a_{10} = 1$, and $a_{20} = 0$.

eigenstates in the loop. Figure 13.8 shows the T_1, T_2, R_1, and R_2 of the double square loop as functions of the magnetic field b for $\varepsilon = 0.5$, $\bar{\alpha} = 1$, $a_{10} = 1$, and $a_{20} = 0$. From Fig. 13.8 we see that the T_1, T_2, and R_2 all oscillate with the magnetic field and the oscillating period is $b = 6.28$. According to the definition of the b in the square loop, the oscillating period corresponds to $\Phi_m = 3.14\hbar c/e = hc/2e$. It is half of that of the single square loop, in agreement with the experimental results [15].

Finally, we consider that electrons in Koga's experiment [15] are not spin-polarized, so we average our results for all spin orientation and get the total transmission coefficient T. Figure 13.9 shows T as a function of α (θ in Koga's papers) for $b = 0$ and $\varepsilon = 0.5$ and 50, corresponding to $E = 0.01$ meV and 1.0 meV for $L = 1200$ nm and $m^* = 0.047\ m_e$, as in Ref. 15. We note that the period is small, just about 1/4 of that in Koga's papers, and the curve is not very regular. So we consider that though Koga et al. got the biggest change of σ, they didn't control $\Delta\theta$ from 0 to 0.75 π. Maybe the variety range of α is just about 1/4 of what they expected.

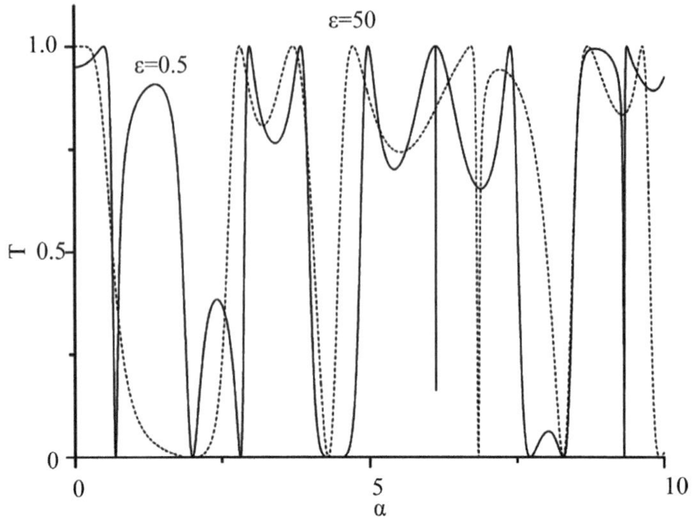

Figure 13.9 T as functions of α (θ in Koga's papers) for $b = 0$ and $\varepsilon = 0.5$ and 50.

13.7 Summary

We studied the spin waveguide transport of electrons with Rashba spin-orbit interaction (RSOI) in the curved circuits. The eigenstates of the circular and square loops were studied by using the transfer matrix method. the transfer matrix $\mathbf{M}(E)$ of a circular arc is obtained by dividing the circular arc into N segments and multiplying the transfer matrix of each straight segment. The energies of eigenstates in a closed loop are obtained by solving the equation $\det[\mathbf{M}(E) - I] = 0$. For the circular ring, the eigenenergies obtained with this method are in agreement with those obtained by solving the Schrödinger equation. For the SL, the analytic formula of the eigenenergies is obtained first. The transport properties of the AB ring, AB SL, and double SL are studied using the boundary conditions and the transfer matrix method. In the case of no magnetic field, the zero points of the reflection coefficients are just the energies of eigenstates in closed loops. In the case of a magnetic field, the transmission and reflection coefficients all oscillate with the magnetic field. The oscillating period is $\Phi_m = hc/e$, independent of the shape of the loop, where Φ_m is the magnetic flux through the loop. Finally, we compared our results with Koga's experiment.

References

1. Datta, S., and Das, B. (1990). *Appl. Phys. Lett.*, **56**, 665.
2. Rashba, E. I. (1960). *Sov. Phys. Solid State*, **2**, 1109.
3. Belluci, S., Carillo, E., and Onorato, P. (2008). *Eur. Phys. J. B*, **66**, 509.
4. Zhang, R. L., Zhang, Z. I., Peng, R. W., et al. (2008). *Appl. Phys.*, **103**, 07B727.
5. Souma, S., and Nikolić, B. K. (2005). *Phys. Rev. Lett.*, **94**, 106602.
6. Shelykh, L. A., Galkin, N. G., and Bagraev, N. T. (2005). *Phys. Rev. B*, **72**, 235316.
7. Yao, J., and Yang, Z. Q. (2006). *Phys. Rev. B*, **73**, 033314.
8. Wang, X. F., Vasilopoulos, P., and Peters, F. M. (2002). *Appl. Phys. Lett.*, **80**, 1400.
9. Wang, L. G., Chang, K., and Chan, K. S. (2006). *J. Appl. Phys.*, **99**, 043701.
10. Földi, P., Molnár, B., Benedict, M. G., and Peters, F. M. (2005). *Phys. Rev. B*, **71**, 033309.
11. Belluci, S., and Onorato, P. (2008). *Phys. Rev. B*, **78**, 235312.
12. Kálmán, O., Földi, P., Benedict, M. G., and Peters, F. M. (2008). *Physica E*, **40**, 567.
13. Aronov, A. G., and Lyanda-Geller, Y. B. (1993). *Phys. Rev. Lett.*, **70**, 343.
14. Nitta, J., Meijer, F. E., and Takayanagi, H. (1999). *Appl. Phys. Lett.*, **75**, 695.
15. Koga, T., Sekine, Y., and Nitta, J. (2006). *Phys. Rev. B*, **74**, 041302(R).
16. Bergsten, T., Kobayashi, T., Sekine, Y., and Nitta, J. (2006). *Phys. Rev. Lett.*, **97**, 196803.
17. Konig, M., Tschetschetkin, A., Hankiewiez, E. M., et al. (2006). *Phys. Rev. Lett.*, **96**, 076804.
18. Liu, D. Y., Xia, J. B., and Chang, Y. C. (2009). *J. Appl. Phys.*, **106**, 093705.
19. Sheng, J. S., and Chang, K. (2006). *Phys. Rev. B*, **74**, 235315.
20. Bolgakov, E. N., and Sadreev, A. F. (2002). *Phys. Rev. B*, **66**, 075331.
21. Koga, T., Nitta, J., and van Veenhuizen, M. (2004). *Phys. Rev. B*, **70**, 161302(R).

Chapter 14

Spin Polarization of a Rashba Electron with a Mixed State

In recent years, much attention has been paid to the field of RSOI [1] in low-dimensional semiconductor structures due to its potential applications in spintronic devices [2–4], which is based on the idea of the possible manipulation of the electron spin by an electric field [5]. Although spin transistors have yet to be achieved, the fundamental interest in understanding the effect and application of RSOI on macroscopic low-dimensional semiconductor structures continues [6, 7]. Many investigations focus on ballistic macroscopic rings [8–11] because a quantum ring exhibits an intriguing spin interference phenomenon [12, 13]. For instance, Chang et al. have studied persistent current in a quantum ring with two kinds of SOIs [9] and have shown that effective periodic potential caused by SOIs results in the weakening of the spin current and the localization of electrons. Ballistic electron transport of a Rashba electron through a chain of quantum circular rings has been investigated by Molnar et al. [10]. They have shown a periodic dependence on the incident electron's energy, through the parameter ka, the magnetic field B, and the strength of the RSOI α. Recently Naeimi et al. have shown that a double quantum ring in the presence of RSOI and a

Quantum Waveguide in Microcircuits
Jian-Bai Xia, Duan-Yang Liu, and Wei-Dong Sheng

ISBN 978-981-4669-85-6 (Hardcover), 978-1-315-36477-3 (eBook)
www.panstanford.com

magnetic flux can work as a spin-inverter [11]. Most investigations on quantum rings with RSOI focus on the circular ring because its Hamiltonian can be written as a one-dimensional model [14]. Without this advantage, spin transport in other shapes of rings is not convenient to calculate.

In previous work the injected electron is in the pure state, but for many cases, we expect a spin polarizer to get a spin polarization current from a nonpolarized state. To achieve this objective, in addition to an electric field, a magnetic field is also required. In this chapter, we study in detail the spin transport of Rashba electrons in an AB square ring with a magnetic flux. In addition, we study the spin polarization and its manipulation by α or B.

14.1 Transfer Matrix of a Rashba Electron in an AB Ring with a Magnetic Flux

In the presence of Rashba spin-orbital interaction (RSOI) and of a magnetic field B perpendicular to the $x-y$ plane, the appropriate Hamiltonian of an electron in the two-dimensional (2D) system in the $x-y$ plane is

$$H=\begin{pmatrix} \frac{\hbar^2}{2m^*}(\mathbf{p}+e\mathbf{A})^2+V(x,y) & \frac{\alpha}{\hbar}\left(ip_x+p_y\right) \\ \frac{\alpha}{\hbar}\left(-ip_x+p_y\right) & \frac{\hbar^2}{2m^*}(\mathbf{p}+e\mathbf{A})^2+V(x,y) \end{pmatrix}, \tag{14.1}$$

where m^* is the electron effective mass, α is the Rashba coefficient, and the Zeeman energy has been neglected [13]. For a one-dimensional (1D) circular ring structure this Hamiltonian can be rewritten as

$$H=\frac{\hbar^2}{2m^*R^2}\left[\left(-i\frac{\partial}{\partial\varphi}+\frac{\bar{\alpha}}{2}\sigma_r-\frac{\phi}{\phi_0}\right)^2-\frac{\bar{\alpha}^2}{4}\right], \tag{14.2}$$

where ϕ is the azimuthal angle, R is the radius, $\bar{\alpha}=\alpha\left(\frac{2m^*R}{\hbar^2}\right)$ is the normalized Rashba constant, $\sigma_r=\cos\varphi\sigma_x+\sin\varphi\sigma_y$, ϕ is the magnetic flux through the ring, and $\phi_0=h/e$. We can introduce the dimensionless Hamiltonian. Then the eigenenergy and eigenstates in this system can be given as

$$E^{\mu} = \left(m + \frac{b}{4} + \frac{1}{2} + \frac{(-1)^{\mu}}{2}\sqrt{1+\bar{\alpha}^2}\right)^2 - \frac{\bar{\alpha}^2}{4} \tag{14.3}$$

and

$$\Phi^{\mu} = e^{im\varphi}\chi^{\mu}(\varphi), \tag{14.4}$$

where $\mu = 1$ and 2, which refer to the up- and down-spin states, respectively, $b = 2eBR^2/\hbar$, and the orthogonal spinors $\chi^{\mu}(\varphi)$ can be expressed in the terms of the eigenvectors $(1,0)^{\mathrm{T}}$ and $(0,1)^{\mathrm{T}}$ of the Pauli matrix σ_z as

$$\chi^1(\varphi) = \begin{pmatrix} \cos\frac{\beta}{2} \\ e^{i\varphi}\sin\frac{\beta}{2} \end{pmatrix} \tag{14.5}$$

and

$$\chi^2(\varphi) = \begin{pmatrix} \sin\frac{\beta}{2} \\ -e^{i\varphi}\cos\frac{\beta}{2} \end{pmatrix}, \tag{14.6}$$

where $\beta \equiv \arctan(-\bar{\alpha})$. These results are obtained from the 1D Hamiltonian Eq. 14.2, but for a variety of 1D ring, such as a square ring or an elliptical ring, we can't find the 1D Hamiltonian. To study a Rashba electron's transport in these structures, we divide a curved line into N segments [15]. For a curved line, such as an elliptical ring or a circular ring, N is large enough and every segment is very small, and then every segment can be approximated to be a line segment along the tangential direction. For every segment we can obtain the eigenstates and we can write the wavefunction in the curve as

$$\Phi = (\psi_1(\theta), \psi_2(\theta))\Psi = (\psi_1(\theta), \psi_2(\theta))\begin{pmatrix} a(l) \\ b(l) \end{pmatrix}, \tag{14.7}$$

where

$$\psi_1(\theta) = \frac{1}{\sqrt{2}}\begin{pmatrix} 1 \\ ie^{i\theta} \end{pmatrix}, \quad \psi_2(\theta) = \frac{1}{\sqrt{2}}\begin{pmatrix} 1 \\ -ie^{i\theta} \end{pmatrix},$$

l denotes the coordinates on the curve line, and θ is the azimuthal angle of the tangent line of the curve. Adopt Ψ to describe the wave function and by using Griffith's boundary conditions [16–18] in each vertex, we can relate the wave function at the two endpoints by

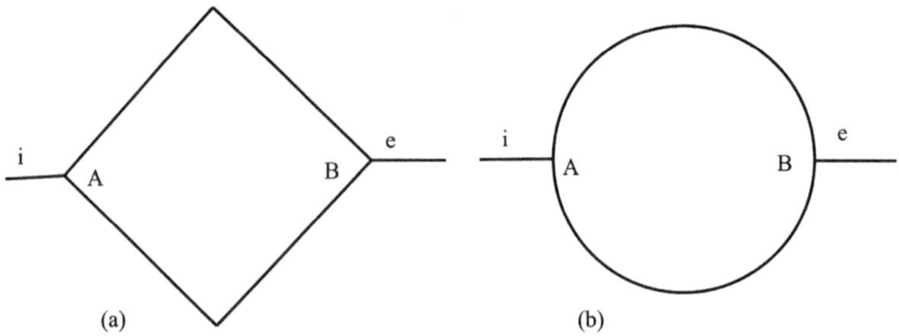

Figure 14.1 Two structures: (a) an AB square ring and (b) an AB circular ring.

a transfer matrix. For a polyline structure, such as a square ring, every lead is a natural line segment, so N is the number of leads. All analyses on the curved line remain correct, and actually a curved line is approximated to be a multistage polyline in our method. In a circular ring this method gave results that are identical to those obtained from 1D Hamiltonian [15], so this method is reasonable.

Consider a 1D square ring as shown in Fig. 14.1a. Here the electron current is injected from circuit i and the output circuit e is on the right side. We assume that at point A the down arm is with the polar angle θ_1 and the up arm is with the polar angle θ_2. Therefore in Eq. 14.7 θ_1 and θ_2 correspond to the corresponding side of the square ring. The side length of the square is denoted by L, and the strength of RSOI in the square is denoted by α_s. In this chapter, we use the dimensionless physical quantities. Similar to R in the circular ring, L can be treated as the size of the square ring. If the energy unit $E_0 = \hbar^2/(2m^* L^2)$, then the energy $\varepsilon = E/E_0$, the magnetic field $b = (\hbar eB/m^*)/E_0$, and the Rashba coefficient $\bar{\alpha}_s = (\alpha_s/L)/E_0 = \alpha_s(2m^* L/\hbar^2)$. Similar to Ref. [15], we can write the state of the electron in every part of the structure. We adopt Ψ to describe the wave function in the two arms of the square ring:

$$\Psi^j_{\text{up}} = \begin{pmatrix} a^j_{\text{up}} & (l^j_{\text{up}}) \\ b^j_{\text{up}} & (l^j_{\text{up}}) \end{pmatrix}, \tag{14.8}$$

$$\Psi^j_{\text{down}} = \begin{pmatrix} a^j_{\text{down}} & (l^j_{\text{down}}) \\ b^j_{\text{down}} & (l^j_{\text{down}}) \end{pmatrix}, \tag{14.9}$$

$$\Phi_i = \begin{pmatrix} a_i \\ b_i \end{pmatrix} e^{ik_0 l_i} + \begin{pmatrix} a_r \\ b_r \end{pmatrix} e^{-ik_0 l_i}, \tag{14.10}$$

and

$$\Phi_0 = \begin{pmatrix} a_\mathrm{t} \\ b_\mathrm{t} \end{pmatrix} e^{ik_0 l_\mathrm{o}}, \tag{14.11}$$

where up and down denote the upper and lower arms of the square ring and $j = 1$ or 2, which correspond to the clockwise and counterclockwise motions of electron through the square ring, respectively. In particular, l_up^1 and l_up^2 or l_down^1 and l_down^2 have opposite directions. According to the transfer matrix method, we can obtain the Ψ of each arm if we know its value at any one point, so there are 12 unknown coefficients in Ψ_up^j, Ψ_down^j, Φ_i, and Φ_0. Using Griffith's boundary conditions [16–18], we can determine all unknown coefficients. We assume that the original points of l_i and l_o are point A and point B, respectively, then when $a_\mathrm{i} = 1$ and $b_\mathrm{i} = 0$, we have $a_\mathrm{r} = r_{11}$, $b_\mathrm{r} = r_{12}$, $a_\mathrm{t} = t_{11}$, and $b_\mathrm{t} = t_{12}$; similarly, when $a_\mathrm{i} = 0$ and $b_\mathrm{i} = 1$, we have $a_\mathrm{r} = r_{21}$, $b_\mathrm{r} = r_{22}$, $a_\mathrm{t} = t_{21}$, and $b_\mathrm{t} = t_{22}$, where $\sigma = 1$ or 2, which denote the spin-up and spin-down states in the z direction. The spin-dependent transmission coefficient of an electron with incoming spin σ and outgoing spin σ' can be written as $T_{\sigma\sigma'} = |t_{\sigma\sigma'}|^2$. For comparison the spin transport in an AB circular ring as shown in Fig. 14.1b is also calculated.

14.2 Description of Spin Polarization of a Rashba Electron

In the above discussion, the injected electron is in the pure state, but for many cases, this condition can't be satisfied. We assume that the rate for spin-up is P_1 and the rate for spin-down is P_2. Then it is convenient to introduce a spin polarization P to describe the difference between the spin-up and spin-down electron transmissions:

$$P = \frac{P_1 - P_2}{P_1 + P_2}. \tag{14.12}$$

Obviously, $-1 \leq P \leq 1$, $P = -1$, and $P = +1$ represent complete spin polarization in the z direction. Now we define

$$Q \equiv P_1/P_2. \tag{14.13}$$

Then $P = (Q - 1)/(Q + 1)$. There is a one-to-one correspondence between Q and P, and Q and P have the same changing trend, so we can study the variation of Q instead of the variation of P. We can obtain the relationship of Q of the injected electron Q^{i} and outgoing electron Q^{o}:

$$Q^{\text{o}} = \frac{T_{11}Q^{\text{i}} + T_{21}}{T_{21}Q^{\text{i}} + T_{22}}. \tag{14.14}$$

First we consider the change of Q though a structure ΔQ. In the condition $Q^{\text{i}} < Q^{\text{fix}}$, we have $\Delta Q < 0$; in the condition $Q^{\text{i}} > Q^{\text{fix}}$, $\Delta Q > 0$, and in the condition $Q^{\text{i}} = Q^{\text{fix}}$, $\Delta Q = 0$, where

$$Q^{\text{fix}} = \frac{-(T_{11} - T_{22}) + \sqrt{(T_{11} - T_{22})^2 + 4T_{12}T_{21}}}{2T_{12}}. \tag{14.15}$$

We can determine that the spin polarization can be changed though a structure, and $Q^{\text{fix}}(P^{\text{fix}})$ is the sign value of $Q(P)$ of the outgoing electron. Because $T_{12} = T_{21}$, Q^{fix} is determined by $(T_{11} - T_{22})/T_{12}$. Another condition we are interested in is the injected electron is totally nonpolarized. In this case $Q^{\text{i}} = 1$, so $Q^{\text{o}} = (T_{11} + T_{21})/(T_{12} + T_{22}) \equiv Q^{\text{sp}}$. In this condition, $P^{\text{sp}} = (Q^{\text{sp}} - 1)/(Q^{\text{sp}} + 1)$ can describe the polarization of the spin of the outgoing electron when the injected electron is nonpolarized.

14.3 Spin Transport in a Square Ring and a Circular Ring with a Magnetic Flux

In this section we present the numerical result for the spin-dependent electron transport in a square ring and a circular ring. The effect of the RSOI strength α, the magnetic field B, and the incident electron energy E are investigated for different conditions, and two structures are compared with each other. Further, we use the dimensionless physical quantities as in section 14.2, but for B, we measure the magnetic flux ϕ in units of $\phi_0 = h/e$.

In Fig. 14.2 we show the spin-dependent electron transmission coefficients T_{11}, $T_{12}(T_{21})$, and T_{22} and the electron spin polarizations

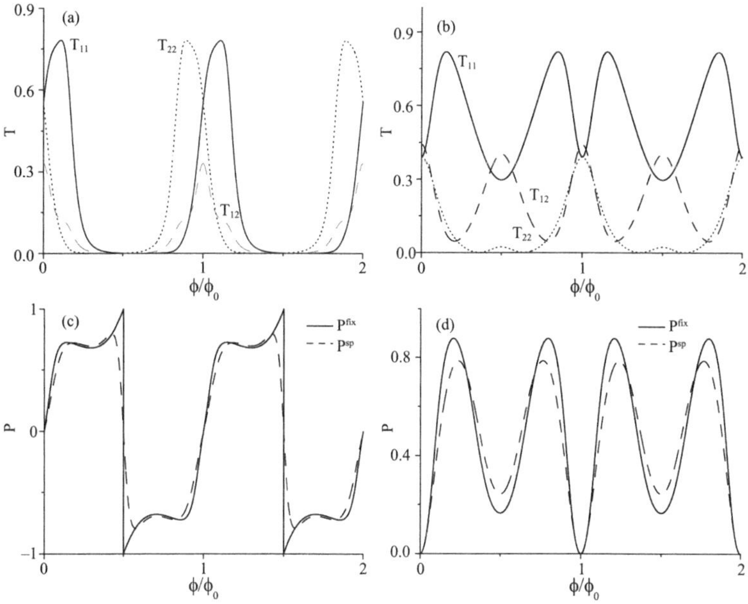

Figure 14.2 (a, c) The spin-dependent electron transmission coefficients T_{11}, $T_{12}(T_{21})$, and T_{22} and (b, d) the electron spin polarizations P^{fix} and P^{sp} of the emergent electron as a function of the magnetic flux ϕ. (a, c) for the AB square ring, and (b, d) for the circular ring.

P^{fix} and P^{sp} of the emergent electron as a function of the magnetic flux ϕ. The relevant parameters in our calculation are that $E = 10$ and $\bar{\alpha} = 1.0$. Figure 14.2a shows the electron transmission coefficients for the square ring in Fig. 14.1a, and Fig. 14.2b shows the electron transmission coefficients for the circular ring in Fig. 14.1b. We can see that for both cases, the electron transmission coefficient curves all oscillate with the magnetic flux ϕ and the oscillating period is $\phi/\phi_0 = 1$. It proves that the AB effect exists in two kinds of AB rings. In these figures, $T_{11} \neq T_{22}$ for any regions in which ϕ/ϕ_0 is not an integer number. According to our theory in Section 14.2, this means that the AB rings can act as spin polarizers in the presence of both the RSOI and the perpendicular magnetic field. In Fig. 14.2c and Fig. 14.2d we show the P^{fix} and P^{sp} as a function of the magnetic flux ϕ for the square ring and the circular ring, respectively. High polarization of spin can be reached in two structures, but there are some differences. In our calculation, in the circular ring, the peak

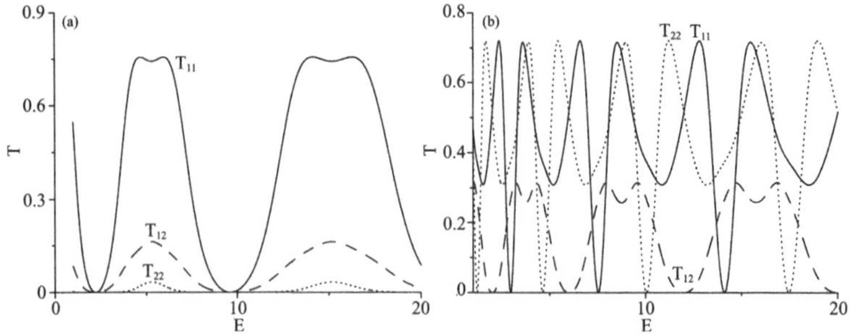

Figure 14.3 T_{11}, $T_{12}(T_{21})$, and T_{22} as a function of the injected electron's energy (a) for the AB square ring and (b) for the AB circular ring.

of P^{fix} or P^{sp} is sharp, while in the square ring, the peak area and the valley area of P is wide. This means that the square ring has a higher stability as a spin polarizer. This fact shows that the geometry of the structure is an important parameter for modulation of the spin transport if other parameters are fixed.

Now we investigate the effects of the energy of the injected electron on the spin transport. Figures 14.3a and 14.3b show T_{11}, $T_{12}(T_{21})$, and T_{22} as a function of the injected electron's energy E for $\bar{\alpha} = 1.0$ and $\phi/\phi_0 = 0.4$ in the square and circular rings, respectively. From Fig. 14.3 we see that the electron transmission coefficients oscillate with the energy, but "the period" increases with increasing E. This result is due to the expression of the eigenenergy of corresponding close rings in Ref. [15]. Comparing the electron transmission coefficients in the two rings, we find that the electron transmission coefficients in the circular ring oscillate more rapidly because the energy-level spacing is smaller in the circular ring. This result shows again that the square ring has a higher stability as a spin device.

Figure 14.4a and Fig. 14.4b show T_{11}, $T_{12}(T_{21})$, and T_{22} as a function of the Rashba strength $\bar{\alpha}$ in the square ring and in the circular ring, respectively. The relevant parameters are $E = 10$ and $\phi/\phi_0 = 0.4$. Again we see that the electron transmission coefficients in the circular ring oscillate much more rapidly, so it means that the stability of the circular ring is worse than the square ring as a spin device.

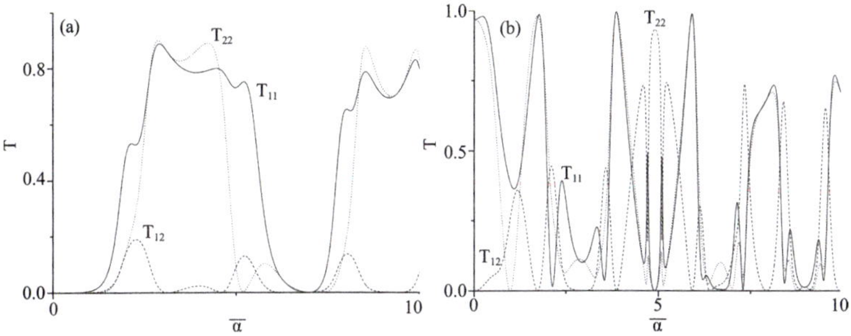

Figure 14.4 T_{11}, $T_{12}(T_{21})$, and T_{22} as a function of the Rashba strength $\bar{\alpha}$ (a) for the AB square ring and (b) for the AB circular ring.

14.4 Spin Polarization of a Rashba Electron in a Quantum Ring

To obtain a higher spin polarization and more effective modulation, we should take account of the effect of more parameters together. In Fig. 14.5 we show the effect of the Rashba strength and the magnetic flux on the spin polarization transport. We focus on the realization of spin polarizer, so the spin current density is as important as the spin polarization. We define the effective P

$$P^{\text{ef}} = \frac{1}{2} P^{\text{sp}} \sum_{\sigma,\sigma'=1,2} T_{\sigma\sigma'}. \tag{14.16}$$

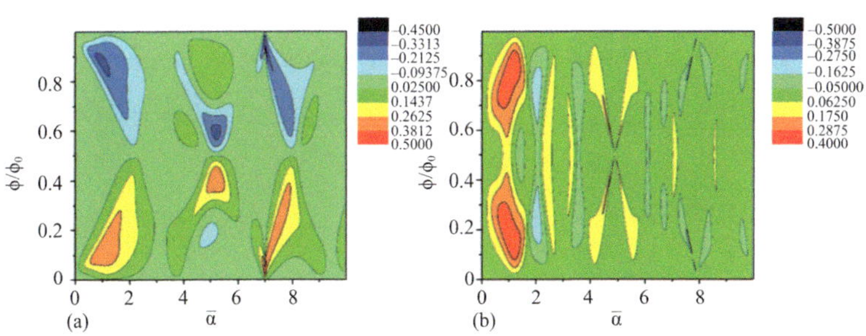

Figure 14.5 Contour map of effective spin polarization P^{ef} as a function of the Rashba strength $\bar{\alpha}$ and the magnetic flux $\phi(a)$ for the AB square ring and (b) for the AB circular ring.

If the injected electron is nonpolarized, the sign of P^{ef} denotes the spin-polarization direction on the z axis and its absolute value contains information of both electron current density and spin polarization of the outgoing electron. Only when both of them reach a higher value, P^{ef} have a considerable value. The contour maps of P^{ef} as a function of $\bar{\alpha}$ and ϕ in the square ring and in the circular ring are shown in Fig 14.5a and Fig. 14.5b, respectively. In our calculation the incident electron energy $E = 10$. As shown in Fig. 14.5, $|P^{\text{ef}}|$ is very small for most of the region of $(\bar{\alpha}, \phi/\phi_0)$, so we must choose suitable parameters for a spin polarizer. For instance, we can set $\bar{\alpha} = 1.0$ and modulate ϕ in both structures. This condition is discussed in Fig. 14.2. Another result is that we don't need large Rashba strength and magnetic field. If the scale of the structure is about 100 nm and $m^*/m_e \simeq 0.1$, then we get $\alpha = \bar{\alpha}\hbar^2/(2m^*L) \simeq 4.0$ meV nm and $B \simeq 0.1$T. Comparing Fig. 14.5a with Fig. 14.5b, we can clearly find that P^{ef} changes more rapidly in the circular ring and there is a wider region of $(\bar{\alpha}, \phi/\phi_0)$ in the square ring, which is useful for modulating the spin polarization. These results are reasonable. Many research studies have indicated that the transport in an AB ring is related to the energy band structures of a corresponding closed ring. Eigenenergies of Rashba states in a square loop are given in Ref. [15], and we can find the energy-level spacing is much larger than that in Eq. 14.3. As a result the spin transport of a Rashba electron in the square ring is not so sensitive to relevant parameters as that in the circular ring. In addition, when the $\bar{\alpha}$ and ϕ/ϕ_0 are the same in two kinds of rings, the arms of the square ring are longer and a spin-dependent quantum interference phenomenon is more likely to occur. This fact may be another reason why the geometry is important.

14.5 Summary

In this chapter, we studied the spin polarization in a square ring and in a circular ring with the RSOI and the magnetic flux. We developed the 1D quantum waveguide theory in straight waveguide systems and applied it in the 1D curve systems. The effects of Rashba strength, magnetic field, and incident electron energy were taken into account. We found that for appropriate values of parameters, both kinds of AB rings can work as spin polarizers and modulation by some parameters is realizable. Comparing the results in two structures, it was found that the spin polarization in the square ring has a wider peak (valley) area and it means that the square ring has higher stability as a spin polarizer.

References

1. Rashba, E. I. (1960). *Sov. Phys. Solid State*, **2**, 1109.
2. Pareek, T. P. (2004). *Phys. Rev. Lett.*, **92**, 76601.
3. Koga, T., Nitta, J., and van Veenhuizen, M. (2004). *Phys. Rev. B*, **70**, 161302(R).
4. Koga, T., Sekine, Y., and Nitta, J. (2006). *Phys. Rev. B*, **74**, 041302(R).
5. Datta, S., and Das, B. (1990). *Appl. Phys. Lett.*, **58**, 665.
6. Simchi, H., Esmaeilzadeh, M., and Mazidabadi, H. (2013). *Physica E*, **54**, 220.
7. Fallah, F., and Esmaeilzadeh, M. (2011). *AIP Adv.*, **1**, 032113.
8. Splettstoesser, J., Governale, M., and Zulicke, U. (2003). *Phys. Rev. B*, **68**, 165341.
9. Sheng, J. S., and Chang, K. (2006). *Phys. Rev. B*, **74**, 235315.
10. Molnar, B., Vasilopoulos, P., and Peeters, F. M. (2005). *Phys. Rev. B*, **72**, 075330.
11. Naeimi, A. S., Eslami, L., Esmaeilzadeh, M., et al. (2013). *J. Appl. Phys.*, **113**, 014303.
12. Mathur, H., and Stone, A. D. (1992). *Phys. Rev. Lett.*, **68**, 2964.
13. Molnar, B., Peeters, F. M., and Vasilopoulos, P. (2004). *Phys. Rev. B*, **69**, 155335.
14. Meijer, F. E., Morpurgo, A. F., and Klapwijk, T. M. (2005). *Phys. Rev. B*, **66**, 033107.
15. Liu, D.-Y., Xia, J.-B., and Chang, Y.-C. (2009). *J. Appl. Phys.*, **106**, 093705.
16. Liu, D.-Y., Xia, J.-B., and Chang, Y.-C. (2010). *Sci. China Ser. G*, **53**, 16.
17. Griffith, S. (1953). *Trans. Faraday Soc.*, **49**, 345.
18. Xia, J. B. (1992). *Phys. Rev. B*, **45**, 3593.

Chapter 15

Two-Dimensional Quantum Waveguide Theory of Rashba Electrons

The first model of spin transistor proposed by Datta [1] working by controlling the strength of Rashba spin-orbit interaction (RSOI) [2] was demonstrated to be feasible in narrow-gap semiconductors [3]. Then many device ideas were brought forward [4–10]. Recently, Koo et al. [11] reported the demonstration of the spin-injected field-effect transistor in a high-mobility InAs heterostructure. They confirmed the Datta's theory [1]—an oscillatory channel conductance as a function of monotonically increasing gate voltage. Besides, a great deal of one-dimensional (1D) devices were proposed [12, 13]. The 1D quantum waveguide theory have been introduced in the previous three chapters. When the width of the waveguide is not narrow enough, the 1D approach cannot work; the transport of the electrons will be in some transverse excited states synchronously, not only the ground state; and the transmission will be concerned with the structure shape.

The two-dimensional (2D) quantum waveguide transport for a spinless electron has been introduced in Chapter 11, but that for a Rashba electron has rarely been studied [5]. In our work for this chapter we applied the 1D quantum waveguide theory of

Quantum Waveguide in Microcircuits
Jian-Bai Xia, Duan-Yang Liu, and Wei-Dong Sheng

ISBN 978-981-4669-85-6 (Hardcover), 978-1-315-36477-3 (eBook)
www.panstanford.com

a Rashba electron to the 2D cases, which can operate the spin flip and the electron block more effectively. We used the transfer matrix method [16, 17] with the boundary conditions derived in Refs. [14] and [15] to study the 2D ballistic transport of Rashba electrons in straight structures of various shapes, including square stub, triangular stub, and periodic structures [19]. We found that the boundary condition for the derivative of the wave functions at the discontinuous interface used by Wang et al. [5] is not reasonable, so it is necessary to formulate the theory and calculate the results correctly. And the 2D quantum waveguide theory for a Rashba electron may be useful for designing the spin-injected field-effect transistor.

15.1 Transfer Matrix Method Considering Spin [19]

The transfer matrix method's general formalism of a spinless situation has been described in Chapter 11 and many papers [16–18]. Now we apply it to Rasbha electrons. If ballistic electrons move along a straight channel in two-dimensional electron gasses (2DEGs) that work in the presence of the Rasbha spin-orbit interaction (RSOI), we can divide the channel into some segments (see Chapter 11) and in each segment the width is constant. If we assume that 2DEGs are in the $x-y$ plane and the channel is in the x direction, in each segment the wave function can be written as

$$\Psi^m(x,y) = \sum_{n=1}^{N} \left[a_{1n}^m \phi_1(0)\, e^{ik_{1n}^m x} + a_{2n}^m \phi_2(0)\, e^{ik_{2n}^m x} + b_{1n}^m \phi_1(0)\, e^{-ik_{2n}^m x} + b_{2n}^m \phi_2(0)\, e^{-ik_{1n}^m x}\right] \varphi_n^m(y), \quad (15.1)$$

where m denotes the m-th segment and ϕ_1 and ϕ_2 are the phases of the Rashba wave functions in Eq. 12.6 [14]. The argument θ in ϕ_1 and ϕ_2 is the azimuth angle of the circuit; in our case $\theta = 0$ or π. k_{1n}^m and k_{2n}^m are the wave vectors [14] depending on the transverse energy of the electron in the m-th segment,

$$k_{1n}^m = k_{0n}^m + k_\delta, \quad k_{2n}^m = k_{0n}^m - k_\delta$$

and

$$k_{0n}^{m} = \frac{m^*}{\hbar^2}\sqrt{\alpha^2 + \frac{2\hbar^2}{m^*}E_{||}^{mn}}, \quad k_{\delta} = \frac{m^*}{\hbar^2}\alpha, \tag{15.2}$$

where α is the Rashba coefficient, $E_{||}$ is the longitudinal kinetic energy

$$E_{||}^{mn} = E - \frac{\hbar^2}{2m^*}\left(\frac{n\pi}{W_m}\right)^2, \tag{15.3}$$

W_m denotes the width of the m-th segment, and n denotes the n-th transverse sublevel. The sum over n includes evanescent modes, that is, k_{0n}^{m} is imaginary.

In this chapter we use dimensionless units of physical quantities. The length of the unit is the width of the input channel W_0, the wave vector unit is π/W_0, and the units of the energy and the Rashba coefficient are

$$\varepsilon_0 = \frac{\hbar^2}{2m^*}\left(\frac{\pi}{W_0}\right)^2 \quad \text{and} \quad \alpha_0 = \frac{\hbar^2}{2m^*}\left(\frac{\pi}{W_0}\right), \tag{15.4}$$

respectively. With the dimensionless units, k_{0n}^{m} and k_{δ} in Eq. 15.2 can be written as

$$k_{0n}^{m} = \sqrt{\left(\frac{\alpha}{2}\right)^2 + E - \left(\frac{nW_0}{W_n}\right)^2} \quad \text{and} \quad k_{\delta} = \frac{\alpha}{2}. \tag{15.5}$$

Then we match the wave function and the current density, J_x left-multiplying the wave function, at each interface of segments, with different widths. J_x is the current density operator (4.12) [14]

$$J_x = -\frac{i}{\hbar}[l, H] = \frac{i}{\hbar}\begin{pmatrix} -\frac{\hbar^2}{m^*}\frac{\partial}{\partial l} & \alpha e^{-i\theta} \\ -\alpha e^{i\theta} & -\frac{\hbar^2}{m^*}\frac{\partial}{\partial l} \end{pmatrix}. \tag{15.6}$$

It is noticed that the result of the operator J_x left-multiplying the wave function is rather simple [14].

$$J_x\Psi_{\sigma n} = J_x\phi_{\sigma}(\theta)\, e^{ik_{\sigma n}x} = \frac{\hbar k_{0n}}{m^*}\Psi_{\sigma n}. \tag{15.7}$$

This means that the current density is independent of spin σ, which is in contrast to the result of Ref. [5], where the authors used the derivative operator instead of the current density operator J_x.

Considering the orthogonality of ϕ_1 and ϕ_2, we divide the Rashba electron wave functions into two parts, spin-up and spin-down. We write the expression of Ψ^m in Eq. 15.1 in the matrix form and adopt a 4N dimensional column vector to describe the wave function in the m-th segment as the following form:

$$\Psi^m = \phi_1(0) \otimes \Psi_1^m + \phi_2(0) \otimes \Psi_2^m \tag{15.8}$$

and

$$\begin{aligned}\Psi_\sigma^m &= \left(a_\sigma 1 e^{ik_{\sigma 1}^m x}, a_{\sigma 2} e^{ik_{\sigma 2}^m x}, \cdots a_{\sigma N} e^{ik_{\sigma N}^m x}, b_{\sigma 1} e^{-ik_{3-\sigma 1}^m x},\right.\\ &\quad \left. b_{\sigma 2} e^{-ik_{3-\sigma 2}^m x}, \cdots b_{\sigma N} e^{-ik_{3-\sigma N}^m x}\right)^T \\ &= \left(A_\sigma^m, B_\sigma^m\right)^T,\end{aligned} \tag{15.9}$$

where $\sigma = 1$ or 2. We assume the hard wall approximation at the edge of channel, hence the transverse wave functions

$$\varphi_n^m(y) = \sqrt{\frac{2}{W_m}} \sin\left[\frac{n\pi}{W_m}\left(y - y_0^m\right)\right], \tag{15.10}$$

where y_0^m is the coordinate of the down edge of the m-th segment. This assumption is adopted in the whole chapter. The boundary conditions of the wave function and the current density at the interface of the m-th and the $(m+1)$th segment are

$$\Psi^m = \Psi^{m+1}$$

and

$$J_x \Psi^m = J_x \Psi^{m+1}. \tag{15.11}$$

Then left-multiplying Eq. 15.11 by $\phi_1(0)$ and $\phi_2(0)$, respectively, we get

$$\Psi_\sigma^m = \Psi_\sigma^{m+1} \tag{15.12}$$

and

$$J_x \Psi_\sigma^m = J_x \Psi_\sigma^{m+1}, \tag{15.13}$$

where $\sigma = 1$ or 2. So it is derived from Eqs. 15.12 and 15.13 that for movement in the straight channel, there is no mixing between the wave functions of spin-up ($\sigma = 1$) and spin-down ($\sigma = 2$) and the transfer matrix, which relates Ψ_σ on two sides of the interface, is independent of σ. In the following we will omit the index σ.

There are two cases: the transverse width of the m-th segment W_m is smaller than W_{m+1} of the $(m+1)$th segment, or vice versa. For the former, we multiply both sides of Eq. 15.12 by $\varphi_n^{m+1}(y)$ and both sides of Eq. 15.13 by $\varphi_l^m(y)$ and integrate over the transverse coordinate range of the $(m+1)$th and m-th segments, respectively. We get

$$\sum_{l=1}^{N}\left(a_l^m + b_l^m\right) S_{l,n} = a_n^{m+1} + b_n^{m+1} \tag{15.14}$$

and

$$k_{0l}^m\left(a_l^m - b_l^m\right) = \sum_{n=1}^{N} k_{0n}^{m+1}\left(a_n^{m+1} - b_n^{m+1}\right) S_{l,n}, \tag{15.15}$$

where $S_{l,n}$ is defined as

$$S_{l,n} = \int_{W_n} \varphi_l^m(y)\,\varphi_n^{m+1}(y)\,dy. \tag{15.16}$$

Now if we adopt the expression of Ψ_m in Eq. 15.8 and Eq. 15.9, we can obtain the transfer matrix connecting the Ψ_m on the left side of the interface and the Ψ_{m+1} on the right side [16]

$$\begin{aligned} \Psi^m &= M_{m,m+1}\Psi^{m+1}, \\ M_{m,m+1} &= \frac{1}{2}\begin{pmatrix} M^+ + M^- & M^+ - M^- \\ M^+ - M^- & M^+ + M^- \end{pmatrix}, \end{aligned} \tag{15.17}$$

$$M^+ = \left(\mathbf{S}^T\right)^{-1}, \text{ and } \quad M^- = \left(K^m\right)^{-1}\mathbf{S}\mathbf{K}^{m+1}. \tag{15.18}$$

K^m is the diagonal matrix with elements k_{0n}^m. For the case of $W_m > W_{m+1}$, we can similarly obtain the transfer matrix.

In the straight m-th segment, the transfer matrix connecting the Ψ_m on the left end and the right end of the segment is the diagonal matrix, dependent on σ.

$$M_{m,\sigma} = \begin{pmatrix} P_\sigma^- & 0 \\ 0 & P_\sigma^+ \end{pmatrix} \tag{15.19}$$

and

$$\left(P_\sigma^-\right)_{nl} = e^{-ik_{\sigma n}^m L_m}\delta_{nl}, \ \left(P_\sigma^+\right)_{nl} = e^{ik_{3-\sigma n}^m L_m}\delta_{nl},$$

where L_m is the length of the m-th segment.

In this chapter, we assume that an incident electron with energy E_0 enters the channel and the state of the incident electron is known.

So the coefficients of the wave functions at the input end and the output end A_σ^{in} are certain and $B_\sigma^{\text{out}} = 0$. The total transfer matrix $\mathbf{M}_\sigma$ is the multiplication of all partial transfer matrices in due order, which is just related with E, σ, and the channel's structure.

$$\mathbf{M}_\sigma = \prod_m \mathbf{M}_{m,\sigma}\mathbf{M}_{m,m+1} = \begin{pmatrix} \mathbf{M}_{\sigma,1} & \mathbf{M}_{\sigma,2} \\ \mathbf{M}_{\sigma,3} & \mathbf{M}_{\sigma,4} \end{pmatrix}. \tag{15.20}$$

From the transfer matrix Eq. 15.20 we can obtain A_σ^{out} and B_σ^{in}.

$$A_\sigma^{\text{out}} = (M_{\sigma,1})^{-1} A_\sigma^{\text{in}} \text{ and } B_\sigma^{\text{in}} = M_{\sigma,3}(M_{\sigma,1})^{-1} A_\sigma^{\text{in}}. \tag{15.21}$$

The transmission and reflection coefficients t_{ij} and r_{ij} are related to the wave function coefficients. Supposing that the incident electron propagates in the ground transverse mode of the input channel [16]

$$A^{\text{in}} = \begin{pmatrix} k_{01}^{-1/2} \\ 0 \\ \vdots \\ 0 \end{pmatrix}, \ B^{\text{in}} = \begin{pmatrix} r_{11}k_{01}^{-1/2} \\ r_{21}k_{02}^{-1/2} \\ \vdots \\ r_{N1}k_{0N}^{-1/2} \end{pmatrix}, \text{ and } A^{\text{out}} = \begin{pmatrix} t_{11}k_{01}^{-1/2} \\ t_{21}k_{02}^{-1/2} \\ \vdots \\ t_{N1}k_{0N}^{-1/2} \end{pmatrix}. \tag{15.22}$$

The total transmission and reflection probabilities T and R equal

$$T_i = \sum_{j=1}^{N} \left|t_{ji}\right|^2 \quad \text{and} \quad R_i = \sum_{j=1}^{N} \left|r_{ji}\right|^2, \tag{15.23}$$

for one electron incident in the i-th transverse mode. The summation is over all the traveling waves in the longitudinal direction. It can be proved that the current density is conserved.

$$T_i + R_i = 1. \tag{15.24}$$

15.2 Spin Interference in Two Kinds of 2D Waveguides [19]

First we studied the transmission probabilities in the stub structure as shown in Figs. 15.1a and 15.1b. We take the dimensionless parameters as $L_1 = L_2 = L_3 = 1$, $W_1 = W_3 = 1$, $W_2 = 1.8$, and $\alpha = 0.5$, and define the effective wave vector of the incident electron,

$$k_{\text{eff}} = \sqrt{\left(\frac{\alpha}{2}\right)^2 + E_0}, \tag{15.25}$$

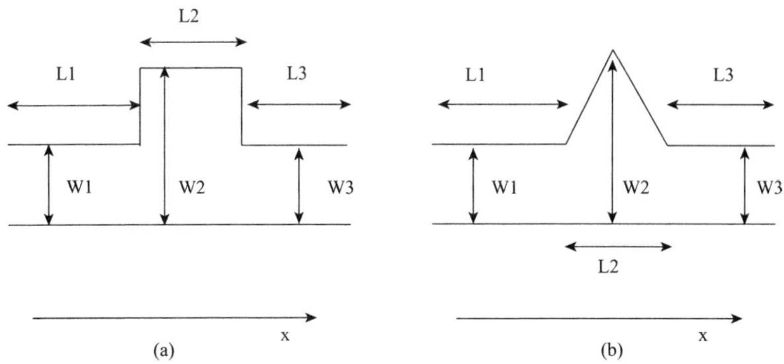

Figure 15.1 Two kinds of waveguides with different stubs: (a) a square stub and (b) a triangle stub.

where E_0 is the energy of the incident electron. For $1 < k_{\text{eff}} < 2$, the transmission probabilities as functions of k_{eff} for two structures are shown in Fig. 15.2. From Fig. 15.2 we see that the T versus k_{eff} relation is independent of σ (=1 or 2, corresponding to $\pm\alpha$). Furthermore, it is also independent of the magnitude of α if we take k_{eff} as the variable. That means the calculated results of the two-dimensional (2D) quantum waveguide transport for the spinless electron published in pervious papers [16–18] are also valid for the Rashba electrons; only the variable k_{eff} is changed from $\sqrt{E_0}$ to Eq. 15.25. In Fig. 15.2 the T curve has a sharp dip at $k_{\text{eff}} = 1.85$ and the position of the dip depends on the length of the stub W_2; here we take $W_2 = 1.8$. If we look at the stub as a gate, over which we make a metal electrode, then the gate length W_2 can be controlled by the gate voltage. So the transmission probability of the electron with a fixed energy E_0 can be controlled by the gate voltage. For square stubs (solid line), all vales have those energies where k_{0n} in Eq. 15.2 equals 1. If we assumed stubs are totally closed, these points correspond with eigenenergies. We can infer that this rule holds true for triangular stubs.

For $2 < k_{\text{eff}} < 3$, the transmission probabilities as functions of k_{eff} are shown in Fig. 15.3. There are two modes of incident electrons: one is at the first sub-band and the other is at the second sub-band. Similarly, there are two modes of outgoing electrons, so the transmission probabilities have four qualities, T_{ij} (i, j = 1 or 2),

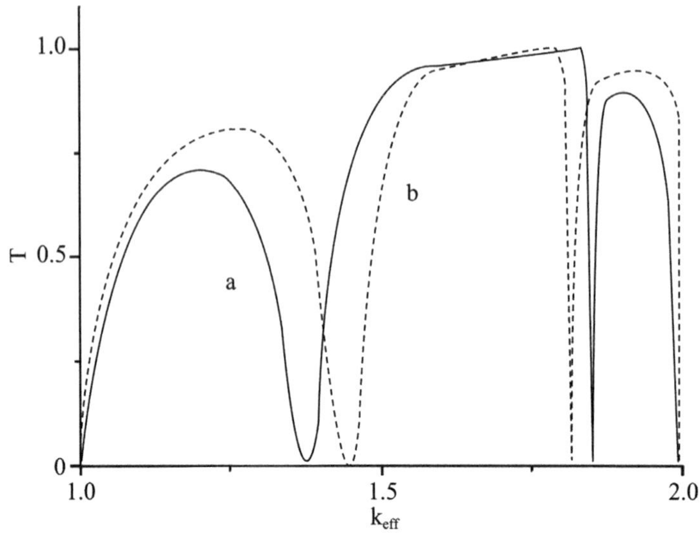

Figure 15.2 T as a function of E in the structure in Figs. 15.1a and 15.1b, when $1 < k_{\text{eff}} < 2$ and $N = 5$.

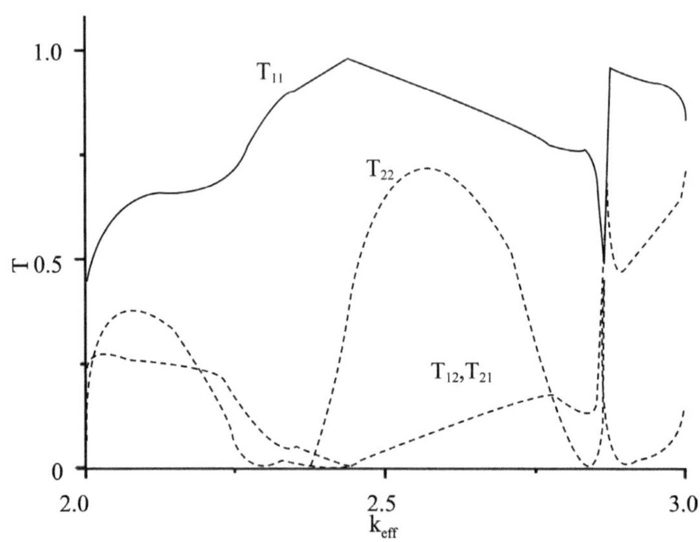

Figure 15.3 T_{ij} $(i, j = 1 \text{ or } 2)$ as a function of E in the structure in Fig. 15.1a when $2 < k_{\text{eff}} < 3$ and $N = 5$.

which denotes the transmission probability from the j-th mode to the i-th mode. From Fig. 15.3 we see that the T_{11} and T_{21} are larger and the T_{12} and T_{21} are smaller, but not zero. This means that in the transport process there is coupling between different modes. We also found that $T_{12} = T_{21}$.

Though the transmission probabilities are independent of the spin orientation (σ), if we put a ferromagnetic contact oriented in the x direction at the output end, which permits only electrons with spin σ_x to pass through, then the spin polarization along the x direction will depend on the Rashba coefficient α and the total length of the structure

$$P = \frac{J_+ - J_-}{J_+ + J_-}, \tag{15.26}$$

where J_+ and J_- are current densities of spin along the $+x$ and $-x$ directions, respectively. Figure 15.4 shows the spin polarizations as functions of α for $k_{\text{eff}} = 1.7$. The coefficients of incident wave function are $A_1^{\text{in}} = 1/\sqrt{2}\,(1, 0, 0\ldots)^T$ and $A_2^{\text{in}} = 1/\sqrt{2}\,(i, 0, 0\ldots)^T$. From Fig. 15.4 we see that the spin polarization of the outgoing Rashba electron can be modulated by the Rashba coefficient and the relation of P and α is immovable even when E or the structure of the waveguide changes.

Figure 15.5 shows the transmission probabilities as functions of the width of the stubs for the structure of Fig. 15.1a with parameters $L_1 = L_3 = 1$, $L_2 = 0.5$, $W_1 = W_3 = 1$, $N = 3$, $\alpha = 0.889$, and incident electron energies $E_0 = 3.4$, 3.5, and 3.6. We choose this value of α for comparing with results of Fig 15.7. From Fig. 15.5 we see that the transmission probability equals zero at a definite width of stub W_{stub}, which is different for different incident electron energies. Figure 15.6 shows the transmission probabilities as functions of the width of the stubs for the same parameters as Fig. 15.5, but $\alpha = 0.5$. Comparing Figs. 15.5 and 15.6, we found that the positions of the transmission probability valleys change with the Rashba coefficient α; when α increases, the W_{stub} of the transmission probability valley decreases. This means that we can control the transmission probability by changing the W_{stub}, that is, changing the gate voltage over the stub, or changing the Rashba coefficient α, that is, changing the perpendicular electric field to the 2DEG.

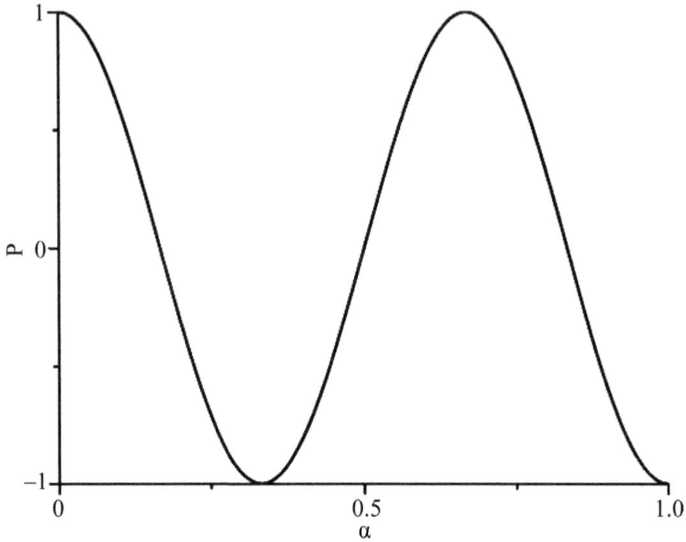

Figure 15.4 P as a function of α; this function is the same as the 1D case and is not related with the structure.

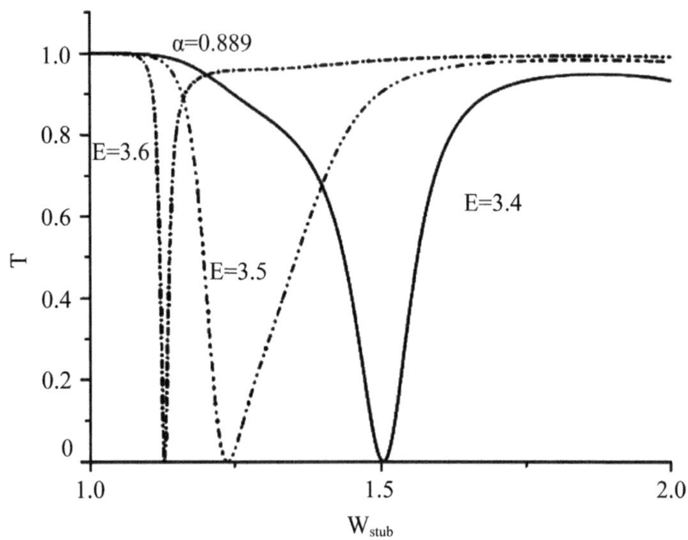

Figure 15.5 T as a function of W_{stub} in the waveguide with a single square stub; the length of the stub is 0.5, $\alpha = 0.889$, and $N = 3$ for $E_0 = 3.4$, 3.5, and 3.6.

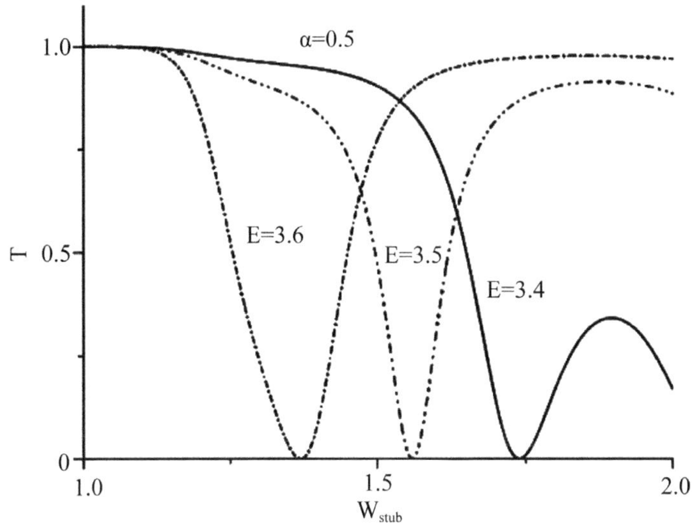

Figure 15.6 T as a function of W_{stub} in the waveguide with a single square stub; the length of the stub is 0.5, $\alpha = 0.5$, and $N = 3$ for $E_0 = 3.4$, 3.5, and 3.6.

Then we investigate the influence of the number of stubs. We investigate the structure where there are three configurations that are the same as the structure of Fig. 15.5, with the parameters $N = 3$ and $\alpha = 0.889$. We select this α value so that $P = 1$. Figure 15.7 shows T as a function of W_{stub} when $E_0 = 3.4$ and 3.8. From Fig. 15.7 we see that the transmission probabilities equal zero at the same W_{stub} as the single stub structure but the half-widths of the valleys decrease greatly. Trends in two curves are similar: $T \approx 1$ in most range of W_{stub}, and T decreases to zero in a very small range. In these regions in which $T \approx 0$, we can completely block the electron. Figure 15.8 shows T as a function of W_{stub} when square stubs are replaced by triangular ones, and $E = 3.4$ and 3.8. From Figs. 15.7 and 15.8 we see that these regions in which $T \approx 0$ depend on the shape of the structure. With the multistub structure we can control the T more effectively. In Fig. 15.8 the dip in the solid line looks strange because it is too sharp to be expressed. And there are some very sharp dips, which can be explained by the (nW_0/W_n) in Eq. 15.5. It make the condition of resonance become unsatisfied rapidly.

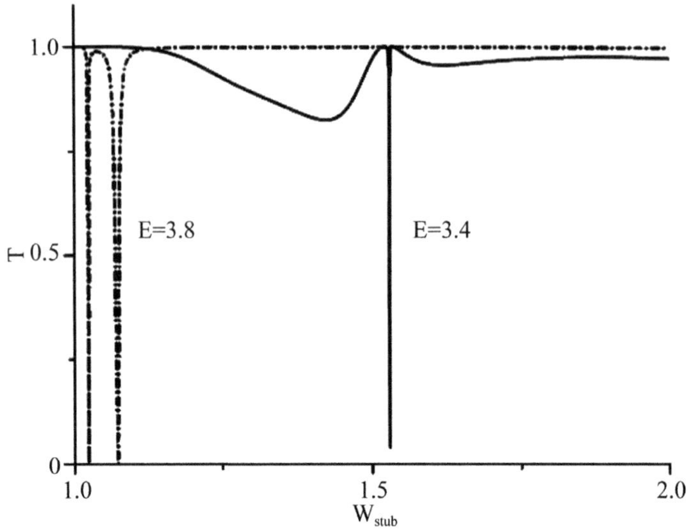

Figure 15.7 T as a function of W_{stub} in waveguides with three square stubs that are the same as Fig. 15.5, for $E_0 = 3.4$ and 3.8.

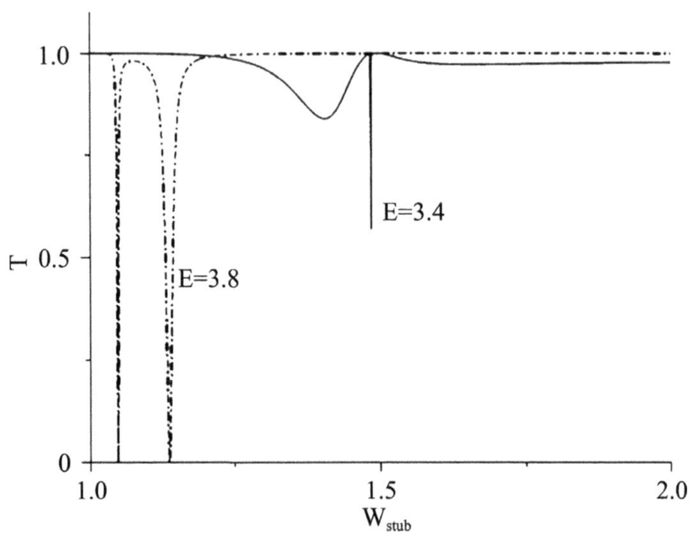

Figure 15.8 T as a function of W_{stub} in waveguides with three triangular stubs that are the same, other parameters are the same as

Physically, in the case of $T = 0$ there is an eigen standing wave state in the stub region between the input and output waveguides for each structure. Figure 15.2 shows that when E is in a small region T decreases rapidly. It is because for these E values there is almost a complete standing wave in the mid-region, so at the interfaces of input and output waveguides between the mid-region, $\Psi \approx 0$, so $R = 1$ and $T = 0$. And the eigenenergy E of these standing waves depends on the E, W_{stub}, and the shape of the structure. So we can select a structure of a suitable shape and parameter and apply gate voltage and perpendicular electric field to block the electron.

15.3 The Unitary Condition [19]

Now we prove that the unitary condition Eq. 15.24 is always tenable. Considering that $\mathbf{M}_{m\sigma}$ are unitary matrices, we just need to prove that currents on the two sides of the interface of the m-th and the $(m+1)$th segment are equal. For every wave function Ψ in the waveguide, the current in the x direction is $\text{Re}(\Psi^{+} J_x \Psi)$. Considering the orthogonality of $\varphi_n^m(y)$ and the express of Ψ^m in Eq. 15.1, $J^m = J_1^m + J_2^m$ and

$$J_\sigma^m = \text{Re}\left[\sum_{n=1}^{N} k_{0n}\left(a_{\sigma n}^m e^{ik_{\sigma n}^m x} + b_{\sigma n}^m e^{-ik_{3-\sigma n}^m x}\right)^* \left(a_{\sigma n}^m e^{ik_{\sigma n}^m x} - b_{\sigma n}^m e^{-ik_{3-\sigma n}^m x}\right)\right]. \quad (15.27)$$

So if we define a new Ψ^m and $J_x\Psi^m$ as Eq. 15.8 and

$$\Psi_\sigma^m = \left(a_{\sigma 1}e^{ik_{\sigma 1}^m x} + b_{\sigma 1}e^{-ik_{3-\sigma 1}^m x}, a_{\sigma 2}e^{ik_{\sigma 2}^m x} + b_{\sigma 2}e^{-ik_{3-\sigma 2}^m x}, \cdots a_{\sigma N}e^{ik_{\sigma N}^m x} + b_{\sigma N}e^{-ik_{3-\sigma N}^m x}\right)^T,$$

and

$$J_x\Psi_\sigma^m = K^m\left(A_\sigma^m - B_\sigma^m\right)^T. \quad (15.28)$$

Then formula $J_\sigma^m = \text{Re}\left[\left(\Psi_\sigma^m\right)^* J_x \Psi_\sigma^m\right]$ remains effective and Eq. 15.14 and Eq. 15.15 can be written as

$$\Psi_\sigma^m = \left(S^T\right)^{-1}\Psi_\sigma^{m+1} \quad (15.29)$$

and

$$J_x \Psi_\sigma^m = S \left(J_x \Psi_\sigma^{m+1} \right). \tag{15.30}$$

Left-multiplying Eq. 15.30 by Hermitian conjugation of Eq. 15.29 and taking the real component

$$J_\sigma^m = \text{Re} \left[\left(\Psi_\sigma^m \right)^+ J_x \Psi_\sigma^m \right] = \text{Re} \left[\left(\Psi_\sigma^{m+1} \right)^+ J_x \Psi_\sigma^{m+1} \right] = J_\sigma^{m+1}. \tag{15.31}$$

So the unitary condition is satisfied in our method.

15.4 Summary

We studied the 2D ballistic transport of Rashba electrons in a straight structure in 2DEGs. We derived the transfer matrix relating the wave functions at the input end and at the output end of the structure and found that for movement in a straight structure, there is no mixing between the wave functions of spin-up ($\sigma = 1$) and spin-down ($\sigma = 2$) and the transfer matrix is independent of σ in the interface. We investigated the influence of the structure on electron transport. It is found that the transmission probabilities as functions of the effective wave vector k_{eff} are independent of the sign and magnitude of the Rashba coefficient α. The transmission probability depends on the shape of the structure, especially the stub width. If we change the stub width by the gate voltage, we can control the transmission probability of the electron with a fixed energy. The transmission probabilities of the electron with an energy higher than the second transverse sub-band include contributions from different sub-bands, which means in the transport process there is coupling between different sub-bands. The spin polarization along the x direction depends on the Rashba coefficient, so we can control the spin polarization of the outgoing Rashba electron by changing the Rashba coefficient, for example, changing the applied perpendicular electric field. For the multistub structure, T decreases rapidly in a certain small region of W_{stub} and T keeps high at the other W_{stub} for a certain Rashba coefficient α. And the anti-resonance is found, where the quasi-confined state is formed in the center part of the structure. So, we can modulate a spin-polarized current by controlling the incident electron energy E_0 and by changing the shape, parameters of the stub, the applied gate voltage, and the perpendicular electric field. With the 2D stub-like structures we can design the spin-injected field-effect transistor. We proved the unitary condition of the transfer matrix, that is, the conservation condition of the current density.

References

1. Datta, S., and Das, B. (1990). *Appl. Phys. Lett.*, **56**, 665.
2. Rashba, E. I. (1960). *Sov. Phys. Solid State*, **2**, 1109.
3. Nitta, J., Meijer, F. E., and Takayanagi, H. (1999). *Appl. Phys. Lett.*, **75**, 695.
4. Kiselev, A. A., and Kim, K. W. (2001). *Appl. Phys. Lett.*, **78**, 775.
5. Wang, X. F., Vasilopoulos, P., and Peeters, F. M. (2002). *Appl. Phys. Lett.*, **80**, 1400.
6. Bulgakov, E. N., and Sadreev, A. F. (2002). *Phys. Rev. B*, **66**, 075331.
7. Sheng, J. S., and Chang, K. (2006). *Phys. Rev. B*, **74**, 235315.
8. Bellucci, S., Carillo, F., and Onorato, P. (2008). *Eur. Phys. J. B*, **66**, 509.
9. Zhang, R. L., Zhang, Z. J., Peng, P. W., et al. (2008). *J. Appl. Phys.*, **103**, 07B727.
10. Souma, S., and Nikolić, B. K. (2005). *Phys. Rev. Lett.*, **94**, 106602.
11. Koo, H. C., Kwon, J. H., Eom, J., et al. (2009). *Science*, **325**, 1515.
12. Bellucci, S., and Onorato, P. (2008). *Phys. Rev. B*, **77**, 075303.
13. Wang, L. G., Chang, K., and Chan, K. C. (2006). *J. Appl. Phys.*, **99**, 043701.
14. Liu, D. Y., Xia, J. B., and Chang, Y. C. (2010). *Sci. China: Phys. Mech. Astron.*, **53**, 1.
15. Liu, D. Y., Xia, J. B., and Chang, Y. C. (2009). *J. Appl. Phys.*, **106**, 093705.
16. Sheng, W.-D., and Xia, J.-B. (1996). *J. Phys. C*, **8**, 3635.
17. Weisshaar, A., Lary, J., Goodnick, S. M., and Tripathi, V. K. (1991). *J. Appl. Phys.*, **70**, 355.
18. Akis, R., Vasilopoulos, P., and Debray, P. (1995). *Phys. Rev. B*, **52**, 2805.
19. Liu, D. Y., and Xia, J. B. (2010). *J. Appl. Phys.*, **108**, 053717.

Index